THE FATEFUL TRIANGLE

THE UNITED STATES, ISRAEL & THE PALESTINIANS

NOAM CHOMSKY

The Fateful Triangle

THE FATEFUL TRIANGLE

The United States, Israel and the Palestinians

Noam Chomsky

SOUTH END PRESS   BOSTON, MA

Library of Congress Card Catalog Number: 83-061480
ISBN: 0-89608-187-7 paper
ISBN: 0-89608-188-5 cloth
Cover design by Ann L. Raszmann
First published in the United States by
South End Press
302 Columbus Ave.
Boston, MA 02116
First published in Great Britain by
Pluto Press
The Works
105a Torriano Ave.
London, England NW5 2RX

TABLE OF CONTENTS

1

Fanning the Flames

In the war of words that has been waged since Israel invaded Lebanon on June 6, 1982, critics of Israeli actions have frequently been accused of hypocrisy. While the reasons advanced are spurious,* the charge itself has some merit. It is surely hypocritical to condemn Israel for establishing settlements in the occupied territories while we pay for establishing and expanding them. Or to condemn Israel for attacking civilian targets with cluster and phosphorus bombs "to get the maximum kill per hit,"[2] when we provide them gratis or at bargain rates, knowing that they will be used for just this purpose.[3] Or to criticize Israel's "indiscriminate" bombardment of heavily-settled civilian areas or its other military adventures,[4] while we not only provide the means in

---

* Through the summer of 1982, the media were flooded with letters of a strikingly similar format, typically asking of critics: "Where were you when. . .?," where the gap is filled by the writer's favorite Palestinian atrocity, often invented. Another typical format was the accusation that it is hypocritical to criticize Israeli atrocities unless one goes on to condemn the Russians in Afghanistan, the Syrians for the terrible massacre in Hama, etc. No similar requirements were imposed when the PLO was bitterly condemned for terrorist atrocities. In fact, it has been a common pretense that the media and others had *not* condemned PLO atrocities or even that the media have been "pro-PLO" (e.g., Leon Wieseltier: "There *is* a scandal, and it is the moral and political prestige of the PLO [in media] coverage of the Middle East"). Entering still further into the world of fantasy, we even find the charge (Robert Tucker) that "numerous public figures in the West, even a number of Western governments" (all unnamed) have "encouraged the PLO in its maximalist course" of "winner-take-all," i.e., destruction of Israel.[1] When the intellectual history of this period is someday written, it will scarcely be believable.

1

abundance but welcome Israel's assistance in testing the latest weaponry under live battlefield conditions—to be sure, against a vastly outmatched enemy, including completely undefended targets, always the safest way to carry out experiments of this sort. In general, it is pure hypocrisy to criticize the exercise of Israeli power while welcoming Israel's contributions towards realizing the U.S. aim of eliminating possible threats, largely indigenous, to American domination of the Middle East region.

Clearly, as long as the United States provides the wherewithal, Israel will use it for its purposes. These purposes are clear enough today, and have been clear to those who chose to understand for many years: to integrate the bulk of the occupied territories within Israel in some fashion while finding a way to reduce the Arab population; to disperse the scattered refugees and crush any manifestation of Palestinian nationalism or Palestinian culture;[5] to gain control over southern Lebanon. Since these goals have long been obvious and have been shared in fundamental respects by the two major political groupings in Israel, there is little basis for condemning Israel when it exploits the position of regional power afforded it by the phenomenal quantities of U.S. aid in exactly the ways that would be anticipated by any person whose head is not buried in the sand. Complaints and accusations are indeed hypocritical as long as material assistance is provided in an unending and ever-expanding flow, along with diplomatic and ideological support, the latter, by shaping the facts of history in a convenient form. Even if the occasional tempered criticisms from Washington or in editorial commentary are seriously intended, there is little reason for any Israeli government to pay any attention to them. The historical practice over many years has trained Israeli leaders to assume that U.S. "opinion makers" and political elites will stand behind them whatever they do, and that even if direct reporting is accurate, as it generally is, its import will gradually be lost as the custodians of history carry out their tasks.

The basic point seems simple enough, and is well-understood outside the United States, including Israel. A dissident Israeli journalist observes that "All this delusion of imperial power would stop if the United States turned off the tap...in anger at some excessive lunacy."[6] The London *Economist* comments:

> Holding up the supply of shiny new weapons is America's traditional slap on Israel's wrist. But an embargo is ineffective unless it is certain to last... Much more effective would be the belief in Israel that this time an American president will stick with his policy, including if need be a lasting embargo on arms and a rethink of the extent of America's aid.[7]

The point, as noted, seems simple enough. Some years ago it was in fact as simple as it seems. It would then have been possible to influence

Israel to join in the international consensus—which has long included the major Arab states, the population of the occupied territories, and the mainstream of the PLO—in support of a two-state political settlement that would include recognized borders, security guarantees, and reasonable prospects for a peaceful resolution of the conflict. The precondition, of course, was for the U.S. itself to join this consensus and cease its support for the adamant rejectionism of the Labor Party and then Menachem Begin's Likud coalition. Though this picture of recent history is remote from the standard version here, it is familiar abroad, and has the additional merit of accuracy.[8]

What seemed simple several years ago, however, has become considerably more complex today. By now it is not at all clear what the effect would be if U.S. policy were to shift towards the international consensus, abandoning the commitment to a Greater Israel that will dominate the region in the interests of American power—a commitment that is expressed in deeds, whatever the accompanying words may be—and terminating its immense material, diplomatic and ideological contributions towards ensuring that the quite reasonable international consensus will not be realized. The question is of no small significance. I will return to the background, the issues, and the current prospects.

What follows is not intended as a comprehensive review or analysis of the network of relations among the United States, Israel and the Palestinians. Rather, its more modest aims are to bring out certain elements of the "special relationship" between the United States and Israel, and of their relationships to the original inhabitants of the land, which I think have been insufficiently appreciated or addressed and often seriously misrepresented, with the consequence that we have pursued policies that are both disgraceful and extremely dangerous, increasingly so.

These remarks will be critical of Israel's policies: its consistent rejection of any political settlement that accommodates the national rights of the indigenous population; its repression and state terrorism over many years; its propaganda efforts, which have been remarkably successful—much to Israel's detriment in my view—in the United States. But this presentation may be misleading, in two respects. In the first place, this is not an attempt at a general history; the focus is on what I think is and has been wrong and what should be changed, not on what I think has been right.* Secondly, the focus on Israeli actions and initiatives may obscure the fact that my real concern is the policies that have been pursued

---

* One of the things that is right is the Hebrew-language press, or at least, significant segments of it. I have relied extensively on the work of thoughtful and courageous Israeli journalists who have set—and met—quite unusual standards in exposing unpleasant facts about their own government and society. There is nothing comparable elsewhere, in my experience. See also *TNCW*, p. 450 (see note 5); Robert Friedman, "The West Bank's brave reporters," *Middle East International*, March 4, 1983. I am indebted to several Israeli friends, primary among them Israel Shahak, for having provided me with a great deal of material from these sources, as well as much insightful comment.

by the U.S. government and our responsibility in shaping or tolerating these policies. To a remarkable extent, articulate opinion and attitudes in the U.S. have been dominated by people who describe themselves as "supporters of Israel," a term that I will also adopt, though with much reluctance, since I think they should more properly be called "supporters of the moral degeneration and ultimate destruction of Israel," and not Israel alone. Given this ideological climate and the concrete U.S. actions that it has helped to engender, it is natural enough that Israeli policies have evolved in their predictable way. Perpetuation of these tendencies within the U.S. and in U.S.-Israel relations portends a rather gloomy future, in my view, for reasons that I hope will become clearer as we proceed. If so, a large measure of responsibility lies right here, as in the recent past.

The essential features of the U.S. contribution towards the creation of a Greater Israel were revealed in a stark and brutal form in the September 1982 massacre of Palestinians in Beirut, which finally did elicit widespread outrage, temporarily at least. I will return to the events and their background later. For now, it suffices to observe that the Israeli invasion of Lebanon was supported by the U.S. and by editorial comment generally, though qualms were raised when it seemed to be going too far (perhaps threatening U.S. interests) or to involve too many civilian casualties. All of this is reminiscent of the U.S. attack on South Vietnam in 1962, then most of Indochina a few years later, to mention an event that did not take place according to standard U.S. journalism and scholarship, just as official Party history recognizes no such event as the Russian invasion of Afghanistan in 1979.

The Israeli occupation of West Beirut on September 15 also elicited no official U.S. criticism, though the Sabra and Shatila massacres that followed aroused angry condemnation. The condemnation was directed in the first place at the Christian Phalange, which was accused of the actual massacre, and in the second place at the Government of Israel, for failing in its responsibility to protect the inhabitants of the camps. A flood of letters and articles in the press contrasted Begin's reliance on force and violence, his deception, his high-handed rejection (at first) of an official inquiry, and his efforts to evade responsibility, with the stand of the opposition Labor Party both now and when it had held power. The "beautiful Israel" of earlier years was disappearing, because of Begin and Sharon.

Col. Eli Geva, who had been dismissed from the IDF* after refusing to lead his troops against West Beirut, was quoted as saying:

---

* Israel Defense Forces; the army of the State of Israel.

The feeling is that the house is on fire. I am referring to a country which is in a type of deterioration, or landslide, and everyone who believes in this country, has to contribute to stopping the landslide.[9]

Many agreed, specifically, many long-time supporters of Israel (in the special sense of the term mentioned earlier), who dated the deterioration from the invasion of West Beirut, or of Lebanon, or perhaps somewhat earlier, though surely after Begin took power.

Within Israel, the Beirut massacre evoked much anguish and an unprecedented wave of protest against the government, including an immense popular demonstration, backed, for the first time, by the opposition Labor Party. There was, however, little evidence of any significant loss of support for Begin and his governing Likud coalition. The strong and often passionate support for the military operation in Lebanon on the part of the majority of the population also appears to have been unaffected by the massacre, though opposition grew in the following months as the costs began to mount.

The response in the U.S. was interesting. After initial sharp condemnation, the general reaction, across quite a broad spectrum, was that the events and the reaction to them highlighted the uniquely high moral standards of Israel. A *New York Times* editorial commented that Israel's anguish "is only appropriate for a society in which moral sensitivity is a principle of political life." Even in journals that are often regarded as taking a critical stance towards Israel, similar sentiments were voiced. *Time*, for example, commenting on protests within the IDF, wrote that it "has from the start been animated by the same righteous anger and high moral purpose that has guided Israel through its tumultuous history."[10] When the Report of the Israeli Commission of Inquiry into the massacres appeared a few months later, commentary was rhapsodic: Israel had sought and attained "salvation"; its achievement was "sublime" (see pp. 397-8).

No state in history merits such accolades; such comments would be dismissed with contempt with reference to any other state (apart from one's own, in patriotic speeches or the more dismal segments of scholarship). But with reference to Israel such references are so common-place as to pass without notice, quite across the board in American journalism and scholarship, with rare exceptions. In contrast, the Palestinians and their organizations, and the Arabs more generally, have been portrayed in terms of violence, terrorism, irrationality, and un-compromising refusal to come to terms with the existence of Israel or to accept the norms of decent behavior. The contrast is clear enough in journalism and scholarship, and it is also familiar in standard media fare, where the Arab terrorist is routinely contrasted with the heroic Israeli. It would, for example, be inconceivable for a TV drama to portray an Israeli or Jewish character in the manner of the standard Arab villain, despite the ample record of Israeli terrorism over many years, effectively concealed in the United States.

Colonel Geva's comment, cited above, may well be accurate, but the question of timing is of some significance, as is the stance—both current and historical—of the Labor Party that dominated the pre-state Zionist movement and ruled from the establishment of the state to 1977. This is a question that will be addressed below. The record shows quite clearly, I believe, that it is a serious error to attribute the deterioration to Begin's Likud coalition. The house was on fire long before, and supporters of Israel have been fanning the flames, a fact long deplored by many true Israeli doves. Those who have watched the "landslide" in silence, or have helped it along, or have successfully concealed it by often vulgar apologetics, or have blamed the Palestinians when they are persecuted or killed in alleged "retaliations," have laid the groundwork for the current conflagration, and for the atrocities in Beirut that finally evoked some temporary protest. The reasons for this judgment will appear as we proceed.

It would be salutary, then, to abandon hypocrisy. Either we provide the support for the establishment of a Greater Israel with all that it entails and refrain from condemning the grim consequences of this decision, or we withdraw the means and the license for the pursuit of these programs and act to ensure that the valid demands of Israelis and Palestinians be satisfied. This can, perhaps, still be accomplished, though the possibilities recede with each passing year as the Greater Israel that we are creating becomes more firmly implanted, and as its military power—now estimated to be surpassed only by the U.S., the USSR and China[11]—continues to grow. A point of no return may soon be reached, with consequences that may be appalling for Israel and the Palestinians, for the region, and perhaps for the entire world.

Notes—Chapter 1
Fanning the Flames

1. Leon Wieseltier, *New Republic*, Sept. 23, 1981; Robert W. Tucker, "Lebanon: The Case for the War," *Commentary*, October 1982.
2. Richard Ben Cramer, *Philadelphia Inquirer*, June 30, 1982. Reprinted in *The Israeli Invasion of Lebanon* (Claremont Research and Publications, New York, 1982), a useful collection of press clippings for June/July 1982. On the extensive scale of Israeli use of cluster bombs in heavily populated areas, see Warren Richey, *Christian Science Monitor*, Nov. 2, 1982, reporting the findings of munitions experts from the nultinational peacekeeping force. Doctors in Beirut reported that other anti-personnel weapons, such as phosphorus bombs, were no less devastating in their impact upon civilians, though the major effect was from the massive air, sea and artillery bombardment itself.
3. It could not be known, of course, that an American marine (Cpl. David L. Reagan) would also be killed by a cluster bomb of the type supplied to Israel by the U.S.; J. Michael Kennedy, *Los Angeles Times*, Oct. 2; *Time*, Oct. 11, 1982.
4. On August 5, 1982, *New York Times* correspondent Thomas Friedman reported "indiscriminate" shelling of West Beirut by Israeli planes, gunboats and artillery. The editors deleted the word "indiscriminate" as inconsistent with the approved image of our Israeli ally. *Washington Post* editors, in contrast, felt that it was permissible to report "indiscriminate" Israeli bombardment on the same day. See Alexander Cockburn, *Village Voice*, Sept. 21, 1982, for discussion and details, including Friedman's protest to the editors for their lack of "courage - guts," for being "afraid to tell our readers and those who might complain to you that the Israelis are capable of indiscriminately shelling an entire city." The solicitude of *Times* editors for Israel during this period—as before—has been remarkable, as we shall have occasion to observe below.
5. Amos Perlmutter describes "the destruction of Palestinian nationalism in any form" as one of "Begin's most extreme and cherished ambitions" (*Foreign Affairs*, Fall 1982). The same was true of his predecessors, who typically denied that it existed and sought to destroy its manifestations. On the measures taken under the occupation to prevent even cultural expression, see my *Towards a New Cold War* (henceforth, *TNCW*; Pantheon, New York, 1982, pp. 277-8).
6. Haim Baram of *Haolam Haze;* cited in the *Manchester Guardian Weekly*, Sept. 12, 1982.
7. *Economist*, Sept. 11, 1982.
8. For ample though only partial evidence, see *TNCW*, chapters 9-12. We return to this matter, and other questions touched on here.
9. UPI, *Boston Globe*, Sept. 26, 1982.
10. Editorial, *New York Times*, Nov. 6, 1982; *Time*, Oct. 11, 1982.
11. The estimate is that of the London-based International Institute of Strategic Studies; *Time*, Oct. 11, 1982. Israelis tend to rank their power one notch higher, describing themselves as the third most powerful military force in the world. See, for example, Dov Yirmiah, *Yoman Hamilchama Sheli (My War Diary*; privately printed, Tel Aviv, 1983, to be published in English translation by South End Press), an important record of the Lebanon war to which we return.

2

The Origins of the "Special Relationship"

1 Levels of Support: Diplomatic, Material, Ideological

The relationship between the United States and Israel has been a curious one in world affairs and in American culture. Its unique character is symbolized by recent votes at the United Nations. For example, on June 26, 1982 the United States stood alone in vetoing a UN Security Council resolution calling for simultaneous withdrawal of Israeli and Palestinian armed forces from Beirut, on the grounds that this plan "was a transparent attempt to preserve the P.L.O. as a viable political force," evidently an intolerable prospect for the U.S. government.[1] A few hours later, the U.S. and Israel voted against a General Assembly resolution calling for an end to hostilities in Lebanon and on the Israel-Lebanon border, passed with two "nays" and no abstentions. Earlier, the U.S. had vetoed an otherwise unanimous Security Council resolution condemning Israel for ignoring the earlier demand for withdrawal of Israeli troops.[2] The pattern has, in fact, been a persistent one.

More concretely, the special relationship is expressed in the level of U.S. military and economic aid to Israel over many years. Its exact scale is unknown, since much is concealed in various ways. Prior to 1967, before the "special relationship" had matured, Israel received the highest per capita aid from the U.S. of any country. Commenting on the fact, Harvard Middle East specialist Nadav Safran also notes that this

9

amounts to a substantial part of the unprecedented capital transfer to Israel from abroad that constitutes virtually the whole of Israel's investment—one reason why Israel's economic progress offers no meaningful model for underdeveloped countries.[3] It is possible that recent aid amounts to something like $1000 per year for each citizen of Israel when all factors are taken into account. Even the public figures are astounding.* For fiscal years 1978 through 1982, Israel received 48% of all U.S. military aid and 35% of U.S. economic aid, worldwide. For FY 1983, the Reagan administration requested almost $2.5 billion for Israel out of a total aid budget of $8.1 billion, including $500 million in outright grants and $1.2 billion in low-interest loans.[4] In addition, there is a regular pattern of forgiving loans, offering weapons at special discount prices, and a variety of other devices, not to mention the tax-deductible "charitable" contributions (in effect, an imposed tax), used in ways to which we return.[5] Not content with this level of assistance from the American taxpayer, one of the Senate's most prominent liberal Democrats, Alan Cranston of California, "proposed an amendment to the foreign aid bill to establish the principle that American economic assistance to Israel would not be less than the amount of debt Israel repays to the United States," a commitment to cover "all Israeli debts and future debts," as Senator Charles Percy commented.[6]

This was before the Lebanon war. The actual vote on foreign aid came after the invasion of Lebanon, after the destruction of much of southern Lebanon, the merciless siege and bombardment of Beirut, the September massacres, and Israel's rapid expansion of settlement in the occupied territories in response to Reagan's plea to suspend settlement in accord with his peace proposals, which Israel rejected. In the light of these events, the only issue arising in Congress was whether to "punish" Israel by accepting the President's proposal for a substantial increase in the already phenomenal level of aid—what is called taking "a get-tough approach with Israel"[7]—or to take a softer line by adding even more to the increases that the President requested, as the Senate and most liberals demanded. Fortunately, the press was sufficiently disciplined so that the comic aspects of this characteristic performance were suppressed. The consequences of this message of approval to Israel for its recent actions on the part of the President and Congress are not at all comic, needless to say.

It should be noted that in theory there are restrictions on the use of American aid (e.g., cluster bombs can be used only in self-defense; development funds cannot be spent beyond Israel's recognized—i.e.,

---

* The General Accounting Office (GAO) has informed Congress that the actual level of U.S. aid may be as much as 60% higher than the publicly available figures. This is the preliminary result of a detailed study of U.S. aid to Israel by the GAO. "A major issue could develop next year [1983] over how much of the GAO study may be made public." James McCartney, *Philadelphia Inquirer*, August 25, 1982.

pre-June 1967—borders). But care has been taken to ensure that these restrictions will not be invoked, though the illegal use of weapons occasionally elicits a reprimand or temporary cut-off of shipments when the consequences receive too much publicity. As for the ban on use of U.S. funds for the settlement and development programs that the U.S. has officially regarded as illegal and as a barrier to peace (i.e., beyond the pre-June 1967 borders), this has never been enforced, and the aid program is designed so that it cannot be enforced: "in contrast to most other aid relationships, the projects we fund in Israel are not specified," Ian Lustick observes, and no official of the State Department or the aid program has "ever been assigned to supervise the use of our funds by the Israeli government."

For comparison, one may consider the U.S. aid program to Egypt (the largest recipient of non-military U.S. aid since Camp David), which is run by an office of 125 people who supervise it in meticulous detail. Many knowledgeable Egyptians have been highly critical of the aid program, alleging that it reflects American rather than Egyptian priorities, financing U.S. imports which must be brought on American ships and U.S. consultants, when trained personnel are available in Egypt for a fraction of the cost. They also note the emphasis on the private sector, "pay[ing] Mid-west farmers for wheat which could be grown at half the price in Egypt" (according to a former AID director), and in general the infiltration of Egyptian society to the extent that some perceive a threat to Egyptian national security.[8]

These examples illustrate the diplomatic and material support that the U.S. provides for Israel. A concomitant, at the ideological level, is the persistence of considerable illusion about the nature of Israeli society and the Arab-Israeli conflict. Since 1967, discussion of these issues has been difficult or impossible in the United States as a result of a remarkably effective campaign of vilification, abuse, and sometimes outright lying directed against those who dared to question received doctrine.* This fact has regularly been deplored by Israeli doves, who have been subjected to similar treatment here. They observe that their own position within Israel suffers because of lack of support within the U.S., where, as General (Res.) Mattityahu Peled observed, the "state of near hysteria" and the "blindly chauvinistic and narrow-minded" support for the most reactionary policies within Israel poses "the danger of prodding Israel once more

---

* Israeli intelligence apparently contributes to these efforts. According to a CIA study, one of its functions is to acquire "data for use in silencing anti-Israel factions in the West," along with "sabotage, paramilitary and psychological warfare projects, such as character assassination and black propaganda." "Within Jewish communities in almost every country of the world, there are Zionists and other sympathizers, who render strong support to the Israeli intelligence effort. Such contacts are carefully nurtured and serve as channels for information, deception material, propaganda and other purposes." "They also attempt to penetrate anti-Zionist elements in order to neutralize the opposition."[9]

toward a posture of calloused intransigence."[10] The well-known Israeli journalist and Zionist historian Simha Flapan describes "the prejudice of American Jewry" as now "the major obstacle to an American-Palestinian and Israeli-Palestinian dialogue, without which there is little chance to move forward in the difficult and involved peace process."[11] In concentrating on the role of American Jewry, these Israeli writers focus much too narrowly, I believe.

To cite one last example, an article in the American Jewish press quotes a staff writer for *Ha'aretz* (essentially, the Israeli *New York Times)* who says that "you American Jews, you liberals, you lovers of democracy are supporting its destruction here by not speaking out against the government's actions," referring to the wave of repression in the occupied territories under the "civilian administration" of Professor Menachem Milson and General Ariel Sharon introduced in November 1981 (see chapter 5, sections 5-8). He goes on to explain the plans of Begin and Sharon: to drive a large number of Arabs out of the West Bank, specifically, the leaders and those with a potential for leadership, "by every illegal means." How?

> You activate terrorists to plant bombs in the cars of their elected mayors, you arm the settlers and a few Arab quislings to run rampages through Arab towns, pogroms against property, not against people. A few Arabs have been killed by settlers. The murderers are known, but the police are virtually helpless. They have their orders. What's your excuse for not speaking out against these violations of Israeli law and Jewish morality?

The settlers, he adds, are "Religious Jews who follow a higher law and do whatever their rabbis tell them. At least one of the Gush Emunim rabbis has written that it is a mitzvah [religious duty] to destroy Amalek [meaning, the non-Jewish inhabitants], including women and children."[12] The *Ha'aretz* journalist adds that his journal has "a file of horror stories reported to us by soldiers returning from occupation duty in the West Bank. We can refer to them in general terms—we can rail against the occupation that destroys the moral fibre and self-respect of our youth— but we can't print the details because military censorship covers actions by soldiers on active duty."[13] One can imagine what the file contains, given what has been printed in the Israeli press. It should be noted, in this connection, that many crucial issues that are freely discussed in the Hebrew press in Israel and much that is documented there are virtually excluded from the American press, so that the people who are expected to pay the bills are kept largely in the dark about what they are financing or about the debates within Israel concerning these matters. Many examples will be given below.

The dangers posed to Israel by its American supporters have consistently been realized, leading to much suffering in the region and repeated threat of a larger, perhaps global war.

2   Causal Factors

2.1   Domestic Pressure Groups and their Interests

The "special relationship" is often attributed to domestic political pressures, in particular, the effectiveness of the American Jewish community in political life and in influencing opinion.[14] While there is some truth to this, it is far from the whole story, in two major respects: first, it underestimates the scope of the "support for Israel," and second, it overestimates the role of political pressure groups in decision-making. Let us consider these factors in turn.

In the first place, what Seth Tillman calls the "Israeli lobby" (see note 14) is far broader than the American Jewish community, embracing the major segments of liberal opinion, the leadership of the labor unions,* religious fundamentalists,[16] "conservatives" of the type who support a powerful state apparatus geared to state-induced production of high technology waste (i.e., military production) at home and military threats and adventurism abroad, and—cutting across these categories—fervent cold warriors of all stripes. These connections are appreciated in Israel, not only by the right wing. Thus Yitzhak Rabin, reputedly a dove and soon to become the Labor Prime Minister, argued against moves towards political settlement after the 1973 war. Israel should try to "gain time," he urged, in the hope that "we will later find ourselves in a better situation: the U.S. may adopt more aggressive positions vis-a-vis the USSR . . ."[17]

Many American Zionist leaders recognize these factors. In December 1980, several of them argued in the American Jewish press that "there is far greater potential commonality of interests among Jews and the Moral Majority than there is among Jews and the National Council of Churches" *(Jewish Week)*. Jacques Torczyner, former President of the Zionist Organization of America and an executive of the World Zionist Organization, wrote that "We have, first of all, to come to a conclusion that the right-wing reactionaries are the natural allies of Zionism and not the liberals"[18]—he is wrong about the latter, mistakenly assuming that they do not join in the cold war consensus whereas in fact they have

---

* Leon Hadar writes: "Along with the organized American-Jewish community, the labour movement has been a major source of support for Israel"; true with regard to the labor union bureaucracy, whatever the membership may think. Hadar quotes ILGWU president Sol Chaikin who condemns Reagan for his willingness "to 'sell' both Israel and the Solidarity movement in Poland . . . to appease his big business friends." Victor Gotbaum discusses the problems posed for Israel's supporters by the Begin government and its "antagonizing" foreign policy decisions: "We couldn't justify [the Golan annexation], so we preferred to remain silent"; many labor leaders find themselves "divorcing their love for Israel from their relations with Begin" (Gotbaum).[15] Such rhetoric has not been heard since the peak days of American Stalinism and Trotskyite "critical support." It is, however, rather common among Western intellectuals with regard to Israel. See *TNCW*, chap. 10, for some examples. More will appear below.

consistently promoted and helped to maintain it. It should furthermore be noted that the American left and pacifist groups, apart from fringe elements, have quite generally been extremely supportive of Israel (contrary to many baseless allegations), some passionately so, and have turned a blind eye to practices that they would be quick to denounce elsewhere. Again, examples will appear below.

There is an interesting expression of views akin to Rabin's in a recent study of "the real anti-Semitism in America" by Nathan and Ruth Perlmutter, respectively, the National Director of the Anti-Defamation League of B'nai Brith and his wife, also an active Zionist leader. In the United States, the Anti-Defamation League is regarded as a civil libertarian organization, at one time, a deserved reputation. Now, it specializes in trying to prevent critical discussion of policies of Israel by such techniques as maligning critics, including Israelis who do not pass its test of loyalty, distributing alleged "information" that is often circulated in unsigned pamphlets, and so on.[19] In Israel, it is casually described as "one of the main pillars" of Israeli propaganda in the United States. Seth Tillman refers to it as part of "the Israeli lobby." We return to some of its public performances (see pp. 284f.). The well-known Israeli military historian Meir Pail, formerly head of the Officers Training School of the IDF and an Israeli dove, might well have had the League in mind when he described the ways in which "Golda Meir and the Labor Party destroyed pluralism and debate within the old Zionist framework," mimicking "Joseph Stalin's tendency towards communist parties all over the world," whose interests were to be "subjugated...to the power interests of the Soviet Union"; "And the Israeli regime's tendency has been similar" as it has "destroyed the very process of dissent and inquiry," beginning (he says) with the Golda Meir labor government.[20] The League has proven a more than willing instrument.

The Perlmutters cite studies showing that whereas anti-Semitism "was once virulent" in the U.S., today there is little support for discrimination against Jews; there may be dislike of Jews, anti-Jewish attitudes, etc., but then much the same is true with regard to ethnic and religious groups quite generally. What then is "the real anti-semitism," which is still rampant, in fact perhaps more dangerous than before? The *real* anti-Semitism, it turns out, lies in the actions of "peacemakers of Vietnam vintage, transmuters of swords into plowshares, championing the terrorist PLO..."* The Perlmutters fear that "nowadays war is getting a bad name and peace too favorable a press..." They are concerned by "the

---

* It is a common claim, perhaps believed by its proponents, that there are many "champions of the PLO" in the U.S., even that the press is "pro-PLO" (see p. 1*). When examples are given, it regularly turns out that these "champions" are critics (often harsh critics) of the PLO who, however, believe that Palestinians have the same human and national rights as Jews.

defamations by the Left of the promptings for our warring in Vietnam and latterly . . . their sniping at American defense budgets . . ." "Beyond oil it is the very ideology of the liberals in which peace, even if it is pockmarked by injustice, is preferable to the prospect of confrontation that today imperils Jews." Similarly, Jewish interests are threatened "by this decade's Leftists, here and abroad, as they demonstrate against and scold the United States for its involvement in Nicaragua and El Salvador." Jewish interests are threatened because the Central American dictators have been friends of Israel—friendship which has been and is being reciprocated with much enthusiasm, though the Perlmutters do not discuss these facts, which help explain why victims of Somoza and the Salvadoran and Guatemalan generals are not friends of Israel, not because of anti-Semitism, but for quite understandable reasons; peasants being massacred with Israeli arms or tortured by military forces who boast of their Israeli training and support are not likely to be friends of Israel. According to the Perlmutters, such groups as the National Council of Churches also threaten Jewish interests by calling on Israel "to include the PLO in its Middle East peace negotiations." "Apologists for the Left—like those for the Right—have frequently rationalized anti-Semitism or indifference to Jewish interests as being merely a transitory phase," but Jews should know better.

Throughout, the argument is that Israel's interests—understood implicitly as the interests of a rejectionist Greater Israel that denies Palestinian rights—are the "Jewish interests," so that anyone who recognizes Palestinian rights or in other ways advocates policies that threaten "Israel's interests" as the authors conceive them is, to paraphrase Stalinist rhetoric of earlier years, "objectively" anti-Semitic. Those who are "innocent of bigotry" are now placing Jews in "greater jeopardy" than traditional anti-Semites, with their advocacy of peace, criticism of U.S. interventionism, opposition to bloodthirsty tyrants and torturers, etc. This is the "real anti-Semitism," and it is exceedingly dangerous. So the Anti-Defamation League has its work cut out for it.[21]

It might be noted that the resort to charges of "anti-Semitism" (or in the case of Jews, "Jewish self-hatred") to silence critics of Israel has been quite a general and often effective device. Even Abba Eban, the highly-regarded Israeli diplomat of the Labor Party (considered a leading dove), is capable of writing that "One of the chief tasks of any dialogue with the Gentile world is to prove that the distinction between anti-Semitism and anti-Zionism [generally understood as criticism of policies of the Israeli state] is not a distinction at all," and that Jewish critics (I.F. Stone and I are specifically mentioned) have a "basic complex . . . of guilt about Jewish survival." Similarly Irving Howe, typically without argument, simply attributes Israel's dangerous international isolation to "skillful manipulation of oil" and that "sour apothegm: *In the warmest of hearts there's a cold spot for the Jews"*—so that it is quite unnecessary to consider the impact of the policies of the Labor government that he supported, for example, the brutality of the occupation,* already fully apparent and sharply condemned in Israel when he wrote.[23]

The Perlmutters deride those who voice "criticism of Israel while fantasizing countercharges of anti-Semitism," but their comment is surely disingenuous. The tactic is standard. Christopher Sykes, in his excellent study of the pre-state period, traces the origins of this device ("a new phase in Zionist propaganda") to a "violent counterattack" by David Ben-Gurion against a British court that had implicated Zionist leaders in arms-trafficking in 1943: "henceforth to be anti-Zionist was to be anti-Semitic."[24] It is, however, primarily in the post-1967 period that the tactic has been honed to a high art, increasingly so, as the policies defended became less and less defensible.

Within the Jewish community, the unity in "support for Israel" that has been demanded, and generally achieved, is remarkable—as noted, to the chagrin of Israeli doves who plausibly argue that this kind of "support" has seriously weakened their efforts to modify harsh and ultimately self-destructive government policies. There is even a lively debate within the American Jewish community as to whether it is legitimate to criticize Israel's policies at all, and perhaps even more amazing, the existence of such a debate is not recognized to be the amazing phenomenon it surely is. The position that criticism is illegitimate is defended, for example, by Elie Wiesel, who says:

I support Israel—period. I identify with Israel—period. I never attack, never criticize Israel when I am not in Israel.

As for Israel's policies in the occupied territories, Wiesel is unable to offer a comment:

What to do and how to do it, I really don't know because I lack the elements of information and knowledge... You must be in a position of power to possess all the information... I don't have that information, so I don't know...[25]

A similar stance of state-worship would be difficult to find, apart from the annals of Stalinism and fascism. Wiesel is regarded in the United States as a critic of fascism, and much revered as a secular saint.

The reason generally offered in defense of the doctrine that Israel may not be criticized outside its borders is that only those who face the dangers and problems have a right to express such criticism, not those who observe in safety from afar. By similar logic, it is illegitimate for Americans to criticize the PLO, or the Arab states, or the USSR. This

---

* It might be noted that to people concerned with the facts, "skillful manipulation of oil" also seems too easy an excuse (while the "sour apothegm" hardly merits comment). See, for example, the discussion by Zionist historian Jon Kimche of how the Labor government's apparent duplicity and rejection of possible peaceful settlement alienated friendly African countries well before the use of the "oil weapon."[22]

argument actually extends a bit more broadly: it is legitimate—in fact, a duty—to provide Israel with massive subsidies and to praise it to the skies while vilifying its adversaries, particularly those it has conquered, but it is illegitimate to voice any critical comment concerning the use of the bounty we provide.

2.2 U.S. Strategic Interests

Returning to the main theme, reference to Jewish influence over politics and opinion seriously underestimates the scope of the so-called "support for Israel." Turning to the second point, the argument much overestimates the pluralism of American politics and ideology. No pressure group will dominate access to public opinion or maintain consistent influence over policy-making unless its aims are close to those of elite elements with real power. These elements are not uniform in interests or (in the case of shared interests) in tactical judgments; and on some issues, such as this one, they have often been divided. Nevertheless, a closer look will illustrate the correctness of the assessment that the evolution of America's relationship to Israel "has been determined primarily by the changing role that Israel occupied in the context of America's changing conceptions of its political-strategic interests in the Middle East."[26] Let us consider some of the relevant historical background, in an attempt to clarify this issue.

Despite the remarkable level of U.S. support for Israel, it would be an error to assume that Israel represents the major U.S. interest in the Middle East. Rather, the major interest lies in the energy reserves of the region, primarily in the Arabian peninsula. A State Department analysis of 1945 described Saudi Arabia as "...a stupendous source of strategic power, and one of the greatest material prizes in world history."[27] The U.S. was committed to win and keep this prize. Since World War II, it has been virtually an axiom of U.S. foreign policy that these energy reserves should remain under U.S. control. A more recent variant of the same theme is that the flow of petrodollars should be largely funnelled to the U.S. through military purchases, construction projects, bank deposits, investment in Treasury securities, etc. It has been necessary to defend this primary interest against various threats.

2.2.1 Threats to U.S. Control of Middle East Oil

At the rhetorical level, the threat from which the Middle East must be "defended" is generally pictured to be the USSR. While it is true that the U.S. would not tolerate Soviet moves that threatened to provide the USSR with a significant role in Middle East oil production or distribution, this has rarely been a realistic concern—which is not to say that ideologists have not come to believe the fantasies they conjure up to serve other needs.[28] In fact, the USSR has been hesitant to intrude on what is recognized to be American turf.

The pattern was set early on in the Cold War, when the U.S. organized its first major postwar counterinsurgency campaign, in Greece in 1947. Entering Greece after the Nazis had withdrawn, Britain had imposed the rule of royalist elements and former Nazi collaborators, suppressing the anti-Nazi resistance—in Athens, under Churchill's order to British forces "to act as if you were in a conquered city where a local rebellion is in progress."[29] The repression and corruption of the British-imposed regime revived the resistance. Severely weakened by the war, Britain was unable to cope with the problem and the U.S. took over the task of destroying the Communist-led peasant and worker-based nationalist movement that had fought the Nazis, while maintaining in power its own favorites, such as King Paul and Queen Frederika, whose background was in the fascist youth movements, and Minister of the Interior Mavromichalis, described by U.S. intelligence as a former Nazi collaborator and given responsibility for internal security. Some Senators found all of this difficult to reconcile with Truman Doctrine rhetoric about supporting "free peoples who are resisting attempted subjugation by armed minorities or by outside pressures," under which the counterinsurgency campaign was mounted. To them, Senator Henry Cabot Lodge explained that "this fascist government through which we have to work is incidental."[30]

The counterinsurgency effort was no small enterprise: in the war that ensued, 160,000 Greeks were killed and 800,000 became refugees. The American Mission set itself the task of eliminating those to whom Ambassador Lincoln MacVeagh referred as "subversive social forces," rooted in the insidious "new growth of class-consciousness and proletarianism"—"an alien and subversive influence," as American chargé Karl Rankin described them, to which "no leniency" should be shown until "the state has successfully reasserted its dominance" and the "bandit uprising has been quelled" (the Ambassador's phrase, standard usage in U.S. documents as in Soviet documents concerning Afghanistan). It was the American Mission and its fascist clients (and, of course, the wealthy and, later, American corporations, who were the real beneficiaries) who represented the "native" element in Greece, as distinct from the "alien" influence of Greek peasants and workers subverted by class-consciousness.

The dedicated savagery with which the U.S. Mission set about the task of liquidating the class enemy was a bit too much even for the British, who are not known for their gentlemanly decorum in such procedures; they were also not too happy about being displaced from yet another outpost of British influence and power. With the enthusiastic approval and direct participation of the U.S. Mission, tens of thousands were exiled, tens of thousands more were sent to prison islands where many were tortured or executed (or if lucky, only "re-educated"), the unions were broken, and even mild anti-Communist socialists were suppressed, while the U.S. shamelessly manipulated the electoral process to ensure that the right men won. The social and economic consequences were grim. A decade later, "between 1959 and 1963, almost a third of the Greek labor force emigrated in search of satisfactory employment."[31] The fascist coup of 1967, again with apparent U.S. backing, had its roots in the same events.

A major motivation for this counterinsurgency campaign was concern over Middle East oil. In his March 12, 1947 speech announcing the Truman Doctrine, the President observed that "It is necessary only to glance at a map" to see that if Greece should fall to the rebels "confusion and disorder might well spread throughout the entire Middle East." A February 1948 CIA study warned that in the event of a rebel victory, the U.S. would face "the possible loss of the petroleum resources of the Middle East (comprising 40 per cent of world reserves)."[32] A Russian threat was fabricated to justify U.S. intervention, but without factual basis; Stalin was trying to rein in the Greek guerrillas, knowing that the U.S. would not tolerate the loss of this Middle East outpost, as Greece was regarded, and not at all pleased at the prospect of a possible Balkan Communist confederation under Titoist influence. Again, it does not follow from the fact that the threat was fabricated that it was not believed in some planning circles; in public as in personal life, it is easy to come to believe what it is convenient to believe. The exaggeration of the Russian threat should be understood as an early example of the functioning of the Cold War system by which each superpower exploits the threat of the great enemy (its "Great Satan," to borrow Ayatollah Khomeini's term) to mobilize support for actions it intends to undertake in its own domains.

The success of the Greek counterinsurgency campaign, both at the military and ideological level, left its stamp on future U.S. policy-making. Since that time there has been recurrent talk about Russia's attempts to gain control of Middle East oil, the Soviet drive to the Gulf, etc. But no serious case has been made that the USSR would risk nuclear war—for that would be the likely consequence—by pursuing any such objective.

A more realistic threat to U.S. dominance of the region has been posed by Europe.* In the 1940s, the U.S. succeeded in displacing France, and to a large extent Britain, in part by design, in part simply as a reflection of the power balance.[33] One consequence of the CIA-backed coup that restored the Shah in Iran in 1953 was to transfer 40% of Iranian oil from British to American hands, a fact that led the *New York Times* editors to express concern that some misguided British circles might

---

* And more recently, Japan, which in 1982 replaced the U.S. as Saudi Arabia's number one trading partner and is also first or second as supplier for most other Gulf oil producers. Still, the Middle East is "the only U.S. foreign market that has experienced any significant growth in the past few years." William O. Beeman, *Christian Science Monitor*, March 30, 1983.

believe that "American 'imperialism'. . . has once again elbowed Britain from a historic stronghold." At the same time, the editors exulted that "underdeveloped countries with rich resources now have an object lesson in the heavy cost that must be paid by one of their number which goes berserk with fanatical nationalism."[34] The costs of the object lesson were indeed heavy, as events were to show, and are still being paid; and many others have been compelled to learn the same lesson since.

Concern over European involvement in the region persisted. The U.S. strongly opposed the attempt by Britain and France to reassert their influence in the area with the 1956 Suez invasion (in conjunction with Israel); the U.S. was instrumental in expelling all three powers from Egyptian territory, though Soviet threats may also have played their part. Henry Kissinger, in his 1973 "Year of Europe" address, warned of the dangers of a Europe-dominated trading bloc including the Middle East and North Africa from which the U.S. might be excluded. Later, he confided in a private meeting that one basic element in his post-1973 diplomacy was "to ensure that the Europeans and Japanese did not get involved in the diplomacy" concerning the Middle East.[35] Subsequent U.S. opposition to the "Euro-Arab dialogue" stems from the same concerns. Today, competition among the state capitalist societies (including now some lesser powers such as South Korea) for a share in the wealth generated by oil production is a matter of growing significance.

2.2.2 The Indigenous Threat: Israel as a Strategic Asset

A third threat from which the region must be "defended" is the indigenous one: the threat of radical nationalism. It is in this context that the U.S.-Israel "special relationship" has matured. In the early 1950s, the U.S.-Israel relationship was decidedly uneasy, and it appeared for a time that Washington might cement closer relations with Egyptian President Nasser, who had some CIA support. These prospects appeared sufficiently worrisome so that Israel organized terrorist cells within Egypt to carry out attacks on U.S. installations (also on Egyptian public facilities) in an effort to drive a wedge between Egypt and the U.S., intending that these acts would be attributed to ultranationalist Egyptian fanatics.*

From the late 1950s, however, the U.S. government increasingly came to accept the Israeli thesis that a powerful Israel is a "strategic asset" for the United States, serving as a barrier against indigenous radical nationalist threats to American interests, which might gain support from the USSR. A recently declassified National Security Council memoran-

---

* The official in charge of these operations, Defense Minister Pinhas Lavon, became Secretary-General of the Histadrut (the socialist labor union). According to the respected Israeli journalist Nahum Barnea, Lavon gave orders that were "much more severe" than those leading to the terrorist operations in Egypt, including an attempt "to poison the water sources in the Gaza Strip and the demilitarized zones" (Davar, Jan. 26, 1979). He does not indicate whether these alleged orders were executed.[36]

dum of 1958 noted that a "logical corollary" of opposition to radical Arab nationalism "would be to support Israel as the only strong pro-West power left in the Near East."[37] Meanwhile, Israel concluded a secret pact with Turkey, Iran and Ethiopia. According to David Ben-Gurion's biographer, this "periphery pact" was encouraged by Secretary of State John Foster Dulles, and was "long-lasting."[38] Through the 1960s, American intelligence regarded Israel as a barrier to Nasserite pressure on the Gulf oil-producing states, a serious matter at the time, and to Russian influence. This conclusion was reinforced by Israel's smashing victory in 1967, when Israel quickly conquered the Sinai, Gaza, the West Bank and the Golan Heights, the last, after violating the cease-fire in an operation ordered by Defense Minister Moshe Dayan without notifying the Prime Minister or Chief of Staff.[39]

The Israeli thesis that Israel is a "strategic asset" was again confirmed by Israel's moves to block Syrian efforts to support Palestinians being massacred by Jordan in September 1970, at a time when the U.S. was unable to intervene directly against what was perceived as a threat to U.S. clients in the Arab world. This contribution led to a substantial increase in U.S. aid. In the 1970s, U.S. analysts argued that Israel and Iran under the Shah served to protect U.S. control over the oil-producing regions of the Gulf. After the fall of the Shah, Israel's role as a Middle East Sparta in the service of American power has evoked increasing American support.

At the same time, Israel aided the U.S. in penetrating Black Africa with substantial secret CIA subsidies—supporting Haile Selassie in Ethiopia, Idi Amin in Uganda, Mobutu in Zaire, Bokassa in the Central African Republic, and others at various times[40]—as well as in circumventing the ban on aid to Rhodesia and South Africa,* and more recently, in providing military and technological aid, as well as many advisers, for U.S. clients in Central America. An increasingly visible alliance between Israel, South Africa, Taiwan and the military dictatorships of the southern cone in South America has also proven an attractive prospect

---

* UPI, *Boston Globe*, May 16, 1982: the item reads, *in toto*, "American-made helicopters and spare parts went from Israel to Rhodesia—now Zimbabwe—despite a trade embargo during the bitter war against guerrillas, the Commerce Department has disclosed." The Labor Party journal quotes the head of South Africa's military industry as saying that Israeli "technological assistance permits South Africa to evade the arms embargo imposed upon it because of its racial policies" (*Davar*, Dec. 17, 1982). *Yediot Ahronot*, citing the *London Times*, reports that "Israeli technicians are helping South Africa evade the French military embargo" by transferring and repairing French armaments in Israeli hands (Oct. 29, 1981). Close relations with South Africa were established by the Rabin Labor government in the mid-1970s and remain warm, because, as Minister of Industry and Commerce Gidon Pat recently stated in Pretoria, "Israel and South Africa are two of the only 30 democracies in the world." Similarly, Gad Yaakovi of the Labor Party "praised the economic and 'other' [i.e., military] relations with South Africa in a television interview" in Israel, Yoav Karni reports, adding that if he had said similar things in Britain, Holland or Sweden he would have lost his membership in the Social Democratic party, though his remarks caused no distress in the Israeli Labor Party.[41]

for major segments of American power.[42] Now, Israel is surely regarded as a crucial part of the elaborate U.S. base and backup system for the Rapid Deployment Force ringing the Middle East oil producing regions.[43] These are highly important matters that deserve much more attention than I can give them here.

Had it not been for Israel's perceived geopolitical role—primarily in the Middle East, but elsewhere as well—it is doubtful that the various pro-Israeli lobbies in the U.S. would have had much influence in policy formation, or that the climate of opinion deplored by Peled and other Israeli doves could have been constructed and maintained. Correspondingly, it will very likely erode if Israel comes to be seen as a threat rather than a support to the primary U.S. interest in the Middle East region, which is to maintain control over its energy reserves and the flow of petrodollars.

Support for the concept of Israel as a "strategic asset" has, then, been considerable among those who exercise real power in the U.S., and this position has regularly won out in internal policy debate, assisted, to some extent, by domestic political pressures. But the position has not been unchallenged. There have also been powerful forces in favor of the kind of peaceful political settlement that has long been possible, a matter to which we turn in the next chapter.

Michael Klare has suggested that a useful distinction can be drawn between the "Prussians," who advocate the threat or use of violence to attain desired policy ends, and the "Traders," who share the same goals but believe that peaceful means will be more effective.[44] These are tactical assessments, and positions may therefore shift. It is, to first approximation, accurate to say that the "Prussians" have supported Israel as a "strategic asset," while the "Traders" have sought a political accommodation of some sort. The point is implicitly recognized in much pro-Israeli propaganda, for example, a full-page *New York Times* advertisement signed by many luminaries (including some who are doves in other contexts), which calls for establishment of a pro-Israel political pressure group (NAT PAC) under the heading "Faith in Israel strengthens America." To support their case, they write: "...if U.S. interests in the Middle East were threatened, it would take months to mount a significant presence there. With Israel as an ally, it would take only a few days." Similarly, Joseph Churba, Director of the Center for International Security, complains that "the left in Israel" lacks appreciation of U.S. and Israeli interests and "many in their ranks, as in the ranks of the American left, are working for the same purpose, i.e., that neither country should function as an international policeman, be it in El Salvador or in Lebanon"—the left in Israel and the U.S., then, are contributing to anti-Semitism, "threatening the interests of Jews," according to the doctrine of "the *real* anti-Semitism" developed by the Anti-Defamation

League, discussed above. Those who understand U.S. and Israeli interests believe, as Churba does, that "Western power" should be "effectively used to moderate Soviet and radical adventurism,"[45] and that the U.S. and Israel should function as international policemen in El Salvador, Lebanon and elsewhere.

The authentic voice of the "Prussians," in both cases.

The same distinction is implicit in the argument as to whether Israel's "Peace for Galilee" invasion of Lebanon strengthened the American position in the Middle East and, in general, served U.S. ends. The *New Republic* argues that this is so; hence the operation was justified. Others believe that American interests in the region have been harmed. Thus Thomas Friedman, after an extensive investigation of opinion in the Arab world, concludes that "not only did respect for many Arab leaders die in Lebanon [because they did not come to the defense of the victims of the Israeli attack, even when a besieged Arab capital was being defended by "a popular movement," as a Lebanese political scientist explained], but so too much of America's respect in the Middle East," because of the perception that "America cannot be trusted" (the director of the Kuwait Fund for Arab Economic Development) and that the U.S. supports Israel "as an instrument of its own policy." A senior Kuwaiti official, echoing widely expressed opinions, stated: "You have lost where it matters most— on the humanitarian level. Whatever respect there was in the Arab world for the United States as a moral authority has been lost."[46]

Who is right in this debate? Both sides are, in their own terms. Those who deride "the humanitarian level" and the concept of "moral authority" can argue, with some plausibility, that Israel's military might enhances the capacity of the United States to rule the region by force and violence, and that the invasion of Lebanon contributed to this end, at least in the short term. Those who have a different conception of what the U.S. role should be in world affairs will draw different conclusions from the same evidence.

2.2.3 Subsidiary Services

After the Lebanon invasion, Israel moved at once to underscore its status as a "strategic asset" and to reinforce its own position by improving relations with its allies (which, not by accident, are U.S. allies) in Africa and Latin America. Renewing relations established under CIA auspices in the 1960s (see above), Foreign Minister Yitzhak Shamir visited General Mobutu in Zaire, informing him that apart from direct military and technical support, "Israel will aid Zaire through its influence over Jewish organizations in the United States, which will help in improving [Zaire's] image."* This is a rather serious matter, since the image of this corrupt

---

* Mobutu is not the only brutal dictator to whom this idea occurred, or was suggested. In an interview with the left-wing journal *Al-Hamishmar* (Mapam), Dec. 29, 1981, Imelda

and brutal dictatorship is not of the highest, and as Mobutu complained, "the main antagonists [of Zaire] in the U.S. are Jewish members of Congress." Shamir's comforting response was: "Jews criticize us too." He went on to explain that "with the cooperation of Israeli groups and with the money that American Jews will contribute, it will be possible to aid Zaire," militarily and materially and in improving its image. General Mobutu expressed his pleasure that Israeli officers are providing military training (specifically, for his Presidential Guard) along with French and Chinese advisers. In January 1983, Defense Minister Ariel Sharon visited Zaire and an agreement was reached that Israeli military advisers would restructure Zaire's armed forces. Sharon "defended Israel's new arms and military aid agreement with Zaire today as a step towards increasing Israeli influence in Africa," UPI reported. Sharon added that the program (which must be secret) would be "a contribution to Israeli exports in arms and equipment" and that it would lead other African countries to turn to Israel for military aid.[47]

A few weeks earlier, Sharon had visited Honduras "to cement relations with a friendly country which has shown interest in connection with our defense establishment." Israeli radio reported that Israel had helped Honduras acquire what is regarded as the strongest air force in Central America, and noted that "the Sharon trip raised the question of whether Israel might act as an American proxy in Honduras." "It has also been reported that Israeli advisers have assisted in training Honduran pilots."[48] A "top-level military source" in Honduras stated that the new Israel-Honduras agreement involved sophisticated jet fighters, tanks, Galil assault rifles (standard issue for state terrorists in Central America), training for officers, troops and pilots, and perhaps missiles. Sharon's entourage included the head of the Israeli Air Force and the director-general of the Defense Ministry; they "were accorded the full measure of honors usually accorded to a visiting head of state." A government functionary stated that Sharon's visit was "more positive" than Reagan's shortly before, since Sharon "sold us arms" while "Reagan only uttered platitudes, explaining that Congress was preventing him from doing more." There is no significant domestic force to prevent Israel from "doing more," a fact deplored by Israeli doves. "The unannounced visit and military accord underline Israel's growing role as U.S. arms broker

---

Marcos, acting as an "international advocate" for her husband, explained their intention of exploiting improved relations with Israel and the influence of American Jews "to improve the tainted image [of the Philippine dictatorship] in the American media, and to combat its unpopularity in the American Congress." Commenting, journalist Leon Hadar reports the opinion of Israeli officials that other third world dictatorships with a "negative image" are also interested in using this device to obtain greater political, economic and military aid from the U.S., and that strengthening of Israel's role in the Third World is one of the "advantages" that Israel will gain from strategic cooperation with the U.S.

and proxy in crisis-ridden Central America." Meanwhile in Guatemala, Chief of Staff Mario Lopez Fuentes, who regards President Rios Montt as insufficiently violent, complained about U.S. meddling concerning human rights; "What we want is to be left at liberty," he said; "It would be preferable if the U.S. were to take an attitude similar to that of other allies such as Israel, he indicated."[49]

Israel's services in Central America have been considerable, including Nicaragua (under Somoza), Guatemala, El Salvador and Honduras, and now apparently Costa Rica since it began to draw closer to U.S. policy in the region after the election of Luis Alberto Monge in February 1982. The Israeli contributions to Guatemalan and Honduran military forces are particularly significant: in the former case, because the military regimes placed in power through U.S. intervention were finding it difficult to resist a growing insurrection while congressional human rights restrictions were impeding direct U.S. military aid to these mass murderers; and in the case of Honduras, because of Reagan's increasingly visible efforts to foment disorder and strife by supporting the Somozist National Guard based in Honduras in their forays into Nicaragua, where they torture and destroy in the manner in which they were trained by the United States for many years.[50] Before the Falklands war, it had been hoped that Argentine neo-Nazis could be employed for this purpose, as well as for improving the efficiency of state terrorism in El Salvador and Guatemala. A more reliable client-ally may be needed to perform this proxy role, however.

Charles Maechling, who led counterinsurgency and internal-defense planning for Presidents Johnson and Kennedy from 1961-66 and is now an associate of the Carnegie Endowment for International Peace, described U.S. trainees in Latin America as "indistinguishable from the war criminals hanged at Nuremberg after World War II,"* adding that "for the United States, which led the crusade against the Nazi evil, to support the methods of Heinrich Himmler's extermination squads is an outrage."[51] Apart from being an outrage, it has become difficult, because of congressional legislation. Hence the importance of Israel's contributions through the 1970s and increasingly today, in support of those who employ the methods of Himmler's extermination squads.

The congressional human rights campaign (often misleadingly attributed to the American presidency) was a reflection of the "Vietnam syndrome," a dread malady that afflicted much of the population in the wake of the Vietnam war, with such terrifying symptoms as insight into

---

* The extensive direct U.S. involvement in state terrorism in Latin America, as Maechling notes, began under the Kennedy Administration, when the mission of the Latin American military was shifted from "hemispheric defense" to "internal security," i.e., war against their own populations. The effects were catastrophic, throughout Latin America. In terms of its impact, this 1961 decision of the Kennedy liberals was one of the most significant ones of recent history. It is little known here.

the ways in which American power is used in the world and concern over torture, murder, aggression, and oppression. It had been hoped that the disease had been cured, but the popular reaction to Reagan's revival of Kennedy-style counterinsurgency showed that the optimism was premature, so Israel's contributions are perhaps even more welcome than before. It has, incidentally, been alleged that the U.S. has been opposed to Israel's Latin American ventures (e.g., that Carter opposed Israel's aid to Somoza), but this is hardly likely. There is little doubt that the U.S. could have prevented any intervention of which it did not approve, and it sometimes did so, though not in Nicaragua, where the Human Rights Administration in fact supported Somoza to the end of his bloody rule, even after the natural allies of the U.S., the Nicaraguan business community, had turned against him.

Israel's services have extended beyond the Middle East, Africa and Latin America, to Asia as well. Thus on one occasion Israel supplied American jets to Indonesia when its arms were depleted in the course of the massacre of Timorese, and the Human Rights Administration, while doing its best to provide the armaments required to consummate this mission, was still reluctant to do so too openly, perhaps fearing that the press might depart from its complicity in this slaughter.[52] Taiwan has been a particularly close ally. The Israeli press speaks of "the Fifth World"— Israel, South Africa, Taiwan—a new alliance of technologically advanced states that is engaged in advanced weapons development, including nuclear weapons, missiles, and so on.[53] We return in chapter 7 to these developments, which may by now be causing some alarm in Washington.

With Reagan's efforts to enflame the Nicaragua-Honduras border and Sharon's trip to Honduras, the Israeli connection became so visible as to call forth some official denials, duly reported as fact in the *New York Times*. Noting that Israel is "enlarging its military training missions and role as a principal supplier of arms to Central America," Leslie Gelb writes that "from every indication, the Israelis are not there, as are most of the others [Americans, PLO, Cubans, East Germans], as participants in a form of East-West confrontation or to engage in revolutionary or counterrevolutionary intrigue." These "indications" turn out to be statements to this effect by Israeli and American officials, none of whom "said that Israel was in Central America to do Washington's bidding or to help out in countries such as Guatemala where the Administration is barred from providing military aid because of civil rights abuses." Naturally, one would expect Israeli and American officials to proclaim any such arrangements openly, so their failure to do so suffices to prove that there is nothing to this canard. A State Department official comments that "we've indicated we're not unhappy they are helping out" in places like Guatemala and Honduras, "but I wouldn't say we and the Israelis have figured out together what to do."[54] Elaborate "figuring out" would seem to be superfluous, given the shared perceptions and interests, not to speak of the extremely close relations at all levels, including the military itself, military industry, intelligence, diplomatic, etc.

It is striking that Gelb assumes as a matter of course that while Israel might be pursuing its own interests (as it no doubt is, one of these being to render services to U.S. power), this could not be true of, say, Cuba, which surely has no reason to feel threatened and therefore could not be trying to break out of its "isolation" (as Israel is, he reports) by supporting friendly governments. One might have expected Gelb, perhaps, to be sensitive to this issue. He was the director of the Pentagon Papers study, which contained the astonishing revelation that U.S. intelligence, over the 20-year period surveyed, was so completely indoctrinated by Cold War propaganda that it was unable to conceive of the possibility that the North Vietnamese might have been motivated by their own perceived interests, instead of simply acting as lackeys of the USSR or China.[55]

3 American Liberalism and Ideological Support for Israel

As noted, the view of the "Prussians" has generally won out in internal policy debate. But the story is more complex. American liberalism has led the way in constructing the "blindly chauvinistic and narrow-minded" support for Israeli policy that General Peled deplores. On the same day that the U.S. and Israel stood alone against the world at the United Nations (see p. 9), the national conference of the Democratic Party "adopted a statement highly sympathetic to Israel's recent attacks in Lebanon, qualifying it only with an expression of regret over 'all loss of life on both sides in Lebanon'." In contrast, the Foreign Ministers of the European Community "vigorously condemned the new Israeli invasion of Lebanon" as a "flagrant violation of international law as well as of the most elementary humanitarian principles," adding that this "unjustifiable action" posed the risk of "leading to a generalized war."[56] This is by no means an isolated case.

In fact, the front page of the *New York Times* on that day (June 27) encapsulates the U.S.-Israel "special relationship" rather neatly. There are three adjacent columns. One is a report by William Farrell from Beirut, describing the effects of Israel's latest bombardments: cemeteries jammed, people buried in mass graves, hospitals in desperate need of supplies, garbage heaped everywhere in stinking piles, bodies decomposing under tons of rubble, buildings little more than shattered hulks, morgue refrigerators full, bodies piled on the floors of hospitals, the few doctors desperately trying to treat victims of cluster and phosphorus bombs, Israel blocking Red Cross medical supplies, hospitals bombed, surgery interrupted by Israeli shelling, etc. The second is a report by Bernard

Nossiter from New York, reporting how the U.S. blocked UN action to stop the slaughter on the grounds that the PLO might be preserved as "a viable political force." The third is a report by Adam Clymer from Philadelphia on the sympathetic support of the Democratic national conference for Israel's war in Lebanon. The three front-page reports, side-by-side, capture the nature of the "special relationship" with some accuracy—as does the lack of editorial comment.

American liberalism had always been highly sympathetic to Israel, but there was a noticeable positive shift in attitudes in 1967 with the demonstration of Israel's military might. Top Israeli military commanders made it clear not long after that Israel had faced no serious military threat and that a quick victory was anticipated with confidence—that the alleged threat to Israel's existence was "a bluff."[57] But this fact was suppressed here in favor of the image of an Israeli David confronting a brutal Arab Goliath,[58] enabling liberal humanitarians to offer their sympathy and support to the major military power of the region as it turned from crushing its enemies to suppressing those who fell under its control, while leading Generals explained that Israel could conquer everything from Khartoum to Baghdad to Algeria within a week, if necessary (Ariel Sharon).[59]

The rise in Israel's stock among liberal intellectuals with this demonstration of its military prowess is a fact of some interest. It is reasonable to attribute it in large part to domestic American concerns, in particular, to the inability of the U.S. to crush indigenous resistance in Indochina. That Israel's lightning victory should have been an inspiration to open advocates of the use of violence to attain national goals is not surprising, but there are many illusions about the stance of the liberal intelligentsia on this matter. It is now sometimes forgotten that in 1967 they overwhelmingly supported U.S. intervention (more accurately, aggression) in Indochina and continued to do so, though many came to oppose this venture for the reasons that impelled business circles to the same judgment: the costs became too high, out of proportion to the benefits that might be gained—a "pragmatic" rather than principled opposition, quite different from the stance adopted towards depredations of official enemies, the Soviet invasion of Czechoslovakia, for example. (In contrast, the central elements of the peace movement opposed aggression in both cases on principled grounds; these facts have been much obscured in the subsequent rewriting of history). Thus the appeal of Israel's efficient and successful use of force was, in fact, quite broad. It was only half-jokingly that people spoke of sending Moshe Dayan to Vietnam to show how to do the job right.

At the same time, the challenge to authority at home was regarded with much distress. A dread image was conjured up of Vietcong, Maoist fanatics, bearded Cuban revolutionaries, rampaging students, Black

Panthers, Arab terrorists and other forces—perhaps on the Russian leash—conspiring to shake the foundations of our world of privilege and domination. Israel showed how to treat Third World upstarts properly, winning the allegiance of many frightened advocates of the virtues of knowing one's place. For some, the military might that Israel displayed induced open admiration and respect, while others disguised these feelings, appealing to the alleged vulnerability of Israel before the forces it had so decisively crushed, and still others were deluded by the effective "'David and Goliath' legend" (see note 58).

Individuals have their own reasons, but tendencies of this nature are readily detectable and go a long way towards explaining the outpouring of "support for Israel" as it demonstrated its capacity to wield the mailed fist. It is since 1967 that questioning of Israel policies has largely been silenced, with effective use of the moral weapons of anti-Semitism and "Jewish self-hatred." Topics that were widely discussed and debated in Europe or in Israel itself were effectively removed from the agenda here, and a picture was established of Israel, its enemies and victims, and the U.S. role in the region, that bore only a limited resemblance to reality. The situation slowly began to change in the late 1970s, markedly so, after the increasingly visible repression under the Milson-Sharon regime in the occupied territories (only partially reported here) and the 1982 invasion of Lebanon, which offered a serious challenge to the talents of propagandists.

The immense popularity that Israel won by demonstrating its military efficiency also offered a weapon that could be usefully employed against domestic dissidents. Considerable effort was devoted to showing that the New Left supported Arab terrorism and the destruction of Israel, a task largely accomplished in defiance of the facts (the New Left, as the documentary record clearly shows, quite generally tended to support the position of Israeli doves).[60]

It is interesting that one of the devices currently used to meet the new challenge is to extend to the press in general the deceptive critique applied to the New Left in earlier years. Now, the insistent complaint is that the media are antagonistic to Israel and subject to the baleful influence of the PLO, motivated by their reflex sympathy for Third World revolutionary struggles against Western power. While this may appear ludicrous given the evident facts, neither the effort (see p. 1*, and further examples below) nor its not insignificant success in containing deviations towards a minimal degree of even-handedness will come as any surprise to students of twentieth century propaganda systems, just as there was no surprise in the earlier successes of those who were fabricating a picture of New Left support for PLO terrorism and contempt for Israel precisely because it is a democracy advancing towards socialism, one of Irving Howe's insights.[61] We are, after all, living in the age of Orwell.

One can, perhaps, offer a more sympathetic psychological interpretation. Those who are accustomed to near total dominance of articulate opinion may feel that the world is coming to an end if their control is threatened or weakened ever so slightly, reacting in the manner of an over-indulged child who is chided for the first time. Hence the wailing about the reflex sympathy of the press for the PLO and its immutable hatred of Israel when, say, there is an occasional report of the bombing of hospitals or beating of defenseless prisoners. Or the phenomenon may simply be an expression of a totalitarian mentality: any deviation from the orthodox spectrum of "support for Israel" (which includes a variety of permissible "critical support") is an intolerable affront, and it is therefore barely an exaggeration to describe slight deviation as if it were near total.

As an illustration (there are many), consider a March 1983 newsletter of the American Professors for Peace in the Middle East—a well-funded organization that is concerned about peace in the Middle East in the same sense in which the Communist Party is concerned about peace in Afghanistan—sent to its 15 Regional Chairmen and its many Campus Representatives. It warns of an "organized, centrally controlled, information plan" on the "Arab side" which is not matched by anything representing "the Israeli position." Their concern is aroused by "a list of speakers who are being toured through the university circuit . . . to present the Arab point of view," giving presentations that "smack more of propaganda than of education." "In order of frequency and virulence the speakers are: Hatem Hussaini, Edward Said, Noam Chomsky, Fawaz Turki, Stokely Carmichael, James Zogby, Hassan Rahman, Chris Giannou, M.D., Israel Shahak, and Gail Pressberg." As any observer of the American scene will be aware, these nefarious figures almost completely dominate discussion of the Middle East in the United States, and "the Israeli point of view" virtually never obtains a hearing, though, the newsletter adds, "there are doubtless many speakers who espouse the Israeli position" and would speak if only there were an opportunity for them to do so. Even if there were some truth to the paranoid concept of "an organized, centrally controlled, information plan," or the belief that these speakers are part of it, or that they "present the Arab point of view,"* it should be obvious that this would be a phenomenon of marginal

---

* Among them are people who have always been harsh critics of all the Arab states and the PLO, for example, the third in order of virulence and others as well, but it is true that no one on the list meets the approved standards of servility to the Israeli government propaganda system, so they might be considered "pro-Arab" by someone who takes this to be the criterion for distinguishing "education" from "propaganda." For the record, virtually every talk I have given on this topic has been arranged by some tiny student or faculty group, as any sane person familiar with the United States would of course know without being told.

significance in the United States and could not begin to compare with the massive pro-Israel propaganda system, of which this organization—which alone surely dwarfs anything on the "Arab side"—is a tiny element. But the frightened little men of the APPME probably believe all of this. Perhaps they are aware that this "information plan" and its agents have virtually no access to the mass media or journals of opinion, but they are right in noting that no way has yet been found to prevent them from responding to invitations at one or another college, a flaw in the American system that still remains to be addressed.

As the invasion of Lebanon proceeded, the list of those who were deliberately falsifying the facts to place Israel in a less than favorable light grew quite long, including the European press and much of the American press and television, the International Red Cross and other relief agencies, American diplomats, and in fact virtually everyone except spokesmen for the Israeli government and selected Americans returning from guided tours. The general tone is conveyed by Eliahu Ben-Elissar, chairman of the Knesset's Committee on Foreign Affairs, who received "the most applause" at the convention of B'nai Brith when he said: "We have been attacked, criticized, dirtied, besmirched... I wouldn't want to accuse the whole world of anti-Semitism, but how to explain this violent outburst."[62] A similar perception, widely shared, was expressed by Israeli Defense Minister Ariel Sharon:

> Today we are in the arena opposite the entire world. It is the people of Israel, a small and isolated people, against the entire world.[63]

This "horrible thing that is now taking place around us in the world" is "no doubt" the result of anti-Semitism, not the Lebanon war or the Beirut massacres a few days before. We return to some details of this intriguing story.

The truth of the matter is that Israel has been granted a unique immunity from criticism in mainstream journalism and scholarship, consistent with its unique role as a beneficiary of other forms of American support. We have already seen a number of examples and many more will appear below. Two examples noted earlier in this chapter offer a clear enough indication of this immunity: the Israeli terrorist attacks on U.S. facilities and other public places in Egypt (the Lavon affair), and the attack on the unmistakeably identified *U.S. Liberty* with rockets, aircraft cannon, napalm, torpedoes and machine guns, clearly premeditated, leaving 34 crewmen dead and 75 wounded in "the Navy's bloodiest 'peacetime' international incident of the 20th century"* (see notes 36, 39).

---

* Richard Smith (see note 39). He notes that the only comparable incident in recent years was the Japanese attack upon the U.S. gunboat *Panay* in 1937 in which 3 were

In both cases, the general reaction of the press and scholarship has been silence or misrepresentation. Neither has entered history as a deplorable act of terrorism and violence, either at the time or in retrospect. In the case of the bombings in Egypt, the Israeli novelist Amos Oz, writing in the *New York Times*, refers to the terrorist acts obliquely as "certain adventurist Israeli intelligence operations"—the standard formulation—in a highly regarded article on the "beautiful Israel" of pre-Begin days.[64] The nature of the attack on the *Liberty* was also evaded not only by the press fairly generally but by the government and by a U.S. Naval Board of Inquiry, though high-ranking figures had no doubt that the official report was a whitewash; former chairman of the Joint Chiefs of Staff Admiral Thomas H. Moorer, for example, states that the attack "could not possibly have been a case of mistaken identity," as officially claimed.[65]

Can one imagine that any other country could carry out terrorist bombings of U.S. installations or attack a U.S. ship killing or wounding 100 men with complete impunity, without even critical comment for many years? That is about as likely as that across the spectrum of mainstream opinion, some country (other than our own) should be depicted as guided by a "high moral purpose" through the years (see p. 5, citing *Time*, a journal regarded as *critical* of Israel), while its enemies are dehumanized and despised, and history is reconstructed to preserve the desired illusions, a topic to which we turn directly.

---

killed, and contrasts the "strangely callous" Israeli attitude with the far more forthcoming Japanese reaction, both at the personal and governmental levels. His conclusion is that nations have no friends, only interests; but he overlooks the fact that Japan could not count upon the American intelligentsia to cover up the incident, a privilege that Israel correctly took for granted.

Notes—Chapter 2
The Origins of the "Special Relationship"

1. Bernard D. Nossiter, *New York Times*, June 27, 1982.
2. *Boston Globe*, June 27; June 9, 1982.
3. Nadav Safran, *Israel: the Embattled Ally* (Harvard, Cambridge, 1978, pp. 576, 110), a study that bends over backwards to provide an interpretation sympathetic to Israel; see *TNCW*, chapter 13, for discussion.
4. G. Neal Lendenmann, "The Struggle in Congress over Aid Levels to Israel," *American-Arab Affairs*, Winter 1982-3 (see chapter 4, note 60); *Boston Globe*, Sept. 26, 1982.
5. For an attempt to assess the actual level of U.S. aid, see Thomas Stauffer, *Christian Science Monitor*, Dec. 29, 1981. For the specific details of the official record, see Yosef Priel, *Davar*, Dec. 10, 1982; Ignacio Klich, *South*, February 1983.
6. Bernard Weinraub, *New York Times*, May 26, 1982.
7. "Senate OK's foreign aid plan with $2.6b for Israel," *Washington Post—Boston Globe*, Dec. 18, 1982.
8. Ian S. Lustick, "Israeli Politics and American Foreign Policy," *Foreign Affairs*, Winter 1982/83; Amanda Mitchison, "Gift horses," *New Statesman*, Feb. 4, 1983.
9. "Israel: Foreign Intelligence and Security Services," reprinted in *Counterspy*, May-June 1982; one of the documents brought by American journalists from Iran, where they were released after the takeover of the American Embassy. Given the circumstances, one cannot be certain of the authenticity of the document, though this tends to be confirmed both by its character and the subsequent discussion concerning it. A former chief of the Israeli Mossad (essentially, the Israeli CIA), Isser Harel, accepted the authenticity of the document but condemned it as "anti-Semitic," "one-sided and malicious," "dilletantish," reflecting a tendency in the CIA to "rewrite history" at the time the report was written in 1979; Yuval Elizur, *Boston Globe*, Feb. 5, 1982, citing an interview in *Ma'ariv*.
10. General (Res.) Mattityahu Peled, *New Outlook* (Tel Aviv), May/June 1975, reporting on a visit to the United States.
11. *New Outlook* editor Simha Flapan, speaking at an October 1979 conference in Washington; cited by Merle Thorpe, Jr., President, Foundation for Middle East Peace, Hearing before the Subcommittee on Europe and the Middle East of the Committee on Foreign Affairs, House of Representatives, 97th Congress, First Session, Dec. 16, 1981 (U.S. Government Printing Office, Washington, 1982, p. 143).
12. See chapter 4, below.
13. Jessie Lurie, *Jewish Post & Opinion*, May 28, 1982.
14. On the political influence of what he calls "the Israeli lobby," see Seth Tillman, *The United States in the Middle East* (Indiana, Bloomington, 1982). Tillman was on the staff of the Senate Foreign Relations Committee with special concern for the Middle East.
15. Leon Hadar, "Labour of Love," *Jerusalem Post*, March 2, 1982.
16. See Stephen Zunes, "Strange Bedfellows," *Progressive*, Nov. 1981. He notes that passionate support for Israel combines readily with fervent anti-Semitism. See also Richard Bernstein, "Evangelicals Strengthening Bonds With Jews," *New York Times*, Feb. 6, 1983, and J. A. James, "Friends in need," *Jerusalem Post*,

Jan. 20, 1983, discussing the "potential importance of Evangelical support" in American politics and the "immense infra-structure" of media at their command, and also the vast wealth that can be tapped. *Davar* reports that the Temple Mount Fund, "established in Israel and the U.S. and financed by Christian extremists," intends to donate tens of millions of dollars to Jewish settlements in the West Bank; Jan. 23, 1983 *(Israleft News Service)*. It is a reasonable surmise— now sometimes voiced in Israel—that an Israeli-Evangelical Protestant alliance may become more prominent in Latin America, following the model of Guatemala, where the Rios Montt regime (which has succeeded even in surpassing its predecessors in its murderous barbarity) is supported by Evangelical Protestant movements and advised and supplied by Israel. See note 42.

17. Cited by Amnon Kapeliouk, *Israel: la fin des mythes* (Albin Michel, Paris, 1975, p. 219). This book by an outstanding Israeli journalist is the best account of Israeli government (Labor Party) policies from 1967-1973. Many U.S. publishers were approached for an English edition, but none was willing to undertake it.

18. Cited by Zunes, "Strange Bedfellows."

19. See, for example, *Pro-Arab Propaganda in America: Vehicles and Voices; a Handbook* (Anti-Defamation League of B'nai Brith, 1983); Thomas Mountain, "Campus anti-Zionism," *Focus* (Brandeis University), February 1983 (thanking the League for what passes as "fact"); and many handouts and pamphlets circulated in colleges around the country, typically without identification, which students distributing them often attribute to the League.

20. Benny Landau, *Ha'aretz*, July 28, 1981; Tillman, *The United States in the Middle East*, p. 65; Jolanta Benal, Interview with Meir Pail, *Win*, March 1, 1983.

21. Nathan and Ruth Ann Perlmutter, *The Real Anti-Semitism in America* (Arbor House, New York, 1982, pp. 72, 111, 116, 136, 133f., 159, 125, 231). The book also contains the kinds of defamation of critics of Israeli policies and distortion of their views that one has come to expect in such circles and that merit no more comment than similar exercises in Communist Party literature.

22. Jon Kimche, *There Could Have Been Peace* (Dial, 1973. pp. 310-11).

23. Abba Eban, *Congress Bi-Weekly*, March 30, 1973; speech delivered July 31, 1972; Irving Howe, "Thinking the Unthinkable About Israel: A Personal Statement," *New York magazine*, Dec. 24, 1973.

24. Christopher Sykes, *Crossroads to Israel: 1917-1948* (Indiana, Bloomington, 1965), p. 247.

25. Interview, *Jewish Post & Opinion*, Nov. 19, 1982. The interviewer, Dale V. Miller, interprets him, quite accurately and it seems approvingly, as holding that the "province" of criticism is "the sole right of the Israelis themselves." On Wiesel's attitudes concerning the September Beirut massacre, see pp. 386-7.

26. Safran, *Israel*, p. 571.

27. Cited by Joyce and Gabriel Kolko, *The Limits of Power* (Harper & Row, New York, 1972, p. 242).

28. For some discussion of this point, see my chapter "What directions for the disarmament movement?," in Michael Albert and David Dellinger, eds., *Beyond Survival: New Directions for the Disarmament Movement*, (South End, Boston, 1983).

29. Cited in Gabriel Kolko, *The Politics of War* (Random House, New York, 1968, p. 188), from Winston Churchill, *Triumph and Tragedy* (Houghton-Mifflin, Boston, 1953, p. 249). For more recent discussion, see Lawrence S. Wittner, *American Intervention in Greece* (Columbia, New York, 1982). The two volumes of the Kolkos' (see note 27) remain invaluable for understanding the general wartime and postwar period, though much useful work has appeared since, including much documentation that basically supports their analyses, in my

view, though the fact is rarely acknowledged; since they do not adhere to approved orthodoxies, it is considered a violation of scholarly ethics to refer to their contributions.

30. Wittner, *American Intervention in Greece*, pp. 119, 88.
31. *Ibid.*, pp. 1, 149, 154, 296; see the same source for an extensive review and documentation.
32. *Ibid.*, pp. 80, 232.
33. For discussion, see *TNCW*, chapters 2, 11, and references cited there.
34. *New York Times*, August 6, 1954; see *TNCW*, p. 99, for further quotes and comment.
35. Cited in *TNCW*, p. 457, from *MERIP Reports*, May 1981; also, *J. of Palestine Studies*, Spring 1981. The source is a memorandum obtained under the Freedom of Information Act.
36. The man in direct charge of these operations, Avri el-Ad, describes them in his *Decline of Honor* (Regnery, Chicago, 1976). See Livia Rokach, *Israel's Sacred Terrorism* (AAUG, Belmont, 1981), for excerpts from the diaries of Prime Minister Moshe Sharett concerning these events and how they were viewed at the time, at the highest level. On the ensuing political-military crisis (the "Lavon affair"), see Yoram Peri, *Between Battles and Ballots: Israeli Military in Politics* (Cambridge, 1983), an important study that undermines many illusions.
37. "Issues Arising Out of the Situation in the Near East," declassified 12/10/81, commenting on NSC 5801/1, Jan. 24, 1958.
38. Michael Bar-Zohar, *Ben-Gurion: A Biography* (Delacorte, New York, 1978, pp. 261f.).
39. *Ibid.*, pp. 315-6; Peri, *Between Battles and Ballots*, p. 80. It has been suggested that the Israeli attack on the U.S. spy ship *Liberty* was motivated by concern that the U.S. might detect the plans for this attack. See James Ennes, *Assault on the Liberty* (Random House, New York, 1979). See also Richard K. Smith, *U.S. Naval Institute Proceedings*, June 1978, who describes how "with the greatest ease...the Israeli pilots [and later torpedo boats] butchered the large, slow-moving, and defenseless *Liberty*," which was clearly and unmistakeably identified, in accordance with "a vital part of Israel's war plan," namely, "to keep foreign powers in the dark" so as to avoid "superpower pressures for a cease-fire before they could seize the territory which they considered necessary for Israel's future security"—a rather charitable interpretation, given the facts about the cease-fire and some questions that might be raised about "security."
40. See *TNCW*, p. 315 and references cited. See also the CIA study cited in note 9, which states that "The Israelis also have undertaken widescale covert political, economic and paramilitary action programs—particularly in Africa." In his report on U.S. labor leaders, Leon Hadar notes that they have been particularly "impressed with Israel's success in establishing links with the Third World, especially in Africa, to resist Soviet influence"—the latter phrase being the usual code word for resistance to unwanted forms of nationalism. That American labor bureaucrats should be pleased by support for Mobutu and the like no longer comes as any surprise. See note 15.
41. Yoav Karni, "Dr. Shekel and Mr. Apartheid," *Yediot Ahronot*, March 13, 1983. On the extensive Israeli relations, military and other, with South Africa, see *TNCW*, pp. 293f. and references cited; Israel Shahak, *Israel's Global Role* (AAUG, Belmont, 1982); Benjamin Beit-Hallahmi, "South Africa and Israel's Strategy of Survival," *New Outlook* (Tel Aviv), April/May 1977; Beit-Hallahmi, "Israel and South Africa 1977-1982: Business As Usual—And More," *New Outlook*, March 1983, with further details on the enthusiasm shown by both Labor and Likud for South Africa though Labor prefers to keep the matter

hidden, on the arrangements to use Israel for transshipment of South African goods to Europe and the U.S. to evade boycotts, etc.; Uri Dan, "The Angolan Battlefield," *Monitin*, January 1982; Carole Collins, *National Catholic Reporter*, Jan. 22, 1982; and many other sources.

42. See *TNCW*, pp. 290f. and references cited; Shahak, *Israel's Global Role;* Ignacio Klich, *Le Monde diplomatique*, October 1982, February 1983; *Washington Report on the Hemisphere* (Council on Hemispheric Affairs), June 29, 1982; *Latin America Weekly Report*, Aug. 6, Sept. 24, Dec. 17, 24, 1982; *El Pais* (Spain), March 8-10, 1983; Steve Goldfield, Jane Hunter and Paul Glickman, *In These Times*, April 13, 1983; and many other sources. It was reported recently that Kibbutz Beit Alpha (Mapam) has been providing equipment to the Chilean army *(Ha'aretz,* Jan. 7, 1983). In particular, Israel is now Guatemala's biggest arms supplier *(Economist,* April 3, 1982), helping the U.S. government evade the congressional ban on arms, and Israeli military advisers are active. The new regime in Guatemala, which has been responsible for horrible massacres, credits its success in obtaining power to its many Israeli advisers; its predecessor, the murderous Lucas Garcia regime, openly expressed its admiration for Israel as a "model" (see p. 290). On the new levels of barbarism achieved by the Rios Montt regime, see Allan Nairn, "The Guns of Guatemala," *New Republic*, April 11, 1983 (ignoring the Israeli connection, which could hardly be discussed in this journal). See references cited, and an unpublished paper by Benjamin Beit-Hallahmi, "Israel's support for Guatemala's military regimes," with information from the Israeli press. We return to further details. On Israel's arms sales as a "U.S. proxy supplier of arms to various 'hot spots' in the Third World," see *SOUTH*, April 1982. Arms sales now constitute a third of Israel's industrial exports *(Dvar Hashavua,* Aug. 27, 1982).

43. See Michael Klare, in Leila Meo, ed., *U.S. Strategy in the Gulf* (AAUG, Belmont, 1981).

44. Michael Klare, *Beyond the 'Vietnam Syndrome'* (Institute for Policy Studies, Washington, 1981).

45. Advertisement, *New York Times*, Oct. 13, 1982; Joseph Churba, letter, *New York Times*, Nov. 21, 1982. See also Steven J. Rosen, *The Strategic Value of Israel*, AIPAC Papers on U.S.-Israel Relations, 1982; AIPAC is the officially-registered pro-Israel lobbying organization in Washington.

46. Thomas L. Friedman, "After Lebanon: The Arab World in Crisis," *New York Times*, Nov. 22, 1982.

47. Tamar Golan, *Ma'ariv*, Dec. 1, 1982; Reuter, *Boston Globe*, Jan. 20, 1983; UPI, *New York Times*, Jan. 22, 1983.

48. *New York Times*, Dec. 6, 1982.

49. Susan Morgan, *Christian Science Monitor*, Dec. 14, 1982; "Guatemala: Rightists on the warpath," *Latin America Weekly Report*, March 4, 1983.

50. For one of many recent examples, see Marlise Simons, *New York Times*, Dec. 14, 1982, citing American Roman Catholic missionaries who report that "the raiders had lately been torturing and mutilating captured peasants or Sandinist sympathizers, creating the same terror as in the past," giving examples. The Somozist National Guard was trained in the U.S. Army School of the Americas in the Panama Canal Zone.

51. Charles Maechling Jr., "The Murderous Mind of the Latin Military," *Los Angeles Times*, March 18, 1982.

52. See *TNCW*, p. 429 and chapter 13, and references cited.

53. Yoav Karni, "The secret alliance of the 'Fifth World'," *Yediot Ahronot*, Nov. 22, 1981. See *TNCW*, pp. 292-3.

54. Leslie H. Gelb, "Israel Said to Step Up Latin Role, Offering Arms Seized in Lebanon," *New York Times*, Dec. 17, 1982.

55. See my *For Reasons of State* (Pantheon, New York, 1973, p. 51), for citation and discussion.

56. Adam Clymer, *New York Times*, June 27, 1982. *Le Monde*, June 11, for the full text; *Christian Science Monitor*, June 11, 1982.

57. For references, see John Cooley, *Green March, Black September* (Frank Cass, London, 1973, pp. 161-2); my *Peace in the Middle East?* (Pantheon, New York, p. 140).

58. The U.S. press appears to have ignored this important discussion among Israeli military commanders, apart from a report by John Cooley, *Christian Science Monitor*, July 17, 1972. For some discussion of what he refers to as "the 'David and Goliath' legend surrounding the birth of Israel," see Simha Flapan, *Zionism and the Palestinians* (Barnes & Noble, New York, 1979, pp. 317f.).

59. *Yediot Ahronot*, July 26, 1973; see *Peace in the Middle East?*, p. 142.

60. See my "Israel and the New Left," in Mordecai S. Chertoff, ed., *The New Left and the Jews* (Pitman, New York, 1971); and *Peace in the Middle East?*, chapter 5, including a discussion of some of the remarkable contributions of Irving Howe, Seymour Martin Lipset, and others. See chapter 5, below, for further discussion.

61. See the references of the preceding note on this and other examples, all presented without a pretense of evidence or rational argument, a stance always available when the targets are outside the approved consensus.

62. *Jewish Post & Opinion*, Nov. 5, 1982.

63. Jerusalem Domestic Television Service, Sept. 24, 1982. Reprinted in *The Beirut Massacre* (Claremont Research and Publications, New York, 1982), from the U.S. government Foreign Broadcast Information Service (FBIS).

64. Amos Oz, "Has Israel Altered its Visions?" *New York Times Magazine*, July 11, 1982. On misrepresentation of these events in scholarship, referring to Safran, *Israel*, see *TNCW*, p. 331.

65. For a rare recording of the facts in the press, see the article by staff correspondents of the *Christian Science Monitor*, June 4, 1982; also Cecilia Blalock, *ibid.*, June 22, 1982 and Philip Geyelin, *Washington Post (Manchester Guardian Weekly*, June 20, 1982). On the events and the cover-up, see references of note 39; also Anthony Pearson, *Conspiracy of Silence* (Quartet, New York, 1978) and James Bamford, *The Puzzle Palace* (Houghton Mifflin, Boston, 1982).

3

Rejectionism
and Accommodation

1 A Framework for Discussion

What have been the attitudes and policies of the major participants in the Arab-Israeli conflict, and those concerned with it, during the period since 1967, when the U.S.-Israel relationship became established in something like its present form? To approach this question sensibly, we should begin by clarifying what we take to be the valid claims of those who regard the former Palestine as their home. Attitudes towards this question vary widely. I will simply state certain assumptions that I will adopt as a framework for discussion. The first of these is the principle that Israeli Jews and Palestinian Arabs are human beings with human rights, equal rights; more specifically, they have essentially equal rights within the territory of the former Palestine. Each group has a valid right to national self-determination in this territory. Furthermore, I will assume that the State of Israel within its pre-June 1967 borders had, and retains, whatever one regards as the valid rights of any state within the existing international system. One may formulate these principles in various ways, but let us take them to be clear enough to serve at least as a point of departure.

1.1 The Concept of Rejectionism

The term "rejectionism" is standardly used in the United States to refer to the position of those who deny the right of existence of the State of Israel, or who deny that Jews have the right of national self-determination within the former Palestine; the two positions are not exactly the same because of the question of the status of Israeli Arabs and of Jews outside of Israel, but let us put these questions aside temporarily. Unless we adopt the racist assumption that Jews have certain intrinsic rights that Arabs lack, the term "rejectionism" should be extended beyond its standard usage, to include also the position of those who deny the right of national self-determination to Palestinian Arabs, the community that constituted 9/10 of the population at the time of the first World War, when Great Britain committed itself to the establishment of a "national home for the Jewish people" in Palestine.* I will use the term "rejectionism" in this non-racist sense. By "accommodation," I will mean the position that accepts the basic assumptions of the preceding paragraph. Each position can take various forms, as regards the manner in which national rights are realized, boundaries, etc.

The doctrine of self-styled "supporters of Israel," which has largely dominated discussion here, holds that the PLO and the Arab states have been undeviatingly rejectionist (apart from Egypt since 1977), while the U.S. and Israel have sought a peaceful settlement that will recognize the valid claims of all. A more recent version is that the "beautiful Israel" of earlier years, which was realizing the dream of democratic socialism and becoming "a light unto the nations," has been betrayed by Begin and his cohorts, a consequence of the refusal of the Arabs to accept the existence of Israel and the unwavering commitment of the PLO—a collection of thugs and gangsters—to the destruction of Israel, the murder of innocents, and the intimidation of all "moderate" opinion in the occupied territories.[1] Like virtually all propaganda systems, this one contains elements of truth. But the real world is rather different, as will quickly be discovered if the historical record is rescued from the oblivion to which it has been consigned.

1.2   The International Consensus

Since 1967, a broad international consensus has taken shape, including Europe, the USSR and most of the nonaligned nations. This consensus initially advocated a political settlement along approximately the pre-June 1967 borders, with security guarantees, recognized borders, and various devices to help assure peace and tranquillity; it envisioned the gradual integration of Israel into the region while it would remain, in essence, a Western European society. This is the way the basic international document, UN Security Council Resolution 242, has been under-

---

* See the next chapter for discussion of the historical backgrounds of the current conflict. Note that there was a pre-Zionist Jewish community in Palestine, consisting largely of anti-Zionist orthodox Jews whose leadership in later years supported the PLO in its call for a democratic secular state in Palestine. Thus virtually all of the indigenous population was anti-Zionist.

stood throughout most of the world, though its actual wording was left vague so that agreement on it could be achieved. As Jon Kimche comments: "Everybody subscribed to it and no one believed in it, since neither Arabs nor Israelis, Russians or Americans could agree on what the Resolution meant."[2] This is not quite accurate, since in fact there was substantial agreement along the lines of the consensus just described.* The official position of the United States, for example, was that only "insubstantial alterations" of the pre-June 1967 borders would be allowed.[4]

Note that this consensus was rejectionist, in that it denied the national rights of Palestinian Arabs, referring to them solely in the context of a refugee problem. For this reason, the PLO has refused to accept the resolution. This refusal may be a tactical error, but it is easy to understand its motivation. One would hardly have expected the World Zionist Organization, in 1947, to have accepted a UN resolution concerning Palestine that referred to Jewish interests only in terms of a refugee problem, denying any claim to national rights and any status to the Zionist movement or its organizations.

The U.S. has refused any direct contacts with the PLO on the grounds of its unwillingness to accept UN 242 and to recognize the existence of the State of Israel, basing this refusal on a "Memorandum of Agreement" concluded with Israel by Secretary of State Kissinger in September 1975. This policy raises two questions. The narrower one is that the status of the Memorandum is dubious. In testimony before the Senate Foreign Relations Committee, Kissinger specified that its terms are not "binding commitments" of the United States and warned against creating such commitments. Furthermore, "Congress specifically dissociated itself from the related memoranda of agreement," including this one.[5] More broadly, whatever one thinks about the attitude of the PLO towards UN 242, it is quite clear, as we shall see, that it has been far more forthcoming than either Israel or the U.S. with regard to an accommodationist settlement. Nevertheless, the refusal of Israel to recognize the PLO, or to accept Palestinian national rights in any meaningful form, is not invoked as a reason to refuse contacts with Israel. Unless we adopt rejectionist assumptions, then, the argument supporting the American refusal to enter into direct contacts with the PLO has no force.

From the mid-1970s, the terms of the international consensus have been modified in one significant respect: the right of the Palestinians to national self-determination has been recognized, and the consensus now includes the concept of a Palestinian state in the West Bank and Gaza Strip, with perhaps some minor border rectifications. The newer form of

---

* The resolution was accepted by Israel, Egypt, Jordan and Lebanon, and in 1972 by Syria, with the condition that Palestinian "rights" must be recognized.[3]

the international consensus overcomes the earlier rejectionism and falls under the rubric of "accommodation" in the sense of this term described above. Within the international consensus, there has been little discussion of whether such a settlement—henceforth, a "two-state settlement"—reflects higher demands of abstract justice; rather, it has been taken to be a politically realistic solution that would maximize the chances for peace and security for the inhabitants of the former Palestine, for the region, and for the world, and that satisfies the valid claims of the two major parties as well as is possible under existing conditions. One can imagine various subsequent developments through peaceful means and mutual consent towards a form of federation or other arrangements.

The existence of this international consensus, and the nature of the rejectionist forces that block its realization, are well-understood outside of the U.S., and are also recognized by knowledgeable observers here. For example, Seth Tillman (see note 5) concludes his recent study of U.S. policies in the Middle East by noting "the emergence of a *consensus* among moderates in the Arab world, the United States, and Europe—with some minority support in Israel as well—on the approximate terms of a viable and equitable comprehensive settlement in the Middle East," namely, along the lines just sketched. He notes that "the essentials of the consensus of moderates are well known, approximating in most respects the *official* policy of the United States" since 1967. "Outside of Israel, the United States, a few 'rejectionist' Arab states, and certain groups within the PLO, support for a settlement along these lines approaches worldwide unanimity," he observes.[6] A simpler but quite accurate formulation would be that U.S.-Israeli rejectionism has consistently blocked the achievement of "a viable and equitable comprehensive settlement."

I will assume the international consensus, as just sketched, to be reasonable in essence. Let us consider, then, three basic positions as points of reference: the international consensus in its more recent form, and the two varieties of rejectionism. Note that I do not mean to imply that these are the only possible solutions that merit consideration. In fact, in my view, they are not optimal. Furthermore, from 1967 to the October 1973 war, there were realistic alternatives that would have been far preferable for all concerned, I believe. These were rejected at the time, and after the 1973 war the short-term possibilities narrowed to essentially those sketched, within the framework of accommodation.[7]

Perhaps I should qualify these remarks, saying rather that I will assume the international consensus to *have been* reasonable in essence during the period under review here. It might be argued that as a result of U.S.-Israeli rejectionism, a peaceful political settlement is no longer possible, that the U.S.-financed program of Israeli settlement in the occupied territories has "created facts" that cannot be changed short of war. If persistent U.S. rejectionism brings about this state of affairs, as sooner or later it will if U.S. policy does not change course, the primary objective for Americans concerned with peace and justice will no longer be to try to bring the U.S. in line with the international consensus, now irrelevant, but to block American support for the next step: expulsion of a substantial part of the Arab population on some pretext, and conversion of Israel into a society on the South African model with some form of Bantustans, committed to regional disruption, etc. I will put these questions aside until the final chapter.

2   The Stands of the Major Actors

Adopting this as the basic framework for discussion, we can turn to consideration of the attitudes and policies of the major actors since 1967, considering in turn the U.S., Israel, the Palestinians under Israeli occupation, and the Arab states and the PLO. I will intersperse this historical account with some comment on the ways in which the history has been interpreted in the U.S., an important matter bearing on the ideological support for Israel discussed earlier, and thus bearing crucially on the development of policy and the prospects for the future.

2.1   The United States

As far as the U.S. is concerned, there has been internal conflict over the issue throughout the period. At one extreme, the Rogers Plan, announced by Secretary of State William Rogers in December 1969, reflected the international consensus of the time. At the other extreme, Henry Kissinger advocated the rejectionist position: a "Greater Israel" should refuse any accommodation, and should maintain control over the occupied territories. This position was never explicitly formulated, at least in publicly available documents, but the policies pursued conform to it quite closely and it even emerges with relative clarity from the murky rhetoric of Kissinger's memoirs, as we shall see directly. Kissinger succeeded in taking control over Middle East affairs by 1970, and the rejectionist "Greater Israel" position became U.S. policy in practice. It has remained so in essence ever since, with post-1973 modifications to which we return. Echoes of these conflicting positions remain today.

As noted in the preceding chapter, major sectors of American corporate capitalism, including powerful elements with interests in the Middle East, have supported the international consensus, as have others. But this position has lost out in the internal policy debate in favor of the concept of an Israeli Sparta serving as a "strategic asset." The persistent policy debate concerns the question of whether the fundamental U.S. interests are better served by this rejectionism, or by a move towards the international consensus, with a peaceful resolution of the conflict. In the latter view, the radical nationalist tendencies that are enflamed by the unsettled Palestinian problem would be reduced by the establishment of a Palestinian mini-state that would be contained within a Jordanian-Israeli military alliance (perhaps tacit), surviving at the pleasure of its far more powerful neighbors and subsidized by the most conservative and pro-American forces in the Arab world, in the oil-producing monarchies, which have been pressing for such a settlement for some years. This would, in fact, be the likely outcome of a two-state settlement. The internal policy debate has certainly been influenced, at the congressional level substantially so, by the highly effective pressure groups described above.

A number of prominent supporters of Israel, particularly in left-liberal circles, have adduced the fact that oil companies tend to favor the international consensus as support for their own rejectionism.[8] This makes about as much sense as the fringe right-wing argument that if Soviet leaders happen to advocate some proposal for their own purposes (say, ratification of Salt II), then we should oppose it. The further claim that Israel is being "sold out" for oil is hardly consistent with the plain facts. The levels of U.S. aid to Israel, apart from all else, tell us just to what extent Israel has been "sold out." In fact, it is the Palestinians who have consistently been "sold out" in the U.S., with no objection from left-liberal proponents of such arguments, in favor of a militarized Israel that will serve the U.S. interest of controlling the petroleum reserves of the Middle East and will provide the subsidiary services noted above. The policy debate in elite circles takes for granted, on all sides, the goal of maintaining U.S. control over Middle East petroleum resources and the flow of petrodollars. The question is a tactical one: how best to realize this goal.

U.S. policy, then, has in practice been consistently rejectionist, and still is, despite continuing internal conflict that is barely reflected in public discourse, with its overwhelmingly rejectionist commitments and assumptions.

2.2 Israel

Within Israel, the policy debate has been much narrower in scope. There are two major political groupings in Israel, the coalition dominated by the Labor Party (the Labor Alignment, *Ma'arach*), and the Likud coalition dominated by Menachem Begin's Herut Party. The Labor Party governed with various partners until 1977, the Likud coalition since then.

2.2.1 The Rejectionist Stands of Labor and Likud

Contrary to illusions fostered here, the two major political groupings in Israel do not differ in a fundamental way with regard to the occupied territories. Both agree that Israel should effectively control them; both insistently reject any expression of Palestinian national rights west of the Jordan, though the Labor Alignment contains a margin of dissidents. Thus, both groupings have been consistently rejectionist. Furthermore, both have departed from the accommodationist assumptions sketched above in another respect as well. The State of Israel, as the courts have determined, is not the state of its citizens. Rather, it is "the sovereign State of the Jewish people," where "the Jewish people consists not only of the people residing in Israel but also of the Jews in the Diaspora." Thus, "there is no Israeli nation apart from the Jewish people," in this sense.[9] Almost 1/6 of the citizens of the State of Israel are not Jews. But let us put this matter aside for now.

The professed reason for the rejectionism of the two major political groupings is security, but from this fact we learn nothing, since every action of every state is justified in these terms. Nevertheless, there is no doubt that Israel faces a serious security problem. As the matter is posed and discussed in the United States, Israel's security problem is the paramount issue. This presupposed framework of discussion again reflects the profound racism of the American approach to the topic. Evidently, the indigenous population also has a "security problem"; in fact, the Palestinians have already suffered the catastrophe that Israelis justly fear. The familiar rhetoric concerning the issue only reveals more clearly the underlying racism. Thus it is argued that the Arabs already have 22 states, so the Palestinians have no valid claim to self-determination, no claim comparable to that of the European Jews who established the State of Israel in 1948; at a similar moral level, a fanatic anti-Semite could have argued in 1947 that there are, after all, many European states, and Palestinians of the Mosaic persuasion could settle there if they were not satisfied with minority status in an Arab region. Another argument is that there are numerous Palestinians in Jordan, even in the government, so *that* should be the Palestinian state—and by similar logic, the problem could be solved by settling Israeli Jews in New York, where there are many Jews, even the Mayor and city officials, not to speak of their role in economic and cultural life. Or it is argued against the Palestinians that the Arab states have not supported their nationalist efforts, a stand that contrasts so markedly with the loving attitude that Europeans have shown towards one another during the centuries of state-formation there. Other familiar arguments are at about the same moral and intellectual level.

Dropping racist assumptions, there are two security problems to be dealt with. The international consensus in fact provides the most satisfactory, if quite imperfect, response to this dual problem in the contemporary period. In the unlikely event that it is realized, a major security problem will remain—namely, for the Palestinian state, confronted with one of the world's major military powers and dependent on the most conservative elements in the Arab world for survival. Whatever security problems Israel would then face do not compare with those it has been in the process of creating for itself by its commitment to expansionism and confrontation, which guarantees endless turmoil and war, and sooner or later, probable destruction.

Though Israel's security concerns—by now, in large part self-generated—are not to be dismissed, they do not provide an impressive basis for U.S.-Israeli rejectionism, even if we were to accept the familiar tacit assumption that the security of the Palestinians is of null import. In fact, there are other motives for Israel's rejectionism that appear to be more compelling. The territories provide Israel with a substantial unorganized labor force, similar to the "guest workers" in Europe or migrant workers in the U.S. They now play a significant role in the Israeli economy, performing its "dirty work" at low pay and without rights (it might be noted that child labor among Arabs, particularly those from the occupied territories, has caused something of a scandal in Israel, though without affecting the practice, but not here). The process of proletarianization of Arab labor in the territories, in part through land restrictions, mimics what happened in Israel itself. Shai Feldman of the Center for Strategic Studies of Tel Aviv University comments accurately that "at present, important sectors of Israel's economy cannot function without manpower provided by the West Bank and the Gaza Strip," including tourism, construction, and to some extent, agriculture. [10]

The territories are also a controlled market for Israeli goods, with export sales of about $600 million per year according to the military government. These sales are paid for in hard currency, since the territories in turn export about $100 million a year in agricultural products to Jordan and the Gulf states and receive hard currencies from them from various payments and remittances. Income to Israel from West Bank tourism may amount to about $500 million, so that the potential loss to Israel of abandoning the territories may come to over $1 billion per year. Noting these facts, Thomas Stauffer of the Harvard Center of Middle East Studies observed that there is a crucial difference between Israel's interest in these territories and in the Sinai, which had little economic value once the oil fields had been returned. [11] In addition, there was of course a major gain for Israel in the Sinai settlement, in that the most powerful state in the Arab world was removed from the Arab-Israeli conflict, so that Israel could pursue its programs in the occupied territories and Lebanon without undue concern over any military deterrence. It is, then, extremely misleading to think of the withdrawal from occupied Sinai as providing any sort of precedent for the West Bank; as for the Gaza Strip and the Golan Heights, they have been virtually excluded from the discussion of potential political settlement, within Israel or the United States.

Furthermore, Israel is now heavily dependent on the West Bank for water, a more significant commodity than oil in the Middle East. Its own water supplies are exploited to the maximum limit, and it is now estimated that about 1/3 of Israel's water is from West Bank sources.[12] An Israeli technical expert writes that "cutting Judea and Samaria [the West Bank, in Israeli parlance] off from the rest of the country" will lead to serious consequences with regard to water management; "There is no solution in sight for the water deficiency problem from the natural water resources of the area," he writes, so that "the eventual solution must be sought in the import of water from external, still unutilized resources, and in brackish and seawater desalination on a large scale" (which to date, has not proven feasible). The only unexploited source nearby is the Litani river in southern Lebanon, which Israel has long coveted and will sooner or later place under its control, quite probably, if the U.S. supports Israel's steps to impose the political arrangements of its choice in southern Lebanon.[13]

One consequence of the Lebanon war was that Israel's national water company took over "total control of the scarce and disputed water resources in the West Bank," an important move towards further integration of the territories. Zvi Barel comments that the decision contradicts the Camp David principle that control over water should fall under the autonomy provisions, and that knowledgeable sources attributed the decision to political factors, not technical considerations as was claimed.[14] It may be that this step was taken in defiance after the announcement of an unwelcome U.S. "peace plan" on September 1, 1982, to which we return. It is, incidentally, noteworthy that the U.S. September 1982 peace plan makes special mention of Israel's rights to "fair safeguards" with regard to West Bank water, the only exception specifically noted to the "real authority" that is to be granted the Palestinian inhabitants.[15]

In the past, there has been considerable conflict over utilization of the waters of the Jordan and its tributaries, and it is likely that this will continue. One potential point of conflict has to do with the Yarmuk River, a tributary of the Jordan. The Israeli press reports that current Jordanian projects will decrease the flow of Yarmuk waters to the Jordan, where they are utilized by the Israeli water system. Chief of Staff Rafael Eitan "travelled yesterday along the border with Jordan near the Yarmuk, opposite the Jordanian water project. It was not possible to learn his reaction to the Jordanian project."[16] It is unlikely that Israel will permit such a project within Jordan on any significant scale.

While the two major political groupings, Labor and Likud, agree in their overall rejectionism, they do differ in the arrangements they prefer for the occupied territories. The Labor governments pursued what has been called the "Allon Plan," proposed by Minister Yigal Allon. Its basic principles were that Israel should maintain control of the Golan Heights, the Gaza Strip, parts of the Eastern Sinai, and much of the West Bank including the Jordan valley, a considerably expanded area around Jerusalem (Arab East Jerusalem was annexed outright by the Labor government over virtually unanimous international protest, including in this case the U.S.), and various corridors that would break up the Arab West Bank and ensure Israeli control over it. In his study of this period, Israeli journalist Amnon Kapeliouk writes that the Allon Plan was "rendered operational" in 1970, and envisioned the annexation of about 1/3 of the West Bank—actually about 40%; see chapter 4, section 4.1. The centers of dense Arab settlement, however, would be excluded, with the population remaining under Jordanian control or stateless so as to avoid what is called "the demographic problem," that is, the problem of absorbing too many non-Jews within the Jewish State. To the present, this remains essentially the position of the Labor Party, as we shall see. Thus former Prime Minister Rabin, interviewed in the Trilateral Commission journal in January 1983, states that "speaking for myself, I say now that we are ready to give back roughly 65% of the territory of the West Bank and the Gaza Strip where over 80% of the population now resides,"[17] a formulation that is less extreme than most. We return to other expressions of this unchanging commitment.

The Allon Plan was designed to enable Israel to maintain the advantages of the occupation while avoiding the problem of dealing with the domestic population. It was felt that there would be no major problem of administrative control or support by Western liberal opinion (an important matter for a state that survives largely on gifts and grants from the West) as long as the second-class Arab citizens remained a minority, though such problems might arise if their numbers approached half the population. As Anthony Lewis writes, actual annexation "will change the very nature of the Jewish state, incorporating within it a large, subservient and resentful Arab population"[18]—in contrast to the 15% minority of today, to which the same terms apply.

In contrast, Begin's Likud coalition has been moving towards extension of Israeli sovereignty over the West Bank and Gaza and has virtually annexed the Golan Heights, though it was willing to return the Sinai in full to Egypt—over strong objections from leading segments of the Labor Party—in the context of the Camp David accords.* Like Labor, Likud also apparently intends to keep the Gaza Strip. Contrary to what is often assumed, Likud has not called for annexation of the West Bank and does

* Former Prime Minister Golda Meir "assailed Prime Minister Begin's government yesterday, calling his peace plan 'a concrete, terrible danger' for Israel," and "accused" Begin of "agreeing to concessions she would never stand for"; "Labor Knesset Member [former Chief of Staff] Mordechai Gur today sharply opposed the continuation of the peace process with Egypt" on the grounds that Sadat would demand return to the 1967 borders. Many Labor leaders were particularly opposed to the return of the northeast Sinai settlements that they had established.[19] See also pp. 112-3, below.

not appear to be aiming for this, at least in the short run. Extension of Israeli sovereignty—the actual announced intent—is a more subtle device, which will allow Israel to take what it wants while confining the Arab population to ever-narrower ghettoes, seeking ways to remove at least the leadership and possibly much of the population, apart from those needed as the beasts of burden for Israeli society. Outright annexation would raise the problem of citizenship for the Arabs, while extension of sovereignty, while achieving the purposes of annexation, will not, as long as liberal opinion in the West is willing to tolerate the fraud.

The logic of the Likud position does, however, appear to be that the Arab population must somehow be reduced, and it has been alleged that then Defense Minister Ariel Sharon "hopes to evict all Palestinians from the West Bank and Gaza and drive them into Jordan."[20] Sharon is not entirely alone in this view, though his position, if correctly reported, is extreme. The idea that the solution to the problem is for the Palestinians to leave—far away — has deep roots in liberal and socialist Zionism, and has recently been reiterated by American "democratic socialists" as well as by Israeli leaders sometimes regarded as doves. We return to various expressions of such ideas, in virtually all shades of Zionist thought, and to current policies in the occupied territories.

While the two major political groupings do differ in the ways in which they formulate their rejectionist positions, neither has been explicit about the matter—which is easy enough to understand, given Israel's dependence on liberal opinion in the West—and it is therefore not easy to formulate this difference clearly. Thus as noted, while the policies of the Likud government have regularly been interpreted as leading to annexation by the Labor opposition and others, in fact, Begin calls for the establishment of Israeli "sovereignty" over the currently occupied territories. Under this Israeli sovereignty, those Arabs who remain would have some form of local autonomy. Presumably, they and their descendants would not receive Israeli citizenship under this arrangement, so that the "demographic problem" would not arise. Or, perhaps, if their numbers are sufficiently restricted they might opt for either Israeli or Jordanian citizenship, while Israeli sovereignty remains in force over the entire territory in question. Surely it is intended by both Labor and Likud that the Jewish settlers will retain Israeli citizenship. Under the Labor Alignment plan, the inhabitants would be Jordanian citizens or stateless, but effectively under Israeli control.

In essence, then, the two programs are not very different. Their difference lies primarily in style. Labor is, basically, the party of the educated Europe-oriented elite—managers, bureaucrats, intellectuals, etc. Its historical practice has been to "build facts" while maintaining a low-keyed rhetoric with conciliatory tones, at least in public. In private, the position has been that "it does not matter what the Gentiles say, what matters is what the Jews do" (Ben-Gurion) and that "the borders [of Israel] are where Jews live, not where there is a line on a map" (Golda Meir).[21] This has been an effective method for obtaining the ends sought without alienating Western opinion—indeed, while mobilizing Western (particularly American) support.

In contrast, the mass base of the Likud coalition is largely the underclass, the lower middle class, and the workforce, the Sephardic population of Arab origin, along with religious-chauvinist elements, including many recent immigrants from the U.S. and the USSR; it also includes industrialists and many professionals. Its leadership is not so attuned to Western styles of discourse and has frequently been willing to flaunt its disregard for the hypocritical Gentile world, often in a manner regarded as openly insulting in the West, including the U.S. For example, in response to Reagan's September 1982 call for a settlement freeze, the Likud leadership simply announced plans for 10 new settlements while Begin sent a "Dear Ron" letter with a lesson on "simple historic truth."[22] Under somewhat similar circumstances in the past, Labor responded not by establishing new settlements but by "thickening" existing ones or by establishing military outposts which soon became settlements, meanwhile keeping to conciliatory rhetoric. The more devious Labor approach is much more welcome to the West, and raises fewer problems for "supporters of Israel."

In the case of the Reagan September 1982 proposals, Labor's response was one of qualified interest. In part, the reason was the traditional difference in style; in part, it reflected the fact that Reagan's proposals, while vague in essentials, could be interpreted as compatible with Labor's ideas in part, though they certainly were not consistent with the Likud demand for total "sovereignty." Furthermore, Labor's show of statesmanlike interest might, it was hoped, strengthen its dismal electoral prospects by discrediting the government. Labor speaks of "territorial compromise" or "trading peace for territory," terms that have a pleasant sound to American ears, though the reality they disguise is not very different from Likud's "sovereignty." In fact, the "compromise" and "trade" are explicitly rejectionist positions. There have already been two "territorial compromises" in Mandatory Palestine: the 1947 UN General Assembly resolution that recommended partitioning Palestine into a Palestinian and a Jewish State, and the 1949 armistice agreement that divided the Palestinian State, with about half annexed by Israel and the rest annexed by Jordan or administered by Egypt (see chapter 4). A further "compromise," in terms of some version of the Allon Plan, simply eliminates the right of Palestinian self-determination.

It is often alleged that there was, in fact, an earlier "territorial compromise," namely, in 1922, when Transjordan was excised from the promised "national home for the Jewish people." In fact, in 1922 "the

Council of the League of Nations accepted a British proposal that Trans-jordan should be exempted from all clauses in the mandate providing for...the development of a Jewish National Home in Palestine," a decision that is difficult to criticize in the light of the fact that "the number of Jews living there permanently in 1921 has been reliably estimated at two, or according to some authorities, three persons."[23]

2.2.2 The Legacy of the Founding Fathers

Both political groupings, then, have been consistently rejectionist, willing to grant no national rights to the indigenous Arab population. Israel's consistent rejectionism is founded on the attitudes expressed by the long-time leader of the Labor Party, David Ben-Gurion, when he stated that the Palestinian Arab shows no "emotional involvement" in this country:

> Why should he? He is equally at ease whether in Jordan, Lebanon or a variety of places. They are as much his country as this is. And as little.[24]

Elsewhere, "Ben-Gurion followed Weizmann's line when he stated that: 'there is no conflict between Jewish and Palestinian nationalism because the Jewish Nation is not in Palestine and the Palestinians are not a nation'."[25] Essentially the same view was expressed by Moshe Dayan at a time when he was a principal spokesman for the Labor Party. The cause of the Palestinians (which he professed to understand and appreciate) is "hopeless," he intimated, so they should establish themselves "in one of the Arab countries." "I do not think," he added, "that a Palestinian should have difficulties in regarding Jordan, Syria or Iraq as his homeland."[26] Like Ben-Gurion, Dayan was asserting that the Palestinians, including the peasantry, had no particular attachment to their homes, to the land where they had lived and worked for many generations, surely nothing like the attachment to the land of the Jews who had been exiled from it 2000 years ago.

Similar views were expressed by Prime Minister Golda Meir of the Labor Party, much admired here as a grandmotherly humanitarian figure, in her remark that:

> It was not as though there was a Palestinian people in Palestine considering itself as a Palestinian people and we came and threw them out and took their country away from them. They did not exist.[27]

Elsewhere, she describes the Palestinian problem as merely an "invention of some Jews with distorted minds."[28]

In accordance with these dominant views concerning the Palestinians, an Israeli court ruled in 1969 that the Palestinians "are not a party to the conflict between Israel and the Arab States," and Foreign Minister Abba Eban of the Labor Party (a well-known dove) insisted that the Palestinians "have no role to play" in any peace settlement,[29] a position that received no major challenge within the Labor Party when it governed or in opposition. Simha Flapan concludes his study of this question with the observation that "The Palestinians were never regarded as an integral part of the country for whom long-term plans had to be made, either in the Mandatory period or since the establishment of the state." This was the most "lasting impact" of "Weizmann's legacy."[30] This appears to be quite a realistic judgment, as far as the mainstream of the Zionist movement was concerned. We return to further discussion in the next chapter.

These positions, which have been consistently maintained, amount to rejectionism in its clearest form, though the matter is rarely seen in this light in the U.S. Both major political groupings in Israel have taken the position that Jordan is a Palestinian state, and that Israel will accept no third state between Israel and Jordan—the "Jordanian-Palestinian Arab State" in the official words of the Labor Party,[31] the "Palestinian State" in Likud rhetoric. This is not, of course, the position of what might reasonably be called the "peace movement," a small but significant minority that adheres to the international consensus. On its actual scale, see chapter 7, section 4.1.1.

2.2.3 The Disguise

The consistent rejectionism of both major political groupings in Israel is disguised in the United States by two main devices. First, as already noted, the concept of "rejectionism" is restricted to the denial of Jewish national rights, on the implicit racist assumption that the indigenous inhabitants of Palestine do not have the human rights that we naturally accord to Jews. Second, it is observed—quite accurately—that Israel has always been more than willing to negotiate with the Arab *states*, while they have not reciprocated this willingness. It requires barely a moment's thought to perceive that Israel's willingness in this regard is strictly rejectionist, since the Palestinians are excluded. When a framework for negotiations has been proposed that includes the Palestinians, Israel has always refused to participate. Thus Israel's apparently forthcoming position with regard to negotiations, much heralded in the U.S., is simply part and parcel of its commitment to the rejection of Palestinian rights, an elementary point that is regularly suppressed in discussion of the issue in the U.S. Like the term "territorial compromise," so also the appealing phrase "negotiated settlement" has become a disguise for outright rejectionism in American discourse.

When these simple points are understood, we can interpret properly the pronouncements of Israel's American propagandists. For example, the general counsel to the Anti-Defamation League of B'nai Brith (see pp. 14f.), Arnold Forster, condemns current U.S. government policy because he sees the U.S. as insisting that an Israel-Lebanon peace must be part of a more "comprehensive" settlement:

> Absurdly, the Israelis are made to appear dreadful simply because they ask of Lebanon open borders, tourism both ways, trade relations, negotiations in their respective capitals[32] and regular political contacts—all the stuff of a healthy, peaceful relationship between countries. Our Government argues that if genuine peace is achieved only between Israel and Lebanon, the pressure would then be off the Jewish state to resolve the West Bank Palestinian problem along the lines of President Reagan's fading peace plan. Secretary Shultz's clever tactic is therefore to deny Israel the peace with Lebanon it hungers for—unless Israel simultaneously withdraws from the West Bank.[33]

This argument will no doubt seem impressive to those who share the assumptions of this well-known civil rights group, specifically, the assumption that Palestinians do not have the same rights as Jews. Dropping these assumptions, we see at once that Israel's proposals, which Forster advocates, would simply take another long step towards the extension of Israeli sovereignty over the occupied territories. In short, Forster is simply presenting a brief for a "Greater Israel" and for the denial of elementary human rights to the Arabs of Palestine. Furthermore, the "healthy, peaceful relationship" that Israel seeks to impose on Lebanon by force would be one that subordinates Lebanon—at the very least, southern Lebanon—to Israeli interests, as a market for Israeli goods, a potential source of cheap labor and water, etc., a fact that is plain when we consider the relations of economic and military power and that was well on its way towards realization as Forster wrote (see chapter 6, section 7.1). This "healthy, peaceful relationship," then, would be of the sort imposed by many other "peace-loving states" during the colonial era, for example, the relationship imposed on India by benevolent Britain (after the destruction of native Indian enterprise) or on China at the time of the Opium Wars, to mention two of many classic examples. All of this is so transparent that it might be surprising that the general counsel of an alleged human rights organization would be willing to make such statements publicly—until one recalls that this is the *New York Times*, with an audience of educated readers for whom the underlying racist assumptions are so firmly implanted that the obvious conclusions will generally not be drawn. As to whether Forster is correct in his belief that the U.S. government is really dropping its rejectionist stance, that is another matter; the increase in aid to Israel, passed by Congress at exactly that time, surely belies this assumption, as already noted.

2.3   The Population of the Occupied Territories

The third party to be considered is the population of the occupied territories, the Gaza Strip and the West Bank—the latter, called "Judea and Samaria" by both the Labor government and Likud, though the U.S. press regularly attributes this usage, which is taken to imply a biblically-endorsed right of possession, to Menachem Begin.* In fact, reference to biblical rights is common in both political groupings. Thus Shimon Peres, the socialist leader of the Labor Party, accepted Begin's rationale for retaining the West Bank, writing: "There is no argument in Israel about our historic rights in the land of Israel. The past is immutable and the Bible is the decisive document in determining the fate of our land." This doctrine apparently causes few raised eyebrows in the Socialist International, in which Peres and his Labor Party are honored members.[35] Nevertheless, Peres advocates "territorial compromise" in accordance with the Allon Plan, to free Israel of an unwanted Arab population which "would eventually endanger the Jewish character of Israel. . ."[36]

2.3.1 Attitudes under Occupation

The attitudes of the indigenous population are generally ignored in the U.S., on the assumption—racist in essence—that they simply do not count. In the early years of the occupation, the Labor government refused to permit any independent political expression on the part of the population, even rejecting the request of pro-Jordanian "notables" to form an anti-PLO grouping, a fact revealed in 1974 by the former military commander of the West Bank, General (now President) Chaim Herzog (breaking government censorship), and arousing no concern among American liberals and democratic socialists, firm supporters of the Labor Alignment.[37]

In 1976, relatively free elections were permitted for municipalities in the West Bank. The elected candidates soon made it clear that they regarded the PLO as their sole legitimate representative. In recent years, the Begin government and others have attributed this outcome to PLO pressure and intimidation. No such claims were made at the time. On the contrary, the elections were regarded as a crowning achievement of the

---

* The same error is made by commentators who should know better, for example, Rabbi Arthur Hertzberg, who describes the terms "Judea" and "Samaria" as those that "the Likud and its sympathizers prefer," in an interchange that exhausts the usual range of tolerable opinion: Hertzberg (with the assent of Irving Howe) representing the position of "Jewish moderates, headed by the Labor Party," and Ivan Novick, President of the Zionist Organization of America, representing the Likud position.[34]

"benign occupation." There was, in fact, interference in the electoral process, namely, by Israel, in favor of more conservative elements. Two nationalist candidates were expelled in violation of the governing military regulations, to ensure the election of more acceptable opponents. The PLO took no position with regard to the elections, Amnon Kapeliouk observes in a detailed commentary on them.[38] He also points out that a significant political structure arose in the territories at the time, regarding the PLO as its representative and prepared to reach a political settlement with Israel. Instead of recognizing the Palestinian right to self-determination alongside of Israel, however, "the Rabin [Labor] government opened the door to Gush Emunim," the fanatic religious-chauvinist settlers in the occupied territories.

Since that time the inhabitants of the occupied territories have made known their support for the PLO, and for an independent Palestinian state, on every possible occasion. To cite only two of many examples, the mayors of West Bank towns sent a letter to Secretary of State Cyrus Vance when he toured the area in 1977, stating that the Palestinian people had chosen as "its sole legal representative, irrespective of the place . . . the PLO under the leadership of Mr. Arafat,"[39] an act of no small courage given the nature of the occupation—people generally regarded as moderates had been expelled for much less. Turning to the present, after the PLO had been evacuated from Beirut in September 1982 (so that alleged PLO intimidation was now a thing of the past), a group of "Palestinian personalities" in the occupied territories were asked for their evaluation of the outlook, among them Elias Freij (the last remaining mayor of a major town, the others having been dismissed by Israel) and Rashad Shawa (the conservative and pro-Jordanian dismissed mayor of Gaza); Freij and Shawa are represented here as leading figures of the "moderate" nationalist alternative to the PLO. They were uniform, including Freij and Shawa, in their support for the PLO, some holding that support for the PLO had in fact increased as a result of the Lebanon invasion (Shawa).[40]

An indication of current opinion in the West Bank (no one doubts that the results would be similar in the Gaza Strip) is given by the results of a poll undertaken by the PORI Institute, a leading public opinion research organization in Israel, in March 1982.[41] The results will come as no surprise to people who have been following developments in the occupied territories since 1967.* 98% were in favor of an independent

---

* The actual wording of the questions is not given. Therefore one does not know exactly how to interpret the *Time* paraphrase: "As might be expected, 98% of the respondents said that they favored the creation of a Palestinian state. Yet only 59% agree with the P.L.O. that such a state should encompass 'all of Palestine' (*i.e.*, including Israel); 27% seem ready to accept a Palestinian state made up only of the West Bank and Gaza Strip" (the actual PLO position, for several years). Surely, however, no sensible person can have much doubt that whatever the preferences of the population, as expressed in the Israeli poll, they would be more than willing to be relieved of Israeli or Jordanian occupation and to exercise their right of self-determination in an independent state—for the large majority of them, a state organized by the PLO—set up alongside of Israel and coexisting with it.

Palestinian state, and 86% said that they wanted this state to be run solely by the PLO. Of other figures, the most popular (68% support) was Nablus Mayor Bassam Shak'a, dismissed shortly before by West Bank "Civilian Administrator" Menachem Milson as part of his general attack on free political expression. Other pro-PLO figures on the West Bank received various degrees of support. At the very bottom was Mustafa Dudin, who received the support of 0.2% of the population. Among Arab leaders, King Hussein of Jordan ranked low, admired by 4%. King Hussein is the U.S. choice for representative of the inhabitants of the West Bank, while Dudin is the choice of the government of Israel and its supporters here. He is the head of the "Village Leagues" created by Israel in an effort to replace the elected leadership, and is claimed to represent the rural majority of the population—the "silent majority." He is regularly described in the U.S. press as a "moderate," and it is claimed that only PLO terror prevents the population from supporting him openly; evidently, fear of the PLO is so great that close to 100% of the population were afraid to state their support for Dudin secretly and anonymously in an Israeli-run poll.

Perhaps we might pause for a moment to consider the two personalities who are, respectively, the most popular (apart from the PLO) and the least popular in the West Bank: dismissed Mayor Bassam Shak'a and Mustafa Dudin. Shak'a was the victim of a terrorist attack in June 1980 in which both of his legs were blown off by an IDF bomb. No progress has been made towards discovering the identity of the assailants, though it seemed a relatively straightforward matter as several Israeli journalists pointed out, if only because the army had records of people who had access to the sophisticated type of explosives used. It is generally assumed that the terrorists were Jewish settlers in the area (see, for example, the comments of the *Ha'aretz* journalist cited above, p. 12). When violent acts are carried out against Jewish settlers, houses of families of suspects are demolished, curfews imposed, subjects interrogated (and, they allege, often tortured), etc., while U.S. journals fulminate about Arab terrorism. In fact, even stone throwing can lead to curfews and other punishments, as, for example, the *Times* casually observes in reporting an incident in which yet another Arab youth was killed by Israeli soldiers firing at his feet.* But in the case of the attack on Mayor Shak'a and others, it was difficult to detect even signs of an investigation, and obvious clues were

---

* The report states that Samir Ghazal Taflak, 19 years old, was killed by a bullet in the chest (another youth was seriously injured) when, according to an army spokesman, Israeli soldiers "had fired at the feet of youths who had hurled rocks at an Israeli bus, smashing one window." Hundreds of students were protesting a curfew imposed on a camp of 12,000 people "after youths threw rocks at Israeli vehicles in the area," one of a series of curfews in the past two months. "The students waved the flag of the Palestine Liberation Organization and photos of its leader, Yasir Arafat, the sources said." "About seven weeks ago a 14-year-old Nablus youth was shot and killed by a [Jewish] settler of nearby Elon Moreh after he had stoned the settler's car."[42]

not pursued.[43] Ze'ev Schiff wrote at the time in *Ha'aretz* that it would be politically impossible for the government to arrest and convict the guilty parties because these West Bank settlers had too much political support.[44] *Ha'aretz* also reported that the suspects were believed to be Jewish extremists who used sophisticated IDF equipment, citing intelligence sources. The bombings (Mayor Karim Khalef of Ramallah was also seriously injured; both were subsequently dismissed by the Milson administration) were praised in the journal *Nekudah* of the religious West Bank settlers, and the spokesman for American Rabbi Kahane's Kach Party announced at a press conference that they were in retaliation for the murder of Israeli settlers in Hebron a few weeks earlier. Six Jewish suspects were under investigation by the Israeli secret police (Shin Bet), but according to Knesset Member Shulamith Aloni, they said that "the Jews responsible are part of a close-knit group that has been impenetrable." Stories about the affair are routinely censored in the Israeli press. Many journalists following the case, including Danny Rubinstein of *Davar*, suspect that a high-ranking government official was involved and that the Shin Bet is part of a cover-up. "Most Israelis were indifferent to the mayors' fates after the attacks anyway," and "there was no public outcry or pressure on the government to conduct a full-scale inquiry."[45]

After the terrorist attack and his subsequent dismissal, Shak'a was subjected to considerable government harassment. He was refused permission to travel to Holland on the grounds that "he will use the visit for the dissemination of false information about Israel and will present Israel as oppressing public figures in the [occupied] territories," according to representatives of the security forces. There have been many other examples, another recent one being the denial of an exit visa to his daughter to enable her to resume her studies at North Carolina State University in October 1982.[46] At the same time, Shak'a's Israeli guards refused to permit journalists from *Ha'aretz* and the *Jerusalem Post* to interview him. A week later, there had been no action by the newspapers or the Press Association, leading one outraged Israeli citizen to compare this "shocking incident" to what happens in the USSR.[47]

2.3.2 The Carrot and the Stick

Let us turn now to the least popular personality in the West Bank, Menachem Milson's protegé Mustafa Dudin, head of the Village Leagues. It should be noted at once that journalists who cover the West Bank for the Hebrew press have no illusions about the support for Milson's Village Leagues. Danny Rubinstein of *Davar* writes that "The vast majority of the Arab population, led by city mayors, leaders of unions and other public figures in the West Bank, recognized the Israeli attempt to undermine the P.L.O.'s authority [by establishing the Leagues], and denounced it in the East Jerusalem newspapers, in conferences and in declarations." He describes the measures adopted by the Sharon-Milson administration to impose the rule of the Leagues by giving them "vast financial support" and compelling inhabitants to turn to them for the needs of daily life.[48]

Exploiting its military success in Lebanon, Israel expanded the Village Leagues and formed them into a regional organization, assigning them the role of representative of the Palestinians in the occupied territories for dealings with Israel. On the invitation of the Israeli authorities in charge, Danny Rubinstein attended the meeting in Hebron where this "political task" was announced publicly for the first time. The representatives came armed and substantial Israeli military forces surrounded the area. Dozens of villagers outside stood up to cheer on command. The speakers praised former Civilian Administrator Menachem Milson, who was responsible for the worst atrocities in the West Bank, for "his service to the inhabitants of the West Bank...his outstanding personality and warm compassion, all in eloquent rhetoric," some so effusive that the audience burst out in laughter. It was, Rubinstein writes, "a sad and oppressive day in Hebron."[49]

Meanwhile in the *Boston Globe*, we read only that Milson "received thunderous ovations at the first conference of the West Bank 'Village Leagues' he helped foster," referring to the same meeting, a sure sign of his great popularity and the support for the Leagues on the West Bank—the immense popularity shown by the PORI Institute poll for the head of the Leagues, Mustafa Dudin, is still another sign. Milson is referred to in the *Globe* as a "Mideast Maverick," who "calls for a Palestinian role in the West Bank," a leading partisan of the oppressed Palestinians, evidently.[50]

This is surely the appropriate characterization, as 1984 approaches, for the man who along with General Sharon initiated the most brutal period of repression in the West Bank, "a reign of terror," in the words of the Israeli dove Uri Avneri, who describes Milson as a poor copy of "his former master, Ariel Sharon": "So far as compulsive lying, boasting and impudence are concerned, he is merely Sharon's pocket edition," Avneri continues, going on to recall the measures he instituted in an effort to break the will of the Palestinians, including formation of "the hated 'Leagues,' which became the representatives of the Israeli conquest for the public," "armed gangs of quislings" largely constituted of "the human refuse of the villages, known hooligans and criminals, who received weapons from the military government in order to create an atmosphere of terror."[51] In short, a true "Mideast Maverick," much to be admired for his defense of Palestinian rights.

To illustrate Avneri's description, Professor Milson, in his *Globe* interview, states that "partly due to my influence, the fact is that no house was demolished in the West Bank." In fact, two weeks after his November 1, 1981 takeover, on November 16, four houses were destroyed in Beit Sahur in a collective punishment, and one house was destroyed in Bethlehem, the home of a man suspected of throwing a molotov cocktail at a bus.[52] Milson assumed, correctly no doubt, that his statement would pass unchallenged in the United States, where he is presented as an advocate of peace and conciliation. He might, however, have argued correctly that the Labor Party resorted to this technique of collective punishment in the case of people suspected of some act of violence (or resistance, depending on one's point of view) far more extensively than he did.

The West Bank correspondent of *Ha'aretz*, Zvi Barel, reports General Sharon's statement that the League members "are not collaborators in the usual sense of the word." Barel agrees, on the grounds that "no past collaborators had enjoyed such wide government support as these people receive." He describes how they are not only provided with arms to terrorize the population, but are even given "the privilege of making the [Israeli] civil administration commit illegal acts to praise the name of the Village Leagues," describing how the administration acts to serve "their desire for revenge." Barel also illustrates how West Bank inhabitants are compelled to submit to the rule of the Milson-Dudin Leagues in order to survive, citing the case of Abu Adnan of the West Bank town of Halhul, whose mayor, Muhammed Milhem (who had called for a peaceful two-state political settlement), was also dismissed by the Milson administration. Adnan had sent his son (born and educated in the West Bank) to Greece for medical studies. His son was not permitted to return on the pretext that he was away when a census was taken; removal of the educated population has been a standard procedure of the occupation since the beginning. Requests to permit his son at least to visit were denied by the Milson administration. Finally, Adnan turned to the Village Leagues, signing a form stating his request to become a member, and offering a "donation" of 500 Israeli shekels. He at once received permission for his son to visit.[53] The Hebrew press contains many similar examples illustrating how the Leagues gain their popularity.

In testimony before Congress, a member of an American study group returning from a Middle East tour reported that "the vast majority" of the population "dislike the Unions" (the Village Leagues) but "feel forced to deal with them" because of the arrangements imposed by the Military Government. The Leagues are "widely feared and are dealt with only as individuals and groups feel pressured to do so." "The greatest fear of West Bankers is that these Union of Villages officials will be selected by the Israelis as the 'moderate' Palestinians who will 'negotiate' autonomy under the Camp David accords, and thus give the appearance of legitimacy to an autonomy agreement." It is this fear that was realized in the subsequent meeting that Rubinstein reported. "Shlomo Gazit, former Chief of Israeli Intelligence, has stated that the setting up of the Village Leagues established a network of quislings to serve the purposes of the government and was not in the interest of Israeli security. He has called for the dissolution of the Village League program."[54] It is good to know that Congress was well-informed when it increased the enormous subsidy to Israel to still higher levels to pay for these admirable measures.

The civilian administration of "Mideast Maverick" Menachem Milson, which gave Dudin a position of power in the occupied territories and a position of prominence as a noted moderate in the United States, began on November 1, 1981. The "reign of terror" that began at once received considerable press coverage in the United States at the time, but, memories being short and prejudices strong, the facts were quickly forgotten. The Israeli *Black Book* (see note 52) gives a detailed account of the first sixth months, along with testimony by Palestinians and Israeli soldiers. "The civil administration orchestrated by Professor Milson," it reports, "is nothing but another attempt to revive an old, well-known colonial method in a new 'original' Israeli form," laying the basis for "an Israeli Bantustan, which imposes on the Palestinians the role of hewers of wood and drawers of water for Israeli society." It "intends to destroy every social institution in the occupied territories in two ways: first, by harassing municipal councils, labor unions, and universities which mold national-political culture, and second, by constructing what seems to be an alternative power center in the shape of the Village Leagues," basing itself on the assumption that the Palestinians are "primitive 'natives' who are easily pacified when the occupier buys off a few notables in their villages." Its techniques are these: "leaders and activists are arrested, inhabitants are expelled, meetings are banned, demonstrators are detained, and the demonstrations themselves are brutally dispersed; curfews and confinements are imposed, houses are blown up, and quislings from the Village Leagues are used in a terror campaign against the population; universities and newspapers are shut down, journalists are detained or prevented from interviewing leaders, who, in turn, are not allowed to be interviewed anyway; censorship is applied to both newspapers and books, and humiliation, harassment, and terror are inflicted on the population by the Jewish settlers in towns and villages alike." The *Black Book* then presents extensive evidence, in a virtually day-by-day account. These practices, in fact, go back to the earliest days of the occupation, but there is no doubt that they escalated to new levels of violence under the regime of the "Mideast Maverick" and his chosen instrument. Small wonder that Dudin's support in the West Bank amounted to 0.2% by March 1982, after six months of Milson's beneficence. We return to the historical context, and some specific illustrations, in the next chapter.

The conception of the Palestinians as primitive "natives" who can easily be bought off has deep roots in Zionist history, and is a natural concomitant to "Weizmann's legacy," as expressed by Ben-Gurion and others (see p. 52, and for more detail, the next chapter). It was observed long ago by visitors to Palestine. The American journalist Vincent Sheean, for example, arrived in Palestine in 1929 as an avid Zionist sympathizer, and left a few months later as a harsh critic of the Zionist enterprise. He found that the Jewish settlers "had contempt [for the Arabs] as an 'uncivilized race,' to whom some of them referred as 'Red Indians' and others as 'savages'," and felt that "We don't have to worry about the Arabs" who "will do anything for money." They looked upon the indigenous population as "mere squatters for thirteen centuries" so that it should "be feasible for the Zionists, by purchase, persuasion and pressure, to get the Arabs out sooner or later and convert Palestine into a Jewish national home," an attitude which he thought was "from their own point of view . . . perilous in the extreme." Sheean "could not believe that the Arabs of Palestine were so different from other Arabs that they would welcome the attempt to create a Jewish nation in their country."[55] These attitudes remain alive today, expressed in the actions of the Milson administration and its predecessors in the occupied territories, in the common view of Israeli leaders and others that the Palestinians can readily find a place in some other Arab land, and in the general disregard in the West—particularly the United States—for Palestinian rights.

It might also be noted that even Mustafa Dudin—the archetypal quisling—has called for total Israeli withdrawal from the occupied territories and the evacuation of all Jewish settlements established there since 1967. How this stand results from PLO intimidation has not yet been explained. Furthermore, well after the expulsion of the PLO from Beirut and southern Lebanon, Palestinian demands for an independent state and rejection of Israeli-imposed "autonomy" remained unchanged, and "with the notable exception of Mustafa Dudin, . . . very few Palestinians think they can reach their objectives by negotiating with Israeli officials." In January 1983, the leader of the Ramallah League, Riyad el-Hatib, called for an independent Palestinian state, and the chairman of the Hebron area Village Leagues, Muhammad Nasser, called upon Israel to freeze settlements, describing them as "an obstacle to peace" between Israel and the Palestinians.[56] In the meeting that Rubinstein attended, representatives of the Leagues called for measures to prevent migration of Palestinians from the West Bank ("a clear anti-government goal," Rubinstein observes), while Dudin and others urged the Israeli military authorities to facilitate the return of Palestinian refugees, primarily from Lebanon, to the West Bank, a position with only the most marginal support within Israel. Again, it seems that the PLO must have a long arm.

2.3.3 The "Peace Process"

Returning to the PORI Institute survey of West Bank opinion, also of interest were the attitudes expressed towards the two Israeli political groupings. 0.9% preferred to see Begin's Likud in power, while 2% preferred the Labor Party. 93% registered complete indifference. As for Camp David, 2% felt it helped the Palestinian cause, while 88% regarded it as a hindrance.

In news reporting as in editorial commentary in the United States, the arrangements set in motion by the Camp David accords are known simply as "the peace process." Evidently, those whose lives are at stake do not share the assumptions that underlie this usage, which simply reflects a tacit acceptance of the U.S. propaganda system by the media and scholarship.

It is also quite likely that the inhabitants of the occupied territories understand some facts about "the peace process" that are little noted here. Specifically, it is plain, on the ground, that the government of Israel never had the slightest intention of joining "the peace process" in anything other than a rhetorical sense, beyond the Sinai agreements, which had the merit of giving Israel a free hand elsewhere by effectively excluding Egypt from the conflict. Not only is this obvious from the settlement program and the internal repression, but it is even clear from the official record, a fact that Abba Eban has pointed out. He cites the official "Government policy guidelines" adopted by the Knesset (by a single vote), which state that "After the transition period laid down in the Camp David accords, Israel will raise its claim and *will act to fulfill its rights* to sovereignty over Judea, Samaria and the Gaza district" (Eban's emphasis). "There is no resource of language," he notes, "that can possibly bridge the gulf" between this decision and the Camp David Agreement, which leaves the status of the territories to be determined after the transition period by negotiations between Israel, Jordan, Egypt, and elected representatives of the inhabitants of the territories, not by Israeli actions. Eban states that he is unable to find any precedent "in the jurisprudence of any government for such a total contradiction between an international engagement and a national statement of policy." Surely an exaggeration,* but nevertheless an understandable reaction to the immediate announcement by the government of Israel that it intended to disregard the Camp David Agreement, to which it pledges (and demands of others) total fidelity.[57]

The poll results reflect the attitudes of those who have learned about the occupation, as conducted by the Labor Party and then Likud, from their own lives. They are deprived of *New York Times* editorials, and therefore—as their low regard for the Labor Party indicates—they are unaware that under the Labor Party the occupation was a "model of future cooperation" and a "nine-year experiment in Arab-Israeli coexistence," or that the Labor Party in 1980 "has taken a giant step toward compromise with the West Bank Palestinians and thus challenged the Arab world to reciprocate with acts of restraint and conciliation"[58]; the

---

* To mention only one obvious case, consider the statement of U.S. government policy by Kissinger and Nixon in January 1973 as they announced the signing of the Paris peace agreements concerning Vietnam, adding in the clearest and most explicit terms that the U.S. intended to violate every obligation to which it had just committed itself. For details concerning the facts, the consequences, and the U.S. reactions, see *TNCW*, chapter 3.

"giant step" was a reiteration, once again, of the rejectionist Allon plan put into effect by the Labor Party ten years earlier.

2.3.4 The United States and the Conquered Population

The hopes and aspirations of the indigenous population are generally ignored in the United States, not because the facts are unknown—the poll just cited, for example, appeared prominently in *Time* magazine—but because the Palestinians are not accorded the human rights that are properly and automatically recognized in the case of Israeli Jews, so that their attitudes are of no account, just as one would not ask the donkeys in the West Bank what their preferences might be. Those who have backed or tolerated U.S. policy towards the region, or who support either of the two major political groupings in Israel, simply announce thereby their complete contempt for the indigenous inhabitants of the former Palestine.

Of course, such attitudes cannot be openly expressed. We therefore read in the *New Republic* that "No means exist of discovering what public opinion may be today [in] the occupied territories, which are the eye of the storm"—although the same author, who simply exudes sympathy for the Palestinians suffering under PLO terror, informs us confidently that Arafat's "extraordinary public relations success has no popular base," and that the "Palestinians *en masse* leave the PLO alone."[59] Evidently, polls carried out by Israel give us no insight into public opinion, just as we learn nothing from the elected leadership and others, even from Israel's favorite collaborator Mustafa Dudin. The same authority explains that there are genuine "moderates" who might "agree to whatever is left of the concept of partition" (presumably he has in mind "territorial comprom- ise" in the sense of the Labor Party). He even tells us who they are: Mayor Freij and dismissed Mayor Shawa (both of whom continue to support the PLO; see p. 55), and Mustafa Dudin who, he informs us, "has met with the disdain of self-appointed Western tribunes for the Palestinians"—though not this tribune, who is unconcerned by the fact that his candidate for "responsible leadership" insists upon a Palestinian state contrary to his claims, and is supported by a rousing 0.2% of the population. Again, the age of Orwell, nowhere better exemplified than in the semi-official journal of American liberalism, as we shall have ample occasion to see below.

It might be added that the sentiments of the Palestinians in the occupied territories regarding an independent state and the legitimacy of the PLO appear to be widely shared among Arab citizens of Israel as well. One of the Arab leaders who has been most closely integrated into Israeli political life, Saif ad-din Zuabi, wrote a letter to Prime Minister Begin protesting the expansion of the "Peace for Galilee" invasion of Lebanon beyond the originally-announced 40km limit. Zuabi, "who is known for his moderate opinions, indicated in his letter that he has never been an admirer of Yasser Arafat, but after the war it became clear to everyone that Yasser Arafat is the most fitting representative of the Palestinian people."[60] Similar conclusions have often been expressed within the Israeli Arab community. We return to more detailed studies of Israeli Arab opinion on these matters in chapter 7, section 4.1.1.

2.4   The Arab States and the PLO

We have reviewed the international consensus and the positions of the U.S., Israel, and the Palestinians in the occupied territories. What about the Arab states and the PLO? The historical record is rather different from what is generally believed in the United States.

2.4.1   The Erosion of Rejectionism and the U.S.-Israeli Response

In the immediate post-1967 period, the Arab states and the PLO took a rejectionist position comparable to the stand that has been consistently maintained by Israel and the U.S. Not long after, this rejectionism began to erode. In February 1970, President Nasser of Egypt declared that "it will be possible to institute a durable peace between Israel and the Arab states, not excluding economic and diplomatic relations, if Israel evacuates the occupied territories and accepts a settlement of the problem of the Palestinian refugees." Amnon Kapeliouk observes that "this declaration received no response at the time in Israel."[61] Note that settlement of the refugee problem within the context of a negotiated peace has been the official position of the U.S., along with virtually the entire world apart from Israel, since 1949, and is regularly endorsed in UN resolutions. Note also that Nasser made no reference to a Palestinian state, in accordance with the international consensus of the time. Nasser also "accepted the [Secretary of State William] Rogers [June 1970] proposals for a cease-fire and subsequent negotiations," a "brave and constructive step" in the words of Zionist historian Jon Kimche.[62]

After Nasser's death, the new President, Anwar Sadat, moved at once to implement two policies: peace with Israel and conversion of Egypt to an American client state. In February 1971, he offered Israel a full peace treaty on the pre-June 1967 borders, with security guarantees, recognized borders, and so on. This offer caused much distress in Israel (it caused "panic," in the words of the well-known Israeli writer Amos Elon),[63] and was promptly rejected with the statement that Israel would not return to the internationally recognized pre-1967 borders. Note that Sadat's offer of February 1971 was more favorable to Israel than what he proposed in November 1977 on the trip to Jerusalem that officially established him as "a man of peace," since he made no mention of Palestinian rights, allegedly the stumbling block in the Camp David "peace process." Sadat's offer was in line with the international consensus of the period, in particular, with the Rogers Plan, which had been angrily rejected by Israel.[64] In internal discussion in Israel, Labor Party doves recognized that a peace settlement was within reach, but recommended against it on the grounds that territorial gains would be possible if they held out.[65]

Israel's only reaction to Sadat's offer, apart from the immediate flat rejection, was to increase settlement in the occupied territories. On the same day that Sadat's offer was officially rejected, the Labor government authorized plans for settlement in the hills surrounding the Arab portion of Jerusalem, well beyond the earlier borders of the city, as part of the process of "thickening Jerusalem." Noting this fact, Edward Witten comments on the similarity to Begin's response to the Reagan plan in 1982: new settlements in response to a request for a settlement freeze (see p. 50; we return to the facts). Witten also points out that Sadat clearly expressed his desire for "coexistence" with Israel at the same time in a *Newsweek* interview, and that Foreign Minister Abdullah Salah of Jordan announced that Jordan too was ready to recognize Israel, if it returned to the internationally-recognized pre-June 1967 borders (February 23, 1971). There appears to have been no Israeli response.[66] In 1972, Israel's Labor government angrily rejected the proposal of King Hussein of Jordan to establish a confederation of Jordan and the West Bank (again, a rejectionist position, denying Palestinian national rights). In response, the Israeli Knesset "determined," for the first time officially, "that the historic right of the Jewish people to the Land of Israel [including the West Bank] is beyond challenge," while Prime Minister Golda Meir stated that "Israel will continue to pursue her enlightened policy in Judea and Samaria . . ." Her political adviser Israel Galili, who was in charge of settlement in the occupied territories, stated that the Jordan River should become Israel's "agreed border—a frontier, not just a security border," the latter term implying the possibility of some form of self-government, however limited, for the indigenous population.[67]

Returning to Sadat's February 1971 offer of a full peace treaty, Israel was backed in its rejection by the United States. Unfortunately for Sadat, his efforts came just at the time when Israel had established in Washington its thesis that it was a "strategic asset" for the U.S. (see chapter 2). Kissinger assumed that Israel's power was unchallengeable, and takes considerable pride, in his memoirs, in his steadfastness in blocking the efforts of his primary enemy—the State Department—towards some peaceful resolution of the conflict. His aim, he writes, "was to produce a stalemate until Moscow urged compromise or until, even better, some moderate Arab regime decided that the route to progress was through Washington . . . Until some Arab state showed a willingness to separate from the Soviets, or the Soviets were prepared to dissociate from the maximum Arab program, we had no reason to modify our policy" of stalemate, in opposition to the State Department.[68]

Kissinger's account is remarkable for its ignorance and geopolitical fantasies, even by Kissingerian standards.* Sadat had explicitly decided that "the route to progress was through Washington," joining Saudi Arabia and others (even when Sadat expelled Soviet advisers in 1972 Kissinger did not see the light). Saudi Arabia was not only willing "to separate from the Soviets" but in fact did not even have diplomatic relations with them. The USSR backed the international consensus including the existence of Israel within recognized (pre-June 1967) borders and with security guarantees.[69]

Apparently under Kissinger's influence, the Nixon Administration decided to suspend State Department efforts aimed at a peaceful settlement in accordance with the international consensus and the explicit proposals of Egypt. An envoy was sent to a conference of U.S. ambassadors in the Mideast to announce the suspension of these efforts. "To a man, the U.S. ambassadors replied that if the countries in the Mideast concluded that the process itself had ended, there would be a disastrous war."[70] Sadat also repeatedly warned that he would be forced to resort to war if his efforts at a peaceful settlement were rebuffed, but he was dismissed with contempt, apparently because of the widespread belief in Israel's military supremacy. Warnings from American oil companies operating in the Arabian peninsula concerning threats to U.S. interests were also disregarded.[71] Nahum Goldmann, long a leading figure in the Zionist movement, observed that Sadat had conducted a "daring" policy by "declaring himself ready to recognize Israel, despite the opposition," and that "if he cannot show that he can obtain results, the army will be compelled to launch a war." Israel listened no more than Kissinger did, and on the same assumptions. After Israel shot down 13 Syrian planes with one Israeli plane lost in September 1973, the editor of one major Israeli journal wrote: "This battle will remind our Arab neighbors that they cannot manage their affairs without taking into consideration who is the true master of this region."[72]

In October 1973, Sadat made good his threat. As a group of Israeli and American-Israeli scholars observe, "After the Egyptian Ra'is [Sadat] had realized that all diplomatic efforts would lead to a dead end, he decided to try a limited military option which, combined with an oil embargo, would lead to a significant Israeli withdrawal from Arab terri-

---

* Kissinger's inability to comprehend what was happening in the Middle East was almost monumental in its proportions. The second volume of his memoirs extends the story. See the review by James E. Akins (U.S. Ambassador to Saudi Arabia from 1973 to 1976), who argues that "the truly tragic consequence of Watergate is that President Nixon was not in a strong enough position to dominate his secretary of state. Weakened and distracted by domestic issues, he allowed Kissinger to frustrate his own Middle East design. Had it not been for Watergate, it is possible, even probable, that Nixon would have achieved a just and lasting peace in the area and that the world would be much safer today." See note 68.

tories."[73] To the great surprise of Israel, the U.S., and virtually everyone else, Egypt and Syria were remarkably successful in the early stages of the war and Saudi Arabia was compelled (reluctantly, it seems) to join in an oil boycott, the first major use of the "oil weapon," a move with considerable long-term implications in international affairs. Primary responsibility for these developments is attributable to Henry Kissinger's ignorance and blind reliance on force.

At that point, U.S. policy shifted, reflecting the understanding that Egypt and the oil-producing states could not be so easily dismissed or controlled. Kissinger undertook his shuttle diplomacy and other diplomatic efforts. Concealed behind the razzle-dazzle was the easily discernible intent, now surely clear in retrospect even to those who could not perceive it at the time, to accept Egypt as a U.S. client state while effectively removing it from the Middle East conflict with a Sinai agreement. Then Israel would be free to continue its policies of integrating the occupied territories—and to concentrate its forces for war on the northern border without concern for the major Arab military force, as when Israel invaded Lebanon in 1978 and again in 1982.

Egypt continued to press for a full-scale peace settlement, now joined by other Arab states. In January 1976, the U.S. was compelled to veto a UN Security Council Resolution calling for a settlement in terms of the international consensus, which now included a Palestinian state alongside of Israel. The resolution called for a settlement on the 1967 borders, with "appropriate arrangements...to guarantee...the sovereignty, territorial integrity and political independence of all states in the area and their right to live in peace within secure and recognized boundaries," including Israel and a new Palestinian state in the occupied territories. The resolution was backed by the "confrontation states" (Egypt, Syria, Jordan), the PLO, and the USSR. President Chaim Herzog, who was Israel's UN Ambassador at the time, writes that the PLO not only backed this peace plan but in fact "prepared" it; the PLO then condemned "the tyranny of the veto" (in the words of the PLO representative) by which the U.S. blocked this important effort to bring about a peaceful two-state settlement. The occasion for Herzog's remarks was the Saudi Arabian peace proposal that had just been announced, which Israel was right to reject, Herzog asserts, just as it correctly rejected the "more moderate" PLO plan of January 1976. According to Herzog, the "real author" of the 1981 Saudi Arabian (Fahd) peace plan was also the PLO, who never seem to cease their machinations.[74]

Israel refused to attend the January 1976 Security Council session, which had been called at Syrian initiative. The Rabin government—a Labor Party government regarded as dovish—announced that it would not negotiate with any Palestinians on any political issue and would not negotiate with the PLO even if the latter were to renounce terrorism and recognize Israel, thus adopting a position comparable to that of the minority Rejection Front within the PLO.[75] The main elements of the PLO had been moving towards acceptance of a two-state settlement, and continued to do so, at times with various ambiguities, at times quite clearly, as in this case.

The Arab states and the PLO continued to press for a two-state settlement, and Israel continued to react with alarm and rejection. In November 1976, the *Jerusalem Post* noted that Egyptian Prime Minister Ismail Fahmy had offered four conditions for a Middle East peace settlement: "Israel's withdrawal to the pre-1967 war frontiers; the establishment of a Palestinian state in the West Bank and the Gaza Strip; the ban on nuclear weapons in the region; and the inspection of nuclear installations in the area." It noted further President Sadat's statement to a group of U.S. Senators "that he was prepared to sign a peace treaty with Israel if it withdrew from all Arab territories captured in the 1967 war, and if a Palestinian state was created on the West Bank and in the Gaza Strip." The Labor Party journal *Davar* quoted Prime Minister Rabin's response to this disturbing "peace offensive":

> But there is nothing new in all of this, in the objectives that the Arabs wish to obtain, stressed the Prime Minister when recalling that back in 1971 Sadat told Dr. Jarring of his willingness to reach a peace settlement as he understood it. On the contrary, he has even made the conditions harder, since then, as opposed to now, he did not link an Israeli-Egyptian agreement with agreements with other Arab countries and did not raise, in such a pronounced manner [in fact, at all], his demand for a Palestinian state in the West Bank and the Gaza Strip.[76]

Thus no Israeli reaction was in order.

The following year, Egypt, Syria and Jordan "informed the United States that they would sign peace treaties with Israel as part of an overall Middle East settlement."[77] The Palestinian National Council, the governing body of the PLO, issued a declaration on March 20, 1977 calling for the establishment of "an independent national state" in Palestine—rather than a secular democratic state *of* Palestine—and authorizing Palestinian attendance at an Arab-Israeli peace conference. Prime Minister Rabin of Israel responded "that the only place the Israelis could meet the Palestinian guerrillas was on the field of battle."[78] The same session of the National Council elected a new PLO Executive Committee excluding representatives of the Rejection Front.[79]

Shortly after, the PLO leaked a "peace plan" in Beirut which stated that the famous Palestinian National Covenant would not serve as the basis for relations between Israel and a Palestinian state, just as the founding principles of the World Zionist Organization were not understood as the basis for interstate relations, and that any evolution beyond a two-state settlement "would be achieved by peaceful means."[80]

Supporters of Israel have long treasured the Covenant as the last line of defense for their rejectionism when all else fails. Israeli doves, in contrast, have always dismissed this last-ditch effort. For example, Elie Eliachar, former president of the Council of the Sephardic Community in Israel and the first person from Jerusalem to represent it at the Zionist Congresses, made the following statement in a lecture at the Hebrew University in 1980:

> On the basis of personal contacts I have had with leaders of the PLO, in London and elsewhere [in] meetings that were held openly, and that interested people know all about, I can say categorically that the idea that the PLO covenant is an obstacle to negotiations is utter nonsense... There is no Arab organization in existence today which can bring about a durable peace in our region, except the PLO, including its extremist factions.

Mattityahu Peled, asked why the PLO does not abandon the Covenant, responded:

> For the same reason that the Government of Israel has never renounced the decisions of the Basle Zionist Congress, which supported the establishment of a Jewish state in the historic land of Israel—including Transjordan. No political body would do this. Similarly Herut and the Irgun [its terrorist forerunner] never abandoned their map [which includes Transjordan, contemporary Jordan; the official slogan of Begin's Herut Party still calls for an Israel on both banks of the Jordan]. We demand a ritual abandonment of the Covenant—a kind of ceremony of humiliation—instead of concerning ourselves with the decisions that were accepted by the PLO from 1974, which support the establishment of a Palestinian state in the territories evacuated by Israel.

It is, in fact, interesting to see how Israeli propaganda has focused on the Covenant with increasing intensity as it is deemphasized by the PLO in favor of subsequent resolutions which drastically modify its terms, for reasons that are hardly obscure.[81] We should note that the Convenant holds a rejectionist view comparable to that of the Labor Party and Likud.

A few months after releasing the 1977 peace plan, the PLO endorsed the Soviet-American statement of October 1977, which called for the "termination of the state of war and establishment of normal peaceful relations" between Israel and its neighbors, as well as for internationally guaranteed borders and demilitarized zones to enhance security. "The United States had, however, quickly backed away from the joint statement under Israeli protest," Seth Tillman observes, adding that "without exception," proposals for superpower collaboration to bring about a settlement and to guarantee it "have been shot down by Israeli leaders and supporters of Israel in the United States, who have perceived in them the bugbear of an 'imposed' settlement"—that is to say, a settlement that is unacceptable (otherwise, no sane person would care whether it was "imposed" or not) because it departs from their rejectionist principles. There were "a few dissenters from the prevailing consensus," Tillman points out, among them Nahum Goldmann, who described the Soviet-American agreement of October 1977 as "a piece of real statesmanship," adding that "it is regrettable that Israel's opposition and that of the pro-Israel lobby in America rendered the agreement ineffective" (Goldmann's words), another piece in the familiar pattern.[82]

2.4.2 Sadat's Trip to Jerusalem and the Rewriting of History

The failure of many such efforts as these led Sadat to undertake his November 1977 trip to Jerusalem, motivated by a desire to convene a Geneva conference of major powers to settle the conflict, according to Hermann Eilts, who was U.S. Ambassador to Egypt at the time.[83] It is also likely that Sadat was motivated by concern over the escalating conflict across the Israel-Lebanon border, initiated by Israeli-Maronite bombing of Nabatiya and culminating in Israeli air raids that killed some 70 people, mostly Lebanese.[84]

The United States has generally been opposed to a Geneva conference, which would include the USSR and the European powers. As Kissinger had explained, his diplomatic efforts were designed "to keep the Soviets out of the diplomatic arena" and "to ensure that the Europeans and Japanese did not get involved in the diplomacy" concerning the Middle East, where the U.S. role is to remain predominant.[85] Israel has also consistently opposed the idea, adamantly so if the PLO participates. The reason was explained by Prime Minister Rabin of the Labor Party after the Knesset had approved a resolution to this effect. If Israel agrees to negotiate "with any Palestinian element," he stated, this will provide "a basis for the possibility of creating a third state between Israel and Jordan." But Israel will never accept such a state: "I repeat firmly, clearly, categorically: it will not be created."[86] The Labor Party's rejection of the right of the Palestinians to any meaningful form of self-determination has been consistent and exceptionless.

Sadat's dramatic visit to Jerusalem did not open the way to negotiations for a comprehensive political settlement involving true accommodation in the sense of the earlier discussion and the international consensus. Rather, the resulting Camp David "peace process," as the U.S. government and the press designate it, consummated Kissinger's earlier efforts. Egypt has, temporarily at least, been incorporated within the U.S. system and excluded from the Arab-Israeli conflict, allowing Israel to continue its creeping takeover of the occupied territories, apart from the Sinai, now returned to Egypt and serving as a buffer zone. Diplomatic efforts remain largely in the hands of the U.S., excluding both the USSR and the rivals/allies of Europe and Japan.

From 1977, the Begin government rapidly extended land expropriation and settlement in the occupied territories while instituting a considerably more brutal repression there, particularly from the fall of 1981, with the Milson-Sharon administration. The U.S. government signalled its approval by increasing the massive aid which, in effect, funded these projects—while also emitting occasional peeps of protest. As noted earlier (see p. 62), the Begin government indicated from the start its rejection of the "peace process," so it is not surprising that it moved at once to "fulfill its rights to sovereignty" by large-scale development projects designed to ensure that the West Bank could not be separated from Israel.

Evidently, the actual historical record—here briefly reviewed up to Sadat's November 1977 trip to Jerusalem—is not exactly in accord with the familiar picture of U.S.-Israel-Arab diplomatic interactions in this period. The preferred story is one of Arab intransigence and U.S.-Israeli efforts at accommodation. Sadat, for example, is regularly portrayed as a typical Arab warmonger who tried to destroy Israel by force in 1973, then learned the error of his ways and became a man of peace under the kindly tutelage of Henry Kissinger and Jimmy Carter. As the *New Republic* puts the matter, Sadat's "decision to make peace" came *after* the 1973 war: "Finally, after the enormous destructiveness of the 1973 war, Anwar Sadat realized that the time had come to replace the conflict of war with law and rights."[87] The other Arabs—particularly the PLO—persist in their evil ways.* Endless references can be cited from the press to illustrate this version of history.[88]

To reconcile the actual history with the preferred picture has been a relatively simple matter. It has only been necessary to resort to Orwell's useful memory hole. The historical record has been so effectively sanitized that even as well-informed a person as Harold Saunders (former Assistant Secretary of State for Near Eastern and South Asian affairs) can write that "As long as no Arab government but Egypt would make peace, Israel saw no alternative to maintaining its security by the force of its own arms."[89]

---

* The *New Republic* goes on to explain that one of the great achievements of the Israeli war in Lebanon is that the destruction of the PLO and "its elimination as an independent *political* force [will] allow those on the Arab side who have no designs on Haifa or Tel Aviv to negotiate free from intimidation" (my emphasis). Prior to 1982, this leading journal of American liberalism would have us believe, no Arabs were "allowed" to consider a settlement that would include the existence of Israel. Compare the record sampled here.

Sadat's pre-1977 peace efforts have been conveniently expunged from the record, like the January 1976 Security Council Resolution and much else. In Israel and Egypt, Sadat's 1971 offer is described as his "famous" attempt to establish a genuine peace with Israel.[90] Similarly, Amnon Kapeliouk describes Sadat's expression of willingness "to enter into a peace agreement with Israel" (the words of the official English text of Israel's recognition of Sadat's offer) as a "historic event in Israel-Arab relations."[91]

Consider, in contrast, the two-page encomium to Sadat by Eric Pace, Middle East specialist of the *New York Times*, after Sadat's assassination.[92] There is no mention here of the real history, as briefly sketched above; indeed in the *New York Times* version, the well-documented facts are explicitly denied. Thus, referring to Sadat's trip to Jerusalem in 1977, Pace writes:

> Reversing Egypt's longstanding policy, he proclaimed his willingness to accept Israel's existence as a sovereign state. Then, where so many Middle East negotiators had failed, he succeeded, along with Presidents Carter and Reagan and Prime Minister Menachem Begin of Israel, in keeping the improbable rapprochement alive.

An elegant example of what has sometimes been called "historical engineering,"[93] that is, redesigning the facts of history in the interests of established power and ideology, a crime of which we justly accuse our enemies.

Such historical engineering is in fact quite widespread. To illustrate more closely how the system works, I will cite one final example, again from the *New York Times*, which is much more interesting in this connection than, say, the *New Republic* or *Commentary*, because of its image and pretensions as an independent journal. After the Lebanon war and the Beirut massacres of September, there was much debate about how Americans, and American Jews in particular, should relate to Israel. The contribution of the *New York Times Magazine* was a discussion by Mark Helprin,* who is identified as a Middle East specialist with service in the Israeli army.[94]

Helprin begins by setting up a framework for discussing the issue. There are two extreme positions: "Among Jews in the United States there

---

* It would be misleading to describe this as just one man's opinion, fully in place in an independent journal. That would indeed be true if the range of permitted opinion extended beyond the rejectionist spectrum, but it does not, contrary to much pretense (the reference of note 111 below being one example). The *Times Magazine* published an interesting letter critical of Helprin's article, by Julius Berman, Chairman, Conference of the Presidents of Major American Jewish Organizations (Dec. 12). Berman held that Helprin rejected the "consensus" of American Jews: that the PLO is excluded as a negotiating partner and that "an independent Palestinian state would be a dagger poised at the heart of Israel." The latter phrase is borrowed from Hitler, who used it with reference to Czechoslovakia.

are those who would see Israel fall, and those who care only for its aggrandizement." These "two extremes," he adds, "have been highlighted in the debate following the massacre of innocents in Beirut." We must reject both of these extremes, he urges, and take the "middle ground," which is described rather vaguely, but is intended to be understood as the position of the Labor Party, it appears.

Now of course, every commentator sees himself as occupying the middle ground between the extremists. The question is: who stands at the two extremes? As the sole example of those "Jews in the United States . . . who would see Israel fall," Helprin cites George Habash, the leader of the rejectionist faction of the PLO. It is not surprising that he offers no other example; it would be difficult indeed to find real cases.

What about the other "extreme," i.e., those who support the policies of Likud. Helprin does not elaborate on the constituency of this group, but others do, for example, Rabbi Arthur Hertzberg, who describes the Zionist Organization of America as (in recent years) "the American wing of the Liberal Party in Israel which, together with Begin's Revisionists, make up the Likud.[95] Thus the two extremes that have been "highlighted" in recent debate among American Jews are not exactly equally represented: one consists of George Habash, and the other, the Zionist Organization of America, and in fact, most others in the organized Jewish community.

Helprin then proceeds to give the version of history as perceived in the "middle ground." Apart from the U.S., we find "the facile rejection of Israel and compassionate overembrace of its enemies by nearly all the world," including Europe, which "hardly reacted" to PLO atrocities in the past, saving its condemnations for Israel—a ridiculous falsification, of course, but one that appears to be widely believed in the U.S. and is sometimes supported with serious misrepresentation; for one example, by Saul Bellow, see *TNCW*, pp. 303-4. As for Israel, while it is not perfect, its "campaign in Lebanon was both late in coming and restrained in character when compared with what any other state, civilized or uncivilized, would do in reaction to the continual shelling of its cities, the murder of its children and the massing of arms against it for years without abatement." Omitted are a few possibly pertinent facts: e.g., that Israel occupies Arab territory from which hundreds of thousands of Palestinians fled or were expelled in 1967 (not to speak of questions that might be raised about earlier years) and that the PLO had scrupulously adhered to the July 1981 cease-fire in the face of constant Israeli provocations, a matter to which we return.

As for the PLO, it "is to the slaughter of men, women and children what France is to wine." Assuming this to be a valid characterization, we may ask what analogy is appropriate for Israel with its far greater slaughters since the early 1950s, long before the PLO was founded, or for the pre-state Zionist terror organizations, which, Simha Flapan writes, "established the pattern of terrorism adopted 30 years later by Al-Fatah."[96]

According to official Israeli army statistics, 106 people died in the course of all terrorist actions in the north since 1967, considerably fewer than the number of victims of a single Israeli bombing raid.[97] Or to take another comparison, the total number of Israeli victims is approximately the same as the number killed when Israel shot down a civilian Libyan airplane over the occupied Sinai in February 1973; the plane had become lost in bad weather and was one minute flight time from the Suez Canal, towards which it was heading, when shot down by the Israeli air force.[98] The total number of Israelis killed in all acts of terror from 1967 is 282,[99] less than the number killed by Israel's air terrorists in Beirut on July 17-8 1981, in "retaliation" after a PLO response to Israeli bombing that broke the cease-fire.[100] What of recent years?*

> According to figures provided by Minister of the Interior Yosef Burg, in 1980 10 Jews were killed by terrorists and in 1981—8. In contrast, we have killed about a thousand terrorists in 1982, and caused the loss of life of thousands of inhabitants of an enemy country. If so, it results that for every 6-8 Jews sacrificed, we kill in return thousands of Gentiles. This is, undoubtedly, a spectacular situation, an uncommon success of Zionism. I might even dare to say—exaggerated.[101]

Israeli terrorist acts over the years, beginning long before the PLO was formed, have undoubtedly claimed far more victims than those of the PLO, and while they are typically described as "retaliation" here, the facts make clear that this is a term of propaganda, not description.[102]

So much for Europe, Israel and the PLO. Next, Helprin turns to the Arab states apart from post-1977 Egypt: "Were the confrontation states and the rejection states to allow that the Jews, too, have a right to political existence, they would get serene open borders and peace treaties... Israel will not listen to the Arabs until they decide to put an end to their 30-year war against it." He adds that "when Arab officials speak of liberating or regaining the occupied territories, they mean all of Israel," although "the Western press has been remiss at sniffing out this verbal trick." The entire history just described—only a small part of the story, which will be extended directly—is completely expunged from the record.

Clearly, all of this is pure Agitprop. How can the *New York Times* and its writers expect to get away with it? The answer is simple enough; it is no trick at all, given overwhelming dominance of the means of articulate expression by one specific point of view. It is difficult to imagine, for

---

* Note that we are taking these Israeli figures at face value, not asking how the victims were killed, though a closer look at the terrorist incidents shows that the question is worth asking.

example, that the *New York Times Magazine* would permit an article to appear reviewing the actual historical facts, at least, as long as the U.S. remains committed to its Greater Israel policies. This example, which is by no means unusual, illustrates very well what Walter Lippmann sixty years ago called "the manufacture of consent," an art which "is capable of great refinements" and will lead to a "revolution" in "the practice of democracy."[103]

3   The Continuing Threat of Peace

The well-known Israeli writer Amos Elon has written of the "panic and unease among our political leadership" caused by Arab peace proposals (see p. 64). "The most extreme instance," he adds, "though not the only one, was in early 1971, when Sadat threw Israel off balance with his announcement, for the first time, that he was willing to enter into a peace agreement with Israel, and to respect its independence and sovereignty in 'secure and recognized borders'."[104] Elon describes the harshly negative reaction of the government, the silence of most of the press, and the convoluted efforts of most Orientalists to prove that Sadat's offer did not mean what it said—rather like Helprin's insight into the devious "verbal trick" of the Arabs when they speak of a settlement in which the occupied territories will be turned over to their inhabitants. The occasion for Elon's article was the "emotional and angry" reaction of the government to the just-announced Saudi (Fahd) peace plan of August 1981, a response which he found "shocking, frightening, if not downright despair-producing."*

Elon had good reason for his despair. The Labor Party journal *Davar* found Israel's reaction—including military flights over Saudi Arabia—to be so "irrational" as to cause foreign intelligence services to be concerned over Israeli bombing of Saudi oil fields.[106] Another well-known journalist described "the frightened, almost hysterical response of the Israeli government to the Saudi plan" as "a grave mistake," adding that if the PLO offered to negotiate with Israel, "the government would undoubtedly declare a national day of mourning."[107] In fact, the PLO had repeatedly expressed a willingness to accept a negotiated settlement and to participate in general peace negotiations, but no call for a day of

---

* Israeli Foreign Minister Yitzhak Shamir stated that "Even the suggestion of Saudi recognition of Israel is not new."[105] The Saudi plan called for a two-state settlement on the 1967 borders, with recognition of the right of all states in the region to exist in peace. It should be noted that many Labor leaders denounced the Saudi peace plan, e.g., Chaim Herzog, who warned that it was prepared by the PLO (see p. 67) and Party chairman Shimon Peres, who "remarked today that the Saudi peace proposal threatened Israel's very existence" *(Ha'aretz,* Aug. 10, 1981; *Israeli Mirror).*

mourning was necessary, since the denial of the facts was still effectively in force.

A few months later, in February 1982, Uri Avneri criticized a similar Israeli reaction to a Syrian proposal calling for "termination of the state of war between the Arabs and Israel..." along with confirmation of the right of the Palestinians to an independent state alongside of Israel in the occupied territories.[108] B. Michael made a similar observation in *Ha'aretz*. Noting the immediate efforts to dismiss the statement of the Syrian Minister of Information that a peace agreement would be possible if Israel were to withdraw to its 1967 borders, he commented sardonically that "We must therefore be careful not to underestimate the danger posed by the Syrian plot, and we must do our best to kill it while it is still small."[109]

In the same month (February 1982), Saudi Arabia's state radio twice "called for direct peace negotiations between the Arabs and Israel, on condition that Israel recognize the PLO as the negotiating partner." These initiatives too were ignored,[110] as was a subsequent Iraqi initiative (see p. 203*).

Israeli propaganda beamed to an American audience, however, regularly speaks of the willingness of "socialist Zionism" to make peace if only some Arab leader would show some sign that Israel may exist in the region,[111] ignoring—in fact, denying—the actual extreme rejectionism of mainstream socialist Zionism and the halting and sometimes ambiguous steps of the PLO and the Arab states over the past years towards a political settlement, which, whatever one thinks of them, clearly go far beyond anything that the Israeli Labor Party has been willing to consider and in fact go beyond what the Israeli "Peace Now" group has proposed. American commentators are still more extreme in their rejection of the historical record, as in the sample of cases cited. In the earlier years, the PLO was no less rejectionist than Israel, and its call for a "democratic secular state" was not what it appeared to be on the surface (see *TNCW*, p. 430). But it simply cannot be denied that from the mid-1970s, the PLO has moved increasingly towards an accommodationist position. While concealing this record, propagandists search desperately for statements by PLO spokesmen that reveal their unremitting hostility to Israel and unwillingness to accept it. Israeli doves have regarded such efforts with contempt, pointing out that the same logic would lead to the conclusion that no one should have any dealings with the Zionist movement or the State of Israel, since its leaders have consistently rejected any Palestinian rights and have repeatedly indicated that they regard any political settlement as a temporary stage leading to further expansion. What is more, they have acted on these principles. We return to the record, which is not without interest and is generally concealed here. That outright propagandists should resort to these deceptive practices is not very surprising; that, after all, is their vocation. It is more interesting that the practice is common across a broad spectrum of Western opinion, particularly in the U.S., as one aspect of the ideological support for Israel.

There have been other examples of missed chances, before and since. Mattityahu Peled alleges that "a historic opportunity was missed to start a dialogue between Israel and the PLO" in 1976, when plans were devised for mutual conciliatory gestures, leading to further peaceful contacts. He states that the plan collapsed because of Israeli military actions in Lebanon. Just at the time when Arafat was scheduled to make a conciliatory statement, as part of the plan, the Israeli Navy began capturing boats belonging to Lebanese Moslems, turning them over to Israel's Lebanese Christian allies, who then killed them.[112]

In the light of American beliefs about the history of terrorism, it should perhaps be observed that along with acts of piracy such as these, Israel has also resorted to hijacking of airplanes, and may indeed have initiated this practice. In December 1954, a Syrian civilian airliner was captured by Israeli military aircraft to obtain hostages for exchange with Israeli soldiers who had been captured within Syria. The Prime Minister of Israel, Moshe Sharett, states in his diary that he was informed by the State Department that "our action was without precedent in the history of international practice." Note that this Israeli action is a direct precedent for much later PLO actions to capture hostages for exchange with captured guerrillas, as in the major terrorist incidents that were widely and properly denounced in the West; at Ma'alot in 1974, for example.[113]

Returning to PLO initatives, by the late 1970s, Seth Tillman concludes, "the evidence seemed persuasive...that Arafat and al-Fatah [the PLO mainstream] were prepared to make peace on the basis of the West Bank-Gaza state and to accept Israel within its approximate borders of 1967," though not to "concede the moral legitimacy of Israel." In November 1978, requesting a dialogue with the United States in a discussion with Representative Paul Findley, "Arafat issued the following statement: 'The PLO will accept an independent Palestinian state consisting of the West Bank and Gaza, with connecting corridor, and in that circumstance will renounce any and all violent means to enlarge the territory of that state. I would reserve the right, of course, to use nonviolent means, that is to say, diplomatic and democratic means, to bring about the eventual unification of all of Palestine'." Tillman reports further that he promised: "We will give de facto recognition to the State of Israel." Neither these statements, nor others of a similar nature that were conveyed directly to the State Department, "elicited a response from the Carter administration."[114]

In its April 1981 session, the PLO National Council unanimously passed a resolution endorsing a February proposal of Soviet President Brezhnev for peace in the Middle East in which Brezhnev—in accordance with what has been consistent Soviet policy—enunciated the following principles:

The inalienable rights of the Arab people of Palestine must be secured up to, and including, the establishment of their own state. It is essential to ensure the security and sovereignty of all states of the region including those of Israel. These are the basic principles.[115]

Citing the unanimous PLO endorsement of the Brezhnev proposal at a Paris press conference on July 14, 1982, Issam Sartawi of the PLO National Council* stated that

From this it follows that the PLO has formally conceded to Israel, in the most unequivocal manner, the right to exist on a reciprocal basis. This eliminates automatically the obstacle placed by Secretary of State Kissinger in the way of U.S. recognition of the PLO and the establishment of U.S.-PLO dialogue.

See p. 41. The statement was welcomed by the British and French governments (with qualifications in the former case) as a recognition of the right of Israel to exist on a reciprocal basis. A joint communiqué issued by Sartawi and Mattityahu Peled on July 20 noted that "The PLO has made its willingness to accept and recognize the state of Israel on the basis of mutual recognition of each nation's legitimate right of self-determination crystal clear in various resolutions since 1977."[116]

One might argue that this exaggerates the clarity of these declarations, but there is no doubt about the general drift of policy of the PLO and the Arab states, the "panic" that this has regularly inspired in Israel, and the reaction of dismissal or simply denial of the facts in the United States.

---

* On April 10, 1983, Sartawi was assassinated at a meeting of the Socialist International in Portugal. Responsibility for the assassination was announced by the Abu Nidal group, which has been at war with the PLO for a decade. In October 1973 Abu Nidal was condemned to death by a Fatah military tribunal. He is assumed to have been responsible for the assassination of several PLO figures in Europe, among them the leading PLO moderate Said Hammami in London in 1978, Naim Khader in Brussels in 1981, and others, and also for murderous attacks on synagogues and Jewish establishments in Vienna and probably in France. He was also responsible for the attempted assassination of Israeli Ambassador Shlomo Argov in London in June 1982, the event that sparked the Israeli invasion of Lebanon to which we return. In an effort to piece together his murky and bloody history, Philippe Boggio describes him as "a dangerous fomentor of antagonisms, an expert agitator who can do a better job than any army of demolishing the PLO's naturally ambiguous relations with a good part of the world," and whose activities have consistently been directed to undermining PLO efforts from the early 1970s "to get all its factions to abandon the terrorist tactics discrediting the organisation." The PLO has charged that he is an Israeli agent, noting that his operations "frequently serve Israeli interests indirectly," a charge that is "one of the assumptions you bear in mind" according to a French secret service specialist. It is generally assumed that he is supported by Iraq, sometimes Syria, where his offices are located and where he appears to have access to considerable funding. Philippe Boggio, *Le Monde*, Oct. 13, 14, 1982; *Manchester Guardian Weekly*, Oct. 31, 1982.

To cite one last example, *Ha'aretz* published an interview with Shafiq el-Hout, official PLO spokesman in Beirut, who stated that "the PLO is prepared to offer peace to Israel on the condition that the Israelis will obey the UN resolutions and will recognize the national rights of the Palestinian people... We are prepared to participate in any official effort aimed at bringing a just and comprehensive peace settlement in the Middle East."[117] Again, perhaps not what Israel is prepared to accept, but hardly consistent with the incessant charge that the PLO is adamant in its refusal to accept the existence of Israel on any terms, that "the backbone of its existence is the philosophy of destruction of Israel, and the road to this is the use of terror" (Yitzhak Rabin).[118]

The concern over evidence of Arab moderation, illustrated repeatedly above, can be traced to the early days of the Zionist movement. Simha Flapan discusses "Weizmann's opposition to negotiations with the Palestinians themselves for a political solution" from the early 1920's, and his concern that the Arabs might be "moderate enough to be likely to agree to [a constitutional settlement] and thereby preclude forever the possibility of a Jewish state." This concern grew when "the moderate trend gained the upper hand among the Palestinians," a "new and moderate trend in Palestinian nationalism" that Weizmann viewed "with grave suspicion."[119] One can understand the reasons. Arab moderation might have stood in the way of Zionist goals at the time, and therefore had to be resisted. Comparable remarks hold today.

In fact, it was not only the Saudi Arabian peace plan and other conciliatory gestures of the Arab states that were causing the familiar "panic" by 1981-82. A still more serious problem was the increasing difficulty in portraying the PLO as merely a gang of terrorists, particularly, in the light of its observance of the U.S.-arranged cease-fire on the Lebanon-Israel border despite much Israeli provocation. There is good reason to believe that this threat was one prime factor impelling Israel to invade Lebanon, as we shall see.

Putting such considerations to the side for the moment, the historical record seems plain enough. It strongly confirms the conclusion that the U.S. and Israel have headed the rejectionist camp, increasingly so as the 1970's progressed. The Arab states that are directly involved in the conflict have approached or joined the international accommodationist consensus, as has the mainstream of the PLO. Irrelevantly to these considerations, it should perhaps be remarked, given the climate of irrationality on this matter in the United States, that this historical record does not show that the Arab states are decent regimes—they most definitely are not— nor does it bear on one's judgments about the merits of the PLO.* It is simply a matter of fact.

---

* Though the matter is of no relevance here, for the record, my own judgments have been consistently harsh, both with regard to their actions and programs. See, e.g., *Peace in the Middle East?*, pp. 99f., 108; *TNCW*, pp. 262, 430; *Socialist Revolution*, April-June 1976.

As for the matter of principle, it seems to me that rejectionist programs are unacceptable, for the reasons already indicated. Furthermore, whatever one's views about these matters may be, there surely is no justification for maintaining the illusions and misrepresentations that are so characteristic of the American literature on this subject, one would think.

Notes—Chapter 3
Rejectionism and Accommodation

1. For examples, see virtually any article or editorial on the topic in the *New Republic;* e.g., for various aspects of the picture, Michael Walzer, "The new terrorists," Aug. 30, 1975; David Pryce-Jones, "The Palestinian pattern," Nov. 8, 1982.
2. Jon Kimche, *There Could Have Been Peace* (Dial, New York, 1973, p. 306).
3. For discussion, see Fred J. Khouri, "The Arab-Israeli conflict," in P. Edward Haley and Lewis W. Snider, eds., *Lebanon in Crisis* (Syracuse Univ. Press, 1979).
4. *U.S. Department of State Bulletin* (January 5, 1970), cited by Khouri, *op. cit.*, p. 299.
5. Tillman, *The United States in the Middle East*, pp. 223f.
6. *Ibid.*, pp. 276-7; emphasis in original.
7. For discussion of these matters, see my *Peace in the Middle East?* and *TNCW*.
8. See, for example, Tom Hayden, *The American Future* (South End, Boston, 1980), for argument in support of his rejectionist position on the Arab-Israeli conflict (roughly, that of the Israeli Labor Party), in essentially the terms described. On his support for the Israeli invasion of Lebanon, which went well beyond the position of the Labor Party, see chapter 6, section 6.4.
9. For references, see *TNCW*, pp. 249, 438.
10. *Foreign Affairs*, Spring 1981.
11. Thomas R. Stauffer, *Christian Science Monitor*, Jan. 13 1982.
12. For a detailed analysis of technical aspects of the problem, see Jehoshua Schwarz, "Water Resources in Judea, Samaria, and the Gaza Strip," in Daniel J. Elazar, ed., *Judea, Samaria, and Gaza: Views on the Present and Future* (American Enterprise Institute, Washington, 1982). Also Thomas R. Stauffer, *Christian Science Monitor*, Jan. 20, 1982. For further references, see *TNCW*, p. 447. See also David Elstein and Sharon Goulds, *New Statesman*, July 10, 1981 and *Middle East International*, July 31, 1981; *Business Week*, Dec. 20, 1982, citing an Israeli estimate that by the year 2000 demand will outrun expected supply.
13. Schwarz, *op. cit.* See Thomas R. Stauffer, *Christian Science Monitor*, Jan. 20, 1982 and *Middle East International*, July 30, 1982, on what he calls "the lure of the Litani."
14. *Economist*, Sept. 11, 1982; Zvi Barel, *Ha'aretz*, Sept. 9, 1982.
15. See "Talking Points," *New York Times*, Sept. 9, 1982.
16. Shaya Segal, *Ma'ariv*, Dec. 7, 1982.
17. Kapeliouk, *Israel*, p. 23; Yitzhak Rabin, interview ('1983: New Opportunities for Peace"), *Trialogue*, Winter 1983.
18. *New York Times*, Nov. 1, 1982. Lewis, who has been one of the most outspoken critics of recent Israeli policies in U.S. journalism, basically supports the Labor Party position, it appears.
19. *Boston Globe*, June 1, 1978; *Ma'ariv*, Oct. 11, 1981; *Israeli Mirror*, London.
20. Amos Perlmutter, *New York Times*, May 17, 1982.
21. Kapeliouk, *Israel*, pp. 220, 21. Ben-Gurion's statement is "known to every child in Israel," according to Kapeliouk.
22. *New York Times*, Sept. 6, 1982.
23. Sykes, *Crossroads to Israel*, p. 48.
24. David Ben-Gurion, *Memoirs* (World, New York, 1970, p. 118).
25. Flapan, *Zionism and the Palestinians*, p. 134, citing a speech of October 12, 1936. For the actual record of Palestinian nationalism, see the outstanding two-volume study by Yehoshua Porath, *The Emergence of the Palestinian-Arab National Movement, The Palestinian Arab National Movement* (Frank Cass, London, 1974, 1977)

26. Kapeliouk, *Israel*, p. 32.
27. *London Sunday Times*, June 15, 1969. For a longer excerpt, see John K. Cooley, *Green March, Black September* (Frank Cass, London, 1973, pp. 196-7). See Porath, *op. cit.*, for a serious discussion of the facts concerning Palestinian nationalism.
28. Kapeliouk, *Israel*, p. 32.
29. Cooley, *Green March, Black September*, p. 197.
30. Flapan, *Zionism and the Palestinians*, p. 83.
31. See *TNCW*, p. 231, citing an official government document. As noted, this state is to incorporate parts of the West Bank, according to Labor Party doctrine.
32. The reference is to Israel's demand, later abandoned, that the negotiations take place in Jerusalem, recognized by virtually no one (specifically, not by the U.S.) as Israel's capital.
33. Arnold Forster, letter, *New York Times*, Dec. 20, 1982.
34. *New York Review of Books*, Nov. 18, 1982.
35. The Socialist International has been unusual, outside of the U.S. and Israel, in often taking a rejectionist stand, denying Palestinian rights, leading to sharp condemnation by Israeli doves. See *TNCW*, pp. 270-1.
36. Cited by Tillman, *The United States in the Middle East*, p. 143, from the *New York Times*, August 6, 1978.
37. See *TNCW*, p. 442, citing the Israeli journal *Emda*, December 1974.
38. K. Amnon (Amnon Kapeliouk), "The 1976 elections in the territories," *Al Hamishmar*, April 16, 1982.
39. See *TNCW*, p. 269.
40. See *The Dawn (Al Fajr)*, Jerusalem, Sept. 3, 1982.
41. The results appear in *Time*, May 24, 1982.
42. "Israeli Soldiers Kill Arab Youth in the West Bank," special to the *New York Times*, Dec. 19, 1982.
43. On the investigation (more accurately, apparent lack of investigation) in the Shak'a case, see *TNCW*, p. 445, citing discussion and protest in the Israeli press.
44. Trudy Rubin, *Christian Science Monitor*, Nov. 18, 1982; see also *New York Times*, same date.
45. Robert I. Friedman, "West Bank Bombings," *Nation*, Dec. 25, 1982; *Middle East International*, Jan. 21, 1983.
46. Nov. 12, 1982 (see the reference of note 52); *Ha'aretz*, Oct. 1, 1982; *Action Alert*, American-Arab Anti-Discrimination Committee (ADC), October 27, 1982. In January 1983, Ms. Shak'a was granted an exit visa, after intervention by the State Department; ADC Bi-Weekly Report, Jan. 31 - Feb. 11.
47. Menachem Golan, letter, *Jerusalem Post*, Nov. 3, 1982.
48. *New Outlook*, June/July 1982. Rubinstein covers the West Bank for the Labor Party journal *Davar*.
49. Danny Rubinstein, *Davar*, Nov. 15, 1982. There is an up-beat account the preceding day by David Richardson in the English-language *Jerusalem Post*.
50. Michael Precker, "A maverick view of the West Bank; Begin's former administrator calls for a role for the Palestinians," *Boston Globe*, Dec. 19, 1982. The quoted phrases appear in the front-page notification of Precker's article-interview.
51. Uri Avneri, *Haolam Haze*, Oct. 13, 1982.
52. For a detailed record of Milson's actual achievements, including these, see *Only Do Not Say That You Did Not Know*, a publication of the Israeli Committee for Solidarity with Bir Zeit (the West Bank university that was closed by Professor Milson 3 days after he took office and kept closed for two months, then repeatedly closed and harassed afterwards), Jerusalem, June 1982, described as "the *Black Book* of the civil administration's actions in the West Bank and Gaza strip." It was published on June 5, 1982, to mark "the fifteenth anniversary of the

Israeli occupation"—and the opening of Israel's "war of aggression against the Palestinian people in Lebanon." A translation is being prepared for publication.

53. Zvi Barel, *Ha'aretz*, 20, 27 August 1982.

54. Testimony of Merle Thorpe, Jr., President of the Foundation for Middle East Peace, Dec. 16, 1981; see chapter 2, note 11. Thorpe testified along with the other members of the study group, two formerly in the State Department, one a former Secretary of Commerce and former President of the World Jewish Congress (Philip Klutznick).

55. Vincent Sheean, *Personal History* (Doubleday, Doran & Co., New York, 1935; sections reprinted in Walid Khalidi, ed., *From Haven to Conquest*, Institute for Palestine Studies, Beirut, 1971).

56. Norman Kempster, *Los Angeles Times*, September 29, 1982; Charles Hoffman, *Jerusalem Post*, Jan. 30, 1983. The first editorial in the new Arabic newspaper put out by the Village Leagues states that they will "work for the national goals of ending occupation and acquiring the right to self-determination, through direct negotiations between Israel and the Palestinians" (Supplement on the Palestinians under Israeli Rule, *Israel & Palestine*, vol. V, no. 110, 1982, citing *Ha'aretz* and the *Jerusalem Post*, June 17, 1982).

57. Abba Eban, "Obstacles to Autonomy," *New Outlook* (Tel Aviv), June/July 1982.

58. *New York Times*, May 19, 1976, Dec. 21, 1980; see *TNCW*, pp. 281f., for fuller discussion.

59. Pryce-Jones, "The Palestinian pattern."

60. *Al Hamishmar*, August 20, 1982. Saif ad-din Zuabi, who has long been associated with the Labor Party, was Vice-President of the Knesset and a high official of the Ministry of Agriculture.

61. Kapeliouk, *Israel*, p. 281, citing an interview with Eric Rouleau, *Le Monde*, February 19, 1970.

62. Kimche, *There Could Have Been Peace*, pp. 288f.

63. Amos Elon, *Ha'aretz*, Nov. 13, 1981; reprinted in *Israleft News Service* (Jerusalem), Nov. 17, 1981.

64. See Kimche, *There Could Have Been Peace*, pp. 286f.

65. See the comments by General Haim Bar-Lev, a cabinet member in the Meir and Rabin governments, in the Labor Party journal *Ot*, March 9, 1972, quoted in *TNCW*, p. 460.

66. Edward Witten, "Cold Silence," *Ha'aretz*, Jan. 6, 1983.

67. See *Peace in the Middle East?*, pp. 120-2.

68. Henry Kissinger, *The White House Years* (Little, Brown & Co., Boston, 1976, pp. 1279, 1291; for further discussion of this curious document, see *TNCW*, chapter 6); James Akins, review of *Years of Upheaval* (Little, Brown & Co., Boston, 1982), in *American-Arab Affairs*, Summer 1982. For some further examples of Kissinger's astonishing inanities, which much impressed many journalists and academics, see *TNCW*, p. 406; also pp. 338f., below.

69. See Tillman, *The United States \in the Middle East*, chapter 6, on Soviet policies. He observes that "The official Soviet position has been consistent since 1948 in support of Israel's right to exist and consistent since 1967 in support of Israel's right to a secure national existence, as called for in Security Council Resolution 242, within its 1967 borders." The USSR has even offered to provide security guarantees (p. 246).

70. Charles William Maynes (editor of *Foreign Policy*), *Boston Globe*, June 15, 1982.

71. For some examples, see *Multinational Oil Corporations and U.S. Foreign*

Policy, Report to the Committee on Foreign Relations, U.S. Senate, January 2, 1975 (U.S. Government Printing Office, Washington, 1975, Part III, Section VII).

72. *Ha'aretz*, June 25, 1973; *Yediot Ahronot*, Sept. 16, 1973. Cited by Kapeliouk, *Israel*, pp. 49-50, along with a range of similar evaluations by Israeli generals (among them, Sharon), intelligence specialists, orientalists, and others.

73. Amos Perlmutter, Michael Handel and Uri Bar-Joseph, *Two Minutes Over Baghdad* (Vallentine, Mitchel & Co., London, 1982, p. 33-4). They argue that Sadat's war aims were limited because of the threat of nuclear retaliation by Israel, and also allege that Israel's threat to use nuclear weapons impelled the U.S. to provide a massive shipment of conventional weapons to Israel. For more on this topic, see *TNCW*, pp. 321, 458. As for the USSR, "Evidence that the Soviet Union did not support President Sadat's decision to go to war is persuasive" (Barry M. Blechman and Douglas M. Hart, "The Political Utility of Nuclear Weapons," *International Security*, vol. 7, no. 1, 1982).

74. *Jerusalem Post*, November 13, 1981. On the January 1976 Arab initiative, which has virtually disappeared from history in the U.S. (it is not even mentioned in the unusually careful review in Tillman, *The United States and the Middle East*, for example), see *TNCW*, pp. 267, 300, 461.

75. For references and discussion, see *TNCW*, p. 268; also p. 70, above.

76. *Jerusalem Post*, Nov. 15, 1976; *Davar*, Nov. 21, 1976; *Israleft News Service*, Dec. 1, 1976.

77. Bernard Gwertzman, *New York Times*, August 21, 1977.

78. *New York Times*, March 21, 1977.

79. Tillman, *The United States and the Middle East*, p. 213. Tillman gives an extensive (though incomplete) record of PLO moves towards accommodation, some of them fairly explicit. See also my articles in *New Politics* (Winter, 1975-6; Winter 1978-9), reviewing many of these developments. See also *TNCW*, chapters 9, 13.

80. David Hirst, *Manchester Guardian weekly*, August 7, 1977.

81. Elie Eliachar, quoted by Merle Thorpe, in the congressional testimony cited in note 54; Mattityahu Peled, interview, *Hotam*, Jan. 28, 1983; the Basle program did not actually refer to a "Jewish state" but rather to the vaguer concept of a national "home". The history of the exploitation of the Covenant would make an interesting research project, which might contain some surprises.

82. Tillman, *The United States in the Middle East*, pp. 217, 271-2, 238.

83. Letter, *New York Times*, Jan. 12, 1982.

84. See *TNCW*, p. 321; also John K. Cooley, "The Palestinians," in Haley and Snider, eds., *Lebanon in Crisis*, pp. 28-9, citing Sadat directly to this effect.

85. See p. 20.

86. Cited by Amnon Kapeliouk, *Le Monde diplomatique*, August 1982, from *Ma'ariv*, Dec. 5, 1975.

87. Editorial, *New Republic*, Nov. 29, 1982.

88. For example, Theodore Draper writes that "Even Mr. Sadat admittedly did not accept [Israel's] existence until he decided to come to Jerusalem" in 1977, and even then his "program called for peace on the most extreme Arab terms, except for those Arab extremists who would be satisfied with nothing but the total destruction of the state of Israel" *(New York Times Book Review*, May 17, 1981; for a longer quote, see *TNCW*, p. 460). Or Mitchell Cohen, Professor of Political Science at CUNY: "We must also note the historical persistence of the Palestinian national movement's insistence on no compromise and no partition, which helped lead it to destruction in 1948 and to Beirut in 1982" *(New Republic*, Oct. 25, 1982). Or Arthur P. Mendel, Professor of History at the University of Michigan: it is now likely "that Hussein will follow Sadat's example and

negotiate with Israel the compromise that most Israelis and Palestinians (in contrast to the P.L.O.) have long wanted" (letter, *New York Times*, Oct. 10, 1982). Or Kenneth Jacobson, director of Middle Eastern Affairs for the Anti-Defamation League: "In fact, the PLO is the major obstacle to Arab-Israeli peace, ideologically committed to Israel's destruction, never moving an iota from that commitment..." *(Christian Science Monitor,* July 13, 1982). Or Ivan Novick, who, with innumerable others, explains that "the core problem of the Arab-Israeli dispute is the failure of the Arab nations to come to terms with the existence of the permanence of the Jewish State"; see note 34). Or Yitzhak Rabin: "the facts speak for themselves"; "the main reason—the heart of the Arab-Israeli conflict—was, and still is, the fact that except for Egypt, there has been no readiness on the part of the Arab leaders to reconcile themselves with the existence of Israel as a viable, Jewish, independent state—regardless of its boundaries"; and as for Egypt, "for 28 years [i.e., until 1977], no one believed that Egypt would make peace with Israel" *(Harvard International Review*, Sept.-Oct. 1982; recall his statement in *Davar,* Nov. 1976, referring to Sadat's willingness to make peace in 1971, p. 68 above, though in that case to an Israeli audience, who could be expected to know the facts). Or, to cite one of 1000 editorials: "the unexpected conquest of the land in 1967 and the Arabs' refusal to reclaim it with a peace treaty have left the Begin-Sharon bulldozers in charge of policy" (Max Frankel, editor, *New York Times*, Nov. 15, 1982). See also note 111. And so on, in an almost endless litany.

89. *New York Times*, June 20, 1982, referring to the situation as of 1982. Note that as in the case of many of the references of the preceding note, this was written well after numerous other Arab initiatives, beyond the pre-1977 ones just reviewed.

90. "...Sadat was the first Arab leader who, a year after coming to power, declared his willingness to make peace with Israel in his famous reply [February 1971] to [UN negotiator] Dr. Jarring's memorandum" (editorial, *Ha'aretz*, October 8, 1981); four days after Sadat's "initiative, later known by his own name, for solving the Middle East problem," Gunnar Jarring presented his "famous report of 8 February 1971...to which Egypt gave a positive reply" (Ghali Shoukri, *Egypt: Portrait of a President,* Zed press, London, 1981, pp. 50-51). See also Mordechai Gur *(Ma'ariv,* Oct. 11 1981; *Israeli Mirror):* "In February 1971 [Sadat] said that he was prepared to make peace with Israel." Also Rabin, p. 68. and many others.

91. Kapeliouk, *Israel,* pp. 59-60.

92. Eric Pace, "Anwar el-Sadat, the Daring Arab Pioneer of Peace With Israel," *New York Times*, Oct. 7, 1981.

93. Frederic L. Paxson, one of a group of American historians who offered their services to the state for this purpose during World War I; see *TNCW*, p. 70.

94. Mark Helprin, "American Jews and Israel: Seizing a New Opportunity," *New York Times Magazine*, Nov. 7, 1982.

95. See note 34. Hertzberg is responding to the President of the ZOA, who alleges that support for his (basically, Likud) position is far broader, excluding only "a tiny, unrepresentative minority of the American Jewish community, a fringe element," in Hertzberg's paraphrase. See also Julius Berman's response to Helprin, p. 72*.

96. Flapan, *Zionism and the Palestinians,* p. 116.

97. As noted by Amnon Kapeliouk, *Le Monde diplomatique,* July 1982; see Shulamit Har-Even, *Ha'aretz*, June 30, 1982 (reprinted in *Palestine/Israel Bulletin*, Sept. 1982); also B. Michael, *Ha'aretz*, June 22, 1982, citing the official IDF spokesman. To cite an example almost at random, a single Israeli air raid on

Beirut in July, before the really massive bombing began, killed 209 people, "almost all of them civilian" (Robert Fisk, *London Times*, July 13, 1982.

98. Kapeliouk, *Israel*, p. 41.

99. B. Michael, *Ha'aretz*, July 16, 1982, citing official police statistics in response to the claim by Defense Minister Sharon that the number of victims was 1392—a number that turned out to include 285 IDF soldiers, 392 Arabs from the occupied territories (some of them killed in preparing alleged terrorist attacks), 326 victims of terrorism of unspecified origin in various other countries, etc. Sharon repeated the same figure in a safer format, a *New York Times* Op-Ed (Aug. 29, 1982), writing that "since 1965, 1,392 civilians have died and 6,400 have been wounded as a result of P.L.O. terrorist raids against our people." Recall Avneri's description of Sharon as a "compulsive liar," like his "pocket edition," Menachem Milson. The characterization is, in fact, not uncommon in the Israeli press, but in the *Times* Sharon is safe from refutation.

100. *TNCW*, pp. 296-7. In this interchange, 6 Israelis and 450 Arabs, nearly all Lebanese civilians, were reported killed.

101. *Migvan* (Labor Party), October/November 1982, quoting Aluf Hareven of the Van Leer Institute, in a debate on "Zionism - 82" held at Tel Aviv University.

102. See *TNCW*, pp. 458f., and discussion below.

103. Walter Lippmann, *Public Opinion* (Allen & Unwin, London, 1932, p. 248; first published in 1921). See *TNCW*, chapter 2, for further discussion in a broader context.

104. See note 64, above.

105. On Israel's immediate rejection of the Fahd plan, see Norman Kempster, *Los Angeles Times—Boston Globe*, Aug. 10, 1981, and the brief story in the *New York Times* on the same day.

106. Daniel Bloch, *Davar*, Nov. 13, 1981. We return to a fuller discussion in chapter 7.

107. Yoel Marcus, *Yediot Ahronot*, Nov. 6, 1981.

108. See *Palestine/Israel Bulletin*, April 1982, citing *Haolam Haze*, February 3, and the *Jerusalem Post*, February 1, 1982.

109. "How Syria's Peace Plan Was Swept under the Carpet," *Ha'aretz*, Feb. 12, 1982; *Israeli Mirror*.

110. *Jerusalem Post*, International Edition, Feb. 14-20, 1982; cited in *Palestine/Israel Bulletin*, April 1982.

111. For example, Amos Oz, "Has Israel Altered its Visions?," *New York Times Magazine*, July 11, 1982 (see chapter 2, note 64). Compare the picture portrayed by Mark Helprin in the same journal; see note 94. See also note 88. See also Amos Oz, "From Jerusalem to Cairo," *Encounter*, April 1982, for an intriguing method of evading the historical record. Oz claims that "there is no symmetry" between Israel and the PLO, because "the PLO resembles the *militant* position in Israel," namely, the position that "disregard[s] the identity of the Palestinian problem" (note that this "militant position," contrary to what he asserts, is the mainstream position in Israel, adopted by both political groupings, and has been such since the days of Weizmann and Ben-Gurion). How does he conclude that the PLO resembles this position? By totally ignoring the record of their actual proposals, as reviewed briefly above, and restricting himself to their unwillingness to recognize the legitimacy of Zionism or to support partition "as a fundamental and right solution," rather than a compromise imposed by circumstances (a stand in which they mimic Ben-Gurion and others, contrary to Oz's claims). He also grossly misrepresents Sadat, claiming that his "visit to Jerusalem" represented "a conceptual revolution." With this technique of presenting a completely false picture of the history of socialist Zionism including the stand of the Labor governments and the current position of the Labor Alignment, and ignoring the

diplomatic efforts of the Arabs including the PLO in favor of irrelevant commentary about the PLO attitude towards the "legitimacy" of Zionism, Oz is able to maintain the pose of the tragic victim, so willing to make peace if only the Arabs were not committed to their militancy. This pose has been a great success among western intellectuals, though Israeli doves naturally find it extremely offensive; and pernicious, in that it makes a major contribution to reinforcing attitudes and policies in the west (primarily, the U.S.) that contribute directly to settlement and oppression in the occupied territories, aggression in Lebanon, and so on.

112. *Jerusalem Post*, March 6, 1981. Rabin, who was Prime Minister at the time, conceded the facts but said that the boats were captured before the proposed gesture, and that this was simply an excuse for the PLO to back out of the agreement. Shimon Peres, who was Defense Minister at the time, declined to comment.

113. See *TNCW*, p. 458, citing Livia Rokach's very important study, *Israel's Sacred Terrorism* (AAUG, Belmont, 1980), based largely on Sharett's *Personal Diary, (Yoman Ishi*, Hebrew, Ma'ariv, 1979).

114. Tillman, *The United States in the Middle East*, pp. 215-8. Congressman Findley was the senior Republican member of the House Middle East Subcommittee. See *New York Times*, Nov. 27, 1978 for a brief report; there is no further mention of the matter in the *Times*. Tillman cites Arafat's statement to Findley with no qualifications, making no mention of the allegation that Findley transmitted it inaccurately or that the PLO retracted it. According to Tillman, "Thwarted by the lack of American response to its signals of willingness to compromise and angered by the Camp David agreement and Egypt's separate peace with Israel, the PLO reverted to bluster and threat and stepped up acts of terror"; p. 218.

115. *Israel & Palestine* (Paris), July-August 1982; Brezhnev's statement is cited from his address to the 26th Congress of the Soviet Communist Party in February 1981. See also Shmuel Segev, *Ma'ariv*, March 2, 1983, noting the re-endorsement of this position at the PLO National Council meeting in Algiers in February 1983. I noticed no reference to these facts (or much else reported here) in the U.S. press, apart from quotes from Arafat and Sartawi in an article from Tunis by Lally Weymouth, special to the *Boston Globe*, Dec. 21, 1982. There is an oblique and inaccurate reference to the facts in the *New York Times* at the end of a story on a different topic by Thomas Friedman, who writes that the Brezhnev plan "indirectly recognized the right of Israel to live in peace," and was endorsed by the PLO; there was nothing "indirect" about it. It is doubtful that even this reference would have appeared in the *Times* had it not been for the context, a story worth emphasis as illustrating PLO intransigence; see note 116.

116. *Israel & Palestine*, July-August 1982. Sartawi's relations with the PLO had been stormy. While he was regularly defended by Arafat against the "radicals" and rejectionists, his conflicts with them were sufficiently harsh so that he occasionally resigned from the National Council, with varying interpretations as to what had in fact occurred. See *TNCW*, pp. 443-4 for a mid-1981 example. See also Thomas L. Friedman, "A P.L.O. Moderate Resigns In Protest," *New York Times*, Feb. 21, 1983, reporting at length Sartawi's resignation from the National Council once again after he was prevented from addressing the group (the resignation was not accepted; see Trudy Rubin, *Christian Science Monitor*, March 11, 1983; it is also worth noting that Labor Party leader Shimon Peres had succeeded in preventing him from speaking at the Socialist International meeting, just prior to his assassination). Some PLO officials stated that Arafat did not object "to the

substance of his ideas but that the P.L.O. leader feared it would lead to a dispute that could upset the entire conference and scuttle his own quiet maneuvering to gain approval for more meetings with Israelis," but Friedman questions this interpretation in the light of the statement by the official PLO representative that Sartawi "did not represent the views of the Palestinian leadership." Peled is far more marginal in Israeli politics than Sartawi was within the PLO. Peled had been associated with the tiny Sheli party, a dovish Zionist party that has no current members in the Knesset, but broke relations with it after the Lebanon war when some of its leaders denounced his meetings with Arafat and gave their support to "crimes against humanity" in Lebanon (Peled, interview; see note 81). These facts are suppressed by those who point to Sartawi's troubled relationship with the central PLO decision-making body as proof of PLO iniquity.

117. *Ha'aretz*, July 10, 1981, cited in a July 1982 publication *(Who will stop them?*, Hebrew), of the Committee Against the War in Lebanon, Jerusalem.

118. *Migvan*, Labor Party Monthly, August 1982. For further discussion of these matters, see *TNCW*, Tillman, *The United States in the Middle East*, and the regular reporting in such journals as the *New Outlook, Israel & Palestine*, and *Palestine/Israel Bulletin*.

119. Flapan, *Zionism and the Palestinians*, pp. 70ff. Within the mainstream, he notes, Moshe Sharett (then Shertok) disagreed with this view, arguing that it was pointless to deny that the leadership is the "legal representative" of the Palestinians and to refuse to negotiate with them (pp. 149-50).

4

Israel and Palestine: Historical Backgrounds

It is widely believed that the Israeli invasion of Lebanon in the summer of 1982 opened a new chapter in the U.S.-Israel "special relationship." That seems dubious; the U.S. remains committed to ensuring Israel's military dominance in the region, so that further aggression resulting from the imbalance of force is not unlikely. No less crucially, the U.S. remains committed—rhetoric aside—to financing Israel's settlement programs in the occupied territories. The latter commitment, however it may be disguised, is expressed with considerable clarity in the aid increases requested by the President and increased further by Congress after the Lebanon war. This U.S. commitment eliminates the possibility for a peaceful resolution of the Israel-Arab conflict and for any recognition of the elementary rights of the Palestinians. It is nevertheless true that the events of summer 1982 shook one pillar of the special relationship, the ideological element in the "support for Israel" (again, I note here the misleading terminology; see p. 4), though the other two major elements, the diplomatic and material support for a Greater Israel, remained unchanged—in fact, were strengthened—as 1982 drew to a close.

Israel's 1982 invasion can only be understood in the context of the Arab-Jewish conflicts in Palestine, then beyond, that developed from what the indigenous population saw as "the Zionist invasion" and what the settlers regarded as "the return to their homeland." These developing interactions were complex, and often tragic. It would take a lengthy and detailed study to do them justice. The preceding chapter was concerned with the attitudes and policies of a broad range of actors within a narrow historical period: following the 1967 war. This chapter will extend the time frame while narrowing the focus to developments within the former Palestine (cis-Jordan). The discussion is, needless to say, far from comprehensive; I will review some facts that seem to me to have a direct bearing on understanding the current situation.[1]

1   The Pre-State Period

The Arabs of Palestine were overwhelmingly opposed to a Jewish state, or to large-scale Jewish immigration, which often led to their dispossession from their lands. "They had not been consulted at any level in the preparation of European plans for the disposal of their homeland and felt in no way bound peaceably to accept their implementation."[2] This attitude is generally described as "intransigence" or even "anti-Semitism" in the American literature, which tends to accept as the natural point of departure the position expressed by Lord Arthur Balfour, author of the Balfour declaration of 1917 which committed Britain to "facilitate" the "establishment in Palestine of a national home for the Jewish people" on the condition that "nothing shall be done which may prejudice the civil and religious rights of the existing non-Jewish communities in Palestine. . . ." Two years later, he wrote a memorandum discussing the contradictions in the various pledges given during the war, noting that a French-controlled administration was simply imposed on the Syrians.[3] Expressing views held widely across the political spectrum, he continued:

> The contradiction between the letter of the Covenant and the policy of the Allies is even more flagrant in the case of the independent nation of Palestine than in that of the independent nation of Syria. For in Palestine we do not propose even to go through the form of consulting the wishes of the present inhabitants of the country, though the American [King-Crane] Commission has been going through the form of asking what they are. The four great powers are committed to Zionism and *Zionism, be it right or wrong, good or bad, is rooted in age-long tradition, in present needs, in future hopes, of far profounder import than the desires and prejudices of the 700,000 Arabs who now inhabit that ancient land.*

The people of "the independent nation of Palestine" never accepted the legitimacy of this point of view, and resisted it in a variety of ways. They repeatedly resorted to terrorist violence against Jews. The most extreme case was in late August 1929, when 133 Jews were massacred. The "most ghastly incident" was in Hebron, where 60 Jews were killed, most of them from an old Jewish community, largely anti-Zionist; the Arab police "stood passively by while their fellow Moslems moved into the town and proceeded to deeds which would have been revolting among animals," and a still greater slaughter was prevented only by the bravery of one member of the vastly undermanned British police.[4] Many were saved by Muslim neighbors.*

---

* The massacre followed a demonstration organized at the Wailing Wall in Jerusalem to counter "Arab arrogance"—"a major provocation even in the eyes of Jewish public

The opposition of the indigenous population to the Zionist project was never a secret. President Wilson's King-Crane Commission reported in 1919 that "the Zionists looked forward to a practically complete dispossession of the present non-Jewish inhabitants of Palestine" and estimated that the latter—"nearly nine-tenths of the whole—are emphatically against the entire Zionist programme." The Commission warned that to subject them to this program "would be a gross violation of the principle [of self-determination], and of the people's rights, though it kept within the forms of law," a conclusion disregarded by the great powers, including the U.S. The Commission, while expressing "a deep sense of sympathy for the Jewish cause," recommended limitation of Jewish immigration and abandonment of the goal of a Jewish state.

The Recommendations had no influence on policy and are barely even mentioned in standard histories. Where mentioned, they are generally dismissed. Thus the ESCO Foundation study (see note 1), while recognizing that the opinions summarized in the Commission report "undoubtedly reflected the prevalent political attitude in Syria and Palestine," nevertheless disparages the report on various grounds; crucially, because "it gave due consideration to only one part of the issue," namely Arab views, and did not give "equal consideration to the Jewish problem." Or to state the facts from a different point of view, the Commission's report gave due consideration only to the views of inhabitants of the land (recall that much of the indigenous Jewish minority was anti-Zionist), without giving equal consideration to the plans of European Zionists.[5]

In 1936-9, the Palestinian Arabs attempted a nationalist revolt after the failure of a long strike, which was ignored and ineffectual. David Ben-Gurion, eminently a realist, recognized its nature. In internal discussion, he noted that "in our political argument abroad, we minimize Arab opposition to us," but he urged, "let us not ignore the truth among ourselves." The truth was that "politically we are the aggressors and they defend themselves... The country is theirs, because they inhabit it, whereas we want to come here and settle down, and in their view we want to take away from them their country, while we are still outside." The revolt "is an active resistance by the Palestinians to what they regard as a usurpation of their homeland by the Jews... Behind the terrorism is a

---

opinion" (Flapan, *Zionism and the Palestinians*, p. 96). See Sheean, in Khalidi, *From Haven to Conquest*, for a detailed eyewitness account. This provocation was organized by Betar, the youth movement of Vladimir Jabotinsky's Revisionist organization, which is the precursor of Begin's Herut, the central element in the Likud coalition. The very name, "Betar," reflects the cynicism of this fascist-style movement, which, in Flapan's words, described Hitler "as the saviour of Germany, Mussolini as the political genius of the century," and often acted accordingly. The name is an acronym for "Brith Yosef Trumpeldor" ("the Covenant of Joseph Trumpeldor"). Trumpeldor was killed defending the northern settlement of Tel Hai from Bedouin attackers; Jabotinsky "opposed the Labour call for mobilisation to help the threatened settlements" (Flapan, p. 104).

movement, which though primitive is not devoid of idealism and self-sacrifice."[6]

The revolt was crushed by the British, with considerable brutality, after the 1938 Munich agreement permitted them to send sufficient military force.[7]

In later years, the indigenous Arab population rejected the idea, accepted as natural in the West, that they had a moral obligation to sacrifice their land to compensate for the crimes committed by Europeans against Jews. They perhaps wondered why a more appropriate response would not have been to remove the population of Bavaria and turn it into a Jewish state—or given the self-righteous moralizing they hear from the United States, why the project could not have been carried out in Massachusetts or New York. Many profess to find their lack of concern for the problems of the Jews incomprehensible or profoundly immoral, asking why the Palestinian Arabs, unlike the Jewish immigrants, were unwilling to accept a "territorial compromise," something less than what they hoped but a fair settlement, given conflicting demands. Perhaps the assessment is legitimate, but it is surely not hard to understand why the indigenous population should resist this conclusion. If someone were to take over your home, then offer you a few rooms in a "fair compromise," you might not be overwhelmed by his generosity, even if he were homeless, destitute, and persecuted.

As for the wretched survivors of Hitler's Holocaust themselves, it is likely that many—perhaps most—would have chosen to come to the United States had this opportunity been offered,* but the Zionist movement, including American Zionists, preferred that they settle in a Jewish

---

* To my knowledge, there has been no serious study of this question. For conflicting opinions, see Lieut.-General Morgan, British Chief of Staff to the Supreme Allied Commander, 1943-44, and Chief of UNRRA (the UN Relief and Rehabilitation Administration) Operations in Germany, 1945-46; and Yehuda Bauer, a well-known Israeli historian. Morgan believes that what "was represented as being the spontaneous surge of a tortured and persecuted people toward their long-lost homeland" was in fact the result of superb Zionist organization and "iron discipline" in the camps, misrepresented by "the skill of the Zionist propaganda campaign." "I fancy that, in reality, there were few among the travellers [Jewish refugees from Eastern Europe] who, of their own free will, would have gone elsewhere than to the U.S.A." His allegations concerning Zionist exploitation of UNRRA for political goals with little concern for the interests of the refugees read remarkably like subsequent Zionist allegations concerning Arab exploitation of its successor organization, UNRWA, in connection with the Palestinian refugees in its charge. Bauer, in contrast, concludes that the vast majority of the refugees preferred to go to Palestine, citing an UNRRA questionnaire indicating that 96.8% preferred to go to Palestine with only 393 of 19,311 wanting to go to the U.S. (pp. 202-3; his source is a Hebrew investigative commission report, published in Tel Aviv in 1946). He also concludes that by late 1947 about half would have preferred to go to the U.S., though after the establishment of the State of Israel in May 1948 "most Jews chose it" (pp. 317-8)—no alternative was in fact available. The Report to President Truman by his envoy Earl G. Harrison on the conditions and needs of displaced persons concluded that Palestine was the first choice of the Jewish DPs, noting however that many want to go there "because they realize that their opportunity to be admitted into the United States or into other countries in the Western hemisphere is limited, if not impossible."[8] Archival sources in Israel might well provide the answer to this question.

state, a story being relived today with Jewish emigrants from the USSR.[9] After the war, tens of thousands of Jewish displaced persons died in camps from miserable conditions and lack of care, and congressional Displaced Persons (DP) legislation gave priority not to Jews but to refugees from the Russian-occupied Baltic states, many of them Nazi sympathizers, including even SS troopers. There was little American Zionist support for legislation intended to bring DPs to the U.S. in contrast to massive support for resolutions calling for the establishment of a Jewish state. Dinnerstein comments: "Unspoken publicly, but in the air privately, was the Zionist concern that fewer European Jews would resettle in Israel if the possibility existed of getting to the United States." Jewish support for the legislation, which was extensive, was from non-Zionist or anti-Zionist groups, overwhelmingly.[10]

Some found this objectionable. Roosevelt's adviser Morris Ernst wrote in 1948 of his shock at the refusal of American Jewish leaders to consider the possibility of giving "these beaten people of Europe a choice," instead of offering them only the option of emigration to Palestine; the program he advanced "would free us from the hypocrisy of closing our own doors while making sanctimonious demands on the Arabs," he wrote, adding that he "was amazed and even felt insulted when active Jewish leaders decried, sneered and then attacked me as if I were a traitor" for suggesting that the survivors of the Holocaust be permitted the choice of emigrating to the United States.[11]

The question remains a sensitive one, not surprisingly. In 1980 a private commission of prominent American Jews was established, headed by former Supreme Court Justice Arthur Goldberg, "to examine the behavior of Jewish organizations in this country at the time of the Nazi campaign to annihilate European Jews." 15 months later the commission had "split up in anger and dissension," with charges and countercharges as to what had gone wrong. The commission's main financial backer alleged that "It became apparent that the vestiges of the old establishment were fighting to protect its name." Goldberg, as well as research director Seymour Finger, denied this charge, claiming that "the promised money wasn't forthcoming." "Commission sources said that [established Jewish groups] had objected to the panel's examining such painful questions as whether thousands, or tens of thousands, of Jews could have been saved if American-Jewish organizations had acted forcefully and applied pressures on the Roosevelt Administration." A draft report stated that it was "incontrovertible" that "the Jewish leadership in America at no stage decided to proclaim total mobilization for rescue." Established Zionist organizations, the draft report continued, were "riveted to postwar plans" and the creation of a Jewish state, so that the "energies of those American Jews who were profoundly concerned were dissipated, when the ground was burning under their feet." One of the leading members of the American Jewish community, Rabbi Stephen Wise, who was also close to

Roosevelt, opposed a congressional effort in 1943 to set up a commission "to effectuate the rescue of the Jewish people of Europe" because the resolution failed to include a provision demanding that the British open up Palestine to Jews. The draft states:

> What is certain is that the exclusive concentration on Palestine as a solution, coupled with its intrinsic pessisimism as to other alternatives, distracted the Zionist movement as well as large segments of American Jews from giving serious attention to various rescue plans offered by the advocates of separating rescue from political or ideological considerations.[12]

These conclusions accord reasonably well with the scholarly literature; see note 10. Note that the mandate of the Goldberg Commission did not extend to the question raised above: the attitude of established Jewish organizations, particularly the Zionist organizations, to Jewish immigration after Europe was liberated, a question touched upon only obliquely in the scholarly literature.

Whether there would have been a way to reconcile competing claims and needs in the former Palestine is not clear. By the time of the Second World War and the Nazi Holocaust, the question had become academic, at least for the large majority of the Zionist movement. In the spring of 1942, the American Zionist movement endorsed the idea of a Jewish state (the "Biltmore program") and in November, "the creation of a Jewish state became the official goal of the Zionist movement" under Ben-Gurion's initiative.[13] Prior to this, the official position had been a commitment to some form of "parity" between Jewish and Arab populations.* This commitment to Jewish statehood preceded the discovery of firm information that the Nazi state was undertaking its Final Solution, though its vicious anti-Semitism had long been apparent.

2   The War of Independence/Conquest

In November 1947, the General Assembly of the United Nations recommended the partition of mandatory Palestine (cis-Jordan) into a Jewish and an Arab state. The recommendation was accepted by the bulk of the Zionist movement—though not by Begin's terrorist army (the Irgun Tsvai Leumi) and LEHI (the Stern Group), the terrorist force com-

---

* Simha Flapan argues that these commitments were tactical maneuvers.[14] See also *TNCW*, pp. 258-9, citing, in particular, Nahum Goldmann's rather cynical interpretation of the outspoken rejection of the concept of a Jewish state by Ben-Gurion and others.

manded by the current Foreign Minister, Yitzhak Shamir* — and rejected with near unanimity by the Arabs of Palestine.[15] General Assembly resolutions are considered to be non-binding; Israel, for example, holds the world record for rejection of subsequent ones. The U.S. remained ambivalent, for a time preferring a trusteeship until Truman recognized the Jewish state established in May 1948.

Civil strife broke out immediately after the partition recommendation, with terror and violence on both sides. As usual, it is the record of Arab violence that remains in popular consciousness, but that is far from the whole story. For example, on December 18 the Palmach—the kibbutz-based strike force of the Haganah (the Defense Force of the Jewish settlement in Palestine, the precursor of the IDF)—carried out a "retaliation" operation against the village of Khissas, killing 10 Arabs, including one woman and four children. Israeli military historian Uri Milshtein writes that this operation, commanded by Moshe Dayan, was contrary to the Haganah policy "not to 'heat up' relatively quiet areas," but was justified by Dayan on the grounds that it had a "desirable effect." Sykes suggests that this operation, three weeks before the first Arab irregulars entered the country, may have "precipitated the next phase of the war."[16]

The better-organized Jewish community had the advantage in the military conflict. By May, its armies had taken over parts of the territory assigned to the Palestinian state. The Irgun-LEHI Deir Yassin massacre in April had already taken place, one major factor in causing the flight of much of the Arab population. This fact was reported with much enthusiasm in official statements of Irgun and LEHI, specifically, by the terrorist commander Menachem Begin, who took pride in the operation in which some 250 defenseless people were slaughtered, including more than 100 women and children, with 4 killed among the attacking forces.

Recently discovered personal testimonies of the leaders of the operation reveal that the majority favored eliminating whoever stood in their way, including women and children, and proceeded to do so, murdering captured and wounded. Begin praised his killers for their humanity, for "acting in a way that no other fighting force had ever done," a refrain that

---

* It has been known for some time that this group, an offshoot of the Irgun, offered to cooperate with the Nazis against the British. The topic has recently been brought to public attention in Israel, where columnist B. Michael published a LEHI proposal of January 1941 to the Nazis (*Ha'aretz*, Jan. 31, 1983; also Feb. 6). The proposal expressed its sympathy for the "German conception" of a "New Order in Europe" and offered to cooperate in the formation of a Jewish state "on a national and totalitarian basis, which will establish relations with the German Reich" and protect Nazi interests in the Middle East. An English version appears in Lenni Brenner, *Zionism in the Age of the Dictators* (Lawrence Hill, Westport Conn., 1983), translated from the original in the Nazi archives, from David Yisraeli, *The Palestine Problem in German Politics* (Bar Ilan University, Ramat Gan, Israel, 1974).

has been echoed after every war, including the 1982 war, and that is loyally repeated by supporters who are much in awe of Israeli "purity of arms," a new phenomenon in the history of warfare. The Irgun command sent an internal message of congratulations on the "wonderful operation of conquest," saying: "As in Deir Yassin, so everywhere... Oh Lord, Oh Lord, you have chosen us for conquest." The Haganah command condemned the operation, including the looting and plunder that appear to have been the objective according to the recently discovered documents, noting that the village was one of those that had avoided any cooperation with the Arab forces. The massacre was also condemned officially by the Palestinian Yishuv (the pre-state Jewish settlement). An official government military history accords the incident 3 lines, giving the date, reporting that combat was "light," and finishing with the statement that "in the course of the conquest of the village about 200 of its inhabitants were killed, including women and children." An additional paragraph then explains how Arab propaganda over what it called "the Deir Yassin massacre" backfired; "there is no doubt" that the affair contributed effectively to the collapse of the Arab forces because of the fear induced concerning "the cruelty of the Jews."[17] By May, about 300,000 Arabs had fled, about 1/3 of them from territories assigned to the Palestinian State.[18]

The armies of the Arab states entered the war immediately after the State of Israel was founded in May. Fighting continued, almost all of it within the territory asigned to the Palestinian state, leading to an eventual further partition, with about half of the proposed Palestinian state incorporated within Israel and the remainder taken over by Jordan (then Transjordan) and Egypt. This arrangement persisted until 1967, when the remainder too was conquered by Israel (along with the Syrian Golan Heights and the Sinai). About 700,000 Palestinians fled or were expelled in the 1948 conflict.

It is common to refer to these events in a manner such as this: "Events during 1947-1948 led to a situation whereby Jordan became the Arab successor state in Palestine."[19] This is inaccurate. The events led to a situation whereby Jordan *and Israel* became "the successor states." The Gaza region was divided between Israel and Egypt, and the remainder of the territory assigned to the Palestinian state was divided between Israel and Jordan. Israel and Jordan, but not Egypt, annexed the territories they occupied. About half the Palestinian state became part of Israel.

For many years, it was claimed that the Palestinians fled in 1948 on the orders of Arab leaders. The basis for this claim was undermined by Erskine Childers in 1961, though one hears it still. In fact, it seems that the Arab leadership tried to prevent the flight, which was encouraged by Israeli terror and psychological warfare, sometimes direct expulsion.[20] Additional thousands of Arabs—citizens of Israel, in this case—were expelled from Israel's Galilee region during the attack on Egypt in 1956,* and hundreds of thousands more fled or were expelled from the conquered territories during and after the 1967 war. In a detailed investigation of the refugee flight, W. W. Harris estimates that of a pre-war population of about 1.4 million, approximately 430,000 left their homes from June to December 1967 (most of them in June), with considerable variation among regions (over 90% of the 100,000 people in the Golan Heights fled, but less than 20% of the 400,000 residents of the Gaza Strip, with other local variations). High population losses in some areas resulted from "a legacy of assorted fears," for example, in the vicinity of Qibya, where Israeli forces commanded by Ariel Sharon had conducted a major massacre in 1953 (see pp. 383f.). Israeli hawks on occasion threaten a new expulsion if the Arabs do not mind their manners, as when Defense Minister Sharon warns that "the Palestinians should not forget 1948." "The hint is clear," Amnon Kapeliouk comments, citing Sharon's statement.[22]

In the U.S., it is commonly argued that the annexation of the West Bank by Jordan was illegitimate. The argument has merit, but then it is difficult to see why it does not apply with equal force to Israel's annexation of half of the designated Palestinian state—though this question is, in fact, academic, and has been since 1949. The argument also overlooks the fact that Israel and Jordan were acting in accord with a secret agreement to partition Palestine in 1947-8, both of them regarding the Palestinian leadership as a primary enemy. Yoram Peri observes that Ben-Gurion's "tacit understanding with King Abdullah of Transjordan, which allowed the latter to move into the territories west of the River Jordan, which had been allotted by the 1947 UN Partition Plan to the Arab Palestinian state,...was not revealed either to the Cabinet nor to the military command," leading to internal conflict when the Southern Commander, Yigal Allon, was prevented from launching an expedition into the West Bank by Ben-Gurion in October 1948. It has been argued further that the entry of the Arab states into the war was in part motivated by opposition to the ambitions of King Abdullah and that ". . . Egyptian intentions were not to invade Palestine, but to find a diplomatic solution to the conflict."[23] Similar beliefs led Nahum Goldmann to recommend against the May decision to establish the State of Israel at the time, on the assumption that a peaceful diplomatic settlement might be possible.

King Abdullah was assassinated by a 19-year old Palestinian in July 1951. This fact is commonly cited as proof that the Palestinians (or Arabs

---

* This fact, previously unknown, was revealed by former Prime Minister Yitzhak Rabin of the Labor Party, who at the time was commander of Israel's northern region, where the expulsions took place. He estimates that 3-5000 Arabs—Israeli citizens—were expelled by the Army to Syria at that time. These Arabs had been expelled from their native villages in 1951 in the course of water diversion projects.[21]

more generally) will not tolerate a "moderate" leadership that will accept the existence of Israel. A closer look at the backgrounds—in particular, the Israeli-Jordanian plan to destroy the planned Palestinian state—suggests a somewhat different interpretation.

As for Nahum Goldmann, he became President of the World Zionist Organization from 1956 to 1968 but remained critical of Israel's diplomacy, including its entry into the Cold War system on the side of the U.S. and its post-1967 rejectionism. He was also critical of the tactic of converting the Holocaust into a device to justify atrocities and murder. At the beginning of the Jewish New Year, in October 1981, he wrote:

> We will have to understand that Jewish suffering during the Holocaust no longer will serve as a protection, and we certainly must refrain from using the argument of the Holocaust to justify whatever we may do. To use the Holocaust as an excuse for the bombing of Lebanon, for instance, as Menachem Begin does, is a kind of "Hillul Hashem" [sacrilege], a banalization of the sacred tragedy of the Shoah [Holocaust], which must not be misused to justify politically doubtful and morally indefensible policies.[24]

Goldmann was also one of those who felt that American "supporters of Israel" were causing it considerable harm. At the January 1981 meeting of the World Jewish Congress in Israel, he spoke of the need "to effect a change in our policy towards the Arabs." "What Israel is doing in this regard is very bad," he added, "and equally bad is the effect of the screams uttered by American Jewry."[25] He was also a sharp critic of the Lebanon invasion. Goldmann died in August 1982, after a lifetime of service to the Zionist cause. Prime Minister Begin did not attend his funeral and "no official statement of grief was issued by the government," the American Jewish press observed, noting that this indicated the "shabby way" in which the Israeli government treats "its opponents." A headline in the *Jerusalem Post* read: "Goldmann's Death is Ignored." PLO chairman Yasser Arafat sent condolences, stating:

> The Palestinians mourn the death of Nahum Goldmann. He was a Jewish statesman of a unique personality. He fought for justice and legitimate rights for all peoples.[26]

3   The Israel-Arab Wars

In the U.S., it is intoned with ritual uniformity that Israel's wars, prior to the 1982 Lebanon invasion, were strictly defensive. Even serious political analysts make such statements, for example, Hans Morgenthau, who wrote that "Four times the Arabs tried to eliminate Israel by war"; it is, furthermore, "an undisputed historical fact" that the wars had to do with "the existence of a Jewish state in the midst of the Arab world."[27] In press reporting, this is also taken regularly as an undisputed historical fact. As one of innumerable examples, consider David Shipler's explanation of why the invasion of Lebanon in 1982 caused "a crisis of conscience" in Israel:

> ...this has been a different kind of war for Israel. Never before did Israel go to war when its actual existence was not threatened. Never before was it clearly responsible for initiating the fighting without being provoked by some Arab military move with devastating potential.[28]

Similarly, Robert Moskin describes Chaim Herzog's history of the Arab-Israeli wars as "a volume that anyone who wants to understand what Israel has endured will have to read or refer to,"[29] implying that the wars have all been "endured" by Israel, a passive victim of Arab aggressiveness.* The assumption that prior to the 1982 Lebanese invasion, Israel's posture was strictly defensive is shared not only by a wide range of political analysts and journalists, but also by people regarded as critics of Israeli adventurism. Jacobo Timerman, for example, published a critique of the Lebanon invasion that is regarded as quite harsh, and in part is. He begins by asserting that Israel's "previous wars were in defense against aggression... The fact that the invasion of Lebanon was the first war launched by the state of Israel could not go unnoticed."[30]

Such statements, which are common, are untrue—indeed, astonishing—certainly with regard to the 1956 Israeli-French-British attack on Egypt and the 1978 invasion of Lebanon (not generally counted as one of the Arab-Israeli wars, perhaps because the aggression was too obvious, or perhaps because only some 2000 Palestinians and Lebanese were killed and 250,000 made refugees, with many towns left in ruins).[31] The 1973 war was a clear case of an Arab attack, but on territory occupied by Israel, after diplomatic efforts at settlement had been rebuffed (see chapter 3). Hence it is hardly "an undisputed historical fact" that in this case the war

---

* Moskin also refers to the role of "Soviet armaments, advisers and agitation" and other Russian conniving as a factor in inciting the militant Arabs, noting that the USSR has supplied weapons (specifically, anti-aircraft missiles) to the Arabs (in contrast, U.S. supply of jet bombers to Israel, used for bombing raids deep within Egypt, merely demonstrates our commitment to peace) and that "In 1970 Soviet pilots were flying combat missions for Egypt" (namely, defensive missions when Israel was carrying out deep penetration bombing raids against civilian targets in Egypt, a fact that he fails to mention). Moskin criticizes Herzog's book because he "remains neutral about the morality or necessity of the [1982] attack beyond the Litani River," tacitly implying that one could raise no question about the invasion of southern Lebanon south of the Litani, an assumption adopted quite generally by the American press, which grants Israel the same right of aggression accorded to the United States itself.

had to do with "the existence of a Jewish state." On Sadat's war aims, see chapter 3, note 73 and text. On the 1948 war, see above.

The 1967 war also involves complexities often ignored by supporters of Israel here. It is, in fact, intriguing to see how the facts are presented. An interesting example is Michael Walzer's investigation of "just wars." Surveying a record of 2500 years, he finds only one example of "legitimate anticipation," that is, legitimate resort to a preemptive military strike in violation of the standard doctrine on this matter as embodied in the United Nations Charter (see note 31): namely, Israel's attack in June 1967. This is, furthermore, a "clear case" of *resistance* to aggression. "It is worth setting down some of the cases about which we have, I think, no doubts: the German attack on Belgium in 1914, the Italian conquest of Ethiopia, the Japanese attack on China, the German and Italian interventions in Spain, the Russian invasion of Finland, the Nazi conquests of Czechoslovakia, Poland, Denmark, Belgium, and Holland, the Russian invasions of Hungary and Czechoslovakia, the Egyptian *challenge* to Israel in 1967."[32]

Walzer offers no argument or evidence to show that the "Egyptian challenge" to Israel stands on a par with the "clear cases" of aggression cited. He simply states that Israel had a "just fear" of destruction—which, even if true, would hardly substantiate his claim. Israeli generals take a rather different view. The former Commander of the Air Force, General Ezer Weizmann, regarded as a hawk, stated that there was "no threat of destruction" but that the attack on Egypt, Jordan and Syria was nevertheless justified so that Israel could "exist according to the scale, spirit and quality she now embodies."[33] Citing corroboratory statements by Chief of Staff Chaim Bar-Lev and General Mattityahu Peled, Amnon Kapeliouk wrote that "no serious argument has been advanced to refute the thesis of the three generals." See p. 28. American intelligence held a similar view.[34] Furthermore, the interactions leading up to the war included provocative and destructive Israeli actions and threats, which Walzer ignores,[35] alongside of Egyptian and other Arab actions such as the closing of the Straits of Tiran, which Egypt claimed to be an internal waterway.

Among others who, unlike Walzer, have doubts about the Egyptian "challenge" as a "clear case" of aggression is Menachem Begin, who had the following remarks to make:

> In June 1967, we again had a choice. The Egyptian Army concentrations in the Sinai approaches do not prove that Nasser was really about to attack us. We must be honest with ourselves. We decided to attack him.

Begin of course regards the Israeli attack as justified; "This was a war of self-defense in the noblest sense of the term."[36] But then, it may be recalled that the term "self-defense" has acquired a technical sense in modern political discourse, referring to any military action carried out by a state that one directs, serves or "supports." What is, perhaps, of some interest is that an American democratic socialist dove goes well beyond Menachem Begin in portraying Israel's actions as defense against aggression. However one evaluates these complex circumstances, it is plainly impossible to regard the "Egyptian challenge" as a "clear case" of aggression, on a par with the Nazi conquests, etc. Rather, this is a "clear case" of the style of apologetics adopted by many supporters of Israel.[37]

Immediately after the armistice agreements of 1949, Israel began encroachments into the demilitarized zones along with military attacks with many civilian casualties and the expulsion of thousands of Arabs, some of whom later formed terrorist bands that carried out what they presumably regarded as reprisals and what Israel and its supporters regard as unprovoked terrorism; the terms "terrorism" and "reprisal," as noted earlier, are to a considerable extent terms of propaganda, not description. These actions set the stage for further conflicts with Egypt and Syria. Israeli raids in the Gaza Strip led to *fedayeen* attacks that served as the pretext for the 1956 invasion, though as is known from captured Egyptian documents and other sources, Egypt was attempting to calm the border region in fear of such an attack.[38] The aggressors concocted an elaborate and largely successful propaganda campaign in an effort to show that it was Nasser who was planning an attack, not they, comparing him to Hitler while they effectively mimicked Goebbels.

Many details are provided by Kennett Love, who was then the Middle East correspondent of the *New York Times*. He describes, for example, how the *Times* failed to publish his interview with Nasser in which Nasser offered to demilitarize the frontier: "distorted versions of Nasser's effort to pacify the frontier were splashed across New York's front pages under headlines representing him as a warmonger," including a *Times* report stating that "Many neutrals say Premier Nasser's statement [on demilitarizing the frontier] was bellicose and is certain to increase tension." Two days after the *Times* killed Nasser's interview it ran a front-page headline, based on distorted news agency versions of the interview, which read: "Gaza War Threat Voiced by Egypt."[39] The aggressors themselves at the same time were attributing fabricated bellicose statements to Nasser, taking earlier writings of his out of context and grossly changing their sense, etc. The distortions of Western propaganda, which in this case reflect a remarkable degree of moral cowardice quite apart from the falsification of the facts, remained effective even after the outright aggression by Israel, France and England. In particular, it is still widely held that Israel's aggression was in fact defensive, at worst a "preemptive strike" in response to Nasser's threats. The incident is an example—one of many—of how facts can be overwhelmed by a powerful propaganda system employing the "free press" as its instrument.

The Israeli occupying army carried out bloody atrocities in the Gaza Strip, killing "at least 275 Palestinians immediately after capturing the Strip during a brutal house-to-house search for weapons and *fedayeen* in Khan Yunis" and killing 111 Palestinians in "another massive bloodletting" at the Rafah refugee camp in "disorders" after "Israeli troops stormed through the hovels, rounding up refugees for intelligence screenings." General E. L. M. Burns, Commander of the UN Truce Supervision Organization (UNTSO), commented that this furnished "very sad proof of the fact that the spirit that inspired the notorious Deir Yassin massacre of 1948 is not dead among some of the Israeli armed forces." The head of the Gaza observer force, Lt.-Col. R. F. Bayard of the U.S. Army, reported that treatment of civilians was "unwarrantedly rough" and that "a good number of persons have been shot down in cold blood for no apparent reason." He also reported that many UN relief officials were missing and presumed executed by the Israelis and that there had been extensive looting and wanton destruction of property. Israel claimed that the killings were caused by "refugee resistance," a claim denied by refugees (there were no Israeli casualties).* Love cites Moshe Dayan's diaries confirming the looting, which caused "much shame to ourselves," and indicating that there had been practically no resistance.[40] The aftermath of the 1982 Lebanon war was similar, though in this case the occupying army left it to its local clients to carry out the worst massacre. It is an unfortunate fact that occupying armies often behave in this fashion,[41] but then, they usually do not bask in the admiration of American intellectuals for their unique and remarkable commitment to "purity of arms."

Encroachments in the demilitarized zones in the north for water diversion projects and agricultural development† led ultimately to the shelling of Israel from the Golan Heights by those described here as "Syrian-killers-for-the-fun-of-it" in a typical misrepresentation of the facts.[42] Swedish UNTSO Commander General Carl von Horn wrote that "it [was] unlikely that these [Syrian guns] would ever [have] come into action had it not been for Israeli provocation," including armed encroachments into areas farmed by Palestinians.[43] General (Res.) Mattit-

---

* For an eyewitness account from an Israeli source of atrocities committed by the Israeli occupying army until "Ben-Gurion himself gave orders to stop the looting, murder and robbery," see Mark Gefen, *Al Hamishmar*, April 27, 1982—a timely (though ignored) report, considering what was to follow shortly.

---

† Israeli encroachments and attacks in this area were in part motivated by a desire to take control of the waters of the Jordan and prevent diversion within Arab territories. This led to conflict between Israel and both the UN and the U.S. The American-planned Johnston project designed to arrange for sharing of the Jordan waters was undermined by Israeli opposition, and "the Israeli raid on Syria in December 1955 annihilated the very wreckage of his work" (Love, *Suez*, p. 277). The occupation of the Syrian Golan Heights in 1967 settled this issue.

yahu Peled points out that after the Israeli conquest of the Golan Heights in 1967, the Syrian artillery was barely moved. There was no subsequent shelling because the cease-fire arrangements were clarified. Prior to 1967, Israel followed a "planned strategy" designed to impose *its* interpretation of the 1949 Armistice Agreements, including settlement in the demilitarized zones which infringed on the rights of the local inhabitants, leading to shelling in reprisal. The conquest of the Heights did not change the military situation, but showed that negotiated settlement is possible, as had been true before too, he argues. If Israel were truly to accept UN Resolution 242, returning the Golan Heights to Syria, demilitarization of the Heights would cause no security problem, he argues further, as the facts he reviews suggest.[44]

It is also generally overlooked that Arabs too have reason to fear shelling from the Golan Heights. By 1970, there were already nearly 100 casualties in the Jordanian city of Irbid resulting from Israeli air attacks and shelling from the Golan Heights.[45]

Syrian shelling served as the pretext for the conquest of the Golan in 1967 in violation of the cease-fire, and for subsequent actions leading to its virtual annexation by the Begin government in December-January 1981-82.[46]

4   After the 1967 Conquest

Apart from the Syrian border, the years following Israel's retreat from the Sinai were relatively tranquil. The Egyptian border was quiet and the Jordanian border, nearly so. Within Israel, vast areas of Arab land were expropriated and converted to Jewish settlement, used in part to settle Jewish refugees who fled or were expelled from Arab countries in the aftermath of the 1947-49 war.[47] Arab citizens were thus compelled to become a work force for Jewish enterprises (including kibbutzim), a phenomenon that became quite noticeable by the 1960s.

4.1   The Settlement Policies of the Labor Governments

Immediately after the 1967 war, the Labor government began its moves to integrate the occupied territories within Israel. East Jerusalem was immediately annexed, and the city's borders were considerably extended into the Arab West Bank (a program called "the thickening of Jerusalem"), with considerable Jewish settlement and expulsion of Arabs from some sections of the Old City. Paramilitary settlements were established, then permanent civilian settlements, in the occupied territories. A harsh military occupation was instituted and has since been maintained.[48]

Settlement in the occupied territories began immediately after the war, sometimes without government authorization, though this regularly came later. Five weeks after the war, a settlement was established on the Golan Heights, and shortly after, at Kfar Etzion in the West Bank. Amnon Kapeliouk observes that by December 1969, the Meir government had established as one of its "essential goals" the "acceleration of the installation of military settlements and permanent agricultural and urban settlements in the territory of the homeland" (the official wording). Secretary of Defense Moshe Dayan, who played a central role in these Labor government projects, stated that "the settlements established in the territories are there forever, and the future frontiers will include these settlements as part of Israel." These future frontiers, then, were to stretch from the Golan Heights in the north to the southernmost part of the Sinai at Sharm el-Sheikh (Israeli "Ophira"; Dayan's statement that he "preferred Sharm el-Sheikh without peace to a peace without Sharm el-Sheikh" later became famous, during the period when the Labor government was evading Arab peace initiatives), and from Gaza and northeastern Sinai to the Jordan river, all areas where settlements were established under the Labor government.

Alongside of the inevitable "security argument," it was commonly held that it would be wrong, perhaps even racist, to deny to Jews the right to settle in these areas (the West Bank, furthermore, was the heartland of "the historic land of Israel"). There was, however, no reciprocity. Arabs in the occupied territories could not settle in Israel; for example, those who had been expelled from Jaffa in April 1948. Arabs could not buy land in Israel, Dayan explained, "because that would disturb the territorial continuity of the Jewish population" (it would be virtually impossible anyway because of the legal devices that effectively restrict land use to Jews, to which we return). But Jewish settlements in the densely-populated Gaza area, in contrast, were designed to "break the territorial continuity" of Arab settlement to prevent "eventual self-determination" for the inhabitants of the Gaza Strip, *Ha'aretz* explained, and the same considerations soon applied in the West Bank as well. Similar arguments were advanced in the course of Labor's program of "Judaization of the Galilee" within Israel proper, where it was felt to be necessary to establish Jewish settlements to break up the concentrations of Arab citizens. In the occupied territories, Israel was to establish "permanent rule," Dayan held.

Foreign Minister Abba Eban, a Labor dove, took note of the fact that according to international law, settlement was permissible only in the name of military security; but he and others recognized that it was not motivated by such considerations, while continuing to support it. Eban rejected "the conception that maintains that the basic criterion for settlement in Judea and Samaria [the West Bank] must be the strict necessity of obtaining secure boundaries," adding that for him the "key expression" was "the territory of the homeland," as indicated in the December 1969 government program. Dayan, with his customary frankness, stated that "from the point of view of the security of the State, the establishment of the settlements has no great importance"; rather, it was necessary to create "political *faits accomplis* on the principle...that no place of settlement or agricultural use will be abandoned." In his extensive study of Israel's post-1967 settlement program, W. W. Harris shows that the Allon Plan, which provided the basic framework for the policy, at first actually envisaged absorption of about 40% of the West Bank and annexation of the Gaza Strip, and by 1977 (ten years after it was first proposed in July 1967) it included some additional encroachments into the West Bank as well as extensive settlement in the Golan Heights (then well-advanced) and an Israeli takeover of a strip of the Sinai from the Mediterranean to Sharm el-Sheikh.[49] Much material of the sort just cited is in Hebrew sources or relatively inaccessible studies and was little noted in the United States, even denied, though the facts of settlement were clear enough to those who chose to be aware of what was happening.

There were, of course, certain problems: "the main difficulty encountered when planning the settlement of Judea and Samaria," Elisha Efrat explains, is that it is inhabited by Arabs "who are not prepared to leave any place of their own free will" and who "are not at the mercy of absentee 'effendi' landowners who are willing to sell their land," as was (conveniently) the case during the settlement of Israel itself.[50] Efrat is a planner with the Israel Ministry of the Interior and a professor at Tel Aviv university, where, he informs us, he prepared a longer study of these problems "in the framework of the Tel-Aviv University Research Project on Peace," a name that Orwell would have appreciated.

In September 1973, the Labor Party approved the "Galili Protocols," which called for extensive additional rural and urban settlement and commercial and industrial development in the territories, including the Golan, the West Bank, Gaza, and northeastern Sinai, where the city of Yamit was to be established (the native population had been brutally expelled, driven into the desert, their settlements levelled). Not even the Labor "moderates" (Allon, Eban) criticized the decision, though Arieh Eliav, the most noted dove, abstained from the vote and criticized the document, as did Shulamith Aloni. Minister of Justice M. Y. Sh. Shapira declared that "this document expresses the hope that with the passage of time we will be able to find a permanent solution for keeping the territories annexed, included, or united to the State of Israel." A month later, Egyptian forces crossed the Suez Canal in a surprise attack, initiating the 1973 war. Sadat had stated that "Yamit means war, at least for Egypt."[51]

The treatment of the inhabitants of northeastern Sinai merits attention, not only because of its character but also in the light of the reaction in the United States, to which we return, when the new Jewish settlers were compelled to leave this Egyptian territory, with handsome compensation, as part of the Camp David "peace process." After initial expropriations in 1969, military forces commanded by General Ariel Sharon, in January 1972, "drove off some ten thousand farmers and bedouin, bulldozed or dynamited their houses, pulled down their tents, destroyed their crops and filled in their wells," to prepare the ground for the establishment of six kibbutzim, nine villages, and the city of Yamit.* Subsequently Israeli bulldozers uprooted orchards (what is called in technical terms "making the desert bloom"), CARE aid from the U.S. was withheld to force landowners to sell their lands, mosques and schools were destroyed, and the one school to escape demolition was turned over to a new kibbutz.[52] The Minister of Housing, Labor Alignment dove Avraham Ofer, visited the area in the summer of 1975 and was disturbed to find that a few hundred Bedouin still remained along the coastline. He demanded that the Israeli army evacuate the area since it was to become a national park to "serve the masses of vacationers and bathers who, it is expected, will flow to the golden coast of Yamit." These Israeli vacationers would naturally be disturbed if there were Bedouin encampments nearby, disfiguring the terrain. In the journal of Mapam (the dovish, kibbutz-based left-wing of the Labor Alignment), Ezra Rivlis reported that Yamit is to be "a Zionist, chalutzic, desert city," much like Tel Aviv, built on the sands in the earliest days of the Jewish settlement—an apt analogy, since in that case too Arabs alleged that their lands had been taken by force. Rivlis describes how "along the barbed wire, on the other side, the Bedouin stare at us wide-eyed, dispossessed, with no arrangements or solutions as yet to their problems." He adds that "in the background of their stubborn refusal to compromise, it is said, lies the hidden incitement of representatives of Sadat and Fatah."[53] What other reason could there be for this stubborn refusal? Dark references to a sinister "hidden hand" when Arabs irrationally refuse some such "compromise" are common in the Israeli press, including the left-wing press, as in this case.

As has so often been the case, the Arabs refused the kind of "compromise" offered to them by their benign adversaries, who even were so kind as to permit them to serve as an underpaid and exploited labor force in the lands from which they had been expelled. It was therefore necessary to resort to force, in the manner just indicated, after the failure of peaceful means, a regrettable necessity, particularly for a state that has always been committed to such sublime moral standards and humanistic principles, from which it is forced to depart by Arab intransigence, as American supporters are quick to inform us. In the American Jewish press, Samson Krupnick described the "most unique and exciting experience" of observing the birth of Yamit and the arrival of the first "Americans, Canadians, Russian olim [immigrants] and some Israelis."[54] In the U.S., there was

---

* Public criticism led to a military commission of inquiry that issued a reprimand to Sharon; Yoram Peri, *Between Ballots and Bullets*, p. 97.

general silence on these matters, which scandalized many Israelis, apart from such expressions of admiration for this unique and exciting experience. In particular, these events elicited no comment from democratic socialists who were singing hymns of praise to Israel while denouncing anyone who dared raise questions about these policies as anti-Semites, bloody-minded radicals who support terrorism and hate democracy, etc. See chapter 2, note 60, and examples below.

4.2   Settlement under Begin and Reagan

4.2.1 Policies

The post-1973 Kissinger diplomacy was designed to exclude Egypt from the Arab-Israel conflict, thus making it possible for the Labor government to pursue its settlement program along the lines of the Allon Plan (see chapter 3). Settlement was accelerated when Begin took power in 1977. There was a further substantial expansion in the settlement program after President Reagan announced that he regarded the West Bank settlements as "legal." This reversal of U.S. government policy (at least at the rhetorical level) set in motion a huge "land grab" operation on the West Bank under a deceitful guise of legality intended to satisfy liberal American opinion. It aroused much protest among Israeli doves, but little comment here at the time.[55]

One opponent of Israeli rejectionism, former Deputy Mayor of Jerusalem Meron Benvenisti, observed shortly after that the settlement program "now completely ruled out a future solution" because of its extent and design, and that the commitment of the Labor Alignment not to withdraw from an area constituting 40% of the West Bank (the original intent of the Allon Plan of July 1967, as noted earlier) also meant "that its alleged aspiration not to rule over Arabs was meaningless."[56] Benvenisti undertook extensive research on the post-Reagan land grab operation. He found that under various ruses, the government had taken over more than half of the West Bank (outside of annexed East Jerusalem), and was planning to settle 100,000 people there by 1986. The nature of the settlement plans had meanwhile changed. The newer concept is to focus on "development of large urban centres which will organically link vital areas of the West Bank to the major Israeli urban centres." These are to be "dormitories for Jerusalem and Tel Aviv." The intent is to create a "dual society": "The Arab towns and villages are to become like ghettos...surrounded by large Jewish dormitory suburbs, settlements, military camps—all served, linked and carved up by fast access highways." The Jewish areas will have "Jewish services and standards...like elections and free speech," while the Arab ghettos will remain under "the military government—or, if you prefer, the civil administration" of Menachem

Milson (who has since resigned). In these ghettos, there is "a low level of service, almost no governmental investment in infrastructure or development." Their boundaries are "sharply defined and no building will be permitted outside them" (there is virtually no room within them). These plans, he notes, are supported by the Labor Party under its current version of the Allon Plan, a fact which "makes nonsense of the [Labor] Alignment plan to keep only those areas where there is low density Arab population."[57]

4.2.2 Reactions

The immediate occasion for Benvenisti's revelations was the recently-announced Reagan Peace Plan, which called for a settlement freeze while stating that "America will not support the use of any additional land for the purpose of settlement." The latter statement was a bit ironic, as the U.S. press was kind enough not to observe, in the light of Reagan's role in setting off the land grab that led to the current situation. The statement is also false, since the Reagan administration moved at once to *increase* aid to Israel, and as noted earlier, the U.S. government has always been scrupulous in avoiding any supervision or other arrangements that might serve to restrict the use of the lavish American funding in conformity with the stated policy of denying support for settlement in the occupied territories. In fact, in his meetings with Begin, Reagan was careful to avoid the question of settlements, a fact brought out in a "well-documented" analysis by Senator John Glenn, whose plausible conviction is "that what heads of government say to each other through emissaries or in public pronouncements is far less important than what they say to each other in private, face to face." "The consent that the Israelis have obviously read into a consistent record of silence on the part of the President over at least a year and a half has carried the de facto annexation of the West Bank by Israel very close to, if not beyond, the point of no return."[58] The message sent by liberal Democrats was still clearer, as they spearheaded the effort to increase aid to Israel even beyond the increases advocated by the Reagan administration.

To put the matter in slightly clearer terms than those employed in the media and other commentary, the U.S. once again expressed its support for further settlement in the occupied territories, on two levels: first, openly, by offering—in fact, increasing—the aid that will enable these programs to be pursued; and second, more subtly, by avoiding any reference to these matters in private discussion, so that it will be even clearer that the public rhetoric is for show, to be ignored in practice, as in the past.

The message is surely understood, a fact recognized by both critics and supporters of Israel's current policies. In the former category, Chaim Bermant writes that there are "two principal arguments for a withdrawal from the West Bank and Gaza." The "moral argument" holds that Israel will not remain a democratic state if it continues to "retain the land of another people and maintain dominion over them." The "practical argument" is that the U.S. "will not tolerate the occupation of the West Bank and Gaza, and if the occupation should continue, all American aid will be reduced and perhaps even stopped altogether." Bermant states that "moral arguments have some force in Israel, perhaps more so than anywhere else, but they are not in themselves enough to effect a withdrawal from occupied territory" or even to check the policy of "galloping annexation." As for the "practical argument," it would have force "if it were at all valid." But it is not, since Begin (like his predecessors, we may add)

> has shown that whatever protests this or that American administration might make against the expansion of Jewish settlement or the infringement of human rights, in the West Bank, he has been able to strengthen his grip on the area without any diminution of American aid. Indeed, he is even anticipating an increase... Indeed the American Government has been financing the very policies it denounces with such consistency that one doesn't have to be an Arab to wonder if the denunciations are sincere.[59]

True; one only has to be committed to elementary rationality and honesty, an observation that has some interesting consequences when applied to commentary on this matter in the United States.

On the other side of the Israeli political fence, Wolf Blitzer, under the heading "Lessons from aid victory," reports the successful outcome of the battle between the Administration, who wanted to "punish" Israel by increasing aid to it, and Congress, which preferred a "softer line," increasing the aid still further. The final outcome, he notes, was that the full aid package sought by the Administration was accepted ($2.485 billion in economic and military assistance), but with "improved terms," with $500 million converted from loans to outright grants. "The entire aid affair clearly represented an important and badly-needed substantive and symbolic victory for Israel," thanks to the crucial assistance of congressional liberals, as he notes.* These loyal supporters were helped by "the reaffirmed vision of Israel as a working democracy, especially following the West Beirut massacres."[60]

---

* Particularly noteworthy, Blitzer observes, was the defeat of Congressmen who "had been targeted by the Jewish community." This lesson has no doubt been carefully noted by Senator John Glenn, a presidential aspirant, who has been similarly "targeted" because of such indiscretions as the one cited on p. 108. See Curtis Wilkie, "Glenn campaign gets a buffeting," *Boston Globe*, Feb. 20, 1983, discussing what *New York Magazine* called Glenn's "significant Jewish problem," a nontrivial one considering traditional Jewish financial support for Democratic candidates, Wilkie notes.

Presumably there is also a lesson here as to how to obtain further victories in Congress. It would be interesting to know how the reported 400,000 people who demonstrated in Israel in protest over the massacres will react to the fact—and fact it is—that the practical outcome of their efforts, given the way things are in the United States, was to accelerate the militarization of Israeli society and its expansion into the occupied territories.

In passing, we might note some curious aspects of Bermant's "moral argument." The argument rests on consequences for the *Jews*, not for the conquered population, whose rights and wishes are null—not an untypical stance among liberal Zionists, or among Western intellectuals generally, as we have seen repeatedly. We might also ask what the basis is for the belief that moral arguments have more force in Israel than elsewhere, also a standard doctrine even among critics of Israeli policies. It would be difficult to justify this conclusion on the basis of the historical record. A more accurate picture is presented by Labor Party Knesset member (Gen.) Chaim Herzog, a military historian and former Israeli diplomat and the successful Labor Party candidate for President in March 1983. He writes that "We must be guided in our [foreign policy] relationships by the one criterion that has guided governments of Israel ever since the establishment of the state, namely: 'Is it good for the Jews?' "[61]

The context for Herzog's observations was his rejection of the (mild and limited) domestic criticism of Israel's support for murderous dictators in Latin America—specifically, recent visits by Israeli high officials to such countries as Argentina, where, *Haolam Haze* reports, "the Israeli foreign minister last week extended a warm handshake to the Generals in Buenos Aires who had murdered about 1000 Jews in Argentina" (exactly as as was done by other high Israeli political and military figures, including those of the Labor Party, while the Argentine massacre was at its height; Jacobo Timerman states that "I saw with my own eyes how Argentine jailers tortured Jews in prison while the Israeli government requested the Jewish community there to remain silent").[62] This Labor dove is also annoyed by the occasional displeasure voiced over the crucial aid offered by Israeli military advisers, arms salesmen and technical experts to the government of Guatemala for counterinsurgency and the hunt for "subversives," helping to implement an anti-guerrilla campaign that "is showing more signs of success than El Salvador's, mainly because it is more brutal," with thousands "tortured, mutilated and killed" and tens of thousands driven to Mexico while "many peasants are herded into protected villages, leaving the countryside as a free-fire zone for the army," a campaign that led to the killing of "at least 5,000 Indians" in the summer of 1982.[63] In this case, unlike Argentina, there are no embarrassing questions as to whether it is "Good for the Jews."

Blitzer's "lessons from the aid victory" emphasize the importance of preventing critical discussion of Israeli policies in the U.S., as when the revered moralist Elie Wiesel explains that it is improper to criticize Israel outside its borders (but not improper to criticize others, e.g., the PLO), and in fact illegitimate to question its policies even within, since only those "in a position of power" possess the relevant information (see p. 16). Apparently on the same assumptions, Israeli physicist Gerald Horwitz of the Hebrew University, in a letter to the *New York Times* (Jan. 9, 1983), condemns Mattityahu Peled for an critical Op-Ed on December 30. He contends that Peled's article "represents an anti-democratic and nationally objectionable act" because there is no justification "in a democratic society such as Israel—where disagreements with the Government can freely be brought to the press, to the polls, and even to the street—to turn to an external government, to an external voting population, to bring about by coercion a change which its proponent cannot succeed in persuading his own countrymen to accept." The very fact that Peled voiced a criticism outside of Israel shows that he "does not understand democratic procedures," which require that Israelis refrain from such "nationally objectionable acts" as criticizing policies of the government—particularly, in the U.S., where the "external voting population" is expected to pay the bills. Apparently, it is legitimate, according to this intriguing concept of democracy, to write in *support* of the government's policies in the U.S., but not to criticize them. He does not explain how we are to deal with another problem, namely, that someone in the U.S. might quote something that Peled writes in Israel. Note that there is also apparently no violation of democratic principles when Americans visiting Israel condemn U.S. policies as "too harsh towards Israel," a common practice.

The same issue of the *Times* contains a slightly more subtle expression of totalitarian attitudes in an Op-Ed by Annette Dulzin of *Yediot Ahronot*, who discusses Israel's "moral strength" as shown by the reaction to the Beirut massacres (presumably such comment is legitimate according to the doctrine of Wiesel, Horwitz and others, particularly in the light of Blitzer's observation about the utility of such testimonies to Israel's moral strength for increasing U.S. military and economic aid). She writes that "The world's news media not only search out Israel's imperfections with a magnifying glass, they also turn their attention to the extremes of its political spectrum," conveying as "representative of the body politic" the views of "people made irresponsible by their hatred of [Begin]" as well as "the most grotesque ideas expressed by Mr. Begin's most mindless worshippers." In fact, in the U.S. at least, the media characteristically ignore even serious "imperfections" and rarely report, let alone convey as "representative," positions at the extremes; but those who regard only total conformity as permissible might well consider the occasional deviation as outrageous, and with a sufficient dose of paranoia, even as typical.

Returning to Benvenisti, his conclusion is that Reagan's peace plan is largely irrelevant in any event because it overlooks the "radical changes" which followed his earlier approval of the settlement policy. The "unilateral implementation of Israel's version of autonomy on the ground" does not require "the odd new settlements" that might be ruled out by Reagan's proposal—which, nevertheless, the Begin government angrily rejected, immediately announcing plans for new settlements. This "unilateral implementation" is in violation of the terms of the so-called "peace process," but then, as Abba Eban observed, Israel had announced at once its rejection of these terms; see p. 62. We return in chapter 6 to the actual impact of Reagan's September 1982 peace plan on West Bank settlement.

Note that Labor's effective endorsement of the new arrangements underscores the hypocrisy of its superficially positive response to the Reagan proposals. Labor's actual policy is explained by Yitzhak Rabin. He notes that until now Jordan has refused to accept the Allon Plan ("territorial compromise") as a basis for settlement and that Reagan's plan is also unacceptable to the Labor Alignment for this reason. He "emphasized" that Labor does not differ from Likud about the "right of settlement" but only about its manner, and that if Jordan does join the negotiations Israel should agree to a 4-6 month settlement freeze, "but not throughout the negotiations, which might be prolonged." As for the PLO, Rabin continued to reiterate the longstanding Labor policy that it cannot be a partner to negotiations "even if it accepts all of the conditions of negotiations on the basis of the Camp David agreements, because the essence of the willingness to speak with the PLO is the willingness to speak about the establishment of a Palestinian state, which must be opposed." A few months later he reiterated the call for a "limited" settlement freeze ("let us say, six months") if Hussein agreed to join the negotiations, though not before, adding that Labor is "in favor of certain settlements in the Jordan Valley, the greater Jerusalem area [which is by now very "great"], Gush Etzion [in the West Bank] and the southern part of the Gaza Strip."[64]

The Labor Party position is elaborated further by Uzi Shimoni of Kibbutz Ashdot Yaakov, head of the propaganda *(hasbara)* branch of the party, in its journal. Israel "has the right to all of the Land of Israel," but it should agree to "relinquish" its rights in part, returning areas of heavy Arab population concentration in the West Bank to Jordan. It should make this concession "not because of the wishes of the Arabs of the territory," which are irrelevant, just as they are irrelevant to American liberal opinion, but so as to avoid the "demographic problem." At the same time, Israel must intensify settlement elsewhere so that it will become impossible to return the territories to the local population and Arab rule, as Begin agreed to do in northeastern Sinai over strong Labor opposition (see p. 48*). "The Likud government's relinquishing defensible borders in the south of the State of Israel makes it even more necessary that any peace agreement must be conditioned on the principle that the Jordan River will be our Eastern border and that the Golan Heights will be part of the State of Israel. . . If Yamit had grown to the size of Netanya, for example, there would have been no agreement to return it to Egypt."[65]

Commenting on Benvenisti's research, Anthony Lewis wrote:

> But it is the Arab leaders who need most of all to understand the meaning of the Benvenisti study. They have maneuvered for years, avoiding negotiation. But unless they move now—unless they accept the fact of Israel and talk about ways to secure the rights of Palestinians in accommodation with that fact—there will be nothing left to negotiate.[66]

Lewis has been unusual in mainstream American journalism in his willingness to reveal some unpleasant truths about Israel's recent policies.* He is right to observe that there will soon be nothing to negotiate. But we learn something important about American intellectual and political culture from the fact that even at the outer fringes of mainstream journalism—thus essentially across the board with very few exceptions— the same illusions are put forth as unquestioned fact. As discussed in chapter 3, it is Israel and the U.S. who have maneuvered to avoid negotiations, while the Arab leaders and the PLO have largely joined the international accommodationist consensus, and have accepted "the fact of Israel" long ago. If there is little left to negotiate, that is primarily the result of U.S.-Israeli rejectionism and the policies of the Labor government, then Likud, in the occupied territories, all subsidized by American munificence and backed by "supporters of Israel." And no mainstream political grouping in Israel offers any basis for negotiations or political settlement apart from the kind of "territorial compromise" that would eliminate the last vestiges of Palestinian rights.

4.2.3 Policies (Continued)

Returning again to Benvenisti (see note 57), he goes on to elaborate the consequences of the current programs being implemented by the Likud government, with tacit Labor backing, indeed, extending Labor's policies when in office. "The economy of the West Bank," he states, "may be characterized as undeveloped, non-viable, stagnant and dependent. It is an auxiliary sector of both the Israeli and Jordanian economies." It is a

---

* Lewis, whose position generally accords with that of the Labor Party, is considered so "anti-Israel" by the American Zionist establishment that their press urges readers to boycott his talks *(Jewish Week*, New York; reported by *Jewish Post & Opinion*, Dec. 3, 1982). Like the regular behavior of the Anti-Defamation League, this is another illustration of the Stalinist character of the American Zionist institutions noted and condemned by Israeli doves; see p. 14.

"captive market" for Israeli manufactures, Israel's largest single market, where 25% of Israel's exports are sold.[67] There is "no capital investment, no government investment in industrial infrastructure, no credit facilities or capital market, no protection from the import of Israeli goods." There are, however, Israeli taxes. The working population increasingly serves as a cheap labor force for Israel, a repetition of what happened to the Arab population within Israel itself; in the terms preferred by Col. (ret.) Sasson Levi, a specialist in Arab affairs who "served in a key capacity in the military government of Judea and Samaria," the Arabs of the territories benefit from "the opportunity given to them to work in Israel."[68] Continuing with the rhetoric preferred by the conquerors, Israeli scholars Sandler and Frisch (see note 67) are euphoric about "the remarkable accomplishments of the territories in the last decade" and "the benefits derived from contact with Israel." Like Col. Levi and many others, they have little to say about why the Palestinians in the territories do not appear to share their enthusiasm. Perhaps this is yet another manifestation of Irving Howe's "sour apothegm: *In the warmest of hearts there's a cold spot for the Jews";* or perhaps, as Levi remarks, the reason is that "the terrorist organizations continued to incite the people."

Israel's policies in the West Bank, Benvenisti concludes, are "an outgrowth of an imperial concept—'I want this'—combined with the ability to go about taking it." It must be stressed again that this "ability" is conferred by lavish U.S. funding, ideological support of the kind described, and diplomatic support; for example, the U.S. veto of an April 2, 1982 Security Council resolution calling on Israel to reinstate the ousted elected mayors Bassam Shak'a of Nablus, Karim Khalef of Ramallah, and Ibrahim Tawil of El Bireh, recent targets of terrorist attack (see pp. 56f.).* The U.S., which stood alone in voting against the resolution (Zaire abstained), regarded it as "one-sided."[69]

In fairness, it should be noted that Israel is not the only state to be accorded such diplomatic protection by the U.S. A few months earlier, the U.S. vetoed a Security Council resolution condemning "South Africa's

---

* On the same day, the U.S. vetoed a resolution which "named no names and made no charges," but "simply repeated United Nations Charter principles opposing intervention in the affairs of other countries and the use of force." It was implicitly directed against U.S. intervention in Nicaragua, which at that time was still being denied. The U.S. objected to the resolution on the grounds that it "breeds cynicism" and "harms the United Nations" because "it undermines the Inter-American system" and "mocks the search for peace." The basis for this charge was that the resolution called upon the Secretary General of the UN to keep the Security Council informed about the crisis in Central America and the Caribbean. Observers could recall no previous occasion when one country cast two vetoes on two different subjects at the same session. Those whose sense of humor inclines them in this direction might be intrigued to look back at the learned discussions by distinguished Western anthropologists on Russian vetoes in the early days of the UN, when the U.S. dominated the organization; the explanation offered was that Russian negativism resulted from the practice of swaddling infants, "diaperology," as the theory was called by the occasional skeptics.

utilization of the illegally occupied territory of Namibia as a springboard for armed invasions and destabilization of the People's Republic of Angola." Other countries too have been afforded such diplomatic protection, for example, Indonesia at the time of its invasion of East Timor, as liberal hero Daniel P. Moynihan relates with much satisfaction in his memoirs, referring to his success in blocking United Nations action to deter the aggression and prevent the subsequent massacre that Moynihan partially and misleadingly acknowledges.[70]

The policies that Benvenisti describes were established by the Labor government shortly after the 1967 conquest, then accelerated by Begin. The consequences were predicted from the start by Israeli doves, who were generally ignored or denounced here in the post-1967 raptures about Israel's unique magnificence—when, for example, Irving Howe was explaining that Israel offers "about as good a model as we have for the democratic socialist hope of combining radical social change with political freedom" (precisely at the time when such hopes, such as they were, were rapidly receding), and issuing vitriolic denunciations of those who attempted to report some of the facts as obsessed by "a complex of values and moods verging on the pathology of authoritarianism,"* among other similar thoughts to which we return.[71] In essence, these policies are supported by both major political groupings and there is no indication, despite the recent Reagan plan, that the American policy of lending them the required support will change. It is possible that the same story will be relived in southern Lebanon—what some Israeli doves now refer to bitterly as "the North Bank"—in coming years. See chapter 6, section 7.1.

Danny Rubinstein points out that there has been opposition within Israel to the settlement policy, but it has been ineffectual because of lack of support from the United States—a complaint of Israeli doves that we have already noted several times. Reagan's reversal of the earlier American stand on the legality of the settlements gave a "dispensation" to the Israeli government to carry out "a massive settlement program," building

---

* See my *Peace in the Middle East?*, chapter 5, for extensive discussion of Howe's virulent attacks on Daniel Berrigan and unnamed "New Leftists" (particularly "New Left students" and "young professors," the main targets of Howe's venom during the years of their active opposition to the Indochina war), and comparison with the facts that he entirely ignores. It is interesting that this style of invective, carefully avoiding fact and argument, is regarded rather highly in the intellectual community—at least, when the targets are active opponents of the violence of some favored state. See pp. 15, 28f. One should bear in mind, in this connection, the mythical picture that has been constructed of the New Left and the student movement, and of the self-designated "responsible" figures who were offended by its principled objection to aggression and massacre. Those who are in a position to design the historical record assure us that they were courageously defending "civilized values" against the excesses of the student movement, as they indeed were, if we include among these values the right of the U.S. to murder peasants in Indochina without any vulgar disruption at home, such as resistance to military service, for example. This is an important story in itself, which would carry us too far afield.

70 settlements in place of the 10 previously announced. "As long as the Americans, our only friends, do not raise problems, then the internal opposition is silent," a "sad fact" that was also proven during the Lebanon war, he notes. Those who think that the Israeli government is bringing about a "catastrophe" for Israel are unable to make harsher criticisms than those heard from Washington. We have reached "the last moment" in the occupied territories, with vast resources (provided by the U.S.) being devoted to settlement there, amounting to virtual annexation. Settlement projects are being carried out across the spectrum: by the construction company of the Histadrut Labor Union (Solel Boneh),* religious groups, Rabbi Kahane's followers who "tell the Arabs that they must get out of here," and so on.[72] Histadrut firms are now also operating stone quarries in Lebanon, supplying cut stone to the "Israeli security forces" (i.e., occupying army), and are engaged in many other projects to "enable the Israeli army to settle down there during the winter months."[73]

4.3   The Demographic Problem and its Solution

The commitment to integrate the occupied territories within Israel in some form raised the "demographic problem" discussed earlier. The only real solution to the problem is some sort of transfer of the population. As noted earlier, it has been alleged that this was Defense Minister Sharon's intent (see p. 49), and some such notion seems implicit in the logic of the Likud moves towards "de facto annexation." It is not surprising, then, to hear the Deputy Speaker of the Knesset, Meir Cohen, say "that Israel had made a grave mistake by not expelling 200,000 to 300,000 Arabs from the West Bank" in 1967. In fact, Labor has had somewhat similar ideas, though they were more delicately put. Prime Minister Rabin had urged that Israel

> create in the course of the next 10 or 20 years conditions which would attract natural and voluntary migration of the refugees from the Gaza Strip and the West Bank to Jordan. To achieve this we have to come to agreement with King Hussein and not with Yasser Arafat.[74]

It has been traditional in Labor Zionism to see the King of Jordan (formerly, Transjordan) as the partner for negotiations, not the local

---

* At a demonstration of "about 2000 Peace Now activists" protesting new settlements, Professor Avishai Margalit, a well-known philosopher at the Hebrew University, "attacked the Histadrut for participating in the massive construction programs in the territories, [a stand] which went against the position taken by most of its [Peace Now's] members who were for a solution involving a territorial compromise between us and the Arabs," i.e., the Labor Party position; *Ha'aretz*, Nov. 28, 1982 *(Israeli Mirror)*. The platform of Peace Now opposes "continued rule over another people" and calls for "partition of the Land of Israel," but is unclear about precisely what is intended.

population; see below, p. 161. Rabin was breaking no new ground in this respect. Furthermore the feeling that ultimately the Arabs must somehow find their place elsewhere has deep roots in Zionist thinking, including such figures as Berl Katznelson, one of the heroes of socialist Zionism (a man who "rose gradually to the status of a secular 'rabbi' for most of the early pioneers"[75]), though he had in mind Syria and Iraq as the ultimate repository for the indigenous population.[76]

The same idea had been advocated by Chaim Weizmann, David Ben-Gurion, and many others. As Ben-Gurion stated, expressing a common view, "there is nothing morally wrong in the idea," even if the transfer is compulsory, i.e., is expulsion.[77] Recall his view that the indigenous population, about whom he seems to have known little and cared less, have no "emotional involvement" in the country, no attachment to their traditional homes.* One hears the same views expressed today. General Aharon Yariv, former head of military intelligence, commented on "widely held opinions" in favor of exploiting a future war situation to expel 7-800,000 Arabs; such a plan exists, he said, and the means to execute it had been prepared.[78] Another former intelligence chief, General Shlomo Gazit (now President of Ben-Gurion University), warned in a lecture at Hebrew University against evacuating any part of "historic Eretz Israel," which must "remain entirely under Jewish control" as "a basically Jewish state." It is therefore necessary to face "the problems of the Arabs of historic Eretz Israel." He explained that "Israel regards this as a humanitarian, not a political problem, and it therefore follows that the solution for them must be found outside historic Eretz Israel."[79] Chalk up another one for Orwell.

Similar thoughts are expressed by Michael Walzer, though in this case with respect to the Arab citizens of Israel proper: since the original inhabitants of the land are "marginal to the nation," their problems might be "smoothed" by the benevolent policy of "helping people to leave who have to leave," he suggests.[80] Walzer (then at Harvard, now at the Institute for Advanced Study in Princeton) is much respected in U.S. intellectual circles as a humanitarian and moral thinker.

All of this is entirely natural on the assumption of Zionists across the spectrum (with some exceptions) that the Arabs have no real ties to their

---

* See p. 51. Another important advocate of removal of the indigenous population was Yosef Weitz, a high official of the Jewish National Fund. When he held this position in the early 1940s, he explained that the proper solution "is the land of Israel, at least the Western Land of Israel [cis-Jordan] without Arabs, because there is no room for compromise." They must be completely removed, leaving "not one village, not one tribe," with the possible exception of Bethlehem, Nazareth, and the Old City of Jerusalem. They must be removed to Trans-Jordan, Syria or Iraq. This plan was widely discussed in the Palestinian Jewish community and was authorized by the top leadership, including Moshe Sharett (then Shertok) and Berl Katznelson, well-known doves. See Israel Shahak, "'They should leave and empty out the region'," letter, *Koteret Rashit*, March 16, 1983, citing Weitz's diaries and letters (published in 1965) and the Sharett diaries. See also *TNCW*, p. 236.

homes in Palestine, and will be just as content—perhaps more so— outside of the land of the Jews. See chapter 3.

4.4   The Workforce and the Labor Alignment

As many Israeli doves had expected and feared, the 1967 war led to radical changes within Israel: a growing reliance on force and violence, alliance with "pariah states" such as South Africa, increased chauvinism, irrationality and religious fanaticism,[81] and grandiose conceptions of Israel's global mission. It has also predictably led to much heavier dependence on the U.S., service to U.S. global interests, and association with some of the most reactionary currents in American society.

At the same time, internal political changes have been taking place within Israel. Menachem Begin succeeded in mobilizing much of the "Oriental" (Sephardic) Jewish population—now a majority and becoming increasingly so—behind his chauvinistic and aggressive policies, though there is much diversity within this community and it is a great over-simplification, as we shall see, to contrast Sephardi hawks to Ashkenazi doves. These segments of the population had long regarded the Labor Party and its institutions as an oppressive bureaucracy, representing management and the hated kibbutzim, often islands of wealth and luxury alongside of "development towns"—notorious for their lack of development—for the Oriental Jews, many of whom serve as the labor force for kibbutz industry. The 1981 election campaign brought these feelings to sometimes violent expression and led to considerable soul-searching on what had gone wrong and some close attention to what was happening in the development towns. It was observed that support for Labor came primarily from the wealthy and educated, while the working class and underclass tended to support Begin. The question was raised why the kibbutz has become "the object of hate" in the development towns, the apparent answer being given by the comparison between kibbutz wealth and privilege and the conditions in working class areas, and by the "master and servant" relation between the kibbutzim and their exploited labor force from the development towns.[82] These attitudes of the working class and underclass, incidentally, began to manifest themselves with considerable clarity just at the time when American democratic socialists, who previously had been remote from the Zionist movement, began to speak of Israel as a "model...for the democratic socialist hope of combining radical social change with political freedom."[83]

Ha'aretz devoted a series of searching articles to the very visible anger of the Oriental community towards the Labor Alignment and their alienation from it, based on discussions with Alignment leaders, kibbutz members, and people in the development towns. This alienation and anger extend across social classes, and are "particularly harsh among the educated youth," an under-represented minority in the Oriental Community. "The alienation between the inhabitants of the development towns and the kibbutzim began to appear visibly in the 1977 elections, but was revealed in all its ugliness in the last [1981] elections."* It is, in fact, striking even within the Labor Alignment itself, where there is strong feeling against the kibbutzim for their "arrogance" and "isolation" from the working classes in the development towns that provide much of their labor force. There is also growing opposition to the Histadrut (the socialist labor union, which plays a major role in Israeli society) on the part of the Oriental Jewish working class, which constitutes the majority of workers, though not officials and managers. Some studies indicate that Oriental Jewish workers consider that Likud represents them better than Labor does, by about two-to-one. Others show that Labor Alignment voters support it with little enthusiasm, for negative reasons, rather in the manner of most of the 27% of American voters who voted for Ronald Reagan, according to electoral analyses here. The leadership is particularly disliked. While 30% of the electorate support the Alignment, only 4% support its leader, Shimon Peres, "a shocking attitude." Among Oriental Jewish workers from the development towns who are employed in the kibbutzim, 70% voted for Likud, as compared with a 60% Likud vote in the Oriental community as a whole, a reflection of the "servant-master" relation between the Oriental Jewish proletariat and "the two socialist institutions that serve as the show-window of the Labor party," the Histadrut and the kibbutzim. The kibbutzim are hated by the working class particularly for their attitudes of "arrogance" and "bossism," and for "the impossibility of establishing real human relations with kibbutz members." The hatred is in fact "increasing" (referring to the development town Beit Shean). In the last elections, the vote for Likud increased beyond the national average in regions where there was a concentration of kibbutzim alongside of Oriental Jewish communities in moshavim (semi-collectivized communities) and development towns.

Another source of bitterness is memories of how the refugees from the Arab countries were received and treated in the *Ma'abarot* (transitional resettlement camps) in Israel. One educated Oriental Jewish businessman who "succeeded in breaking out of the circle of poverty and distress" (a 1951 immigrant from Libya) recalls that in his *Ma'abara*, "all the managerial positions were held by Ashkenazim [Europeans]. The bosses were only Ashkenazim." "When we arrived in the *Ma'abara,*" he reports, "there were many Poles and Rumanians among us, but after a few

---

* The timing is inexact. It began to appear, quite visibly, in the late 1960s. In fact, it was always reasonably clear. I recall personal incidents reflecting this antagonism in 1953, when I lived for a time in a kibbutz in Israel.

months you would see how whole communities of them disappeared, while we remained stuck in place." The Ashkenazim were associated with the Labor Party (Mapai). "They treated us like third class citizens. They subjected us to extensive brainwashing, and wanted to break our connection with our culture and our traditions [a long-standing and frequently expressed complaint]. Our social structure broke down—it was their fault." "There is real hatred, hatred for what was done by the Alignment, which is seen by a whole generation as the successor to Mapai from a cultural, economic and social class standpoint." "Mapai also destroyed us from the point of view of our self-image. That will not be forgotten easily." He complains, characteristically, that the Labor Party organized the lives of the Oriental Jews in the *Ma'abarot* "the way they organize the lives of the Arabs in Gaza today." When the immigration of Russian Jews began, these tensions became far worse, because of the comparison between the "de luxe" treatment of these European immigrants and the long-standing oppression and impoverishment of the Jews from Arab countries.[84]

Tamar Maroz presents a detailed and illuminating record of working class and lower middle class attitudes as expressed in the Oriental communities, among a group that she regards, with some plausibility, as "the silent majority." The lines are rather sharply drawn: Begin is a "messiah," a "hero," "one of us," "honest," a man of the people who lives simply in a rented apartment, a "real Jew." Peres, the head of the Labor Party, is a "capitalist," a commonly repeated insult; the people of the Labor Alignment are swindlers, bureaucrats, the "establishment," "careerists." Likud is "anti-establishment." Begin "is concerned for the workers"; Labor, in contrast, is not. Its "development towns" were constructed as working class slums for kibbutz industry, where the rich kibbutzniks are the managers and "do nothing." Begin cares about the Oriental community; Labor has contempt for them. Defense Minister Sharon is also a hero, who doesn't fear and pander to the Americans, as Labor does; he should be the next head of the government, and it is a disgrace that he was forced to resign as Defense Minister. There can be no peace with the Arabs: "if we don't fight, they will destroy us"; "a good Arab is a dead Arab." Peace Now are traitors and have contempt for the religious values of the people. "Begin is our father, and 'Peace Now' is our enemy." The Likud "lifted up the weak, for whom the Alignment (Ma'arach) showed no concern." The opinions she records verbatim are forceful, and have an ominous ring.[85]

The contempt of Europe-based Labor Zionism for the Oriental Jews and their "Arab culture" is notorious. It may reflect the widely-expressed fear of "Levantinization" in what the settlers anticipated would be a modern European society, as well as the felt need to denigrate Arab society and culture in general as a justification for taking back "the Land of Israel" from its temporary occupiers and the parallel need to demonstrate that the Oriental Jews were rescued by Zionism from a miserable existence. Whatever the causes of these attitudes towards the "human dust," as they were sometimes called, a serious price is now being paid by the Labor Alignment.

The development towns were generally established in remote areas, often along the border, where they were not only neglected but also subject to vicious (and, furthermore, tactically idiotic) terrorist attacks by the PLO, particularly in the early 1970s. Michael Elkins described one such "frontline settlement," Avivim, after a particularly brutal attack on a school bus in which 12 children were killed (20 Lebanese civilians were killed in retaliatory shelling of the Lebanese town of Bint Jubeil, which appears to have been selected at random). He describes the "rubble-strewn road that is Avivim's main street" where he talked with "a ragged, pinched-faced kid," and the "jerry-built shacks thrown together in 1963 when the Jewish Agency—following Israel's policy of populating its borders—settled about 60 families of unskilled immigrants from the Atlas Mountains of Morocco in this inhospitable place" where the settlers live "out of sight and out of mind of most Israelis." One "typical" story of suffering was told by a settler who said: "We starve here, we get sick here. I don't want to stay here—nobody wants to stay. It is an awful place, nobody cares about us." Israeli officials allege that "this negative attitude was the result of the shocking school-bus incident—and strictly a temporary phenomenon." But Elkins's "own feeling was that many Israelis living in the frontier villages are profoundly unhappy with their lot—and not primarily because of the Arab commando attacks, but because of what the settlers judge to be the lack of concern for their welfare by other, more affluent Israelis." He quotes one who says: "We won't be driven out of this area by the Fatah...but the cold hearts of our own people in Tel Aviv—that can drive us out."[86]

Similar stories can be told concerning the larger towns established for the Oriental Jews, who support Begin in what they see as revenge against their oppressors of the Labor Alignment. The bitterness and violence of the 1981 electoral campaign, which evoked memories of Germany and Austria in the early 1930s among older citizens,[87] was a reflection of these conflicts. The bitterness is so great that Labor Party leader Shimon Peres was literally unable to speak in the northern city of Kiryat Shemona, even with hundreds of security officers present to maintain order. Crowds shouting "Begin King of Israel"[88] and other slogans drowned him out, and the few supporters—"hated visitors from the nearby kibbutzim"—were barely in evidence.[89]

In the older cities too there is serious disaffection within the Oriental Jewish community. Anti-Ashkenazi hatred erupted in a dramatic fashion when police arrived with a bulldozer to demolish a room added without a permit to a small house in a Tel Aviv slum, leading to the fatal shooting of one member of the family. In response, swastikas were painted on houses in wealthy Ashkenazic neighborhoods, along with such slogans as "Ashkenazim to Auschwitz, Treblinka and Dachau," "The Sephardic Revolution Has Begun," and the like. In an investigation of the situation in Tiberias, Leah Etgar found a group of about 300 young men of Moroccan origin, mostly unemployed and preparing for violence—murder if necessary—directed against Arabs and Jews who employ them. In general, they "love Begin, because he is a great man—and hate the Labor Alignment, which during its rule did nothing for the Moroccans while now there is at least food, television, and stereophonic radios." Again, the kibbutzim are a prime irritant. One man fired from Kelet Afikim "hates the kibbutzim." He claims that they discriminate against the Moroccan Jews. "They ask if they are Moroccans and if they voted for the Likud, and that is the end of the job... They hate us and we hate them." But the primary hatred is directed against Arabs, their competitors in the job market who agree to accept work for very low wages or that Jews do not want, as servants or in hotels, or jobs that require work on the Sabbath, excluded for these men from religious families. "Only the Arabs have money and they go to the movies and your heart breaks." Your "heart also breaks" when you are compelled to ride by bus and see Arabs in their private cars. "Something really tears you up inside." Others complain that Arabs not only take their work but steal their girl friends. "What girl will go out with a Jewish man who has no work, honor or livelihood. They even take our women, the scoundrels." One can see "the hatred in the eyes." All agree that there is "no solution" except "to exterminate the Arabs, because they are ruining the lives of the Jews." These men feel that "they have no choice, except to proceed to violence." They have already demonstrated at the town buildings against the increase in the Arab population in the city, and they now want to gather arms, and are preparing "to pick up boards and sticks and to break the heads of the others [the Arabs]."

A similar story is reported by Michal Meron from the town of Netivot near Gaza ("ugly," "dirty," largely inhabited by Sephardis). This was in March 1983, after the dismissal of Sharon as Defense Minister; the young men here "no long call Begin King, now Sharon is King of Israel." Meron interviews many of them, lounging around billiard parlors, dressed in designer jeans and leather jackets, virtually all unemployed and refusing the employment (for example, packing fruits and vegetables) that is offered to them. They despise the Ashkenazim and the Peace Now activists; one is sorry that he did not have the chance to throw the grenade that killed a Peace Now demonstrator in Jerusalem in February. But their hatred for the "Araboushim" (a term of contempt for Arabs, with connotations similar to "kike" or "nigger") is far deeper and more intense. "I hate Arabs because on account of them I am unemployed," because they work at "half the wages" we would accept and "twice as hard." "For money they will do anything." "The Arab has no honor and the Jew does, that's the problem." "With my own hands I would kill all of them, they are animals," one man says while the others laugh, "their hatred of Arabs uniting them in a special manner." "A good Arab is a dead Arab," they repeat.[90]

Cases of attacks on Arabs are sometimes reported in the press—e.g., the beating of an Arab hospital worker in Gedera by two armed men who threatened "to do much worse things if he does not leave Gedera."[91] Some who have close contacts with the Arab community allege that such incidents are not uncommon, but are generally unreported (in this case, the victim was threatened with death if he went to the police). It has also been widely observed that attitudes are more reactionary among the young* — the universities, for example, have been dominated by student groups that engage in such activities as breaking up Arab social events with clubs and chains[92]—so that the prospects are for an intensification of chauvinism and violence. The tendencies since 1967 are rather clear, as are their causes.

5   The Ways of the Conqueror

5.1   The West Bank

The religious settlers in the West Bank, operating freely with army support, take pride in creating a pogrom-like atmosphere among the Arabs, who must be trained not to "raise their heads," this being the only way to treat Arabs, who "adore power" and will live in peace with the Jews only when "we show him that we are strong." How? "We enter a village, shoot a bit at windows, warn the villagers and return to the settlement. We don't kidnap people, but it can happen that we catch a boy who had been throwing stones, take him back with us, beat him a bit and give him over to the Army to finish the job." The same West Bank settler also explains how official investigators act to protect Jews who shoot to hit and to kill (including firing at children). This particular interview ended because the settler—a friend of the journalist—"was in a hurry to get back home before the Sabbath."[93]

The settlers are quite open about the measures they take towards Arabs and the justification for them, which they find in the religious law and the writings of the sages. In the journal of the religious West Bank

---

* To mention another indication, a recent poll shows that 40% of 14-15 year-olds oppose equal rights for Communists, Arabs, and released prisoners. *Davar*, Aug. 6, 1982. In fact, 65% of the population favor imposing further constraints on reporting in radio and television; *Davar, Al Hamishmar*, March 20, 1983.

settlers we find, for example, an article with the heading "Those among us who call for a humanistic attitude towards our [Arab] neighbors are reading the Halacha [religious law] selectively and are avoiding specific commandments." The scholarly author cites passages from the Talmud explaining that God is sorry that he created the Ishmaelites, and that Gentiles are "a people like a donkey." The law concerning "conquered" peoples is explicit, he argues, quoting Maimonides on how they must "serve" their Jewish conquerers and be "degraded and low" and "must not raise their heads in Israel but must be conquered beneath their hand ... with complete submission." Only then may the conquerers treat them in a "humane manner." "There is no relation," he claims, "between the law of Israel [*Torat Yisrael*] and the atheistic modern humanism," citing again Maimonides, who holds "that in a divinely-commanded war [*milhemet mitzvah*] one must destroy, kill and eliminate men, women and children" (the rabbinate has defined the Lebanon war as such a war). "The eternal principles do not change," and "there is no place for any 'humanistic' considerations."[94] We return to a further examination of this phenomenon, which has its counterparts throughout the Middle East region.

A recent device for protecting settlers who attack Arabs is to transfer all investigation of the illegal use of arms by settlers from police to the military. Settlers simply refuse to cooperate with police, who do not "dare question or arrest Jewish suspects," even one "seen on television shooting directly into a crowd of demonstrating Arabs while soldiers stood behind him and were holding their fire" (the head of the district council of a Jewish settlement near Ramallah, in this case).[95]

When Palestinians are beaten or detained by settlers, Arab policemen are afraid to intervene. "Palestinian lawyers say: the settlements are so formidable that the Arab police and courts never dare to serve a summons or make a search, leaving settlers beyond the law when it comes to conflicts with Arabs." The general character of the occupation is indicated by an incident in an Arab village in March 1982. Four settlers claimed that a stone was thrown at their car in this village. They fired "into the air," shooting one boy in the arm. Another boy was kidnapped, beaten, locked in the trunk of the car, taken to a Jewish settlement and locked in a room where he was beaten "on and off during most of the day," then taken to the military government compound in Ramallah, where the boy was held while the settlers went on their way.[96] A standard bit of black humor in the occupied territories is that Arabs should stop flying and begin walking on the ground so they won't be shot so often when settlers fire into the air.[97]

Children and teen-agers are often the main victims, since they are generally the ones involved in protests and demonstrations. Danny Tsidkoni reports from Gaza that informants in an Arab village told him that several very young children threw stones at a car driven by armed settlers, who broke the leg of one boy and the hand of one girl in "retaliation."[98] A soldier reports that 30 12-13 year-old children were lined up facing a wall with their hands up for five hours in Hebron one very cold night, kicked if they moved. He justified the punishment because they are not "all innocent lambs as they look now, with their hands up and their eyes asking pity. . . . They burn and they throw stones and participate in demonstrations, and they are not less harmful than their parents." Afterwards, the children were taken to prison at an Army camp. Parents began to arrive to find out what had happened to their children, including one old man "with the dignity of a Christian saint." He did not ask to see his son, but only wanted to know whether he was there and to bring him a coat. "The guard at the gate simply looked him up and down, and cursing him, ordered him to leave." The old man stood all night waiting, in the freezing cold. In another case, a settler suspected of murdering an Arab boy "already had a criminal record for breaking the arm of an eleven-year-old boy who allegedly had thrown a stone at an Israeli vehicle."[99]

The aged are also not spared. "For five days an elderly Arab woman has lain unconscious in a Jerusalem hospital after being brutally beaten in the small flat in which she lives with her husband in the Muslim quarter of the Old City." She was attacked by religious Jews from a nearby Yeshiva (religious school) while her 85-year-old husband was praying in the Al Aqsa mosque. He heard that Jewish settlers had killed his wife, rushed home, but could not enter his apartment because, he said, "the Jews were on the roof of our building hurling bricks and bottles." An Arab youth who tried to save the woman was also brutally beaten, and lies next door in the hospital. He "identifies his attackers as the Jewish zealots from the Yeshiva." They "scarcely bothered to deny the attack." When questioned about it, "an American zealot blandly talked of the need to cleanse the area of 'terrorists'." The group "is known to to the police as 'the blessing of Abraham,' a Yeshiva comprised mostly of European and American-born Jews who have returned to their faith with a burning desire to reclaim land lost to the Arabs." Several years ago they established the Yeshiva in an old Arab area; eighteen Arab families had since moved out, and this couple was the only one remaining as the "Jewish zealots" sought "to 'redeem' property that had once been inhabited by Jews as long ago as the 16th century." The couple had rejected cash offers which were followed by threats of violence; "there is no doubt that those threats were carried out this week." The police arrested a few of the Jewish extremists but they are to be charged only with "riotous behavior." "The assault on Mrs Mayalleh and the fact that she and her husband are now homeless seemed to be accepted as a *fait accompli* by the police," which is typical of the "indulgent attitude by authorities." "The vicious attack scarcely rated a mention in the local press."[100]

One not untypical issue of a Palestinian weekly contains two stories on the front page. The first deals with the week-long curfew imposed on the Dheisheh refugee camp after an Israeli observation post was burned and stones were thrown at an Israeli vehicle. It reports that inhabitants lacked food and that Israeli authorities raided houses, confiscating large numbers of books, magazines and tapes with national songs, while the men were forced to stand outside the police station during the cold nights. Soldiers searched the house of a man who had died two months earlier and "burned his private library and the school books of his children." The second story cites *Ha'aretz* (Zvi Barel, Oct. 31): "Two Arab youths were injured by an Israeli time bomb in the stands of Hebron's Hussein School football field... The explosion occurred minutes before the beginning of the game... The Israeli army which searched the area discovered another time bomb."[101] There are no curfews or collective punishment (standard practice for Arab communities) in the neighboring Jewish settlement, which has often been the source of violence and racist gangsterism. One wonders whether there was even an investigation. Other stories are still more grim, for example, the allegation by a Rakah (Communist Party) Knesset Member that there was "confirmed information" of the disappearance, torture and murder of convicts in various prisons,[102] or the detailed testimony of prisoners concerning torture under interrogation,* sometimes with the cooperation of medical personnel, for many years.[103]

The extensive reports of torture by Arab prisoners have generally been dismissed in the U.S., just as little notice is taken of reports of Palestinian refugees, or in general, of the travail and concerns of the Palestinians. Reports by prisoners or refugees of course have to be carefully evaluated; in particular, the conditions of transmission must be carefully considered, as well as the fact that they may have a stake in exaggerating or falsifying, or in suppressing the truth out of fear of their interrogators or guards. But surely such reports should be taken seriously. These remarks are truisms, characteristically disregarded in two cases: where refugees or prisoners have a tale to tell that is useful for ideological or propaganda purposes (e.g., atrocity reports about some enemy), in which case all caution is thrown to the winds; or where their stories reflect badly on some revered state, in which case they are disregarded.[104]

In the case of Palestinian prisoners in Israel, particular care has been taken to ensure that little is known here, though it has become more difficult over the years to meet this requirement. One interesting example was the unusually careful study conducted by the *London Sunday Times*

---

* This testimony comes primarily from Arab prisoners. MK Shulamit Aloni, one of Israel's leading civil libertarians, reported that Jewish prisoners in military prisons allege that conditions are so severe that some were driven insane. MK Charley Biton, a Sephardi, added that 90% of those in military prisons are from the Oriental Jewish community. *Davar*, Jan. 24, 1983.

Insight team which, after a lengthy investigation, found evidence of torture so widespread and systematic that "it appears to be sanctioned at some level as deliberate policy," perhaps "to persuade Arabs in occupied territories that it is least painful to behave passively."[105] The study was offered to the *New York Times* and *Washington Post* but rejected for publication and barely reported. A study by the Swiss League for the Rights of Man (June 1977), presenting similar material, received no notice here. The same is true of the reports of torture by Israeli journalists.[105] Various Israeli rebuttals were published though not, to my knowledge, the devastating *Sunday Times* response.

More interesting than the attempt at rebuttal, however, was the conclusion that torture of Arabs by Israelis is legitimate, a position expressed, perhaps not surprisingly, in the *New Republic*, the semi-official journal of American liberalism, where Seth Kaplan concludes that the question of how a government should treat people under its control "is not susceptible to simple absolutism, such as the outright condemnation of torture. One may have to use extreme measures—call them 'torture'— to deal with a terrorist movement whose steady tactic is the taking of human life."[106] To my knowledge, this is the first explicit defense of torture to have appeared in the West* apart from the ravings of the ultra-right in France during the Algerian war.

No less interesting was the response of the Israeli judiciary. Amnesty International raised the question whether the remarkably high level of confessions of Arab prisoners might suggest inhumane treatment. To this, Israeli Supreme Court Justice Moshe Etzioni responded that "the Arabs in any case—if they are arrested—do not take much time before they confess. It's part of their nature"—a comment that we may place along-side of Martin Peretz's "Arabs exaggerate" and others of the same ilk concerning Jews and other oppressed peoples over the years. It is perhaps of some interest to note that the genetic defect of Arabs noted by Justice Etzioni appears to be somehow contagious, since by now Jewish prisoners are confessing to crimes that they did not commit after police interroga-

---

* See also Michael Levin, "The Case for Torture," *Newsweek*, June 7, 1982. A professor of philosophy at City College of New York, Levin plays a game familiar from every Phil. 1 course, constructing an outlandish case where torture might be "morally mandatory" (a terrorist has hidden an atomic bomb on Manhattan Island, etc.), then noting that "once you concede that torture is justified in extreme cases, you have admitted that the decision to use torture is a matter of balancing innocent lives against the means needed to save them"; finally, he advocates torture "as an acceptable measure for preventing future evils," rejecting talk about "terrorists' 'rights'," assuring us that Western democracies will not "lose their way if they choose to inflict pain as one way of preserving order," etc. This should be understood in the context of the hysteria being whipped up at the time concerning "international terrorism," defined so as to include "retail terrorism" conducted by enemies but not "wholesale (or retail) terrorism" conducted by friends (or by us). On this matter, see Herman, *The Real Terror Network*.

tion, including cases of interrogation by police investigators previously identified by Arabs as torturers.[107]

Amnesty International, incidentally, is not very popular in Israel, at least since it published a rather mild and understated report on treatment of suspects and prisoners in 1979. An editorial in *Ha'aretz*, entitled "Amnesty is at it again," commented that the organization had "turned itself into a tool of Arab propaganda by publishing the document," criticizing among other things its reliance on the "distorted and malicious report" in the *London Sunday Times*. The left-wing Mapam journal took a different tack. An editorial observed that "Experience tells us that it is extremely difficult to effectively defend oneself against terrorists or even ordinary criminals without bringing great pressure to bear on the suspects, in order to eventually bring them to trial at all," and recommended that "constant vigilance" be exercised to determine that there are no "excesses" in the use of the required "great pressure."[108]

Quite apart from alleged torture under interrogation, the conditions of Arab political prisoners are horrifying, not a great surprise, perhaps, when we consider the scale of arrests in the occupied territories: some 200,000 security prisoners and detainees have passed through Israeli jails, almost 20% of the population, which has led to "horrendous overcrowding" and "appalling human suffering and corruption."[109]

The occasional trials of military offenders sometimes shed light on practices in the occupied territories. A number of reserve officers connected with the Peace Now movement threatened to make charges against soldiers public unless there was an investigation, leading to a trial that "brought forth evidence of methodically brutal treatment of the local townspeople last spring" (1982), at the peak of the atrocities carried out under the Milson-Sharon administration. Reuters reports that at the trial, Maj. David Mofaz, the deputy military governor of Hebron at the time of the alleged atrocities, testified that "Israeli soldiers were given orders to harass and beat up Palestinian residents" and that they "viciously struck and kicked defenseless young Arab prisoners." He testified that "he personally was ordered to beat up Arabs by the West Bank military commander," but he knew that "the orders came from higher up, from the chief of staff." He said that "the army had orders to harass the West Bank population in general, not just those involved in anti-Israeli demonstrations," giving examples. An Israeli captain testified that he had personally beaten Palestinian detainees and that "Israeli soldiers routinely beat up Palestinian detainees on the occupied West Bank with the knowledge of senior officers."[110]

On the same day, another brief report in the same American journal describes how Turkish women, "suspected leftists," are placed in coffin-like boxes "in an attempt to extract information during questioning," one minor example of a systematic pattern of torture and repression that also evokes little interest here, though perhaps the same report from another military dictatorship (say in Poland), might have elicited some comment.

According to the *Jerusalem Post*, "a military court has allegedly heard evidence that Defence Minister Ariel Sharon urged Israeli soldiers to beat Arab schoolchildren in the West Bank," referring to the same trial of soldiers "accused of brutally mistreating Arab youths in Hebron last March," a trial that "has attracted almost no publicity in Israel"—though it did shortly after. The source is a major in the reserves who told the court that the military governor had quoted Sharon to this effect. At the trial, soldiers reportedly told the court that they had beaten Arab high school students while the major stood by and watched, hitting them as hard as they could. One said: "Afterwards, I left the shed where this was happening because I couldn't stand beating up people who couldn't fight back."

The Hebrew press reports the testimony of the vice-commander of the Judea region, who reports that in a meeting with Civilian Administrator Menachem Milson, General Sharon gave instructions as to how to deal with demonstrators: "Cut off their testicles." The Chief of Staff went a step further, telling soldiers on the northern front that "the only good Arab is a dead Arab," as reported by Abraham Burg, son of the Minister of Interior. The vice-commander reports also that his superior officer General Hartabi led troops into a Hebron school where they beat the students with clubs. In another incident, Hartabi imposed a curfew on the Dheisha camp after a stone was thrown at his car and ordered his troops to fire in the streets and at the rooftop solar water tanks, destroying the hot water supply and also making a terrifying racket. Another curfew was imposed on the Dhahriyeh camp south of Hebron on January 30 after youths stoned Israeli vehicles passing through the town. An Israeli woman was injured, and later died. A report in the U.S. press three weeks later notes that the curfew is still in effect, because "it is necessary for the investigation," an Israeli military source said, adding: "It prevents people from working and causes financial losses. But it also gives them an incentive to help us find the people who carried out the attack. The sooner we find them, the sooner all this will be over." Meanwhile the people are allowed out of their homes only two hours a day, schools are closed, and there is no employment. The treatment is somewhat different when Israeli West Bank terrorists go on a rampage. A minor fact, not noted in the press accounts, is that two weeks before the demonstrators unaccountably began to stone passing Israeli vehicles, 20,000 dunams of land used for orchards and grain were expropriated by Israeli military authorities.[111]

The trial of the soldiers did receive publicity later on, particularly when the defense established its claim that the orders to brutalize prisoners and impose collective punishments came directly from Chief of Staff Eitan. He was called to testify before the military court and confirmed that he had ordered such punishments as expulsion, harassment of inciters, the establishment of detention or exile camps "even without regular prison conditions" (which are grim enough), and a wide variety of collective punishments against towns where there had been resistance to the conquerors (primarily, stone throwing) and against families of pupils who "caused disturbances" (this device "works well with Arabs," he testified). The Chief of Staff opposed calling leaders in for warnings. "We demean ourselves," he said: "Instead of conversations, we should carry out arrests." He also said that Jewish settlers must travel armed and feel free to open fire when attacked, say, by children throwing stones. The military court sentenced four soldiers to several months imprisonment,* but ruled that Eitan's orders were legal.

Maj. Mofaz, the highest ranking officer charged, was released; his lawyers had held—accurately it appears—that he and others were "merely following the orders and guidelines laid down by their superiors," Edward Walsh reports. Apart from beating of Arab detainees and civilians, charges included forcing people to crawl on all fours and bark like dogs, laud Begin and Border Guards (who were allegedly responsible, though not punished), slap one another (children were ordered to slap their parents), along with other punishments that work well with Arabs. Maj. Mofaz ordered soldiers to write numbers on the arms of prisoners on the Day of the Holocaust, but the military court accepted his defense that this order was only given in jest (though it was carried out).[112] The New Republic, democratic socialists, Elie Wiesel and others have not yet rendered their judgment as to whether these practices fall within the range of those that are acceptable for dealing with terrorists; the same silence has held for many years in similar circumstances, though there has been no shortage of praise for Israel's remarkably high moral values and sympathy for its travail under the burdens of occupation imposed upon it by Arab intransigence.

⁂   Aharon Bachar writes of "the things that are being done in my name and in yours": "we will never be able to escape the responsibility and to say that we did not know and we did not hear." He describes a meeting between Labor Alignment leaders (including some of the most noted

---

* For comparison, "An Israeli military court sentenced seven West Bank Arab teenagers to jail terms ranging from six to nine months and fined them $650 each yesterday for stoning an Israeli police chief in his car in the occupied territory" (Washington Post—Boston Globe, March 18, 1983). Later, Chief of Staff Eitan expressed his views on proper punishment again, this time to the Knesset's Foreign Affairs and Defense Committee. For every incident of stone-throwing by Arab youths, he said, ten settlements should be built: "When we have settled the land, all the Arabs will be able to do about it will be to scurry around like drugged roaches in a bottle." Defense Minister Moshe Arens was asked by opposition Knesset members to reprimand Eitan for this remark, but declined because Eitan "has great achievements to his credit" during his tenure as Chief of Staff—in fact, two great achievements, intensification of the repression in the conquered territories and destruction of the virtually defenseless Palestinian society in Lebanon. Gad Becker, Yediot Ahronot, April 13, 1983; David K. Shipler, New York Times, April 14, 20, 1983.

hawks, such as Golda Meir's adviser Israel Galili) and Menachem Begin, where they presented to Begin "detailed accounts of terrorist acts [against Arabs] in the conquered territories." They described the "collective punishment in the town of Halhul," in these words:

> The men were taken from their houses beginning at midnight, in pajamas, in the cold. The notables and other men were concentrated in the square of the mosque and held there until morning. Meanwhile men of the Border Guards [noted for their cruelty] broke into houses, beating people with shouts and curses. During the many hours that hundreds of people were kept in the mosque square, they were ordered to urinate and excrete on one another and also to sing *Hatikva* ["The Hope," the national anthem of Israel] and to call out "Long Live the State of Israel." Several times people were beaten and ordered to crawl on the ground. Some were even ordered to lick the earth. At the same time four trucks were commandeered and at daybreak, the inhabitants were loaded on the trucks, about 100 in each truck, and taken like sheep to the Administration headquarters in Hebron.
>
> On Holocaust Day, the 27 of Nissan [the date in the Jewish calendar], the people who were arrested were ordered to write numbers on their hands with their own hands, in memory of the Jews in the extermination camps.

The report continues, detailing how prisoners are beaten, tortured and humiliated, how settlers are permitted into the prisons to take part in the beating of prisoners, how the settlers brutalize the local inhabitants with impunity, even in the case of a settler who killed an Arab, whose identity is known, but who is not arrested.[113] All legitimate, presumably, by the standards of the *New Republic*, as quoted above. The same correspondent reports similar stories a few weeks earlier, presented to top government officials who did not even take the trouble to check the information, provided by an Israeli soldier.[114]

A week later, Yoram Peri again published sections of the report transmitted to Begin by the Labor Party delegation. There had been no question raised in the Knesset concerning it, he noted, and the matter had been passed over silently elsewhere. But, he added bitterly, why be surprised? "After all, who are they [the victims]? Araboushim, two-legged beasts" (the latter a reference to Prime Minister Begin's characterization of "terrorists"). He writes that the "frightening metamorphosis that is coming over us . . . places in question the justice of the Zionist movement, the basis for the existence of the state," but it receives no attention in the Knesset, the World Zionist Congress (then in session in Jerusalem), or elsewhere. It is time to recognize, he concludes, that "there is no such thing as an enlightened occupation, there cannot be a liberal military administration." The pretenses of the past 15 years are simply lies. By now, 3/4 of a million young Israelis who have served in the IDF "know that the task of the army is not only to defend the state in the battlefield against a foreign army, but to demolish the rights of innocent people just because they are Araboushim living in territories that God promised to us."[115]

Writing identification numbers on the arms of prisoners is a practice that many have naturally found particularly shocking. It is apparently common, and the circumstances just described are not unique. Peace Now military officers describing the daily "brutality and violence" of the IDF and the settlers in the territories, the "repression, humiliation, maltreatment and collective punishment," report that soldiers regularly write the numbers of Arab IDs on the wrists of Arab prisoners, and one recalls a particularly "appalling incident" of this sort that he witnessed—again, on the Day of the Holocaust. Another describes an incident in which a group of fresh recruits were issued clubs and told: "Boys, off you go to assault the locals." He describes the treatment of Arab prisoners, who are required to clean the soldiers' rooms, mess halls and latrines. "At night, they are put into a small room and beaten up" so badly that "many of them cannot even stand up"—"youngsters,...most of whom have not been tried, people who will be released due to lack of evidence." Aharon Geva writes in *Davar* that "Some of us Israelis behave like the worst kind of anti-Semites, whose name cannot be mentioned here, like the very people who painted a picture of the Jew as a sub-human creature..."[115] In fact, what has been happening in the occupied territories for many years is all too familiar from Jewish history.

Stories such as these, which abound, have constituted the daily lives of those subjected to Israeli rule for many years. Outright murders by Israeli soldiers or settlers are sometimes reported in the U.S., but the regular terror, harassment and degradation pass unnoticed among those who are paying the bills. It is, for example, most unlikely that an American newspaper would print the report by Aharon Bachar, which appeared in a mass-circulation Israeli journal, on the atrocities reported to the Prime Minister by a high-level (and generally hawkish) Labor Alignment delegation. The few people who have tried to transmit some of the facts reported in the mainstream Hebrew press have either been ignored, or subjected to a campaign of lies and vilification that is reminiscent of Stalinist practices.

5.2   The Golan Heights

Until December 1981, the Golan Heights had been spared this treatment. Over 90% of the population had fled or were expelled at the time of the Israeli conquest of the Heights in 1967. Israeli settlements were then established, but the Druze population generally "accepted the authority and jurisdiction of the military government," according to a report by a leading Israeli civil rights association.[117] On December 14, the day after martial law was declared in Poland, the Knesset passed a law extending civilian law and administration to the Golan Heights—in effect, annexation. In January, new regulations were imposed requiring that the inhabitants carry Israeli IDs. There was overwhelming opposition to this integration into Israel. On February 13, four leading members of the Druze community were placed under administrative arrest and a general strike was called, supported by "the overwhelming majority" of the population. The Israeli military command closed the area, forbidding villagers to move between villages and preventing journalists, lawyers and medical staff from entering. Expressions of solidarity in the Israeli Galilee and the West Bank were suppressed and organizers were placed under house arrest. No supplies were allowed to enter. All telephones were disconnected (reports of a similar policy in Poland at the same time caused great outrage here). Residents who were imprisoned after a "summary trial" were denied legal aid. For three days before the closure was lifted in April, "all villagers were restricted to their homes (they were even forbidden to visit the toilets which are in outhouses)," and "allegedly, forbidden to go out on balconies or to open windows." A woman who was sent to a hospital by a local doctor after the closure was lifted was refused exit by the military when—like most others—she refused to accept an Israeli ID. Inhabitants reported shooting and other physical violence; one was hospitalized with bullet wounds and others still carried scars or fresh wounds when the Israeli civil rights delegation visited after the closure was lifted, having previously been denied entry.

The press reported many more details, for example, the case of a three-year-old boy who was beaten with a club by a soldier after he threw an Israeli ID card to the floor; his mother was shot when she came to his aid. The national water company reduced water supplies. Jewish settlements (including kibbutzim) complained because they were deprived of their normal workforce of Golan Druze.[118] A lead article in *Ha'aretz* observed that there was no protest in the Knesset apart from Rakah (Communist) and that editors did not protest the prohibition of entry of journalists. "In the general Israeli Jewish public the indifference is shocking. Only some few hundreds of meters away from the besieged Druze village, young Israelis enjoy the sun, take photos in the snow, eat and gossip. On one side, barbed wire and human beings in a cage, on the other, people skiing, going up and down in lifts. In the middle, the Israeli Army."[119] Subsequently, former Supreme Court Justice Chaim Cohen described the Golan Law as "the law of the barbarians."[120] One reason for objections of the Druze to the Golan Law was "the great fear of expropriation of their lands." They "know well that most of the lands of the Druze in

Israel [whose loyalty to the state is so unquestioned that they regularly serve in the armed forces] were expropriated in the last 30 years and handed over to Jews."[121]

All of this, and much more, care of the American taxpayer, who must be kept uninformed, and generally has been, quite successfully.

5.3   The Attack on Palestinian Culture

Throughout this period, the Arab intelligentsia have been a particular target of attack, in accordance with "the clear plan of Sharon to drive out and destroy any sign or element with an Arab national character, to bring about full Israeli control in the territories."[122] Bir Zeit university in the West Bank has been one of the favorite targets, with "night raids on women's and men's dormitories, and on student and faculty apartments," disruption of classes by military checkpoints, confiscation of students' ID cards making it illegal for them to travel, and in general, "daily humiliation inflicted on students [which] placed them under psychological pressure that made the normal functioning of the University difficult"[123]—an understatement, as more detailed reporting shows.

More recently, much of the foreign faculty has been expelled for refusing to sign a statement that they will not offer support for the PLO (as does the overwhelming majority of the West Bank population), eliciting a protest from the State Department.[124] Secretary of State George Shultz condemned the Israeli loyalty oath as "an abridgment of academic freedom" and as "totally unnecessary" for Israel's security, a clear infringement "of freedom, freedom of thought," and called upon "people in the intellectual community particularly...to speak up" in protest. That American intellectuals should suddenly become exercised over violations of academic freedom under Israeli occupation seems unlikely, given their dismal record of "support for Israel." There was, however, a statement of protest by two hundred Israeli academics, organized before the Shultz statement.[125] The expulsion of foreign faculty (by November, 22 had been expelled, including the President of al-Najah University in Nablus, and many more had been banned from teaching and were facing expulsion) is particularly harmful, since "many talented West Bankers educated abroad are unable to get Israeli work permits."[126]

One aspect of the problem, noted by David Richardson, is illustrated by the case of Mohammad Shadid, an American-trained political scientist at al-Najah university, one of those banned from teaching and facing expulsion. He lost the right to return to the West Bank, where he was born, because he happened to be out of the country studying when a census was taken in 1967; requests by his family to allow him to return under a "family reunion scheme" were simply ignored, and he is now an American citizen. Richardson observes that what the civil administration is trying to do is to suppress the local intelligentsia, and to "make political use" of the signed statements as part of the effort to undermine support for the PLO in the occupied territories. Furthermore, a degree for a West Bank student is a "passport to emigration," since "most of the young graduates cannot hope to find employment in their own society"—as Israel is reconstructing it.[127] In fact, Israeli policy in the occupied territories has clearly been designed to remove elite groups, either by direct expulsion ("moderates" have been a particular target) or by eliminating the possibility of meaningful employment, in the hope that no nationalist or cultural leadership will remain.[128] After Shultz's protests, the anti-PLO pledge was technically "withdrawn," in fact transferred in virtually the same terms to the general work permit.[129]

Mohammad Shadid is no unique case. President Salah of al-Najah University, who was expelled in October, is also a native of the West Bank, born in Nablus, who was studying abroad in 1967 and is therefore considered a "foreigner" by the Israeli government; in its brief story on the expulsion, the *New York Times* refers to him as "a Jordanian national," technically correct but missing a rather important point. In a press conference on the morning of his expulsion, unreported here to my knowledge, Dr. Salah stated that Israel's

> strategy is to destroy the infrastructure of the universities, as it is to destroy the infrastructure of Palestinian society. This started with the municipalities. Now they've come to a second attempt after the first one failed. Their ultimate aim is to destroy any Palestinian infrastructure in the homeland.[130]

Danny Rubinstein reports that most of the "foreign lecturers" at the University "are not really 'foreigners,' but rather Palestinians, natives of the West Bank, who do not have Israeli identity cards (from the military administration) so that the authorities can revoke their residence permits and expel them from the country." He also notes that the harassment of the West Bank universities, of which the latest expulsions are only a part, elicits little interest in the Israeli academic community. The same is true of Israeli journalists with regard to restrictions on Arab colleagues, publishers with regard to censorship, lawyers with regard to legal issues, and so on. At a time when the academic community in Israel went on strike over wages, no academic organization raised any question about the regular harassment of the West Bank universities. Those who have been concerned are "very few and without influence on the course of events."[131]

The former acting president of al-Najah University, W.F. Abboushi (a professor of political science at the University of Cincinnati), faced continual harassment, he reports, alleging that his protest over similar practices on an earlier occasion at Bir Zeit university had led to beating by Israeli soldiers. From his experience, he believes that "it is impossible to run a Palestinian university under Israeli occupation" and that "generally, life in the West Bank has become almost unbearable, particularly for the students who are constantly subjected to harassment, including arbitrary search and arrest, imprisonment, beating, and sometimes even severe physical abuse." The worst has been since the takeover of the "civil administration" by Professor Menachem Milson, the "Mideast maverick" praised here for his advocacy of a Palestinian role in the affairs of the West Bank (see p. 58). Abboushi says that "perhaps over one-third of our student body had been in Israeli jails," where they were "routinely beaten." Like much of the faculty and administration, most of the so-called "foreign students" at al-Najah were in fact Palestinian Arabs who had lost their right of residence because they were out of the area when the 1967 census was taken. The situation worsened after the invasion of Lebanon, when Israeli soldiers "attacked the university using real bullets" to disperse a demonstration protesting the invasion.[132]

In his article "A threat to freedom" (note 127), David Richardson observes that just as the Israeli academic community has by and large showed "indifference" to the treatment of their Arab colleagues under the military occupation, so Israeli journalists have for the most part remained (purposefully) "ignorant of the fact that three West Bank editors have been confined to their places of residence for almost two years and thereby prevented from pursuing their professions properly." Boaz Evron investigated this matter, visiting the three editors in violation of his resolve not to enter the occupied territories. The three editors were confined to their West Bank villages three years ago, he reports. No reason was given. None of them had ever been accused of any crime, and the security services refused to provide their lawyers with any charges. As editors, they are responsible for what appears in their journals, published in Jerusalem, but they are unable to see these journals, since distribution is forbidden in the West Bank areas where they are confined: "the Kingdom of the Absurd." "If this were happening to Jewish journalists, we would be raising a cry to the heavens," he observes, "but here we accept it all peacefully. What is so terrible? Is anyone being killed?" The technique of the occupation, in this case, is "to keep them on a short leash," not to act brutally, but to make sure that they recognize always "that the whip is held over their heads."[133]

The treatment of the editors of the Jerusalem journal *Al Fajr* illustrates what Arab intellectuals may expect if they "raise their heads," in the terminology of the West Bank settlers—if they try to act with a measure of intellectual independence.* One was picked up by the police and kept in

---

* For an account of harassment and arbitrary arrest, detention and alleged beatings of journalists from *Al Fajr*, harassment of other Arab journals, and the forms taken by Israeli

solitary confinement for 17 days. He was made to stand for 24 hours with a bag over his head and his arms bound, until he fainted. He was then charged with possessing two copies of a PLO journal. A second has been prevented for a year from visiting the occupied territories, where his family and friends live and where his professional responsibilities are focused. A third was kept in jail for a week for failure to change the license on a new car. A fourth was confined for two and a half years in Ramallah. The journal is subjected to heavy censorship, often not permitted to republish material from the Hebrew or more conformist Arabic press. It is even prevented from publishing factual information about such matters as the opening of a school that had been closed, or events in the occupied territories. Journalists from *Al Fajr* are continually taken for interrogation, degraded, threatened, arrested. "If things like this happened to your journalists," one editor said to an Israeli reporter, "all the world would respond with great anger. You shout about the suppression of intellectuals in the USSR, but you close your eyes to what is happening to the intellectuals in the West Bank, right under your noses."[134]

Michal Meron, who reports these facts, writes that *Al Fajr* "is not an example of what it is possible to call free journalism." The reason is that those who participate in the journal "see in their task a national mission, and their pen is ready to serve only the Palestinian interest." The editors, in fact, are outspoken about their political commitments. One states to Meron that "we see in the PLO our sole representative, and therefore we support its point of view. We are in favor of the establishment of a Palestinian state alongside of the State of Israel." Perhaps some might see in this a justification for the constant harassment of a journal that does not really merit the appellation "free press." One might ask how such a stand differs in principle from that of Soviet authorities with regard to Zionist publications within the USSR. Or we might ask just what one should expect of honest journalists working under military occupation and living in what they—and virtually the entire world, including the U.S. government—regard as occupied East Jerusalem.

Other questions arise as well. While Meron was disparaging *Al Fajr* because of its commitment to "the Palestinian interest," the *Jerusalem Post*, highly regarded within Israel and elsewhere, was celebrating its

censorship, see Robert I. Friedman, "No Peace for West Bank Press," *CPJ Update*, Committee to Protect Journalists, January 1983. Israeli officials defend the censorship on the grounds that "It's no secret that Palestinians in general, and the Arab press, support the PLO" (it is kept a secret in some circles in the U.S., where the fact is consistently denied, e.g., in the *New Republic*; see p. 63), and Israel is "in a state of war with the PLO." Israeli journalists who have investigated the censorship allege, however, that it is politically motivated, and often entirely arbitrary (e.g., love poems have been censored though they had no reference to the national question). Words are censored that Israeli officials find objectionable, e.g., the word "sumud," referring to the steadfastness of the *samid* who chooses the "third way," neither resistance nor capitulation; see below, section 6.

Jubilee. Editor Erwin Frenkel published an article in the Jubilee issue just a week before Meron's article on *Al Fajr* appeared, in which he explained that the goal of the paper today is "the same as it was from the start" 50 years ago: "the fulfilment of Zionism." Its predecessor, the *Palestine Post*, was founded under the British Mandate "for a purpose that was political"; and under conditions far less onerous than those faced by the Arabs under Israeli occupation, it maintained this purpose, even after the state was founded. The journal also exercised self-censorship. Readers of the Israeli press can hardly fail to notice that the English-language *Post* is more cautious in what it publishes than is the Hebrew press. The reasons are obvious, and editor Frenkel states them clearly: "Both within the newspaper and without, it was generally presumed that Hebrew was a private language of the Jews, in which they addressed only each other... English, on the other hand, was public. It enabled access from the outside, the Gentile world, the Arab foe. In short, what could be written in Hebrew could not necessarily be exposed in English." Frenkel claims that this posture was modified in the 1960s, that "the old constraints of English" were abandoned and "English would no longer inhibit expression."[135] I do not believe that this is true, judging by my own limited exposure to the Hebrew and English-language press, and I would guess that a systematic investigation would support this conclusion. But even if the earlier constraints were dropped, the journal by its own admission remains subject to the critique that Meron applies to *Al Fajr*, and surely did even more so before the alleged abandonment of "the old constraints," without the justification that it is attempting to survive with extremely limited resources under a harsh military regime where it attempts to express the aspirations of a conquered and oppressed people.

A few days earlier, the Congress of Jewish Journalists from the Diaspora opened, with 60 journalists from 14 countries. The deputy chairman of the Zionist Congress in Israel, Yitzhak Koren, informed the gathering "that anti-semites today blamed every Jew, wherever he might live, for Israel's actions, and that it was therefore extremely important for the Jewish press to show Israeli policies in a positive light."[136]

The constant and sometimes almost fanatic harassment of West Bank intellectuals and educational institutions, along with the general fear of permitting independent cultural expression, suggests that Israel's leaders may be recalling some lessons from their own history, to which they frequently appeal. Every Israeli schoolchild knows the story of Rabbi Jochanan Ben Zakkai, who foresaw the destruction of the Temple in 70 AD when Jerusalem was under Roman siege. He opposed the final resistance and sought a way to save his people from destruction by an appeal to the Roman commander. Not being permitted to leave Jerusalem by its defenders, he had his disciples pretend that he was dead and carry him out in a coffin for burial. He reached the Roman camp and was granted his request to open a school in the small town of Yavneh. The famous Jewish historian Heinrich Graetz relates that the Roman commander "had nothing to urge against the harmless wish of Jochanan, for he could not foresee that by this unimportant concession he was enabling Judaism, feeble as it then appeared, to outlive Rome, which was in all its vigor, by thousands of years."[137] Most of the scholars of the next generation were his pupils. According to the tradition, he consoled them for the destruction of the Temple with a quote from the Prophet Hosea: "For I desire mercy, not sacrifice." Both the appeal to the prophetic tradition and the significance of maintaining a school to keep the culture alive may well have a certain resonance today.

Israeli Arab citizens are, incidentally, also frequently denied the right of cultural expression. To cite one recent example, the High Court of Justice upheld the government's refusal to permit Najwa Makhoul, a lecturer at the Hebrew University with a Phd degree from MIT, to publish an Arabic political-literary journal, citing undisclosed "security reasons." "The security of the state has silenced yet another Arab," B. Michael observes, adding that Israeli intellectuals, professors, writers and poets have nothing to say. The journal was "envisioned as a forum for serious analyses of Palestinian-Israeli society, as well as more general articles written [in] a Third World context...[with] a scientific, Marxist and feminist perspective." It would have been the only publication based in the Galilee, where most Israeli Arabs live, and not connected with a political party, and would have provided jobs for Arab university graduates, no small problem in Israel.[138] This scandal was not reported in the U.S. to my knowledge, and at the time of writing has evoked no protest, though the facts have been known for many months to individuals and organizations devoted to intellectual freedom throughout the world. The "security reasons" are no doubt comparable to those used by other states to prevent groups that are "marginal to the nation" (in Michael Walzer's phrase) from having an independent cultural and political life.

As for the lack of interest here, that should be no more surprising than the fact that there is no protest when the well-known Palestinian poet Mahmoud Darwish, invited to take part in a UNICEF poetry reading, is denied a visa "under a section of immigration law that allows the State Department to bar people for certain ideological reasons"—as the State Department confirmed. If an Israeli poet were denied entry to the United States for "ideological reasons"—assuming this to be possible—there would be no limits to the outrage and indignation, the charges of a return of Nazism, etc. In this case, there is no response at all. Similarly, when Israeli censors banned the play "The Patriot" by the Hebrew writer Hanoch Levin, there was considerable protest in Israel, widely reported here as further proof of the deep commitment to democratic principles in Israel. A few months before, the police banned a play by a Druze writer,

Salman Natour, describing the life and opinions of a young Israeli Arab, and arrested the director. There was virtually no protest in Israel, and nothing was reported here. The same was true in early 1983 when an Arab from Nazareth was arrested "for publishing a newspaper without permission"—four information leaflets. He appealed to the responsible Israeli government authority in the Galilee, Israel Koenig, but his petition was rejected.[139] Examples are numerous; the silence here is unbroken.

5.4   "The Opportunity to Work in Israel"

As one might expect, the experiences of those who enjoy "the opportunity given to them to work in Israel" (Sasson Levi; see p. 114) are also not entirely delightful. One problem that they face is that they are not permitted to spend the night within Israel. Since employers do not want to pay the costs of shipping workers back and forth, some have adopted the idea of locking them into factories at night, a practice that became public knowledge when several were found burned to death in a locked room after a fire in a small Tel Aviv factory. Others have been kept under armed guard behind barbed wire in factory detention camps, including one owned by Histadrut, the socialist trade union. These practices aroused some protest in Israel where, for example, Natan Dunvitz wrote in *Ha-'aretz* that "it is unacceptable to treat Arab workers as Black slaves were treated in American cotton fields." There was no mention here, to my knowledge, apart from a letter of mine,[140] and the facts were not considered worthy of notice by those who were celebrating Israel's advance towards democratic socialism. One might ask, incidentally, what the reaction would be if it were learned that Jewish workers were burned to death in a locked room in a Moscow factory or kept in factory detention camps because they are not permitted to spend the night in Russian areas. Praise for Russia's march toward democratic socialism and its high moral purpose, perhaps?

The same regulation leads to other problems. Two moshavim (semi-collective settlements) were recently condemned by the Moshav movement for arranging "decent housing" for seasonal agricultural workers, instead of bringing them from their homes in the Gaza Strip 200 km away every morning and returning them there in the evening, as required by law. Their work day thus ran from 3AM to 8PM, and they were found to be tired, strangely. The phrase "decent housing" appears in the English-language press account. The Hebrew press tells a different story, with pictures to illustrate: the "decent housing" consisted of barns, store-houses, abandoned buildings where they are crammed into rooms, old buses; the headline in *Haolam Haze* reads: "Too far away for any eye to see, hidden in the orchards, there are the sheep pens for the servants, of a sort that even a state like South Africa would be ashamed of." Amos Hadar, Secretary General of the Moshav movement, strongly opposes providing housing for the workers, which is in any event illegal. If they are given housing, he says, "after a short while the workers from the territories will bring their families and house them in camps. That would be Arab settlement on land of the Jewish National Fund. That cannot be." Journalist Aryeh Rubinstein adds sarcastically: "his children will help with the picking and his wife will clean the 'master's' house." Hadar is asked whether he agrees to the use of Arab labor, "but only on condition that they will live in subhuman conditions, degraded, and not under human conditions, more or less." "Correct," he answers, conceding that "really, there is a difficult question here." "There is no choice but to employ Arabs," he says. They must be brought from Gaza in the morning and returned there in the evening. "It is hard, it is costly, it is problematic from an economic standpoint—but there is no other solution, if Jews in the State of Israel are unable to pick the oranges and grapes."

Another officer of the Moshav movement concedes that hired labor troubles him: "But I am troubled far more by the fact that we, with our own hands, are establishing settlements for Arabs within the Green Line [the pre-June 1967 borders]." As for the problem of bringing in workers from such a distance, he asks: "What are 200 kilometers in comparison with the loss of the justice of our struggle for the land?"—especially when others are doing the travelling, with a work day from 3AM to 8PM. But the problem will apparently soon be resolved, since the Border Guards have been ordered to evacuate the Arab workers from the camps set up for them.[141] Further steps towards "the democratic socialist hope."

This only skims the surface. There is also, for example, the issue of child labor, of children aged six or seven trucked in by labor contractors at 4 AM to work on private or collective farms for "a meager subsistence wage," though "often they are cheated on that." Again, the matter has not been discussed in the United States, to my knowledge. And there is the matter of Arab trade unions, long a target of repression, again with little notice here from democratic socialist supporters of Israel, American union leaders who tell us how much they "love" Israel (see p. 13*), or others. To cite only one recent case, the club of the Ramallah trade union was closed by orders of the military governor in December 1982, all written materials were seized, and its secretary, Bassem Barguti, was arrested, held for a month and then sentenced to two months in prison on charges of possessing forbidden material of political significance, including, according to the charges, some that was literally "obscene" (a publication that included the colors of the PLO flag) and some that was defamatory of the Israeli army (a calendar with a demand for release of prisoners in the Ansar concentration camp in Lebanon).[142]

5.5   Israeli Inquiries and American Suppression

Coverage of events in the occupied territories is far more comprehensive in Israel than in the U.S., but it too is impeded, in part by censorship, in part by "internal censorship." See p. 12. TV journalists (including Rafik Halabi; see note 48) complain that they are kept away from 90% of the serious demonstrations in the territories and that they are not permitted to film much of what is happening, including soldiers firing at demonstrators, etc.[143] "Only a small part of the actions of the settlers, in or out of uniform, reaches the Israeli press," Amnon Kapeliouk reports: "facts about harassment and maltreatment of Palestinians are not published," sometimes, because editors feel that they are "too hard to bear," as one decided when "settlers caught an old man who had protested when his lands were taken and shaved off his beard—just what Polish anti-Semites did to Jews."[144]

A great deal of information about human rights violations, particularly in the occupied territories, has been made available by the Israeli League for Human and Civil Rights. Its Chairman from 1970, Dr. Israel Shahak, has compiled a personal record of courage and commitment to human rights that few people anywhere can equal, and has been untiring in exposing the facts about the occupation and circulating information, much of it from the Hebrew press, where several outstanding journalists (frequently cited above) have attempted to provide an honest record—sometimes, some say, using material provided by Arab journalists who hope to be able to reprint the stories from the Hebrew press. The work of the League is little known here, in part, because human rights organizations prefer not to know the facts. The League had been an affiliate of the New York-based International League for Human Rights, but was suspended in 1973 on the interesting grounds that the governing Labor Party had attempted to take over and destroy the League by methods so crude that they were quickly blocked by the Israeli Courts; on similar grounds, it would be proper for Amnesty International to suspend a Moscow chapter attacked by the government. One professed civil libertarian, Professor Alan Dershowitz of Harvard Law School (who had already distinguished himself by defending preventive detention in Israel and denouncing political prisoners in jail*—a particularly despicable practice, as

---

* The particular target of Dershowitz's slanders was the Israeli Arab writer Fouzi el-Asmar, held for 15 months without charges under administrative detention. On the basis of information provided to him by the Israeli secret police, Dershowitz arrived at the "personal conviction" that he was a terrorist "commander," as he proceeds to assert without qualification, so that the detention was legitimate. There is, by now, little pretense in Israel or elsewhere that there was any substance to these charges, but it is interesting that in the U.S. it is not considered that Dershowitz's stand represents any departure from civil l̶i̶b̶e̶r̶t̶a̶r̶i̶a̶n̶ standards. The attitude within the American Communist Party to Soviet

would be at once recognized in any other context)— attempted to cover up the disgraceful Labor government takeover attempt with gross misrepresentation of the facts and slanderous accusations directed against Shahak, who has, in fact, been bitterly attacked by American Zionists who are horrified at his belief that Palestinians are human; see his entry in the Anti-Defamation League "enemies list," for example.[145] Again, these facts fall under the ideological aspect of the "special relationship," as discussed earlier.

6   The Testimony of the Samidin

The account given above is primarily from Israeli sources. There is ample testimony from the victims, but it is virtually unknown here. Suppose that some American intellectual who expressed his undying love for the Soviet Union were to return from a visit there and write that Jews are prosperous and generally content apart from some youthful rabble-rousers and Zionist terrorists who try to incite them, basing his conclusions on discussions with Russian experts on Jewish affairs, government officials, and Russian academics and taxi drivers. It is an understatement to say that such a person would be dismissed with contempt and disgust. Comparable practices are quite common, however, in the case of Western visitors to Israel.[146] The standard practice of dismissing Arab sources falls into the same category. It is simply an expression of racist attitudes so deeply entrenched as to be quite unrecognized, one aspect of the amazing double standard with regard to Israeli Jews and Palestinian Arabs that we have observed throughout, and that would be apparent to any observer of the American scene with even a pretense of rationality.

I have mentioned the reports of Arab prisoners, available only to the most dedicated researcher and excluded from mainstream journalism and scholarship. The same is true, by and large, of the writings of Palestinian intellectuals. For example, much insight into the lives of Israeli Arabs is provided in a personal memoir by Fouzi el-Asmar (see p. 142*).[147] It is an important and, I think, shocking fact that this material is essentially unavailable in the U.S., which bears a major responsibility for what has happened to the indigenous inhabitants of the former Palestine. The same can be said about material produced by Palestinian intellectuals from the occupied territories. It is, for example, fairly safe to predict that the thoughtful and revealing study by Raja Shehadeh, his "journal of life in the West Bank," will remain unknown in the United States (see note 48). That would be a shame—indeed, a scandal, given the crucial American role in perpetuating the conditions he describes.

judicial proceedings is similar. See Alan Dershowitz, "Civil liberties in Israel," in Howe and Gershman, eds., *Israel, the Arabs & the Middle East*, and the responses in *Commentary*, July 1971, to the original article. See also note 107.

Shehadeh distinguishes three ways of responding to occupation. The first is that of "blind hate," the second, "mute submission." To the captive population, the first way is that of the freedom fighter, the second, that of the quisling. To the conqueror, the first way is that of the terrorist, the second, that of the moderate. The paymasters keep to the rhetoric of the conqueror, naturally. What then is "the third way"? That is the way of the *Samid*, "the steadfast one," who watches his home turned into a prison. "You, *Samid*, choose to stay in that prison, because it is your home, and because you fear that if you leave, your jailer will not allow you to return. Living like this, you must constantly resist the twin temptations of either acquiescing in the jailer's plan in numb despair, or becoming crazed by consuming hatred for your jailer and yourself, the prisoner." To be *Samid*

> is like being in a small room with your family. You have bolted the doors and all the windows to keep strangers out. But they come anyway—they just walk through the walls as if they weren't there. They say they like your room. They bring their families and their friends. They like the furniture, the food, the garden. You shrink into a corner, pretending they aren't there, tending to your housework, being a rebellious son, a strict father or an anxious mother—crawling about as if everything was normal, as if your room was yours for ever. Your family's faces are growing pale, withdrawn—an ugly grey, as the air in their corner becomes exhausted.
>
> The strangers have fresh air, they come and go at will—their cheeks are pink, their voices loud and vibrant. But you cling to your corner, you never leave it, afraid that if you do, you will not be allowed back.

The strangers are advised by specialists, "'experts on Arab mentality' churned out by the Hebrew University and called 'advisers on Arab affairs'."[148] If need be, they can use the means of violence that they monopolize, to whatever degree is required, ensuring that the *Samidin* will be no more than drugged roaches in a bottle, in the graphic phrase of Chief of Staff Eitan. See p. 130*.

Shehadeh gives examples, from his personal experience as a lawyer attempting the hopeless task of working within a legal system devised to ensure failure to protect the rights of the vanquished, and from his life as a *Samid*. There is the example of "a criminal who was sentenced to life, and released soon after by the Israelis and given a gun," well-placed in what passes for a courtroom alongside of "the Israeli's man in court," who has also chosen the second way. There are the Israeli soldiers who herd demonstrating students into a bus, then shave each one down the middle of his head, "branded"—each one "a new fida'i" ("freedom fighter" or "terrorist," according to one's point of view). And the soldiers who find slogans painted on a wall, who "wait until night and then wake up all the people on the street and make them whitewash the wall,...mainly old people wrapped in dressing-gowns, shivering, bewildered, some cursing" after the soldiers have broken into their houses to get them out. There is the military governor who closes an exhibition of Palestinian art, plays, fashion shows of Palestinian dress at Birzeit college on the grounds that "expressions of Palestinian culture are dangerous political acts." And the Arab policemen at one of the innumerable roadblocks who have standing orders from the Israeli military "to take in for questioning any Jewish woman seen with an Arab." Roadblocks carry their own terror when manned by Israeli military, many of whom rejoice in the opportunity to humiliate defenseless Arabs in accordance with the doctrine of "purity of arms." They can also be dangerous, as for Shehadeh's uncle who was stopped by some soldiers just after the 1967 war, marched off to a nearby field and shot along with his companion, their bodies then set on fire and found days later.

There is also the case of the Arab lawyer who was engaged to contest the sale of land of a nearby village to the Jewish National Fund, whose representatives had frightened an old woman into signing documents selling the land (purchased by charitable tax-deductible contributions by Americans, and then reserved for Jewish use). He was warned by the military government to keep off the case, and when he refused, was arrested "on suspicion of driving without a licence" and sentenced to six months in prison and a fine of 7500 Israeli pounds. The Jewish National Fund is represented by a West Bank lawyer, one who has chosen the second way, "so that it can never be said that the land was taken against our will," an important consideration for Americans called upon the explain why all of this is right and just. There is the client who "has clearly been severely tortured," and many other images that shape the world of the *Samid.*

There are other experiences that entice the *Samid* to undertake the first way, as the conquerer would no doubt prefer, so as to rid himself of the troublesome intruder in the Land of Israel. For example, the case of Hani, shot by an Israeli soldier during a demonstration against the racist American Rabbi Meir Kahane, who openly calls for driving the Arabs out of the Land of the Jews, and acts accordingly, with particular effectiveness while he is performing his duties in the occupied territories in the military reserves. Hani says that he was not taking part in the demonstration, but since he was shot, he was a participant by definition, "throwing stones and petrol bombs at soldiers" and injured when he fell, as he was instructed by the soldier standing over him after he was shot. An ambulance arrived from Ramallah hospital, but the soldiers insisted that he first be taken, bleeding from his wounds, for questioning at the military headquarters. He was finally taken to Ramallah hospital for surgery, but the soldiers decided that he must be taken to Israel's Hadassah Hospital on Mt.

Scopus in Jerusalem instead. There, he could not be admitted to the emergency room because, he was told, "there is no room." He was taken to the Hadassah branch hospital at the other end of town. Seven hours after he was shot, he was admitted to a hospital. His mother must borrow "vast sums to pay for his hospitalization in Hadassah," despite the promises that the military government would pay the bill. At the hospital, "the hostility and coldness were marked...and nurses did not bother to conceal their animosity," perhaps because of a subsequent shooting of Jews at Hebron. Hani's calls went unanswered, and he "would be left unfed for whole days on end." Hani's mother fears to appeal the decision of the Israeli military that "not enough evidence was found to incriminate anyone," knowing "that if she files charges, her son will be charged for participating in the demonstration against Kahane," or he will simply be picked up on some charge and beaten by soldiers, like others. All of this is part of the life of the *Samid*.

The *Samid* sees "many Israeli faces fly by," but "three stand out":

First, the slightly pudgy, bespectacled face of the Ashkenazi intellectual; around him his Sephardi and Druse imitators. They look at me with the arrogance of colonizers. Their eyes express surprise mingled with anger that I, the native, should dare to think that I understand what they are up to. Then comes the gross, almost unlined face of Ariel Sharon and his gang of thugs: a petrifying combination of retardation and power: they mean evil and will succeed. Their faces are blank, completely free of even a twinge of conscience. And last, and in some way more disturbing than any: the weak face of the 'beautiful Israeli' who is upset by the occupation, not because it is evil, but because it ruins his looks. And he has every right to be concerned, because the lines on his face are ugly: those of a pampered narcissist who sees in his ever-present mirror his beauty fading—and begins to pout.

It is not too difficult to attach names to the faces, though there are other Israelis too, as Shehadeh eloquently describes—to one of whom I am indebted for sending me a copy of his book.

The faces of Israel seen by the *Samid* are rather different from those depicted by the admiring American visitor: Saul Bellow, for example, who sees an Israel where "almost everyone is reasonable and tolerant, and rancor against the Arabs is rare," where the people "think so hard, and so much" as they "farm a barren land, industrialize it, build cities, make a society, do research, philosophize, write books, sustain a great moral tradition, and, finally create an army of tough fighters"[149]; or Irving Howe, whose Israelis are busy realizing "the democratic socialist hope of combining radical social change with political freedom." Evidently, things look a bit different from the wrong end of the club.

7   The Cycle of Occupation, Resistance, Repression and Moral Degeneration

These developments in Israel and the occupied territories were a direct consequence of the 1967 military victory, which a number of perceptive Israeli observers saw as a long-term defeat for the society they cherished, not without certain illusions of their own, in some cases. They were aware of what Eric Rouleau of *Le Monde* described in the early days of the occupation as "the classical chain reaction—occupation, resistance, repression, more resistance," and of further links in the chain: Israeli journalist Victor Cygielman wrote in 1968 that "One thing is sure, terrorism will not succeed in wrecking Israel, but it may succeed in ruining Israeli democracy," referring to the demoralizing effect of "such measures of collective punishment as the blowing up of houses, administrative arrests and deportation to Jordan." At the same time, Uri Avneri noted further that the "steep spiral of terror and counter-terror, killing and retaliation, sabotage and mass deportation...will bring undreamt-of miseries to the Palestinian people...[while] turning Israel into an armed and beleaguered camp forever," leading ultimately to "Semitic suicide."[150]

7.1   Americans Hear the News

Similar warnings have repeatedly been voiced through the years by Israelis and others who called for an end to the occupation. By late 1982, the message had even reached the *New York Times*. Editor Max Frankel noticed that Israeli "dissenters fear endless cycles of Palestinian terror and Israeli war—and the degradation of Israeli society as it grows dependent on the manual work of...a permanent 'guest population'"[151]; those who had been making the same point for 15 years had been given short shrift by the *Times*, which was extolling the occupation as "a model of future cooperation," an "experiment in Arab-Jewish coexistence" (editorial, May 19, 1976) as the spiral of violence and repression mounted ever more steeply.

Others too had begun to hear the news by mid-1982. Irving Howe, who for years had been berating the bearers of unwelcome tidings as "elitist," anti-democratic, subject to "the pathology of authoritarianism," and worse, reviewed Rafik Halabi's *West Bank Story* (see note 48) in the *New York Times Book Review*, discovering to his sorrow that all was not well, primarily because of Menachem Begin.[152]. His comments caused much distress in Israel, even eliciting an article in the Labor Party journal *Kol Hair* reporting that "the former diplomat Zvi Rafiach recently returned [from the U.S.] quite shaken, bringing with him the issue" with Howe's review. The journal comments, a bit unfairly, that "in fact Howe had little to say in criticism concerning the new book; he only knew how to speak and weep about himself." But the matter is serious, the article continues, since "only with difficulty did he find a good word to say about the country that he loves." And Howe is no ordinary admirer of Israel: "All America recognizes Howe, and knows that he is a lover of Israel. When no more supporters of Israel will remain in the United States—he will still be waving the blue and white flag." "Who else will we lose because of you, Likud government?," the writer laments.[153]

In his review, Howe writes that Halabi's commentary on life under the military occupation, "though open to dispute at some points, is strong enough to disturb even the most ardent supporters of Israel. At least, it disturbed this one." The book "fills me with a deep dismay—let me be candid and say pessimism," even when we correct for Halabi's exaggerations, as when he says that the occupation has a "corrupting effect...on the moral and social fiber of Israeli society" ("Let us be a little cautious and say instead a coarsening effect"). Howe learned from the book that "the Begin Government's intention has been the gradual takeover of the West Bank and that its vision of 'autonomy' is little more than an enforced Arab docility." This, in May 1982. He suggests instead that Israel "should announce its readiness to withdraw, provided satisfactory security arrangements are worked out," but fears that this policy cannot be adopted "as long as Mr. Begin remains in office." Equally, it could not be adopted if the Labor opposition that Howe supports were in office, as the record of the past 15 years, and Labor's current positions, make crystal clear. Howe also learned that Labor had stumbled into "error" in its occupation policy, and that "Labor's incoherence was replaced by Menachem Begin's coherence." But in fact Labor's rejectionism and pursuit of the Allon Plan were clear from the start and were not in the least "incoherent" to those who chose to look at the facts. And the brutal and repressive character of the occupation in the West Bank was clearly apparent under the Labor government, a fact well recognized by Israeli doves in the late 1960s, as we have seen, not to speak of the repression in the Gaza Strip in the early 70s or Labor's brutal treatment of the Sinai Arab farmers at the same time; see pp. 105f. The kind of "ardent support" that Howe was providing—in particular, his personal attacks on those who knew what he is now beginning to learn, Daniel Berrigan for example—was a not insignificant factor in helping to establish the "errors" that he is now beginning to perceive with dismay, exactly as Israeli doves and others have been pointing out, with little effect, for many years; it might have been in place for Howe to address this point, which he heard years ago.

Howe is concerned that Begin's policies will "threaten the Jewish character of Israel"—would we have similar concern about the Islamic, or

Christian, or White character of some state? In the same context, he speaks of the "underpopulated Galilee," to which development funds should be allocated instead of the West Bank. The concept "underpopulated Galilee" is common in Israel, with a particular interpretation: there is a large population of Arab citizens, but there are too few Jews there (recall that many Arabs fled or were expelled from the Galilee in 1948, and that thousands more were expelled during the 1956 attack on Egypt; see p. 97*). The many Arabs, Israeli citizens, are excluded from the "national lands" (reserved for Jews). Their own lands have often been expropriated for Jewish settlement, they are unable to build for their expanding populations because of restriction of land use to Jews, and they have therefore been compelled to find work in Jewish enterprises. There is much concern in Israel over their "land robbery," over the "invasion" of "national lands" by Israeli citizens of the wrong ethnic affiliation. It was for such reasons that the Jewish Agency, under the Labor government, established the program of "Judaization of the Galilee," to reverse this specific form of "underpopulation." It was in response to the same problems that Israel Koenig of the Ministry of Interior, whose jurisdiction covers this region, issued the notorious "Koenig memorandum" in 1976 (under the Labor government), calling for measures to "thin the concentrations of existing Arab population," reduce employment and educational opportunities for Arabs and otherwise encourage their emigration, undermine their organizations by covert means, etc.— policies that some Israelis described as reflecting "fascist values." Koenig retained his position after the exposure of this secret memorandum and is still applying his values; see p. 140. In short, Howe's concept "underpopulated Galilee" conceals a tale.[154] Howe also reviews some minor examples of the harsh practices that have been in force for 15 years and their "coarsening" effects—on the Israelis—and expresses his dismay as one of those "who admire and think of ourselves as partisans of Israeli society," indeed an "ardent supporter," and who continues to support the Labor Party, which was responsible for initiating these practices, with no detectable qualifications.

It is not entirely clear how to reconcile Howe's self-description as an "ardent supporter"—still less, the picture presented in *Kol Hair*—with his earlier account of his stand: "I have never been a Zionist; I have always felt contempt for nationalist and chauvinist sentiments" (see note 83). This account is perhaps plausible, pre-1967, but what about more recent years? A closer look at some of Howe's writings may help dispel the mystery, while providing some insight into the nature of post-1967 support for Israel in significant circles, as discussed in chapter 2. We may begin, perhaps, with Howe's explanation of why unnamed "New Left intellectuals" oppose Israel—namely, because of their "growing distaste" and "downright contempt" for "the very idea of democracy," so that they "despise Israel not because of her flaws but because of her virtues," because of Israel's commitment to "combining radical social change with political freedom." Howe explains that to regain the favor of these "New Left intellectuals," whoever they may be, Israel would have to institute a fascist-style dictatorship in a bloody revolution. Then, he writes, this is what we would see:

> Everywhere the New Left rejoices. Brigades of youth from Scarsdale, Evanston, and Palo Alto race to Israel to help with "the planting." The *New York Review* plans a special issue. And Jean-Paul Sartre and Mme. de Beauvoir take the next plane to Israel, prepared to write a thousand pages in four weeks on *The Achievements of the Israeli Revolution* (while getting the street names of Tel Aviv wrong).[155]

In fact, Sartre was honored by the Hebrew University in recognition of his support for Israel, the *New York Review* has always been strongly pro-Israel, and the mainstream of the New Left tended towards the positions of Israeli doves. But facts are really irrelevant here, which is why Howe feels free to ignore them in his writings on this topic. The point is to destroy one's enemies, relying on a useful convention of political discourse: slander and abuse are quite legitimate and argument and evidence are superfluous when the targets are activist elements of popular dissident movements. It is convenient to have one's political enemies committed to the destruction of Israel and bloody fascist revolutions, so they are, whatever the facts. Note that Israel is really irrelevant to this drama, except insofar as the overwhelming support for Israel is used as a stick to beat the student movement, the New Left, peace activists, etc. Hence the possibility that someone who has "never been a Zionist" might appear to be such an "ardent supporter" of Israel—perhaps even to himself as well, after only a few years of playing the role—that he will still be waving the blue and white flag when everyone else has deserted the cause. From 1967, many others have adopted the same device, which has proven a useful and highly effective one; see chapter 2 and references cited for further discussion of the phenomenon illustrated here, which is of some significance in the development of the "special relationship" in the 1970s, particularly in its ideological aspect.

7.2   The Rise of Religious-Chauvinist Fanaticism

The predictable cycle of repression, terror, and violence continues to arouse much concern in Israel, particularly among older, more Europe-oriented segments of the population, who recognize all too clearly what is happening. The first warnings came from Professor Yeshayahu Leibovitz, one of Israel's best-known scholars, who has continued to speak out forcefully against the occupation (also against the war in Lebanon), a fact that has won him little praise. Amnon Rubinstein, former Dean of the Tel Aviv University Law School and a Knesset member, describes a series of actions by "extremist and racist elements," including military rabbis, adding that "an ill wind is blowing against the direction of the Zionist vision, against the character of humanistic Judaism, against all that we had wanted Israel to become." "Perhaps the worst sign of this," he adds, "is that it is becoming hard to distinguish between the lunatic fringe and the mainstream of our political life." He describes anti-Arab terrorism by student leaders at the Hebrew University who threatened the university authorities with violence if they were disciplined, attacks by "unknown cowardly inhabitants of Kiryat Arba [the religious settlement at Hebron] on the house of an Arab widow," the failure of the authorities to react, the refusal of a construction company to rent an apartment in Jerusalem to a Christian couple, the sentiment among youth that the Arabs must be expelled, etc., concluding that "what we are witnessing is not the action of minor and marginal fringe movements." As internal conflict intensified in Israel in the wake of the Lebanon war, Rubinstein—among many others—warned in still clearer terms of the consequences of the "Nazi storm trooper style" of the agents of "criminal violence," now fortified by "a political ideology of violence" with tacit government support and overt support from Gush Emunim Rabbis who publicly "incite to kill Arab civilians." Again he described how right-wing students "use their fists to control the campuses of the Jerusalem and Tel Aviv universities," using "not only fists but clubs and iron chains," and threatening violence if the university were to attempt disciplinary action. "Large areas of Israel are simply closed to anyone who is not from the Likud" because of the violence of the supporters of Begin and Sharon, which they make no attempt to control (see p. 121). Those who oppose the Likud are threatened with murder, or silenced "by shouting, screaming and threats," and are attacked if they attempt to distribute their materials. Perpetrators of overt violence "are rarely caught." He warns of a sorry fate if these tendencies continue.[156]

What Rubinstein and others fear is a virtual civil war, in which elements of a fascist character are increasingly visible—a fact that they do not disguise. But quite apart from the scale of the verbal and physical violence and its socioeconomic, ethnic and religious-cultural roots, there are other indications to support Rubinstein's judgment that the "ill wind" is a serious phenomenon, not confined to the lunatic fringe.[157] The Director General of the Israel Broadcasting Authority (radio and television), who "is a long-time admirer of South Africa and a frequent visitor there," wrote an "emotional article" in 1974 expressing his preference for South Africa over Black Africa, complete "with citations of research proving the genetic inferiority of blacks"—a view which "seems to reflect the feelings of many in the Israeli elite." The journal of Mapam (the left-wing of the Labor Alignment) is capable of publishing an explanation of the superiority of Israeli pilots, based on American research which has "proven" that Blacks (including, apparently, Arabs) are inferior in "complex, cognitive intelligence" (which is why "American Blacks succeed only in short-distance running"). The same journal also devoted 2 full pages to racist idiocies tracing genetic differences between Jews and Gentiles to Abraham, and explaining the alleged cultural ascendance of the U.S. over Europe in terms of the change in the proportion of the Jewish populations. The article begins by noting that "in the atmosphere prevailing today in the Holy Land, everything is possible, even racist doctrine . . .," but then proceeds to give a rather sympathetic portrayal of the author of the example they provide, letting the interested reader know how to obtain more information. In the Labor Party journal, we read about "genetic experiments" that have shown that "the genetic differences among Jewish communities [Poland and Yemen are cited] are smaller than those between Gentiles and Jews" (the medical correspondent, reporting research conducted at Tel Aviv University), while the Ministry of Education sponsors a creationist congress organized by Orthodox scientists from Ben-Gurion University in which the theory of evolution is dismissed as "speculation," "secular dogma" and "myth" while most of the participating scientists "reaffirmed their belief in divine creation."[158] It is not too surprising, then, to discover that Israel's Christian Maronite allies in Lebanon are really Syrian Jews in origin[159]—though it is likely that they lost this status after the Beirut massacres, a few days after this information appeared.

It is, however, primarily in religious circles that such "Khomeinism" (as it is now sometimes characterized in Israel) is to be found. These circles are increasingly influential as a result of the social and demographic processes noted earlier. There also appear to be efforts to support Islamic fundamentalism in the occupied territories in opposition to secular (and hence more dangerous) forms of Palestinian nationalism. Commenting on this phenomenon in both the West Bank and Gaza, Danny Rubinstein observes that the military authorities—who generally clamp down on demonstrations with an iron hand—allowed busloads of "Islamic fanatics" to pass through IDF roadblocks to join demonstrations at Bir Zeit and al-Najah Universities, one sign of their support for Islamic fundamentalism against left and "nationalist" (read: pro-PLO) trends.[160]

"The uniting of religious fanaticism with extremist nationalism is not an unknown phenomenon in Israel in the past few years," Eliahu Salpeter writes, citing as one example the pronouncements of a young Rabbi on the "filth" of mixed marriages and the "hybrid children" they produce, "a thorn in the flesh of the Jewish society in Israel" that may become a real catastrophe unless proper measures are taken—he recommends total school segregation and exclusion of Arabs from the universities. The Rabbi denies that he is prejudiced against Arabs, insisting that he has "close Arab friends"—a remark familiar to Jews, Salpeter comments. Salpeter cites other examples of the dangerous religious-nationalist brew: e.g., the failure to find those responsible for the terrorist attack on Arab mayors, the difference in treatment of Arabs who throw rocks and religious Jews who stone people who drive on the Sabbath.[161]

In earlier years, the Rabbinate had cited biblical authority to justify expulsion of the Arabs (a "foreign element") from the land, or simply their destruction, and religious law was invoked to justify killing of civilians in a war or raid.[162] After the 1973 war, the highly-respected Lubavitcher Rabbi (New York) deplored the failure to conquer Damascus.[163] He also warned against abandoning any of the conquered territories, condemning those "who for the sake of miserable money and honors, and especially in order to be well-regarded by the big Goy [Gentile] in Washington, are ready to threaten the security of the Holy Land by giving up territories against the opinions of military experts," which is "against the Jewish Religion . . ."[164] Another American Rabbi* explained that the religious law empowers Israel to "dispossess" the Arabs of the conquered territories: "As long as the war which initiated the conquest was conducted under instructions from the Israeli government, who halachicly [by religious law] possesses the same powers as the biblical king, all territories captured as a result of this war belong to Israel." As for "the argument that by not surrendering the territories, we might be heightening the possibility of a future war," this is "not valid" under religious law which "indicates that, on the contrary, we must start a war to prevent even the possibility of permanent settlement nearer our borders than heretofore."[165] After Sadat's visit to Jerusalem, a group of leading Rabbis and religious authorities in Israel and the U.S. warned the government that it is "forbidden" to return any territories of the Land of Israel,[166] and the Supreme Rabbinical Council of Israel later reiterated this judgment, citing biblical obligations and religious law.[167]

The chief Rabbis also gave their endorsement to the 1982 invasion of Lebanon, declaring that it conformed to the Halachic (religious) law and that participation in the war "in all its aspects" is a religious duty. The military Rabbinate meanwhile distributed a document to soldiers containing a map of Lebanon with the names of cities replaced by alleged

---

* Rabbi Isaac J. Bernstein, who is identified as "spiritual leader of Manhattan's Jewish Center, . . . an executive member of the Rabbinical Council of America and a lecturer in Talmud at Stern College."

Hebrew names taken from the Bible, along with the explanation that much of Lebanon belonged to the Hebrew tribe of Asher. They also provided a strategic analysis of the Lebanon war under the heading "Joshua son of Nun to the clearing of the nests of the enemies in Lebanon," referring to the biblical account of the conquest of the Land of Canaan[168]—the phrase "clearing the nests of terrorists" is now a standard way of referring to operations against Palestinian vermin. Speaking to soldiers under the auspices of the *hasbara* ("propaganda"; literally, "explanation") officer, a military Rabbi in Lebanon explained the biblical sources that justify "our being here and our opening the war; we do our Jewish religious duty by being here".[169]

Such pronouncements are by no means novel, and since 1973 at least, they have been taken seriously in significant circles. In the mass-circulation journal *Yediot Ahronot* in 1974, Menahem Barash wrote with much admiration about the teachings of Rabbi Moshe Ben-Zion Ushpizai of Ramat-Gan, who used biblical texts and traditional commentary to explain how Israel should deal with the Palestinians, "a plague already written in the Bible." "With a sharp scalpel and convincing logic" the Rabbi uses the writings of the "greatest sages" to elucidate the commandments, still binding today, as to how to "inherit the land" that was promised by God to Abraham. We must follow the doctrines of Joshua, he explains, referring to the genocidal texts that appear in the book of Joshua and elsewhere. "The biblical commandment is to conquer the land of Israel in its detailed borders, to take possession of it and to settle it." It is "forbidden" to "abandon it to strangers" (Gentiles). "There is no place in this land for the people of Israel and for other nations alongside it. The practical meaning of [the commandment to] possess the land is the expulsion of the peoples who live in it" and who try to prevent the Jews of the world from "settling in our land." It is "a holy war, commanded in the Bible," and it must be fought against Palestinians, Syrians, Egyptians "or any other people in the world" who seek to block the divine commandment. There can be no compromises, no peace treaties, no negotiations with "the peoples who inhabit the land." "You shall destroy them, you shall enter into no covenant with them, you shall not pity them, you shall not intermarry with them," the divine law dictates. Whoever stands in our way must be annihilated, the Rabbi continues with his "convincing logic," citing numerous traditional authorities. All of this is reported quite seriously, and with much respect.[170]

After the Beirut massacres of September 1982 there was a renewed outpouring of militant support for the war in religious circles. The influential Gush Emunim group, which spearheads West Bank settlement, published a statement praising Begin, Sharon, and Chief of Staff Rafael Eitan, describing the war as a "great act of sanctification of God's name." The statement also spoke of "the return of the territory of the tribes of Naftali and Asher to the boundaries of Israel," and of Israel's "responsibility to act to the limits of its ability to destroy the foundations of evil in the entire world."[171] Two months before, Rabbi Elazar Valdman of Gush Emunim wrote in the journal *Nekudah* of the religious West Bank settlers:

> We will certainly establish order in the Middle East and in the world. And if we do not take this responsibility upon ourselves, we are sinners, not just towards ourselves but towards the entire world. For who can establish order in the world? All of those western leaders of weak character?[172]

In Israel, one does not take pronouncements of Gush Emunim lightly. Their influence has been considerable, and they have regularly created policy (with state support) by their actions in the occupied territories. This statement therefore caused some consternation. One of the founders of the movement, Yehuda Ben-Meir, sharply denounced it, stating that "according to Gush Emunim, we must conquer not only Syria and Turkey but with the blood of our children we must become the guardian of the entire world."[173] It may seem odd that such ludicrous pronouncements are taken seriously, but in the current atmosphere of spreading "Khomeinism" among significant circles of the fourth greatest military power in the world, they cannot be disregarded, and are not, by serious Israeli commentators. We return to further indications of this grandiose self-image, and its implications.[174]

Those who really deserve the name "supporters of Israel" will not be unconcerned over such developments. Within Israel itself, they have often led to near despair. Boaz Evron writes that "the true symbol of the state is no longer the Menorah with seven candlesticks; the true symbol is the fist."[175] In conformity with his judgment, when West Beirut was invaded, IDF Chief of Staff Rafael Eitan announced:

> What must be destroyed—we will destroy. Whoever must be imprisoned—we will imprison.[176]

Aharon Meged writes of his sadness with regard to "the new 'Zionist mentality'," which is coming to reign and "cannot be stopped": "the age of military Zionism." "The old fear of a 'Sparta'—is changing to fear of a 'Prussia'." Like Danny Rubinstein (see note 172), he is much concerned over the ravings of Rabbi Valdman, and offers the hope that return of the territories can still overcome this fate, citing Chief Sephardic Rabbi Ovadiah Yoseph, who agreed that return of territories is legitimate if it would lead to peace. It may incidentally be noted that his Ashkenazi counterpart, Chief Rabbi Shlomo Goren, drew the opposite conclusion from religious law, holding that retaining "Judea and Samaria" takes precedence over the religious duty to save life ("pikuach nefesh"). He "rejects categorically" the idea that achievement of peace would justify territorial compromise.[177] The example once again illustrates the fact that one should be rather cautious in contrasting Ashkenazi doves with Sephardi hawks.

8 Conflicts within Israel

8.1 Within the Jewish Community

During the war in Lebanon, the conflict between two communities— roughly, the older, West Europe-oriented, wealthier and more educated sectors, and the working class and lower middle class (mostly Sephardic) Jews joined by much of the youth and by religious-chauvinist elements, many from the recent U.S. and USSR immigrations—became increasingly sharp. In a study of the protest against the war, sociologist Benjamin Beit-Halahmi of Haifa University observed that "it is clear that the opposition to the 1982 war is that of a minority of the Israeli population," the "elite." The Sephardic community and the youth were less represented, and in general supported the war—as did some leaders of the traditional peace groups, he notes. The favorable publicity given to the opposition by the press is misleading, since the journalists too tend to belong to the elite. "Opposition to the 1982 war increased even further the alienation of the traditional Ashkenazi elite, which identifies with a progressive tradition in Zionism. This group is in the midst of a process of alienation, which has been growing stronger since 1977 [when Begin's Likud took power], and each development since then causes this alienation to deepen." As for the war itself, "the price of the direct military victory and of political and human oppression is paid not only by the vanquished, but by the victors as well."[178]

The lines of the conflict were drawn still more sharply after the Lebanon war (see p. 151), a matter to which we return.

8.2 Non-Jews in the Jewish State

The conflict between the two communities has long been simmering within Israel. There is, of course, a still deeper internal conflict. Israel has been and remains a vibrant democracy on the western model for its Jewish citizens, but it has always embodied a fundamental contradiction, as noted earlier (see p. 45). Israel is a Jewish state with a minority of non-Jewish citizens. It is not the state of its citizens, but of the Jewish people, those in Israel and in the diaspora. There is no Israeli nationality. While it is commonly argued that Israel is Jewish only in the sense that England is English, so that those who (vainly) insist on the facts are uniquely rejecting the rights of Jewish nationalism, that is a flat falsehood. A citizen of England is English, but a citizen of Israel may not be Jewish, a non-trivial fact, much obscured in deceptive rhetoric.[179]

The legal structures and administrative practice of the state and society reflect these principles, again, a fact consistently suppressed in the voluminous literature concerning Israel and in particular in admiring left-liberal commentary; and also by Israelis writing for an American audience. Thus Amos Oz asserts that "To this day, only about 5 percent of the land is privately owned; the rest is public property, in one way or another," including the lands of the kibbutz in which he lives. He presents this fact (the actual figure appears to be about 8%) as one indication that:

> ...Israel could have become an exemplary state, an open, argumentative, involved society of unique moral standards and future-oriented outlook, a small-scale laboratory for democratic socialism—or, as the old-timers liked to put it, "a light unto the nations." But at that point, when everything seemed ready for such an emergence, crisis set in.[180]

The "vision" is being lost, though it may still be resurrected by "a growing tendency on the part of young Israelis" (mythical, to judge by available evidence) to recover "the ideological, ethical and political propositions of the early Zionists."*

But Oz and others who advance such arguments do not present accurately the "propositions" of the early Zionists—for example, the transfer proposals discussed earlier—or the "one way or another" in which the land remains "public property," a rather significant matter. Through a complex system of legal and administrative arrangements, public land is under the control of the Jewish National Fund, an organization committed to use charitable funds (specifically, tax-free contribu-

---

* In the U.S., Oz is regarded as a spokesman for the "peace forces" in Israel. See, for example, Hayden, *The American Future*, or Oz's interview with Eugene Goodheart, *Partisan Review*, #3, 1982. Here he recommends that Israel "make a generous proposal which will no doubt be rejected by the Palestinians right now" (what it should be, he does not say). "So far there has been a firm and consistent rejection by the Palestinians of any such proposals from Israeli moderates and doves." "There is," he says, "no Palestinian equivalent to the Israeli Peace Now movement." The "so-called reasonable Palestinians ...do hint or suggest that they will accept the idea of partition, accept the existence of Israel under certain terms and are ready to negotiate," but to their own people, they "are just as extremist as Arafat"—who, in fact, has urged negotiations and a two-state settlement for years, going beyond even the Israeli Peace Now movement (which is vague about these matters), let alone the Labor Party, in a search for a peaceful settlement (see p. 116* and chapter 3). It is an interesting commentary on left-liberal American intellectuals that this is taken seriously here. Predictably, Oz also grossly misrepresents the positions of critics of Israeli policies. See also chapter 3, note 111.

tions from the United States) in ways that are determined to be "directly or indirectly beneficial to persons of Jewish religion, race or origin." Much of the development budget is in the hands of the Jewish Agency, which has similar commitments. These and other "national institutions" serve the interests of Jews, not citizens of Israel, 15% of whom are non-Jews. The consequences of these arrangements and others like them for the lives of non-Jewish citizens are considerable,[181] putting aside here the activities of these and other "national institutions" in the occupied territories. We would hardly regard similar arrangements in a "White State" or a "Christian State" as an illustration of "unique moral standards" and "democratic socialism" of the highest order. The notorious UN Resolution identifying Zionism as a form of racism can properly be condemned for profound hypocrisy, given the nature of the states that backed it (including the Arab states), and (arguably) for referring to Zionism as such rather than the policies of the State of Israel, but restricted to these policies, the resolution cannot be criticized as inaccurate.

The devices that are used to perpetuate discriminatory practices are sometimes remarkable. For example, the state offers benefits to large families, but some way must be found to ensure that Arab citizens are excluded. The standard method in such cases is to restrict benefits to families of those who have served in the armed forces, hence not to Arab families. But there is still a problem, since religious Jews are exempt from army service. The legislation therefore incorporates a special provision for families of students in yeshivas (Jewish religious schools). There are numerous similar examples. It might also be noted that Israel is perhaps the only western democracy in which there is legal discrimination against Jews. To cite one recent example, in 1983 the Knesset again defeated a bill that would have given Reform and Conservative Jews equal rights with those of Orthodox Jews, not a small matter given the role of the Rabbinate in civil life in Israel.[182]

Given the founding principles of the state, it is a crucially important matter to maintain a clear distinction between Jews and non-Jews. "The officials of the Ministry of the Interior are very tough with any members of the Israeli minorities who try to change their names, because they are afraid that they may want to try 'to appear in public as Jews,' and this may bring about mixed marriages, God forbid," it is reported in an article critical of these practices. Repeatedly, Arabs have been condemned by the courts for pretending to be Jews. In 1977, an inhabitant of Kafr Kassem was sentenced to a year in prison "for pretending to be a Jew in order to marry a [Jewish] woman," after "he had tried to convert—but did not succeed."[183] The sentence might have been expected to cause some embarrassment—but apparently did not—in the light of the history of this criminal's village, where 47 Arabs were murdered by Israeli Border

Guards in 1956.[184] This was recognized to be a crime. The office responsible for the orders by the court was fined one piaster (ten cents) for a "technical error." Gabriel Dahan, who was convicted of killing 43 Arabs in one hour, served just over a year, the longest sentence served, and was then promptly engaged as officer for Arab affairs in Ramle.* Note that his crime was considered by the courts to be approximately equal in severity to that of the inhabitant of the village who pretended to be a Jew.

To cite only one further example, the city of Denver has a sister city: Karmiel, in the Galilee. The citizens of Denver who relax in Karmiel Park are surely unaware that their sister city has excluded Arab citizens of Israel; even a 20-year Druze veteran of the Israeli Border Guards was denied the right to open a business there. Furthermore, this "magnificent example of Zionism at its successful best," as it is described by an admirer,[185] is built on the lands of an an Arab village, expropriated under a cynical ruse in the mid-1960s.[186] In short, the citizens of Denver are victims of a clever propaganda trick, which can be successful—and is— because of the "ideological support" for Israel noted earlier, which protects it from scrutiny.

Quite generally, when one looks beneath the surface, one finds that the utopian vision has always been seriously flawed. Americans who now write ruefully about contemporary Israel as a "Paradise Lost"[187] are victims of considerable delusion and very effective propaganda, though they are right in feeling that much that was praiseworthy in the society, sometimes uniquely so, was lost (as many predicted) as a result of the 1967 military victory. While it is convenient (and not totally false) to shift the blame to Arab intransigence, honesty should compel us to recognize that the primary source lies elsewhere: in the policies of the Labor governments and their successor and the support offered to these policies by the United States, crucially including the attitudes and activities of alleged "supporters of Israel," who have much to answer for, if truth be acknowledged.

The fundamental internal contradiction in the commitment to a "democratic Jewish State" has always been present, but it becomes more

---

* See Tom Segev, "Kafr Kassem Remembered," *Ha'aretz*, Oct. 23, 1981, for a rare report in the Israeli literature, reconstructing the events, which, Segev notes, are not taught in Jewish or Arab schools and are not known to many Israelis. Meir Pail is quoted as saying that "only a pathological hatred of the Arabs" made the massacre possible. Former Prime Minister Sharett said that the massacre "had made one thing clear: To spill Arab blood was permissible for Jews." Segev reports the attempts to cover up the atrocity, the special privileges accorded the prisoners, and their successful subsequent careers, particularly that of Issachar Shadmi, who was in charge and had told the soldiers under his command that "it was 'better to kill someone' (or, according to another version, 'several people') than to get bogged down by arrests." The victims had technically violated a curfew, which they knew nothing about since it was imposed after they had left the village for work; they were killed on their return that evening, cold-blooded premeditated murder. On expropriation of the lands of the village, both before and after the massacre, see *TNCW*, p. 465.

difficult to suppress with steps towards integration of the occupied territories, one reason why the Labor Alignment—more concerned with the
democratic socialist image than Likud—has always been opposed to
absorbing the Arabs of the occupied territories within the state proper. In
the earlier history of Zionism, the issue was sometimes frankly addressed.
As noted earlier, it was not until 1942 that the Zionist movement was
officially committed to the establishment of a Jewish state. Earlier, its
leaders—particularly those from the labor movement that dominated the
Palestinian *Yishuv* (Jewish settlement)—forcefully opposed the concept
of a Jewish state on the explicit grounds that "the rule of one national
group over the other" is illegitimate. David Ben-Gurion and others
declared that they would never agree to a Jewish state, "which would
eventually mean Jewish domination of Arabs in Palestine."[188] With the
coming of the war and the Nazi genocide, these currents were reduced to a
minority, though they persisted until the UN partition resolution of
November 1947. Since the establishment of the State of Israel, the issues
have generally been suppressed while the prospects feared have been
realized; and in the U.S., they have been concealed by means that hardly
do credit to those responsible.

9   The Zionist Movement and the PLO

In the pre-state period, the nuclei of the two present political groupings were in often bitter conflict, in part, class conflict. The Labor Party
was a party of Jewish workers (NB: not workers; in fact, it opposed efforts
by the Mandatory government to improve the conditions of Arab
workers* while urging a boycott of their labor and produce),[189] while the
Revisionists, the precursors of Begin's Herut, were in fact an offshoot of
European fascism, with an ideology of submission of the mass to a single
leader, strike-breaking, chauvinist fanaticism, and the rest of the familiar
paraphernalia of the 1930s.[190]

---

* Few leaders of the pre-state Labor Party were so concerned with justice for the Arabs as
Chaim Arlosoroff, who was assassinated in 1933 (by Revisionists, Labor alleged). It is
therefore interesting to consider his views on this matter. In a 1932 memorandum to Chaim
Weizmann, he wrote that a major problem was that the British administration was
"considerate of the sensibilities of the Arabs and Moslems," and "it would be very hard for
them to depart from this practice to the extent of becoming responsive to our demands."
Another problem was that the Mandatory authorities might promulgate "regulations for the
protection of tenant farmers," etc., all harmful to the Zionist enterprise. He therefore
proposed "a transition period during which the Jewish minority would exercise organized
revolutionary rule." On the powerful influence of Bolshevik ideas on the Labor Party,
particularly its leader David Ben-Gurion, see Yoram Peri, *Between Ballots and Bullets*. The
left wing of the Labor Alignment, Mapam, was predominantly Stalinist until the
mid-1950s.

9.1 "The Boundaries of Zionist Aspirations"

The two factions also differed in their political tactics when the prospects for a Jewish state became realistic. Supporting a British partition proposal of 1937, Labor Party leader David Ben-Gurion stated that:

> The acceptance of partition does not commit us to renounce Transjordan; one does not demand from anybody to give up his vision. We shall accept a state in the boundaries fixed today, but the boundaries of Zionist aspirations are the concern of the Jewish people and no external factor will be able to limit them.[191]

Ben-Gurion, and the large majority of the Zionist movement, reacted with similar pragmatism to the partition proposal of 1947.

In contrast, even after the state was established in 1948, Menachem Begin declared that:

> The partition of the Homeland is illegal. It will never be recognized. The signature of institutions and individuals of the partition agreement is invalid. It will not bind the Jewish people. Jerusalem was and will forever be our capital. Eretz Israel [the Land of Israel] will be restored to the people of Israel. All of it. And forever.[192]

Echoes of these conflicting positions remain today.

It might be noted that the "boundaries of Zionist aspirations" in Ben-Gurion's "vision" were quite broad, including southern Lebanon, southern Syria, today's Jordan, all of cis-Jordan, and the Sinai.[193] This was, in fact, one of Ben-Gurion's constant themes. In internal discussion in 1938, he stated that "after we become a strong force, as the result of the creation of a state, we shall abolish partition and expand to the whole of Palestine... The state will only be a stage in the realization of Zionism and its task is to prepare the ground for our expansion into the whole of Palestine by a Jewish-Arab agreement... The state will have to preserve order not only by preaching morality but by machine guns, if necessary." The "agreement" that Ben-Gurion had in mind was to be with King Abdullah of Jordan, who would be induced to cede areas of cis-Jordan under his control, while many of the Arab residents would leave.[194] Earlier, Ben-Gurion had explained to Arab interlocutors that "our land" included Transjordan, and that it extended from the Sinai to "the source of the Jordan."[195] In internal discussion he urged that "we do not suggest now to announce the final aim," which is "far-reaching," even more so than the aim of those who were opposing partition. "I am unwilling to abandon...the great Jewish vision, the final vision," he added. This vision, here unspecificied in scale, "is an organic, spiritual and ideological component of my Jewishness and my Zionist aspiration," Ben-Gurion explained.[196]

Zionist leaders were sometimes quite open about the matter in public discussion. The Twentieth Zionist Congress at Zurich in August 1937 took the official position that "the scheme of partition put forward by the Royal Commission [the British Peel Commission] is unacceptable," but, nevertheless, the Congress indicated a degree of support for the idea. In particular, Ben-Gurion and Weizmann favored it. In a press interview concerning the deliberations at the Congress, Ben-Gurion explained:

> The debate has not been for or against the indivisibility of Eretz Israel. No Zionist can forgo the smallest portion of Eretz Israel. The debate was over which of two routes would lead quicker to the common goal.

The "two routes" were rejection of partition, or acceptance on the assumption that circumstances would later permit a further expansion of the borders of the Jewish state to all of the territories that fell within "the boundaries of Zionist aspirations," as Ben-Gurion understood them.* Chaim Weizmann, asked about the exclusion of the Negev from the proposed Jewish state, responded: "It will not run away."[197] In a similar vein, Labor dove Chaim Arlosoroff wrote to Weizmann in 1932 that "the desire to establish national sovereignty in a part of Palestine . . . contains a core of sound thinking," since "state power" in this region "could become a strategic base for potential future progress."[198]

In a letter to his son, discussing partition, Ben-Gurion wrote that

> A partial Jewish state is not the end, but only the beginning. . . I am certain that we will not be prevented from settling in the other parts of the country, either by mutual agreement with our Arab neighbors *or by some other means*. . . [If the Arabs refuse] *we shall have to speak to them in a different language. But we shall only have another language if we have a state.*

In May 1948, feeling quite confident of Israel's military superiority (contrary to the "David and Goliath legend" discussed earlier), Ben-Gurion presented the following strategic aims to his General Staff:

> . . . we should prepare to go over to the offensive with the aim of smashing Lebanon, Transjordan and Syria . . . The weak point in the Arab coalition is Lebanon [for] the Moslem regime is

* After the 1967 war, long after he had left office, Ben-Gurion changed his views and came to oppose the expansionist policies he had always advocated and pursued while in a position of authority, thus isolating himself completely from his former Labor Party associates. By some remarkable logic, this fact is regularly adduced by Labor supporters here to show how conciliatory Labor Zionism really was. See p. 381, below, for one of many examples.

artificial and easy to undermine. A Christian state should be established, with its southern border on the Litani river [within Lebanon]. We will make an alliance with it. When we smash the [Arab] Legion's strength and bomb Amman, we will eliminate Transjordan too, and then Syria will fall. If Egypt still dares to fight on, we shall bomb Port Said, Alexandria, and Cairo.

An interesting portent.

After the Armistice Agreement was signed in February 1949, Ben-Gurion decided to establish another *fait accompli.* He ordered two brigades to Eilat, on the Gulf of Aqaba, which they took with no resistance on March 10. Violation of cease-fires has been a standard practice; recall the attack on the Golan Heights in 1967 (see p. 21). Shortly after, Ben-Gurion was touring the border with a young general, whom he asked, "How would you take those hills?," pointing to the Mountains of Edom beyond the Jordanian border. The general made some suggestions and then said, "Why do you ask? Do you want to conquer those hills?" Ben-Gurion responded: "I? No. But *you* will conquer them." He also maintained what his official biographer calls "his dream of annexing the Sinai Peninsula." After the 1956 conquest of the Sinai,* Ben-Gurion announced the founding of "the Third Kingdom of Israel," and informed the Knesset that "Our army did not infringe on Egyptian territory . . . Our operations were restricted to the Sinai Peninsula alone."[199]

9.2   Moderates and Extremists

Pre-state Zionism exhibits a number of striking similarities to divisions within the PLO between the Rejectionists, who refuse to accept any compromise, and the mainstream around Yasser Arafat, who have joined the international consensus on a two-state settlement (see chapter 3), though they too do not abandon their "dream" of a unitary democratic secular state, a goal to be achieved, they now say, through a process of peaceful interaction with Israel. The fact that the accommodationist elements that dominate the PLO refuse to abandon their "dream" has been exploited regularly as an argument that it is impossible to have any dealings with them. For example, David Krivine describes "the agony which Jewish Israelis are going through at present in seeking a solution to the problem of the Palestinians," discussing a seminar on that subject in Jerusalem. The "agony" is caused by the fact that there is no one to speak

---

* Menachem Begin "swore" before the Israeli Knesset that David Ben-Gurion had proposed the conquest of the West Bank in 1956 in a discussion with his co-conspirator in the attack on Egypt, French Socialist Prime Minister Guy Mollet, who was allegedly receptive. Mordechai Basok, "Begin's 'scoop'," *Al Hamishmar*, Sept. 9, 1982. If this is true, then the operation was presumably aborted as a consequence of Eisenhower's unexpectedly harsh response to the invasion of Egypt. One might also wonder whether there was a more general plan involving the Arabs of the Israeli Galilee as well; see p. 97.

to: not even Meir Pail's plan for a two-state settlement "had any chance of acceptance by the Arabs"—which is of course false: a similar plan was "prepared" by the PLO, proposed at the UN, rejected by Israel and vetoed by the U.S. as far back as January 1976, as we have seen. It is this alleged refusal of the PLO to accept "even that" that is "the real holdup, which has shattered the complacency of all Israeli disputants, left-wing and right-wing." The problem is "that the PLO—in all its factions—has only one aim, to retrieve the whole of Palestine; that is, to eliminate Jewish statehood."[200] See also chapter 3, note 111.

By the same logic, British anti-Semites might have argued in 1947— and perhaps did—that it was impossible to deal with the "moderate" Zionists who accepted partition, given the nature of their "dream," a point that is regularly and conveniently ignored.

Elsewhere, incidentally, Krivine has put the matter a bit more honestly, explaining that:

> the one group we won't talk with, it is true, is the PLO—but not because they are nasty people. The obstacle is the subject on the agenda. It can only be the creation of a Palestinian state on the West Bank, and that we can't agree to.[201]

Quite generally, the PLO has the same sort of legitimacy that the Zionist movement had in the pre-state period, a fact that is undoubtedly recognized at some level within Israel and, I think, accounts for the bitter hatred of the PLO, which, rational people must concede, has been recognized by Palestinians as "their sole representative" whenever they have had the chance to express themselves. Israeli doves have not failed to take note of this fact, and have also observed that "Those who shall sober up from the collective intoxication will have to admit that the Palestinians are the Jews of our era, a small, hunted people, defenseless, standing alone against the best weapons, helpless . . . the whole world is against them."[202].

9.3   The Use of Terror

The similarities extend to the use of terror. Commenting on the PLO's resort to terror, Noah Lucas observes that though this "earned it little sympathy in the world, it nevertheless succeeded in establishing the image of its cause as the quest of a victimized people for national self-determination, rather than a neglected refugee problem as it had hitherto been widely regarded." He adds that "There is no escaping the analogy with Zionism in the late forties."[203] Recall that the current Prime Minister of Israel and its Foreign Minister are former terrorist commanders, with a bloody record of atrocities to their credit including the killing of Jews* as

---

* Barnea and Rubinstein state that "the Hagana archives contain the names of 40 Jews who were killed by Irgun and LEHI (Stern Group) men in the course of their underground work

well as Britons and many Arabs, while the Secretary-General of the Jewish Agency until 1981 (Shmuel Lahis) was a man who murdered several dozen Arab civilians under guard in an undefended Lebanese village during the land-clearing operations of October 1948; he was immediately amnestied after receiving a seven-year prison sentence, then granted a second amnesty which "denies the punishment and the charge as well" and later granted a lawyer's licence by the Israeli Legal Council on the grounds that his act carried "no stigma."[205]

As noted earlier, the self-defense forces based in the labor movement (the Haganah) also engaged in terrorist violence, though to a more limited extent than the outright terrorist groups—against Arabs, and also against dissident Jews, including a religious Jew organizing among the largely anti-Zionist native Jewish inhabitants of Palestine who was assassinated by two Haganah agents "as he left the small synagogue in the 'Shaarey Tsedek' hospital" in June 1924. The official history of the Haganah describes this "special activity" matter-of-factly, justifying the order "to remove the traitor from the land of the living" on the grounds of the "pathological character" of his anti-Zionist activities (furthermore, he was alleged to be a homosexual, the history reports). As one proof of the inveterate evil of the Palestinians, or perhaps all Arabs, David Pryce-Jones, the *New Republic* specialist on this topic, cites the fact that King Abdullah of Jordan "was killed while leaving Friday prayers in the Mosque of Omar in Jerusalem." So different from the Zionists, with their fabled "purity of arms" and "sublime" moral sensibilities, much lauded in this journal.[206]

The record is long and bloody, as in the case of most nationalist movements; in the single month of July 1938, for example, the Irgun killed 76 Arabs with bombs in market places and the like.[207] The official history of the Irgun makes little pretense that these actions were retaliatory, as is often alleged, referring proudly, for example, to the murder of 27 Arabs to prevent celebration over the British White Paper limiting Jewish immigration, the murder of 52 more Arabs when an Irgun member was arrested by the British, etc.[208] The record is generally suppressed in the U.S., where cynics refer to terror and intimidation as an invention of the PLO. In the years after the state was established, there was also ample resort to terrorism, a few examples of which have already been cited.

---

or in the context of settling internal accounts," reviewing the record.[204] This does not include Jews killed by terrorist attacks aimed at others, as in the King David Hotel bombing. The official history of Begin's Irgun describes how they drowned a member who they thought might give information to the police, if captured; see Shahak, *Begin And Co.* The Haganah Special Actions Squads undertook "punitive actions against informers within the Jewish community" as one of its tasks (Bar-Zohar, *Ben-Gurion*, p. 99). A Haganah prison in Haifa contained a torture chamber for interrogation of Jews suspected of collaboration with the British, the Haifa weekly *Hashavua Bair* revealed in its 35th anniversary issue (April 1983), in an interview with a high military officer of the Haganah. In his review of Halabi (see note 152), Irving Howe attributes the alleged assassination of "a few of these [Village League] quislings" in the West Bank to the "fratricidal violence that seems so frequent in *Arab* politics" (my emphasis).

It is noteworthy that former terrorists are honored in Israel, as the examples of Begin, Shamir, and Lahis indicate; there is "no stigma" attached to their murderous deeds, again, a standard feature of nationalist movements. There are many other examples. The Israeli Cabinet recently decided to issue a new series of stamps in memory of Zionist heroes, including Shlomo Ben-Yosef, who was hanged by the British for shooting at an Arab bus; the murderers of Lord Moyne in 1944; and two men "executed for their part in the 1955 Cairo security mishap"[209]—this, a rather coy reference to the terrorist bombings (actually, 1954), which were a "mishap" in that the perpetrators were caught.

Since terrorism is considered to have been an honorable vocation, it is not surprising that its perpetrators have been protected by government authorities. For example, one of the suspected assassins of UN mediator Count Folke Bernadotte in 1948 was a close friend of Ben-Gurion's,* but he kept secret the fact that his friend had confessed the murder.[210] Efforts have been made to suppress the record in other ways as well. After the 1954 "mishap," the Israeli government angrily rejected the Egyptian charges against the captured terrorists, denouncing the "show trial. . . against a group of Jews. . . victims of false accusations." The journal of the governing Labor Party accused the Egyptian government of "a Nazi-inspired policy," though the government was well aware of the facts.[211] There are numerous other examples.

Perhaps the most remarkable illustration of the ability to efface atrocity concerns Deir Yassin, where 250 people were murdered by Begin's Irgun and LEHI in April 1948 (see pp. 95-6). A year later, Ha'aretz reported the "settlement festival" for religious settlers who were founding Givat Shaul Beth (now part of Jerusalem) in "the former village of Deir Yassin." Ha'aretz reports further: "President Chaim Weizmann sent his greetings in writing. . . the chief Rabbis and Minister Moshe Shapira took part in the ceremony. . . the orchestra of a school for the blind played. . ."[212] In 1980, the remaining ruins were bulldozed to prepare the ground for a settlement for Orthodox Jews. Streets were named after units of the Irgun which perpetrated the massacre, and of Palmach, the kibbutz-based strike force of Haganah, which took part in the operation but not the massacre. These units were to be "immortalized on the site," in the words of the Israeli press.[213] More recently, most of the Deir Yassin cemetery was bulldozed to prepare the ground for a highway to a new Jewish settlement.[214]

---

* Barnea and Rubinstein (see note 204) write: "according to the accepted version, the present Foreign Minister, Yitzhak Shamir, was one of those who planned the murder." They also note that Shamir has refused many requests to explain his role in the murder of Eliahu Giladi, a LEHI officer condemned to death by the LEHI command (headed by Shamir) in 1943.

Nahum Barnea writes that "at first Deir Yassin was forgotten. Now it is celebrated." He describes a (to him, horrifying) tour to Deir Yassin organized by the Society for the Protection of Nature, perhaps, he suggests bitterly, because "nature was the only thing not destroyed there on April 9, 1948." The tour (an annual event) was led by a former Irgunist, who whitewashed the operation before a largely passive audience. The actual site of the village is now a mental hospital, as is the Acre prison, site of another Irgun operation.[215]

None of this is particularly surprising, or unique to the Jewish national movement. It can, furthermore, be explained in terms of the circumstances in which the Zionist movement developed and won its victories, which were hardly propitious. The actual record does, however, highlight the cynicism of the constant denunciation of the PLO as a movement unique in its inexplicable commitment to terror, guilty of such acts as intimidating "moderates," along with major crimes against innocents that contrast so strikingly with the standards of its enemy. The actual record also helps to explain the feelings and attitudes of Palestinians who have fled or been driven from their homes, or who live under military occupation, or who remain as second-class citizens in a land that not long ago was their own. To explain is not to justify, but if circumstances can help to explain the resort to terror in pre-state Zionism and increasingly in subsequent years, then the same is true with regard to those who see themselves, not unreasonably, as the victims of Zionist success.

10   The Problem for Today

It is often argued that it is hypocritical for Americans or Europeans to condemn Israel for its treatment of the native population, considering the history of European colonization, which was surely vastly more barbaric than anything that can be attributed to the Jewish settlers. If the argument has merit, then the same is true of earlier resort to similar efforts; for example, when Japanese imperialists in the pre-war years argued that what they were doing in Manchuria was based on a European model. Or suppose that Israel were to enslave the Arab population, arguing in justification that, after all, the American colonists indulged in literal human slavery for a century after their independence. Whatever merit the charge of hypocrisy may have, the fact is that brutal and inhuman practices that were tolerated when the plague of European civilization spread over much of the world no longer are. Israelis often complain that they are held to higher standards than others. If they have in mind those who massacred American Indians and enslaved Blacks they are quite right, for the little that that observation is worth. In the real world of today, however, they have been largely immune from serious critical analysis, at least in the United States, where the true history is little known and they are depicted as guided by uniquely high moral principles though surrounded by barbarians whose sole aim is to murder innocents and to deny them their rightful home.

The conflict over Palestine has sometimes been depicted as one of "right against right," an arguable—and in my view, defensible—proposition, though naturally not one that the Palestinians are likely to accept as morally valid. It is not clear that there is much to be gained by pursuing this question. Israel is a reality, a fact that few now contest despite increasingly desperate pretense to the contrary on the part of its numerous supporters and apologists. The same obviously cannot be said for the Palestinians, whose right to national self-determination is denied by the leaders of the rejectionist camp, Israel and the United States, whose power is dominant in the region. That is the primary topic that Americans must address.

Notes—Chapter 4
Israel and Palestine: Historical Background

1. There is a substantial literature on this topic, the overwhelming mass of it from the Zionist point of view. One useful study is Noah Lucas, *The Modern History of Israel* (Weidenfeld and Nicolson, London, 1974). Another, for the earlier years, is Sykes, *Crossroads to Israel.* On interactions between Jews and Palestinians, see, among many others, Porath, *Emergence of the Palestinian National Movement, The Palestinian National Movement;* Flapan, *Zionism and the Palestinians;* Khalidi, ed., *From Haven to Conquest;* David Hirst, *The Gun and the Olive Branch* (Harcourt Brace Jovanovich, New York, 1977); Edward W. Said, *The Question of Palestine* (Times Books, New York, 1979); Barry Rubin, *The Arab States & Palestine* (Syracuse, 1981). On the earlier years, there is much valuable material in the ESCO Foundation Study, *Palestine: a Study of Jewish, Arab, and British Policies* (Yale, New Haven, 1947), with the collaboration of a distinguished group of scholars, generally liberal Zionist in complexion. There are useful bibliographical notes in the books by Lucas and Said.
2. Lucas, *The Modern History of Israel*, p. 101.
3. Sykes, *Crossroads to Israel*, p. 5. My emphasis.
4. *Ibid.*, pp. 109-10, 123.
5. Vol. I, pp. 218, 221. The Recommendations of the Commission are reprinted in George Antonius, *The Arab Awakening* (G.F. Putnam's Sons, New York, 1946, Appendix H); also Khalidi, *From Haven to Conquest.*
6. Flapan, *Zionism and the Palestinians*, pp. 141-2, citing a 1938 speech.
7. See Porath, *The Palestinian National Movement*, for a careful analysis of the revolt.
8. Frederick Morgan, *Peace And War: A Soldier's Life* (Hodder and Stoughton, London, 1961; relevant parts reprinted in Khalidi, *From Haven to Conquest).* Yehuda Bauer, *Flight and Rescue: Brichah* (Random House, New York, 1970). The Harrison Report is reprinted as an appendix in Leonard Dinnerstein, *America and the Survivors of the Holocaust* (Columbia, New York, 1982).
9. See *TNCW*, p. 433. In this case, preferences are clear, since a choice is available. Despite extensive pressures to compel immigration to Israel, most, particularly from European Russia, now prefer immigration to the U.S. Another relevant case is that of the Ethiopean Jews (Falashas), who have been subject to savage persecution with little attempt on Israel's part to do anything for them or to "gather them in." They of course are Black; also, Israel had close relations with Ethiopia through much of the worst period of persecution. For some recent comment, see Simcha Jacobovici, alleging that "for at least six years all major Jewish organizations, uncharacteristically adhering to Israel's line on a diaspora matter, have suppressed information about the Falashas' plight and have refused to undertake major initiatives to save them," in sharp contrast to Russian Jews (Op-Ed, *New York Times*, April 23, 1983).
10. Saul S. Friedman, *No Haven for the Oppressed* (Wayne State, Detroit, 1973, pp. 222f.); Dinnerstein, *op. cit.*, p. 223 and elsewhere; Alfred Lilienthal, *The Zionist Connection* (Dodd, Mead & Co., New York, 1978, p. 56). On the reluctance of American Zionists to consider resettlement of Jews outside of Palestine during the war years and before, see Henry L. Feingold, *The Politics of Rescue* (Rutgers, New Brunswick, 1970, pp. 13f., 69ff., 109, 123f., 237f., 264f., 298f.). See also Yehuda Bauer, *American Jewry and the Holocaust* (Wayne State, Detroit, 1981. pp. 123f.); Uri Davis, *Israel: Utopia Incorporated* (Zed, London, 1977, pp. 24-5); *TNCW*, p. 466, among others. There is a scathing indictment of the policies of the

Zionist leadership in Rabbi Moshe Shonfeld, *The Holocaust Victims Accuse: Documents and Testimony on Jewish War Criminals, Part I* (Neturei Karta of USA, Brooklyn, 1977); the publisher is affiliated with the Jerusalem Neturei Karta, the organization of Orthodox anti-Zionist Jews that has its roots in the pre-Zionist Jewish settlement and that now supports secular democracy rather than a Jewish state.

11. Morris L. Ernst, *So Far So Good* (Harper & Brothers, New York, 1948, pp. 175-6).

12. Bernard Weinraub, *New York Times*, Jan. 4, 1982. For further discussion and controversy over this matter, see Bernard Weinraub, *New York Times*, Jan. 20; Richard Bernstein, *New York Times*, Feb. 9, 1983.

13. Lucas, *Modern History of Israel*, p. 192.

14. Flapan, *Zionism and the Palestinians*.

15. There is interesting discussion of the interactions among the various Arab and Jewish parties during this period in Flapan, *Zionism and the Palestinians*, and Rubin, *The Arab States & Palestine*.

16. Uri Milshtein, *Davar*, Oct. 23, 1981; Sykes, *Crossroads to Israel*, p. 337. For a contemporary record of Irgun-LEHI terrorism in December 1947, see *Peace in the Middle East?*, pp. 64-5, citing a report by the Council on Jewish-Arab Cooperation, which concludes that these actions were undertaken to create conflict in peaceful areas. See *TNCW*, pp. 464-5 and references cited for additional examples of Zionist terrorism, including major massacres. Little of this is known here; the information appears in standard Israeli (Hebrew) sources.

17. Israel Segal, "The Deir Yassin File," *Koteret Rashit*, Jan. 19, 1983; *Toldot Milhemet Hakomemiut*, prepared by the Historical Branch of the General Staff, Israel Defense Forces (Ma'arachot, Israel, 1959; citation from the 14th edition, 1966, p. 117). English translations of a number of other documents concerning the Deir Yassin and other Irgun massacres are provided in a privately printed anthology by Israel Shahak, *Begin And Co. As They Really Are* (Jerusalem, 1977). This was, in fact, only one of a number of such massacres, though it was the worst. See also *TNCW*, pp. 464f. Units of Palmach participated in the attack, though not in the massacre. The village "had refused permission for foreign Arab volunteers to use it as a base for operations against the Jewish life-line into Jerusalem" (Jon Kimche). On the massacre, see the report from the scene by Jacques de Reynier, head of the International Red Cross delegation in Palestine, and remarks by Zionist historian Jon Kimche, reprinted in Khalidi, *From Haven to Conquest;* also Israeli military historian Meir Pail, an eye-witness, cited in *TNCW*, p. 465, and much more extensively in Shahak, *Begin And Co.* See also pp. 166-7.

18. Lucas, *Modern History of Israel*, pp. 252, 460.

19. Mordechai Nisan, Professor of Political Science in the School for Overseas Students of the Hebrew University, in Elazar, ed., *Judea, Samaria and Gaza*, p. 193. Nisan is an admirer of the use of terror (against Arabs). See *TNCW*, p. 304.

20. Erskine Childers, *Spectator*, May 12, 1961; reprinted in Khalidi, *From Haven to Conquest*. See also his essay in Ibrahim Abu-Lughod, ed., *The Transformation of Palestine* (Northwestern, Evanston, 1971), citing mainly Zionist sources on the terror and expulsion, and reviewing some of the remarkable propaganda exercises undertaken to disguise the facts.

21. Eli Tabor, *Yediot Ahronot*, Nov. 2, 1982.

22. *Al Hamishmar*, April 16, 1982. See p. 49 and note 49 below. On the 1948 and 1967 expulsions, see Hirst, *The Gun and the Olive Branch*. About 200,000 fled across the Jordan in 1967.

23. Yoram Peri, *Between Battles and Ballots*, p. 58; Flapan, *Zionism and the Palestinians*, p. 337. Flapan gives a detailed account of these interactions; see also Rubin, *The Arab States & Palestine*. Michael Widlanski reports from Jerusalem that recently discovered British diplomatic documents reveal that Britain exerted pressure on Transjordan, Egypt, Syria and Iraq to refrain from coming to formal or informal peace agreements with Israel after the 1949 armistice, fearing that peace might lead to an Israeli-dominated neutralist bloc (at this time, Israel had not yet chosen sides in the Cold War system) that might oppose British interests in the Middle East. The documents also allegedly show that Britain used the Arab League to limit the influence of the USSR, France, the U.S. and Israel at the time. Michael Widlanski, Cox News Service, *Winnipeg Free Press*, Jan. 24, 1983. On conflicts between the U.S. and Britain in the Middle East at the time, see *TNCW*, introduction and chapters 2, 11, and references cited.

24. *Shalom Network Newsletter* (Berkeley), Oct./Nov. 1981, reprinted from the London *Jewish Chronicle*. See p. 386*.

25. Reprinted in *Israel & Palestine* (Paris), Oct./Nov. 1981.

26. World Jewish Congress *News & Views*, Sept. 1982; *Jewish Post & Opinion*, Sept. 17, 1982; SOUTH, November 1982.

27. *New Leader*, Dec. 24, 1973. For a fuller quote, see my *Peace in the Middle East?*, p. 187.

28. David K. Shipler, "A Crisis of Conscience Over Lebanon," *New York Times*, June 18, 1982. One expects such a version of history from outright propagandists; e.g., Nathan I. Nagler, Chairman of the New York Region, Anti-Defamation League of B'nai Brith, who refers to the "five attempts at military means" of the Arabs who "invaded Israel, bent on her destruction" (letter, *New York Times*, June 19, 1982). It is more interesting that it is regularly expounded by serious journalists and scholars.

29. J. Robert Moskin, review of Chaim Herzog, *The Arab-Israeli Wars, New York Times Book Review*, Nov. 28, 1982. The *Times* weekly book review section appears to be reserved for "supporters of Israel" as a matter of editorial policy, a topic that merits a special study, particularly, in the light of the role of the *Review* in influencing the distribution of books in U.S. libraries, bookstores, etc.

30. Jacobo Timerman, *The Longest War* (Knopf, New York, 1982; lengthy sections appeared in the *New Yorker*, Oct. 18, 25). Timerman also repeats other standard myths, and sometimes fabricates new ones. We return to some examples in the next chapter.

31. The attack was in response to a PLO terrorist operation that left 34 Israelis dead in an interchange of fire on a coastal road after a bus had been seized. Putting aside the question of proportionality or of the merits of the principle of international law (binding on members of the United Nations) that the use of force is permissible only in the case of self-defense against armed attack, the Israeli retaliation was irrelevant to the terrorist incident that provoked it since the terrorist operation by seaborne commandos was launched from a point north of the area invaded by Israel. The border had previously been relatively quiet, apart from Israeli-provoked military interchanges. See the next chapter.

32. Michael Walzer, *Just and Unjust Wars* (Basic Books, New York, 1977, p. 292), my emphasis.

33. *Ha'aretz*, March 29, 1972; for a more extensive quote, see Cooley, *Green March, Black September*, p. 162.

34. *Le Monde hebdomadaire*, June 8-14, 1972; Kimche, *There Could Have Been Peace*, p. 258..

35. See Cooley, *Green March, Black September*; Charles Yost, *Foreign Affairs*, January 1968; and many other sources.

36. Menachem Begin, August 8 speech at the National Defense College, excerpts in the *New York Times*, Aug. 21, 1982, reprinted from the *Jerusalem Post*.
37. For a number of other examples from the same pen, see *TNCW*.
38. See *TNCW*, pp. 331, 463, and sources cited, particularly, Ehud Yaari, *Egypt and the Fedayeen* (Hebrew; Givat Haviva, 1975), based on captured Egyptian documents; Kennett Love, *Suez: The Twice-fought War* (McGraw-Hill, New York, 1969, pp. 92f., 408f); Donald Neff, *Warriors at Suez* (Simon & Schuster, New York, 1981). See Rokach, *Israel's Sacred Terrorism*, for information from Prime Minister Moshe Sharett's diaries. There is also important material in the memoirs of the commanders of the UN forces on the borders, who characteristically took up this post sympathetic to Israel but ended their tours quite critical of its encroachments and resort to unprovoked violence.
39. Such reconstruction of unwanted facts is not unusual. For another example of skillful re-editing, by which the *Times* succeeded in converting a *London Times* report with an unwanted message into its precise opposite (to be picked up in the *Times* version by *Newsweek* with some additional fillips and to enter official history), see N. Chomsky and Edward S. Herman, *The Political Economy of Human Rights* (South End, Boston, 1979, vol. I, pp. 135f.). The same section gives numerous other examples of successful news management, of particular interest in this case because of their efficacy in enabling the Human Rights Administration to participate actively in one of the major acts of mass murder in recent years. These two volumes give many other examples of behavior which is, in fact, fairly systematic, though not exceptionless, as explained and illustrated there. See also *TNCW*, chapters 3,4 and elsewhere, and references cited. For more on this subject, and particularly discussion of the mechanisms, see Edward S. Herman, *The Real Terror Network* (South End, Boston, 1982).
40. Neff, *Warriors at Suez*, pp. 420-1; Love, *Suez*, pp. 551f.
41. To cite one case that has not exactly become common knowledge in the U.S., the American occupying army in Japan engaged in rape, pillage and murder, according to Japanese sources (see Saburo Ienaga, *The Pacific War*, Pantheon New York, 1978, pp. 236f.). For discussion of other examples of the treatment of prisoners, collaborators, and other victims of liberation by the U.S. and its allies, also largely unknown here, see Chomsky and Herman, *The Political Economy of Human Rights*, vol. II, pp. 32-48.
42. Alfred Friendly, "Israel: Paradise Lost," *Manchester Guardian weekly*, July 11, 1982.
43. Carl Van Horn, *Soldiering for Peace*, cited along with other evidence from UN and Israeli sources by Fred J. Khouri, *Arab Perspectives*, January 1982. See also Hirst, *The Gun and the Olive Branch*.
44. Mattityahu Peled, "A burden rather than an asset," *Ha'aretz*, Oct. 30, 1980.
45. John K. Cooley, *Christian Science Monitor*, Jan. 30, 1970.
46. See p. 21, and section 5.2, below.
47. For documentation, see Sabri Jiryis, *The Arabs in Israel* (Monthly Review, New York, 1976). On the possible role of Israeli terrorism in the flight from Iraq, see *TNCW*, p. 462, referring to reports in the Israeli press by Iraqi Jews and the account by Wilbur Crane Eveland, who was military attaché in the U.S. Embassy in Baghdad at the time, in his *Ropes of Sand* (Norton, New York, 1980, p. 48). See also Rabbi Moshe Schonfeld, *Genocide in the Holy Land* (Neturei Karta of the USA, Brooklyn, 1980, pp. 509ff.); see note 10.
48. For discussion and references, see *TNCW*, chapter 9 (1974, 1982); also Rafik Halabi, *The West Bank Story* (Harcourt Brace Jovanovich, New York, 1981) and references of note 1. There are important personal accounts by Raymonda Tawil (*My Hope, My Prison*, Holt, Rinehart and Winston, New York, 1980)

and Raja Shehadeh (*The Third Way*, Quartet, London, 1982); Shehadeh, a West Bank lawyer, is also the principal author of an informative study of the legal devices and practices of the military administration: Raja Shehadeh, assisted by Jonathan Kuttab, *The West Bank and the Rule of Law* (International Commission of Jurists, Geneva, 1980). See also Emanuel Jarry, *Le Monde diplomatique*, Sept. 1981, and Danny Rubinstein, *New Outlook*, June/July 1982. On the sharp intensification of repression under the Sharon-Milson repression from November 1981, see *Only Do Not Say That You Did Not Know;* chapter 3, note 52.

49. For specific references and much further discussion, see Kapeliouk, *Israel*. On "the Judaization of the Galilee," see *TNCW*, chapter 9. The most detailed study of the settlement program is William Wilson Harris, *Taking Root: Israeli Settlement in the West Bank, the Golan and Gaza-Sinai, 1967-1980* (Research Studies Press, Wiley, New York, 1980).

50. Elisha Efrat, "Spatial Patterns of Jewish and Arab Settlements in Judea and Samaria," in Elazar, ed., *Judea, Samaria and Gaza.*

51. Kapeliouk, *Israel*, p. 65, pp. 44-5, pp. 296f.

52. Amnon Kapeliouk, *Le Monde*, May 15, 1975, translated in *Middle East International*, July 1975.

53. *Al Hamishmar*, Aug. 22, 29, 1975; A. Droyanov, *Sefer Tel Aviv*, 1936, vol. 1, sections reprinted in *Matzpen*, July 1975. See my article "The Interim Agreement," *New Politics*, Winter, 1975-6, for these and other references.

54. *Jewish Post & Opinion*, Sept. 26, 1975.

55. See *TNCW*, pp. 280-1, for discussion.

56. Danny Rubinstein, *Davar*, March 16, 1981. See also Benvenisti's proposal for "mutual recognition of the national aspirations of Israelis and Palestinians" in the *Jerusalem Post*, April 7, 1981. Benvenisti was then a candidate for the Knesset on the Citizens Rights List.

57. David Richardson, "De facto dual society," interview with Meron Benvenisti, *Jerusalem Post*, Sept. 10, 1982. For more details on Benvenisti's research and conclusions, see David K. Shipler, *New York Times*, Sept. 12, 1982. Shipler gives the figure of 55-65 percent of the West Bank under Israeli government control. See also Ian Black, *Manchester Guardian Weekly*, Sept. 19, 1982; Anthony Lewis, *New York Times*, Nov. 1, 1982, reporting on a briefing by Benvenisti in Washington. See also Lesley Hazelton, "The Israelis' 'Irreversible' Settlements," *Nation*, Dec. 18, 1982, describing the vast extent of the settlement projects and noting, *inter alia*, that Labor "is trying to prove itself as settlement-conscious as Likud." Government officials agree that Benvenisti's data are accurate, Hazelton reports. See also Amos Elon, "Ariel for example," *Ha'aretz*, Nov. 11, 1982, describing a new town south of Nablus.

58. Philip Geyelin, "On Israeli Settlements, Reagan Really Isn't Trying," *Los Angeles Times*, Dec. 27, 1982.

59. Chaim Bermant, "Financial Influence," *Jerusalem Post*, Dec. 19, 1982.

60. Wolf Blitzer, "Lessons from aid victory," *Jerusalem Post*, Dec. 24, 1982. For detailed background, see G. Neal Lendenmann, "Aid Levels to Israel," *American-Arab Affairs*, Winter 1982-3.

61. Chaim Herzog, "Good for the Jews?," *Jerusalem Post*, Dec. 24, 1982.

62. Interview with Jacobo Timerman in the dissident journal *Haolam Haze*, Dec. 22, 1982. On earlier Israeli relations with the Argentine neo-Nazis, including military aid, see *TNCW*, pp. 291-2.

63. *Economist*, Nov. 13, 1982; Feb. 19, 1983. See chapter 2, section 2.2.3.

64. *Davar*, Nov. 11, 1982; interview in *Trialogue*, journal of the Trilateral Commission, Winter 1983.

65. Uzi Shimoni, "The Allon Plan—an expression of Zionist and security activism," *Davar*, Dec. 21, 1982.

66. Anthony Lewis, *New York Times*, Nov. 1, 1982.
67. And sold for hard currency; see p. 46. The figure that Richardson cites seems too high. Shmuel Sandler and Hillel Frisch, in Elazar, ed., *Judea, Samaria and Gaza*, give the figure of about 12%.
68. Sasson Levi, in Elazar, ed., *Judea, Samaria and Gaza*.
69. Bernard Nossiter, *New York Times*, April 3, 1982.
70. *New York Times*, Sept. 1, 1981. See *TNCW*, chapter 13, for details and references.
71. Irving Howe, "The Campus Left and Israel," *New York Times* Op-Ed, reprinted in Howe and Carl Gershman, eds., *Israel, the Arabs, and the Middle East* (Bantam, New York, 1972).
72. Danny Rubinstein, *Davar*, Nov. 5, 12, 1982.
73. *Ha'aretz*, Nov. 18, 1982; *Israeli Mirror*.
74. David K. Shipler, *New York Times*, April 4, 1983, citing Meir Cohen's remarks to the Knesset's Foreign Affairs and Defense Committee on March 16 (the *Jerusalem Post* commented that the lack of reprimand by his Herut party "inevitably" gives the impression that "he articulates the tacit premises of official policy"; cited by *Jewish Post & Opinion*, March 30); Francis Ofner, "Sketching Rabin's Moves towards Peace," *Christian Science Monitor*, June 3, 1974, dispatch from Tel Aviv. See *TNCW*, p. 234, for more on Rabin's views.
75. Amos Oz, "Has Israel Altered its Visions?," *New York Times Magazine*, July 11, 1982.
76. See *TNCW*, p. 235-6, for quotes and reference.
77. See Flapan, *Zionism and the Palestinians.*, pp. 69f., 82, 222, 259ff., for extensive discussion.
78. *Ha'aretz*, May 26, 1980.
79. *Yediot Ahronot*, Jan. 15, 1982; *Israeli Mirror*.
80. Michael Walzer, "Nationalism, internationalism, and the Jews: the chimera of a binational state," in Howe and Gershman, eds., *Israel, the Arabs and the Middle East*.
81. See *TNCW*, pp. 255f., 286f., for some examples, and my articles in *New Politics*, Winter 1975-6, Winter 1978-9, for more.
82. See Amos Elon, *Ha'aretz*, Sept. 28, 1981 (on the development town Beit Shemesh); Shevach Weiss, *Al Hamishmar*, Oct. 2, 1981; Z. Dorsini, *Davar*, Sept. 21, 1981; Avshalom Ginat, *Al Hamishmar*, Sept. 18, 1981. See Davis, *Israel: Utopia Incorporated*, for some useful background, and *The Dawn (Al Fajr*, Jerusalem), Nov. 5, 12, 1982, for informative discussion. Also the extensive discussion by Ellen Cantarow, "A Family Affair," *Village Voice*, Jan. 25, 1983; and David K. Shipler, *New York Times*, April 6, 7, 8, 1983.
83. Irving Howe, see above. Howe states: "I have never been a Zionist; I have always felt contempt for nationalist and chauvinist sentiments" ("Thinking the Unthinkable About Israel: A Personal Statement," *New York Magazine*, Dec. 24, 1973). We return to the matter.
84. Ze'ev Yaphet, "No Lessons were Learned, Nothing was Done," "The Exhaustion of the Kibbutz Movement," *Ha'aretz*, Oct. 15, 22, 1982. Also "Mapai destroyed us," *Ha'aretz*, Oct. 15, 1982.
85. Tamar Maroz, *Ha'aretz*, Feb. 25, 1983.
86. Michael Elkins, *Newsweek*, June 8, 1970.
87. Jerusalem Mayor Teddy Kollek, for example, who "expressed his horror at the growth of fascism in Israel," noting that "the events he was now observing in Jerusalem were familiar to him from his experiences in Europe of the 1930s" (in Vienna) and "would also be familiar to anyone who had recently arrived in Israel from Latin America." *Al Hamishmar*, June 22, 1981; *Israeli Mirror*.

88. This is one of the standard slogans, reflecting the almost hysterical love for Begin in large circles. Americans inclined to ridicule such "Kim il-Sungism" on the part of the Israeli underclass might turn to some of their own sophisticates, e.g., the review by left-liberal social critic Murray Kempton of a book by Joseph Alsop on FDR. Kempton describes the "majesty" of Roosevelt's smile as "he beamed from those great heights that lie beyond the taking of offense. . . Those of us who were born to circumstances less assured tend to think of, indeed revere, this demeanor as the aristocratic style. . . [We are] as homesick as Alsop for a time when America was ruled by gentlemen and ladies." Roosevelt and Lucy Mercer "were persons even grander on the domestic stage than they would end up being on the cosmic one," and met the crisis in their lives, a secret love affair, "in the grandest style." "That Roosevelt was the democrat that great gentlemen always are in no way abated his grandeur. . .[though] this majesty had its notes of condescension to be sure. . . [His blend of elegance with compassion] adds up to true majesty." He left us with "nostalgia" that is "aching." His "enormous bulk" stands between us "and all prior history. . .endearingly exalted. . .splendidly eternal for romance," etc., etc. Incidentally, FDR took such complete command that he "left social inquiry. . .a wasteland," so much so that "ten years went by before a Commerce Department economist grew curious about the distribution of income and was surprised to discover that its inequality had persisted almost unchanged from Hoover, through Roosevelt and Truman. . ." But no matter: he brought us "comfort. . .owing to his engraving upon the public consciousness the sense that men were indeed equal." Murray Kempton, "The Kindly Stranger," *New York Review of Books*, April 15, 1982. The article called forth one comment: in the June 10 issue, Noel Annan referred to "the encomium that Murray Kempton justly bestowed on Roosevelt."

89. *Yediot Ahronot*, Oct. 31; Shimon Weiss, *Davar*, Nov. 1, 1982.

90. David K. Shipler, "Ethnic Conflict Erupts in Israel," *New York Times*, Dec. 29; Leah Etgar, "The Arabs took our jobs and are running Tiberias," *Yediot Ahronot*, Dec. 10, 1982; Michal Meron, "Town without pity," Supplement to *Yediot Ahronot*, March 11, 1983.

91. *Ha'aretz*, Nov. 26, 1982.

92. See *TNCW*, pp. 287f., for some examples.

93. Zvi Barel, "Talking to a settler," *Ha'aretz*, April 20, 1982. On the immunity of the settlers, see *TNCW*, p. 279.

94. Yedidia Segal, *Nekudah*, Sept. 3, 1982.

95. Amnon Rubinstein, *Ha'aretz*, April 5, 1982; *Ha'aretz*, April 4, 1982; Danny Rubinstein, *Davar*, April 9, 1982, who observes that with the police and the civilian authorities removed, the settlers "can act as they wish in the territories," giving many examples.

96. David Shipler, *New York Times*, March 22, 21 1982.

97. Barel, "Talking to a settler."

98. Danny Tsidkoni, *Davar*, May 18, 1982.

99. Michal Meron, *Yediot Ahronot*, March 29, 1982; Amnon Kapeliouk, *Al Hamishmar*, March 26, 1982.

100. James McManus, *Guardian* (London), April 7, 1983.

101. *The Dawn (Al Fajr)*, Nov. 5, 1982.

102. MK Tawfiq Toubi, reported in *The Dawn*, Dec. 3, 1982.

103. For one recent example, see the report by Felicia Langer, the Israeli Communist lawyer who defends many Arabs, quoting an Arab prisoner who recounts in detail what he says happened to him under interrogation in the "Sarafand" interrogation center, leaving him in such a condition that the Nablus prison authorities refused to admit him without a doctor's report from a military

hospital. He specifically implicates Israeli doctors. *The Dawn (Al Fajr)*, Dec. 31, 1982. See Langer's book *With My Own Eyes* (Ithaca, London, 1974), and the more extensive Hebrew original *Bemo Eynay* for many examples. There is ample further evidence. For a few examples, see *TNCW*, p. 447.

104. For extensive evidence concerning both categories, see Chomsky and Herman, *Political Economy of Human Rights*. Predictably, our insistence that refugee reports be taken seriously and considered with the same caution and concern whatever their origin has repeatedly been interpreted as apologetics for some official enemy, a matter that merits little comment apart from an inquiry, which might be illuminating, into some of the techniques typically adopted by those whom Bakunin aptly called the "state worshipping" intellectuals; in the West, those who pretend to be anti-Communist while mimicking Stalinist practice.

105. *London Sunday Times*, June 19, 1977. There is considerable further evidence in the testimony of Paul Eddy and Peter Gillman of the *Sunday Times* before the UN Special Committee to Investigate Israeli Practices Affecting the Human Rights of the Population of the Occupied Territories (A/SPC/32/L.12, 11 Nov. 1977), including also interesting analysis of the efforts at rebuttal on the part of David Krivine of the *Jerusalem Post* and the Israeli government. See *TNCW*, p. 447.

106. Seth Kaplan, *New Republic*, July 23, 1977.

107. Amnesty International *Newsletter*, Sept. 1977; Martin Peretz, *New Republic*, Aug. 2, 1982; Amnon Rubinstein, *Ha'aretz*, Feb. 27, 1981; *TNCW*, p. 454. For another remarkable example of a "confession," regarded by the *Washington Post* as a "vindication of Israel's system of justice" and given a stamp of approval also by "civil libertarians" Monroe Freedman and Alan Dershowitz, see Chomsky and Herman, *Political Economy of Human Rights*, vol. I, p. 381.

108. *Report and Recommendations of an Amnesty International Mission to the Government of Israel*, including the Government's response and Amnesty International's comments (London, 1980); *Ha'aretz*, Sept. 3, 1980; *Al Hamishmar*, Sept. 3, 1980 *(Israeli Mirror)*.

109. Mattityahu Peled, *Ha'aretz*, Aug. 8, 1980; see references to the U.S., British and Israeli press on conditions in the prisons in *TNCW*, pp. 446-7.

110. *Jerusalem Post*, Dec. 24, 1982; Reuters, *Los Angeles Times, Boston Globe*, Dec. 29, 1982; *Boston Globe*, Jan. 5, 1983.

111. *Jerusalem Post*, Dec. 12, 1982; "'Cut off their testicles,' Sharon said with regard to demonstrators in the West Bank" *Yediot Ahronot*, Dec. 29, 1982; *Ma'ariv*, Feb. 18, 1983, quoting Avraham Burg; *The Dawn (Al Fajr)*, Jan 21, Feb. 4, 1983, on the expropriation and the curfew; Michael Precker, *Dallas Morning News—Boston Globe*, Feb. 17, 1983. The expropriation was noted by Trudy Rubin, *Christian Science Monitor*, March 4, 1983.

112. Zvi Barel, *Ha'aretz*, Jan. 20, 1983 *(Israleft News Service;* Barel, *Ha'aretz Weekly*, Feb. 6-11, 1983; Edward Walsh, *Washington Post—Boston Globe*, Feb. 18; David Richardson, *Jerusalem Post*, Feb. 18; Barel, *Ha'aretz*, Jan. 30 (translated in *The Dawn (Al Fajr)*, Feb. 11); Eitan Mor, *Yediot Ahronot*, Feb. 18, 1983; Reuven Padhatzur, *Ha'aretz*, March 11, 1983, explaining how the defense "broke the rules of the game" by building its case on the demonstration that IDF policy is responsible for the atrocities; the defense was successful, since higher officers, who gave the orders, could not be (and were not) tried. See also Marcus Eliason, AP, *Boston Globe*, Jan. 22, 1983, reviewing Eitan's orders and also his statement, which is correct, that the practice of demolishing houses in collective punishment and deportation was practiced much more extensively by his Labor predecessors. Also *New York Times*, Feb. 10, 18. The sanitized *New York Times* accounts may usefully be compared to those cited from other American journals, particularly the detailed account of Eitan's testimony by Norman Kempster, *Los Angeles Times*, Feb. 10, 1983.

113. Aharon Bachar, "Do not say: We did not know, we did not hear'," *Yediot*

Ahronot, Dec. 3, 1982.

114. Aharon Bachar, *Yediot Ahronot*, Nov. 5, 1982.

115. Yoram Peri, *Davar*, Dec. 10, 1982.

116. "Peace Now officers recount atrocities," *Al Hamishmar*, May 11, 1982; Aharon Geva, *Davar*, April 4, 1982 *(Israeli Mirror)*.

117. "Human Rights Violations on the Golan Heights: February-May, 1982," Report of the Association for Civil Rights in Israel, Israel Office of the American Jewish Committee (1982). The following account and quotes are from this study. The events discussed were reported by some of the Israeli press, despite efforts by the authorities to prevent journalists from discovering the facts or even entering the area.

118. *Ha'aretz*, April 16; David Richardson, *Jerusalem Post*, April 16; Emmanuel Elnekaveh, *Yediot Ahronot*, Feb. 25; Yoram Hamizrahi, Feb. 25; Nahum Barnea, *Davar*, April 13, 1982.

119. *Ha'aretz*, March 15, 1982.

120. *Ha'aretz, Jerusalem Post*, April 16; see also editorial, "Shame on the Golan," *Jerusalem Post*, April 16, 1982.

121. Amos Elon, *Ha'aretz*, April 13, 1982.

122. Danny Rubinstein, *Davar*, April 12, 1982. See *TNCW*, pp. 277-8, for some examples, including even the closing of art exhibits.

123. *Jerusalem Post*, July 13, 1982; *Israleft News Service*. The harassment of Bir Zeit apparently began with the Likud takeover in 1977. For some early discussion, see Manfred Ropschitz, ed., *Volunteers for Palestine Papers 1977-1980* (Miftah, Kfar Shemaryahu, 1981).

124. UPI, *Boston Globe*, Nov. 17, 1982.

125. *New York Times*, Nov. 20, 23, 1982; Benny Morris, *Jerusalem Post*, Nov. 21, 1982. *Israleft News Service*, Dec. 1, 1982, contains a detailed chronology and material from the Israeli press. See the advertisement of the Ad Hoc Committee for Academic Freedom, *New York Times, Christian Science Monitor*, April 1, 1983.

126. *Christian Science Monitor*, Nov. 16, 1982.

127. David Richardson, "A threat to freedom," *Jerusalem Post*, Nov. 19, 1982; Norman Kempster, *Los Angeles Times*, Nov. 20, 1982.

128. See, among others, Danny Rubinstein, *Davar*, May 16, 1980; *TNCW*, p. 274.

129. *Boston Globe*, Nov. 22; *New York Times*, Nov. 23, 1982.

130. *New York Times*, Oct. 21; *The Dawn (Al Fajr)*, Nov. 12, 1982.

131. Danny Rubinstein, *Davar*, Nov. 19, 1982.

132. W.F. Abboushi. *Christian Science Monitor*, Nov. 30, 1982.

133. Boaz Evron, *Yediot Ahronot*, Dec. 3, 1982. Shortly after, the restrictions on one of the editors (and several other people) were lifted; *Jerusalem Post*, Dec. 21, 1982 *(Israleft News Service)*.

134. Michal Meron, *Yediot Ahronot* (supplement), Dec. 10, 1982.

135. Erwin Frenkel, "A newspaper's loyalties," *Jerusalem Post Jubilee Supplement*, Dec. 1, 1982.

136. *Ha'aretz*, Nov. 29, 1982.

137. H. Graetz, *History of the Jews* (Jewish Publication Society, Philadelphia, 1893, vol II, p. 324). See *The Universal Jewish Encyclopedia* (New York, 1942, vol. 6).

138. Press Release, Association for Civil Rights in Israel, Oct. 27, 1982; *Ha'aretz*, Oct. 28, 1982 *(Israleft News Service*, Nov. 15). B. Michael, *Ha'aretz*, Nov. 7, 1982. *The Dawn (Al Fajr)*, Dec. 10, 1982.

139. *Boston Globe*, Nov. 27, 1982, under "Names and Faces," where brief odd items involving various personalities are presented; *Al Hamishmar*, Nov. 16, 1982; *Ha'aretz*, March 8, 1983.

140. Letter, *New York Review of Books*, March 17, 1977. See *TNCW*, p. 283, for references from the Israeli, British and Swedish press.

141. Aharon Dolav, *Ma'ariv*, Dec. 10, 1982; Ben-Tsion Tsitriv, *Haolam Haze*, Dec. 22, 1982; Yigal Bichkov, *Ha'aretz*, Dec. 9, 1982. There is a watered-down version in the English-language press: Aryeh Rubinstein, "Sleeping scandal," Yitzhak Oked, "Arab labourers' housing to be probed," *Jerusalem Post*, Dec. 26, 1982.

142. Ian Black, *New Statesman*, Sept. 29, 1978 (for further references from the Hebrew press, see Chomsky and Herman, *Political Economy of Human Rights*, vol. II, p. 360; *TNCW*, p. 283); Felicia Langer, Report of the Israeli League for Human and Civil Rights, Jan. 19, 1983 (Langer was the lawyer representing Barguti).

143. *Hotam*, Feb. 19, 1982.

144. "The Gangrene of the Occupation," *Al Hamishmar*, Feb. 19, 1982.

145. For details, see *Peace in the Middle East?*, pp. 196-7, and references cited, and Adnan Amad, ed., *Israeli League for Human and Civil Rights (The Shahak Papers)* (Palestine Research Center, Beirut, 1973); the latter also contains documentation provided by the League on a wide range of serious human rights violations under the Labor government. See also Shahak, *The Non-Jew in the Jewish State* (a collection of documents, mostly from the Israeli press; privately printed, Jerusalem, 1975), and much else. See *Pro-Arab Propaganda in America: Vehicles and Voices*, Anti-Defamation League of B'nai Brith (New York, January 1983). This book (including this entry) contain numerous falsehoods and slanders, as one would expect in the "enemies list" of an organization now largely dedicated to defamation. See p. 14.

146. Saul Bellow and Stephen Spender, to mention two examples; see *TNCW*, pp. 302, 454. Still worse, in my view, are those who give similar stories on the basis of alleged statements by unidentified "Arab friends," in the *New Republic* style sampled several times above, and again in the next chapter.

147. Fouzi el-Asmar, *To be an Arab in Israel* (Francis Pinter, London, 1975; Institute for Palestine Studies, Beirut, 1978); translated from the Hebrew original.

148. For discussion in a far more general context, see Edward Said, *Orientalism* (Pantheon, .New York, 1978). Also Kapeliouk, *Israel*, on some of the pronouncements of Israeli Orientalists.

149. Saul Bellow, *To Jerusalem and Back* (Viking, New York, 1976). See *TNCW*, chapter 10, for further samples from this classic contribution to a familiar 20th century genre.

150. All cited in a 1969 essay included in my *Peace in the Middle East?*, pp. 61, 55.

151. Editorial Notebook, *New York Times*, Nov. 16, 1982.

152. *New York Times Book Review*, May 16, 1982.

153. "Minus One Friend," *Kol Hair*, June 4, 1982.

154. For references and more on these matters, see my articles in *New Politics*, Winter 1975-6, 1978-9, and *TNCW*, pp. 285ff., 436-7.

155. Irving Howe, "The Campus Left and Israel." Howe cites no Tel Aviv street names, but he does illustrate by giving Minister Yigal Allon the wrong first name.

156. "Mainstream chauvinism," *Ha'aretz*, March 19, 1982; "This is not verbal violence," *Ha'aretz*, Feb. 13, 1983.

157. See *TNCW*, chapter 9 and Afterword for many examples.

158. Benjamin Beit-Hallahmi, "Israel and South Africa," *New Outlook*, March/April, 1983; *Hotam*, April 18, 1975, Oct. 1, 1982; *Davar*, Sept. 8, 1981; Charles Hoffman, "A monkey trial, local style," *Jerusalem Post*," March 22, 1983. This kind of material is common in religious circles. For example, the Habad organization of the Lubavitcher Rabbi, much respected here and in Israel, explains that "the body of a Jew is of an entirely different type than that of a non-Jew"; they are, in fact, "two entirely different species" *(Likutey Sihot*, 1965). For some background discussion, see Israel Shahak, *Khamsin*, nos. 8-9, 1981.

159. *Yediot Ahronot*, Sept. 14, 1982; a response to a query in a column called: "Soldiers ask."

160. Danny Rubinstein, "Religion against Nationalism," *Davar*, March 12, 1982.

161. Eliahu Salpeter, *Ha'aretz*, Nov. 4, 1982.

162. For examples from publications of the military Rabbinate, see *Peace in the Middle East?*, pp. 108-9; Shahak, *Begin and Co.*; Said, *Question of Palestine*, p. 91; *TNCW*, p. 305.

163. *Ha'aretz*, May 16, 1974.

164. *Al Hamishmar*, Jan. 4, 1978.

165. Rabbi Isaac J. Bernstein, *Dialogue* (New York), Winter 1980.

166. *Yediot Ahronot*, Dec. 9, 1977.

167. Menachem Barash, *Yediot Ahronot*, March 29, 1979.

168. Francis Cornu, *Le Monde*, July 2, 1982; Yoela Har-Shefi, *Al Hamishmar*, July 25, 1982.

169. Haim Handwerker, *Ha'aretz*, July 15, 1982. See chapters 5, 6, on the nature of such *hasbara*.

170. Menachem Barash, *Yediot Ahronot*, Dec. 20, 1974.

171. *Ma'ariv*, Oct. 3, 1982.

172. Cited by Danny Rubinstein, *Davar*, Oct. 8, 1982, in an article expressing concern over the intentions of the movement.

173. *Yediot Ahronot*, Oct. 4, 1982.

174. There was something similar in the wake of the 1967 victory; see *Peace in the Middle East?*, chapter 4, and particularly Kapeliouk's *Israel*, which investigates in detail how Israel's grandiose self-image contributed to the near disaster of 1973.

175. "Strength, Strength, Strength," *Yediot Ahronot*, Sept. 10, 1982.

176. Military correspondent Ze'ev Schiff, "War Crime in Beirut," *Ha'aretz*, Sept. 20, 1982. This article, commenting on the Beirut massacre, was widely quoted in the U.S. press, but not this remarkable statement by the Chief of Staff.

177. *Davar*, Sept. 3, 10, 1982. Also Aviezer Ravitzky, *Ma'ariv*, Oct. 21, 1982 (*Israeli Press Briefs*).

178. Benjamin Beit-Hallahmi, "The Consensus that Never Was," *Migvan*, Aug. 1982. An abbreviated version appears in the *New Outlook*, October 1982.

179. See *Peace in the Middle East?*, pp. 132f., 172ff., *TNCW*, 240f., for discussion of some examples from the left-liberal segment of the political spectrum.

180. Oz, "Has Israel Altered its Visions?"

181. For discussion of these matters, see Ian Lustick, *Arabs in the Jewish State* (Texas, Austin, 1980); *TNCW*, chapter 9 and Afterword, and sources cited there, including Jiryis, *The Arabs in Israel*. See also Elia T. Zureik, *The Palestinians in Israel* (Routledge & Kegan Paul, London, 1979).

182. *Jewish Post and Opinion*, March 30, 16, 1983. The family benefits legislation is currently before the courts.

183. *Yediot Ahronot*, April 20, 1979; *Ha'aretz*, July 28, 1977. Had the pretender succeeded in the ruse, he would have been a bigamist, but it is clear that "attempted bigamy" was not the major charge. In another case, "an inhabitant of the West Bank was convicted of pretending to be a Jew," also with the intent of marrying a Jewish woman *(Ma'ariv*, April 27, 1976). Note that the charge was not that he attempted to pass as an Israeli, but that he pretended to be a Jew.

184. For details on the events and the legal process, see Jiryis, *The Arabs in Israel*, chapter 6.

185. Professor Raphael Jospe, "Report on Visit to Karmiel as Scholar in Residence," report to the American Zionist Federation, April 1, 1982, circulated by the

Zionist Academic Council as part of its educational program in American universities.

186. For some facts concerning Karmiel, see *TNCW*, pp. 247f., and references cited.

187. Alfred Friendly, "Israel: Paradise Lost."

188. See *TNCW*, pp. 257f., for citations and further references. See also note 14, above.

189. See *TNCW*, p. 439, for some references. For the Arlosoroff memorandum, published in 1948 in the Labor Party journal *Jewish Frontier*, see Khalidi, ed., *From Haven to Conquest.*

190. For quotes from some contemporary documents, see *Peace in the Middle East?*, p. 88. See also Flapan, *Zionism and the Palestinians*, chapter 2.

191. Speech of 1937, cited in *New Outlook* (Tel Aviv), April 1977, from Ben-Gurion's *Memoirs.*

192. Menachem Begin, *The Revolt* (New York, Schuman, 1951, p. 335). See Shahak, *Begin And Co.*, for extensive documentation from official sources on the positions taken by Begin's terrorist army (Irgun Tsvai Leumi) and the political party (Herut) that was formed from it.

193. Report to the World Council of Poalei Zion (the forerunner of the Labor Party), Tel Aviv, 1938; cited by Israel Shahak, *J. of Palestine Studies*, Spring 1981.

194. Flapan, *Zionism and the Palestinians*, pp. 265-6.

195. David Ben-Gurion, *My Talks with Arab Leaders* (Third Press, New York, 1973, pp. 27, 52), reporting talks of 1934 and 1936 with Musa Alami and George Antonius.

196. Speech of Oct. 13, 1936, Ben-Gurion, *Memoirs*, vol. 3, 1936, p. 467 (Hebrew).

197. Sykes, *Crossroads to Israel*, pp. 174-5.

198. Arlosoroff memorandum; see note 189.

199. Michael Bar-Zohar, *Ben-Gurion: A Biography* (Delacorte, New York, 1978, pp. 91-2, 166, 186-7, 249-50). All emphases in original.

200. David Krivine, "The Palestinian puzzle," *Jerusalem Post*, Feb. 20, 1981.

201. David Krivine, letter, *Economist*, July 10, 1982.

202. "Liberated Territory No. 20," *Ha'aretz*, June 13, 1982, advertisement.

203. Lucas, *Modern History of Israel*, p. 437. Though his analogy is in part correct, I do not think he is correct in suggesting that it was the resort to terror—which was real enough—that established this image for the Zionist movement.

204. Nahum Barnea and Danny Rubinstein, *Davar*, March 19, 1982.

205. *Al Hamishmar*, March 3, 1978; *Jerusalem Post*, Feb. 28, 1978 (a somewhat sanitized version).

206. *Toldot Hahaganah*, vol II (Ma'arachot, pp. 251f.); see *TNCW*, pp. 461-2; David Pryce-Jones, *New Republic*, Year-end Issue, 1982. See p. 97.

207. For a small sample, see *TNCW*, pp. 463f. and references cited, among them the rather admiring account of Irgun-LEHI atrocities by J. Bowyer-Bell *(Terror out of Zion*, St. Martin's, New York, 1977). See also the books by Hirst, Sykes, and others cited earlier, and for the later years, also Rokach, *Israel's Sacred Terrorism*. Recall Flapan's comment on the Irgun model for PLO terrorism, many decades later, cited above, p. 74.

208. See Shahak, *Begin And Co.*, for translations from the Hebrew original.

209. *Jerusalem Post*, Feb. 15, 1982. See chapter 2, note 36 and text.

210. Bar-Zohar, *Ben-Gurion*, pp. 180-1.

211. Rokach, *Israel's Sacred Terrorism*. See p. 20.

212. Cited by Nahum Barnea, *Davar*, April 9, 1982.

213. See *TNCW*, p. 465, for references.

214. *The Dawn (Al Fajr)*, Jerusalem, Sept. 24, Oct. 1, 1982.

215. *Davar*, April 9, 1982, the anniversary of the massacre.

5

Peace for Galilee

Since 1949, Israel has sought to remove the displaced Palestinian refugees from the border areas and to destroy their emerging political and military structures. The 1982 invasion of Lebanon was a further stage in these efforts. Their general character over the years was indicated by Chief of Staff Mordechai Gur in an interview in the Israeli press after the 1978 invasion of Lebanon, which drove another quarter-million Arabs from their homes with heavy casualties, in retaliation for a PLO terrorist attack in Israel. Gur observed that "For 30 years, from the War of Independence [which Palestinians call "the War of Conquest"] until today, we have been fighting against a population that lives in villages and cities," noting such incidents as the bombing of the Jordanian city of Irbid, the clearing of all inhabitants from the Jordan valley by bombing, driving a million and a half civilians from the Suez Canal area during the 1970 "war of attrition," and other examples, all undertaken in alleged retaliation against Arab attacks. His remarks were accurately summarized by the noted Israeli military analyst Ze'ev Schiff:

> In South Lebanon we struck the civilian population con-
> sciously, because they deserved it...the importance of Gur's
> remarks is the admission that the Israeli Army has always
> struck civilian populations, purposely and consciously...the
> Army, he said, has never distinguished civilian [from military]
> targets...[but] purposely attacked civilian targets even when
> Israeli settlements had not been struck.[1]

These remarks, in 1978, apply with considerable accuracy to the Lebanon invasion four years later, and with still more force.*

1   The Rational Basis for Attacking the Civilian Population

The motive for Israel's attacks against civilian populations to the north and east was dual: to disperse the Palestinian refugees, and to embitter relations between them and the local population in the areas to which they had been driven. As explained by Labor Party dove Abba Eban: "there was a rational prospect, ultimately fulfilled, that affected populations would exert pressure for the cessation of hostilities." Eban was writing in condemnation of an article by Prime Minister Begin which reviewed attacks against civilians under the Labor government,† presenting a picture, according to Eban, "of an Israel wantonly inflicting every possible measure of death and anguish on civilian populations in a mood reminiscent of regimes which neither Mr. Begin nor I would dare to mention by name."[2] Eban does not contest the facts that Begin reviewed, but criticizes him for stating them, thus contributing to Arab propaganda. He also does not mention that his own doctrine, just quoted, represented the standard practice of the regimes he does not "dare to mention by name." Recent events in Lebanon again confirm Eban's judgment about the "rational prospect."

On the current scene, it is not only in Lebanon (earlier, Jordan) that Eban's "rational prospect" has met with a certain success. A "veteran Western observer," commenting on the tactics of the Afghan resistance, states that "They'll come through a village, expect people with hardly any food themselves to feed them, then they'll use the village—with or without permission—as a staging point to attack a passing Russian patrol. After

---

* The military doctrine of attacking defenseless civilians derives from David Ben-Gurion, who was quite explicit about it, though not in public of course. In a January 1, 1948 entry in his Independence War Diary, he writes:

> There is no question as to whether a reaction is necessary or not. The question is only time and place. Blowing up a house is not enough. What is necessary is cruel and strong reactions. We need precision in time, place and casualties. If we know the family—[we must] strike mercilessly, women and children included. Otherwise the reaction is inefficient. At the place of action there is no need to distinguish between guilty and innocent. Where there was no attack— we should not strike.

The latter qualification was not observed, frequently, in the pre-state period and increasingly in later years (as, for example, at Qibya). Excerpts from these diaries, to be published, appear in *Yediot Ahronot*, April 17, 1983, the independence day edition.

---

† Begin's review of atrocities under Labor Party rule was in response to Labor criticism of the recent bombing of Lebanon, which left hundreds dead. For further quotes and discussion, see Herman, *The Real Terror Network*, pp. 76f.

the guerrillas leave, the Russians come back and pulverize the area in retaliation." It is partly for this reason, he alleges, that "A small but growing number of Afghans...have chosen the [Russian-established] militia as the only alternative to starvation and to more death at the hands of the Russians."[3]

In short, the fulfilment of Eban's "rational prospect," as in Lebanon.

Other similarities have been noted. In Pakistan, local political activists describe the "recent Israeli incursion into Lebanon...as an indication of what could happen if the [Afghan] refugees and resistance assume a permanent presence in Pakistan, a sort of Asian version of the Palestinian problem." Local residents speak of the Afghan guerrilla group that is favored by the Pakistani government "as troublemakers with licence to interfere in provincial politics," a fact that is "keenly exploited by local political activists to stir up fear and animosity among their followers towards Afghans in general." Bombing of refugee concentrations in Pakistan (what the Russians, perhaps, call "cleaning out nests of terrorists") surely contributes to these efforts.[4] Those acquainted with the recent history of Lebanon will recognize the pattern. With many local variations, it is, in general, a familiar story. Military tactics in the course of U.S. aggression in Indochina (or to keep to the Party Line, "the defense of South Vietnam") are another case.

2   The Northern Border of Greater Israel

With regard to Lebanon, Israel is now realizing plans that have early antecedents in Zionist thinking. It had long been hoped that Israel's boundaries would ultimately extend to the Litani River in southern Lebanon, one part of Ben-Gurion's "vision" (see p. 161). In 1932, a Jewish Agency emissary visited Beirut to discuss "a joint company for using southern Lebanon's Litani River for electricity and irrigation." The Zionists regarded the Christian Maronites as a natural ally and sought to form "a symbiotic alliance" with them against the "common enemy: Islamic-oriented Arab nationalism." The majority of the Maronites, however, "chose the alternative of peace with the Muslims," establishing the 1943 National Pact which "succeeded in preserving Christian predominance and prosperity for three decades." They recognized that "the only alternative to a pact with Lebanese Muslims was civil war and since the resulting agreement was quite satisfactory for Christian interests, this posed little temptation"—in the mid-40s. Only 30 years later "did the main Maronite parties accept alliance with Israel."[5] By then, years of communal strife resulting largely from the inequities suffered by the Muslim majority and later exacerbated by the Palestine presence (siding with the Muslims) had led to the breakdown of the National Pact and a vicious civil war, with Syrian and Israeli participation.

Ten days after the establishment of the State of Israel in May 1948, Ben-Gurion presented his General Staff with his plan to establish a Christian state north of the Litani river with which Israel would form an alliance (see pp. 162-3). In the mid-1950s, plans were considered at the highest level to dismember Lebanon, establishing a Christian state with Israel annexing the territory south of the Litani. Chief of Staff Moshe Dayan felt that this could be achieved by finding "an officer, even just a Major," who could be bribed or won over and would then "agree to declare himself the savior of the Maronite population," after which Israel would invade and realize its plans.[6] These plans had to be put in abeyance from 1956, when Israel was allied with France, which saw itself as "the protector of Lebanon." But they were taken up again in the 1970s and were partially realized with the establishment of Major Saad Haddad's "independent state" in southern Lebanon in 1979, after the 1978 Israeli invasion, in territory handed over to him by the Israeli army in defiance of the United Nations after Haddad had deserted from the Lebanese army.

3   The Background in Lebanon

3.1   The PLO and the Civil War

In 1970, many Palestinians were driven from Jordan after a bloody conflict in which thousands were killed by King Hussein's forces. In Lebanon, they joined hundreds of thousands of refugees from the 1948 war. The PLO at first attempted to keep clear of Lebanon's internal strife. Furthermore, after vicious terrorist attacks in Israel in the early 1970s, PLO tactics began to change. John Cooley observes that "During 1974 [and in fact, thereafter] there was a strong tendency by Arafat's PLO leadership, al-Fatah, to curb cross-border activity," though this did not prevent "'wildcat' actions" by other groups in the PLO.[7] The PLO was, however, drawn into the civil war, initially, by an April 1975 Phalange attack on a bus killing 27 Palestinians and Lebanese who were travelling to Tel al-Zaatar from the Sabra and Shatila camps—a grim portent. At first, the PLO role was largely limited to arming some Muslim and leftist groups and helping defend Muslim districts that were under Christian (largely Maronite Phalange) attack. The PLO took a more active role in January 1976, when Christian militias blockaded Palestinian camps. "By this time," Cooley writes, "such events as 'Black Saturday' on December 6, 1975, when over 200 Muslim hostages were taken and murdered by the Phalange in reprisals for murders of four Phalangist militiamen, and a new leftist offensive against the fortified [Christian] hotels, had consummated the partition of Beirut and Lebanon as a whole into two well-defined zones: the eastern Christian and the western, 'Islamo-Progressivist' or leftist sector." (The alliances were actually fairly complex, but I will keep to the oversimplified familiar terms, noting here that they are a bit misleading.) The Muslim Karantina slum was overrun by Christian forces with large numbers massacred, then "burned and razed . . . with bulldozers." The Christian (Chamounist) town of Damour was then taken by "the leftist-Palestinian coalition and . . . occupied, looted, and destroyed." The propaganda of Israel and its American supporters regularly refers to the last of these atrocities as proof that the PLO was conducting a murderous war against the Lebanese; what preceded is regularly omitted.

3.2   Syria and Israel in Lebanon

Syria entered the war in support of the Christians against the leftist-Palestinian coalition, an act that Kissinger called "constructive" and that was tacitly backed by Israel, though Israel insisted that the Syrian army remain north of the Litani. By July 1976, a Syrian-led "peace-keeping force" had intervened under an Arab League mandate, still in support of the Christians. In August, the Tel al-Zaatar Palestinian camp was overrun after a long siege. Thousands were massacred by Christian forces using Israeli arms, armored personnel carriers and tanks, "still with Israeli Defense Forces markings in Hebrew," Cooley writes, adding that "By early summer considerable transfers of tanks, vehicles, artillery, and other military equipment had been made by Israel to the rightists [Maronites]." Israeli military forces now operated regularly in southern Lebanon to establish rightist control. Syria launched another major offensive against the leftist-Palestinian alliance in September. By October 1976, the "peace-keeping forces," largely Syrian, numbered 30,000.

Subsequently, Syria turned against the Christian right. The Maronite Phalange under Bashir Gemayel established its dominance within the Christian-right alliance by murdering opposition elements. The PLO continued to engage in murderous conflict with Israeli-supported Christian elements and, later, with local Muslim groups in the south, while frequently acting to protect Muslim elements from Christian massacres. Israel meanwhile conducted regular military attacks in Lebanon, including bombing and shelling of refugee camps, bombardment of coastal cities by gunboats, terrorist raids in Beirut and elsewhere, the outright invasion of 1978, and finally the occupation of large parts of Lebanon in the summer of 1982. See also p. 77.

Israeli sources give further information about early Israeli-Maronite contacts. In *Hotam* (Mapam), Chaim Margalit reports that in February 1976 a boat with Maronite leaders was received secretly in Haifa. He quotes Amos Eran, then General Manager of the office of Prime Minister Yitzhak Rabin of the Labor Party, who explains further that the Maronites were divided into a group that wanted to undertake joint actions with Israel and those who saw Lebanon as part of the Arab world. The Rabin government supported the former group, the Phalangists and

Chamounists. The early contacts were at a low level and were kept secret, though they were widely known; and at the time, Eran reports, "the Americans were not in the picture." A "qualitative change" took place when the Begin government took power—in fact, other evidence suggests, after Sharon became Defense Minister in July 1981. The "exploitative character" of the Maronites was well-known, Margalit continues, "just as we knew that they would not hesitate to arrange provocations in order to bring Israel in to fight for them." He claims that the conflict with the Syrians over the air defense missiles in the Bekaa valley "began with a provocation of the Phalange soldiers," a view corroborated by other sources (see chapter 6, section 2.2). Eran asserts that Bashir Gemayel, who was elected President in August 1982 under Israeli guns and later assassinated, was no friend of Israel: "If Bashir Gemayel were alive and President of Lebanon, he would be no better [meaning, no more friendly to Israel] than his brother Amin [who was elected President after the assassination]. Those who knew him are ready to say that it is reasonable to assume that he would have been even worse than his brother with regard to Israel and its requests," a matter to which we return.[8]

3.3   The Population under the PLO and the Phalange

As Israeli forces conquered southern Lebanon in 1982, many stories began to circulate about the violence and terrorism of PLO rule (in contrast, little was said about the treatment of Palestinians in areas controlled by Israeli-backed Christian forces, but then, there is little to say, since those who were not killed outright were simply expelled; the treatment of Muslims by these forces has also received little notice, and again, the same comment holds). A number of journalists attempted to verify these reports. A respected Israeli Arab journalist, Attallah Mansour (himself a Maronite), travelled through the territories that had been under PLO and Lebanese Muslim control. He observes that of all the forces in Lebanon, only the Maronite Phalange and the extremist Christian "Guards of the Cedars," also allied with Israel, practiced policies based on communal exclusivism, simply removing or destroying their local enemies. "In the left-Muslim-Palestinian camp there were communal militias, but most of these organizations profess a universalist Arab, Lebanese, or socialist ideology," and their practice reflected the fact: Christian communities are found throughout the area under their control, in contrast to the Phalangists, "who drove out of the areas they controlled in Beirut, Junieh, and other areas almost all the non-Christian population." The well-known Muslim atrocities (Damour, Aishiye) "apparently were revenge for similar actions carried out by 'Christians' in Karantina, Tel al-Zaatar, and in the Beirut area and Khiyam (near [Israeli] Metullah)." In contrast, throughout the areas held by the Muslim-Palestinian forces there are "lively Christian communities" of various sects, as Mansour found in a tour through the area, including Christian cities and towns and isolated villages deprived of any Phalange protection. He heard stories of oppression and occasional atrocities—"the Christians were not fortunate at all, but it is doubtful that many people were fortunate in Lebanon from 1975 apart from murderers and robbers." A relative he met in a Christian town near Sidon (under Muslim-Palestinian control) told him that he had "read too many newspapers and believed the politicians." Mansour's general conclusion was that life for the Christians in these areas was no bed of roses, but that it went on in relative peace, in sharp contrast to what happened in the areas dominated by the murderous Israeli-backed Christian forces.[9] Note the unusual, perhaps unique credibility of Mansour's account, given his reputation, background, and access to sources.

Two *Jerusalem Post* reporters also toured south Lebanon to investigate the stories of PLO terror and atrocities. Despite considerable effort, they "could find little or no substantive proof for many of the atrocity stories making the rounds," and eventually concluded that they were "exaggerated." A close reading of their discoveries suggests that this may be an understatement, particularly when we correct for the extreme bias that they barely attempt to hide. Thus they say that in Tel al-Zaatar "many Palestinians were *reportedly* killed by the Christian forces"—my emphasis— and they open their article by saying that life in southern Lebanon was "so unpleasant that a large part of its population fled north to escape the PLO," later giving evidence that the population fled massive Israeli attacks; and so on, throughout.

In the town of Hasbaya, they found that "the PLO appears to have behaved more or less correctly with the people"; they were also told that 49 people were killed there by Israeli shelling though the PLO "never came closer than two kilometers" except for "brief shopping forays," and "fear of the IDF was, the notables imply, far greater among Hasbayans than their fear of the PLO," an observation from which they draw no conclusions with regard to terrorism. In other towns and villages they found that officials and others knew "nothing" about allegations of PLO atrocities or misbehavior. They visited Nabatiye, allegedly one of the areas of the worst PLO atrocities. The police chief there told them of "about 10 cases of disappearance," though he was unable to provide any details. As for the 50,000 people who fled from this town of 60,000, they fled "mostly because of fear of the [Israeli] shelling," the police chief told them (200 were killed by Israeli attacks, including a "reprisal," which destroyed much of the Palestine refugee camp after the terrorist raid in Ma'alot). He also denied that there had been any cases of rape or extortion, though the PLO took goods from shops whose owners had fled. Others confirmed this impression, insisting that they knew of no cases of murder or rape, including residents of Ansar, to which they were specifically directed by an IDF colonel who heard that they were "investigating PLO rule and atrocities." Here, the only story they elicited was of the killing of five local inhabitants who had "opposed the PLO, fought against them, with arms," during or after a firefight, according to residents. They visited the Greek Orthodox Archbishop of Tyre, Georges Haddad, to ask him about life under the PLO, but he "prefers to expatiate on the problem of the thousands detained by the IDF in southern Lebanon," and when asked about "PLO anarchy or rule in Tyre" he responded by speaking of "IDF destruction of buildings in his city." Finally, under repeated prodding, he said ("exasperated") that there were some atrocities by "extremist" elements, specifically, by the Syrian-backed Sa'iqa in revenge for the Phalangist massacre in Tel al-Zaatar, where thousands were murdered. Also, "The PLO was inclined to persecute and strike out against persons who disagreed with or resisted them, or were identified as agents of Major Sa'ad Haddad or Israel." The general impression these two Israeli reporters received was that the PLO were often oppressive, but that atrocities were rare. In southern Lebanon, fear was "never far below the surface— fear of the PLO's arbitrary law of the gun and, in several cases, the even greater fear of Israeli air strikes and artillery barrages."[10]

After what is officially termed their "liberation" from PLO terror, the inhabitants of Hasbaya—where the PLO had behaved correctly and 49 people were killed by IDF shelling—apparently began to raise some problems for their liberators. In November 1982, the IDF banned all political activity in Hasbaya and other villages of the region "after arms caches were discovered in the offices of these parties in the town of Hasbaya." The parties banned were "the pro-Syrian party, the pro-Iraqi party, the Communist Party, and the party of Walid Jumblatt" (the Druze leader whose father, assassinated in 1977, had headed the now disbanded Muslim-Palestinian Lebanese National Front), a party affiliated with the strongly pro-Israel Socialist International. The Israeli commander also ordered that pictures of party leaders be removed from the walls of houses. The day after these reports appeared, the IDF denied them, alleging that the ban was instituted by Major Haddad, the Israeli client who was given jurisdiction over this area after the Israeli conquest; a distinction without a difference.[11]

3.4   Israeli Military Operations in Lebanon in the 1970s

Israel's attacks in Lebanon over the years were generally described in the U.S. as retaliation against PLO terrorism. As usual, the categories of "terrorism" and "reprisal" are more ideological than descriptive. One might, for example, raise the question of what the Palestinians were doing in Lebanon in the first place; they did not move there because they liked the scenery. The comparable question would not be regarded as irrelevant in the case of some official enemy conducting "retaliatory" or "preemptive" strikes against "terrorism," say, attacks by the Russian-sponsored Afghan army against Afghan refugees in Pakistan (see note 4). Other questions also arise. For example, two days before the PLO terrorist attack in Ma'alot in May 1974, where 20 teen-age Israeli hostages from a paramilitary youth group *(Gadna)* were killed during an attempt to rescue the hostages after Israel had rejected negotiation efforts (the terrorist unit, from Hawatmeh's Democratic Front, had previously killed five other Israelis, including 2 Arabs), an Israeli air attack on the village of El-Kfeir in Lebanon killed four civilians. The PLO raid is (properly) described here as terrorism, but not the Israeli air attack—which, in fact, is known (though barely known) here only because it happened to be the native village of the parents of U.S. Senator James Abourezk. According to Edward Said, the Ma'alot attack was "preceded by weeks of sustained Israeli napalm bombing of Palestinian refugee camps in southern Lebanon" with over 200 killed.[12] It might also be noted that the taking of hostages in order to exchange them for prisoners, as at Ma'alot, is not without precedent. Recall the Israeli hijacking of a civilian airliner, 20 years earlier, with the same intent (see p. 77).

In the mid-1970s, as the PLO began to turn away from cross-border terrorist raids and the Labor government intensified its attacks, Israel shifted the grounds from "retaliation" to "prevention." Thus, on December 2, 1975, 30 Israeli warplanes bombed and strafed Palestinian refugee camps and nearby villages, killing 57 people (Lebanese military communiqué; Palestinian press service). "Israeli officials stressed that the purpose of the action had been preventive, not punitive." Two days earlier, over Israel's angry objections, the UN Security Council had "paved the way for participation by the Palestine Liberation Organization in talks on the over-all Middle East situation . . ."—namely, in the session devoted to the Arab initiative for a full-scale peaceful two-state settlement "prepared" by the PLO (according to Israel's UN representative) and vetoed by the U.S.[13] One might conjecture that the "preventive" strikes in fact constituted Israel's retaliation against the UN Security Council. Israel's right to undertake such "preventive" massacres was rarely questioned here.

In fact, Israeli attacks in Lebanon were covered only sporadically in the press, and then often in side comment, in part, perhaps, because of the difficulties faced by journalists attempting to travel in southern Lebanon, in part from indifference. The story of these operations has yet to be told. They did receive occasional notice.[14] *Newsweek* reported in 1970 that "By conservative estimate, the escalating border war has already forced out one-fifth of the 150,000 Lebanese Moslems in the area, and the rest live gripped in a steady terror." In the words of one Christian villager, the population is "caught in the middle" between the Palestinians, who "want back their land," and the Israelis, who "don't want to give it up." "Both are determined to fight," an accurate statement as of 1970.[15]

After a visit to Lebanon in 1974, correspondent Philip Bowring wrote:

Although foreigners feel safe enough from the raids of the
Israelis in central Beirut, if they take the trouble to leave the
tourist haunts they will see why the locals live with fear. The
Lebanese view is that the raids are less an effort to satisfy Israeli
domestic blood lusts than an attempt to blow Lebanon's fragile
political unity apart, setting Christians and Muslims against
each other and the Palestinians against everyone. It could
happen.[16]

It did happen, in accord with the "rational prospect" explained by Abba
Eban, but Americans, who were funding the operation, rarely "took the
trouble" to see.

That Israel has (again rationally) been intent on fostering internal
strife in Lebanon has also been argued, for example, by Walid Khalidi,
who suggests that Israeli initiatives leading to the intensive Israeli bombardment of November 1977 and the 1978 invasion may have been in part
motivated by the desire to disrupt a recent agreement between the Lebanese government, Syria and the PLO (the Shtaura accord), which
imposed a freeze on Palestinian cross-border operations and offered some
possibility for a settlement of the civil conflict. Shortly after the surrender
of heavy armaments by the PLO in the first phase of the accord, the
Israeli-controlled Haddad militia launched an offensive with Israeli military support, disrupting the government's plans to deploy the Lebanese
army in the south. Edward Mortimer suggests that similar concerns may
have influenced the timing of the 1982 invasion, about which, more below.
Discussing Israel's policies after the 1982 invasion, David Hirst concludes:

Israel's policy, in so far as it has a coherent one, appears to be to
divide and rule, to seize, opportunistically, on all available
means of reinforcing military control with political manipulation, to bring rival communities into collision with each other
and into dependence on itself.[17]

A close look at the facts tends to lend credibility to these conclusions, as
we shall see in the next chapter.

One of the rare articles on the bombing of Lebanon in the early 1970s
was written by Judith Coburn, after an investigation of several months.
One Christian Arab village was "a near ghost town" after five straight
days of bombing in May 1974 (the same month as the Ma'alot terrorist
action, which in contrast to this one, is very well-known). She found
scores of villages like it, bombed since 1968 and attacked "almost daily in
recent months . . . by airplane, artillery, tanks and gunboats," and invaded
by Israeli commandos who blow up houses, kill villagers, and take prisoners. "The Israelis are using the full range of sophisticated savagery known
to our own military in Indochina: shells, bombs, phosphorous, incendiary
bombs, CBUs and napalm," much of it supplied by the U.S. The Lebanese

government says that 301 Lebanese civilians have been killed; diplomats in Beirut and UN officials estimate 3500 killed in Lebanon, Syria and Jordan in Israeli raids. There are no figures for Palestinian civilians, "but observers estimate they must be at least twice as high as for the Lebanese." Palestinian towns and camps have been almost levelled. "Most Lebanese and some diplomats in Beirut believe that the Israelis are pursuing a 'scorched earth' policy in southern Lebanon designed to drive all population from the area and establish a DMZ," reporting burning of crops, destruction of olive groves, and so on. "The bombing has become so routine that it goes largely unreported in the American press"[18]—though Palestinian terror attacks were always front-page news and (again, properly) elicited outraged condemnation.* If the figures cited are correct, then by 1975 Israel had killed about 10 times as many Palestinians and Lebanese in attacks on Lebanon as the total number of Israelis killed in the course of cross-border Palestinian attacks through 1982. See p. 74.

London Guardian correspondent Irene Beeson reports that "150 or more towns and villages in South Lebanon . . . have been repeatedly savaged by the Israeli armed forces since 1968." She describes the history of the village of Khiyam, bombed from 1968. By the time Israel invaded ten years later, only 32 of its 30,000 inhabitants remained. "They were massacred in cold blood" by the Haddad forces that Israel had established in the south.[19] After the Beirut massacres in September 1982, the story of Khiyam was recalled in the Israeli press. Moshe Hazani wrote that "we knew about the Christian atrocities of 1978—and we were silent." "The silence fell on other villages, where there were events similar [to those of Khiyam], and perhaps still more terrible. . ." "Our hands spilled this blood," he writes, adding that the Beirut massacres could have been no surprise to the IDF, which knew the history well.[20]

Those who are paying the bills have yet to show similar honesty. Note that a decade of bombardment that drove out much of the population still goes unmentioned.

Before the Lebanese army disintegrated in 1976, it had given a figure of 1.4 Israeli violations of Lebanese territory per day from 1968-74, with 17 per day in 1975, when the tally ended. By October 1977 it was estimated that the total number of refugees from the south (mostly impoverished Shiite Lebanese Muslims) had reached 300,000.[21] Many were brutally expelled from their slum dwellings in West Beirut after the conquering Israeli army (or as some prefer, "their liberators") had handed control over to the Phalange; see chapter 6, section 7.3.

In November 1977 an Israeli-initiated exchange of fire caused several casualties on each side, and finally Israeli bombing "in which some 70 people, nearly all Lebanese, were killed."[22] As noted earlier, the fear of a

---

* American correspondents in Beirut report privately that the New York office of a major television network suppressed a 1975 documentary on Israeli military actions in southern Lebanon.

still greater war at this time may well have been one of the factors that impelled Sadat to offer to visit Jerusalem. In March 1978, Israel invaded Lebanon in retaliation for a terrorist attack by PLO guerrillas, who reached Israel by sea from near Beirut, leading to the death of 34 Israelis in an exchange of fire on a coastal road. The invasion was violent and destructive, with many areas left in ruins, some 250,000 refugees, and 2000 dead.[23] The raiders had come from a point well north of the area invaded by Israel; the border had been relatively quiet since the November 1977 interchange initiated by Israel.

In 1979, heavy Israeli bombardment continued, generally ignored in the U.S., though some of the worst atrocities were reported. John Cooley reports: "Despairing over apparent Western indifference to the ongoing carnage in Lebanon, Lebanese Prime Minister Selim al-Hoss has compiled a list of Lebanese men, women, and children killed or wounded in Israeli attacks inside Lebanon since last April," to be dispatched to Washington by the U.S. Embassy. The purpose was to "show the magnitude of purely Lebanese casualties—nearly 100 killed and wounded in one day's air raids last April alone."[24] The Lebanese government list is reported to have detailed "the names, ages and occupations of 969 Lebanese civilians killed and 224 wounded by Israeli air strikes and shelling."[25] Cooley reports further that the Lebanese Prime Minister, "a mild-mannered man educated in the United States, reacted angrily to a U.S. State Department statement that the American administration did not know whether U.S.-made planes had bombed Lebanon recently," asking: "Does the American spokesman expect to convince us that Israel's military capability, being used to pound populated areas mercilessly and daily, is not provided by the United States, despite all the American economic and military aid Israel is receiving?" Eyewitnesses "report homes, farms, livestock, automobiles, and boats in the port of Tyre destroyed" in the latest fighting, which included firing by U.S.-supplied heavy artillery from inside Israel and from inside Major Haddad's southern Lebanese enclave, Cooley continues.

Israeli bombardment was regarded as so ordinary and unremarkable that it was sometimes merely noted in passing, as when Pranay Gupte mentioned in a *New York Times* article on Lebanon that Israeli warships "lobbed shells into the port city of Tyre, a Palestinian center"[26]— incidentally, a Lebanese city; the "Palestinian center" was in Rashidiyeh, south of Tyre. All of this designed to achieve Eban's "rational prospect." One suspects that regular Palestinian bombardment of Israeli cities and towns might have been treated somewhat less casually, and might even have been regularly reported, perhaps even eliciting editorial comment, perhaps even criticism. One may recall, at this point, the common complaint by some Israeli commentators and many supporters of Israel here, several already quoted, that Israel's "imperfections" are scrutinized under a magnifying glass by the Western media, while PLO atrocities are ignored.

4 From July 1981

4.1 The July Bombardments and the Habib Cease-Fire

In July 1981, Israeli planes once again initiated hostilities after a period of peace, striking Palestinian targets in southern Lebanon. Palestinian retaliation elicited extensive Israeli bombing, ultimately the terror attacks of July 17-8 on Beirut and other civilian targets leaving hundreds dead. After Philip Habib's negotiations on behalf of the U.S. government, a cease-fire was put into effect, but it was clear that "sooner or later, Israel will probably find a pretext for another invasion of Lebanon in an effort to administer the coup de grace to the PLO and to disperse the refugees once again."[27] The subsequent history is illuminating.

4.2 The Occupied Territories

A series of important events took place from summer 1981 to the Israeli invasion a year later. Menachem Begin was re-elected and appointed as his Defense Minister General Ariel Sharon, who at once began to plan for the invasion, as he later explained. In November, a new and far harsher regime was instituted in the West Bank and Gaza, under the direction of Sharon and Menachem Milson, the new Civilian Administrator. The shift to "civilian administration" was widely understood as a move towards a form of annexation. In December and January, the Golan Heights were in effect annexed to Israel.

4.3 The Sinai Withdrawal

In April 1982, Israel completed the withdrawal from the Sinai as arranged at Camp David, evacuating the town of Yamit in northeastern Sinai with a "national trauma" that appears to have been largely staged for a domestic and American audience.[28] Amnon Kapeliouk described the Yamit evacuation as "one of the largest brain-washing operations conducted by the government in order to convince the Israeli people that they have suffered a 'national trauma the effect of which will be felt for generations'" and which will create "a national consensus opposed to similar withdrawals in the remaining occupied territories." He quotes General Chaim Erez, commander of the Yamit evacuation, who says that "Everything was planned and agreed from the beginning" with the settlers who were to offer a show of resistance. Thus, Kapeliouk writes, "While the hospitals of the West Bank were full of scores of Palestinian victims of 'trigger happy' Israeli soldiers, a miracle occurred in Yamit: no demonstrators required even first-aid attention."[29]

Meanwhile, the other intended audience here was treated to heart-rending accounts of Jewish settlers, many of them recent immigrants from the U.S. and USSR, forced to leave their homes. As discussed in the preceding chapter (see pp. 105-7), the former Arab settlers had been displaced by force and violence not long before with little notice here, driven into the desert, their houses, mosques, schools, cemeteries, crops, orchards destroyed. Most then performed menial labor for the new settlers on their former lands. The *New York Times* reported that "local Arab labor is cheap," not troubling to explain why. Some lived only a few hundred yards away, but they were not even provided with water from the pumping stations built for the modern town of Yamit, one of the proud achievements of the Labor Party.[30] This was only one phase in the expulsion of the Bedouin from their lands in Israel and across the borders, beginning in 1950, when some 3500 were expelled from the demilitarized zones with air and ground attacks.[31]

The Bedouin had anticipated that after the completion of the Sinai evacuation, they would be able to move into the town of Yamit that had been constructed on the lands from which they had been driven. This was not to be, however. Yamit and the other Jewish settlements in the area were destroyed by the departing Israeli forces, leaving what Uri Avneri called a "monument commemorating the Israeli vandal."[32] David Shaham describes how Israel expelled the 6000 Bedouin of the area, destroying everything they had built and cultivated, and then introduced 2000 Jewish settlers with billions of dollars of investment (paid for by the usual generous donor). He then adds:

> Now again we have uprooted trees, demolished the buildings, pulled out the water pipes, torn down electricity lines and introduced the desert. In the long run we will have only been an episode. Now the Bedouins will come back, they will dig water holes, build shacks and live in them, plant trees, grow vegetables— the area will truly return to what it was before we came in. But where shall we take our shame?[33]

This is in fact standard Israeli practice. Recall the destruction of Kuneitra a few years earlier when the Israeli army withdrew from parts of the Golan Heights. Or 1956, when Israel was compelled to withdraw from the Sinai after its attack on Egypt in collusion with France and Britain and Israeli forces "systematically destroyed all surfaced roads, railway tracks and telephone lines" and destroyed "all buildings in the tiny villages of Abu Ageila and El Quseima," prompting UN Commander General Burns to comment: "God had scorched the Sinai earth, and His chosen people removed whatever stood above it."[34]

The Sinai was evacuated in April, as scheduled. Egypt and Israel now enjoyed more or less normal arrangements, and, crucially, Egyptian military forces were excluded from the Arab-Israeli conflict, so that Israel could concentrate its attention (and its military forces) on the occupied territories and the northern border.

4.4   Israeli Provocations and the U.S. Response

Through early 1982 Israel carried out a series of provocative actions in southern Lebanon, including the sinking of Lebanese fishing boats in Lebanese territorial waters,* "training exercises" in southern Lebanon with extensive gunfire by the Haddad forces (in effect, part of the Israeli army), military maneuvers in southern Lebanon that were described by the UN as "intensive, excessive, and provocative," repeated deployment of military forces at potential invasion routes, and—from August 1981 to May 1982—2125 violations of Lebanese airspace and 652 violations of Lebanese territorial waters.[35] None of these actions succeeded in eliciting a PLO "provocation" that could serve as a pretext for the planned invasion. In February, *Time* reported, an Israeli "assault was narrowly averted. . .though perhaps not for long." In January, Defense Minister Sharon had met with the commander of the Christian Phalange forces, Bashir Gemayel, in an Israeli gunboat off the Lebanese coast, to plan an invasion "that would bring Israeli forces as far north as the edge of Beirut International Airport,"[36] a precise description of the operation launched in early June. The Israeli and international media carried many other reports of the impending invasion,† but the PLO was uncooperative and supplied no suitable pretext.

On April 21 Israel broke the nine-month truce with a still more provocative action, bombing alleged PLO centers in coastal areas south of Beirut. This time there had been a PLO "terrorist act": an Israeli soldier had been killed when his military jeep struck a land mine—in southern Lebanon! There was still no PLO response. Israel's position that its bombing was retaliatory was accepted in the U.S. by the "pro-PLO" and "anti-Israel" press. The *Washington Post*, for example, responded to these events as follows:

So this is not the moment for sermons to Israel. It is a moment

---

* *AJME News* (Beirut, April 1982) cites a report of the rightist "Voice of Lebanon" radio on March 9 that a Lebanese freighter was dynamited by Israeli frogmen at Tyre (there is a picture of the damaged ship).

---

† Ze'ev Schiff cites an NBC television report by John Chancellor, "known for his contacts in Washington," on April 8, 1982, which was so accurate that it "amounted to a virtual exposure of the Israeli war plans," including the plans for attacking Beirut and confronting the Syrian forces in the Bekaa valley, one of a series of indications that Washington was "duly informed" about Sharon's plans "that went beyond southern Lebanon," contrary to subsequent pretense. "Green Light, Lebanon," *Foreign Policy*, Spring 1983.

for respect for Israel's anguish—and for mourning the latest victims of Israeli-Palestinian hostility.[37]

Typically, it is *Israel's* anguish that we must respect when still more Palestinians are killed in an unprovoked Israeli terrorist attack—again, one imagines that the reaction might have been somewhat different if the PLO had bombed coastal towns north of Tel Aviv, killing many people, in retaliation for the death of a Palestinian guerrilla in northern Israel, an Israeli "provocation." The reference in the *Post* to "Israel's anguish" has to do with the difficulty of "suppressing" Palestinian nationalism in the occupied territories, and the "great pain" caused by the evacuation of the Yamit settlers in what the Israeli press called "Operation National Trauma '82" (see note 28). Note that "the latest victims" were not victims of Israeli air raids, but of the more abstract "Israeli-Palestinian hostility."

Emboldened by such signals as this, Israel prepared for the next "provocation." On May 9 Israel again bombed Lebanon in retaliation for the discovery of land mines in Israel and the bombing of a bus in Jerusalem.[38] This time, there was a light PLO rocket and artillery response, directed away from settled areas, with no reported casualties.

Three days later, the military correspondent of *Ha'aretz*, Ze'ev Schiff, wrote:

> With regard to the war in the North, Israel is now at one minute before midnight . . . It is not true that—as we tell the Americans—we do not want to invade Lebanon. There are influential forces, led by the Defense Minister, which, with intelligence and cunning, are taking well-considered steps to reach a situation that will leave Israel with no choice but to invade Lebanon even if it were to involve a war with Syria.

The war would aim to "root out" the PLO and to make Israel the "policeman of Lebanon," able "to decide even how the members of the Lebanese parliament vote when it comes to the election of the next Lebanese president"[39]—an election scheduled for the coming August. It is inconceivable that the U.S. government was unaware of all of this.

4.5   The Pretext for the Invasion of Lebanon

On June 3, a terrorist group that had been engaged in a running battle with the PLO for a decade and whose head (Abu Nidal) had been condemned to death by the PLO attempted to assassinate Israeli Ambassador Shlomo Argov in London. The facts were reported at once by the British police and government, with the further information that PLO leaders were on the "hit list" of the attackers, but the insistence of the PLO that it had nothing to do with this act was rejected by the Israeli government, with much of the U.S. press in line as usual.* The *Washington Post* commented that the assassination attempt was an "embarrassment" for the PLO, which "claims to represent all Palestinians, but...tends to be selective about accepting responsibility for acts of Palestinian violence."[40] By the same logic, it would be legitimate to bomb Israel when any Jew carries out a violent act against Palestinians, for example, the Jewish Defense League in New York, or an American immigrant who went berserk at the Al Aqsa Mosque in Jerusalem, or the "Jewish Armed Resistance" in Rome (see below). Recall that the Israeli courts have determined that Israel is the State of the Jewish people, which includes the Jews of the diaspora (see p. 45, and chapter 4, section 8.2, for the meaning of the fact). If the *Post* were to make a similar comment about Israel and Jews, it would rightly be condemned for outrageous anti-Semitism and advocacy of terrorism.

In "retaliation" for the attempt to assassinate the Israeli Ambassador, Israel carried out heavy bombardment of Palestinian and Lebanese targets in Lebanon (where the Abu Nidal group does not even have an office). Again the official Israeli version was accepted by the press; the bombings were unfortunate, perhaps excessive, but "retaliation" or "reprisal."[41] The Palestinian refugee camps of Sabra and Shatila (later to become famous as the site of the September massacres) were bombed for four hours. The local (Gaza) hospital was hit. Over 200 people were killed, according to the eyewitness account of an American observer.[42] Recall that the total number of Israelis killed in the course of PLO terrorist cross-border actions in 15 years was 106.

This time, there was a Palestinian response, shelling of northern settlements, and Israel launched its long-planned full-scale invasion, Operation "Peace for Galilee," to "protect the northern border." For 11 months, there had been no Palestinian action on the northern border apart from the May and June retaliatory shellings, and in July 1981 it had been Israel's initiative that shattered the peace along the border, not for the first time, as we have seen.

A number of Israelis expressed shock over the "retaliation" after the attempt to assassinate Ambassador Argov. One asked that "we imagine that the British would have bombed Tel Aviv or Netanya in retaliation for the murder of Lord Moyne [by a group directed by the current Foreign

---

* The three attackers were caught and given 30-35-year sentences. The leader, who was deputy commander of Abu Nidal's special operations section, was identified as a Colonel in the Iraqi Intelligence Service. The assassination may have been ordered by the Iraqi government in the expectation that Israel would attack Lebanon in "reprisal," offering Iraq the opportunity to end the war with Iran in the name of unity against Israel, as it proposed to do on June 10. Iran refused, giving exactly this analysis of what had happened. Ian Black, *Manchester Guardian weekly*, March 13, 1983. Black suggests further that Britain and the U.S. downplayed the incident because of their interest in improving trade and diplomatic relations with Iraq. See p. 203*. Also p. 78*.

Minister of Israel] or the hanging of the [British] Sergeants" by Begin's terrorist army, asking: "Wouldn't we have called it barbarism?"[43] And what would we have called it if Lord Moyne had been killed by an *anti-Zionist* terrorist group, instead of by Zionist terrorists, to correct the analogy? The same might be asked about the assassination of two Palestinians in Rome in June 1982 by a group called the "Jewish Armed Resistance," which appears to have been in contact with the Jewish Defense League,[44] whose leader calls for the expulsion of Arabs from the Land of Israel when he is not beating and shooting at them as part of his regular army service on the West Bank—but in this case, the question was not raised in the United States, in accordance with the normal double standard. The PLO allegation that Israel was involved in the Rome assassinations was denounced by Israeli officials in Rome as tantamount to "an appeal to the assassination of members of the embassy of Israel." In contrast, the Israeli claim that the PLO was responsible for the Argov attack was not tantamount to an appeal for assassination; rather, it was the prelude to the Israeli assassination of thousands of Palestinians and Lebanese in the "retaliatory strikes" and the subsequent full-scale invasion. Again, the obvious questions were not raised here.

4.6   The Reasons for the Invasion of Lebanon

4.6.1   The Imperatives of Rejectionism

The Israeli claim to be acting in legitimate self-defense was accepted by the U.S. government and large segments of the press and intelligentsia, though in this case, an unprecedented negative reaction developed in the U.S. One obvious purpose of the Israeli attack, as predicted long before, was to disperse the refugees once again and to destroy the organization that represents Palestinian nationalism, to ensure, as one senior Israeli diplomat said, that "They [the PLO] are dead people politically."[45] Recall the U.S. veto of the June 26 Security Council Resolution calling for an end to hostilities on the grounds that it was "a transparent attempt to preserve the P.L.O. as a viable *political* force."[46] With the Palestinian counterpart to the Zionist Organization eliminated, it was hoped that Israel could proceed with its plans to suppress any meaningful form of Palestinian self-determination within the occupied territories without any concern for Palestinian opposition in the international arena or for what Palestinians might regard as "retaliation" from southern Lebanon for further oppression and brutality in the territories ("unprovoked terrorism," in western lingo). At the same time, destruction of the PLO might serve to demoralize the Palestinians in the territories and elsewhere, in accordance with the assumption of General Sharon that "quiet on the

West Bank" requires "the destruction of the PLO in Lebanon"[47] and the advice of *New Republic* editor Martin Peretz, on the eve of the invasion, that Israel should administer to the PLO a "lasting military defeat" that "will clarify to the Palestinians in the West Bank that their struggle for an independent state has suffered a setback of many years."[48] Then, Peretz explains, "the Palestinians will be turned into just another crushed nation, like the Kurds or the Afghans," and the Palestinian problem—which "is beginning to be boring"—will be resolved.*

Sharon's war had long been anticipated within Israel, and the reasons for it were clearly understood. Three months earlier, in March, Yoel Marcus had written in *Ha'aretz:*

> Behind the official excuse of "we shall not tolerate shelling or terrorist actions" lies a strategic view which holds that the physical annihilation of the PLO has to be achieved. That is, not only must its fingers and hands in the West Bank be amputated (as is now being done with an iron fist), but its heart and head in Beirut must be dealt with. As Israel does not want the PLO as a partner for talks or as an interlocuter for any solution in the West Bank, the supporters of confrontation with the PLO hold that the logical continuation of the struggle with the PLO in the territories is in Lebanon. With the loss of its physical strength, in their opinion, the PLO will lose not only its hold over the territories but also its growing international status.[49]

Marcus correctly identifies two concerns: the hold of the PLO over the territories—or more accurately, the support for the PLO on the part of the overwhelming majority of the population—and its growing international status. Both factors stood in the way of the rejectionist commitments of the two major political groupings in Israel.

The latter concern recalls the familiar "panic" described by Amos Elon whenever the threat of a peaceful political settlement becomes

---

* In this interview in *Ha'aretz*, Peretz urges "slightly better" treatment of the Arabs in the West Bank than is contemplated under Begin's "autonomy," which, he notes, will allow them no more than the right to collect garbage. He thinks that the "enlightened and liberal" occupation policy followed until 1981 was probably a mistake, and that his "old friend" Menachem Milson may be right in his view that "strongarm policies"—such as those discussed in the preceding chapter—should have been instituted from 1967, not just from 1981. We return directly to his thoughts concerning the press and "the Arab national character" (pp. 200, 283). The interview is interesting as a rather crude expression of the right-wing Labor viewpoint, barely distinguishable from that of Likud hard-liners. It may also be usefully compared to what Peretz addresses to an American audience in the *New Republic*. It is interesting that this advocate of an overwhelming assault on "the PLO" in Lebanon felt no shame in serving as a sponsor for an Oxfam "Urgent Humanitarian Appeal for the People of Lebanon" that described "The grim count of civilian casualties in Lebanon" with "thousands killed" and "hundreds of thousands of people homeless" (*New York Times*, June 20, 1982).

difficult to contain (see chapter 3). In fact, this panic was again rising in 1981-2, as we have already seen, with the Saudi Arabian peace plan (the "real author" being the PLO, according to President Chaim Herzog) and subsequent Syrian and Saudi initiatives. But now there was a still more ominous development: the PLO was scrupulously observing the cease-fire, despite many Israeli provocations. The struggle to portray the PLO as nothing more than a terrorist gang had already largely been lost in Europe, but the U.S. was still holding the line. But how long could American opinion remain under control if the PLO persisted on this dangerous course?

One might note again, in this connection, the curious beliefs of supporters of Israel about the "pro-PLO press" and the "numerous public figures" in the West and even Western governments that "encourage" the PLO in its "maximalist course" of destroying Israel; see p. 1*. Similarly Martin Peretz explained to his Israeli audience that one of Israel's problems in the U.S. is "Obviously—the press." "The press you have lost years ago" because "most journalists are young people of the Vietnam generation whose sympathy is always granted to anyone who calls himself 'a guerrilla' or a 'freedom fighter'," and television simply "makes the problem worse."[50] A similar and equally plausible view of the press as Communist-dominated is common among the extreme right-wing in the U.S.

The dangers posed by PLO passivity were subsequently elaborated by Yehoshua Porath, one of Israel's leading scholars and the author of major works on the Palestinian national movement, cited earlier. Commenting on the motives for the Israeli invasion, Porath dismisses at once the contrived excuse concerning the London assassination attempt as well as the claim that the purpose was to protect Israeli settlements in the Galilee, noting that the PLO had respected the July 1981 cease-fire. But Porath argues that the many commentators who have criticized Israeli propaganda on these grounds are missing the point. "It seems to me," he writes, "that the decision of the government (or more precisely, its two leaders [Begin and Sharon]) *flowed from the very fact that the cease-fire had been observed.*" Arafat had succeeded in imposing discipline on the many PLO factions, thus maintaining the cease-fire that had been achieved under U.S. auspices. His success in this constituted "a veritable catastrophe in the eyes of the Israeli government," since it indicated that the PLO "might agree in the future to a more far-reaching arrangement,"[51] in which case Israel could no longer evade a political settlement on the grounds that the PLO is nothing but "a wild gang of murderers." "It was this eventuality that the Israeli attack was primarily designed to prevent":

The government's hope is that the stricken PLO, lacking a logistic and territorial base, will return to its earlier terrorism: it will carry out bombings throughout the world, hijack airplanes, and murder many Israelis. In this way, the PLO will lose part of the political legitimacy that it has gained and will mobilize the large majority of the Israeli nation in hatred and disgust against it, undercutting the danger that elements will develop among the Palestinians that might become a legitimate negotiating partner for future political accommodations.[52]

Other commentators made the same point. Danny Rubinstein wrote in *Davar* that "The PLO as an orderly political body is more terrifying to the government of Israel than the powerful terrorist PLO." This is the reason why "the government of Israel planned the Lebanon war for the entire past year (as Sharon has testified) and planned to reach Beirut (as all the commanders have testified)." Israel's security had never been so great, but Arafat's success in maintaining the cease-fire was a greater danger than any security threat because of the "political power that the PLO had developed," so that "fear was growing" that it could not be excluded from negotiations, and negotiations would undermine Israel's rejectionism, leading to Palestinian self-determination, i.e., a Palestinian state. The PLO must be forced back to "murderous terror" to overcome the danger of pressure from Western liberal opinion and the U.S. government (a dubious prospect) in favor of a two-state settlement.[53]

Always the same "panic" that there might be a peaceful political settlement, so that Judea, Samaria and Gaza would have to be abandoned, an intolerable prospect to both major political groupings. In line with this rather plausible analysis, one can expect that much of the U.S. press (the *New Republic, New York Times*, etc.), will eagerly seize upon any indication of PLO "radicalism," which may indeed develop in the wake of the disaster that the Palestinians suffered in Lebanon, though by early 1983 there was as yet no sign of this much hoped-for development. See chapter 3, notes 115, 116 and chapter 6, section 3.1.

Some political commentators in the U.S. have argued that Israel's intention to destroy the PLO is against its better interests, since success in this venture might provoke a return to terrorism among the scattered Palestinians, a danger to Israel and its citizens and indeed to much of the world. But as Porath, Rubinstein and others suggest—and their analysis is well-supported by the historical record that has been effectively suppressed in the U.S.—this interpretation misses the essential point: Israel's goal is precisely to achieve this end, fending off the catastrophe of a political settlement in which both Palestinians and Israelis might live in peace and security. As was evident at the time, the Camp David accords and Kissinger's earlier arrangements provided Israel with the opportunity for further moves to incorporate the occupied territories, and to facilitate such actions as the invasion of Lebanon undertaken in large part for the same ends.

In the latter connection, former military intelligence chief Shlomo Gazit observes that "behind the Lebanon victory lie the peace accords with Egypt," which permitted Israel to concentrate its military forces in the north without fear of military retaliation by the Arab states.[54] To underscore the seriousness of this point, Israel warned Egypt during the Lebanese war that if Egypt were to respond by severing diplomatic links, "the Israeli army would be used against Egypt." This was reported by Labor Party chairman Shimon Peres at a meeting of Labor Knesset members, and "aroused anger among the ruling coalition, but has not been denied by any government spokesman."[55] The warning was presumably thought necessary because of the impact of the Israeli invasion in Egypt. Egyptian critics of the Camp David agreements were not surprised by the invasion. "Is it really amazing," one said, "that Israel, supported by America, is implementing the American peace design, after it has separated Egypt from the Arab world?... We objected to the Camp David Accords since we perceived them as a trick to pull Egypt out of the Arab circle, and to make it easier for America and Israel to strike against the Palestinians and the Arab countries who refused to follow Egypt's way." It is primarily among supporters of the "peace process" that bitter anger is expressed. The editor of an Egyptian magazine, who backed the Camp David agreements, told a group of Israeli journalists: "You turned peace into something hated for the Egyptians." The journalists discovered the truth of his statement from their own observations among officials, journalists, taxi drivers, salesmen and others. Unlike those who were skeptical from the start, "the advocates of peace with Israel feel defeated, deceived and scorned." The editor quoted above says: "I perceived the peace with Israel to be the cornerstone for a comprehensive peace in the Middle East. But for you peace was merely a trick to neutralize us so as to more easily strike at the Palestinian people."[56]

The critics of the "peace process" have been proven correct in their analysis by what has happened in the occupied territories and in Lebanon since, though the fact is almost completely unrecognized in the United States, where—by definition—whatever happens is the fault of the PLO, or perhaps Begin's unanticipated excesses.

Israeli commentators are often clear enough about the central points; for example, David Krivine of the *Jerusalem Post*, quoted earlier, who observes accurately that Israel will not talk to the PLO "not because they are nasty people" but because "the subject on the agenda" can only be a Palestinian state, to which Israel will never agree because it must retain "part of" the West Bank. Similarly the leader of the Labor Party, Shimon Peres, explains that "Israel cannot conduct negotiations with the PLO; not only because of the PLO's past but because of the geographical map of Israel itself."[57] See also p. 75*. The reference to the PLO's past can hardly be taken seriously considering the history of Zionism and the State of

Israel, which Peres knows very well. And outside of the U.S., it is doubtful that many people would take very seriously Peres's claim that the world's fourth most powerful military force, which had just once again demonstrated its might, would be threatened by a Palestinian state—or his further claim that Jordan too would be threatened by this emerging superpower (in fact, Jordan's King Hussein is more likely to feel threatened by Israeli leaders who refer to a potential Palestinian state as "an additional Palestinian state," as Peres does here, in the light of the implications of this view). But for an American audience it can pass. The more serious reasons for Israel's insistence on maintaining effective control over the West Bank, we have discussed in chapter 3, section 2.2.1. Recall also the explanation given by Peres's predecessor, Yitzhak Rabin, as to why Israel could never negotiate with any Palestinians: such negotiations could only lead to Palestinian self-determination in a separate state, which Israel will never accept (see p. 70).

Many other Israeli commentators have emphasized the political goals of the operation. Former chief IDF education officer Mordechai Bar-On writes that "there is no doubt that the [war's] central aim was to deal a crushing blow to the national aspirations of the Palestinians and to their very existence as a nation endeavouring to define itself and gain the right to self-determination." And Ze'ev Schiff, Israel's most respected military correspondent, wrote that the decision to enter West Beirut in September in defiance of earlier promises was not motivated, as claimed, "by the desire to prevent a state of anarchy and to save the city." Rather, "the truth is that it was meant to further a different goal: to influence the election of Lebanon's next president and the country's future political path... It was an additional proof of the fact that the goals of the war have been, for a long time now, political and are not directly connected with Israel's security,"[58] as is constantly claimed and loyally repeated by American supporters of Israel.

Meanwhile much of the American press, either through naiveté or cynicism, writes of the great opportunities that the Israeli invasion has offered, including the prospects for a territorial compromise in the West Bank that will lead to genuine recognition of Palestinian national rights now that the PLO military force has been destroyed and PLO intimidation of "moderates" will no longer be possible in the occupied territories.

The truth of the matter, it seems rather clear, is somewhat different: the necessity to destroy the PLO politically—and along with it, organized Palestinian existence in Lebanon—flowed directly from the increasing isolation of the leaders of the rejectionist camp. As we have seen, the U.S. and Israel stood virtually alone (apart from a few holdouts such as Libya and Iraq,* and the minority Rejection Front of the PLO) in opposing a

---

* It had been assumed that at least Iraq would hold the line, but once again it appears that the Arabs cannot be trusted. On January 3, 1983, the Iraqi news agency released the text of

two-state settlement with recognized borders and security guarantees. To evade possibilities for a peaceful negotiated settlement would not be possible forever, it seemed. It was therefore necessary for the U.S. and Israel to resort to force, the dimension along which they reign supreme, to establish their own rejectionist terms as the framework for any potential settlement. This policy required the destruction of the organization that most Palestinians regard as their sole legitimate representative, or at least, impelling it towards random terrorism or a rejectionist stance of its own rather than still further political evolution. With this end achieved, Israel and the U.S. might pursue their respective—and somewhat different— rejectionist policies: for Israel, extension of sovereignty over the occupied territories; for the Reagan Administration, the September 1 proposals that reject a Palestinian state and exclude the PLO, i.e., that reject Palestinian self-determination. The U.S. press and intelligentsia could be counted on to characterize this rejectionist program as the soul of moderation and honor, the basis for any further discussion among humane people, thus eliminating the international consensus, which was becoming something of a nuisance, as an irrelevance. Given the overwhelming U.S.-Israeli control over the means of violence and the obedience of the intellectual community, there was every reason to expect success in these endeavors, and in fact, it has very largely been achieved.

Leaving no doubts as to its intentions in the Lebanon war, Israel quickly proceeded to dissolve the elected city councils of Nablus and Dura in the West Bank and to dismiss the mayors of Jenin and Gaza, also arresting city employees in Jenin. Previously, other elected mayors of major towns had been dismissed or deported, leaving only Mayor Elias Freij of Bethlehem. Mayor Shawa of Gaza had been appointed by the Israeli military government and was known as a supporter of King Hussein of Jordan; he reports that he had been subjected to severe economic pressures by the military government in an effort to induce complete

---

an August 25 statement by President Saddam Hussein to Rep. Stephen Solarz in which Hussein recognized Israel's "need for a state of security," stating also that "no Arab leader has now in his policies the so-called destruction of Israel or wiping it out of existence." Israel at once dismissed the statement as meaningless, the reflex reaction to peace threats. Foreign Minister Shamir stated "that there has been no change in Iraq's attitude towards Israel"; perhaps he had in mind a *New York Times* report (Dec. 4, 1976) that all the Arab states, even Libya and Iraq, had accepted "the principle of a West Bank state" alongside of Israel. Sharon also dismissed the Iraqi statement, adding for good measure that Israel would not agree to negotiations that include any members of the PLO in a Jordanian delegation or even West Bank Palestinians who support the PLO. For more on the matter, see Eric Rouleau's interview with the Deputy Prime Minister of Iraq, Tariq Aziz, who observes that Iraq "went along with the Fez resolutions" of September 1982, which advocated negotiations to establish a Palestinian state alongside of Israel and "to work out arrangements with Israel for guaranteeing the existence and security of all the states in question" (Aziz), including Israel and the Palestinian state. Iraq is also "urging Yasser Arafat to coordinate his diplomatic strategy with King Hussein's." Rouleau also notes a recent low-interest $450 million loan to Iraq from the U.S., part of the "cooperation with the United States [which] is developing in every field."[59] See p. 197*.

conformity. Shortly after, Israel set up a new Village League near Nablus, with a substantial grant for a water supply project, regularly denied to democratically elected officials. Under the Sharon-Milson regime, standard procedure for imposing the rule of the selected quisling leadership is to channel subsidies for development to them, require merchants to apply to them or join them to obtain licenses, etc. (supply of arms is another device). Indeed, such measures are necessary given the minuscule support for the official "moderates"; see chapter 3, section 2.3. As noted there, the Leagues were then united in a regional organization with the "political task" of representing the West Bank in negotiations with Israel. Meanwhile, student protests over the invasion of Lebanon at Bir Zeit University led to tear-gassing by Israeli soldiers and many arrests, beating and harassment of students (according to the university president), and finally closing down of the university—once again. From mid-June, demonstrations and a general merchant strike (in the usual manner, merchants were forced by the occupying army to open shops) were met by firing with injuries. Two inhabitants of Nablus were killed during a demonstration in which Israeli soldiers opened fire (the government claims they were not killed by soldiers), and members of the Village Leagues, armed by Israel, killed and wounded a number of West Bank opponents.

As the Lebanon war proceeded, West Bank organizations and associations, including religious circles, insistently repeated their support for the PLO, in sermons given in mosques and in public statements. The Supreme Islamic Council of Jerusalem, normally apolitical, sent a letter to the United Nations rejecting the Camp David "peace process" and recognizing the PLO as the sole legitimate representative of the Palestinian people, and stated publicly its "support for the PLO in its heroic attempt to reach a noble solution for the Palestinian problem," calling upon the Palestinian people to donate one day's salary "to our sons and brothers in Lebanon." West Bank and Gaza municipalities issued a communiqué denouncing the war in Lebanon and declaring that the PLO remains the sole legitimate representative of the Palestinian people (June 20). A supporting statement, announcing once again "our full support for the Palestine Liberation Organization, the sole legitimate representative of the Palestinian people in the homeland and the diaspora," was issued by a broad group of West Bank unions. Amnon Kapeliouk, who covers the occupied territories for the Israeli journal *Al Hamishmar*, wrote that there is near unanimity in opposition to the invasion (apart from the Village Leagues "fostered by the civilian administration") and in reiterating the previous stand that "for any political negotiation it is necessary to address the PLO in Beirut." Correspondingly, it was next to impossible to find quisling elements to replace deposed officials. In Dir Dabouan, the eighth town to have its elected administration removed since March, not one inhabitant was willing to serve in the new Israeli-imposed administration. Kapeliouk reports that apart from three people in the city of Jenin, no collaborators were found during the intensive summer repression undertaken "to exploit the opportunity" (in the government's phrase) to "break the current local leadership."[60]

In the *New York Times*, David Shipler quoted the spokesman for the Israeli administrative authority in the West Bank who states: "We're conducting a political war against the P.L.O. The army is conducting a military war." "Taking advantage of the P.L.O.'s weakened position in Beirut," Shipler adds, "Defense Minister Ariel Sharon has stepped up political and economic assaults on the organization's adherents and admirers in areas occupied by Israel since 1967," giving a number of details.[61]

Protests continued throughout the summer, despite the harsh military repression. On September 3, one person was reported killed and three injured in Nablus when Israeli soldiers fired into a demonstration, and another Palestinian was killed near Tulkarm during a "combing process" carried out by the Israeli army searching for a person who had fired at Israeli soldiers. Another was killed by a settler during "violent student demonstrations" on October 26, and two were wounded in clashes with Israeli settlers, among other incidents.[62] Recall that even the "moderates" (Freij, Shawa, etc.) continued to express their support for the PLO throughout the Lebanon invasion, and some in fact felt that support for the PLO had *increased* during the invasion (see p. 55). A number of Israeli observers, among others, also observed the significant impact of the heroic PLO resistance against overwhelming odds. See section 8.3.1.

None of this fits too well with the preferred picture of the West Bank Palestinians, intimidated by the PLO for many years, who presumably should have been celebrating their liberation through the summer of 1982. Americans who might have been dismayed by the events in the real world could be comforted by turning to the pages of the *New Republic*, where they would be reassured to learn that what was taking place in the West Bank did not happen. As the journal's specialist on the Palestinians, David Pryce-Jones, explained, "the PLO has had little success in inciting public disturbance on the West Bank and in Gaza" (this has been the case since 1967, he assures us). "As in earlier cases, Palestinians declined the PLO's appeals to action," the reason being that the Palestinians "have been under much more immediate and sustained threat from the PLO itself" than from "Israel, Jordan, and the Lebanese Christians," who they merely "resent," while they are terrified of the PLO.[63] In short, Israel's repression in the occupied territories and its destruction of Palestinian camps in Lebanon, the Black September killings in Jordan, the Tel al-Zaatar and Sabra-Shatila massacres, etc., cannot compare to the terrorism launched against the suffering Palestinians by the PLO. This no doubt explains the total quiescence in the West Bank apart from the outpouring of joyous acclaim for Israel, Jordan, and the Lebanese Christians by the population of the West Bank and Gaza now that they had at last been rescued from their PLO tormenters by Israel's army of liberation.

Returning to the real world, it comes as little surprise that Israel followed its invasion of Lebanon by heightening the repression in the occupied territories, targeting even pro-Jordanian elements (e.g., Mayor Shawa, who, as noted earlier, also recognizes the PLO as the sole legitimate representative of the Palestinian people). Recall that under the Labor government, even pro-Jordanian notables who intended to form an anti-PLO grouping were denied the right to organize (see p. 54), while Palestinian moderates, such as Bir Zeit President Hanna Nasser, were expelled or repressed, a fact long noted by Israeli journalists in the occupied territories; for example, Danny Rubinstein, who observed that some of the earliest choices for expulsion were pro-Jordanian figures, and more recently, elected officials regarded as moderates. Arab leadership "in fact cannot exist" under Israeli rule, he wrote well before the Sharon-Milson regime was established, even "moderate traditionalists."[64]

The Begin government has simply been extending the policies initiated by the Labor government, with increasing harshness, and continued to do so during and after the Lebanon war. On October 29, 1982, the civil administration in the West Bank (which is subordinate to the military) issued a directive instructing administrators "to keep up pressure on 'extremist mayors' while trying to neutralize pro-Jordanian Palestinians" in an effort "to curtail Jordanian influence in the area and to increase the area's dependence on the Israeli administration there." In the words of the directive: "The pressure must not be let up on them [the "extremist mayors"] after dismissing them from their positions," and with regard to pro-Jordanian elements, policy "must be a maximum continuation of neutralizing them and bringing them to great dependence on the administration." Support should be provided for "pragmatic, moderate people," Village League heads who "we have begun to cultivate," although "It should be stressed that the aim of cultivation is not for its own sake but rather for the purpose of achieving a political end."[65]

It is, in fact, difficult to distinguish pro-PLO from pro-Jordanian elements, as the case of ex-Mayor Shawa indicates. Thus when security forces detained three Hebron political figures in mid-June for "trying to organize support for the Palestinians in Lebanon," it turned out that one was a former director of the local agricultural department who ran social services during the Jordanian administration and another was director of education during the same period.[66]

Some argue that the spirit of Palestinian nationalism in the occupied territories and support for the PLO there cannot be destroyed by demolishing the organized Palestinian community in Lebanon and employing the strong-arm methods carried out by Sharon, Milson and others and advocated by Martin Peretz and the like (see p. 199*) in the occupied territories. This seems to me questionable. The strength and courage of the *Samidin* have been truly impressive, but people have their limits, and conquerors in the past have succeeded in breaking their will.

After the repression of June and early July described above, one supporter of the Israeli invasion, Robert Tucker, wrote that "The Israeli action was, quite clearly, an anticipatory measure, taken to forestall the prospect of serious injury" to Israel, hence legitimate; by this moral code, preemptive strikes are now justified, and there can be no rational objection, say, to the Russian invasion of Hungary or Czechoslovakia, given the dangers posed to the USSR by NATO, or perhaps even to Hitler's moves to blunt the Czech dagger pointed at the heart of Germany.* But, Tucker adds, "if, despite the destruction of the P.L.O. as a military force, and perhaps as a political force as well, the Israeli Government uses its victory to harden further its policy in the occupied territories, the case made today by critics of the war will be made more persuasive."[68] One wonders what would count as "hardening of policy," since evidently the actions undertaken from the first days of the invasion, or those of the preceding months, do not—perhaps mass expulsion of Palestinians, though no doubt an appropriate moral code could be devised to justify this as well, and perhaps yet will be.

The destruction of the PLO in Lebanon will require new prodigies of apologetics from "supporters of Israel," who have been stoutly maintaining that Israel has long sought political accommodation but has been blocked in this effort by the PLO, and that only PLO terrorism has prevented West Bank "moderates" from seeking conciliation with Israel—which will, of course, grant them the right of true national self-determination when they are liberated from PLO tyranny. Early efforts appeared by mid-summer 1982, taking the interesting position that of course the Palestinians have national rights and even the right to a state of their own in the occupied territories, but that the PLO cannot play any part in this process. We must "eliminate the PLO, and enfranchise the Palestinians."[69] In short, we are naturally in favor of self-determination for the Palestinians, but *we* will determine who represents them, meanwhile giving full support to Israel, where both major political groupings have long rejected any meaningful form of self-determination or even negotiation with any Palestinians on any political issue, while looking forward to their "departure" in some manner.

---

* Recall that Hitler's 1937 plan for an operation against Czechoslovakia was justified in internal documents "in order to parry the imminent attack of a superior enemy coalition" and in public by the Czech threat and "terror" against Germans.[67] Recall also that Hitler's conceptions have struck a responsive chord in current Zionist commentary; see p. 72*.

In Israel, it is recognized that "American Jews have their work cut out for them." Elmer Winter outlines their task in the *Jerusalem Post*: "They need to place Israel's incursion into Lebanon, and the resulting new opportunities, into proper perspective, and not be deterred by editorial writers who criticize Israel for overkill, expansionism, arrogance, etc." He then proceeds to suggest an appropriate "course of action," the prime element being to stress that "Israel's decision to push the PLO back from the Israeli-Lebanon border came after 11 months of escalating terrorist attacks against its northern towns and villages" which the UN forces were unable to prevent.[70] In fact, the number of these attacks was zero, apart from retaliatory strikes in May and June, and what the UN was unable to prevent was the Israeli invasion through their lines, a fact little discussed here, but not overlooked in the European countries that had provided those troops. Winter proceeds with his instructions in the same vein, and, predictably, many have risen to the occasion, and will continue to work to overcome the actual history, as in the past, continuing to imitate their Stalinist models. See p. 14.

4.6.2 Achieving National Unity

While the occupied territories were the prime target of the Israeli invasion, it had other motives as well. There were, in the first place, domestic political factors. A Hebrew University historian writes that

> The decision to launch and expand the Lebanese war can probably best be seen at this moment as a military quasi-coup in Israel carried through by peaceful means against the previously existing political order. As Bismark demonstrated so brilliantly in the 1860's, there is no better way to pulverize political opposition and to silence recalcitrant colleagues than to initiate short, victorious wars against weak neighboring armies.

A similar point is made by military historian (Col., Ret.) Meir Pail, former Director of the IDF Military Academy for officer training. He writes that some military adventure was needed by the Begin government "to strengthen their position in the Israeli public and to unite the people under their leadership." Why pick Lebanon? "There was to be found the weakest enemy, it would seem, guaranteeing a clear-cut military victory," and furthermore, "American support would be forthcoming" in this case, as indeed it was.[71]

Even short of "victorious wars against weak neighboring states," the same devices can be used to shore up a tottering national consensus, as the Reagan administration has illustrated with its absurd posturing about Libyan hit-men, Libyan aggression and threats, etc. In February 1983, for example, the administration was beginning to be concerned about the defection of its "conservative" (meaning, statist militarist) constituency who were charging it with insufficient militancy. The administration responded by boldly confronting an alleged Libyan threat to the Sudan, sending an aircraft carrier into disputed waters off the Libyan coast, providing AWACS to Egypt, etc. Shortly after, Secretary of State George Shultz was able to announce that "Col. Muammar el-Qaddafi, the Libyan leader, 'is back in his box where he belongs' because President Reagan acted 'quickly and decisively'" against this threat to world order.[72] The racist character of the phrase was no more perceived (by the mainstream media, that is; others commented on it) than the shallowness of the evidence of the "threat" (null, so far as has been made public), or the relation to the immediate background circumstances. In fact, the entire episode was quietly dropped as soon as the needs of the state had been served.

To cover up the weakness of Israel's enemy, it was necessary to concoct stories about the immense military power of the PLO. Impressive tales were circulated about the huge arsenals of captured weapons, repeated with much awe in the U.S. and ridiculed by military commentators in Israel. The military correspondent of *Ha'aretz*, Ze'ev Schiff, reported that "the imagination is given full reign as in the stories of *A Thousand and One Nights*." The captured arms were perhaps sufficient to equip one division with "light weapons," mostly rifles. Some tanks were captured, a few perhaps belonging to the PLO, the rest Syrian. In the *Jerusalem Post*, military correspondent Hirsh Goodman concluded that to regard the PLO as a potential military threat "would be pushing the matter to absurdity." Meir Pail estimated that weapons in the hands of the PLO were approximately equal to the quantities in the hands of the Haddadists and Phalangists (largely provided by Israel), and were intended to maintain the balance of terror within Lebanon. Labor Knesset member Yossi Sarid "wanted to know who had authorized senior IDF officers to tell Jewish fund-raisers from abroad that enough PLO arms had been seized to equip a million terrorists," an obvious absurdity.[73] Former Prime Minister Yitzhak Rabin (Chief of Staff during the June 1967 war) dismissed the idea that the PLO was a threat to Israel, adding that the captured weapons were primarily light arms, intended for "terrorists," not for an army.[74]

4.6.3 A New Order in Lebanon

There were other reasons for the invasion as well. IDF Chief of Staff Rafael Eitan had stated not long before: "Since I have constructed a military machine costing billions of dollars, I am obliged to use it... Tomorrow I may be in Beirut."[75]

A motive of broader scope and greater historical depth was to place Israel in a position to dictate the terms of any political settlement in Lebanon, exactly as Ze'ev Schiff had pointed out prior to the invasion (see above, pp. 196, 203). The timing of the invasion may well have been influenced by the fact that the mandate of the Syrian Arab Peacekeeping force was to expire in late July, while elections were scheduled for August-September.[76] The political situation was therefore fluid, and some observers believed that there was a chance for a political agreement among Lebanese.[77] Israel preferred rule over Lebanon by the Phalange, or as an alternative, some form of partition with Maronite domination of at least the central regions and the southern portions associated in some form with Israel, perhaps under the rule of its client, Major Haddad. Right-wing Israelis have been quite explicit about the matter. The well-known physicist Yuval Ne'eman, former president of Tel Aviv University and a Knesset member from the Tehiya Party, urged that Israel "establish a new order in Lebanon."* The Israeli army "must be prepared for a long stay in Lebanon," during which "Israel will have an opportunity of reaching a stage of socio-economic or technological development in the nearby region which, geographically and historically, is an integral part of Eretz Yisrael." Possibly there could be "an agreement on border rectification," in which "Israel could integrate the strip south of the Litani, with its friendly citizens, into Israel's development plans"[78]—thus taking a long step towards realizing the traditional "vision" of Ben-Gurion and others, which remained quite alive at least through the mid-1950s, and has a strong motivation in terms of economic and resource factors, as we have seen.

A few weeks later, Ne'eman was appointed to the cabinet to head the new Ministry of Science and Technology. "The primary mission of the Ministry of Science headed by Professor Yuval Ne'eman is the development of the Jewish region in the territories beyond the Green Line" (the pre-1967 borders). In an interview, Ne'eman stated that "only this mission impelled Tehiya to join the governing coalition."[79] He may well have his eye on the "North Bank" as well. His new Ministry is also "authorized to concentrate on creating an infrastructure for factories, especially sophisticated scientific industries, in the new Israeli settlements of the West Bank." The government's goal, Ne'eman stated, is "to settle so many Jews that the West Bank and Gaza can't be given back to the Arabs."[80] We return to some of the activities of the new Ministry in the next chapter.

As noted earlier, a kind of balance of terror had been achieved in the course of the bloody civil war in Lebanon between the Palestinian-Muslim National Front coalition and the Phalangist-dominated Christian right. To achieve its two primary aims in Lebanon—namely, to demolish any organized form of Palestinian existence and to impose a "new order"—it was imperative for Israel to destroy this balance and to

---

* The phrase is common in the Israeli press. It is again curious to see how readily the terminology of the Nazis has been adopted in Israeli and American Zionist rhetoric; see p. 72*.

leave power completely in the hands of the Phalangists, and in the south, its Haddadist client or perhaps new ones, to be created. This goal was easily achieved, given Israel's immense military superiority. The end result is expected to be "a conservative alliance dominated by Maronite Christians but also including Moslem privileged classes," now that the Palestinians and their local Muslim allies have been destroyed and disarmed.[81]

In the *Jerusalem Post*, David Bernstein observed that "When Israel invaded Lebanon earlier this year and routed that country's PLO-Moslem alliance it totally destroyed the balance of forces between Moslem and Christian that had prevented either from gaining absolute control over the country," leaving the Phalange and Haddad as the dominant military forces. "The country's large Moslem and Palestinian refugee populations were left almost completely defenceless, at the mercy of their Christian foes and dependent on the ability of the Israel Defence Forces and the largely ineffectual Lebanese Army to protect them," though "for a reason or reasons yet to be adequately explained, the IDF proved unequal to the task" in Beirut in September—curiously, the only task to which it proved unequal, though Bernstein does not speculate as to why.[82] We return to the question. Whatever the mysterious reasons for the sudden and unusual incompetence of the IDF, the goal of placing power in the hands of Israel's allies while the Muslim and Palestinian population is left defenseless against forces that have long proven their skill at massacring defenseless people (with Israel's backing) appeared to have been achieved by late August 1982.

Apart from having "completely destroyed the partial and delicate equilibrium that had existed in Lebanon," the Israeli invasion, as intended, demolished the basis for organized social life among the half million or so Palestinian refugees. "Everyone now knows that in Lebanon the PLO had, to all intents and purposes, set up a Palestinian state: a state with its own army, with a system of civil administration, welfare and educational institutions and even the characteristics of its own economy, which was only partially integrated with that of their host country" and which existed in "a certain equilibrium" with it,[83] not without periodic and sometimes bitter conflict, in part, through the fulfilment of Abba Eban's "rational prospect." This too is gone.

The invasion had some other merits as well. As noted earlier, Israel is now heavily reliant on military exports. While the bombing of Beirut was at its height, the Israeli military industries *(Ta'as)* "came out with an extensive publicity campaign in the international press [*Aviation Week*, etc.] to extend the scope of sales of its bombs." The main feature was a display showing a jet plane dropping bombs with the heading: "Bombs you can count on to do what they're supposed to do. That's the only kind of bomb we make."[84]

4.7   The Green Light from Washington

While Israel may indeed be the world's fourth greatest military power, as the experts claim, this can be true only insofar as it is an appendage to the United States—it would not be quite fair to speak of it as a 51st state as some do, since none of the 50 states receive comparable benefits from the federal government. Despite the weakness of the enemy, the invasion of Lebanon too was predicated on American support, which was quite clearly forthcoming. As Meir Pail writes, "All signs indicate that the U.S. gave reasonable political backing to the IDF invasion of Lebanon, even when it became clear that it was delivering quite a heavy blow both in land and air to the Syrians in Lebanon."[85] The Reagan administration recognized that there were "strong feelings among members of Congress as well as the American people" against the Israeli invasion, in the words of White House counselor Edwin Meese; "this is a problem to be solved," he added, though there would be no "recriminations" by the Administration against Israel because it had "good reasons" for going into Lebanon.[86] Note that it was not a matter of the "pluralist consensus" dragging the government reluctantly towards support of Israel's aggression; rather, the problem was to *create* a consensus in favor of the invasion that the government supported (though less fervently than the Democratic opposition). Supporters of Israel recognized the problem, and regularly appealed to the contribution of Israel to fortifying U.S. power in the region in their attempts to garner support for the invasion in newspaper ads, letters, editorial statements (e.g., in the *New Republic*, repeatedly), and so on. A number of examples have already been given. It is interesting that among the signers of such statements were some who in other contexts have expressed a degree of concern over the manifestations of U.S. power. Another intriguing argument was that Israel had strengthened the U.S. by demonstrating the superiority of U.S. over Russian arms, from which it should follow that the immense "defense" build-up should be re-examined, though this conclusion, having only rationality in its favor, was not drawn.

It is probable that the occasional show of displeasure by the President was one of the means selected to solve the problem of the shaky domestic consensus. Knowledgeable Israeli observers did not take this display very seriously—nor should they, as long as the diplomatic support is steady and aid continues to flow. "Ronald Reagan played his part well," the Labor Party journal *Davar* wrote, commenting on the visit to the U.S. by Foreign Minister Yitzhak Shamir that ended with a photograph at the White House with Reagan looking somber instead of smiling at his guest, a symbolic "message" that elicited much commentary by Washington watchers in the U.S. media—the counterpart of Kreminologists who pore over pictures of Soviet rulers to try to determine who is in favor today. Israeli Washington watchers interpreted the message differently, and more realistically. "I think that [Shamir's] visit was extremely positive," the Washington correspondent of *Davar* continued, even though it offered the U.S. administration the opportunity to "come down on Israel" in public. "This fact in itself—though it is not comfortable and pleasant—does not harm us from a practical point of view. The [U.S.] government is compelled to make a public show of a hard line towards Israel—in part to respond to public pressure and also to deflect the pressures from the Arabs—and to use the same opportunity to extricate itself from the image of a participant in the Israeli operation." In private discussions with government officials and Congress (including Defense Secretary Caspar Weinberger, who is reputed to be the Administration's sharpest critic of Israel), the *Davar* correspondent claims, Shamir was told that it is time to "finish quickly with this matter of West Beirut." The expert opinion conveyed to Shamir by his American contacts was that a quick military blow will be acceptable in Washington. "This is the background for the decision of the Israeli government to carry out, starting yesterday, what its leaders prefer to call 'different means' for solving the Beirut problem"—more intensive bombardment, presumably.[87]

The conclusion seems eminently reasonable, given what is now known. Recall also Reagan's careful avoidance of the issue of settlements in his private discussions with Menachem Begin, one of the ways of signalling that public rhetoric on that issue is not to be taken very seriously either.[88] The more significant component of the message is obviously the increasing flow of aid, as already discussed.

Immediately prior to the Israeli invasion, General Sharon visited Washington where, he claims, he informed Defense Secretary Weinberger that Israel "must act in Lebanon." Pentagon figures "reveal a massive surge of military supplies from the United States to Israel in the first three months of [1982]—as Israel planned the invasion of Lebanon," plans that were perfectly evident, as already noted. Delivery of military goods was almost 50% greater than in the preceding year, including equipment effectively used in Lebanon. Pentagon spokesmen confirm that these deliveries continued through June at a very high level (though not subsequently, it is claimed), including "smart bombs," used with "devastating" effect in Beirut; one such bomb caused the instant destruction of an entire building killing 100 people in an apparent effort to finish off Yasser Arafat, who was thought to be there.[89]

The last example is instructive in itself, and also because of the way it came to be used by Israeli propagandists here. According to *Ha'aretz*, the bomb, which instantly destroyed an 8-story building in West Beirut, was a "blast bomb" or "vacuum bomb" of a type denied to Israel by President Carter but apparently supplied by Reagan. *Ha'aretz* proceeds to explain that the bomb ignites aviation fuel in such a way as to cause a vacuum, creating "immense pressure" and causing a large building to implode, destroying everything within.* Apart from its destructive capacity, the bomb is useful as a terror weapon. The use of such "illegal" terror weapons is described in *Al Hamishmar* as an expression of a "fascist tendency."[90]

The *New Republic* devoted an article to deriding a UPI report (no publication cited) that Israel had used a "vacuum bomb" to destroy the building. The article, by Laurence Grafstein, alleges that UPI was "snookered by a pro," and that the vacuum bomb "exists only in the mind of [the Soviet news agency] Tass," quoting an unidentified "Pentagon spokesman." Editor Martin Peretz then used the UPI dispatch to show that "it's easy to get an anti-Israeli story published," another example of the anti-Israel bias of the press, repeating that "there's no such thing as a vacuum bomb" and that the "tale" that there is "had been exposed" in Grafstein's article.[91] Both Grafstein and Peretz are careful to conceal the fact that a description of the nature of the device, reporting its use on this occasion, and a condemnation of its use, appeared in the mainstream Israeli press, which presumably is neither "anti-Israel" nor "pro-PLO" (I say "presumably," because it is not clear that Peretz would accept this conclusion, given that it is denied by extreme chauvinist elements in Israel, as we shall see). What the example shows, as usual, is not that the American press is "anti-Israel"—a charge too ludicrous to discuss—but that it is highly protective of Israel, failing to report atrocities amply covered in the Israeli press. It is interesting that the fact is illustrated by the very example selected by "supporters of Israel" to demonstrate the contrary, once their deception is exposed.

Returning to the U.S. government attitude towards the invasion, after a briefing by national security adviser William Clark, Jimmy Carter refused to divulge its contents but stated that "The only thing I can say is that the word I got from very knowledgeable people in Israel is that 'we have a green light from Washington'." Alexander Haig, who was Secretary of State at the time, angrily denied this charge ("a grotesque and outrageous proposition," "totally untrue") and then proceeded to confirm it, saying: "The Israelis had made it very clear that their limit of toleration had been exceeded, and that at the next provocation they were going to react. They told us that. The President knew that." It is unlikely that even the Secretary of State was totally unaware of the facts concerning "provocation" and "toleration" in 1981-2. The State Department press office, asked to supply some evidence for the official stance that Washington did not back the invasion, was unable to cite a single official statement opposing it apart from the support, quickly withdrawn, for the first UN Security Council Resolution calling on Israel to terminate its aggression.[92]

---

* The *Ha'aretz* account is cited in *Libération* (Paris), Aug. 12; Jean Gueyras describes the use and psychological effect of this "terror" weapon in *Le Monde*, Aug. 11. I noticed no discussion of the weapon, or the Israeli reports concerning it, in the American press.

The affair is reminiscent of the U.S. backing for the 1975 Indonesian invasion of East Timor and the subsequent near-genocidal massacre. In that case too the U.S. government pretended ignorance of the invasion plans and also claimed that the U.S. had imposed an embargo on arms after the aggression. The latter claim was false (furthermore, under the Human Rights Administration the arms flow, which had never been reduced, was substantially increased to enable Indonesia to consummate the slaughter), and the former, always incredible (except to the U.S. press), has since been thoroughly demolished. In that case too the U.S. blocked UN action to stop the aggression, a story that UN Ambassador Daniel P. Moynihan recounts with pride in his memoirs. Diplomatic cables that have since surfaced reveal that the U.S. Ambassador to Jakarta expressed his hope, several months earlier, that if Indonesia intervened as planned it would do so "effectively, quickly and not use our equipment," very much the reaction to the Israeli invasion of Lebanon; the concern over the use of U.S. equipment is farcical in both cases given the dependence of the aggressors on U.S. supplies, and is to be understood as a hope that Congress will not act to enforce treaty obligations that these weapons are to be used only in self-defense.*

5   War is Peace

On June 6, 1982, a massive Israeli expeditionary force began the long expected invasion, Operation "Peace for Galilee," a phrase "which sounds as if it comes directly out of the pages of *1984*," as one Israeli commentator wrote:

> Only in the language of *1984* is war—peace and warfare— humane. One may mention, of course, that only in the Orwell- ian language of *1984* can occupation be liberal, and there is indeed a connection between the "liberal occupation" [the Labor Party boast] and a war which equals peace.[93]

Excuses and explanations were discarded almost as quickly as they were produced: the Argov assassination attempt, defense of the border settle- ments, a 25-mile limit. In fact, the army headed straight for Beirut and the Beirut-Damascus highway, in accordance with plans that had long been prepared and that were known in advance to the Labor opposition (see section 6.3). Former chief of military intelligence Aharon Yariv of the Labor Party stated: "I know in fact that going to Beirut was included in the original military plan,"[94] despite the pretense to the contrary, dutifully repeated by the U.S. government, which could hardly have been in much doubt about the facts if U.S. intelligence was not on vacation.

---

* See *TNCW*, chapter 13. See Ze'ev Schiff, "Green Light, Lebanon," for further discussion of the tacit authorization from Washington of the invasion it knew to be imminent.

5.1   Extermination of the Two-Legged Beasts

The first target was the Palestinian camp of Rashidiyeh south of Tyre, much of which, by the second day of the invasion, "had become a field of rubble." There was ineffectual resistance, but as an officer of the UN peace-keeping force swept aside in the Israeli invasion later remarked: "It was like shooting sparrows with cannon." The 9000 residents of the camp—which had been regularly bombed and shelled for years from land, sea and air—either fled, or were herded to the beach where they could watch the destruction of much of what remained by the Israeli forces. All teen-age and adult males were blindfolded and bound, and taken to camps, where little has been heard about them since.[95]

This is typical of what happened throughout southern Lebanon. The Palestinian camps were demolished, largely bulldozed to the ground if not destroyed by bombardment; and the population was dispersed or (in the case of the male population) imprisoned. Reporters were generally not allowed in the Palestinian camps, where the destruction was worst, to keep them from witnessing what had happened and was being done. There were occasional reports. David Shipler described how after the camps were captured the army proceeded to destroy what was left. An army officer, "when asked why bulldozers were knocking down houses in which women and children were living," responded by saying: "they are all terrorists."[96] His statement accurately summarizes Israel's strategy and the assumptions that underlie it, over many years.

There was little criticism here of Israel's destruction of the "nests of terrorists," or of the wholesale transfer of the male population to prison camps in Lebanon and Israel—or to their treatment, discussed below. Again, one imagines that if such treatment had been meted out to Jews after, say, a Syrian conquest of Northern Israel, the reaction would have been different, and few would have hesitated to recall the Nazi monsters. In fact, we need not merely imagine. When a PLO terrorist group took Israeli teen-age members of a paramilitary *(Gadna)* group hostage at Ma'alot, that was rightly denounced as a vicious criminal act. Since then, it has become virtually the symbol of the inhuman barbarism of the "two-legged beasts." But when Israeli troops cart off the Palestinian male population from 15 to 60 (along with many thousands of Lebanese) to concentration camps, treating them in a manner to which we return, that is ignored, and the few timid queries are almost drowned in the applause—to which we also return—for Israel's display of humanitarian zeal and moral perfection, while aid is increased in honor of this achievement. It is a scene that should give Americans pause, and lead them to raise some questions about themselves.

Israel's strategy was to drive the Palestinians to largely-Muslim West Beirut (apart from those who were killed, dispersed or imprisoned), then to besiege the city, cutting off water, food, medical supplies and electricity, and to subject it to increasingly heavy bombardment. Naturally, the native Lebanese population was also severely battered. These measures had little impact on the PLO guerrilla fighters in Beirut, but civilians suffered increasingly brutal punishment. The correct calculation was that by this device, the PLO would be compelled to leave West Beirut to save it from total annihilation.[97] It was assumed, also correctly, that American intellectuals could be found to carry out the task of showing that this too was a remarkable exercise in humanity and a historically unique display of "purity of arms," even having the audacity to claim that it was the PLO, not the Israeli attackers, who were "holding the city and its population hostage"—a charge duly intoned by *New York Times* editors and many others. (See section 8.2.3.)

Dan Connell, a journalist with wartime experience and Lebanon project officer for Oxfam, describes Israel's strategy as follows:

> The Israeli strategy was obvious. They were hitting a broad belt, and they kept moving the belt up toward the populated area and pushing the people in front of it. The Israelis forced an increasing concentration of people into a smaller space, so that the casualties increased geometrically with every single shell or bomb that landed.

The attackers used highly sophisticated U.S. weapons, including "shells and bombs designed to penetrate through the buildings before they explode," collapsing buildings inwards, and phosphorus bombs to set fires and cause untreatable burns. Hospitals were closed down or destroyed. Much of the Ain el-Hilweh refugee camp near Sidon was "flat as a parking lot" when Connell saw it, though 7-8000 Palestinians had drifted back—mostly women and children, since the men were "either fighting or arrested or dead." The Israelis bulldozed the mosque at the edge of the camp searching for arms, but "found 90 or 100 bodies under it instead, completely rotted away." Writing before the Beirut massacres but after the PLO had departed, he notes that "there could be a bloodbath in west Beirut" if no protection is given to the remnants of the population.[98]

The Israeli press also reported the strategy of the invading army. One journalist observing the bombardment of Beirut in the early days describes it as follows:

> With deadly accuracy, the big guns laid waste whole rows of houses and apartment blocks believed to be PLO positions. The fields were pitted with craters... Israeli strategy at that point was obvious—to clean away a no-man's land through which Israeli tanks could advance and prevent any PLO breakout.[99]

The military tactics, as widely reported by the Israeli and foreign press, were simple. Since Israel had total command of the air and overwhelming superiority in firepower from land, sea and air, the IDF simply blasted away everything before it, then sent soldiers in to "clean out" what was left. We return to some descriptions of these tactics by Israeli military analysts. The tactics are familiar from Vietnam and other wars where a modern high technology army faces a vastly outmatched enemy. The difference lies in the fact that in other such cases, one rarely hears tales of great heroism and "purity of arms," though to be accurate, these stories were more prevalent among American "supporters" than Israeli soldiers, many of whom were appalled at what they were ordered to do.

Economist Middle East correspondent G. H. Jansen describes Israel's tactics in the first days of the war as follows: to surround cities and towns "so swiftly that civilian inhabitants were trapped inside, and then to pound them from land, sea and air. After a couple of days of this there would be a timid probing attack: if there were resistance the pounding would resume."* "A second striking aspect of Israeli military doctrine exemplified in the Lebanese campaign," he notes, "is the military exploitation of a cease-fire. Israel has done this so often, in every one of its wars, that perhaps one must assume that for the Israeli military 'cease-fire' only means 'no shooting' and is totally unconnected with any freezing of positions on the ground along a 'cease-fire' line." We have, in fact, noted several earlier examples of exploitation of cease-fire: the conquest of Eilat in 1949 and of the Golan Heights in 1967. "The Israelis, in this war, have refined their cease-fire-exploitation doctrine by declaring cease-fires unilaterally, at times most advantageous to them. This has left them free to switch cease-fires on and off with a show either of peaceful intent or of outraged indignation. For the Israelis the cease-fire is not a step towards a truce or an armistice, it is simply a period of rest, reinforcement and peaceful penetration—an attempt to gain the spoils of war without fighting."[100] Such tactics are possible because of the huge military advantage that Israel enjoyed.

---

* Israeli troops in fact often warned inhabitants to leave before the land, sea and air pounding, but many report, not surprisingly, that they were unaware of the warnings; see Michael Jansen, *The Battle of Beirut.* Furthermore, the leaflets sometimes were dropped well after the bombardment of civilian targets began, as in Sidon (see *Israel in Lebanon*, p. 72, citing "the detailed diary of a reputable representative of a relief organisation" among other evidence). It has repeatedly been claimed that Israel suffered casualties because of the policy of warning inhabitants to leave, but it remains unexplained how this came about in areas that were sure to be next on the list, warning or not, and how casualties could be caused by the use of the tactics just described, which are repeatedly verified in the Israeli press (see p. 218 and below, for many examples). Danny Wolf, formerly a commander in the Paratroopers, asks: "If someone dropped leaflets over Herzliya [in Israel] tomorrow, telling the civilians in hiding to evacuate the town within two hours, wouldn't that be a war crime?" (Amir Oren, *Koteret Rashit*, Jan. 19, 1983). It would be interesting to hear the answer from those who cite these alleged IDF warnings with much respect as proof of the noble commitment to "purity of arms."

Since the western press was regularly accused in the United States of failing to recognize the amazing and historically unique Israeli efforts to spare civilians and of exaggerating the scale of the destruction and terror—we return to some specifics—it is useful to bear in mind that the actual tactics used were entirely familiar and that some of the most terrible accounts were given by Israeli soldiers and journalists. In Knesset debate, Menachem Begin responded to accusations about civilian casualties by recalling the words of Chief of Staff Mordechai Gur of the Labor Party after the 1978 invasion of Lebanon under the Begin government, cited on p. 181. When asked "what happens when we meet a civilian population," Gur's answer was that "It is a civilian population known to have provided active aid to the terrorists...Why has that population of southern Lebanon suddenly become such a great and just one?" Asked further whether he was saying that the population of southern Lebanon "should be punished," he responded: "And how! I am using Sabra language [colloquial Hebrew]: And how!" The "terrorists" had been "nourished by the population around them." Gur went on to explain the orders he had given: "bring in tanks as quickly as possible and hit them from far off before the boys reached a face-to-face battle." He continued: "For 30 years, from the war of independence to this day, we have been fighting against a population that lives in villages and in towns..." With audacity bordering on obscenity, Begin was able to utter the words: "We did not even once deliberately harm the civilian population...all the fighting has been aimed against military targets..."

Turning to the press, Tom Segev of *Ha'aretz* toured "Lebanon after the conquest" in mid-June. He saw "refugees wandering amidst swarms of flies, dressed in rags, their faces expressing terror and their eyes, bewilderment..., the women wailing and the children sobbing" (he noticed Henry Kamm of the *New York Times* nearby; one may usefully compare his account of the same scenes). Tyre was a "destroyed city"; in the market place there was not a store undamaged. Here and there people were walking, "as in a nightmare." "A terrible smell filled the air"—of decomposing bodies, he learned. Archbishop Georges Haddad told him that many had been killed, though he did not know the numbers, since many were still buried beneath the ruins and he was occupied with caring for the many orphans wandering in the streets, some so young that they did not even know their names. In Sidon, the destruction was still worse: "the center of the town—destroyed." "This is what the cities of Germany looked like at the end of the Second World War." "Half the inhabitants remained without shelter, 100,000 people." He saw "mounds of ruins," tens of thousands of people at the shore where they remained for days, women driven away by soldiers when they attempted to flee to the beaches, children wandering "among the tanks and the ruins and the shots and the hysteria," blindfolded young men, hands tied with plastic bonds, "terror and confusion."

Danny Rubinstein of *Davar* toured the conquered areas at the war's end. Virtually no Palestinians were to be found in Christian-controlled areas, the refugee camps having been destroyed long ago (see the description by Attallah Mansour, pp. 186-7). The Red Cross give the figure of 15,000 as a "realistic" estimate of the number of prisoners taken by the Israeli army. In the "ruins of Ain el-Hilweh," a toothless old man was the youngest man left in the camp, among thousands of women, children and old men, "a horrible scene." Perhaps 350-400,000 Palestinians had been "dispersed in all directions" ("mainly women, children and old men, since all the men have been detained"). The remnants are at the mercy of Phalangist patrols and Haddad forces, who burn houses and "beat the people." There is no one to care for the tens of thousands of refugee children, "and of course all the civilian networks operated by the PLO have been annihilated, and tens of thousands of families, or parts of families, are dispersed like animals." "The shocking scene of the destroyed camps proves that the destruction was systematic." Even shelters in which people hid from the Israeli bombardments were destroyed, "and they are still digging out bodies"—this, in areas where the fighting had ended over 2 months earlier.[101] An Oxfam appeal in March 1983 states that "No one will ever know how many dead are buried beneath the twisted steel of apartment buildings or the broken stone of the cities and villages of Lebanon."

By late June, the Lebanese police gave estimates of about 10,000 killed. These early figures appear to have been roughly accurate. A later accounting reported by the independent Lebanese daily *An-nahar* gave a figure of 17,825 known to have been killed and over 30,000 wounded, including 5500 killed in Beirut and over 1200 civilians killed in the Sidon area. A government investigation estimated that 90% of the casualties were civilians. By late December, the Lebanese police estimated the numbers killed through August at 19,085, with 6775 killed in Beirut, 84% of them civilians. Israel reported 340 IDF soldiers killed in early September, 446 by late November (if these numbers are accurate, then the number of Israeli soldiers killed in the ten weeks following the departure of the PLO from Lebanon is exactly the same as the number of Israelis killed in all terrorist actions across the northern border from 1967). According to Chief of Staff Eitan, the number of Israeli soldiers killed "in the entire western sector of Lebanon" —that is, apart from the Syrian front—was 117. Eight Israeli soldiers died "in Beirut proper," he claimed, three in accidents. If correct (which is unlikely), Eitan's figures mean that five Israeli soldiers were killed in the process of massacring some 6000 civilians in Beirut, a glorious victory indeed. Israel also offered various figures for casualties within Lebanon. Its final accounting was that 930 people were killed in Beirut including 340 civilians, and that 40 buildings were destroyed in the Beirut bombings,* 350 in all of Lebanon. The number of PLO killed was given as 4000.[103]

---

* Since one of these was Beirut's only synagogue, we may conclude that 39 buildings of terrorists were destroyed. Despite considerable effort, representatives of the World Zionist

The estimates given by Israel were generally ridiculed by reporters and relief workers, though solemnly repeated by supporters here. Within Israel itself, the Lebanese figures were regularly cited; for example, by Yizhar Smilanski, one of Israel's best-known novelists, in a bitter denunciation of Begin (the "man of blood" who was willing to sacrifice "some 50,000 human beings" for his political ends) and of the society that is able to tolerate him.[104] In general, Israeli credibility suffered seriously during the war, as it had in the course of the 1973 war. Military correspondent Hirsh Goodman reported that "the army spokesman [was] less credible than ever before." Because of repeated government lies (e.g., the claim, finally admitted to be false, that the IDF returns fire only to the point from which it originates), "thousands of Israeli troops who bear eye-witness to events no longer believe the army spokesman" and "have taken to listening to Radio Lebanon in English and Arabic to get what they believe is a credible picture of the war." The "overwhelming majority of men—including senior officers"—accused Israeli military correspondents of "allowing this war to grow out of all proportion to the original goals, by mindlessly repeating official explanations we all knew were false." The officers and men "of four top fighting units...accused [military correspondents] of covering up the truth, of lying to the public, of not reporting on the real mood at the front and of being lackeys of the defence minister." Soldiers "repeated the latest jokes doing the rounds, like the one about the idiot in the ordnance corps who must have put all Israeli cannon in back to front. 'Each time we open fire the army spokesman announces we're being fired at...'" Goodman is concerned not only over the deterioration in morale caused by this flagrant lying but also by Israel's "current world image."[105] About that, he need not have feared too much. At least in the U.S., Israeli government claims continued to be taken quite seriously, even the figures offered with regard to casualties and war damages.

As relief officials and others regularly commented, accurate numbers cannot be obtained, since many—particularly Palestinians—are simply unaccounted for. Months after the fighting had ended in the Sidon area inhabitants of Ain el-Hilweh were still digging out corpses and had no idea how many had been killed, and an education officer of the Israeli army (a Lieutenant Colonel) reported that the army feared epidemics in Sidon itself "because of the many bodies under the wreckage..."[106] Lebanese and foreign relief officials observed that "Many of the dead never reached hospital," and that unknown numbers of bodies are believed lost in the rubble in Beirut; hospital figures, the primary basis for the Lebanese calculations cited above, "only hint at the scale of the tragedy." "Many bodies could not be lodged in overflowing morgues and were not included in the statistics."[107]

Organization were unable to convince the Jews of West Beirut to immigrate to Israel. "'Why should we leave,' they asked? Here are our houses and our friends."[102] Or what is left of them.

The Lebanese government casualty figures are based on police records, which in turn are based on actual counts in hospitals, clinics and civil defense centers. These figures, according to police spokesmen, do "not include people buried in mass graves in areas where Lebanese authorities were not informed."[108] The figures, including the figure of 19,000 dead and over 30,000 wounded, must surely be underestimates, assuming that those celebrating their liberation (the story that Israel and its supporters here would like us to believe) were not purposely magnifying the scale of the horrors caused by their liberators. Particularly with regard to the Palestinians, one can only guess what the scale of casualties may have been.

A UN report estimated 13,500 severely damaged houses in West Beirut alone, thousands elsewhere, not counting the Palestinian camps (which are—or were—in fact towns).[109] As for the Palestinians, the head of the UN Agency that has been responsible for them, Olof Rydbeck of Sweden, said that its work of 32 years "has been wiped out"; Israeli bombardment had left "practically all the schools, clinics and installations of the agency in ruins."[110] Israel made much of the fact that one UNRWA school had been converted to a PLO military training center, unknown to UNRWA. "The Israelis are entitled to be indignant," the London *Economist* observed. "Their protest would carry more weight if they had not looted the college's educational equipment, reduced its student roll to about 150 and reduced the nearby refugee camp, from which many of the students were drawn, to a mass of rubble."[111] Some older Israelis must have winced at the show of indignation, those who recalled UNRWA's earlier incarnation as UNRRA, established to care for other refugees. The Chief of UNRRA Operations in Germany, 1945-6, writes in his memoirs that "Military training of Jewish D.P.'s was taking place in [UNRRA] camps, presumably in preparation for active participation in the war of liberation from the British Mandate on their arrival in Palestine. Instructors were found to be N.C.O.s from British and U.S. armies, in uniform, absent without, but I fancy sometimes with, leave from their units."[112] All illegal, a violation of UNRRA's commitment, and one of the proud moments in the history of the foundation of the State of Israel. It is, once again, uncanny to see how history is being replayed, with a change in the cast of characters that will become still more macabre before we conclude, with future chapters that one hesitates to imagine.

John Kifner reported that "there was not much left standing" in the Palestinian camps after Israel's bombardment, and that in the south, "the Israelis have bulldozed refugee camps to make them uninhabitable.[113] Contrary to a standard propaganda claim, reporters found "no heavy artillery or well-fortified positions" in the Sabra, Shatilla and Bourj al-Barajneh camps in Beirut, which had "taken a terrible pounding" since June 6 (actually, June 4), causing the flight of half of their 125,000 population in the first few weeks of the war.[114] The areas to which they escaped, particularly the Fakhani quarter in Beirut, were also mercilessly bombed. Since Palestinians are by definition all terrorists, or mothers of terrorists, or future terrorists—so different from Begin, Shamir and Sharon for example—whatever was done to them was regarded as legitimate.

5.2   Beirut: Precision Bombardment

Repeatedly, Israel blocked international relief efforts and prevented food and medical supplies from reaching victims.* Israeli military forces also appear to have gone out of their way to destroy medical facilities—at least, if one wants to believe Israeli government claims about "pinpoint accuracy" in bombardment. "International agencies agree that the civilian death toll would have been considerably higher had it not been for the medical facilities that the Palestine Liberation Organization provides for its own people"[116]—and, in fact, for many poor Lebanese—so it is not surprising that these were a particular target of attack.

In the first bombing in June, a children's hospital in the Sabra refugee camp was hit, Lebanese television reported, and a cameraman said he saw "many children" lying dead inside the Bourj al Barajneh camp in Beirut, while "fires were burning out of control at dozens of apartment buildings" and the Gaza Hospital near the camps was reported hit.[117] This, it will be recalled, was in "retaliation" for the attempt by an anti-PLO group with no base in Lebanon to assassinate Ambassador Argov. On June 12, four bombs fell on a hospital in Aley, severely damaging it. "There is nothing unusual" in the story told by an operating room assistant who had lost two hands in the attack; "That the target of the air strike was a hospital, whether by design or accident, is not unique either," William Branigan reports, noting that other hospitals were even more badly damaged. Fragments of cluster bombs were found on the grounds of an Armenian sanitarium south of Beirut that was also "heavily damaged during the Israeli drive."[118] A neurosurgeon at the Gaza hospital in Beirut "insists that Israeli gunners deliberately shelled his hospital," it was reported at the same time.[119] A few days later, Richard Ben Cramer reported that the Acre Hospital in Beirut was hit by Israeli shells, and that the hospitals in the camps had again been hit. "Israeli guns never seem to stop here," he reported from the Sabra camp, later to be the scene of a major massacre: "After two weeks of this random thunder, Sabra is only a place to run through."[120]

---

* The International Red Cross, World Vision International, UNICEF and other relief agencies report long delays in supply of food and medicines caused by Israeli interference.[115] This is confirmed by Israeli officials responsible for relief, as we will see directly.

The Acre hospital was again hit on June 24, along with the Gaza hospital and the Islamic Home for Invalids, where "the corridors were streaked with blood." The hospitals were short of supplies because Israel was blocking tons of medical supplies ready for shipment in Cyprus, according to the International Red Cross.[121] By mid-August, the Islamic Home had been repeatedly shelled, only 15 of 200 staff members remained, and "several of the retarded children have died of starvation for lack of someone who has the time to feed them properly." At the Palestinian Hospital for the Disabled (perhaps the same institution), "a visitor walking the gloomy corridors is approached by stumbling figures crying 'Food, food' in Arabic"; 800 patients remained, all mentally ill, half of them children, cared for by a dozen nurses.[122]

A French doctor reported witnessing "an intense Israeli bombing raid around and against the [Gaza] hospital, which forced the evacuation of the hospital at the time."[123] When the Beirut mental hospital was hit shortly after, "800 patients varying in condition from senile dementia to violent schizophrenia were released into the streets of Beirut." The hospital, clearly marked by Red Cross flags, was hit by artillery and naval gunfire, including four phosphorus shells. Medical personnel reported that the patients, including children with mental problems whose nursery was hit by rockets that set beds on fire, were 90% Lebanese. No military target was found within a half-mile. The hospital was, however, "precariously located near the Palestinian ghettoes of Sabra and Shatila, frequent targets of Israeli bombardment," though the "immediate surroundings are residential" (i.e., not Palestinian slums).[124]

Most of this was before the bombing escalated to new levels of violence in August. By August 4, 8 of the 9 Homes for Orphans in Beirut had been destroyed, attacked by cluster and phosphorus bombs. The last was hit by phosphorus and other rockets, though clearly marked by a red cross on the roof, after assurances by the International Red Cross that it would be spared.[125] On August 4, the American University hospital was hit by shrapnel and mortar fire. A doctor "standing in bloodstained rags" said: "We have no more room." The director reported: "It's a carnage. There is nothing military anywhere near this hospital."[126] The hospital was the only one in Beirut to escape direct shelling, and even there, sanitary conditions had deteriorated to the point where half the intensive-care patients were lost and with 99% of the cases being trauma victims, there was no room for ordinary illnesses. "Drive down any street and you will almost always see a man or woman with a missing limb."[127]

The Red Cross reported that by August 6, "there were 130 beds available in west Beirut out of a total of about 1,400." The American University Hospital was admitting only "those who look salvageable" on bad days, the staff reported. The Berbir hospital was "just an underground dormitory with generators churning away to give the few patients air." At the Hotel Bristol, hit by an Israeli phosphorus shell, the Red Cross had set up an underground hospital. "The majority of the doctors and nurses working in the city have fled."[128] "Even the Red Cross delegation has been shelled twice. In an Israeli naval bombardment on July 30, six shells struck the building and on Aug. 5 it was again hit by two artillery shells." The Berbir hospital was already seriously damaged by mid-July, with trails of blood in the corridors, many of the patients removed from the wreckage, and the mortuary full of corpses until the remaining doctors were able to leave the building to bury the unidentified bodies in a communal grave when the shelling and air attacks temporarily stopped.[129]

One of the true heroes of the war is Dr. Amal Shamma, an American-trained Lebanese-American pediatrician who remained at work in Beirut's Berbir hospital through the worst horrors. In November, she spent several weeks touring the U.S., receiving little notice, as expected. She was, however, interviewed in the *Village Voice*, where she described the extensive medical and social services for Palestinians and poor Lebanese that were destroyed by the Israeli invasion. For them, nothing is left apart from private hospitals that they cannot afford, some taken over by the Israeli army. No medical teams came from the U.S., although several came to help from Europe; the U.S. was preoccupied with supplying weapons to destroy. She reports that the hospitals were clearly marked with red crosses and that there were no guns nearby, though outside her hospital there was one disabled tank, which was never hit in the shellings that reduced the hospital to a first-aid station. On one day, 17 hospitals were shelled. Hers "was shelled repeatedly from August 1 to 12 until everything in it was destroyed." It had been heavily damaged by mid-July, as already noted. Hospital employees stopped at Israeli barricades were told: "We shelled your hospital good enough, didn't we? You treat terrorists there."[130] Recall that this is the testimony of a doctor at a Lebanese hospital, one of those liberated by the Israeli forces, according to official doctrine.

An American nurse working in Beirut, who was appalled by the "watered-down descriptions in American newspapers," reported that Israel "dropped bombs on everything, including hospitals, orphanages and, in one case, a school bus carrying 35 young schoolgirls who were traveling on an open road"; she cared for the survivors.[131] The U.S. Navy Lieut. Commander in charge of removing unexploded ordnance in Beirut reports that "we found five bombs in an orphanage with about 45 cluster bombs in the front yard. We were called there after five children were injured and four killed." About 3-5% of the shells and bombs failed to go off and are considered highly dangerous, he said.[132] This particular orphanage, then, must have been heavily bombed.

One of the most devastating critiques of Israeli military practices was provided inadvertently by an Israeli pilot who took part in the bombing, an Air Force major, who described the careful selection of targets and the precision bombing that made error almost impossible. Observing the effects, one can draw one's own conclusions. He also expressed his own personal philosophy, saying "if you want to achieve peace, you should fight." "Look at the American-Japanese war," he added. "In order to achieve an end, they bombed Hiroshima and Nagasaki."[133]

The precedents this pilot cited can be placed alongside of others offered by Prime Minister Begin in justification of the war: Dresden and Coventry, for example. The reference to Coventry particularly amazed Israeli listeners; "We know who carried out the bombardment of Coventry," Abba Eban wrote—commenting also on the "delegations of diaspora Jews [who] came to Israel, or rather to Lebanon, and applauded the decision to make war as enthusiastically as they would have applauded a decision not to make it," and the "embarrassing vulgarity in holding [United Jewish Appeal] fundraising appeals" in occupied Lebanon. These precedents give some insight into the mentality of the Israeli political leadership and segments of the officer corps, and also of American supporters who appeal to the same precedents, for example, former Supreme Court Justice and UN Ambassador Arthur Goldberg. In his interesting comments in support of the invasion, to which we return, he cites the precedent of the bombing of Dresden and more generally, the war "against the demented barbarian who sought to enslave the world." "Is not the government of Israel faced with the same terrible dilemma in view of repeated PLO acts of terrorism against Israeli civilians and the bombing of its northern settlements?"[134] Recall the actual scale of PLO terrorism and the comparison to Israeli terrorism, already discussed, and the fact that there had been no unprovoked bombardment of northern settlements for a year, none at all for 10 months despite extensive Israeli provocation, including bombing in April.

Goldberg's notion that Israel's invasion of Lebanon is comparable to the war against Hitler was also invoked by Prime Minister Begin in a letter to President Reagan in which he portrayed himself as marching to "Berlin" to liquidate "Hitler." To the Labor Party spokesman on foreign affairs, Abba Eban, this seemed "a dark and macabre fantasy," "one of the most bizarre documents in recent diplomatic history," an example of "losing touch with reality."* Other Israeli commentators also ridiculed this comparison, suggesting that it raised questions about Begin's sanity. I

---

* Eban remarks that "Arafat's ideology and rhetoric, repulsive as they are, are identical with those of Anwar Sadat until a few months before Begin embraced him in the Knesset."[135] There is some truth to what he says, though not in the sense that he intended his audience to understand, as we see when we recall Sadat's rebuffed efforts to make peace with Israel for over six years before his visit to Jerusalem, and Arafat's moves towards the accommodationist international consensus, also regularly rebuffed, from the mid-1970s. See chapter 3. Eban surely knows all of this, and more, very well. He is able to exploit his reputation as a dove to conceal the historical record with considerable effectiveness.

noticed no comment here on Goldberg's sanity. It is, perhaps, not too surprising that a liberal American hero should surpass the "macabre fantasies" of Israel's Nobel Peace Prize winner in his own ruminations on the topic.

5.3   Caring for the Victims: Prisoners, Patients, Refugees

Not only hospitals, but also medical personnel seemed to evoke particular fury. One eyewitness saw a Palestinian doctor, unconscious, "his hands and neck tied to a post, his face bloodied and covered with flies."[136] Palestinian hospitals were closed down, their staffs arrested, removed to prison camps, and brutalized.

In Sidon, the Israeli army closed down the Palestinian Red Crescent Hospital. A Dutch nurse working there told a reporter: "I was in Holland during World War II. I know what fascists are like. It's terrible that all these women and children are being killed. Tell that to the world."[137] On the same day, the *New York Times* reported a Jerusalem news conference in which Imri Ron, a Mapam Knesset member (from Kibbutz Mishmar Haemek) and paratroop major, "spoke from a combination of political and military authority" about the "clean fight" the Israeli army had fought, "taking extraordinary precautions to save civilians."[138] Apart from the U.S. military itself, only an Israeli officer would be accorded such "authority" in the U.S. press. Ron's authority is undiminished by the fact that he was such an enthusiast for the war that he volunteered to take part in it, though as a Knesset member he was not called up.[139] We return to some of his further "authoritative" observations, comparing them to those of a different breed of Israeli military officers.

A Belgian doctor at the closed Sidon hospital, who "struggled to cope with wounded men, women and children" (victims of this "clean fight"), stated that "We had a good operation here. We were doing surgery and everything" before almost the entire staff was arrested by the Israeli army.[140] Shipler reported the same events in the *New York Times*. He quotes the Israeli Major who is military governor of Sidon and who closed the hospital because, he said, "It's obvious it's not a good hospital." Therefore, "At 11 A.M. today I had all the patients moved out to a good private hospital, the Labib Medical Center," not tainted by a Palestinian connection. He added that he had not ordered the arrest of a Norwegian nurse, though "she is a member of the P.L.O.," because "we are democratic" and therefore "we are not taking women"—whether or not this was true at the time, it is false for the subsequent period, as we shall see. A Canadian and Norwegian doctor, along with Palestinian doctors, will be taken to Israel for interrogation and possible imprisonment, the Major added. Shipler visited the "good private hospital," where no one seemed "pressed for time" and the director angrily refused to take patients from the closed hospital, explaining to his guests that "The first case I got from there, she had gangrene all over her body." He will take only "good cases." Meanwhile one Belgian doctor remained in the closed Palestinian hospital to take care of 58 patients, some badly wounded, amidst "a stench of filth and rotting flesh." The director of the "good private hospital" is, incidentally, the son of a millionaire orange grove owner, who was quite pleased to be liberated by the Israeli army.[141]

None of this merited any editorial comment, apart from the regular tributes to Israel's sublime moral standards, which are a wonder to behold. One may recall, perhaps, the reaction in the *Times* and elsewhere when the peasant army of Pol Pot evacuated the hospitals of Phnom Penh—without first reducing them to ruins, however.

The Canadian and Norwegian doctor, along with a Norwegian social worker, were indeed arrested and taken to Israel, then released after protests from their governments. Their testimony received a brief notice in the *New York Times*, divided between Canadian surgeon Chris Giannou's testimony before Congress that he had seen prisoners beaten to death by Israeli soldiers and other atrocities, and the Israeli government denials and allegations that Giannou was a liar suspected of working for the PLO, that the hospital he reported being bombed "was hit only because the P.L.O. used it for fighting," etc.[142] This admirable show of balance in reports of atrocities is not familiar from other cases.*

In his congressional testimony, Giannou reported that he was "a witness to four prisoners who were beaten to death" (reduced to two by the *Times*). He also witnessed "the total, utter devastation of residential areas, and the blind, savage, indiscriminate destruction of refugee camps by simultaneous shelling and carpet bombing from aircraft, gunboats, tanks and artillery," leaving only "large blackened craters filled with rubble and debris, broken concrete slabs and twisted iron bars, and corpses"; "hospitals being shelled," one shell killing 40-50 people; the shelling of the camp after Israeli soldiers had permitted women and children to return to it; the use of cluster bombs in settled areas; "the calcinated, carbonized bodies of the victims of phosphorus bombs"; 300 cadavers in one area while he was evacuating the Government Hospital; and much more. He saw "the entire male staff" of the hospitals being taken into custody, leaving patients unattended, and "savage and indiscriminate beatings" of prisoners with fists, sticks, ropes with nuts and bolts tied to them. He saw a Palestinian doctor hung by his hands from a

---

* Not surprisingly, Giannou merits an entry in the Anti-Defamation League Enemies List of people dedicated "to undermine American support for Israel" (see chapter 4, note 145). The *Handbook* of "pro-Arab propagandists" repeats Israel's charges that Giannou "was detained because of his close connection to the PLO and his apparent sympathy for the terrorist organization," sufficient reason by ADL standards, and states that his "public accusations against the Israelis" are "not authenticated."

tree and beaten and an Iraqi surgeon "beaten by several guards viciously, and left to lie in the sun with his face buried in the sand," all in the presence of an Israeli Colonel who did nothing about it. He watched prisoners "being rehearsed by an Israeli officer to shout 'Long Live Begin'," others sitting bound in "stifling heat" with "food and water in short supply." He was forced to evacuate his hospital and bring the patients down to the seafront. The Norwegians confirmed his story and said that they had seen at least 10 people beaten to death, including an old man who was crazed by the lack of water and intense heat as the prisoners were forced to sit for hours in the sun; he was beaten by four or five soldiers who then tied him with his wrists to his ankles and let him lie in the sun until he died.[143] Another demonstration of courage and purity of arms.

Little of this was reported here in the mainstream media, but Giannou's testimony obviously did impress Congress, as we can see from its decision, shortly after, to improve the terms of Reagan's proposed increase of military and economic aid to Israel.

The Norwegian doctor and social worker told the story of their captivity in a report issued by the Norwegian Department of Foreign Affairs.[144] Under Israeli captivity, they were forced to sit, hands tied, for 36 hours without permission to move, while they heard "screams of pain" from nearby. In an Israeli prison, they were forced to lie for 48 hours, blindfolded and handcuffed, on the interrogation ground. They report "extensive violence" against prisoners, including beatings by thick table legs, batons, plastic tubes "often with big knots in the ends" and clubs with nails. Officers were present during severe beatings, but did nothing. One of the most sadistic Israeli guards told them he was from a kibbutz where an Austrian girl had been killed by rocket fire. Prisoners were tied with tight plastic straps with sharp edges, "causing pain." The Norwegians were given "preferential treatment." Arab prisoners were subjected to constant brutality and degradation.

Dr. Shafiqul-Islam from Bangladesh, who was on the staff of the Palestinian hospital in Sidon, reports that he was arrested by the IDF while operating on a 12-year-old Palestinian boy with severe internal shrapnel injuries. He was not permitted to complete the operation, but was arrested, beaten mercilessly, forbidden to ask for food or water for 4 days, denied drugs or dressings for other prisoners on the grounds that they were "all terrorists," and so on.[145]

The treatment of prisoners gives a certain insight into the nature of the conquering army and the political leadership that guides it, as does the very fact that it was considered legitimate to round up all teen-age and adult males and to ship them off to concentration camps after they were identified as "terrorists" by hooded informants. Similarly, the fact that all of this was generally regarded as quite unremarkable here—search *New York Times* editorials, for example, for a protest—gives a certain insight into the society that was funding this operation, the paymasters and coterie of apologists.

Little is known about the fate of those who were imprisoned, in part, because Israel has blocked access to the camps. For over a month, Israel refused even to permit the Red Cross to visit the camps, prompting unaccustomed protest by the ICRC, which later suspended its visits in apparent protest against what it had found within (as a matter of policy, the ICRC refrains from public criticisms). Five months after the war's end, Israel was still refusing to permit reporters to visit the Ansar camp in Lebanon, as was discovered by one of the rare journalists (William Farrell) who tried to do so on the strength of the statement in an official IDF publication that "the camp is open to visiting journalists throughout the day and newsmen may interview detainees on camp grounds."[146] He was told ("politely"): "You may not enter."* More than half of the estimated 15,000 prisoners were reported to be in prisons or camps in Israel, where the Red Cross stated that it was still denied any access to them, many months after the war ended (see p. 221 and chapter 6, section 6.5).

Some information has come from released prisoners, and more from Israeli sources to which we turn directly. The few released prisoners interviewed by the press report "sardine-like" overcrowding, with prisoners required to lie on the ground day and night. Some report that they were required to hold their hands over their heads and forced to "bark like the dogs you are" and shout "Long live Begin, long live Sharon." Jonathan Randal, who reports these facts, states that "there appear to be virtually no Palestinian men between the ages of 16 to 60 free in southern Lebanon," an observation confirmed by other reporters and visitors. Released prisoners allege that many prisoners died of torture. One, who was in Ansar for 155 days, reported in an interview with *Libération* (Paris) that prisoners were laid "on special tables that have holds for legs and arms," then beaten with sticks and iron rods. He claims to have seen deaths as the result of torture. A *London Times* inquiry reported in *Yediot Ahronot* led to the discovery of 7 young men apparently killed in an Israeli detention camp near Sidon in the early weeks of the invasion, their bodies found with hands tied and signs of severe beatings. Independent Lebanese witnesses gave similar accounts; one claimed to have seen one prisoner beaten to death by an Israeli guard. Israeli authorities first denied the

---

* Possibly in response to Farrell's article, Israel then allowed two reporters to enter the camps. Edward Walsh reports that prisoners continue to be brought to Ansar, sometimes as many as 20 a week. The head of the prisoners' committee says: "At first this place was hell. Then there were improvements... I will not say that this is Auschwitz, but it is a concentration camp." He also says that "There is no torture now in Ansar." See also Uri Avneri's report on the Ansar "concentration camp," including interviews with guards who regard the prisoners as "subhuman," etc.; and Mary Arias, reporting degrading conditions, electric torture, efforts to induce psychological disorientation by various measures, etc.[147]

allegations, then confirmed that the bodies had been found and that an investigation was proceeding. One died from a heart attack, they claimed. The *Times* reports that five were Lebanese citizens of Palestinian origin, one was a Palestinian refugee, and one an Egyptian.

A lengthy account of the experiences of one prisoner in Israel and in Ansar appears in the German periodical *Der Spiegel*. This man, a Lebanese Shiite Muslim (the largest religious group in Lebanon), was taken prisoner on July 2, when his village was officially "liberated" by the IDF. At 4:30 AM the village was awakened by loudspeakers announcing that all inhabitants from ages 15 to 75 were to gather in the village center at 5 AM. IDF troops with tanks and armored personnel carriers surrounded the village while, to the amazement of the villagers, a network of collaborators within the village, clearly established in advance, appeared with IDF uniforms and weapons, prepared for their task, which was to select the victims. Each person received a notice, "guilty" or "innocent"; this man was "guilty," with a written statement describing his "crime"—in Hebrew, so he never did find out what it was. The guilty were blindfolded and taken to a camp in southern Lebanon. There they were interrogated while being beaten with heavy clubs. Teachers, businessmen, students and journalists received special treatment: more severe beatings. The interrogation-beating sessions lasted from 10 minutes to half a day, depending on the whims of the liberators. Prisoners slept on the ground, without blankets in the cold nights. Many were ill. They were forced to pass before Lebanese informants, and if selected, were sent to Israel.

For no reason that he could discern, this man was one of those selected. Their first stop in Israel was Nahariya, where Israeli women entered their buses, screaming hysterically at the bound prisoners, hitting them and spitting at them while the guards stood by and laughed. They were then driven to an Israeli camp where they were greeted by soldiers who again beat them with clubs. They were given dinner—a piece of bread and a tomato. Then soldiers came with four large shepherd dogs on chains, who were set upon the prisoners, biting them, while those who tried to defend themselves were beaten by soldiers. "Particularly the young boys, aged 15 and 16, began to cry from fear," leading to further beatings.

"Each day brought with it new torture." Many were beaten with iron bars, on the genitals, on the hands, on the soles of the feet. One had four fingers broken. This man was hung by his feet "and they used me as a punching bag." When prisoners begged for water they were given urine, provided by the liberators. One day they were taken to the sports stadium of a nearby village where the inhabitants came to throw bottles and other objects at them. Prisoners were forced to run like cattle, beaten with clubs. Once they were made to sit for a solid week, most of the time with hands on their heads. The worst times were Friday night and Saturday, when the guards celebrated the Sabbath by getting drunk, selecting some prisoners for special punishment "to the accompaniment of laughter, full of hate."

After the war ended this man was taken back to Lebanon, to the Ansar concentration camp, where there were then about 10,000 prisoners. There the terror continued. One day they saw many Lebanese women outside the camp. They waved to them and shouted. To stop the turmoil, the guards shot in the direction of the women, and the prisoners, angered, threw stones, and were fired on directly with 28 wounded, eight seriously. One night, at 1 AM, he was told that he was free; 225 men were freed, all Lebanese. He was sent to Nabatiye, where an officer told him: "We wish you all the best. We had to mete out justice. It was a long time indeed, but justice triumphed anyway." "I do not know what he meant," this man adds, concluding his story.[148]

The story was translated into Hebrew and appeared in *Ha'aretz*, but curiously, it was missed by the *New York Times, New Republic*, and other journals that were lauding the "purity of arms" and magnificent moral standards of the liberators. Apparently, it was not deemed of sufficient importance to be communicated to those paying the bills.

According to other reports, prisoners were held blindfolded and bound in barbed wire compounds; while Lebanese prisoners were kept with arms tied, Palestinians were kept naked, blindfolded, with arms tied. Despite daily appeals from June 6, the ICRC was permitted to see only 18 injured Palestinians in a hospital in Israel until July 18. Wealthy Lebanese detainees who say that they had "fought the PLO" describe beatings and humiliation, confirming the reports of others.[149] One reads an occasional description, usually in the foreign press, of "the agitated crowd of Arab women gathered in the shade of a neighbouring wall to see whether any of their relatives could be spotted,"[150] but the torment of the families is of as little interest to the paymasters as is the fate of the prisoners themselves.

The Greek Orthodox Archbishop of "demolished Tyre," Monsignor Haddad, described "the arbitrary arrests" as "an insuperable barrier to the establishment of a just peace," expressing his certainty "that 95 percent— if not 99 percent—of the people arrested are innocent."[151] It might be added that some questions also arise about the concept "guilt," as applied by a conquering army.

Correspondents in Lebanon provide more information. One Reuters reporter gives this eyewitness account after seeing prisoners under guard:

> Flicking a two-thonged leather whip, an Israeli soldier moved through the lines of suspected guerillas squatting on a lawn outside the Safa Citrus Corporation. Nearby, a row of eight men stood with their hands in the air as a green-bereted Israeli border guard, an Uzi sub-machinegun slung over his shoulder, inspected them. "This is where they bring our men. It is the

Israelis' interrogation center," said a sobbing woman in a small crowd on the pavement opposite. The border guards, a force renowned for their toughness, barked out orders in Arabic and refused to let journalists linger at the gates of the corporation, a depot on the southern outskirts of Sidon. Through the bars, about 100 prisoners could be seen on the lawn while a queue waited to enter the depot, apparently for questioning. Those able to satisfy the Israelis that they were not PLO guerillas were put onto a bus and driven to an open space in the town for release. As the men left the bus, soldiers stamped a Star of David on their identity cards to show they had been cleared. Those who had no card were stamped on their wrists.

A picture above the story shows the top half of the body of an unidentified man, killed during the bombing of a school building in Sidon a week earlier, lying in the ruins where residents say that more than 300 died. A woman who was personally acquainted with several men who were released says she was told that "they had to stand or sit in the sun all day. The only water they got was poured on the ground, and they had to lap it up like animals." "Other Lebanese residents of Sidon told the same story." Adult males had been rounded up after the occupation, taken to the beaches, and passed before men wearing hoods who pointed some of them out, "and then the Israelis took them away."[152]

Again, it is useful to ask ourselves what the reaction would be in the United States if an Arab army had conquered half of Israel, leaving a trail of destruction in its path, sending all males to prison camps where they were beaten, murdered, humiliated, while their families were left to starve or be harassed or killed by terrorist bands armed by the conqueror.

William Farrell visited the same school 7 months later, reporting again that "several hundred refugees were killed" when the school's shelter was hit. This one shelter, then, contained more corpses than the total number killed in all of Sidon, according to the Israeli official responsible for the population in the territories that were "liberated," Minister of Economic Coordination Ya'akov Meridor, who reported to the Israeli Knesset that 250 people were killed in Sidon,* "including terrorists and their hostages"—which presumably translates as "Palestinians and Lebanese."[153] Farrell interviewed the assistant principal of this French-language elementary school: "there are problems with some of the students, he said, who still shudder when they hear planes overhead. 'It will take a long time to take this impression from them,' he added."[154]

---

* For the accounting by those who were celebrating their liberation, see note 103. Recall that the actual numbers are unknown, and that months after the battle ended corpses were still being found and the IDF feared that epidemics might break out because of those still buried under the rubble. See pp. 221, 222.

More information about the prisons comes from Israeli sources. Dr. Haim Gordon, an IDF educational officer, describes his visit to what he calls the Ansar "concentration camp." Prisoners are not permitted to leave their tents, but must lie on the ground. There are no showers, in the burning July sun. "The terrible stink 'maddens' the Israeli guards." One prisoner is an 83-year-old man who "collaborated" with the PLO, renting a field to Palestinians who allegedly used it for an ammunition dump. He is therefore "a terrorist," and "we must frighten him so that in the future he will not collaborate," Gordon was informed by a guard.

Amnon Dankner reports testimony by an Israeli soldier who served as a prison guard. He too describes the terrible smell, intolerable to the Israeli guards; and "the cries of pain of those under interrogation." He describes the pleading women who kiss your hands and show you a picture, begging you to tell them whether you have seen their husband or child, whom they have not seen or heard from for three months. And the military police officer who shoots into a crowd of prisoners (see p. 233), the blood streaming from the wounds of those who are hit, the roadblocks where you must stop and send back a woman about to give birth or an old man in terrible pain, trying to reach a hospital. And finally, the suicide of an Israeli soldier, who, it seems, could bear no more.[155]

Within Israel, the matter has elicited some concern. Knesset Member Amnon Rubinstein brought up in the Knesset the issue of "terrifying incidents in Ansar," alleging that "intolerable conditions that are a stain on Israel's reputation" prevail in the camp: "Prisoners walk about barefoot in the severe cold and there have been many incidents of assaults against them."[156] In the United States, little has been said about the topic. We return to the Israeli response to an Amnesty International appeal on the matter.

Israeli soldiers returning from duty in Lebanon in the reserves add more to the picture. One, a student at Tel Aviv University, reports what he saw in *Koteret Rashit* (a new journal with Labor support, including many Labor doves). In 1978, he had been arrested in Argentina on suspicion of spying and had spent ten days in an Argentine prison, but had seen nothing there to compare with what he found in the IDF headquarters in Sidon in January 1983, where he spent a month. At least 10 people were arrested each day and forced to perform menial labor for the IDF and the Israeli Border Guards, cleaning latrines and private quarters, washing floors, etc. In a letter of complaint to the Defense Ministry, this man and two other reservists, reporting their experiences, state that the IDF is becoming "an army of masters." Prisoners in this military base were held only on suspicion, and many were released after a brief stay. In the base they were brutalized by the Border Guards; "whoever is caught will be punished," these reservists were told by the commanding officer. They witnessed degradation and beating of prisoners who were bound and blindfolded, forced to crouch on the floor for long hours, then often released. Even worse than the behavior of the Border Guards (with the knowledge of their officers, who did nothing) was that of the Haddad forces who had free access to this IDF base. They beat prisoners brutally, again, with the knowledge of IDF officers. In one case a young woman, "completely bound...and crying from pain wherever they touched her," was repeatedly raped by Haddad soldiers who also attempted to force her to copulate with a dog. Then "they returned her to imprisonment." "Naturally there was no investigation" of what had happened within this IDF military base; the responsible IDF officers "explained to me that this is how they behave in Lebanon..." The soldiers had hoped to present their complaints to Chief of Staff Eitan, who arrived on a tour, but were unable to contact him. His visit had some good effects, however: the prisoners were given mattresses and blankets for the first time, after having been forced to work extra hours to clean the building in preparation for Eitan's visit. This soldier, who seems completely apolitical and is certainly no dove, is unwilling to return to Lebanon but does not want to join the hundreds who have refused service there (many others have refused service at Ansar). He is thinking of emigrating, as several of his friends have done.[157]

It might be noted, incidentally, that brutal treatment of helpless prisoners is an old Begin specialty. After the Deir Yassin massacre, survivors were paraded through the streets of Jerusalem by Irgun soldiers proud of their achievement. Colonel Meir Pail, who was communications officer for the Haganah in Deir Yassin and an eye-witness, describes how Begin's heroes loaded 25 survivors into a truck and drove them through Jewish neighborhoods of Jerusalem, then taking them to a quarry where they were murdered, while others were driven off to be expelled beyond Israeli lines. And after Begin's troops had finished with their "orgy" of looting and destruction in Jaffa in April 1948, they also paraded blindfolded prisoners through the streets of Tel Aviv, "to the disgust of a large section of the public."[158] Many of those driven from Jaffa in 1948 found their way to the Sabra and Shatila refugee camps, where their families were subjected to the gentle ministrations of Israel's local adjuncts in September 1982; see p. 370.

In other respects too, the IDF did not break new ground in Lebanon; recall its massacre of defenseless civilians in the Gaza Strip in 1956 (see p. 102) and its behavior at the end of the 1967 war, when after the fighting "Israel coldly blocked a Red Cross effort to rescue the human ruins staggering and dying in the desert under the pitiless midsummer sun."[159] As already noted, the military doctrine of attacking defenseless civilians, described once again by Menachem Begin in connection with the 1982 invasion of Lebanon, derives from longstanding practice and was enunciated clearly by David Ben-Gurion in January 1948 (see p. 182*).

Many Israeli soldiers were appalled by the nature of the war, a fact
that may be reflected in the "psychiatric casualties," particularly among
reservists, which were twice as high as the norm (including the 1973 war)
in comparison to physical casualties.[160] Many of these soldiers reported
what they had seen on their return, giving a picture of the war that was
rather different from what had passed through Israeli censorship, and
contributing substantially to growing opposition to the war in certain
circles.

One important case was Lieut. Col. Dov Yirmiah,* the oldest soldier
to serve in Lebanon, whose military career goes back to the pre-state
Haganah days.[161] Col. Yirmiah served with a unit that had responsibility
for the captured population. After he returned from his first tour of duty,
he made public some of the facts about its activities, or lack of activities.
He was then dismissed from the army of which he was one of the founders,
as punishment for this misdeed, on August 6.

Yirmiah reports that the care for the captured population was "not
serious, to use an understatement." The behavior of his unit was governed
by "hatred of Arabs, particularly Palestinians, and a feeling of revenge,"
and disregard for the needs of both Palestinians and Lebanese. He
describes how tens of thousands of people (100,000, according to the
estimate of the military commander, 50,000 according to others) were
concentrated on the beaches near Sidon for two days or more, in "terrible
heat," without even water (the city's water system had been destroyed and
no plans had been made for a substitute). When he tried to arrange for
assistance, he was told that there was "no hurry." His unit was not
permitted to care for the needs of Palestinians at all. Only after a week
were supplies brought for the population, and then nothing for the
Palestinians. Supplies gathered in Israel were not permitted entry.
Christians were permitted to sit in the shade; Palestinians and Muslims
forced to sit in the sun.

When the chief Israeli administrator, Cabinet Minister Ya'akov
Meridor, came to inspect and was asked what they were to do with the
Palestinians, his answer was:

"You must drive them East, towards Syria...and not let them
return."

Yirmiah subsequently spoke at a meeting in Tel Aviv with a number
of soldiers and university professors who opposed the war, including

* Yirmiah has compiled an honorable record over many years. It was he, incidentally, who
exposed the story of Shmuel Lahis when this mass murderer was appointed to the highest
executive position in the World Zionist Organization, a fact that merited no comment in the
United States; after all, as the Israeli High Court had determined, his murdering several
dozen old men, women and children under guard in a mosque was an act carrying "no
stigma." See p. 165. Yirmiah had been his commanding officer at the time of the massacre.

soldiers who refused to return to Lebanon and also one of Israel's most prominent military commanders, General (Res.) Avraham Adan, who participated, though he opposed the refusal to serve in Lebanon. Yirmiah explained that as soon as he entered Lebanon he realized that the purpose of the military operation was not "to kill terrorists—few terrorists were killed—but to destroy the [Palestinian] camps." After 3 months, virtually nothing had been done for the tens of thousands of people whose camps (actually, towns) were destroyed, and Israel refused to take any responsibility for them. Even in his service in the European theatre during World War II, Yirmiah said, he saw nothing comparable to the destruction of the Ain el-Hilweh camp. He also described his visit to one of the concentration camps for Palestinian men and boys. He saw prisoners with their hands tied beaten by soldiers, one struck repeatedly in the face with the heel of a shoe, others beaten with clubs all over their bodies—on orders, they claimed. Appeals to higher officers went unanswered. "Everything that is happening is the result of 15 years of conquest," Yirmiah concluded plausibly, referring to the post-1967 occupation.[162]

At the same time, Imri Ron, whose "authority" was so respected by the *New York Times* (see above, p. 228), reported that there were "no signs of beating or ill-treatment" in a prison camp he visited near Sidon, where the prisoners were "smoking and conversing, on the grass . . . definitely a humane attitude"—rather like a college campus in the spring, by his account.[163]

In his published diary and elsewhere, Yirmiah gave further details.[164] He described how military authorities blocked shipments of food, blankets, medical supplies and tents requested by the Mayor of Sidon (the supplies were delayed for several weeks, arriving only on July 5, because of the insistence of the Israeli military that they be shipped through Israel or Christian East Beirut, and they had not been distributed as of early August). A ship arrived with 700 tons of supplies for the people of Sidon, who were in desperate need, sent by a Lebanese millionaire. The IDF command refused to allow it to land, pretending that there were mines in the harbor. The real reason was that it was sent by "foreign and hostile factors who would defame Israel"; and besides, the IDF command said, "they are all Arabs, and they all aided the terrorists in one way or another." Furthermore the IDF command claimed that they had ample provisions in their houses, stored "according to the Arab custom"—in houses that were destroyed, or to which they could not gain access, Yirmiah adds. The IDF command refused to offer any help; "the 'Araboushim' can wait," Yirmiah comments. There was reconstruction, carried out by local people, without IDF assistance. "We know how to destroy, let others build," Yirmiah observes.

The commanding officer ordered that with regard to UNICEF, "we must disrupt all their activities." As for the International Red Cross, it is "a hostile organization" and orders were given to "prevent all its activities in the region." Relief gathered by Israelis was not distributed or was given to Lebanese army units. Milk collected in Haifa was not distributed in Tyre on the grounds that "they (the Arabs) ruin their stomachs with our milk." The IDF command refused to permit huge army water carriers to be used for the tens of thousands of people suffering from thirst and hunger for days on the Sidon beaches. "I will not send one IDF vehicle or driver into that mob," Yirmiah was told by the commanding officer, who also refused to allow him to enter Sidon to help because there might be danger: "It is better that 1000 Arabs should die and not one of our soldiers," the commanding officer said.

Refugees from camps that were flattened were forbidden to pitch tents, though these were in plentiful supply (later, Israeli authorities were to place the blame on the Lebanese and international organizations for this), a decision that is "evil and inhuman, and it teaches us the meaning of the 'humanitarianism' that [the military commander] boasts of on television." Travelling near Tyre, Yirmiah came across the refugees from Rashidiyeh who were camping in citrus groves near their destroyed town. A military commander ordered that they be driven away because "they are being filmed too much." "It is important to preserve the beautiful face of Israel," Yirmiah comments. He hears reports on the Israeli radio of the wonderful humanitarian efforts of the IDF and the Israeli population: "evidently, we learned something from the fascist propagandists in Europe," Yirmiah comments in despair, from the scene. He reports the fakery and invention of ridiculously low numbers of casualties and destroyed buildings, and the lies about humanitarianism and "purity of arms." "The Jewish soldier, the Israeli, who is crowned by hypocritical commanders and politicians as the must human in the world; the Israeli army that pretends to observe the purity of arms (a phrase that is sickening and false)—is changing its image" (Yirmiah is not above certain illusions about the past).

All of this refers to the treatment of the Lebanese, those who were liberated (Yirmiah accepts the official version that the IDF entered Lebanon to "liberate" the Lebanese and to fight "the terrorists"). As for the Palestinians, "the attitude towards the noncombatant Palestinian population recalls the attitude towards cockroaches that swarm on the ground." Ain el-Hilweh was savagely bombed though it was known that many women and children were cowering in the shelters. The women and children must be "punished," because they belong to the families of terrorists; recall General Gur's principles, cited by Prime Minister Begin (p. 220), though he was ordering "punishment" of all inhabitants of southern Lebanon, not just Palestinians. Even the limited aid offered the Lebanese was denied the remnants of the Palestinians.

Some of Yirmiah's most terrible stories concern the prisoners. Lebanese and Palestinians were taken over and over again for "identification" before hooded informers, many from the underworld—"so that they should know what awaits a terrorist, and will be careful in the future," the official explanation ran. He tells story after story of prisoners savagely and endlessly beaten in captivity, of torture and humiliation of prisoners, and of the many who died from beatings and thirst in Israeli prisons or concentration camps in Lebanon. On the bus trip to an Israeli prison, one 55-year old man, a diabetic with heart disease, felt ill and asked for air; he was thrown out of the bus by a soldier, fell and died. His son heard his cries and tried to help him, but he was stopped with "severe beatings." The son was still in Ansar, as of January 1983. The long and repeated interrogations were accompanied by constant beatings, or attacks by dogs on leashes, or the use of air rifles with bullets that cause intense pain but do not kill: "this gets all the secrets out of those under interrogation," Yirmiah was told by an IDF officer who exhibited this useful device. New loads of clubs had to be brought into the camps to replace those broken during interrogation. The torturers were "experts in their work," the prisoners report, and knew how to make the blows most painful, including blows to the genitals, until the prisoners confessed that they were "terrorists"—though when the Red Cross was finally permitted entry to Ansar in August, things improved somewhat. Prisoners were placed in "the hole," a tin box too small to permit them to sit or lie down, with gravel and pieces of iron on the floor; there they would be kept for hours until they fainted and were covered with wounds on the soles of their feet. Prisoners were forced to sit with their heads between their legs, beaten if they moved, while guards shouted at them: "You are a nation of monkeys, you are terrorists, and we will break your heads: You want a state? Build it on the moon." The stories closely resemble those told by other released prisoners, specifically, the death from beatings and harsh treatment of "at least seven prisoners" who were buried in the Muslim cemetery near Sidon; see pp. 231-2.

Yirmiah served in the Allied forces in World War II. He compares the incredible brutality of the IDF with the behavior of Allied troops in Italy, where German POWs were treated honorably and decently and if there were violations, they were stopped at once, while the IDF officers simply observe the atrocities and do not intervene.

Reporting his experiences in June—in the early stages of the war—Yirmiah describes the bombed hospitals, the shattered population wandering in the ruins of Tyre and Sidon and the camps, the terrorism of Phalange hoodlums brought in by the IDF, the cries of the bereaved, the massive weaponry so out of proportion to any military need. "It seems that there are many soldiers in the IDF to whom it matters and who are pained that we have become a nation of vicious thugs, whose second nature is fire, destruction, death and ruin." He sees religious soldiers celebrating the Sabbath amidst the horrors: "I am ashamed to be part of this nation," he says, "arrogant, boastful, becoming more cruel and singing on the ruins." And he asks, finally: "What will become of us," acting in such ways?

5.4   The Grand Finale

Israel's attack continued with mounting fury through July and August, the prime target now being the besieged city of West Beirut. By late June, residential areas had been savagely attacked in the defenseless city. Robert Fisk writes that "The Israeli pilots presumably meant to drop their bombs on the scruffy militia office on Corniche Mazraa, but they missed. Instead, their handiwork spread fire and rubble half the length of Abu Chaker Street, and the people of this miserable little thoroughfare— those who survived, that is—cannot grasp what happened to them... Abu Chaker Street was in ruins, its collapsed apartment blocks still smoking and some of the dead still in their pancaked homes, sandwiched beneath hundreds of tons of concrete... The perspiring ambulance crews had so far counted 32 dead, most of them men and women who were hiding in their homes in a nine-storey block of flats, when an Israeli bomb exploded on its roof and tore down half the building." One old man "described briefly, almost without emotion, how [his daughter's] stomach had been torn out by shrapnel." "This was a civilian area," he said. "The planes are terrorizing us. This is no way for soldiers to fight."[165] This was before the massive air attacks of late July and August.

On one occasion, on August 4, the IDF attempted a ground attack, but withdrew after 19 Israeli soldiers were killed.[166] The IDF then returned to safer tactics, keeping to bombing and shelling from land and sea, against which there was no defense, in accordance with familiar military doctrine (see pp. 220, 256, 312, 315). The population of the beleaguered city was deprived of food, water, medicines, electricity, fuel, as Israel tightened the noose. Since the city was defenseless, the IDF was able to display its light-hearted abandon, as on July 26, when bombing began precisely at 2:42 and 3:38 PM, "a touch of humor with a slight hint," the Labor press reported cheerily, noting that the timing, referring to UN Resolutons 242 and 338, "was not accidental."[167]

The bombings continued, reaching their peak of ferocity well after agreement had been reached on the evacuation of the PLO. Military correspondent Hirsh Goodman wrote that "the irrational, unprovoked and unauthorized bombing of Beirut after an agreement in principle regarding the PLO's withdrawal had been concluded between all the parties concerned should have caused [Defense Minister Sharon's] dismissal," but did not.[168]

The 11-hour bombing on August 12 evoked worldwide condemnation, even from the U.S., and the direct attack was halted. The consensus of eyewitnesses was expressed by Charles Powers:

> To many people, in fact, the siege of Beirut seemed gratuitous brutality... The arsenal of weapons, unleashed in a way that has not been seen since the Vietnam war, clearly horrified those who saw the results firsthand and through film and news reports at a distance. The use of cluster bombs and white phosphorus shells, a vicious weapon, was widespread.

> The Israeli government, which regarded news coverage from Lebanon as unfair, began to treat the war as a public-relations problem. Radio Israel spoke continually of the need to present the war in the "correct" light, particularly in the United States.

> In the end, however, Israel created in West Beirut a whole set of facts that no amount of packaging could disguise. In the last hours of the last air attack on Beirut, Israeli planes carpet-bombed Borj el Brajne [a Palestinian refugee camp]. There were no fighting men left there, only the damaged homes of Palestinian families, who once again would have to leave and find another place to live. All of West Beirut, finally, was living in wreckage and garbage and loss.

> But the PLO was leaving. Somewhere, the taste of victory must be sweet.[169]

6   The Taste of Victory

6.1   The Victors

For some, indeed, the taste of victory was sweet, in particular, for "the Christians of east Beirut [who] drove wildly through the streets in cars draped with [newly-elected President] Mr. Gemayel's portrait, firing into the air in an outburst of glee that left 5 dead and 19 wounded."[170] Previously they had been enjoying the spectacle of West Beirut in flames from the hotel verandas where they were sipping drinks or the beaches where they were sunning themselves, urging the Israeli army on to more violent attacks on the impoverished Muslims and Palestinians who "now live like moles, between destroyed houses," awaiting the next blow. These rich Lebanese "regard us as mercenaries who are working for them," military correspondent Ze'ev Schiff commented after observing this scene of "dolce vita and death."[171]

The *New Republic* described the same scene in rather different words. Its editors complained that among the many crimes of the press, it did not show "pictures of the Lebanese Christian women who demonstrated in east Beirut to celebrate—truly celebrate—the departure of those who had destroyed their lives and killed their loved ones." And "where are the pictures of the weeping mothers of the Israeli war dead?" There is no concern for them in the cynical American press, entranced by the "theatrical flourishes" of the PLO which has displayed such skill in manipulating American "opinion leaders," particularly those—found everywhere in the United States—who revel in "anti-Israel hysteria."[172]

One recalls earlier days, the Spanish civil war, for example, when George Orwell reported from the front lines, where he was serving with the POUM (anti-Stalinist) militia, that "In the *New Republic* Mr. Ralph Bates [assistant commissar of the 15th International Brigade] stated that the P.O.U.M. troops were 'playing football with the Fascists in no man's land' at a time when, as a matter of fact, the P.O.U.M. troops were suffering heavy casualties and a number of my personal friends were killed and wounded" and the Communists were withholding arms from the front, where the troops were predominantly anarchist.[173] Other days, other heroes, other villains, the same integrity—though there is nothing in the history of this journal to compare with what it has become under the current owner and editor. The *New Republic* celebrated the close of 1982 with an article praising Orwell by Irving Howe, in its Year-End edition.

The taste of victory was also sweet for most—not all—Israelis; and for the "supporters of Israel" here, who could look forward to the establishment of the anticipated "New Order" of their dreams in Lebanon and the imposition of Israeli control over the demoralized occupied territories, where Israel could now proceed to implement the "strong arm tactics" so admired by *New Republic* editor Martin Peretz, eliminating the danger of "a dagger poised at the heart of Israel" (see pp. 199*, 72*). The sweet taste was not, however, to linger long. We return to the aftermath in the next chapter.

6.2 The Liberated

There are, of course, Lebanese other than those whom Ze'ev Schiff and the *New Republic* editors described in their differing ways. What was the taste of Israel's victory to them? This question was rarely asked, perhaps because the answer was obvious. After all, former Supreme Court Justice Arthur Goldberg had pronounced that "Lebanese hail Israel's action as liberation" while the editors of the *New York Times* explained early on that they were being granted their "liberation from the Syrians and the P.L.O.," anticipating by several weeks the announcement by Ariel Sharon that "Israel's troops entering Lebanon were greeted as liberators for driving out the terrorists who had raped and pillaged and plundered." And surely the Lebanese were grateful for the fact that "no army in the history of modern warfare ever took such pains to prevent civilian casualties as did the Israel Defense Forces," as Sharon explained (echoing Begin's words after Deir Yassin; see p. 95), observing the "Jewish doctrine" of *tohar haneshek* (purity of arms) "scrupulously" while "attacking only predetermined P.L.O. positions and in bombing and shelling buildings only when they served as P.L.O. strongholds"* —the mental hospital in West Beirut, the school shelter in Sidon, and so on.[174]

Despite these assurances, let us nevertheless, if only out of idle curiosity, inquire further into the attitudes of Lebanese towards their liberation, beyond those who were freely expressing their opinions to visiting Americans guided by an Israeli army escort in occupied Lebanon. An obvious place to start would be the statements of the official representative of the Government of Lebanon at the United Nations, Mr. Ghassan Tueni, a Christian, the owner of the highly-respected Beirut journal *An-nahar*, later the Lebanese government's coordinator of negotiations with the liberators. In fact, he had a good deal to say on behalf of the government of Lebanon, though one has to search a little to discover what it was; his name does not appear in the *New York Times* index for this period, for example.

Mr. Tueni gave a major address at the highly-publicized United Nations conference on disarmament on June 22, a few blocks away from the editorial offices of the *Times*, just two weeks after the liberation began. He asked to be excused if the representative of Lebanon had "no words on universal disarmament, save the pious prayers that it should happen soon enough for his country to survive," a country that was then being "martyred and crucified." "The atomic holocaust of tomorrow," he said, "becomes a problematic danger, remote and almost unreal, to those who are living an actual holocaust: the holocaust of their mother earth, of men, women, and children physically destroyed along with the cities they built and loved." The choice for the Lebanese is "between today and tomorrow," "between surviving immediate death, and thinking—but only thinking—of preventing ultimate destruction." Recall that he was speaking well before the siege of Beirut and the indiscriminate bombing of heavily-populated civilian areas that reached its peak in late July and August. He asked that the General Assembly not "be diverted by abstract testimonies for peace... Concerned as we all are with the necessity of halting the race towards the atomic holocaust of tomorrow, let us remember the no less apocalyptic realities of today."

The official (Christian) spokesman for the country that was then being liberated by Israel may, perhaps, be excused for lapsing into hyperbole.

---

* Sharon also cited the figure of 1392 civilians killed by PLO terrorist raids, a fabrication that set off the inquiries by Israeli journalists that elicited the actual official figures, cited above; see p. 74.

Mr. Tueni called for the "immediate and unconditional withdrawal of Israeli forces from Lebanon," citing UN Security Council Resolution 509, "which clearly and unequivocally establishes the criteria of Israeli withdrawal: that it should be both immediate and unconditional." He deplored the fact that the UN peace-keeping forces were unable "to defend [Lebanon] against aggression," adding that "it is the very future of peace-keeping operations which is now at stake," given the inability of the United Nations to stop the Israeli attack—and, though he was too polite to add this, the support for this aggression by the U.S. government, which rendered the UN impotent. Ungratefully, he offered Israel no thanks for his liberation.[175]

It is perhaps worthy of note that one has to go to Tel Aviv to discover from the press what the representative of Lebanon was saying in New York.*

The Lebanese Ambassador did reach an American audience—though not the press—at a later stage of the liberation. Writing in *Foreign Affairs*, he commented on the name given "to the Israeli invasion: 'Peace for Galilee'." "To occupy almost half of a country, destroy its capital, disrupt its economy, ferociously kill its civilian population by the thousands—for the sake of 'Peace for Galilee'—is indeed a very strange notion of peace!" And of liberation. He also expressed some concern for the future:

> Zionist literature has consistently maintained that the Jewish National Home, and later Israel, needed the water of the Litani and the land south of it. And Israel itself has dealt with the issue as if the population living there—which is Arab not Jewish, and in its majority, Muslim not Christian—were a negligible entity, eventually disposable, not significant, and almost nonexistent."[176]

Perhaps he had in mind some other areas that had been liberated before. Tueni reviews the problems that Israel would face if it attempted to "absorb" this new area.

The Lebanese Ambassador also expressed concern over the intentions of Syria, but we need not dwell on that in the present context, since in the United States there are no "opinion leaders"—or others—who extol Syria for its "liberation" of Lebanon, though more muted expressions of approval were heard when Syria entered Lebanon in 1976 to combat the Muslim-Palestinian National Front coalition in the civil war. On the

---

* There is a brief reference to Tueni's speech at the end of an article on Lebanon in the *Boston Globe*, June 24, 1982. Tueni's impassioned condemnations of the Israeli invasion were occasionally seen on television, which American supporters of Israel have denounced even more bitterly than the "pro-PLO" print media for its alleged anti-Israel attitudes, a matter to which we return.

contrary, what we are told by such luminaries as Arthur Goldberg, in his statement published by the American Friends of Israel (see note 134), is that after Hussein expelled the PLO from Jordan in 1970, "when Syria and the PLO invaded and occupied Lebanon later that year [1970], the killing, maiming and destruction was so wanton and the occupation so pervasive that Lebanon virtually ceased to exist as an independent country." The actual facts of the matter have already been reviewed. The idea that Syria invaded and occupied Lebanon in 1970 is an original contribution by Mr. Goldberg and his sponsors, but apart from that, his sentiments are familiar. We return to his further thoughts on the matter, which do break some new ground.

Putting aside the observations of Lebanon's representative to the United Nations, let us search elsewhere. Another obvious place to turn would be the Lebanese press, just as we naturally turn to the Israeli press if we are interested in the attitudes of Israelis. This possibility also seems not to have occurred to those who inform us with much confidence about what the Lebanese think and feel. Fortunately, the task is not too difficult, even without access to the Arabic or French press; it should be noted, incidentally, that daily translations from the Arabic press are readily available in Beirut *(Middle East Reporter)*. There is an independent English-language weekly published in West Beirut: *Monday Morning*. It is open to a wide spectrum of opinion ranging from Phalangist to PLO, from Nahum Goldmann and U.S. Middle East specialist William Quandt to representatives of the Arab states and movements. In particular, its treatment of Israel's Phalangist clients and of the Phalangist government elected under Israeli guns was sympathetic and free from rancor, so that it passes the basic test of acceptability for an American audience. It contains a regular and detailed factual review of the week's events in Lebanon, along with analytic articles by local Western journalists and others, and broad coverage of the international (including Israeli) media. The tenor of its reporting did not change detectably as one military force replaced another, so it seems plausible to suppose that it was not published at gunpoint, as is obvious enough from the range and character of the material that appeared. Whatever they may have been in the past (about which I do not know), its standards were quite respectable through 1982. It certainly compares quite favorably to Western journals. It is likely that this journal offers as good a reflection of what many educated Lebanese were thinking during this period as any single journal could do, and this is a segment of the population that we do not ordinarily disregard in discussing other societies. Let us then consider what it has reported about Lebanese attitudes to the war, beginning with its first week.

Immediately after the initial Israeli bombardments, the journal reports, Ambassador Tueni informed the Security Council on June 5 that Israeli commandos had landed on the coastal road between Sidon and

Beirut and had opened machine gun fire on cars and buses in which civilian refugees were fleeing from the south—the first attack, after the initial bombings, on "predetermined P.L.O. positions" and "P.L.O. strongholds" in the terms pronounced appropriate by General Sharon (see above), and adopted by Israel's American supporters, and an early example—in this war—of how the IDF never aims at civilian targets, as Begin explained while recalling the familiar military doctrine of punishing the civilian population (see p. 220). "This action is of the utmost gravity," Ambassador Tueni said, "and my government earnestly hopes that the Council is not thus confronted with yet another preemptive act by Israel." He requested that the Security Council act "to stop the aggression against Lebanon," "the wanton bombardment of positions in Lebanon by Israel . . ." The Security Council responded by unanimously passing a Resolution calling for a cease-fire at 6AM on June 6, to which Israel responded in turn by launching the invasion on June 6. Perhaps mindful of the warning by the representative of Lebanon that Israeli aggression was a "catastrophe" for Lebanon and perhaps for international peace and security as well, the Security Council unanimously passed a further resolution on June 6 that "Demands that Israel withdraw its military forces forthwith and unconditionally to the internationally recognized borders of Lebanon." This too was disregarded by the liberators. On June 8, the U.S. vetoed a Security Council resolution that "Condemns the non-compliance" of Israel with the earlier resolutions, calling for immediate cessation of hostilities and withdrawal of Israeli forces.[177]. By this act, the U.S. gave its official blessing to the liberation, a stance that it then maintained, with the general approbation of the media, while stoutly denying the fact.

In an article entitled "Different Lebanese React Differently," the journal reported that "With the exception of the rightist Lebanese Front, officials, politicians and party leaders unreservedly condemned Israel's invasion of Lebanon and vowed to resist it, accusing the United States of responsibility for the savage aggression and denouncing the Arabs' failure to throw their full weight behind Lebanon and the Palestinians." Among those joining in the condemnation was Prime Minister Shafik Wazzan, speaking in the name of the Council of Ministers. Wazzan was again chosen to head the new government by Phalangist President Amin Gemayel after the liberation was completed in September and thus should qualify as a legitimate spokesman for the liberated population, by the standards of the *New York Times* and others. Also joining in the condemnation were Christian Foreign Minister Fuad Butros; Shiite House Speaker Kamel Asaad; a number of former Prime Ministers; Nabih Berri, head of the Shiite militia (Amal) that fought alongside the Palestinians;*

---

* In mid-June, Robert Fisk reported, Nabih Berri, "the leader of the Amal Shia movement, which fought so bravely with the Palestinians against the Israelis south of Beirut, ordered

spokesmen for both the Sunni Islamic Grouping and the Higher Shiite Council (that is, the two major Muslim religious groups); Druze leader Walid Jumblatt, son of the assassinated leader of the Lebanese National Movement (the Muslim-Palestinian coalition); former President Suleiman Franjieh, a Maronite who condemned "the barbaric Israeli invasion"; and others. The invasion was supported only by "the Lebanese Front, which groups the main rightist Maronite parties," specifically, by Front leader Camille Chamoun (who had requested the U.S. marines to land in 1958) and Phalangist Party Chief Pierre Gemayel and his son Bashir Gemayel, who headed the Phalange militia.[179]

Reuters correspondent Patrick Worsnip described the "Phalangist-Israeli cooperation" as "a nightmare come true for Lebanese leftists and Palestinians," noting that the Phalangists had opposed the Palestinians because "they feared the new arrivals could tilt the confessional balance in favor of their Moslem rivals and threaten their own political supremacy" in a country in which they were the minority, and noting also that "many Lebanese Christians, especially non-Maronite sects, reject Phalangist policies." Meanwhile, Israel's main ally in Lebanon, Pierre Gemayel, expressed his reservations concerning the liberation in an interview. He described it as "a catastrophe for Lebanon, the Palestinians and the Arab world," which might even lead to "an international war." The "Israeli presence is going to ruin this Lebanese formula, much to Israel's joy"— where the "Lebanese formula" is the "association between two civilizations," Christian and Muslim; and it will lead to the division of Lebanon into "who knows what [sectarian] states." In short, something less than unreserved pleasure, even from this quarter.[180]

Protests mounted as the invasion-liberation ground on. By late June, Prime Minister Wazzan and Walid Jumblatt stated that they could not continue the negotiations to remove the PLO from Beirut because of the unremitting Israeli attacks. Wazzan stated:

> Every time we reach some kind of understanding, we run into a new escalation as if designed to pressure us. You can quote me: this is an international conspiracy against Lebanon and the Lebanese. You want me to remain silent while Philip Habib watches the bombardment of residential areas? As if we were rats in this country! Shafik Wazzan cannot accept this... Therefore, I have informed President Sarkis that I cannot continue shouldering my responsibility under this blackmail and escalation.[181]

---

his men to lay down their guns," further resistance being hopeless. He and Walid Jumblatt, who also regarded further resistance as hopeless, joined the new "Committee of National Salvation" formed by President Sarkis as an executive in the emergency. Jumblatt counselled "passive resistance," given the overwhelming force of the invaders. Berri later stated that "An Israeli attack on West Beirut will not be the end of the war but the beginning of another one which will spread to the entire country," accusing the U.S. and some Arab states "of having encouraged the Israeli aggression on Lebanon."[178]

His continuing protests in this vein were occasionally reported in the U.S. On July 27, the government of Lebanon once again protested the continuing invasion "in the strongest possible terms" and called upon the Security Council "to seek practical ways and means under the charter to ensure the implementation" of the earlier resolutions, an option that was regularly blocked by U.S. veto.

On July 30, Camille Chamoun issued a statement demanding that "this cruel and unjustifiable treatment of innocent civilians should stop," referring to Israel's blockade of West Beirut. On August 11 he condemned Israel for sending its forces into the Christian hinterland, including areas north of Beirut, saying that "There is no explanation for this."[182] By the end of July, then, condemnation of the liberation was unanimous among Lebanese political elites, including even Pierre Gemayel and Camille Chamoun—who, nevertheless, continued to support the invasion for the reasons already explained by Ze'ev Schiff: they were pleased to have Israeli mercenaries win the civil war for them and reestablish their supremacy over the Muslim majority of the population.

Muslim leaders were far harsher in their condemnations throughout, including Shafik Wazzan, former Prime Minister Saeb Salam, and others. Apart from condemning the merciless attacks on the civilian population, as he did throughout, Salam expressed his outrage over "the phosphorus bombing that gutted the 1,000-year-old mid-city pine woods in and around the now-destroyed horse race track." "The pine forest, the pride of Beirut, the whole forest was burned with phosphorus bombs," he told reporters on August 2.* Subsequently, he demanded that Israel pay reparations, which is "the practice in war." "With the savage way the Israelis have acted, I think it's the least of things to demand of the aggressor," he told a news conference in which he also blamed the U.S. for "backing Israel blindly."[184] Salam and Wazzan lived in West Beirut, where they endured the terror; Chamoun and Gemayel watched from East Beirut.

On August 30, Yasser Arafat departed from Beirut, effectively terminating an organized Palestinian presence in Lebanon. The day began with an emotional farewell meeting with Druze leader Walid Jumblatt. Arafat was then accompanied to Prime Minister Wazzan's office by Jumblatt, Shiite Amal militia commander Nabih Berri and Lebanese Communist Leader Mohsen Ibrahim. "Brother Arafat," as Prime Minister Wazzan referred to him, was seen off from Beirut by Wazzan, four former Prime Ministers, religious leaders, and representatives of President Sarkis,

---

* The destruction of the forest, "a children's park," "the pride of Beirut," was reported (with TV clips) on NBC TV news, Aug. 2. James Compton reported that "There were Palestinian positions here. They have long been abandoned... Most fortified Palestinian positions have been abandoned under Israel's relentless barrage."[183]

many of whom "were in tears as the single smokestack Atlantis, gleaming white in the sunlight, pulled out of the port."[185]

There were, indeed, many who had reason to fear what the future held, and these fears were soon borne out: the Palestinians and Muslims in Beirut, who were left defenseless, with power now in the hands of their Phalange enemies; the population of the south, subject to the whims of Major Haddad and whomever else Israel might choose to arm; the Druze of the Chouf region, which had escaped the civil war, who "were worried and scared last weekend as the Phalangist militias moved in behind the advancing Israelis"; and perhaps also those who remembered the West Bank while they pondered such scenes as the entry to Lebanon of the followers of the New York Lubavitcher Rabbi, equipped with a press to print copies of the *Tanya*, expounding their doctrine, photographed carrying out their work near the Presidential Palace in the hills above Beirut.[186]

The attitudes of Lebanese in Beirut did not go unnoticed in the American press. *Time* Bureau Chief William Stewart reported that by mid-August there

> had been a remarkable transformation of opinion in this beleaguered city. Instead of desperately wanting the P.L.O. to leave in order to avoid further bloodshed, Lebanese civilians we talked to all over West Beirut now want to see Israel defeated. The Israeli attacks were directed not just against Palestinian military positions but at hospitals, schools, apartment houses, government offices and shipping centers. Everything became a target, and so did the people of West Beirut in what has become known as "the great siege."[187]

The consummation—temporarily—of Operation "Peace for Galilee," the "liberation of Lebanon."

Although the commentary on the matter that is standard here is hardly very persuasive, nevertheless it is reasonable to suppose that many Lebanese were pleased to see the PLO depart, for quite sound reasons. The first was that Abba Eban's "rational prospect" (see p. 182) had been amply fulfilled for many years, leading to vast suffering, and had again been fulfilled in Beirut, as Stewart observes. Furthermore, Lebanese across the political spectrum want to see the Palestinians in Palestine, not in their own country. While these feelings were complicated by Palestinian support for the Muslim majority in the civil war, nevertheless the sentiment is no doubt widely held, understandably enough. Just as even the most sympathetic Pakistanis want to see the Afghan refugees return to Afghanistan—particularly when, as in Lebanon, their presence and military actions call forth "retaliatory" strikes—so the Lebanese favor the return of Palestinians to their land. In this regard, they share views held throughout the Arab world. Propagandists here made much of the reluctance of the Arab states to take in the PLO fighters, crowing about this alleged demonstration that even the Arab states despise and reject the PLO. While it is true enough that the elites that rule the Arab states dislike the PLO—and, quite generally, nationalist currents in the Arab world that might threaten their power—one can hardly demonstrate the fact on these grounds, at least if we add one factor commonly ignored: that they regularly stated that they did not want to contribute to a new dispersal of the Palestinians, whom they prefer to see in a state of their own in Palestine in accordance with the international consensus. In the same context, we may take note of the common charge that the Arab states have contributed to the plight of the refugees by refusing to take them in,* a claim that ignores, as usual, the wishes of the Palestinians themselves, who have insisted on maintaining their national and cultural identity and their hope to return to their native land. Finally, while the charges that have circulated in the U.S. concerning the behavior of the PLO in Lebanon appear to be vastly exaggerated, at least to judge by investigations carried out by Israeli journalists, Jewish and Christian Arab, and while there seems little doubt that the behavior of the Israeli-backed Phalange was more brutal than anything attributable to the PLO, it nevertheless remains true that the PLO behaved in a disgraceful and stupid fashion in southern Lebanon, alienating much of the population.

6.3   Israelis

It is, then, a shade less than obvious that Lebanese were uniformly celebrating their liberation through the summer of 1982. As for Israel's reactions, the war had initially received overwhelming support there, including many critics of the drift towards religious-chauvinist fanaticism. For example, Amnon Rubinstein, a Knesset member from the *Shinui* ("Change") Party and a civil libertarian of sorts,† wrote after a

---

* The charge is so common as to make reference almost superfluous. It was, for example, repeated in an unusually accurate ABC *Closeup* report on the Beirut massacres, Jan. 7, 1983, in apportioning the blame for the massacres.

† As for many others (notoriously, Harvard Law Professor Alan Dershowitz), Rubinstein's civil libertarian commitments quickly fade in connection with Israeli dissidents. See *TNCW*, p. 434, and p. 142 and note 107. The point illustrated by Dershowitz, *et al.*, is familiar enough. Thus, many Stalinists really did struggle courageously for civil rights in the United States, while taking a rather different stance with regard to their Holy State. The same is true, to a lesser but nonetheless quite substantial degree, of supporters of the murderer of Kronstadt, the man who called for the militarization of labor in a "labor army," who dismantled the Soviets and factory councils and destroyed the anarchist movements after they were no longer needed to defend Bolshevik rule while assisting in establishing the institutions of the Soviet dungeon. It is a curious feature of the contemporary intellectual scene in the U.S. that former Trotskyites are now commonly described as having fought the good fight against totalitarian oppression.

month of war that "only a small radical minority demands immediate withdrawal" from Lebanon, an accurate appraisal apart from the term "radical," familiar in a similar context from the days of U.S. aggression in South Vietnam. "Israel is rightly not ashamed of its alliance with the Christian minority in Lebanon," Rubinstein added. "The negative attitude toward the Lebanese Christians almost universally expressed in the Western media . . . [is] a mixture of ignorance and insanity that characterizes some segments of the international scene." Even France, which the Maronites regard as a "second homeland," has "completely forsaken them" and in its "frenzied courtship of Palestinians," overlooks the rights of the Lebanese Christians including the Haddadists, as does the West more generally, he argued.[188]

Turning to the facts, it was a convenient pose, hardly to be taken seriously, that Israel's alliance with pro-Israeli segments of Christian society was undertaken to defend a persecuted minority (namely, the privileged group that dominated the Muslim majority). Israel's concern for the rights of the oppressed—adequately illustrated by its behavior with regard to South Africa, Zaire, Somoza's Nicaragua, Guatemala, etc., not to speak of the territory it controls directly and those it has driven from their homes* — is basically no different from that of any other state with interests to pursue in the international arena. The reference to the "frenzied courtship of Palestinians" in the West gives an interesting indication of the state of mind and grasp of reality on the part of many liberal Israeli intellectuals.

What Rubinstein describes as a "mixture of ignorance and insanity" with regard to Israel's Christian allies spread over Israel as well, as soldiers and journalists began to learn about them from evidence more direct than Israeli propaganda. Included were some of the most respected correspondents in Israel, for example, Ze'ev Schiff, whose description of Israel's Maronite allies enjoying the fun was cited above, and Colonel Dov Yirmiah, who recounts stories of Phalange atrocities in June (see p. 240). Or consider the report by this soldier, after the Beirut massacres:

---

* Recall that many of the Palestinian refugees were expelled outright, while many others fled in terror after Israeli atrocities, and that since 1948 Israel has refused any settlement that might involve permitting their return apart from limited cases. Israel's colossal gall in this regard—or more accurately, its perception of the integrity of its supporters and its colossal contempt for them—has repeatedly been demonstrated, for example, in a flyer distributed (with no identification) by the Israeli consulate with the heading "Who Cares About Refugees?" Its purpose is to compare Israel's profound humanitarian concern for refugees, its "care about refugees" deriving from Jewish historical experience, with the callousness of the Arab states. The proof is that Israel has been enthusiastic in helping *Cambodian* refugees. By the same logic, Soviet Party Liners, if they had the audacity, could demonstrate the deep commitment of the Soviet leadership to civil liberties by citing their outrage over miscarriages of justice in the United States, the case of the Wilmington 10, for example. Again, the Age of Orwell.

A storm was aroused in the state concerning the Phalangists in connection with the Sabra and Shatila affair. It was only necessary to become acquainted with the Phalangists to know that they were capable of doing what they did. At least I, a simple soldier, understood this, when I was in Beirut before it all happened. I happened to make friends with one Phalangist. Until today, I cannot forget two pictures that he showed me with real pride. In one he stood in a heroic pose holding in his hands two full jars—ears of terrorists! He told me that he had cut them from the bodies of terrorists recently [that is, after the IDF had turned the "terrorists" over to Phalange control]. In the second, I saw him standing holding in each hand a head that had been cut off, and between his legs a third! He explained to me with great self-importance that these were the heads of Palestinians he had decapitated.[189]

Another case is the story of the Druze Sheikh Sami Abu-Said in the Chouf, quiet during the civil war but enflamed by the entry of the Phalange in the trail of the IDF. He was captured in a Phalange ambush and killed with an axe. His body was mutilated and his limbs cut off, then placed in a box and sent to his village, setting off one of the many postwar incidents in the region.[190] There are many other examples.

In fact, Rubinstein is being a bit disingenuous. There was ample evidence about the character and behavior of Israel's allies and clients long before, from the days of Karantina, Tel al-Zaatar and Khiyam (see pp. 184-5, 191), for example. The facts were simply suppressed in Israel when it was convenient to suppress them—and brought forth, to a degree, when it became useful to do so, in particular, by September 1982, when evidence began to mount that the Phalangists would not be the docile allies that Israel had expected, and after the Sabra-Shatila massacres, when it became necessary to appeal to the "Arab character" to explain away what had happened under the control of the IDF. Rubinstein himself would surely not have written about the Phalange in October the way he did in July, nor would he have condemned the "ignorance and insanity" of those in the West who were critical of the Phalange, not because the Phalange had changed, or because his knowledge about the Phalange had changed, but because Israel's relations with them had changed. One may also recall the forbidden point that however terrible the behavior of Israel's allies had been, it hardly compares with what Israel itself had done in its war of terror in southern Lebanon for many years; consider the full story of Khiyam, for example.

Rubinstein's is a voice from the critical end of the spectrum of mainstream political and intellectual life in Israel. A month later, as the battering of Beirut reached new heights of savagery, Begin's popularity correspondingly soared to record heights. A mid-August poll showed that Begin's Likud would capture 66 seats in the 120-member Knesset if elections were held then (up from 48 in the 1981 elections), while Labor Party support dwindled to 35 seats (47 in 1981).* More than 80% supported the invasion of Lebanon (which was supported, publicly at least, by the Labor opposition), and 64% approved of the decision to go beyond the 25-mile zone announced in early propaganda, though it was already clear that the costs to Israel would not be small.[191] A few weeks later, another poll showed that 60% of Israelis opposed negotiations with the PLO while 5% supported the establishment of a Palestinian state in the West Bank (N.B.: not including the Gaza Strip).[192] Presumably, Israel's population largely agreed with Begin's assertion that Israel "never attacked the civilian population in Beirut," and with the statement of Defense Minister Sharon that "I would not be exaggerating by saying that there is no other country in the world that can boast of such a capacity for confrontation and such successes with such supreme universal moral value as little Israel." The Knesset voted 50-40 to accept Sharon's statement, rejecting by 52-38 a Labor Party statement that "the military advantage gained by the heavy bombing and shelling of Beirut 'did not justify *the damage caused Israel*'," obviously the only relevant consideration.[193] None of this affected judgments here concerning Israel's sublime moral standards. Recall the "pragmatic" critique of America's aggression and atrocities in Indochina which was predominant by far among "the intellectual elite" even at the height of opposition to the Vietnam war.[194]

As explained by Gideon Hausner, Israel's war against the PLO ("the centre of a cancerous growth which has metastasized all over the world," a "gang of thugs") proved "again" Israel's "power and its respect for human values. Not for the first time in our history, an outstanding Jewish contribution is being first begrudged, then gradually acknowledged and ultimately acclaimed"—acclaimed as a "victory for humanity."[195] Hausner was the prosecutor of Adolf Eichmann and is the chairman of the *Yad Vashem* Holocaust Memorial Center.

Hausner's choice of terms can hardly fail to call to mind other episodes of Jewish history, when Jews or Zionists were the centers of various "cancerous growths." Again it is interesting to see how some supporters of Israeli policies seem intent on fulfilling a curious self-image as spokesmen for states that we do not "dare to mention by name," in Abba Eban's phrase, with insistent mimicry of their phraseology: a "new

---

* Asked to state their preference for head of the government, 54% selected Begin in August, the next highest (14%) being Rabin and the next, then President Yitzhak Navon (4%). Begin's popularity dropped to 45% by October (and Rabin's to 11%) after the events to which we return, while Navon's rose to 18%. By February 1983, Begin's popularity was 45%, Navon's 23%, and Rabin's 5% (about 20% not responding throughout). Shimon Peres, head of the Labor Party, stood at about 3.5% throughout. *Ma'ariv*, Feb. 18, 1983. See also p. 451*.

order" imposed by Israeli arms; a Palestinian state as "a dagger poised at the heart of Israel"—not to speak of "two-legged beasts" inhabiting "nests" like vermin, etc. There is something indeed perverse in this pose. The significance of such phrases as "cancerous growth" and "gang of thugs" becomes clearer when we bear in mind the status of the PLO among Palestinians in the occupied territories and elsewhere, and the fact, clear enough to many Israeli soldiers fighting in Lebanon, that "every Palestinian is automatically a suspected terrorist, and by our definition of that term it is actually true. . .[since] we are confronting a comprehensive [PLO] organizational structure," including youth clubs, health services and a functioning economy, and everyone connected with them (i.e., all Palestinians) "is now a terrorist by our definition."[196] Recall Ya'akov Meridor's reference to the casualties in Sidon as "terrorists and their hostages"—a phrase that can only be interpreted as meaning "Palestinians and Lebanese," in the perverse Israeli idiom.

This picture of Israel's war in southern Lebanon, and of the nature of the cancer that was excised, was confirmed by many others, for example, Mordechai Bar-On, formerly the IDF's chief education officer and a Jewish Agency official, whose remarks were partially quoted earlier (p. 203).* "Of all the declared, implied and hidden objectives of the war in Lebanon," he writes, "there is no doubt that the central aim was to deal a crushing blow to the national aspirations of the Palestinians and to their very existence as a nation endeavouring to define itself and gain the right to self-determination." The goal was achieved:

> Anyone who visited Southern Lebanon during and even after the fighting would see that the war was fought not just against terrorist organizations and the PLO, and not even solely to destroy the PLO's military infrastructure in the region. It was fought against the very existence of the Palestinians as a com-

---

* This leading Peace Now activist describes the PLO as "a malicious and extremist movement" which has "to a great extent employed intimidation and terror amongst the Palestinians themselves" (a claim that is not too easily reconcilable with the results of Israeli polls in the West Bank and that also overlooks too easily some elements of the history of Zionism); it is "a vicious and cruel organization" with "extremist positions" refusing any compromise with Israel, reflecting the "obstinacy, blindness and folly of the Palestinians." It would require "a radical internal reform" for the PLO to "lead the Palestinians to realize their aspirations through compromise with Israel." Again, we note how Bar-On, a respected dovish intellectual, erases from history the record of PLO moves to realize Palestinian aspirations through compromise since the mid-1970s, which happen to have been publicized repeatedly in the very journal in which he writes. Comparable remarks by a PLO leader concerning Israel would be eagerly seized upon by Israeli propagandists as proof that the PLO cannot be considered a possible partner for negotiations. Recall that Peace Now (which, in fact, has done important and courageous work) is commonly put forth as an ideal that has no counterpart among the Palestinians. See p. 157* and chapter 3, note 111.

munity with its own way of life, which had been evolving in Lebanon since 1948, and at an enhanced rate since 1975... [against the] health and educational services, political and social organizations, judicial and self-management systems, etc. Now that all these autonomous social systems have been utterly destroyed, the Palestinian refugees have once again become a faceless mass of people, uprooted, evacuated and torn away from any form of collective life.[197]

Bar-On may incidentally be right in saying that "anyone who visited Southern Lebanon" could see the facts that he describes, the results of what Meir Pail calls "the 'smash-up' technique" used "to raze" the areas to be occupied "in various ways: in air, naval and artillery bombardment, and with tanks, rockets and mechanical equipment."[198] But it is also true that many who visited the area explicitly denied these facts and condemned the American media as dupes or liars or worse for partially reporting them.

In any event, so Eichmann's prosecutor informs us, the "gang of thugs" has now been replaced by the Phalange and Haddad—the humanists of Tel al Zaatar, Khiyam, and other noteworthy incidents—backed by the IDF, which has some tales of its own to tell, and the cancer has been removed. As for the terror that had "metastasized" throughout the world, there were early claims that Israel had captured innumerable "international terrorists" from Europe and elsewhere who were being groomed by the PLO. The careful reader of the press was later to learn, in the small print buried in other stories, that these much-publicized reports were false. Israeli intelligence officials conceded that "they had seized no Western European or Japanese terrorists, only 28 Turks, in their occupation of Palestinian camps and bases"; "despite some erroneous statements in the early days of the war that European terrorists had been taken prisoner, no member of a major international terrorist organization was captured by the invading Israeli army,"* an Israeli specialist on terrorism reported, speculating that they might have left in May, "when war appeared imminent."[199]

---

* There is more to the story of terrorism in Europe than what is reported in the U.S. The Palestinian role has been very widely publicized, but it is barely known here that Israel has been accused of direct involvement in terrorism in Europe, and that the Israeli secret services have been condemned for terrorist acts in the courts in Norway and Italy (in the former case, for killing the wrong person in error, and in the latter, in connection with the murder of Palestinian poet Wael Zuaiter). It has also been reported that right-wing European terrorists have had close dealings with the Phalange and have spent time in Phalange and Haddad areas (see, e.g., *Economist*, Oct. 11, 1980, citing the Bavarian Ministry of the Interior; *Zu Haderekh* (Rakah, Communist), July 29, 1981, quoting from the West German journal of former anti-Nazi resisters; the same report alleges that terrorists who were identified as trained by the PLO were in fact captured by the PLO when they left Phalange territory). In their recent spate of confessions, leading Red Brigadists have alleged that the Israeli Mossad sought to assist them, providing them with information

The comparisons brought to mind by Gideon Hausner's words did not go unnoticed in Israel, for example, by the paratrooper just quoted (note 196), who "cannot help remembering what was done to my people during the Second World War," and by a fair number of others who expressed their dismay in the press or in demonstrations. For many, there were chilling reminders of not-so-distant history when roles were reversed, extending concerns that had already been aroused, and clearly articulated, over developments in Israel and the occupied territories in the past few years (see chapter 4). In a huge government-sponsored demonstration in support of Operation "Peace for Galilee," one sign particularly struck reporters, standing out from the others with red letters and in many copies: "One people, One Army, One Government." A Hebrew-speaking journalist from a German television company "immediately translated it to her friends, pointing out its similarity to the Nazi slogan: 'Ein Volk, Ein Reich, Ein Fuehrer'," the Labor Party journal reported.[200] Letters appeared in the press from the generation of Holocaust survivors expressing fear and concern over what they felt was happening. One, Dr. Shlomo Shmelzman, was forbidden by the directors of the *Yad Vashem* Holocaust Memorial Center to conduct a hunger strike there—his son was serving with the paratroopers in Lebanon. He wrote a letter to the press announcing his hunger strike in protest against the Lebanon war:

> In my childhood I have suffered fear, hunger and humiliation when I passed from the Warsaw Ghetto, through labor camps, to Buchenwald. Today, as a citizen of Israel, I cannot accept the systematic destruction of cities, towns, and refugee camps. I cannot accept the technocratic cruelty of the bombing, destroying and killing of human beings.
>
> I hear too many familiar sounds today, sounds which are being amplified by the war. I hear "dirty Arabs" and I remember "dirty Jews." I hear about "closed areas" and I remember ghettos and camps. I hear "two-legged beasts"* and I remember

about targets of assassination as part of what an Italian judge called a "diabolic plan" to destabilize Italy. A Radical Party (i.e., liberal) parliamentarian charged that the Mossad "was not at all disinterested in the elimination of Aldo Moro, considered by Israel as an excessively 'pro-Arab' statesman." Cited by Lisa Palmieri-Billig, *Jerusalem Post*, Feb. 1, 1982, as evidence of "vilification of Israel" in Italy; another example of such "vilification," according to the *Post*, was a statement by President Pertini expressing support for Israel but also calling for a Palestinian "homeland." On the testimony of Red Brigadists, see *Panorama*, January 11, 1982 (Italian). For more information, see Livia Rokach, "Israeli Terror in Europe," *The Dawn (Al Fajr)*. Oct. 16, 1981. An Italian parlimentary inquiry confirmed Mossad efforts to aid the Red Brigades in an apparent effort to destablize Italy. Roger Cohen, Reuter, *Boston Globe*, June 4, 1983.

---

* The reference is to Menachem Begin's statement in the Knesset, widely quoted in Israel and Europe since, interpreted as a description of Palestinians as "two-legged beasts." The government of Israel protested that this is a misinterpretation, and that Begin's "description is applicable to whosoever sinks to such moral depths that by killing or threatening to kill a *Jewish* child, he proves himself bereft of any semblance of humanity" (my emphasis). This clarification elicited several bitter rejoinders, raising the obvious question.[201]

"Untermenschen." I hear about tightening the siege, clearing the area, pounding the city into submission and I remember suffering, destruction, death, blood and murder... Too many things in Israel remind me of too many other things from my childhood.[202]

Many agreed with Meir Pail, who saw "disturbing signs that we are becoming spiritual slaves to the culture of physical force," or with Boaz Evron, who wrote that "the true symbol of the state is no longer the Menorah with seven candlesticks; the true symbol is the fist."[203]

Such voices will not be heard if "supporters of Israel" have their way, and those who choose not to see will continue to be responsible for much grief and suffering.

Like Colonel Dov Yirmiah and many other soldiers, the paratrooper quoted above derides the "talk about the purity of our arms and about our humane fighters" (see Yirmiah's comments cited on p. 239 on the "false" and "sickening" phrase "purity of arms" and the "cynical" lies about the "humane" Israeli soldier), repeated with much respect by Americans taken on guided tours by the Israeli military; for example, the inimitable Martin Peretz, who presents this Truth on the authority of selected Israeli soldiers and an IDF education officer, dismissing evidence to the contrary on the grounds that "Arabs exaggerate" and the media are committed to "deceit" or are simply anti-Israel.[204] A comparable conclusion based on such evidence would be dismissed with ridicule in the case of any other state (always apart from one's own).

But let us look further. The IDF education officer on whose testimony Peretz bases his conclusion about "purity of arms" is Shlomo Avineri, whom Peretz presents as a critic of Begin's policies, hence highly credible in this regard. What is more, this critic of Begin was invited to conduct "'fully free and open' discussions with officers and ordinary soldiers [at the front] on various vexing topics, including whether it would be right or wrong for Israel to move against West Beirut." "The army doesn't fear these discussions," Avineri informed Peretz, "even though it knows that the officers who conduct them, being mostly intelligentsia, are mostly critics of the government or actually on the left." The fact that such a strong critic of Begin's policies as Shlomo Avineri is invited to discuss such "vexing topics" as an invasion of West Beirut surely demonstrates the uniquely democratic and open character of the Israeli army, according to Peretz.

Unfortunately, there are some problems in this demonstration, and in reliance on Avineri as an authority on "purity of arms." peretz neglects to report the opinions of this critical dove. Others have, for example, Meron Benvenisti (see chapter 4, section 4.2), who, as an IDF lecturer, sat through Avineri's "training sessions" for these lecturers and reports their contents in an open letter accusing Avineri of "lack of intellectual honesty." Avineri informed the IDF lecturers in July that "under the given conditions there is no alternative to the conquest of Beirut by force," thus joining the hawkish wing of Likud and setting himself in opposition to the Labor Party. When asked about the political and human cost, he responded that "this question is no concern of the lecturers." He furthermore explained "that the Americans would agree after the fact to the conquest of West Beirut by force." When participants objected to his "shocking presentation," he "burst out and insisted that whoever is unable to go out and to encourage soldiers to perform their duty (that is, the conquest of West Beirut) is not entitled to appear before them."[205] Once again, the facts that Peretz suppresses are highly relevant to the point he is attempting to establish (recall the incident of the "vacuum bomb"; p. 215). Knowing the contents of Avineri's instructions to the IDF lecturers one might draw a rather different conclusion about the significance of his being invited to discuss such "vexing topics" as the invasion of West Beirut, and about his credibility as an authority on "purity of arms."

It is worth noting that Peretz's demonstration of Israeli adherence to the doctrine of "purity of arms" is taken quite seriously in the U.S., even among liberal doves. Few have been so outspoken in criticism of Israeli expansionism as Rabbi Balfour Brickner, a member of the Advisory Committee of the peace group Clergy and Laity Concerned (CALC) and a peace activist for many years. In the CALC journal he writes of his anguish over what happened in Lebanon in 1982, but not before establishing the ground rules:

> But, I believe every word of what others have reported re Israel's conduct of the war and PLO atrocity (the most persuasive of these reports was Martin Peretz's "Lebanon Eyewitness"...)...
> I am persuaded that Israel's soldiers practiced "tohar haneshek"—the morality of arms—with zeal and extreme sensitivity. I am convinced that they took great care to avoid abusing the strength their weapons gave them.

Note that he remained "persuaded" even after the terror bombing and siege of West Beirut, and that the "others" who have reported do not include Israeli soldiers returning from the front or Israeli journalists, some already cited. He also writes that within the PLO only "a small moderate element" is "prepared to support a two-state solution" (clearly false) and that "though the cease fire was holding and had held for over a year, terrorists did continue to rain rocket fire on Israel's northern border communities"; the second of these two inconsistent statements is false, except with reference to the clearly retaliatory strikes of May and June 1982, the first symbolic and after extensive Israeli provocation, including murderous bombardment, here unmentioned. As for the IDF soldiers, "In the annals of military combat, their behavior is unique," with "no abuse of civilian populations," "no reported instances of looting...[and]

a care not to needlessly destroy civilian property."[206] We have reviewed evidence bearing on the veracity of most of these claims, and will turn to the remainder in section 8.1.

Though Shlomo Avineri's views on the war, as presented to the IDF lecturers, are essentially those of Begin and Sharon, he is regularly presented here as a critical dove. A look at what he actually says is interesting. Writing to an American audience, this noted scholar explained that "the Palestinians have always adopted the line of maximum no-compromise with Zionism and with Israel" (on the facts, see chapter 3), though their current willingness to consider a cease-fire "may be the first sign of sanity" (as contrasted with their strict observance of the July 1981 cease-fire, which caused such distress in Israel). "With the decimation of the PLO in Lebanon, Israel can now afford to be more self-assured and more generous," achieving its "legitimate Jewish liaison with Judea and Samaria" and allowing "the bulk of the West Bank and Gaza" to be attached to Jordan, while the East Bank becomes "the area in which the Palestinian refugees could be rehabilitated." He subsequently explained that "as long as the PLO held sway in Beirut, moderate Palestinians were effectively deterred by PLO threats and terrorism from coming forward with plans that did not mesh with the ideology calling for the destruction of Israel" (such as, for example, the January 1976 plan for a peaceful two-state settlement prepared by the PLO). Others often regarded as doves agreed, for example, Raanan Weitz, the head of the rural settlement department of the Jewish Agency, who proposed that "water can be brought from the Litani River, in Lebanon, to arid regions in the West Bank and the Gaza Strip," while Jewish settlement remains at least along the Jordan River, "constituting a part of the state of Israel," and presumably in other areas of the West Bank and Gaza being settled under the auspices of the agency that he directs.[207]

As for the government of Israel, it held fast throughout to its resolution "that the fight against the PLO permits no compromise—because the PLO wants it that way" (compare the facts reviewed in chapter 3), that the PLO threat is "political no less than military," and that the PLO must not be permitted to exist as a "political body." The PLO men who "have entrenched themselves in the heart of residential West Beirut" have "again...created acute danger to the safety of the Lebanese as well as Palestinian men, women and children from behind whom these PLO forces are sending out volleys of artillery and small-arms fire against the Lebanese and Israeli forces in East Beirut and beyond" in "blatant violation of the rules of warfare."[208] The emphasis on the "threat" posed by the existence of the PLO as a "political body" is quite appropriate. One may plausibly read this as confirming evidence, from the highest source, for the thesis of Porath and others concerning the origins of the war, already discussed; reading this quite typical statement, one may also recall the regular indignation over the alleged refusal of the PLO (and the Arabs generally) to accept the existence of Israel, the heart of the Middle East problem, it is commonly argued. One might have hoped, however, that the government of Israel would at least have stopped short of accusing the PLO of attacking Israeli forces in Beirut.

Perhaps one can expect nothing more of the government. What then was the role of Israel's opposition party throughout the war? There should be few illusions in the light of its record when in office, particularly in the bloody 1950s and the expansionist post-1967 period. Amiram Cohen gives a detailed accounting of the deliberations of the Labor Party leadership during the critical events of 1982, based on interviews with high level officials, including the leadership itself.[209] Prior to the war, the leadership strongly opposed the military action that every knowledgeable observer knew was being prepared. Chaim Bar-Lev stated on April 9 that "the present conditions do not justify military action that will engage us in war," and Mordechai Gur, another former Chief of Staff, wrote in *Ma'ariv* that current tensions are not related only to terrorist activities but to "the intention to change the political map of Lebanon." Yitzhak Rabin warned against actions that would disturb the cease-fire and opposed "a massive attack against the terrorists in Lebanon." Israel should observe the cease-fire strictly, he wrote in *Davar* on May 14, "as long as the terrorist organizations are observing it."

Two months before the war, Begin informed the Labor Party leadership of the "large plan": conquest of southern Lebanon up to the Beirut-Damascus highway and a link-up with the Phalangists. A month later they were presented with the "small plan": the pretense concerning a 25-mile security zone. Labor agreed to support Operation "Peace for Galilee," though "when the tanks began to move it was well-known to the leadership where they were heading...just as the officers and the soldiers knew." On June 5, Peres outlined to the Labor leadership the content of the "large plan," which he and others knew was to be implemented. While some conveyed their objections internally, apart from Yossi Sarid and Shulamith Aloni Labor voted with Likud to support the operation, knowing perfectly well that the official explanation about the 25-mile limit was a fraud (at least, the leadership knew). For the first two weeks of the war, Labor was silent. They continued to support the war, with two qualifications: Labor opposed conflict with the Syrians—an aspect of the war to which I will turn in the next chapter—and the entry into Beirut, though even in this regard there were exceptions, among them, Chaim Bar-Lev, Secretary-General of the Labor Party, who approved the invasion of West Beirut after the Gemayel assassination in September.[210]

Throughout, Cohen continues, Labor anticipated that the consequences of the war for Israel would be grim in all respects, but they kept silent. One factor was their conviction that "the U.S. gave the green light and Haig was able 'to live' even with an entry into Beirut." See section 4.7.

Apart from that, "nothing succeeds like success." Labor temporized, waiting to see "how things would turn out." To oppose the war was considered politically impossible, given poll results indicating that 98% of the Likud and 91% of the Labor Alignment supporters backed the war and regarded it as justified. The Labor Alignment refused to take to the streets in support of those who demonstrated against expansion of the war. Rabin regarded the war as justified after "the terrorists bombarded the Galilee settlements" (in retaliation for the heavy bombing of Lebanon on June 4-5; such retaliation, after the unprovoked murder of several hundred people, evidently proves that "the terrorists" continue to be "two-legged beasts," in Begin's rhetoric). Chaim Herzog (elected President in March 1983) went so far as to favor even the conquest of Beirut.

Gur was the strongest opponent of the war among the top leadership. He issued a public denunciation of the Labor leadership and the entire operation on August 20, in *Ha'aretz*. The attack on Beirut, he said, would prove to be an ineradicable stain, and the entire war, as it was conducted, was unjustified. The presence of the IDF, he wrote, was the "primary factor in the election of Bashir Gemayel" to the presidency of Lebanon, "and whoever activates the IDF to such aims is capable of doing the same tomorrow in Israel as well," a concern about Defense Minister Sharon that had been voiced frequently before, even by Begin, it has been alleged. Yossi Sarid, along with Shulamith Aloni and parts of Mapam, opposed the "large plan" strenuously and called for withdrawal of Israeli armed forces from all positions that had no direct connection with the security of the Galilee. But the leadership in general remained silent, apart from its general opposition to the conquest of Beirut. When things began to go wrong later, after the Sabra-Shatila massacres, the Labor leadership changed its tune, as we shall see.

All of this will again evoke memories among opponents of American aggression in Indochina. It is difficult to conjure up a picture of Labor as constituting a meaningful opposition. though one might reasonably argue that support for Labor is nevertheless justified when one considers what Begin and his cohorts are likely to do in the future.

Cohen writes that "if anyone thinks in error that from Abba Eban there will come salvation for the doves—disappointment awaits him." True, Eban's views are "extremely dovish." But he will not use his international prestige to express them in public. In fact, in his article in *Socialist Affairs* cited above (see note 135), Eban writes that Begin "solemnly promised the Knesset on June 8 that when we reach the 40km. limit, 'the fighting will cease'," a sign of his duplicity. Surely Eban knew that the "small plan" had never been seriously entertained and that the Labor leadership was well aware of this fact from the start.

6.4   The American Scene

We have sampled the "taste of victory" among Lebanese and Israelis—it is superfluous to discuss further the reaction of the Palestinians. What of the United States? As noted earlier, Israel's direct aggression evoked only limited criticism within the U.S., though when the true objectives and the costs of the war became clear, the situation began to change. Some went so far as to claim that Syria and the PLO "were the aggressors" in Lebanon, not Israel, which simply "uprooted them from where they had no right to be,"[211] though this commentator—Henry Fairlie—does not tell us where the Palestinians had a "right to be."* Others did, for example, historian Barbara Tuchman, who explained that although "the invasion of Lebanon seems to me out of proportion" and may not be "the wisest course," nevertheless: "Let us put the responsibility for a solution where it lies... Let the Arabs solve the problem of the Palestinians," not those who occupy their former homes.[212] Since the Palestinians were the "aggressors" when Israel invaded Lebanon, it must be that Israel was acting in a "peace-producing role"—and so we are informed by ex-Senator Jacob Javits, who also points out that once before Israel had "serve[d] in this peace-producing role" in Lebanon, namely, in 1958, when Israel provided logistical support at the Haifa port for the landing of U.S. marines in Lebanon.[213]

Michael Walzer, the noted social democratic theorist of "just wars," explained that "I certainly welcome the political *defeat* of the PLO, and I believe that the limited military operation required to inflict that defeat can be defended under the theory of just war." Under his concept of "just war," with its special provisions for the State of Israel discussed above (see pp. 100-1), his conclusion is surely correct. Walzer also assures us that Israel's military practice in the south "was a good example of proportionate warfare"—the proof is that Israeli soldiers so informed him—and if later operations in Beirut put civilians "at risk," we must understand that "the responsibility for the risks lies with the PLO,"[214] the official position of the Begin government and yet another notable contribution to contemporary moral doctrine by this highly-regarded social democratic humanist.*

---

* He also avoids mention of the fact that Syria was present under an Arab League mandate that was to expire in July 1982, and that the U.S. and Israel at least tacitly supported the original Syrian intervention in opposition to the Palestinians and their Muslim allies.

---

* A review of his latest book (*Boston Globe*, March 20, 1983) describes Walzer as "something of a national treasure": "No reader [of these essays], even one profoundly opposed to his democratic socialist politics, could fail to appreciate his humanism." In his previously-cited *Just and Unjust Wars*, Walzer also relies on the testimony of Israeli soldiers to demonstrate the high moral level of the IDF—perhaps not the most objective source. It should be unnecessary to stress that evidence from the combatants of some military force is highly relevant when it is critical of its practices, of limited significance otherwise. No one would credit reports by Russian soldiers on their "purity of arms" in Afghanistan, though critical comment offered freely should be taken quite seriously.

Morris Abram, formerly U.S. representative at the UN Commission on Human Rights, explained that "the moral culpability for the loss of innocent lives in Lebanon, as in Dresden, Germany, and Normandy, in France, during World War II, rests primarily on those who initiated the terror rather than on those who ended it"—that is, on the PLO, whose terrorism, surely to be condemned, hardly matched that of Israel. "The pain of west Beirut was caused by the grip of the guerrillas who held it hostage." The war was "regrettable," but it "would never have occurred" if the Arab states had resettled the Palestinians—who, in fact, insisted on their right to return to their homes, always failing to comprehend the point, so clear to American Zionists, that they had forfeited this right by their flight and expulsion, and must put the past behind them, while the Jewish people returns to the homeland from which it was exiled 2000 years ago.[215]

Just at the point when the siege and bombing of Beirut were reaching their peak of savagery, the well-known liberal columnist William Shannon expressed "some distress" over the "terrifying violence" while noting that "something positive" may yet come out of it; namely, the PLO and "their Syrian patrons" may be "forced to recognize reality." "Reality" is that "the PLO has sabotaged every effort to make some diplomatic or political headway on the problems of the Palestinian people" and that "the PLO has murdered or intimidated into silence independent-minded Palestinians who wanted to explore different political possibilities," "tolerat[ing] no divergence from its political line, tiresomely reiterated, that Israel is unacceptable and must be destroyed":

> But it is not Israel's fault that a defeated PLO chose to hole up in West Beirut and use women and children as shields. For a generation, the PLO has been the aggressor against Israel, using every tactic from terrorist bombings to diplomatic stonewalling. Any nation placed in Israel's predicament would put an end to this aggression if it were within its power to do so.[216]

As we have seen, reality is rather different from Shannon's "reality." In the real world it is the U.S. and its Israeli client that have rejected every effort—including PLO efforts—to reach a peaceful political settlement in accord with the international consensus, and it is hardly accurate to say that the PLO "chose to hole up in West Beirut," to which it was driven by Israeli violence. These lies are particularly ugly ones, coming at the time they did and thus providing a justification for Israel's terrorist attack on the defenseless civilian population then held within its grip.*

---

* Shannon's gross errors of fact were immediately brought to his attention, with extensive documentation, but he had no interest in correcting them. As for the "Syrian patrons" of the PLO, who had entered the Lebanese civil war to attack the PLO, it was hardly necessary to provide Shannon with evidence; the same issue of the *Globe* contained a report by Michael Kennedy of the *Los Angeles Times* on battles between the PLO and Syria just prior

Soldiers who had participated in the attack on Beirut had a rather different picture of what was happening. We may, for example, compare Shannon's version with this one, from the scene:

> One Friday we stood on a high hill overlooking the Beirut airport. We had hundreds of cannons that we used according to plan, to bombard the refugee camps of south Beirut. Everything was calculated. Each unit received a definite area to bombard. For four hours we bombarded the refugee camps which at the same time were being bombarded from the air and the sea. It is difficult for me to return to those four hours and to recount what I felt. From our position we could see our artillery strikes with the naked eye. We could see the sparks of fire every second. It was a terrible scene.[217]

Evidently, things looked a little different from Boston.

Once again, we should recognize the familiarity of the practice of Fairlie, Walzer, Abram and the rest throughout the history of the modern state-worshipping intellectuals, the annals of Stalinism being only the most obvious example. Recall Elmer Winter's admonition in the *Jerusalem Post* that "American Jews have their work cut out for them"; it is perhaps unfair to fault them—and others—for performing their tasks; see pp. 209, 14.

Editorials in the nation's press took a similar stance. Echoing the wording of the Israeli Embassy, cited above, the *Washington Post* argued that "The PLO made [West Beirut] an involuntary battleground; Israeli guns did most of the damage to it: a deadly 'partnership'." Employing similar logic (putting aside differences in the circumstances irrelevant to the point at issue), one might argue—perhaps some Nazis did—that the British made Calais and Dunkirk an involuntary battleground, in a "deadly partnership" with Hitler's armies. The *Post* continues: the PLO must now "find a political course that is reasonable and realistic"—in contrast to its former proposals for a peaceful two-state settlement in accordance with the international consensus.[218]

In the eyes of the *New York Times* editors, "American weapons were justly used to break the P.L.O." The Lebanese must understand that their "liberation from the Syrians and the P.L.O. is no license to resume civil war," and Israel must understand that though "America will extricate them from Lebanon, and let its aid cover the costs," they must have "respect for American interests in the Middle East...and yield something to America's view of the 'full autonomy' jointly promised at Camp

---

to the Israeli invasion. Naturally, this and much similar evidence was also dismissed as irrelevant to Higher Truths. For another no less amazing example of the ruminations of this distinguished liberal columnist, see *TNCW*, p. 87, this one in the *New York Times* and concerned with the righteousness of another Holy State.

David." The Israeli invasion "opened some promising political paths" (as did the Argentine invasion of the Falklands at the same time, though for some reason this fact was not adduced here in support for it), but the U.S. should not "reward [the PLO for] the biggest hijacking in history—half of Beirut is the hostage—in a coin they do not possess, the Israeli-held West Bank" (the Gaza Strip seems to have been tacitly consigned to Israel). "The civilians [the PLO] are using for cover are Moslem innocents; the P.L.O.'s final bet is on Israel's humanity and the sensibilities of civilized nations," and they must respect their "enemy's restraint." "When the P.L.O. holds half a city hostage and shouts 'Pay my ransom or shoot your way past these innocents,' there is no special virtue in cease-fires that let the talks drag indefinitely." The U.S. recognition that the PLO demands as its "ransom" should be denied, since it "would strengthen the P.L.O's extremists" and "would destroy the chances of negotiating true autonomy with fairly elected Palestinians in the West Bank" (though the dismissed elected mayors and even Israel's chosen quislings reject this "true autonomy" and insist upon an independent Palestinian state along with 98% of the population, who furthermore overwhelmingly advocate that this state be run by the PLO). With the final cease-fire, "the P.L.O. fighters who have held west Beirut hostage will finally evacuate without goading the Israeli attackers into ferocious house-to-house fighting that would have vastly increased the carnage."[219] Etc., etc.

Particularly of note—since the remainder is fairly routine in this style of journalism—is the notion that of course the U.S. taxpayer must willingly pay Israel for its achievements in Lebanon.

Not everyone approved. Nathan Glazer and Seymour Martin Lipset described the war as "ill-advised" and urged that Israel grant the Palestinians "real self-determination" in the West Bank and Gaza.[220] Some used stronger terms, though they remained a distinct minority. In fact, across a broad spectrum of articulate opinion, Israel's aggression received strong support. Crucially, it received the direct material and diplomatic support of the U.S. government. The Democratic Party expressed its sympathetic support still more forcefully. The Administration stood by its recommendation for an increase in aid to Israel, and Congress, under the prodding of liberal Democrats, demanded still further increases. The Labor Union bureaucracies strongly supported the war, as did most conservative columnists. The national press did too, though with some reservations. The familiar principles of official doctrine concerning Israel and the PLO were continually reiterated as in the few examples just cited, truth being dismissed as the usual irrelevance.

At the extreme left of mainstream politics, support for the invasion was no less fervent. The Santa Monica City Council, regarded as virtually a socialist enclave, passed a resolution "in essence, to support the right of Israel to defend its borders by invading Lebanon." The same resolution "questions the Reagan Administration's 'drifting away from commitment to the Camp David process,' challenges the appointment of George P. Shultz as secretary of state 'at such a grave time in Israel's existence' and calls upon Sen. Alan Cranston (D-Calif) 'to carefully examine at the Senate Foreign Relations Committee hearings Mr. Shultz's ties to the Bechtel Corporation and his ties and Bechtel's ties to Saudi Arabia* and Saudi Arabian support for the PLO'."[221] The idea that it is *Israel's* existence, not the national (or simply human) existence of the Palestinians, that is threatened as Israeli military forces are systematically demolishing Palestinian society with U.S. support should be carefully noted, not merely dismissed on the grounds of patent absurdity; it reflects, in the clearest possible form, the deep-seated racist assumptions that extend across a broad spectrum of U.S. opinion, including much of the left.

Others too felt that Shultz might be a problem. Seymour Martin Lipset, speaking at the Hebrew University, warned that "Israel's biggest problem is likely to be that Shultz is a 'do-good Christian' with sympathy for the underdog and the oppressed. Israel's policies in Lebanon and in the territories are likely to arouse his 'moral indignation'."[222] One can understand the concern over these possible character flaws.

Few surpassed Tom Hayden and Jane Fonda in their support for the invasion. Well before, Fonda had announced that "I identify with Israel unequivocally." This was on the occasion of her "special prize" from the Hebrew University "for her contribution to freeing the prisoners of Zion in the USSR and for the freedom of immigration for Jews there." Fonda announced on this occasion that she is "making every effort. . . to explain to the government and the general population" in the U.S. that "world peace and certainly the security and future of Israel" are threatened by moves in the U.S. "to establish friendly relations with a state such as Saudi Arabia." "I operate according to my conscience, and am attempting to convince President Reagan that the U.S. interest is bound up with friendship with democratic Israel, and not with feudal Saudi Arabia." This is one aspect of her commitment "to continue with my work for human rights."[223] The ceremony took place just at the moment when the Sharon-Milson oppression had reached its peak of violence; see chapter 4, section 5. If her "work for human rights" extended to those then being shot, beaten, humiliated a few miles from where she was speaking, the fact remained unrecorded.

In July 1982, Fonda and Hayden toured Israel and Lebanon as guests of the Israeli Organization for the Soldier (in effect, the Israeli USO),

---

* The demand to examine Mr. Shultz's various ties would be fair enough, were it coupled with a demand to investigate the ties of others to Israel or to countries that support Israel, a meaningless demand given the U.S. role, thus highlighting the true significance of the concern over Mr. Shultz.

reaching as far as Beirut, where they "watched the shelling" from Israeli positions. Fonda "expressed her identification with Israel's struggle against Palestinian terror, and her understanding for the Israeli invasion in Lebanon, which would remove the terror, and her support for Israel's struggles for its existence and independence"—all feelings that naturally come to the fore as one travels past (probably not seeing) the rubble of Ain el-Hilweh and witnesses the bombardment of Beirut. "Israel has the right to defend herself from anyone who threatens to destroy her," she said, "and not only when they are attacking her." "Tom Hayden blamed the PLO for causing the 'Peace for Galilee' operation," presumably, by its regular and unprovoked shelling of the Galilee in the preceding year and its adamant refusal to consider a political settlement, despite Israel's enthusiastic efforts in this regard. "The couple Fonda-Hayden expressed their hope that the PLO would indeed leave Beirut; that further bloodshed would be avoided there and that the affair will lead to a solution of the Palestinian problem in the spirit of Camp David," thereby taking their stand in explicit opposition to virtually all the inhabitants of the occupied territories.[224]

Hayden laid the blame for the present crisis on the PLO, stating that the PLO, by "its tragic refusal to recognize Israel's existence as being compatible with Palestinian nationalism, by its repeated calls for annihilation of the Zionist state and by its use of terrorism, has made the current Israeli response inevitable"—compare the actual facts, discussed in chapters 3, 4 above—though he said that he did not "turn a blind moral eye to reports of massive and excessive civilian casualties" or the use of cluster bombs, the familiar stance of many liberal supporters of American aggression in Indochina. He further stated that a direct Israeli invasion of Beirut would be "understandable," thus lining up with Begin's Likud against the Labor Party, which opposed this final step; and he held that "Israel won't be able to...pull back without a PLO withdrawal."[225] As quoted, at least, he did not explain why the refusal of Israel to have any dealings with the political representative of the Palestinians does not justify Palestinian military action against Israel, given that the Israeli invasion is justified by the failure of the PLO to recognize Israel, putting aside the fact, which does not appear to be entirely irrelevant, that the PLO has long agreed to the establishment of a separate state alongside of Israel, a position rejected across the mainstream of Israeli politics.

At a luncheon at the Beverly Hilton for the new president of a "fraternal organization which seeks to link American and Israeli Jewry," Fonda gave him "a small menorah she had bought in Hebron [that is, in Kiryat Arba in the occupied West Bank, the settlement of the Gush Emunim racist-chauvinist fanatics who at that very moment were carrying out the pogroms described in chapter 4] during her visit to the Jewish state." The new president then joined with Vidal Sassoon and a number of

Rabbis in a strong endorsement for Hayden for State Assembly, noting the praise he had received from officials of the Begin government and the Labor opposition in Israel, and his views "against the PLO" and for Israel "as a Zionist and Jewish state"[226]—that is, a state based on the principle of discrimination against the ethnic-religious minorities, a principle that is effectively applied in the Jewish state, as we have seen, though the facts have been equally effectively suppressed in the country where one may make tax-free donations to these discriminatory programs.*

At a meeting in New York after the war, Fonda "announced her unqualified support for Israel and condemned the hypocrisy with regard to Israel in connection with the Lebanon war," which she attributed to anti-Semitism and to the subservience of liberals to third world states, both phenomena of great moment in the United States. "I love Israel," she said, "and I believe that Israel is a loyal ally of the United States," and thus deserving of support, apparently with no further questions asked. "She spoke with great emotion about the prisoners of Zion in the USSR"—but not, as reported, about those who might be called "prisoners of Zion" in another sense of the phrase: in Ansar in Lebanon or in the West Bank villages terrorized by the settlers who were selling her a menorah, Halhul for example (see p. 131). "Israel rarely makes mistakes," she said, "and when Israel makes a mistake—everyone, particularly Jews, shouts and screams." She asked: "Who ever made a criticism of Yasser Arafat, the head of the PLO?"—surely no one in the American press—"and who does he represent anyway?"—a question to which she might have heard some answers on her visit to Hebron, had she chosen to mingle with the local population, apart from her gracious hosts. She concluded "that it is easy to sit here, Jews and non-Jews, and to make criticisms." "But we do not live on the Lebanon border and we were not attacked for 12 years by the Palestinian terrorists," so we have no right to criticize.[227] And by the same

---

* One might note, in this connection, Irving Howe's distress over "Jewish boys and girls, children of the generation that saw Auschwitz, [who] hate democratic Israel and celebrate as revolutionary the Egyptian dictatorship," some of whom "go so far as to collect money for Al Fatah. . . . About this I cannot say more; it is simply too painful" ("Political terrorism; hysteria on the left," in Chertoff, ed., *The New Left and the Jews*). He gives no evidence that any such examples exist. If they did, they were sufficiently marginal as to pass unnoticed except by those seeking some means to discredit the activist movements of the 1960s, and surely did not typify the New Left, which was hardly enamored of Nasser and was largely dovish Zionist (see my article in the same volume for documentation). It is interesting to compare Howe's reaction to the alleged collection of funds by Jewish boys and girls (or anyone in the U.S.) for Fatah, with his reaction to their by no means imaginary collection of charitable funds for Israel's "national institutions," to be used for purposes deemed "directly or indirectly beneficial to persons of Jewish religion, race or origin" (not to citizens) including measures that effectively exclude Arab citizens from 92% of the land, legalized robbery of Arab lands, channelling development funds to Jewish rather than Arab citizens, etc. This is not "too painful to discuss" for an ardent (post-1967) supporter of Israel, though in this case the phenomenon is quite real. See chapters 2, 4 and references cited for discussion of the background for all of this.

logic, those who have not lived in Palestinian refugee camps surely have no right to criticize the PLO.

Not everyone in Israel is entranced by these observations, though most of the press, including the left-wing press cited, is quite pleased. The well-known Israeli dove Uri Avneri, for example, writes: "I have learned to despise Jane Fonda, who gained a reputation as a fighter for peace and human rights, and who now sells this name to various fascists, among them Israelis, in order to advance her career and that of her husband . . . ," along with some far harsher comments.

A "partial list of events in the vicinity of Hebron," about which Fonda could have learned with ease on her visit there, is presented by Rafik Halabi, who notes that "until now their perpetrators have not been revealed and no one has come to trial for any of them." Included are a 1976 incident in which "tens of [Arab] youths and students from Hebron" were held prisoner in Kiryat Arba, set upon by dogs so that several required hospitalization; the 1976 expulsion of a judge of a Muslim religious court by the Kiryat Arba settlers after they publicly humiliated him; killings, destruction of vineyards, looting and destruction of property in the house of a leading Muslim family, throwing of grenades at Arab houses, destruction of houses, etc.; alongside of events of the sort described in chapter 4, section 5. Chaim Bermant, an orthodox Jew himself, describes Fonda's Hebron hosts as orthodox Jews for whom "Hate Thy Neighbour" has become a "creed" and a general "philosophy": "The knitted *kippa* [skullcap; their symbol], in Arab eyes, has become the badge of the bully and the thug, and I'm afraid I'm beginning to see it in the same light myself."[228]

At the opposite extreme of California politics, newly-elected rightist Senator Pete Wilson, virtually quoting Jane Fonda a few days earlier, said that "he intends to follow a strongly pro-Israel line in the Senate because Israel is 'the only real hope that we enjoy of a strong, determined ally' in the explosive Middle East."[229] On the views of California's other Senator, liberal Democrat Alan Cranston, see p. 10. In short, considerable unity, across the board.

Jane Fonda is, of course, not alone in her contention that criticism of the war in Lebanon is an expression of anti-Semitism. Norman Podhoretz, among many others, makes the same allegation.* Critics of the

---

* Podhoretz is the editor of *Commentary*, which I have avoided discussing here. For an example of what it contains, see Robert W. Tucker, "Lebanon: The Case for the War," October 1982, which begins by denying that Israel had any "well-developed plan" to destroy the PLO presence in Lebanon (rather, the IDF was, "one might almost say pulled" to Beirut by unexpected lack of "effective opposition"), carefully avoiding extensive and quite compelling evidence to the contrary from Israeli sources, some cited earlier, and continuing at the same level of concern for fact (see, e.g., p. 1*). Tucker rejects the "moral critique" of Israel's aggression, writing that "what has so often been presented as hard-headed political analysis is, when its surface is once scratched, moral preference masquerading as political

invasion, he holds, deny to the Jews "the right of self-defense," which they exercised by invading Lebanon: "What we have here is the old anti-Semitism modified to suit the patterns of international life. Why should Americans lend themselves to this disgusting maneuver?"[230] Or Israelis; for example, those who pointed out the absurdity of appealing to the right of self-defense when in fact the PLO had scrupulously observed the July 1981 cease-fire. Others concocted lurid tales of how Lebanon was "dismembered by Soviet-armed PLO terrorists and Syrian forces who have used its towns and villages as a battleground," leading to the death of 100,000 civilians; the world stood by in silence "while the PLO imposed a seven-year reign of terror on Lebanon" and now condemns Israel for its "recent campaign to uproot the terrorists from their bases" despite its "extraordinary precautions" to prevent civilian casualties. And of course the bottom line: "vital American interests are at stake."[231] The signers speak of "the campaign of lies and distortions mounted by the terrorists and their supporters," an apt description of their own statement.

It is easy enough to ridicule such pronouncements by comparing them with the undisputed facts about the civil war in Lebanon, or with the descriptions by Israeli soldiers, journalists and military experts. But to do so would be to miss the more important point, the efficacy of the Big Lie when the media are effectively disciplined and the illustration, yet again, of how easy it is for intellectuals to believe anything, however fantastic, in the service of some Holy State and to produce apologetics for its atrocities, phenomena of no small significance in this terrible century.

Some attempted more original arguments, for example, Arthur Goldberg, who offered this one:

> Free from the illusion, now demonstrated to be without foundation, that the PLO has the coherence, strength and support to act as the "sole representative of the Palestinian people," and liberated from its terroristic acts and blackmail against Palestinian leaders, inhabitants of the West Bank, and other Arab countries, it should be possible to conclude an autonomy agreement with all deliberate speed.[232]

It is not entirely clear who is said to be now "free" and "liberated" in this semi-coherent statement, but the idea appears to be that by successfully employing its overwhelming military might to smash the PLO, Israel has

---

analysis." He gives no examples, but the judgment holds of his affectation of "hard-headed political analysis," a largely muddle-headed expression of his "moral preference" for the doctrine that "there is nothing in reason or morality that enjoins a government to refrain from taking action against a threat to the state's security," that is, to engage in aggressive war, even in a case such as this, where "the threat that united virtually all Israelis" turns out to be the threat "of a PLO state in the West Bank." His position is a familiar one; Hitler and Goebbels, for example, gave a similar justification for their resort to force. See p. 208*. It is not unusual for this moral stance to be represented as "hard-headed political analysis."

demonstrated that the PLO cannot claim to represent the Palestinian people, specifically, those in Lebanon and the occupied territories who support it even though it is not the world's fourth strongest military power. With a bit more understanding of the facts, and a rather different moral stance, Meir Pail put the point in these terms, presenting what he suggests may have been "the real aim of the invasion," conveyed in the following "message of vital import to the Palestinians" in the occupied territories:

> "Beware you Palestinians living under Israeli rule! All that we have done to the refugee camps, the cities and towns and villages of south Lebanon, on the coast of the Mediterranean between Rashidiye, Tyre and Beirut we can do to you in Gaza, Judea, Samaria...and even perhaps in Um-el-Faham and Nazareth [within Israel proper]. And we can do that now, especially, given that there is no P.L.O. or any other legitimate organized body that could be seen to represent the Palestinian cause. If you will bend down and follow our rules, it would be best that you accept the limited autonomy offered you as defined by Begin-Sharon-Milson; if not, your fate will be that of Rashidiye (near Tyre), Ein-Hilwa (near Sidon), or Beirut."[233]

This "message" is a more literate version of what Goldberg is apparently trying to say, stripped of the deceptive rhetoric that only barely conceals the true meaning of his words.

The former Supreme Court Justice and UN Ambassador has produced a most impressive contribution to contemporary thought: if some political entity can be destroyed by force, that demonstrates its illegitimacy and the right of the conqueror to determine the fate of those whom it had pretended to represent. This idea has not previously been advanced, to my knowledge, though its usefulness is evident; for example, to justify the Nazi conquests. Goldberg's article would also delight structuralist literary analysts with its intriguing formal properties. Thus it begins by berating the media for joining the PLO in speaking of "an invasion" when "Israeli troops encircle Beirut" (how odd for them to do so), and it ends, with charming consistency, by referring to Israel's "justified invasion of Lebanon."

There appears to be one striking exception to this picture of a broad spectrum of American discussion, namely, the publication here of Jacobo Timerman's harsh criticism of Begin's Israel, *The Longest War*, and the reception accorded to it.[234] An earlier version was published in the *New Yorker*, a mass circulation journal that reaches a liberal intellectual audience, and it has been extensively reviewed, critically but also with respect, a most unusual occurrence with regard to a book that is critical of Israel, since 1967. This is true even in the *New Republic*, where passages in the book are described as "stuff and nonsense" and "faintly nauseating," but it is nevertheless taken to be "an eloquent personal testimony, and a contribution of lasting significance to the great debate on Israel."[235] The latter comment is a radical departure from the normal style of this journal in the case of people who presume to criticize policies of Israel, except within the limits of the tolerated form of "critical support." More typical are the terms applied to Alexander Cockburn, whose detailed factual and analytic commentary on the war and the Sharon-Milson repression, in the *Village Voice*, was unique in American journalism in its insight, detail, and accuracy and was thus a major irritant in *New Republic* circles: he is "a nasty piece of work," "despicable," with a "double moral standard," "admiration for the P.L.O. and extreme tolerance of the Soviet Union,"[236] charges flung without a shred of evidence or argument, and with the veracity that we expect in comparable descriptions of political enemies in the *Daily Worker*. Elsewhere too, reviewers and journals that rarely tolerate critical discussion of Israel have praised Timerman's book for its balance and integrity (while generally dismissing its contents). Why such exceptional treatment? Does this show that the spectrum of approved opinion is indeed far wider than I have suggested, in mainstream intellectual circles?

The comment cited from the *New Republic* gives a clue to the mystery. The book is, indeed, a "personal testimony," and can be tolerated as "a contribution of lasting significance to the great debate on Israel," in fact as virtually the sole critical discussion to be admitted to this canon, precisely for this reason. It contains few facts and little analysis, but is primarily a cry of anguish, often quite harsh and eloquent. It is, therefore, fairly safe: one man's impressions, to be understood in terms of his personal history and psychology, and therefore an excellent choice to represent the side of the critics in the "great debate." A further clue is given by the reference in every review to the book's "balance." The *New Republic*, for example, begins by noting Timerman's "strong criticism of some modes of condemning Israel and of supporting the Palestinians," and his "devastating indictment of the P.L.O. sympathizers and the effect of their sympathy," quoted at length. These examples are cited as "sharp bursts of shrewd insight," the only ones so honored. It is not easy to know to whom Timerman is referring in these "sharp bursts of shrewd insight," since this impassioned "personal testimony" is rather short on specifics, but there is little doubt that this "balance" contributes to rendering his criticism tolerable, alongside of the restriction to personal impressions and feelings. A closer scrutiny of the features of the book that permit it to be admitted into the "great debate" yields some insight into the contemporary ideological scene.

As already noted, Timerman repeats standard myths about Israel, for example, that the 1982 Lebanon war "was the first war launched by Israel" (see p. 99). This is one notable contribution to "balance," and there are numerous others. Consider the statement that the PLO "started the 1975 war" in Lebanon—by arranging to have a busload of Palestinians killed by the Phalange in April (see section 3.1). Or the claim that the Peace Now demonstrators on July 4 were "ready to withdraw this very day from Lebanon and negotiate this very day with the Palestinians, regardless of who represents them, for the establishment of an independent sovereign state on the West Bank," a serious misrepresentation of the facts; with some exceptions, the demonstrators took no such position, nor did Peace Now as an organization, but the picture is a useful contribution to images of Israel that are welcome here, regardless of the facts. Or consider the injunction to the Palestinians to abandon their "terrorist strategy" and "sterile diplomacy" and to "organize politically"—unaccompanied by any account of just how they were to "organize politically" under the regime imposed by the Labor Party and then Begin, or why their willingness to accept a two-state settlement in accordance with the international consensus is "sterile diplomacy" (indeed it is, given U.S.-Israeli rejectionism, but that is not Timerman's point). Such assertions, which help establish the "balance" that renders his condemnation of Israeli policies tolerable, go part of the way towards explaining the relatively favorable reception of the book. But let us look further.

The book begins with a moving description of a lunch with Michael Walzer at the Institute for Advanced Study in Princeton three months before the outbreak of the war, when the repression in the West Bank had reached its peak (a fact not mentioned). Both men knew that "Sharon's war" was soon to come. What could they do to stop it? Timerman suggested "that if the two of us decided to commit suicide and explained in our wills that we were killing ourselves to stop Sharon's war, perhaps we could succeed in stopping it." But the idea was rejected, since Sharon would not "have found in his heart the images of so many Jews who believed in moving the conscience of mankind by the generous surrender of their own lives... What would the world, or Israel, or General Sharon himself, have done with our two bodies?... We cut pathetic and ridiculous figures, Michael Walzer and I, in our search for logic and sober judgment," pathetic in their inability to find a way to prevent the tragic events that they foresaw. For Timerman, "Sharon's War began that very day."

There are certain difficulties in this account. First, Walzer supported the war as a "just war," as we have seen. Thus it is not clear why he should have contemplated suicide to prevent it. Indeed, in the light of his record, it is difficult to imagine circumstances in which he would take any action in opposition to policies of Israel, or even deign to recognize unpleasant truths about the state that he so loyally defends. Second, one can think of some less extreme measures that might have been useful, for example, writing an article warning of what lay ahead, an option that neither man undertook though they have access to a wide audience denied to others who had the same perception. In fact, Timerman considered the idea of organizing a petition among "the men of Princeton" but rejected it on the grounds that Sharon and his associates would not "pay attention to these men of Princeton who have written so many books and shared so many discoveries with mankind," which seems a bit facile, even if it would have been possible to mobilize "the men of Princeton" in an advance warning against the war.

Let us turn to the "devastating indictment of the P.L.O sympathizers" which so impressed the *New Republic* reviewer. Timerman bitterly condemns "the Harvard, Princeton, and Columbia professors who went along with [the PLO] for years"; they were "allies or accomplices," or simply "vain and frivolous academics who wanted to prove a thesis." "The principal task of the academics should have been to confront Palestinian terrorism with a clear and convincing picture of the political reality," but instead "they preferred to feel important glorifying an obsolete and reactionary image, that of terrorist *machismo*"; "more than one U.S. scholar considered it a privilege to review the world situation with Arafat." "They seized upon the idea of the historical inevitability of a Palestinian state," while failing to work "with the moderates among the Palestinians and the Arab world within the bounds of a political strategy." And with others (e.g., Western Europeans), "they allowed the PLO to avoid the issue with ambivalent insinuations that not even the goodwill with which some of us in Israel heard them could convince us that they accepted anything less than the destruction of our country." Had these miserable academics met their responsibilities, "they could have forced the creation of a Palestinian state despite the obstructions of Israeli reactionary groups."

Again, there are some problems. First, note the typical falsifications with regard to Arab "moderates" and "political strategy"; thus it is unexplained, for example, why PLO support for a two-state settlement since the mid-1970s drove Israel into such a panic, and failed to convince those with Timerman's "goodwill" that "they accepted anything less than the destruction of our country." And as well, the typical falsifications with regard to Israeli opinion: it was not certain "Israeli reactionary groups" that opposed the creation of a Palestinian state, but the Labor Alignment, along with the Likud. As of 1980, only about 1/10 of the Jewish population in Israel "unconditionally accepted Israel's recognition of a Palestinian nation" while half that number agreed to the establishment of a Palestinian state, and under 3% of the population (and 1/5 of the "Dovish Leaders") agreed to "recognition of the PLO as the Palestinians' representative"—even fewer, presumably, would have been willing to recognize a PLO-run Palestinian state in accordance with the wishes of the vast majority in the occupied territories.[237] We have already noted how images of the "beautiful Israel" have been cynically manipulated by

American liberals to increase military support for Begin's policies of settlement and aggression (see p. 109). Timerman's fables about Israeli attitudes lend themselves to exploitation for these ends in exactly the same way, not his intent surely, but a part of the explanation for the relatively favorable reception of his critique.

Still other questions arise. Just who are these vile professors? No names are mentioned. I cannot think of a single "U.S. scholar," a single professor at Harvard, Princeton or Columbia—or elsewhere — to whom Timerman's description even remotely applies, except insofar as some Palestinian scholars did presumably discuss the world situation with Arafat, hardly a crime, one would think, particularly when one eliminates Timerman's fanciful constructions about the views expressed. Recall Robert Tucker's astonishing fantasies; p. 1*.

There is one important qualification to this remark: Timerman's description does apply, rather accurately in fact, if we replace a few words: "Israel" for "PLO," "Golda Meir" for "Arafat," etc. This is an important fact that could hardly be comprehended within the American intellectual community, apart from a few, or by Timerman, it would appear. But let us keep to his version.

Timerman claims that these disgraceful academics, who "risked nothing," pandered to the Palestinian (or Third World) taste for terrorism instead of patiently explaining to the PLO that this would lead to disaster. Again, some references would have been helpful. I know of none—though possibly a diligent search would yield a marginal example in some Maoist journal. These professors, Timerman says, were "obsessed by their competition with academics who supported Israel" (who are subjected to no criticism by Timerman), as if there were some "great debate" in academic circles, or anywhere in the United States, between "supporters of Israel" and "supporters of the PLO," a ludicrous picture, as anyone familiar with the U.S. would know at once, including his editors and reviewers, if not Timerman himself. There were, in fact, a handful of critics of Israeli policies within the academic profession, no one of whom questioned the right of existence of Israel, to my knowledge. These few, who incidentally had few opportunities to publish here on these matters, consistently warned the PLO of the dangers of its resort to terrorism while sharply condemning this practice, and condemned the early rejectionist diplomacy of the PLO as intolerable on moral grounds as well as self-destructive. They needed no instruction from Timerman on this score.

I was in fact one of these few, so I will keep to my own writings on the subject, though there are few enough critics so that a full record would not be difficult. My first article on the topic appeared in *Liberation* and the *New Outlook* (Tel Aviv) in 1969, and is reprinted in *Peace in the Middle East?* as chapter 1. It contains an extensive discussion of the "suicidal" and deeply immoral character of the resort to terror, drawing from Israeli doves who were making the same point. My next article (reprinted as chapter 2 of the same book) was a talk given at a conference of the Association of Arab-American University Graduates (AAUG) in 1970, where I condemned the PLO reliance on "armed struggle" on moral and political grounds, emphasizing precisely its "suicidal" character for the Palestinians given the actual balance of forces, warning against "romantic illusions about these matters," and also condemning the official PLO rejectionist program, which, even if it could succeed—which, as I emphasized, it could not—would be "intolerable to civilized opinion." Exactly the same remained true in subsequent years (see p. 79*), and is true of the handful of other critics of Israel's policies whose writings or public talks are familiar to me. Timerman's story is fantasy from beginning to end.

But useful fantasy, of a sort illustrated several times above. Like Irving Howe and others, Timerman is relying on the convention that critics of established doctrine can be freely denounced without argument or evidence, or even explicit reference. Like Mark Helprin in the *New York Times Magazine* and numerous others, he invents a "great debate" and lambasts the non-existent advocates of the point of view of the enemy. This creates "balance" and allows the author to take "the middle ground" of sanity while proceeding with the illusions and fabrications of current propaganda concerning the U.S., Israel and the Palestinians. Timerman accuses Begin of "girding himself for a typical Israeli political debate in which accusations require no proof and weigh more than ideas or analysis." I do not know whether this is a fair comment with regard to Israel, but it surely holds with regard to its supporters here, and to Timerman himself.

It should, however, be noted that in the case of Timerman, these concoctions are, in a strange way, a contribution to truth. Had he not presented and emphasized them, his book, with its impressionistic but sometimes accurate critique of Begin's Israel, would have suffered the usual fate of work that lies outside the bounds of mainstream ideology or that presents factual material that tends to undermine it. The text would certainly not have appeared in the *New Yorker* or any other journal that reaches a substantial audience, and could not have been accepted as a contribution to the "great debate," were it not for its tales about pro-PLO academics and its reiteration of familiar fabrications about Israel and the Palestinians; nor could it have been regarded as "a contribution of lasting significance," or even recognized as existing. So, in a certain sense, one should welcome this remarkable record of falsification, given the ideological climate in the United States.

For completeness, I should note that when we escape the confines of the U.S. ideological system, the contributions of this critical tract to Israeli propaganda do not go unnoticed. Thus in London, Elfi Pallis observes that Timerman "falls victim to Israeli mythology":

> Looking at the land of Kibbutz Gesher Haziv in Galilee, he
> reflects "how in the past this was a desert." Galilee, of course,
> has never been a desert, and Kibbutz Gesher Haziv farms the
> fields that used to belong to the Palestinian villagers of al-Zeeb,
> now refugees in Lebanon.

"Two-legged beasts" living in "nests of terrorists" that must be "cleansed,"
we may add. And again in London, David Gilmour comments on
Timerman's belief "that Israel's crimes only began with Begin and that
before him its moral integrity remained intact," listing a series of earlier
examples that demonstrate the contrary, a few of them mentioned above.
Gilmour also cites Timerman's statement that "for the first time Israel has
attacked a neighbouring country without being attacked," commenting
accurately that "Even Begin no longer pretends that" (see p. 100). He also
takes note of Timerman's approval of a letter that Professor Jacob
Talmon wrote to Begin in which he said: "However lacerating are the pain
and the shame we feel for the affronts that our perverse and anachronistic
policy, which is devoid of a future, causes among our neighbors, *much
greater* and even [decisive] is the fear of the consequences of such behavior
for us, the Jews; for our dream of a social and moral rebirth... "[238]
Gilmour comments: "there is something a little ridiculous about the sight
of Ashkenazi intellectuals earnestly debating their own identity while
Israeli aeroplanes are destroying Beirut with phosphorus bombs."[239]

Timerman's personal statement is not without value, and should be
read, but it lends little support to the belief that a "great debate" is raging
in the United States, or that more than a very narrow spectrum of opinion
is represented here among the articulate intelligentsia.

These examples give some idea of the range of opinion expressed as
Israel conducted its attack on Lebanon, or, if one prefers the *New York
Times* version, its "liberation" of Lebanon. These examples, however,
illustrate the attitudes of elite "opinion-makers" and may not be a
reflection of prevailing attitudes among the population that is the
intended target for indoctrination. Indeed, there is reason to believe that
popular attitudes are rather different, to judge by personal experience and
also poll results. One poll indicates that there appear to be "two U.S.
publics," one described as "better informed" and the other as "less
informed." The "better informed" feel that the invasion of Lebanon was
justified, by 52 to 38 percent; the "less informed" hold that it was not
justified, by 43 to 28 percent. One recalls the attitude studies that showed a
correlation between educational level and support for the Vietnam war, or
the current ones that show that nearly 3/4 of the general population
regard the war as "more than a mistake; it was fundamentally wrong and
immoral," a position held by only 45% of "opinion makers" and probably
by a far smaller proportion of the "elite," to judge by earlier studies.[240]

Such results are subject to various interpretations. One, which I think is plausible, is that the term "better-informed" should be construed as "more effectively indoctrinated," i.e., more subject to the distortions of the ideological system. People who are less susceptible to its influences, perhaps because of lack of exposure, are more readily able to perceive aggression and massacre as aggression and massacre, not understanding them to be, in reality, self-defense and extraordinary precautions to safeguard civilians. As a case in point, consider the standard attitude towards the Russian invasion of Afghanistan. Few people know much about it, but it is overwhelmingly understood to be exactly what it is: a case of brutal aggression and massacre. Those subjected to effective Communist indoctrination will regard this view as naive and deluded, as "moral preference masquerading as political analysis" (see p. 270*), accepting the more sophisticated interpretation that the leader of the socialist camp is fulfilling its internationalist duty to defend freedom and human rights from terrorists serving the interests of the CIA and Western imperialism. Our own systems of indoctrination, while quite different in form and technique, often have the same kind of effect on sophisticated opinion.

A poll conducted by Decision/Making/Information, a research institute directed by White House pollster Richard B. Wirthlin, indicated that 3/4 of the population favored the establishment of a Palestinian state—in accordance with the international consensus and in sharp opposition to the rejectionist stands of Israel and the U.S. government. 65% felt that there would be no peace in the Middle East unless a Palestinian state is established.* The poll also revealed a sharp decline in sympathy for Israel (down from 59% a year earlier to 39%) and increase in sympathy for the Palestinians (up from 13% to 23%). 69% disapproved of the Israeli invasion of Lebanon, and of those who felt that the invasion was justified by the PLO presence in Lebanon, nearly half changed their minds when told that the Palestinians had observed the cease-fire while Israel had not. 35% felt that the U.S. should take unspecified "disciplinary measures" against Israel because of its invasion of Lebanon. 50% said "no" when asked if the U.S. "should give aid to Israel," and the 44% "yes" vote decreased when in a follow-up question the actual quantities of aid were cited.[241] It would be interesting to see what the responses would be if it were known for what purposes the aid is used, or if information were

---

* Popular support for a Palestinian state has been expressed before. For example, a survey of participants in the Foreign Policy Association's "Great Decisions '76" program showed that 66% approved of the right of Palestinians to an independent state while 19% objected (*New York Times*, July 11, 1976). There is a survey of a number of polls by Allan C. Kellum, publisher of the Washington report *Mideast Observer*, in *The Link* (AJME, New York, Dec. 1982). Polls taken after the Beirut massacres showed that 50-60% were in favor of suspending or reducing arms sales to Israel, while over half favored a Palestinian state.

provided about the nature and uses of tax-free charitable contributions, or other devices that are used to funnel aid to Israel.

This poll was taken after the Beirut massacre, and State Department "experts say it is not clear whether the shift in American attitudes is transitory or whether it is part of a more lasting trend."[242] It is, however, clear enough that the specialists in what Walter Lippmann called "the manufacture of consent" have their work cut out for them.

These results are particularly striking in the light of the fact that virtually no one who can gain access to a large public advocates the positions that appear to be backed by most of the population: abandonment of U.S.-Israeli rejectionism, and reduction or suspension of aid, particularly military aid. On the contrary, at this very time Congress was debating whether to increase aid to Israel even beyond the increase already proposed by the Reagan Administration; if there was any articulate criticism of this strange spectacle, it was that the Reagan Administration was "politicizing" the aid process by placing barriers before even further increases. And while the public appears ready to accept the international consensus on a two-state settlement, the government and most of articulate opinion continue to maintain the traditional rejectionist position, either supporting the Labor Party or Reagan's September peace plan. As noted earlier, public opposition to the Lebanon invasion was regarded by the Reagan administration as "a problem" that had to be somehow overcome (see p. 213). It is rare for such a gulf to exist between articulate opinion and policy on the one hand, and public opinion on the other. The question merits a closer study, and may be suggestive for people who would like to see the issue truly enter the arena of democratic politics.

7   The Critique of the Media

7.1   The American Media

One interesting feature of the ideological scene in the summer of 1982 was the attack on the media as pro-PLO and anti-Israel. The charge had often been made before (see pp. 1*, 200, for some examples on the part of current *New Republic* editors), but it was renewed with considerable vigor as the Lebanon war began to appear on television screens and front pages. Television was a particular target of attack, particularly, for its insistence on showing scenes of the siege and bombing of Beirut, not counterbalanced by equivalent scenes of the siege and bombing of Tel Aviv or of parts of Lebanon where peace reigned under military occupation (on the same grounds, one could criticize the British press after the bombing of Coventry for not featuring pictures of parts of the city that remained intact). In a rational world, one would simply dismiss the charge of pro-PLO and anti-Israel bias as absurd or paranoid, noting the overwhelming evidence of "support for Israel," racist dismissal of the Palestinians, and suppression of unwanted history across most of the spectrum of opinion and analysis. But we live in this world, so let us consider the matter.

Criticism of the media is certainly a legitimate undertaking, rarely pursued in a serious and intellectually responsible way. But the criticism in this case had some unusual aspects. Critical discussion of the media generally centers on editorializing, in explicit opinion pieces (including editorials) and more important, internal to news reports, where it is often manifested in more subtle ways; or on the selection of items to appear, the emphasis given to various topics, the uncritical acceptance of material that serves ideological needs, the incredible standards of evidence that are erected in the case of material that runs counter to these needs, and so on. There is ample material of this sort, and its significance is vastly underrated, in my opinion. But the criticism in this case was of a novel type. I do not recall a previous charge that correspondents on the scene were systematically misrepresenting what was happening before their eyes. On the contrary, even the harshest critics of the press in the past have always emphasized the generally highly professional standards of foreign correspondents in presenting what they found—though what they were looking for, and how they interpreted it, are often another matter.

In the present case, however, we find such criticisms as this, emblazoned on the front cover of the *New Republic:*

> Much of what you have read in the newspapers and newsmagazines about the war in Lebanon—and even more of what you have seen and heard on television—is simply not true.[243]

So we are informed on the authority of Martin Peretz, who was there—on a guided tour with an Israeli military escort. It is, of course, possible that the news presented here was contrived so skillfully that much of what we had actually seen, and what we had read in the reports of usually reliable correspondents, did not happen, but was fabricated for the occasion. One would want some rather strong evidence before accepting this conclusion, something stronger than "I was there"—or the authority of Israeli soldiers (carefully selected, since as noted many such soldiers gave harrowing reports going well beyond what was published here), his reports of what he was told by Lebanese, "Arab friends" who "coyly" explained that "Arabs exaggerate," noted doves such as Shlomo Avineri (see pp. 258f.), and his own observations, which are credible to the extent that he has demonstrated himself to be a credible commentator and observer.

On the latter issue, we have already seen some pertinent evidence.[244] Recall, for example, his treatment of the very examples he selected to demonstrate the perfidy of the press, the "vacuum bomb" story (pp. 214-5) and the case of Professor Avineri. This article contains much more. Note simply the scrupulous avoidance, once again, of the Israeli press, with its reports—some quoted above—by journalist, military experts and soldiers. Or the integrity (or, to be more charitable, the gullibility) of someone who can report that "Whomever I talked to on the streets—and there are many eager to talk, Christian and Moslem, in French or English or Arabic—pointed out that what the Israelis had targeted were invariably military targets"; an incredible falsehood, from the first day of the bombings just prior to the actual invasion, and a claim startlingly at variance with the reports of Israeli observers. Recall the observation by the former chief education officer of the IDF, Mordechai Bar-On, that "anyone who visited Southern Lebanon during and even after the fighting" could see that the target was not merely "the PLO's military infrastructure" but rather "the very existence of the Palestinians as a community." At the very time that Peretz reported that the IDF was scrupulously limiting itself to only military targets, military historian Col. (Ret.) Meir Pail, former head of the IDF officers training school, was writing that the region that Peretz visited "looked as though it had suffered a major earthquake in the 'best' tradition of the destruction of the Vandal conquests in ancient times or of the Mongols in the Middle Ages," a scene of "destruction and ruin" that "will be the haunting memorial which points to Israel and the IDF as the inheritors of the Mongols in the Middle-East."* There are numerous other examples, some cited earlier from Israeli soldiers, military analysts and journalists; not to speak of the bombardment of Beirut, the character of which was already evident when Peretz wrote. Peretz seems to have visited a different country from the one these Israeli "Lebanon eyewitnesses" were describing (unless they too were secretly "pro-PLO" or intent on defaming Israel). To believe on the basis of Peretz's claims that large segments of the American and European media were systematically lying would require quite a leap of faith—one easily taken by some American doves (see p. 259).

As we have seen (p. 200), even before the war Peretz felt that Israel had "lost" the press years earlier, because most correspondents were so afflicted by the Vietnam experience that they always sympathize with those who call themselves "guerrillas" or "freedom fighters." A person who could read the American press in this way has some credibility problems to start with. These mount further when we proceed to his indictment of television, in the same interview, because it fails to give the

---

* Pail argues that "there was a reasonable military explanation" for all of this, given the goals of the invasion, as already described, and that the IDF observed "the principle of purity of arms on its low and minimal scale," in the sense that "there was no deliberate killing of civilian population," though there was "contempt of that same principle on the national scale," for example, when the airforce was directed "to drop its bombs on unspecified targets, to devastate and raze the city and, apparently, to destroy the houses together with their terrorist residents," etc.[245] A number of soldiers quoted in the Hebrew press made the same point.

relevant background when it shows an Israeli soldier "beating the head of a Palestinian boy with a club"—one aspect of the "strongarm methods" that Peretz recommended, as implemented by his friend Menachem Milson, which he thinks should perhaps have been instituted from the start instead of the "liberal enlightened administration" of the preceding years. Peretz's criticism is that TV reporting, so tainted by superficiality, fails to "explain that the Arab national character tends towards violence and incitement and that thousands would be massacred if the PLO ruled in the West Bank." Without tarrying any longer over the reports of someone who is capable of speaking in this way about "the Arab national character," and who holds that this belief of his about the PLO somehow justifies the scene portrayed, and who is responsible for material of a sort already described sufficiently, it should be noted that if Peretz is to be believed, the Israeli government regards him as too harsh a critic! Peretz asserts that the Israeli Embassy in Washington contacted him with a request to circulate his "Lebanon Eyewitness," but requested first that he eliminate "critical passages."[246]

Peretz did not restrict his criticism to the media. He also extended it to opponents of the invasion, in ways that also reflect on his credibility. Take just one example. He refers to the fact that he signed an ad for Oxfam with the honorable goal of helping to "alleviate the suffering of those Lebanese caught in the fighting" (recall that this ad by "unexceptionable humanitarians" contained the figures on casualties and refugees that he later claimed to have been fabricated by the anti-Israel media, a fact that raises some interesting questions that might have been addressed somewhere; see p. 199*, also p. 221). But

> that is not the purpose of a new committee...[that] rounds up the usual suspects: pro-PLO hardline in America (Edward Said, former Senator James Abourezk, Noam Chomsky);* old-line Communist fellow-travellers (Pete Seeger, Paul Robeson Jr.); and the predictable goofies (Ramsey Clark, Dr. John Mack, Daniel Berrigan). The signatories seek relief money not for all the victims of the war in Lebanon, *but only for those* "trapped in West Beirut without water, essential services, and medical supplies." What an odd humanitarian impulse to aid just West Beirut!

The statement of the pro-PLO hardliners, fellow-travellers and predictable goofies in fact reads as follows: "Help the victims *including* hundreds

---

* On my "pro-PLO hardline" position see pp. 79* and 276 and references cited. For Peretz, the position that Palestinians have a right to select whom they wish as their representatives— that is, the position that they have the same human rights as Jews—is what is intolerable, and counts as a "pro-PLO hardline" position.

of thousands trapped in West Beirut without water, essential services and medical supplies."[247]

More interesting than this convenient bit of rewriting is what follows:

> Who exactly is holed up there? There are none "trapped" but the PLO. So this is what I.F. Stone, after all his agonizing about bloodshed, has finally come to: asking his admirers to put up money so that the PLO can continue to fight, not simply against Israel, but against the possibility of a peaceful Lebanon.

In fact, there were hundreds of thousands of people "holed up there," either because they had nowhere to flee, or because the local forces under Israeli control would not let them leave (see section 8.2.3)—or because it was their city, or because they stayed to help the victims. But to provide food or medicine to those who are being deprived of it by an Israeli siege while the IDF is in the process of blasting them to bits is obviously an intolerable act, more evidence of a "double standard" and a "pro-PLO bias," if not outright anti-Semitism, in the eyes of the editor of this leading journal of American liberalism—a fact that passes without comment here, again yielding some insight into the American cultural scene.

Another major critique of the media was produced by the Anti-Defamation League of B'nai Brith (ADL) in October. This time TV was the villain. The report consists of a documentary record of TV broadcasts with critical observations, and an analysis by the ADL. Subsequently, this was referred to by supporters of Israel as an indictment of the media, but a review of the documentation presented leads to no such conclusion. In fact, the study has its comic aspects. The primary criticism of the early evening news programs to which the study is restricted is that they gave reports with sources the ADL regards as inadequate. Thus on June 14, ABC and NBC cited casualty figures, attributing them respectively to the "Lebanese police" and "the Lebanese government." "Who are 'Lebanese police'," "Who is the 'Lebanese government'," the ADL analysts ask? Apparently, their concept is that in reporting the crimes of their Holy State in a TV clip one must provide an extensive scholarly apparatus. Similarly, CBS cited "international relief officials" in Beirut who reported casualty figures from Sidon. The ADL asks: "Who are these 'international relief officials,' and if they are in Beirut, how could they be reporting on casualties in Sidon?" (could they have received a message from Sidon?). If such standards were applied generally to TV reporting, the 6PM news would last until midnight if it could appear at all; someone who proposed that such standards should be met in any other connection would be regarded as quite mad. The ADL also criticizes the figures cited from Sidon because "this figure was later proven to be a gross exaggeration, yet no retraction was forthcoming." They do not provide the "proof," but it appears to be Israeli government claims to the contrary, cited above. The ADL does not explain why Israeli government announcements "prove" that the figures provided by the Lebanese police and government and by relief officials are false, a conclusion that is particularly curious when we recall that the Lebanese sources were celebrating their liberation by Israel, according to ADL doctrine.

The analysis continues at the same intellectual level. In fact, a review of their material shows, as would be expected, that American TV treated Israel with kid gloves. The ADL study contains one major specific charge of TV turpitude, namely, a June 13 report that there were 600,000 refugees in southern Lebanon, attributed to the Red Cross. The Red Cross later gave an estimate of 300,000 homeless but, the ADL study states: "No network reported this update." Two sentences later we read: ". . . on June 16, John Chancellor of NBC reported a Red Cross estimate of 300,000 homeless." The example reveals rather nicely the contempt of the ADL for its intended audience. The next sentence reads: "Yet on June 19, Jessica Savitch, also of NBC, reported a figure of 600,000 homeless," showing that NBC was persisting in its evil ways. In this case, we do not have self-contradiction within three sentences; rather, gross misrepresentation. Turning to the documentary record supplied as an appendix, we find that in this report Jessica Savitch stated: "It is now estimated that 600,000 refugees in south Lebanon *are without sufficient food and medical supplies.*" (my emphasis). Recall that these are the only specific and marginally serious criticisms that appear in the report.

The ADL study proceeds to criticize the networks for giving inadequate coverage to "Israeli relief efforts (an extraordinary departure from the usual behavior of combatants and certainly newsworthy)." It is quite true that the "Israeli relief efforts" described by Col. Yirmiah were "inadequately covered" and "newsworthy," but this fact merely reveals the normal pro-Israeli bias of the media, as the evidence cited earlier from Israeli sources shows clearly enough (see pp. 237f). This conclusion will simply be fortified when we return, directly, to further reports from the Israeli press about these "extraordinary" efforts. The study also criticizes the networks because "not enough attention was devoted to the fact that the overwhelming majority of Israelis solidly supported the Begin government." This criticism is interesting, given that the media were also regularly accused of failing to report Israeli dissent against the war, which revealed that Israel had not lost its high moral values. How these requirements are to be jointly met has not yet been adequately explained. The ADL study concludes finally that TV coverage was unfair because "the main sentiment which emerged from the coverage was one of revulsion at the violence which was implicitly and explicitly associated with Israel"; "Scenes of violence were inevitably and reflexively linked to Israel, however inadvertently and however understandably in a situation where the media competes for 'scoops' and graphic depiction of violent events"; "a majority of human interest stories shown were those which depicted scenes of great devastation and human suffering."[248] Comment seems unnecessary, except, perhaps, to recall once again Meir Pail's observation on the Stalinist character assumed by the Zionist organizations under the influence of Golda Meir and the Labor Party in the post-1967 period; see p. 14.

While the ADL study itself is merely embarrassing, it is of some interest, perhaps, that this document was taken quite seriously by the media. I saw no critical analysis of it, though its absurdity is obvious on even superficial reading, even putting aside the assumptions that underlie it. The *Times* had a fairly lengthy news report on its release, simply summarizing its allegations without analysis and quoting some responses by TV executives, e.g., Reuven Frank, president of NBC news, who characterized the study as "careful and quietly stated."[249]

Earlier, Frank had commented, more accurately, that "What Israel sees today is not an anti-Israel bias in the news coverage," but "a reduction in the pro-Israel bias." He referred to the attack on the U.S. media by "the pro-Israeli PR establishment, partly the [Israeli] government, partly Martin Peretz," and said he is willing to bet that "somebody in New York" instructed David Shipler of the *New York Times* to write a critical piece "on the PLO occupation of Lebanon" (cited above, note 10).[250]

It is interesting to ask why the media did not expose the self-contradictions, falsehoods and intellectual vacuity of the ADL critique and the astonishing moral values implicit in it. Perhaps they simply did not want to be charged with anti-Semitism or to be subjected to the kind of defamation and slander in which the ADL specializes. But there may be something else involved. It almost appears that the media relish this kind of criticism. There is evidence that that is so, in fact. The incident recalls an earlier one, a massive two-volume critique of the media by Peter Braestrup produced under the auspices of Freedom House, demonstrating (by the standards of its sponsor) that the media were unfairly critical of the American war in Vietnam, contributing to the failure of the U.S. to achieve its (by definition, noble) aims. The study impressed commentators in the press as "conscientious" and "painstakingly accurate" (*New York Times*); "with its endless attention to accuracy," Dean John Roche of the Fletcher School commented in the *Washington Post*, it constitutes "one of the major pieces of investigative reporting and first-rate scholarship of the past quarter century" and should lead to a congressional investigation of the press (see note 251). Harvard political scientist Michael Mandelbaum wrote (*Daedalus*, Fall 1982) that "Peter Braestrup's exhaustive study of the American media's coverage of the Tet offensive does show that the public received a distorted picture of the event." Others reacted similarly.* In fact, the first volume, containing the analysis, grossly falsifies the evidence presented in the second volume, containing the supporting documentation, so even on internal grounds the study would at once be dismissed by any rational commentator. Furthermore, crucial documentary evidence is omitted and the study fails to raise even the most obvious questions (e.g., how did news reporting compare with intelligence analyses, available from the Pentagon Papers and elsewhere?). When these elementary inadequacies are overcome, we see from Braestrup's own evidence—and what he omits—that the media accepted the framework of state propaganda and were more optimistic about the prospects for American arms than internal intelligence documents, not too surprising since the media tended to rely on public government statements, not knowing then what was being transmitted internally. The Freedom House case is narrow to begin with—that the press was too "pessimistic." By Freedom House standards, one must conclude, the press must not only accept the assumptions of the state propaganda system but must do so in an upbeat and enthusiastic spirit in its news commentary and editorial analysis. When the shoddy and incompetent treatment of documentary evidence is corrected, nothing remains even of its remarkable charge: excessive pessimism.[251]

What is interesting in the present context is that there was no exposure of any of this (apart from the reference of note 251, which was ignored). Rather, both the media and scholarship regarded the study as exemplary, even those who argued against its conclusions concerning the media; many agreed with the Freedom House sponsors that Braestrup's impressive results provide cause for concern about the anti-establishment commitments of the media. Even the simple fact of falsification of evidence, easily demonstrated, was considered irrelevant. One can readily understand why conformist scholarship should take this position. As for the media, one may perhaps conclude in this case too that the criticism was in a way a welcome one.

Why should this be so? Anyone who has attended a university commencement or similar event where a spokesperson for the press elaborates on its awesome tasks will understand why. Criticism of the press as "anti-establishment" and too critical of the government or of

---

* See, e.g., Col. Harry G. Summers, *New Republic*, Feb. 7, 1983, a review-article based on the Yale University press reissue, which typically regards the study as definitive, raising no questions about it. Summers claims that "Braestrup was widely attacked" both by supporters and opponents of the war and by "the journalistic profession," citing no examples and giving no indication that there was any favorable reception prior to his own; he also, incidentally, expresses a point of view concerning the war and the U.S. involvement in it that merits attention. The review predictably ends with a comparison to the "media coverage of the recent war in Lebanon": "As was true with Tet, the most damaging aspect of this reporting has been its effect on weakening the community of interest that is the bedrock of the American-Israeli alliance."

standard ideology (e.g., "anti-Israel," "pro-PLO") provides an occasion for orations on the duty of the Free Press courageously to examine and confront established power and doctrine, and if it sometimes goes too far, we must understand that this is a problem inherent in our system, which encourages the media to undertake this crucial challenge, etc. On the other hand, a more accurate critique of the media as tending to be subservient to external power and established doctrine is most unwelcome, and is certain to gain no hearing.

There is an obvious further point. If the conformist media and intelligentsia can be represented as "anti-establishment" and fiercely critical, then any genuine critical discussion, any attempt to approach our own society and institutions and practice with the same rational standards that we are permitted to invoke in the case of others, is at once undercut. There is, then, good reason on all sides to maintain the pretense. As I have documented extensively elsewhere, the device of feigned dissent has made an impressive contribution to indoctrination in the democratic societies. See *TNCW* and references cited for discussion.

There was, in fact, another study of the media and the Lebanon war by a different anti-defamation group, namely, the American-Arab Anti-Discrimination Committee (ADC), written by Eric Hooglund of the ADC Research Institute. Hooglund presents evidence of "a consistent pro-Israeli bias" in press coverage of the Lebanon war, shown by such phenomena as reference to the invasion as a "reprisal" (*New York Times*, June 5; obviously false); emphasis on Israel's right to protect its border towns from being "indiscriminately shelled" (*Washington Post*, June 7; recall the facts concerning the cease-fire and the violations of it); dehumanization of the Palestinians, including racist cartoons that would arouse charges of a revival of Nazism if the targets were Jews; and so on. I noticed no comment in the press apart from a column by *Washington Post* Ombudsman Robert J. McCloskey (Oct. 6, 1982), who referred to the study, ignoring its contents while noting the symmetry of the charges from the Jewish and Arab communities, from which the reader is to understand that "We must be doing our job," in the words of "cynical editors."

Still another study, this time of both print and TV media coverage, was carried out by Roger Morris. His conclusion is that there is no evidence to establish the charges of a "double standard" levelled against the media—referring to the charges by Norman Podhoretz, Martin Peretz, the ADL, and the like. This conclusion he establishes with ease. The material he presents does, however, support the conclusion that there was a rather different double standard; namely, the overwhelming tendency, from the first day, to adopt the point of view and the general interpretations provided by the aggressor. Morris's own assumptions are revealed by his conclusion that TV news "for the most part struck the balance carefully"—between the aggressor and the victim—though there were a few "lapses", for example, an "emotional portrayal" on ABC news that left the impression "that the Israelis were dropping the brutal weapons on civilians." But, Morris adds judiciously, "if noncombatants were now dying in the city, ABC at this early stage had an obligation to remind its viewers pointedly that the PLO had retreated into the heart of West Beirut, bringing the war with them like a plague"—just as British troops had retreated to Dunkirk, "bringing the war with them like a plague," as any fair-minded reporter had an obligation to emphasize in depicting scenes of Nazi bombing.[252] It would be a revealing exercise to take this defense of the media for their balance, replace a few names, and consider how it would read as applied to other wars.

The charge that the American media were "pro-PLO" or "anti-Israel" during the Lebanon war—or before—is easily unmasked, and is in fact absurd. It suffices to compare their coverage of the occupied territories, the war, the treatment of prisoners, and other topics, with what we find in the Hebrew press in Israel, a comparison always avoided by those who produce these ridiculous charges. Again, the annals of Stalinism come to mind, with the outrage over Trotskyite "critical support" for the "workers' state." Any deviation from total obedience is intolerable to the totalitarian mentality, and is interpreted as reflectng a "double standard," or worse.

7.2   The "Broad-scale Mass Psychological War" against Israel

In Israel too there was concern and surprise over the way the war was depicted. Reporting from Jerusalem, Norman Kempster observes that "Israelis, almost universally [a considerable exaggeration], were shocked to learn that large segments of world public opinion considered the nation's war effort to be highhanded, aggressive bullying and excessive." Blame was placed on journalists, whom Begin accused of "hatred for Israel and anti-Semitism" (his words in a Knesset speech). "Critics say Israel's version of the war was not told effectively because of a failure of *hasbara*, the Hebrew word that means literally 'explanation' but in usage comes out somewhere between 'publicity' and 'propaganda'."[253] Among others, former chief of military intelligence Aharon Yariv commented that he could not understand "why so much ground in the *hasbara* battle was lost so quickly to the other side."[254]

The head of the *Hasbara* department of the Foreign Ministry, Moshe Yegar, wrote a spirited defense against the charge of *"hasbara* failure," which was voiced early on, accusing correspondents of violating "the most elementary norms of fairness and professional ethics in their reports and commentary. Some of them were busy spreading propaganda instead of writing fair, objective reports." The international media, he charged, "suppressed information about the unparalleled IDF efforts to avoid or minimize...civilian losses, even at the expense of its own soldiers" (note that this was written after the terror bombings of Beirut). And "Most foreign correspondents ignored what they were shown about the return of normal life in Southern Lebanon and the warm reception given the IDF." Furthermore:

> Unfortunately, international relief organizations helped dis-
> seminate these malicious anti-Israel reports, sometimes in order
> to stimulate contributions in their home countries. Communist
> and leftist elements played a conspicuous role in stirring up
> hostility.

The behavior of the international media amounted to a "media pogrom," though in certain Latin American countries "there was understanding, even sympathy and support." Presumably this was true in Chile, the recipient of much Israeli military aid; and in Guatemala, where the army Chief of Staff under the Nazi-like Lucas Garcia regime thanked Israel for the military aid it was providing, adding that "The Israeli soldier is a model and an example to us,"* while the new Rios Montt regime, which is estimated to have murdered at least 5000 Indians during the period of the Lebanon war while forcing over 200,000 to leave their homes, stated that "we succeeded [in the military coup that brought them to power] because our soldiers were trained by the Israelis."[255] Yegar singles out Martin Peretz for his "deeper analysis of the phenomenon of distorted reporting," namely the one discussed above, which, as noted, was still too critical by the standards of the government.[256] Even Peretz was unable to resist Communist influence completely, it appears.

The director-general of the Department of Information of the World Zionist Organization, Yochanan Manor, agreed with the head of the *Hasbara* department of the Foreign Ministry about the Communist hand in this "media pogrom." Manor comments on a symposium in December 1982 on "War and the Media" organized by the *Jerusalem Post*. The

---

* Among Israel's gifts to the people of Guatemala under Lucas Garcia was a computerized system designed to monitor the use of water and electricity in private homes so as to detect the possible presence of anti-government elements, who could then be dispatched to their proper fate (Aharon Abromovitz, *Ma'ariv*, Dec. 10, 1982). Benjamin Beit-Hallahmi observes that "The Peace Now movement would not dream of protesting Israeli involvement in Guatemala, Haiti or the Philippines," because "what others regard as 'dirty work"—aiding the Chilean junta or South Africa in Namibia, for example—"Israelis regard as a defensible duty and even, in some cases, an exalted calling"; "the role of regional and global policeman is something that many Israelis find attractive, and they are ready to go on with the job—for which they expect to be handsomely rewarded," not unreasonably, considering that Washington is "severely limited by world public opinion" in such cases and therefore has every reason to appreciate Israel's contributions, which it sees as given with "aplomb, enthusiasm and grace." Benjamin Beit-Hallahmi, Op-Ed, *New York Times*, Jan. 6, 1983. See also chapter 2, notes 41, 42, 50; p. 110.

symposium had its good points, for example, in bringing out the "strong inclination" of TV "towards fabrication." But it missed a central fact. It concentrated on the shortcomings of professional journalists, but failed to understand that "the difficulties journalists encounter in covering a war as professionally as possible—and this was especially true of the war in Lebanon and Israel Television—are a direct result of the machinations of other professionals," namely, those "involved in psychological and propaganda warfare," organized by the Kremlin. "One participant hinted at this when he stated that the world press often falls victim to well-oiled systems of disinformation," but this hint was not taken up properly. In fact, the Soviet leadership immediately launched "an extensive worldwide effort of psychological warfare" using "a classical strategy": "First, to disqualify the Israeli military operation ('bloody war,' etc.); second, to provoke a vast reaction of disgust, triggering a peripheral pacifist reaction; and third, to search for ways of disseminating this pacifist reaction to vital Israeli centres, leading to a general paralysis and a closing of the options supposedly opened up by the operation itself." "These 'active measures' (a code word used by the Soviet leaders) were carried out through the vast network of organizations operated by the international section of the party and the International News Services of the Central Committee of the Communist Party of the Soviet Union," abetted by an alliance with the powerful and nefarious organization Wafa (the official PLO news agency). "The outburst last summer of a campaign which is not simply one of intimidation or of disinformation, but which has steadily assumed the dimension of an actual broad-scale mass psychological war, gives rise to serious concern," the director-general explains.[257] The phrase "media pogrom" thus understates the scale of the aggression against Israel in the summer of 1982; it was a "psychological war."*

Now we can understand why the American and world press and television gave such an incredibly distorted picture of the war, one so unfair to Israel. How could one expect simple western journalists to resist the skillfully coordinated machinations of Wafa and the CP news services, or even to be aware of the dark forces that were controlling and manipulating them. Recall the *New Republic* exposé of how UPI was "snookered by a pro" (the Soviet news agency) when it gave a watered down version of the vacuum bomb story that was presented in detail in the mainstream Israeli press, sure proof of the anti-Israel bias of the U.S. media, as editor Martin Peretz triumphantly proclaimed (see p. 215).

The director-general of the Department of Information relies heavily on an amusing book by Annie Kriegel, which appeared in Paris in the fall

---

* Compare the discussion of the alleged success of North Vietnamese propaganda in "exploiting" the "vulnerability" of American opinion in the *New Republic* review of Braestrup's study (see p. 282*), an interpretation favored by a number of people who were seriously frightened by the partial breakdown of ideological controls in the 1960s.

of 1982. He identifies Kriegel (whom he mistakes to be a man) as "a professor of sociology and an internationally known specialist on Communist affairs." He does not add that she is a long-time functionary of the French Communist Party who recently took the familiar, and quite short step to the extreme right. Manor was cautious enough not to refer in the English-language *Post* to her theory of the Sabra-Shatila massacres, to which we return, fearing perhaps that this would be taken as some bizarre form of Parisian parody by an American audience (the Hebrew press has, as usual, been less circumspect). Reading Manor's commentary and the book on which it is based, one who shares Manor's conception of the power of the International Communist Psy-War System (especially when allied with Wafa) might be tempted to conclude that Kriegel is still working as an underground Party agent, with the task of making the enemies of the Kremlin appear to be utter fools.

There were, however, those who felt that even Manor understated the case, among them, Professor Moshe Sharon, chairman of the Department of History of Islamic Countries of the Hebrew University. Manor assumed that it was the Wafa-CP alliance that was responsible for the pogrom, or war, to which Israel was subjected in the summer of 1982, but Sharon points to a still more powerful agency: the U.S. government (presumably nothing is left but God). He suggests that it was "the American delegation in Beirut" that was "responsible for the exaggerated news reports that emerged" from the Sabra-Shatila massacres in September. "One may also ask if the same delegation was not responsible for sending to the camps representatives of the American and world media who were already pumped-up against Israel. Who, one may ask, was responsible for spreading like wildfire through the world press the exaggerated and imaginative claim that thousands of women and children were killed in the camps?" (no references are given to these stories that flooded the world press; perhaps they were written in invisible ink, a still more insidious psy-war device).

Sharon explains that it is entirely natural for the U.S. government to engage in such anti-Israel operations. After all, "If one examines American attitudes towards Israel from 1948 until now, one finds that the Americans have almost constantly acted against the Jewish state, forsaking it in times of need and following what may be termed a 'Saudi policy,' which goes back to 1945," though this "Saudi foreign policy" is "very well disguised so as to appear evenhanded." To add to the list of Sharon's rhetorical questions, we may ask why the U.S. gives such phenomenal quantities of aid to Israel. Could it not be that this is part of the "disguise," a devious attempt to cover up its consistent opposition to the Jewish state?

We may recall, in this connection, the accusation by Defense Minister Ariel Sharon in early August 1982 that U.S. special envoy Philip

Habib and Robert Dillon, U.S. ambassador to Lebanon, "had misled the State Department and Reagan with false and exaggerated reports of Israeli military actions during the past few days," another demonstration of Professor Moshe Sharon's thesis concerning the unremitting efforts of the U.S. to undermine Israel.[258]

It should be observed that the articles by Yegar, Manor and Moshe Sharon appear in the *Jerusalem Post*, a journal directed to an international audience, and that the writers are people of some standing in the government, Zionist institutions, and academic community; Yegar and Manor are, respectively, the chief officials in charge of information for the State of Israel and the World Zionist Organization. This fact reveals something about current developments in Israel that might cause a little concern among people who really have its welfare at heart.

By late June, concern over the *"hasbara* failure" was already considerable: "Ya'acov Meridor, who is in charge of Israeli relief efforts in Lebanon, accused the Western press of 'poisonous lies' in its accounts of the destruction, and Health Minister Eliezer Shostak asserted that the International Red Cross [was] deliberately inflating casualty figures to tarnish Israel's name."* U.S. television coverage was blamed for Begin's (allegedly) hostile reception in the Senate, and the director of the Israeli government press office, Ze'ev Chafetz, accused European news agencies of "disseminating 'propaganda'" because of their "Palestinian bias," also stating "that some U.S. reporting had been inaccurate and harmful to Israel's cause."[259] His predecessor as government press chief, however, saw things differently:

> There was news management. It flopped miserably because it was impossible to manage news under these conditions. But the government thinks it flopped because it was not skillful enough. They keep looking for technical explanations.[260]

Meridor was particularly incensed about what he called the "lies"

---

* See p. 290. In the *Jerusalem Post* (July 15, 1982), Rabbi Professor Eliezer Berkovits explained further that "The self-righteous international condemnation of Israel should be treated with contempt; it has no moral significance. Nor should the International Red Cross be excluded from our contempt. Their monstrous propaganda lies against Israel have the familiar ring of medievalism." The criticism of Israel "is explained by the moral decay engulfing the West," where "everything is for sale, newspapers, TV stations, universities, national policies, ideals, the human conscience, the very future of man." As for Israel, "There has never been an army in human history that has acted as humanely as the Israeli Defence Forces have in Lebanon...Those concerned with the truth will agree that the military action against the PLO was a classic case of self-defence...not for nothing have [the IDF] been enthusiastically welcomed by the Lebanese as liberators," etc. Rabbi Professor Berkovits is identified as "the author of many articles and books on Jewish philosophy. Theology and Halacha." Recall also that the IDF regarded the ICRC as a "hostile organization" whose relief activities must be blocked, as reported by Col. Yirmiah; see p. 238.

reported by the media with regard to "the bodily injury and physical damage caused by the Israeli attack, and insinuated that this is part and parcel of the media's regular policy of toeing the PLO line." He reported the total number of Lebanese civilians killed in the war in the South, now completed, to be 314: 10 in Nabatiye, 54 in Tyre and 250 in Sidon, "including terrorists and their hostages" (his words). He stated that fewer than 20,000 Lebanese lack shelter, and the IDF is looking after them, cooperating fully with the Lebanese authorities.[261] On how the IDF was looking after them, see the reports by Col. Dov Yirmiah, who was in the unit that was supposed to be caring for the population, pp. 237f. Recall that it was Meridor whose sole orders concerning the Palestinians were "Drive them East."

There surely was news management, leading to a debate in the U.S. concerning censorship. IDF officials in charge of press contacts report that they divided foreign correspondents into "positive" and "negative" (whose number "was greater than the number of the 'positive ones'"). The "negative" ones who were judged "hostile to Israel" were given "special treatment," either prohibited from entering the IDF-held areas completely or given "unattractive" travel conditions.[262] These procedures are likely to be considerably more effective than direct censorship, which is highly visible and therefore harmful in its impact. Journalists presumably learn to be careful to avoid being categorized as "negative," thus denied the opportunity to do their work. The greatest problem faced by the news managers, however, was that the war was also covered from the other side, where they had no control.

As if the iniquity just surveyed were not enough, it turns out that Amnesty International had also joined in the international conspiracy to defame Israel, not for the first time (see p. 128). An AI letter requesting the government of Israel to conform to international standards in treatment of prisoners received the following response from the Attorney General of Israel:

> It is somewhat surprising that AI, as an impartial worldwide movement, independent of political grouping and ideology, has chosen to base its approach to the Government of Israel upon press reports, especially when it has become patently evident that such reports have been grossly and, to a certain extent, even deliberately exaggerated and fabricated... Accordingly we find it difficult to accept this reliance by AI upon such reports and consider them as not warranting substantive or serious reply.[263]

To summarize, it is difficult to fault the *hasbara* efforts, given the nature of the forces engaging in a "pogrom" or "psychological war" against Israel in the summer of 1982: the Kremlin and its immense international information system, the powerful and devious Wafa, the

American and world press and television which were deliberately fabricating reports when they were not being deluded by the Wafa-Kremlin psy-war campaign, AI and the international relief agencies that were consciously falsifying the facts to raise more money, the U.S. government still pursuing its traditional "Saudi policy" with a fraudulent pretense of "even-handedness." Small wonder, then, that much of the world thought that there had been a "bloody war" in Lebanon, not a humanitarian rescue effort to liberate innocent people held hostage by "a gang of thugs."

The *hasbara* campaign was far from a total failure, however. Norman Kempster mentions Peretz's article "Lebanon Eyewitness" as a "spectacular" result of "the showpiece of the *hasbara* effort," namely, "the guided tour of Lebanon" in which "visitors were shown the war from the Israeli point of view," citing his statement, quoted above, that "Much of what you have read in the newspapers and newsmagazines about the war in Lebanon—and even more of what you have seen and heard on television—is simply not true." Kempster notes that the guided tours were "superbly done," at least "from the standpoint of the public-relations professional," avoiding signs of damage and arranging talks with selected Lebanese in Christian towns. See note 253.

One staple of the criticism of the media was that the early casualty figures were derived from the PLO ("we know now that the source was the PLO, which spread these figures as part of its psychological warfare campaign").[264] It was also commonly alleged that the media relied on the Palestinian Red Crescent, which it either failed to acknowledge as part of the PLO or confused with the Red Cross. These charges are false, as can easily be determined by reviewing the press record (see, for example, the Claremont Research collection cited above, note 36). The usual source for figures was the Lebanese government or police, or international relief agencies. Palestinian sources were rarely used, and where used were clearly identified. Perhaps there were exceptions, but nothing has been produced to suggest a pattern of error or deception, as claimed. In contrast, Israeli sources were generally regarded as reliable (not by Israeli soldiers, however; see p. 222) and sometimes even considered "authoritative" (see, for example, p. 228); I noticed no charge that Israeli sources should be dismissed. Furthermore, as noted earlier, it now appears that the early figures were generally accurate, and summary estimates that confirm them are now cited in the Israeli media. Recall also that all the figures are very likely to be underestimates, given that months after the fighting ended bodies were still being dug out of the rubble, and that many, particularly Palestinians, were killed without record, not buried or buried in mass graves. This conclusion seems quite plausible, unless we are to believe that the Israeli sources cited above, and the Lebanese government and police, are also part of the international conspiracy to defame Israel. With regard to the Lebanese, the assumption does not square too well with the doctrine concerning their joy at being liberated, as already noted, unless perhaps we invoke some Peretz-style musings about the "Arab national character."

The storm over *"hasbara* failure" elicited some ridicule in the Israeli press. An article in *Haolam Haze* asked: "How are we to explain that an Arab child weeping next to his mother's body proves our justice"? It goes on to comment on the use of the word "hasbara" ("explanation") for what is ordinarily called "propaganda" or "psychological warfare." The assumption behind this curious usage, which appears to be rare among the nations of the world, is that

> obviously the Israeli government is right in all that it does. Therefore, all we have to do is to "explain" its motives and then any sensible person shall support it. Anyone who won't be persuaded by the *hasbara* is anti-Semitic (if he is a Gentile) or self-hating (if he happens to be Jewish), like [Austrian Prime Minister] Bruno Kreisky, for example. This blind belief in the power of *hasbara* is typical of all the Israeli establishment. If the Gentiles don't wholeheartedly support Israeli government actions and policies, then something must have gone wrong with *hasbara*. *Hasbara* is at fault. Therefore the *hasbara* must be changed, just as one changes a sparkplug in a car. It reminds me of the cheated husband who catches his wife making love to his friend on a couch in his house—and decides to burn the couch.[265]

The problem, however, is that "no *hasbara* can change basic facts," though much effort is devoted—often successfully, at least for an American audience—to proving otherwise.

Israeli satirist B. Michael wrote a column expressing his views on the *hasbara* campaign. The occasion was a celebrated incident in which President Reagan was reported to be distressed by a picture of a severely injured child, even placing it on his desk. The child was allegedly found, only slightly injured, a proof of the anti-Israel bias of the media and a great triumph for *hasbara*. Michael's column is entitled: "The Miracle Child":

> Mr. Reagan! Mr. Reagan! Look what we have found! A little boy with two hands! A perfect child! A real sweetie! He's like new! Just a little burned in the face, and one shoulder is out of joint. He was the best we could find. Now can you see what liars the Arabs are? We knew right away they were frauds and we decided to prove it to you. Do you realize how much time we spent searching among the bodies, until we had found a little boy in such excellent condition? We did it all for you.

This boy has not suffered one bit, on the contrary, he enjoyed all the noise and the fireworks. Just ask his father about it. No, sorry, don't, because his father was killed by the same bombardment that did not do any harm to this little boy. Ask his mother! She knows the truth. Only don't look for her in her home. Look for her in some other place, because her home was reduced by the bombardment that was such fun for the boy to the rubble which buried her husband.

This will teach you to believe the media, Mr. President. You should have known that they are controlled by international petro-dollar consortiums. Now go and put on your desk the new picture of the cute little boy who not only has two whole arms, but even two whole legs. Each time you are going to look at him, Mr. President, you are going to remember that nobody was killed in this war, no stone was loosened by it, no children were hurt and no homes were destroyed. You will recall that not a single family was made homeless by us; it's all propaganda. There were just a few traffic accidents, some people had heart attacks and a crumbling building happened to collapse because of the weight of the ammunition stored on its roof. There was nothing else. And next time anyone sends you any nasty picture of a wounded baby, please let us know right away. We will send you by return mail a color photograph of a jolly, healthy child.[266]

Perhaps if this had been taken as a model for reporting, even the *New Republic, Commentary*, Jane Fonda, and the Anti-Defamation League would have been satisfied that the menace of anti-Semitism has been at least partially overcome.

7.3   The Israeli Media

The Israeli media too were the target of attack; from two sources, in fact. As we have already seen, military correspondents were bitterly criticized by soldiers at the front for repeating government lies (see p. 222). At home, the media were denounced for the opposite reason. The diplomatic correspondent of the *Jerusalem Post* writes that

Mr. Begin reportedly took heart from a warm reception he received from worshippers at a Jerusalem synagogue on Yom Kippur [September 27, shortly after the Beirut massacres]. His devotees may have drawn encouragement, too, from the report that a crowd of angry stallholders and shoppers in the Jerusalem vegetable market the previous day mobbed [an Israeli] radio van, chanting "Begin, Begin," and pouring out their wrath upon the media for bringing Israel to its present sorry state.[267]

The press reports the same incident:

> The rioters kicked the [Israeli Radio] van and then attacked the
> three radio employees inside. "How much were you bribed to do
> the job for them?," they shouted at one of the reporters. Radio
> technician Mordechai Maimoni, who had been held prisoner by
> the al-Amal forces in Lebanon, said that "the terrorists treated
> us better than did this mob." The mob blamed the radio repor-
> ters for the incidents in Beirut and cursed them for reporting the
> mass demonstrations of Peace Now.[268]

The "incidents" in question were the massacres at Sabra and Shatila.
Maimoni's use of the term "terrorists" for the Lebanese Shiite militia that
was resisting the Israeli invasion alongside of the PLO deserves special
notice. In fact, Lebanese who resisted the Israeli invasion did become
"terrorists" officially, which makes sense, given that it was an operation to
liberate the Lebanese from terrorism. It is, then, not too surprising to
learn that many of the prisoners at the Ansar prison camp described
earlier are Lebanese, almost half according to *Le Monde*.[269]

8   The Image Problem

8.1   In Lebanon

There were certain *hasbara* problems in Lebanon too, or rather, there
would have been, if anyone had cared. Israel's image was not improved, at
least for the Lebanese, by the behavior of the forces that occupied Beirut.
The entire 25,000 volume library of the PLO Research Center was stolen,
along with a printing press, microfilms, manuscripts, archives, telephones
and other equipment, while what remained was smashed. "They have
plundered our Palestinian cultural heritage," the director, Sabri Jiryis,
said; Jiryis is a well-known Palestinian moderate, actually an Israeli Arab
who left Israel when it was made clear that the alternative was one or
another form of detention. The research center, established with the
approval of the Lebanese government, had diplomatic immunity.[270] In the
same building, Israeli soldiers broke into the apartment of Prof. Khalidi,
chairman of the department of biochemistry at the American University
of Beirut. They looted extensively, taking art objects, ancient pottery,
cooking pots, tools, etc. Sculptures were thrown into the street. Lecture
notes and books that were not stolen were put on the floor, then soldiers
"defecated on them" and "broke raw eggs on the pile." The looting and
vandalizing were stopped only through the intervention of Malcolm Kerr,
the president of American University. The apartment of Khalidi's 84-
year-old mother was also looted and vandalized, as were others, as well as
schools and stores. The urology office of a Lebanese doctor was looted

and about $30,000 in Lebanese pounds was stolen. As Israeli soldiers were allegedly searching for weapons, "Israeli trucks loaded with household appliances and furniture were seen driving south toward Israel," while flatbed trucks loaded cars, taking them "presumably to Israel." Eyewitnesses reported that appliance and television shops were cleaned out, and the director of Lebanon's airline alleged that "even the airport's computer reservation system was stolen."[271]

At the College of Science of the Lebanese University, there was "wanton destruction and looting of scientific laboratories and classrooms by Israeli soldiers." Lebanese report that private homes, universities, hospitals, and at least one mosque were looted and damaged. "And in its thoroughness and the particularity of its targets, the vandalism seems to many Lebanese to have gone beyond what might ordinarily be expected from troops in wartime, living with both fear and boredom." The head of a study commissioned by the Lebanese Information Ministry gave a preliminary estimate of perhaps $100 million in damage. Apart from "random looting and damage," he said, "all major institutions connected with governments unfriendly to Israel—including homes, embassies, cultural centers, banks, etc.—were damaged in some way, either by being hit, looted, burned or otherwise damaged." An American diplomat confirmed that the U.S. government had been asked to intercede to have a $375,000 bulldozer returned to the Lebanese company from which it was stolen. American marines joined in a "massive cleanup effort" at the Lebanese University campus, but after two weeks, "piles of garbage and broken glass lay five feet high in the corridors of the fifth floor" and many laboratories were littered with files that had been taken from drawers and thrown down, while laboratories were bare of equipment, "much of it, according to professors at the college, having been taken or destroyed by the Israelis who moved into the college between June 15 and 20." Apart from destroying lab equipment, the soldiers took the entire scientific library at the college, along with its archives, while taking much scientific material, including the contents of the only polymer laboratory in Lebanon. At the Berbir Hospital, which Israel had repeatedly shelled, "doctors' clinics and apartments were ransacked during a four-day period of Israeli occupation, according to doctors there." Chairs were broken, dirt and food spread everywhere, soldiers had drawn on carpets with lipstick, defecated in pots and pans, stolen lecture tapes, cameras, etc. A mosque on the main east-west thoroughfare was desecrated. "Many of its rugs were stolen, others were defecated upon and beer cans were scattered about the floor," according to people who live near the mosque.[272]

Conquering armies are rarely well-behaved, even those able to enter a virtually undefended city after it had been mercilessly bombarded and besieged (see chapter 4, note 41). Few such armies, however, are provided with a corps of admirers in the country that finances their operations who marvel at their unique moral standards, purity of arms, incredibly polite behavior "with no reported instances of looting" (Rabbi Balfour Brickner, who is far to the critical end of the American spectrum, in a religious pacifist journal; see p. 259), etc. The behavior of this conquering army will no doubt be long remembered by the liberated Lebanese alongside of the treatment of captured prisoners, the bombardment of undefended civilian areas, and the denial of food, water and medicine to civilians.

8.2 Solving the Problem

The "image problem" was a rather serious one in the United States, naturally enough, given Israel's dependence on the U.S. for financing its settlement activities in the occupied territories and its selfless efforts to liberate its neighbors. The measures that were taken to deal with the problem are of some interest. We conclude this discussion of Operation "Peace for Galilee" by reviewing several of them.

8.2.1 Extraordinary Humanitarian Efforts

From the beginning of the war, occasional concerns were voiced in the U.S. over Israel's harsh treatment of the population that was theoretically being "liberated." In the first few days of the war, the press reported that "Israeli military authorities have ordered the United Nations peace-keeping force in Lebanon to stop donating and delivering food to Lebanese civilians caught in the fighting." "From Sunday to Tuesday, the Israeli Army refused to allow any United Nations relief convoys to cross the border into Lebanon, and the civilians' situation became desperate, according to United Nations officials." The UN stated that "Unifil [UN peacekeeping forces, largely West European] teams trying to help and assess the needs of victims were told to pull out, and that all humanitarian questions would be handled by Israel." UN observers "provided detailed accounts of civilians, including small babies, stranded without food and water." "One reason for the Israeli decision to bar the United Nations appeared to have been to prevent reports of the situation from getting out," including reports of "the immense suffering that appears to have been inflicted on the Lebanese population."[273] As to how Israel handled the "humanitarian questions" in south Lebanon, we have seen the reports of Col. Dov Yirmiah, who served with the military force responsible for the civilian population (see pp. 237f.). The image problem only became worse as the war went on, particularly with the siege of Beirut, where too many journalists were present for the facts to be controlled by *hasbara*.

One of the devices used to deal with this problem was to focus attention on the efforts organized within Israel to respond to the needs of war victims in Lebanon. As noted, the Anti-Defamation League objected to the failure of the TV networks to give proper attention to these "extraordinary" efforts. Letters also appeared in the press objecting to the failure of the media to report them: "little has been noted about Israel's humanitarian efforts for the Lebanese people," the National President of "the largest volunteer women's organization in Israel" wrote in several newspapers. Describing these efforts, she wrote that "there is no greater demonstration of Israel's eagerness to live in peace with its neighbors than this 'people to people' effort to help repair the ravages of war."[274]

It is quite true that little was reported about these programs. For example, I noticed no report here that the Israeli army had blocked distribution of supplies collected by humanitarian groups in Israel (see the testimony of Col. Dov Yirmiah, pp. 237-9). There was also no notice of the fact that Kibbutz Dalya sent a parcel of clothing and household items to Tova Neta, a Jewish woman who was discovered in the destroyed Rashidiyeh camp, after the Israeli press had published "the story of Tova and her husband Abdullah, who had lost all their belongings and the roof over their head when their home was destroyed in the war" (by some unknown hand), a package received "with joy and excitement," the left-wing Israeli press informs us.[275]

There was, however, occasional notice. A dispatch from Haifa reported that ten 10-ton trucks set out in a convoy on June 16 to distribute blankets and clothing for refugees, returning the same night "after a mixed reception." "In the Rashadiya refugee camp [the first target of Israel's assault], the distribution was disrupted by women whose relatives had been detained by the Israelis as suspected terrorists. 'We don't want your clothes,' they screamed. 'We want our sons.' The mission left the camp with the rest of its stock and turned it over to a welfare agency and two orphanages in Tyre and Sidon for distribution."[276] Nothing is said about the reaction of Tova Neta and her Arab husband.

Turning to the Hebrew press, we find a somewhat fuller account of this episode, under the title "the Jewish heart functioned without common sense."[277] This humanitarian endeavor of the Magen David Adom (the Israeli equivalent of the Red Cross) suffered numerous "disappointments."

> The first disappointment awaited us a few kilometers south of Tyre, in the Rashidiyeh refugee camp. There was no intention to stop in this camp [since it contained the remnants of a Palestinian community, not Lebanese, and it was not yet known that there was a Jewish woman there], but after we met a foreign television crew across the border, it was decided that it would be a good idea if TV would film the distribution of supplies in a refugee camp.

In the camp, where "purification from terrorists lasted four days," the IDF was preventing the refugees from returning to their homes (or what was left of them). Almost all the men had been taken to Israel for "interrogation and identification," and the women and children who remained lived in a nearby orchard—from which they were later driven when the army became concerned that they were being filmed by TV crews, as Col. Yirmiah reported. (See p. 239). Refugees approached the convoy, leading to the first of many "scenes that put us to shame." The refugees refused to permit the Israelis to distribute supplies even when the Magen David Adom's own TV cameraman asked them "to open at least one package." "Then began the tumult. Women gathered around and began to shriek and to curse: 'We do not want your supplies, take them back, we do not need anything, we only want our husbands and brothers back'." "With much embarrassment, the representatives of the Magen David Adom decided to depart from this place, leaving a few packages of clothes." One person whispered to the journalist that they would sell the clothes to buy food, which they badly needed. The embarrassment, of course, was caused by the presence of the foreign TV crew for whom this humanitarian effort was staged.

A few kilometers away, the head of the convoy decided to stop at a Magen David Adom installation. At that point a little girl about five years of age appeared among the trucks. Soldiers said that she shows up now and then to beg for military rations:

> "Who knows, perhaps even in Sidon they will refuse to accept the packages, so we had better film the little girl with the clothes so that there will at least be pictures," the Magen David Adom people say, and do so. First, they look for a suitable place for the picture. Dan Arnon [head of the International Office of the Magen David Adom] requests that the picture be taken against the background of an ambulance that was a gift from England, so that it will be possible to send them the picture. They take a large box from the trucks and the photographers move the girl into every possible position to record the historic moment for eternity. They load her up with clothes until they cover her face, though the package that was opened includes womens' clothes, slips, dresses and bathing suits. But what will one not do for a good picture!
>
> The child seemed amused at the symbolic role that was assigned to her, but soon she ran away carrying the large pile of clothes, dropping them one by one along the road. It occurred to no one to pick them up, but in a few minutes three other children came by and the picture repeated. The representatives of the Magen David Adom said, perhaps seriously or perhaps as a joke: "We already have pictures. Now we can return to Tel Aviv."

The picture of the little girl holding the clothes appears along with the article, under the heading: "The little girl who served as an 'example' and held clothes for the purposes of a picture."

A picture of one of the children holding the clothes appears in the *Jerusalem Post*, but with no account of the actual events. This, of course, is an English-language journal, which will be reach an international audience. As we have seen several times, it is not uncommon for the *Post* to present a sanitized version of what is reported in the Hebrew press, and in fact in its Jubilee edition the *Post* observes that this was its earlier practice (see p. 138). Much the same, incidentally, is true of the documentary record published in Hebrew. The Diaries of Prime Minister Moshe Sharett, cited several times above, are one example; there was concern in Israel when it was learned that these were to appear in English, since there are many unpleasant revelations, but the concern was misplaced, since their contents have been suppressed in American journalism and scholarship with the single exception of the 1955 proposal by Chief of Staff Moshe Dayan (in accordance with Ben-Gurion's ideas) to create a "Haddad" as a device to take over southern Lebanon and establish a Christian protectorate in what remains—too good to overlook, apparently. Similarly, the important study by Ehud Ya'ari, *Egypt and the Fedayeen*, based on captured Egyptian documents that reveal Egypt's efforts to avert the impending Israeli attack in 1956 by keeping the border quiet, has been loyally disregarded by American scholars. The same is true of official military histories and much else.[279]

The practice is common elsewhere as well, of course. Consider, for example, the fate of the *Pentagon Papers*, an unusually revealing record of high-level government planning, therefore largely ignored in respectable scholarship, except for its bearing on tactical questions of limited significance.*

Returning to the mission of mercy, after the somewhat unfortunate efforts to impress the foreign TV crew near Rashidiyeh, the convoy went on to Tyre (the *Jerusalem Post* reports that "the closer the convoy got to the city of Tyre, the more impressive the destruction grew. Everything along the road had been burned, wrecked, crumpled, blown to pieces").

---

* The Beacon press edition of the 4 volume Gravel edition is the only readibly accessible source for something close to the full record (plus some additional material). It contains an index volume (volume 5, with critical essays and an index), which is obviously indispensable for anyone expecting to use the documents. By the end of 1982, 2700 copies of this volume had been sold, many, presumably, to people who were interested in the analytic articles by American, Vietnamese and French scholars and journalists. The conclusion is that even universities, let alone others, do not intend to have the material available for research. Quite apart from its insight into Vietnam war planning, this material is quite unusual for what it tells about the workings of government and long-term strategic planning. Material of this sort is rarely available until many years have passed or at all, apart from captured enemy archives.[280]

But they found no recipients, so Arnon instructed that packages be left in the center of Tyre "in some ruin." The convoy went on to Sidon. In the light of the earlier "bitter experience," Arnon decided to avoid the refugee camps. Eight trucks were still full, and he announced that "we will not return with them to Tel Aviv." It was finally decided to distribute the supplies at an orphanage. At one, no clothes were needed but they were left anyway. At the second, the orphans said "Who needs clothes? We need food." So the mission ended.

It is true that this impressive story was not properly reported by the American media, another indication of their anti-Israel bias, or perhaps their control by Wafa and the International Communist Conspiracy.

8.2.2 Flowers and Rice

Another contribution to the "image problem" was the story, widely reported and generally accepted at face value in the United States, that the Lebanese greeted their Israeli liberators with warmth and enthusiasm. In continental Europe, which has some experiences of its own, reactions were often a bit different. In Copenhagen, for example, Knesset Member Yosef Rom told a television audience "that Israeli soldiers were greeted in Lebanon with flowers and rice." The interviewer interrupted him with the following words: "Do not tell us in Denmark about flowers and rice. Nazi Germany also had pictures of how the Danish people greated the April 1940 conquest with flowers..."[231] (See also p. 228).

The story was also regarded with some skepticism in Israel. Soldiers described the Lebanese villagers who waved to them "with a frozen expression." One was reminded of a scene from Joseph Heller's *Catch 22* where an old man says that he is not interested in politics: "He is willing to become a Communist, a Fascist or a Capitalist, as long as his life is not in danger," the soldier said, "and those villagers are the same."[282] Colonel Dov Yirmiah, reporting his experiences travelling through the streets of Beirut in June, writes that "the looks that accompany us are not particularly friendly, [but are] indifferent or hostile, only the Phalangists wearing IDF uniforms play the game of faithful collaborators. My impression is becoming stronger that all the talk and our propaganda about the enthusiasm of the Lebanese for our presence in their land and about the 'liberation' that we brought are only our own heart's desire."*

One of the rare skeptics to be published in the United States was Jacobo Timerman, who describes his tour through Tyre with the Israel military escort provided to all visitors in these terms:

---

* See his *War Diary*, cited in note 164. Recall that Yirmiah wanted very much to believe this story. He reports the complaint of Lebanese who were initially cooperative that "you are destroying all of our good will, why?"—and asks himself: "What can I answer? That we have become animals?" This was on June 23, in a discussion about the brutal treatment of prisoners who were Lebanese, not Palestinian.

Those of us who have been in prison know how to speak with our eyes so that we can be understood when forced to talk in the presence of guards. This is how I know that what a cordial and pleasant Lebanese is saying is contradicted by what I see expressed in his eyes. His English is clumsy, his phrases stereo-typed. Whoever has been a prisoner or been forced to surrender knows how degrading this moment can be.

Describing the scene of people who "greet us with shouts of 'Shalom' in Hebrew," Timerman writes:

Throughout the ages, how many times have people learned the language of the conquerors, imitated their gestures, and tried to divine their intentions and moods? How many times must the Jews have done this?... I do not fraternize with those I have subdued by force.[283]

These are the remarks that were described by Conor Cruise O'Brien in his *New Republic* review cited above as "faintly nauseating" and "stuff and nonsense," in contrast to Timerman's impressive insights about PLO sympathizers in the United States. O'Brien's own conclusion is that "most Lebanese—including Muslims and Druses, as well as Christians—were glad that Israel invaded Lebanon," and regarded "the damage and loss of life incurred" as "unavoidable"—"most people did not refer to these at all," presumably regarding them as a small price to pay for the pleasure of being attacked by Israel. In his "Lebanon Eyewitness," Martin Peretz asserts that "everyone I did meet [including no one rich] was relieved that the Israelis had lifted from them the burden of the PLO." That everyone he met expressed gratitude to Israel is quite possibly true—perhaps a tribute to the "spectacular" effectiveness of the public relations stunt that was the "showpiece" of the *hasbara* campaign; see p. 295. That the attitudes expressed to Peretz and O'Brien are in fact the attitudes of the Lebanese they spoke to (let alone "most Lebanese") would seem perhaps questionable, though again one should not underestimate the effective-ness of the means used to achieve Abba Eban's "rational prospect" as well as other factors we have reviewed.

As for the true attitudes of Lebanese approached by Westerners—especially those whose passionate pro-Israel sentiments were surely not difficult to discern—who arrived with an Israeli military escort in a country under Israeli military occupation, we can only speculate. Evi-dently, the difference in the perceptions of Timerman and the Israeli soldiers cited on the one hand, and O'Brien and Peretz on the other, are uncertain matters of judgment; a person who describes a perception different from his own on this matter as "faintly nauseating" and "stuff and nonsense" simply expresses thereby his intent to disqualify himself as a serious commentator, given the nature of the evidence, the circumstances, and the ratio of fact to interpretation.* It might be true that those who have undergone the experiences of the war are pleased that Israel invaded, or perhaps they feel that it would be best, under military occupation, to say one thing with the voice and another with the eyes, when confronted by a Peretz or an O'Brien. It may be that the attitudes articulated over a broad range of Lebanese opinion, as reviewed in section 6.2, do not reflect the real feelings of many Lebanese; or one may draw a different conclusion.

I once spent many hours interviewing refugees in Laos who had just been flown by the CIA to a miserable refugee camp near Vientiane after a CIA mercenary army had overrun the Plain of Jars, where they had "lived," if that is the correct word. There were few young men among them, presumably because most were with the Pathet Lao guerrillas. They had been subjected to years of "secret" American bombing ("secret," in that it had been concealed by the U.S. press despite ample evidence) so intensive that they were unable to leave their caves and holes in the ground to farm, except sometimes at night. Everything in the area had been destroyed by the time it was overrun. Virtually every refugee told me that they hated the Pathet Lao, who were oppressive, for no reason, perhaps because "they are just crazy." Some said that they did not mind the bombing at all, even when their homes were destroyed and their children killed. They also assumed that I was an American soldier in civilian clothes.[284] Perhaps they really did hate the Pathet Lao and enjoyed being plastered with bombs and rockets, or perhaps something else was in their minds. Again, it is a matter of perception and judgment; in Laos, in Lebanon, in Afghanistan, in the Russian Gulag, and many other places where very much the same differences of perception may be found among foreign observers, including those who feel entitled to determine what is best for the natives by invading their country and leaving a trail of ruin and destruction with tens of thousands killed and wounded, all for their own good.

There is something farcical about a debate conducted in the U.S. or Europe as to whether or not the Lebanese welcomed their liberation. The assumption underlying the debate, presumably, is that if they were really "glad that Israel invaded Lebanon," as the *New Republic* would have us

---

* O'Brien's clinching argument to prove that most Lebanese welcomed the Israeli invasion is a statement by a British journalist that the invasion brought peace to Beirut by ending the civil war, though "in the thankless manner of human beings, few Lebanese want the Israelis to reap the political prize of a Lebanon under Israeli influence," an unfortunate character flaw. From this we are to conclude, apparently, that the Muslims of West Beirut are delighted that Israel destroyed their homes, killing and maiming thousands and placing power in the hands of their bitter enemies who proceeded at once to acts of kindness to which we return. Recall the assessment of the *Time* bureau chief on the scene that "all over Beirut" Lebanese "want to see Israel defeated." See p. 250.

believe, then the invasion was justified. Let us assume that they did welcome the invasion, all of them: the orphans wandering in the streets of Tyre; the children at the Sidon school where hundreds were killed in a shelter who still shudder, 7 months later, when planes fly past; the people digging for bodies in Sidon two months after the fighting stopped; the members of the Amal Shiite militia who fought alongside the PLO; the Druze who were allied with the PLO in the civil war and turned to "passive resistance," given the force of the Israeli attack; the impoverished Shiite refugees from the south who were driven out of their hovels by those presented with the victory in the civil war; the cripples searching the rubble of their homes in Beirut to try to discover who may have survived; the doctors whose homes were looted and vandalized after their hospitals were destroyed by bombing; the patients driven from the hospitals closed down by the liberators; the Lebanese prisoners being clubbed by Israeli guards in concentration camps; the children wandering in the blood-stained wreckage of the bombed mental hospital in Beirut. Let us suppose that all of them welcome the liberation, just like B. Michael's Miracle Child. Does this justify the invasion? No one will claim that Israel was invited in by the government to accomplish this necessary task; on the contrary, the invasion was bitterly condemned from the start by the representatives of the government, including the Christian UN Ambassador who saw his country "martyred and crucified," the Muslim Prime Minister who was reappointed after the liberation, the Druze leader Walid Jumblatt, the Sunni leader Saeb Salam who called on Israel to provide reparations for its "savage aggression," the spokesmen for the two major Muslim religious groupings. So we are therefore asked to believe that it was legitimate for Israel to invade Lebanon, in the face of outraged condemnation by those being liberated, on the grounds that passionate Western supporters of Israel later determine, to their own satisfaction, that the invasion was welcomed.

Still assuming that their judgment is correct, let us proceed with the argument. On these grounds, it is legitimate for Israel to demolish the society of the Palestinians, killing thousands of them and imprisoning the adult male population, dispersing the refugees and leaving them without homes, food, defense, social services or any prospects for an organized existence; even the most fanatic supporters of Israel do not claim that *they* welcomed their liberation.*

Let us put aside international law, which makes no provision for judgments by the conqueror (or his cheering section) concerning the attitudes of those he decides he is liberating. Then the military action is

---

* Unfortunately, the statement is not quite correct. Recall the assurances of David Pryce-Jones in the *New Republic* concerning the attitudes of Palestinians towards the PLO, the Israelis and the Christians. (See p. 206).

justified, on the assumptions just granted, if we add one further principle: the Palestinians are *Untermenschen*, with only superficial resemblance to human beings, not even deserving of the treatment accorded to animals. They sacrificed any possible right to be considered human by fleeing in terror from their homeland or being driven from it by a superior race, and therefore whatever is done to them is legitimate. On this assumption, perhaps the argument justifying the invasion goes through, but not otherwise, even if we grant everything to its proponents.

Whatever the facts may have been about the reception of Israeli soldiers in the areas to which the guided tours were taken, the situation a few months later was characteristically described by soldiers and Israeli journalists in a rather different way. "It is not pleasant today to be a soldier in Lebanon," Yaakov Erez writes. Even in Tyre and Sidon, or the Christian town of Damour where Israel's Chamounist allies were restored by the IDF,

> a convoy of IDF soldiers is necessary, pointing their guns outwards during the journey to anticipate any possibility of an ambush or snipers. Israelis in the various sections of Lebanon are subjected to much tension. The Lebanese inhabitants, Christians and Druze, Muslims and Palestinians, do not present smiling receptions. Our soldiers feel as if in an enemy country.[285]

Meanwhile, "the number of daring attacks on Israeli soldiers in Lebanon is increasing weekly, as are the casualties," Trudy Rubin wrote in January 1983. Since Israeli troops pulled out of West Beirut at the end of September, 17 Israelis had been killed and more than 90 wounded (not considering the building collapse in Tyre in which 76 Israelis were killed, allegedly as a result of a gas leak). The incidents are increasing in intensity, with half of the casualties since December 1, and 13 incidents in the first week of January 1983. "The perpetrators are reportedly Palestinians infiltrating back into south Lebanon, Lebanese leftists, as well as, in one case, Lebanese Shiite muslim adherents of Iranian leader Ayatollah Khomeini."[286] Hirsh Goodman reports that "the IDF is conducting live fire patrols...to ensure that no terrorists are waiting in ruins or in orchards along the way"—that is, shooting randomly as they drive along Lebanese roads in what is called "defense against terrorism" by occupying armies.[287] The U.S. marine commander in Lebanon criticized this "reconnaissance by fire" in the southern Beirut sector patrolled by his troops. He stated that for the last two months Israeli soldiers had "come down the Sidon highway and, without having been fired upon, they just fire great numbers of rounds," endangering his troops. "We told them to cease and desist the indiscriminate fire," he said, so they now fire only on the side of the highway away from U.S. marines. A Lebanese official "said at least five civilians had been killed by indiscriminate Israeli fire."[288] The number of Israelis killed in Lebanon in just over 3 months after the war's end is approximately the same as the number of Jews killed in the course of terrorist operations in the two-year period 1980-81, according to Israeli figures (see p. 74) and approaches the number killed from 1967, if we add to the account those killed in the Tyre explosion. We return to the immediate aftermath of the war in the next chapter.

8.2.3 "The Biggest Hijacking in History"

Perhaps the most elegant device designed to deal with the *hasbara* problem was the image of the PLO holding Beirut "hostage" and hiding behind its civilian population, a popular one among American commentators on the war, as we have seen. *New York Times* columnist Flora Lewis even went so far as to allege that "Yasser Arafat, never quite direct, almost admits he is holding the people of West Beirut hostage to win points for his cause; the P.L.O's familiar tactics but on an unimaginable scale."[289]

This intriguing notion illustrates a familiar technique of the manufacture of consent, employed in a rather clumsy way by Goebbels and Stalin and refined to a more subtle art in the democratic societies: when you have absolutely no case at all, accuse your enemies of the crimes you carry out or support; to put it a shade more crudely, if you are caught with your hand in someone's pocket, cry "Thief!, Thief!" This may at least shift the terms of the debate. Thus when the U.S. attacks the peasant society of South Vietnam, debate rages over the profound question of whether it is wise and proper to *defend* South Vietnam from North Vietnamese aggression; and we solemnly debate the question of whether the American defense of South Vietnam is justified under the right of collective self-defense against armed attack, established by international law. It is a matter of minor consequence of concern only to "emotional extremists," those who indulge in "moral preference" rather than "hard political analysis" in Robert Tucker's contemptuous words, that there were no North Vietnamese troops engaged in this aggression when the U.S. air force began extensive bombardment and defoliation in South Vietnam in 1962, or, so far as was known, when the U.S. initiated the bombardment of North Vietnam and (at three times the level) the regular bombardment and then direct invasion of South Vietnam in early 1965. There are many other examples, no less noteworthy.

In the present case, America's Middle East client had driven the PLO, along with hundreds of thousands of Lebanese and Palestinian refugees, to West Beirut, then surrounded it, shelled it mercilessly, and cut off food, water, electricity and medical supplies, holding the city hostage in an effort to compel the PLO to withdraw completely, as it did, to save the city from total destruction. In short, "the biggest hijacking in history—half of Beirut is the hostage," in the words of the *New York*

Times editors. What then is more natural than that these editors and others should accuse the PLO of the very crime they supported—holding West Beirut hostage—while assuring Israel that we will graciously fund this endeavor if Israel would only be so kind as to recognize our interests in the region; see p. 265.

We would be falling into the usual trap by discussing the merits of the case that it was the PLO that was holding the city and its population hostage, but, exactly as one was compelled to do in the comparable case of aggression in South Vietnam, and many others where power sets the rules of the game, let us proceed to do so.

To establish the argument, it would be necessary to show that the PLO, having elected to concentrate its forces within West Beirut, refused to let the population escape, so that it could hold them hostage for its nefarious design of preserving itself as a political force (what U.S. spokesmen said they could not tolerate, as we have seen). Unfortunately for this thesis, there is no evidence that the PLO blocked the escape of the population. On the contrary, the reports of Western journalists in Beirut and others indicate that people could freely leave—if the besiegers would permit it—and that they did not consider themselves PLO hostages.[290] There is, however, evidence that Israel blocked their exit by means of the forces it armed and controlled. At the same time, it claimed to want civilians out of West Beirut so that "the area can be attacked with less hesitation." But, Trudy Rubin continues, "a large number of west Beirut residents have proven resistant to departure. While thousands have fled, others have stayed to protect their homes and businesses or simply because they have nowhere else to go." "Almost all Palestinians trying to exit west Beirut are being turned back or detained by authorities in east Beirut," John Yemma reported.[291] Phalangists were regularly observed "turning back Palestinian civilians, although in any case most Palestinians here vividly remembering the bitter civil war, would be afraid to venture into territory controlled by the Christians." "Israeli officers were standing off to one side of the checkpoint" where Palestinians were refused exit and "Phalangist militiamen [threw] out bottled water, fresh fruit and bread that people were attempting to take back into the besieged section of the city."[292] Marvine Howe reported that the Phalangists refused exit to anyone "without friends or relatives in [Christian] east Beirut," and that "no Palestinians, either civilians or Palestinians with Lebanese passports, were being allowed out of west Beirut."* "When asked why Palestinian women and children were not allowed to leave, Amin Gemayel [now President], whose car was the only one allowed through the crossing,

---

* Recall that while the Israel-backed Christian forces virtually eliminated Palestinians and Muslims from the areas they controlled, in the PLO-controlled areas Christian villages remained in sometimes uneasy coexistence (see pp. 186-7).

shortly before noon, said with bitterness: 'Ask the Israelis; they are the ones who command here,' deciding when and if to open the crossing point and for how long." UNICEF left, however, because the lack of food, electricity and water were intolerable and they were prevented from bringing in food or other relief by the liberators.[293]

But it was the PLO who were holding West Beirut hostage, according to the official version.

A number of Israeli commentators observed that this was a strange sort of hijacking. B. Michael remarked that the concept, invented by an American journalist (presumably referring to Martin Peretz), is "very pleasant for my government." But, he said, there is something "extremely strange" about it. "The rescuers inform the hijackers that if they do not yield at once, they, the rescuers, will massacre the hostages . . . a remarkable innovation in the theory of hijacking." Meanwhile the rescuers kill and starve the hostages, warning the hijackers that still worse is to come "if you continue to be stubborn"; we will continue until "none will be left, and we will be freed of concern for the lives of the miserable victims, the innocents whom you have captured and we have killed." "And then—we will kill you too, miserable and evil creatures that you are, without any fear that, God forbid, the hostages will be harmed in the course of the operation."[294] Nothing similar disgraced the American press, to my knowledge.

There was still worse infamy, though again, the American reader was thoughtfully spared. In an interview on the siege of Beirut in early August, military historian Meir Pail compared it with the Arab siege of Jerusalem in 1948 in which 2000 Jews were killed, about a third of all those killed in the war. He estimated—fairly accurately, as it turned out—that about 5000 must have been killed by then in Beirut by the vastly heavier firepower used by the IDF, including 10,000 artillery shells in one day (not to speak of bombing, naval and tank shelling). During the Jerusalem siege in 1948, "the Israeli Army also prevented civilians from leaving the town, and there too military centers were situated in the midst of the civilian population"—a response to another familiar canard.* Note that the word "also" is out of place in this statement, according to the eyewitness reports of western journalists, quoted above. Pail pointed out that "Naturally military headquarters are at the center," i.e., in populated areas, something that was "especially true" of the Haganah under the British mandate, "when the Israeli military network . . . was pushed under the cover of the legal civilian center, such as the Jewish Agency and the Histadrut [labor union]." Military orders were "that everyone should remain in the

---

* In this connection, G. H. Jansen states that the PLO "first moved anti-aircraft guns into the camps because in the late 60s, when the PLO had little relative strength, these camps had become particular targets for the Israeli air force."[295]

city." The army prevented civilians from escaping, because "civilians are an organic part of the city just as its buildings are." Haganah posts were placed on the roofs of houses, and drew hostile fire. Most of the residents of Jerusalem were from "the old community," people who "fought very little and caused much trouble" (in fact, many were anti-Zionist; recall that the first recorded terrorist act of the Haganah was the murder of a religious Jew organizing among them in 1924—see p. 165). Out of 100,000 inhabitants, "the Haganah managed to organize only two battalions of 800 men each." Israel's tactics in Beirut, he observes, are the standard ones, those used by the Red Army in World War II, for example: surround the city and pound it, hoping for surrender, because urban fighting leads to too many casualties for the attacking troops. See p. 220. Jerusalem was a "disappointment" to the Arab besiegers because the city did not surrender. "Beirut is a disappointment similar to the Arab disappointment with us in 1948 in Jerusalem."[296]

The resistance during the siege of Jerusalem is one of the heroic stories of the founding of Israel. The resistance during the siege of Beirut reveals the miserable cowardice of the PLO, whose "gunmen hold a civilian population hostage" in "the biggest hijacked plane in history" while the cowardly PLO hides behind women and children.[297] So is history designed by its architects, sitting in safety, far away, laboring in the service of their favored state.

8.3   The Image of the Fighters

8.3.1 The Palestinians

From close by, things looked different. Israeli soldiers described their admiration for the Palestinians as "brave fighters."[298] In a June 26 entry of his *War Diary* (see note 164), Colonel Yirmiah writes that "the terrorists fought with a stubbornness that is unlike anything that preceded in Israel's wars with the Arabs. . . In this war a new generation was born and a new era opened that will be remembered in the history of the Palestinian world as a heroic era, in the light of which the coming generations will be taught." Mordechai Bar-On, former IDF chief education officer and no admirer of the PLO (see p. 255*), observed that "the PLO's desperate and heroic fight has, in addition to its other accomplishments, brought it glory in the eyes of the Palestinians. . . it is already clear that even those moderate leaders who had been somewhat reserved towards the PLO leadership and methods, today feel impelled to express their admiration for the heroism of their brothers in Lebanon."[299] As we have seen (p. 55), reactions in the occupied territories after the war tend to confirm this judgment. Israeli journalist Victor Ciegelman drew the same conclusion from his survey of opinion in the occupied territories.[300] The London Bureau chief of *Newsweek* gave his impressions from Beirut at the war's end as follows:

The Palestinians leave here as victors in their own minds and in the eyes of the Arab world. As all of their leaders have said, they fought off one of the most powerful armies in the world. I have no doubt, having seen the intensity of the bombing and shelling of West Beirut, that the Israelis wanted to get into West Beirut to kill or drag the PLO fighters off into captivity. Despite what Ariel Sharon the Israeli defense minister might say, I do not think Israel spent billions of dollars, sacrificed hundreds of its young men and blackened its name in the civilized world just so that Yaser Arafat and George Habash and their men could fly off as heroes to the capitals of the Arab world.

TRIUMPHANT

The guerillas now spreading out across that Arab did what all the combined Arab armies have never been able to do: they denied Israel its victory. For the first time after an Israeli-Arab war, the ending is not recorded in pictures of long lines of Arab troops marching off to captivity and humiliation with their arms over their heads. The world is seeing triumphant soldiers carrying their arms and their flags to new battles. For the first time an Arab-Israeli war has produced a cadre of veterans who know what it is like to face the full strength of the Israeli army, navy and air force—and to stop them dead in their tracks.[301]

Earlier, Chris Drake of the BBC, describing the ferocious bombing of August 1, referred to "The PLO—which can rightfully claim to have fought a tremendous battle against overwhelming military opposition..."[302] An Israeli journalist, a reserve sergeant in the paratroops, wrote that "the PLO fighters fought bravely in Beirut confronted with the Israeli machine of destruction. They continued to fight, in spite of the fact that they had no military chance, just as was the case for the Jewish fighters 40 years ago in the Warsaw ghetto,* in 1943."[303] When Israeli troops overran the Ain el-Hilweh refugee camp after 5 days of fighting, they are reported to have "found many of the defenders had committed suicide, a grisly Palestinian replay of the fate of the ancient Jewish warriors of Massada."[304]

---

* The Warsaw Ghetto and similar images were repeatedly invoked in Israel during the war. Critics objected bitterly that the analogy is inaccurate, as it is, in many respects. Israel evidently cannot be compared to Nazi Germany; its armies are, furthermore, in a sense mercenary armies, since they are supplied and financed by a foreign power that funds their military operations generously. There are also points of similarity, to which those who invoke the analogies want to draw attention.

Courageous American editors deride the PLO for its "theatrical flourishes" and "guerrilla theater": "Egged on by the camera crews in Beirut. . .the PLO now playacts the rituals of victory because it has little else to show for its defeat and its expulsion from Lebanon."[305] Nothing is easier, of course, than to march in step behind the big battalions, singing their praises. Much of the world, including the people of the occupied territories and many Israeli soldiers at the front, appear to have seen a war that barely resembles the one concocted by the editors of the *New Republic* and the like.

Whether the PLO will be able to maintain the image of heroism with which it left Beirut is another question. It may be that dispersed and controlled by various Arab states, it will become discredited, just as it was in a sense discredited by the massacres in Beirut after it departed in the naive belief that U.S. promises were to be trusted: it had failed to protect its people from the murderous gangs organized by the conqueror and sent into the camps as soon as they were left undefended. Furthermore the often sordid and politically stupid behavior of the PLO in southern Lebanon, and the failures of its diplomacy (for which it bears only partial responsibility), may in the long run discredit it further. Or, as Israel and its partisans desperately hope, the PLO, under conditions of dispersal and disarray, may return to random terrorism and abandon its dangerous posture of political accommodation. About these matters, we can now only speculate.

If the PLO is eventually discredited and nullified by the vastly superior military forces ranged against it, we can safely predict that in some circles this consequence will be taken to have demonstrated the validity of the new Arthur Goldberg theory of political legitimacy: a crushing defeat by superior military force demonstrates that the vanquished had no political standing. See pp. 271-272.

8.3.2 The IDF

Putting aside until later the Syrian phase of the war and longer-term consequences, consider finally just the military aspects of the attack on the Palestinians. Israeli assessments indicate that even in these narrow terms the war was less of a triumph than it appeared to be at first. Military historian Martin van Creveld of the Hebrew University presented a detailed and rather pessimistic analysis in the *Jerusalem Post Magazine*. He concludes that "the IDF's performance in Lebanon was not the unqualified success it first appeared to be," despite the fact that from a military point of view, "the war in Lebanon was a relatively easy one." Israeli forces "enjoyed overwhelming numerical superiority" throughout, both against the Syrians and, obviously, against the Palestinians. "The Israeli superiority in equipment was even more overwhelming" in both the Syrian and, again obviously, the Palestinian phases of the war. As for the latter, "the PLO (despite official Israeli attempts to prove the contrary) possessed very few of the heavy weapons crucial to the conduct of modern war and hardly any of the logistic and technical infrastructure required to maintain and deploy them," the general conclusion of serious military analysts, as noted earlier. "Yet in spite of this, as the casualty figures show, the campaign was no walkover." He states that the casualties "during the active phase of operations" were at about the same level as on the Egyptian front in 1967, where Israel was facing major armed forces. The IDF's overwhelming military superiority dictated its tactics: "Wherever problems arose in the war, the IDF solved them by the application of overwhelming firepower—why waste men, or even thought, if you have a virtually unlimited supply of shells to fire and bombs to drop." It was "possible to avoid any kind of military thought" while "spew[ing] forth vast amounts of ammunition to destroy the country which the IDF had allegedly come to save," a familiar phrase from Vietnam days. In human terms, however, the results were "disappointing." "The traditional superiority of individual Israel troops and crews over their opponents took a nosedive." One cannot prove this conclusively, he says, because "the Defence Ministry [is] naturally anxious to hide the shortcomings of Israel's most unpopular war to date." But it is "indisputable," he believes, "that the IDF's morale in Lebanon has been lower than during any other Israeli campaign," a fact reflected in the very high number of psychiatric casualties already noted. "Some aspects of the IDF's performance should serve as a warning rather than as an example," he concludes.[306]

This is the complementary side to the interpretation of the war that appeared to be current among the Palestinians, and others, as it came to an end, still considering only the narrowest aspect of the "Peace for Galilee" campaign. We return to broader aspects in the final chapter.

Notes—Chapter 5
Peace for Galilee

1. *Al Hamishmar*, May 10, 1978; *Ha'aretz*, May 15, 1978.
2. *Jerusalem Post*, Aug. 16, 1981.
3. David Kline, "Inside the Afghan Resistance," *Boston Globe Magazine*, Nov. 7, 1982.
4. John Fullerton, *Far Eastern Economic Review*, Oct. 29, 1982. See Jamal Rashid, "Unpopular refugees," *Middle East International*, Nov. 12, 1982, for further discussion of conflicts between Afghan refugees and the local population, and the fear of "another Beirut." See Robert G. Wirsing and James M. Roherty, *International Affairs*, Autumn 1982, on "the first violation of Pakistan territory by Afghan ground forces" in September 1981, and reports of strafing and rocket attacks in border areas by "Afghan helicopter gunships." The reference is, of course, to the military forces of the Russian client government, carrying out what they call "retaliatory strikes."
5. Barry Rubin, *The Arab States and the Palestine Conflict*, pp. 45, 138f.
6. See Livia Rokach, *Israel's Sacred Terrorism*, citing the diaries of Prime Minister Moshe Sharett. See *TNCW*, p. 285, for some quotes. This suggestion of Dayan's has occasionally been quoted in the U.S. in the past year, but with no reference to Rokach's important research, without which it (and much else) would be unknown. As noted earlier, it is one of the conventions of respectable journalism and scholarship that research that does not adhere to accepted doctrine must remain unmentioned, as if under a taboo, even when it is exploited.
7. John Cooley, "The Palestinians," in Haley and Snider, eds., *Lebanon in Crisis*, p. 33, a detailed discussion of the Palestinian involvement in the Lebanese civil war from which the following account and quotes are drawn unless otherwise indicated.
8. Chaim Margalit, *Hotam*, Dec. 9, 1982. Both Margalit and his high-level informant repeat widespread myths about the Syrian involvement, claiming that the Rabin government in early 1976 armed the Maronites to enable them to defend themselves "against the joint attacks of the Syrians and the PLO," and that the Syrians were invited in by the Christians "in fear of PLO retaliation after the Tel al-Zaatar massacre." In fact, the Syrians were fighting with the Maronites against the Muslim-PLO coalition, and were invited in by the Christians before the Tel al-Zaatar massacre. The actual history has been substantially rewritten within Israel, and far more so, by supporters of Israel here.
9. Attallah Mansour, *Ha'aretz*, July 27, 1982.
10. Benny Morris and David Bernstein, *Jerusalem Post*, July 23, 1982. See also David K. Shipler, *New York Times*, July 25, 1982.
11. *Ha'aretz, Davar*, Nov. 21; *Davar*, Nov. 22, 1982.
12. Edward Said, *Question of Palestine*, pp. 172, 249. See below, pp. 190-1. On the Ma'alot attack, see Hirst, *The Gun and the Olive Branch*, pp. 329-30.
13. See p. 67; James M. Markham, *New York Times*, Dec. 3; Paul Hofmann, *New York Times*, Dec. 1, 1975.
14. See James M. Markham, *New York Times*, Aug. 17, 1975, reporting shelling, abduction and killing by Israeli forces.
15. Milan Kubic, *Newsweek*, June 8, 1970. See p. 121 for the background.
16. Philip Bowring, *Far Eastern Economic Review*, Aug. 9, 1974.
17. Walid Khalidi, *Conflict and Violence in Lebanon* (Center for International Affairs, Harvard, Cambridge, 1979, pp. 125f.); Edward Mortimer, *New Statesman*, June 11, 1982; David Hirst, *Manchester Guardian Weekly*, Nov. 7, 1982.
18. Judith Coburn, *New Times*, March 7, 1975 (a short-lived mid-70s journal).

19. For extensive quotes from her article in *AJME News* (Americans for Justice in the Middle East, Beirut, April 1981), see *TNCW*, pp. 396-7. There is, incidentally, an error in her citation from *Newsweek*, June 8, 1970, included in the quote in *TNCW*. Her figure of 150,000 refugees driven out by 1970 should be "one-fifth of the 150,000 Lebanese Moslems in the area" driven out, "by conservative estimate." See above, p. 189.

20. Moshe Hazani, *Yediot Ahronot*, Sept. 30, 1982.

21. Khalidi, *Conflict and Violence*, pp. 115, 124 (citing the *New York Times*, Oct. 2, 1977).

22. *Economist*, Nov. 19, 1977. While the facts were partially reported here, the interchange was generally described as (unfortunate) Israeli retaliation.

23. For some references and details, see *TNCW*, pp. 295-6.

24. John K. Cooley, "Israel's U.S. arms kill many civilians, Lebanon charges," *Christian Science Monitor*, Aug. 24, 1979. See *TNCW*, p. 296, for further comments and references.

25. Kevin Danaher, *J. of Palestine Studies*, Summer/Fall 1982. Danaher is identified as a professor of Government at American University in Washington.

26. Pranay B. Gupte, *New York Times*, April 11, 1981.

27. *TNCW*, p. 297, sent to press in July 1981.

28. For extensive and often sardonic discussion in the Israeli press of what *Ha'aretz* (April 27, 1982) called "Operation National Trauma '82," see *Israleft News Service*, May 20, 1982.

29. Amnon Kapeliouk, "Conjuring up a trauma," *New Statesman*, May 7, 1982.

30. *Palestine/Israel Bulletin*, February 1982, citing reports by Amnon Kapeliouk in *Le Monde* (May 15, 1975), Clive Robson in *Middle East International, New York Times*, Jan. 11, 1978, and other sources. See pp. 105-7f., and my articles in *New Politics*, Winter 1975-6, Winter 1978-9, for more extensive quotes and discussion.

31. See *TNCW* on this and a number of other examples. See Lesley Hazelton, *New York Review of Books*, May 29, 1980, for some discussion of the treatment of Bedouin citizens of Israel, restricted, however, to the Begin period. See Shulamit Aloni, *New Outlook*, Dec. 1976 for a report of a conference of Israeli Bedouins demanding an end to discrimination, land expropriation, etc. A number of Israeli civil rights groups have taken up the issue in recent years. See p. 349-50.

32. Cited by Kapeliouk (see note 29).

33. David Shaham, *New Outlook*, June 1982. Shaham's final phrase is now commonly used in Israel. See, for example, Amos Oz, "Where shall we hide the shame," *Davar*, June 22, 1982, decrying the failure of the Labor opposition to oppose the Lebanon invasion (and meanwhile, repeating the familiar falsehood: "For the first time in our wars we have gone to war not in order to fight for our existence").

34. Neff, *Warriors at Suez*, p. 435.

35. Robin Wright, "Israeli 'provocations' in southern Lebanon fail to goad PLO—so far," *Christian Science Monitor*, March 18, 1982; Alexander Cockburn & James Ridgeway, *Village Voice*, June 22, 1982, citing UN records.

36. *Time*, Feb. 15, 1982; reprinted in *The Israeli Invasion of Lebanon* (Claremont Research and Publications, New York, August 1982), a collection of press clippings primarily from June and July, containing a number of the documents cited below.

37. Editorial, *Washington Post*, April 22, 1982.

38. See Joseph C. Harsch, "An Arab-Israel chronology," *Christian Science Monitor*, June 10, 1982. For eyewitness reports of the bombings, see *AJME News*,

May 1982, which alleges that at least 25 people were killed in the April raid and 36 in the May raid, Palestinians and Lebanese.

39. Ze'ev Schiff, *Ha'aretz*, May 12, 1982; cited by Jonathan Frankel, *Dissent*, Winter 1983.

40. *Washington Post*, June 7, 1982; cited by Eric Hooglund, *U.S. Press Coverage of the Israeli Invasion of Lebanon*, ADC Issue No. 10, American-Arab Anti-Discrimination Committee, Washington, 1982.

41. Hooglund, citing the *New York Times, Washington Post, Baltimore Sun, Chicago Tribune*. On the outright racist reaction of the tabloid press, see my "Reflections on Israel in Lebanon," *Middle East International*, July 16, 1982, *Inquiry*, August 1982.

42. Cheryl Rubenberg, Assistant Professor of Political Science at Florida International University, *J. of Palestine Studies*, Summer/Fall 1982.

43. Dr. David Zemach, letter, *Ha'aretz*, June 16, 1982.

44. *New York Times, Boston Globe*, June 18, 1982.

45. Henry Kamm, *New York Times*, July 17, 1982.

46. Bernard D. Nossiter, *New York Times*, June 27, 1982, my emphasis. See chapter 2, note 1.

47. Ze'ev Schiff, *Ha'aretz*, May 23, 1982. Sharon's further view, according to this well-informed correspondent, is that destruction of the PLO in Lebanon will lead the way to "the conversion of Jordan to Palestine," thus eliminating the Palestinian issue. This is one of the many articles discussing Sharon's invasion plans, before the fact.

48. Benny Landau, interview with Martin Peretz, *Ha'aretz*, June 4, 1982.

49. Yoel Marcus, "The War is Inevitable," *Ha'aretz*, March 26, 1982. See also Schiff's remarks, p. 196.

50. See p. 199*.

51. My emphasis. It is interesting that even an outstanding historian of Palestinian nationalism cannot bring himself to recall the actual PLO efforts to reach a more far-reaching arrangement, though the facts are familiar in Israel and are often discussed, not only by doves, as we have seen in chapter 3.

52. Yehoshua Porath, *Ha'aretz*, June 25, 1982. See preceding note.

53. Danny Rubinstein, "A political PLO is more dangerous than a powerful PLO," *Davar*, Sept. 6, 1982. A version of the same article appeared as an Op-Ed in the *New York Times*, Sept. 14, 1982.

54. *Yediot Ahronot*, June 18, 1982; cited by Amnon Kapeliouk, "The liquidation of the Palestinian obstacle," *Le Monde diplomatique*, July 1982.

55. *Yediot Ahronot*, Oct. 17, 1982; *Israeli Mirror*.

56. Amnon Kapeliouk, *New Outlook*, August/September 1982.

57. See p. 164; Shimon Peres, "Why Israel's Labor Party Accepts the Reagan Plan," *Washington Post (Manchester Guardian Weekly*, Sept. 26, 1982). The title of Peres's article is misleading, though it is true that Labor hopes to convert the rather vague Reagan plan into something resembling its own rejectionist position.

58. Mordechai Bar-On, "The Palestinian Aspects of the War in Lebanon"; Ze'ev Schiff, "Who Decided, Who Informed" *(New Outlook*, October 1982); see note 39. We return to Bar-On's views on the PLO, p. 255*.

59. *Los Angeles Times*, Jan. 4, 5, 1983; David Shipler, *New York Times*, Jan. 12, 1983; Eric Rouleau, *Le Monde (Manchester Guardian Weekly*, Jan. 23, 1983).

60. *New York Times*, July 6-11; *Boston Globe*, July 7, 9, 10, 11; *Christian Science Monitor*, July 12; *Le Monde*, June 13-4, July 7; *The Dawn (Al Fajr)*, July 2; Kapeliouk, *Le Monde diplomatique*, July; K. Amnon (Amnon Kapeliouk), *Al Hamishmar*, June 25; *Al Hamishmar*, July 12; Kapeliouk, *Al Hamishmar*, July 12.

61. David K. Shipler, *New York Times*, July 11, 1982.
62. *The Dawn (Al Fajr)*, Sept. 10; *Los Angeles Times*, Oct. 27; *Boston Globe*, Oct. 27, 1982.
63. David Pryce-Jones, *New Republic*, Nov. 8, 1982. See p. 63 for his further ruminations on this subject.
64. Danny Rubinstein, *Davar*, May 16, 1980.
65. William E. Farrell, *New York Times*, Nov. 24, 1982. The anti-Jordanian actions aroused some concern in Washington, because of the conflict with American diplomacy.
66. *Jerusalem Post*, July 14, 1982.
67. See William L. Shirer, *The Rise and Fall of the Third Reich* (Simon & Schuster, New York, 1959, p. 417).
68. Robert W. Tucker, "A Reply to Critics: Morality and the War," *New York Times*, July 15, 1982. For Tucker's postwar assessment, see below, p. 270*. On his views concerning the legitimacy of the resort to military force to attain American objectives, including not only "needs" but also "wants," see *TNCW*, chapter 8. On his grasp of reality, see p. 1*.
69. Leon Wieseltier, *Los Angeles Times*, July 25, 1982; also Michael Walzer, *New Republic*, Aug. 16, 1982.
70. Elmer Winter, "The task facing American Jews," *Jerusalem Post*, June 18, 1982.
71. Jonathan Frankel, *Jerusalem Post*, June 27, 1982; Meir Pail, "A Military Analysis," *New Outlook*, Aug./Sept. 1982. Similar observations are made by Beit-Hallahmi, "The consensus that never was" (see chapter 4, note 178), and many others.
72. Bernard Gwertzman, "Shultz Asserts Libyan Threat Has 'Receded'," *New York Times*, Feb. 21; William Beecher, "Khadafy is 'back in his box'—but for how long?," *Boston Globe*, Feb. 25, 1983. See Reuters, *New York Times*, Feb. 22, reporting Egypt's statement "that it has seen no sign of a crisis" and denial "that it had asked for American help." Richard Halloran reports the same day that the American plan was "to lure Libya into striking and then to destroy as much of its air force as possible," or if Libya failed to seize the bait, "to assert that prompt help to Egypt had deterred Libya," which "was, in effect, what Mr. Shultz said Sunday" (as quoted on Feb. 21). The goal of the plan, "according to American officials," was "to improve chances of using Egyptian bases for the Rapid Deployment Force," aimed at the Gulf. From Khartoum, James Dorsey reports that "U.S. intelligence officials appear to be the only source for reports" on the alleged Libyan moves, which are unknown to diplomats or to Sudanese or Egyptian intelligence and officials; *Christian Science Monitor*, Feb. 22, 1983.
73. Ze'ev Schiff, *Ha'aretz*, July 18; Hirsh Goodman, *Jerusalem Post*, July 9; Pail, "A Military Analysis"; *Jerusalem Post*, July 13 *(Israleft News Service)*.
74. Interview in *Migvan*, August 1982. After the capture of West Beirut there was another major show of captured arms, much of it identified as Syrian; "enough to equip three or four divisions" (James Feron, *New York Times*, Oct. 12, 1982). A few days later, in the *News of the Week in Review*, this had become "enough *Palestinian* equipment for three or four divisions" *(New York Times*, Oct. 17; my emphasis).
75. *Yediot Ahronot*, May 14, 1982; cited by Amnon Kapeliouk, *Le Monde diplomatique*, July 1982 (also David K. Shipler, *New York Times*, May 26, 1982); Eliahu Salpeter, *Ha'aretz*, May 17, 1982.
76. Marvine Howe, *New York Times*, July 28, 1982.
77. See Edward Mortimer, *New Statesman*, June 11, 1982. See also p. 190.
78. Yuval Ne'eman, "Israel's options in Lebanon," *Jerusalem Post*, June 24, 1982.
79. Ze'ev Strominsky, economics correspondent of *Davar*, Aug. 3, 1982.

80. *Wall St. Journal*, July 28, Aug. 26, 1982.
81. Thomas L. Friedman, "Christians Won Vast New Power in Lebanon War," *New York Times*, Nov. 2, 1982.
82. David Bernstein, "No quick getaway" (not a great surprise, one would think), *Jerusalem Post*, Sept. 21, 1982, written directly after the Sabra-Shatila massacres.
83. Yuval Elizur, *Maariv*, Oct. 17, 1982; translated in *Israel Press Briefs* (Tel Aviv).
84. Aharon Abramovitz, *Ma'ariv*, Aug. 20, 1982. A picture is appended. The reporter is appalled.
85. Meir Pail, "A Military Analysis."
86. Bernard Gwertzman, "U.S. and Israel: A Quest for Flexibility," *New York Times*, June 24, 1982.
87. Yoseph Priel, *Davar*, Aug. 5, 1982 (dispatch from Washington).
88. See p. 108.
89. Claudia Wright, *New Statesman*, Aug. 20, 1982; *In These Times*, Sept. 8, 1982.
90. *Ha'aretz*, Aug. 11, 1982, with a technical description; Ruvik Rosenthal, *Al Hamishmar*, Aug. 11.
91. Laurence Grafstein, "The Implosion Plot," *New Republic*, Sept. 6; Martin Peretz, *New Republic*, Nov. 15, 1982.
92. Joe Stork and Jim Paul, *MERIP Reports*, Sept./Oct. 1982; Carter's remark is quoted from the *Washington Post*, Aug. 21. Haig's response is in an interview with the *Boston Globe*, March 2, 1983.
93. Beit-Hallahmi, "The consensus that never was."
94. Charles Hoffman, Interview with Aharon Yariv, *Jerusalem Post*, Sept. 24, 1982.
95. Ingela Bendt & James Downing, *We Shall Return* (Lawrence Hill, Westport, 1982). The authors are freelance journalists who spent several months in the camp. Their account is based on the testimony of refugees, which, as always, must be evaluated with care. In this case, there is ample independent verification of the practices described. In contrast to refugees who have a more useful story to tell, Palestinian refugees have been generally avoided by the press. On this matter, see p. 126 and *MERIP Reports*, Sept./Oct. 1982.
96. David K. Shipler, *New York Times*, July 3, 1982.
97. There is a useful account of the war by Michael Jansen, *The Battle of Beirut* (Zed, London, 1982; South End, Boston). See also *The Israeli Invasion of Lebanon*, cited in note 36, for June and July, and Part II, extending the record from August into 1983. A more extensive collection of press clippings appears in *Mideast Press Report*, also published by Claremont Research and Publications. For a fairly extensive summary of these press reports, see "Chronology of the Israeli Invasion of Lebanon," *J. of Palestine Studies*, Summer/Fall 1982. One of the best sources is the regular weekly reporting, using local resources and also drawing extensively from the international press, in the English-language journal *Monday Morning*, published throughout the war (with some issues missing when publication was impossible) in West Beirut. See also *Israel in Lebanon*, Report of the International Commission to enquire into reported violations of International Law by Israel during its invasion of the Lebanon, Sean MacBride, Chairman (Ithaca press, London, 1983).
98. Dan Connell, *MERIP Reports*, Sept./Oct. 1982.
99. John A. Callcott, "'Deadly accuracy' of Israeli guns blasts coastal plain," *Jerusalem Post*, June 23, 1982.
100. G. H. Jansen, "Terror tactics," *Middle East International*, July 2, 1982.
101. Knesset debate cited in *Journal of Palestine Studies*, Summer/Fall 1982; Tom Segev, *Ha'aretz Supplement*, June 18, 1982. Danny Rubinstein, *Davar*, Sept. 3; reprinted in *Memorandum on Human Rights Conditions*, ADC Background Paper #9 (American-Arab Anti-Discrimination Committee), October 1982.

102. *New York Times*, Aug. 12, 1982.; *Yediot Ahronot*, July 19, 1982.

103. *Newsweek*, June 28; *New York Times*, Sept. 2; *Christian Science Monitor*, Nov. 18, Dec. 21; *Los Angeles Times*, Aug. 23; *Boston Globe*, Sept. 3; *Yediot Ahronot*, Sept. 6, 1982, reporting a government announcement. For Eitan's figures, see Asher Wallfish, *Jerusalem Post*, Jan. 19, 1983. The Lebanese government reported 1100 people killed in Sidon before June 14; AP, *Los Angeles Times*, June 21, 1982. The fact that the attacks had little effect on the guerrillas was regularly reported (e.g., John Kifner, *New York Times*, Aug. 14, 1982).

104. Yizhar Smilanski, *Davar*, Sept. 5; also Levi Yitzhak Hayerushalmi, same issue. Both cite Israeli radio reports that coincide with the Lebanese estimates just given.

105. Hirsh Goodman, "Doubts at the front," *Jerusalem Post*, June 28, 1982.

106. Shimon Weiss, *Davar*, Sept. 2; Dr. Haim Gordon, *Ha'aretz*, Aug. 19, 1982.

107. Alan Philps, Reuter, *Boston Globe*, Aug. 21, 1982.

108. *Monday Morning*, Sept. 6-12; Robert Fisk, "The ugly reality of war Israel is trying to hide," *London Times*, July 13, 1982.

109. John Yemma, *Christian Science Monitor*, Nov. 18, 1982.

110. Bernard Nossiter, *New York Times*, Aug. 19, 1982.

111. *Economist*, Nov. 6, 1982.

112. Gen. Frederick Morgan, *Peace and War;* see chapter 4, note 8.

113. John Kifner, *New York Times*, Aug. 14, 1982.

114. David Lamb, *Los Angeles Times*, June 28, 1982.

115. See Christopher Walker, *London Times*, June 18; *New York Times*, Aug. 12; T. Elaine Carey, *Christian Science Monitor*, Aug. 13; UPI, *Boston Globe*, Aug. 19, 1983.

116. David Lamb, *Los Angeles Times—Philadelphia Inquirer*, June 18, 1982.

117. Wire services, *Boston Globe*, June 5, 1982. See p. 197.

118. William Branigan, "Israeli Bombing of Hospitals," *Washington Post (Manchester Guardian weekly)*, June 27, 1982.

119. Hal Piper, *Baltimore Sun*, June 21, 1982.

120. Richard Ben Cramer, *Philadelphia Inquirer*, June 24, 1982.

121. William E. Farrell, *New York Times*, June 27, 1982.

122. T. Elaine Carey, *Christian Science Monitor*, Aug. 13; *Newsweek*, Aug. 16, 1982. The latter contains an extensive account of the massive devastation of civilian sectors of West Beirut.

123. David B. Ottaway, *Washington Post*, June 27, 1982.

124. *Financial Times* (London), July 9, 1982; Robin Wright, "The horror shelling of a defenceless hospital," *Sunday Times* (London), July 4, 1982 (with a picture of dead children and patients wandering in the wreckage).

125. T. Elaine Carey, *Christian Science Monitor*, Aug. 4, 1982.

126. Wire Services, *Boston Globe*, Aug. 5, 1982.

127. J. Michael Kennedy, *Los Angeles Times*, Aug. 19, 1982.

128. T. Elaine Carey, *Christian Science Monitor*, Aug. 13, 1982.

129. *New York Times*, Aug. 12, 1982; Robert Fisk, *London Times*, July 13, 1982.

130. Alexander Cockburn & James Ridgeway, *Village Voice*, Nov. 30, 1982. See also Colman McCarthy, "A Witness to Our Weapons' Efficiency," *Washington Post* (*Manchester Guardian Weekly*, Jan. 23, 1983), reporting "a long conversation" with Dr. Shamma on her effort "to dispense some strong medicine to her fellow Americans" concerning the effect of the supply of advanced weapons to Israel; an effort that was in vain.

131. *Keene Sentinel*, New Hampshire, Aug. 17, 1982.

132. *New York Times*, Dec. 12, 1982.

133. James Feron, *New York Times*, Aug. 25, 1982.

134. Arthur J. Goldberg, "Lebanese Hail Israel's Action as Liberation," *New York Times*, Aug. 15, 1982; a full-page advertisement reprinting an article from the *Jerusalem Post* and *Ma'ariv*, published by The American Friends of Israel. For Eban's comments, see his harsh condemnation of the expansion of the war to Beirut—and of the "'gallant' supporters abroad who advocated [an attack on Beirut], usually from positions of physical non-involvement"—in the *Jerusalem Post*, reprinted in the *Jewish Post & Opinion*, August 27, 1982.

135. Abba Eban, *Socialist Affairs* (journal of the Socialist International), 5/82, reprinted from the *Jerusalem Post*. Eban's remarks are cited along with a range of other Israeli reactions to Begin's "macabre fantasy" by Michael Precker, *Boston Globe*, Aug. 10, 1982.

136. Jonathan C. Randal, *Washington Post*, June 19, 1982.

137. Michael Precker, *Boston Globe*, June 20, 1982.

138. David K. Shipler, *New York Times*, June 20, 1982.

139. Gideon Spiro, "The kibbutznik runs to war," *Haolam Haze*, Aug. 18, 1982. Spiro discusses other cases, notably Lieut. Col. Ran Cohen, one of the leaders of the peace group *Sheli* and a member of Kibbutz Gan Shmuel, who had volunteered for the 1978 invasion and described in a press interview how in 1982 he had fought with "almost diabolical coolness" as a "professional fighter," as he "fired thousands of shells on West Beirut," an act requiring great courage. Spiro believes that "the Likud continues to fulfill the unwritten agreement, inherited from the Labor Alignment, according to which the kibbutz movement shall continue to supply cannon fodder for every war adventure and in return shall receive economic benefits from the state." He also maintains that most of the participation from the kibbutzim in anti-war protests was by people who had moved to the towns.

140. Precker, see note 137.

141. David K. Shipler, *New York Times*, June 15; Randal, see note 136.

142. Judith Miller, *New York Times*, July 14, 1982.

143. Testimony of Dr. Chris Giannou before the House Subcommittee on Europe and the Middle East, July 13; *Toronto Star*, June 21; Canadian Broadcasting Company interview with Norwegian doctor Steinar Berge, June 23, reprinted in *The Israeli Invasion of Lebanon; Guardian* (London), June 24; Alexander Cockburn, *Village Voice*, July 27, 1982.

144. Reprinted in the *J. of Palestine Studies*, Summer/Fall 1982.

145. Testimony, October 31, at Hearings in Oslo.

146. William E. Farrell, "South Lebanon: Rejected, Neglected and Occupied," *New York Times*, Jan. 17, 1983. Others report the same experience, among them, American journalist Charles Glass in December 1982 (personal communication).

147. Edward Walsh, *Washington Post—Boston Globe*, Jan. 25, 1983; Uri Avneri, *Haolam Haze*, Dec. 15, 1982; Mary Arias, "Calvario Palestino," *Cambio* (Spain), Dec. 20, 1982.

148. Jonathan C. Randal, *Washington Post*, July 28, 1982; *The Dawn (Al Fajr)*, Jan. 14, 1983, citing interviews in the Lebanese journal *Al Safir* and the Paris journal *Libération; Yediot Ahronot*, citing the *London Times*, March 18, 1983; *Ha'aretz*, March 18, 1983 (translated from *Der Spiegel*, March 14, 1983).

149. *Times* (London), June 16; Randal, *Washington Post*, June 19; David Blundy, *Times* (London), July 18; Trudy Rubin, *Christian Science Monitor*, Aug. 5; *New York Times*, June 21, 1982.

150. Christopher Walker, *Times* (London), June 23, 1982.

151. Jacobo Timerman, *The Longest War*.

152. Earleen F. Tatro (AP) and David Rogers (Reuters), *Monday Morning* (Beirut), June 28-July 4, 1982.

153. Aryeh Rubinstein, *Jerusalem Post*, June 24, 1982.
154. William E. Farrell, "South Lebanon."
155. Dr. Haim Gordon, *Ha'aretz*, Aug. 19, 1982; Amnon Dankner, "A shot on the last day" (the suicide), *Ha'aretz*, Nov. 5, 1982. On December 3, the *Boston Globe* reported (from wire services) that two Palestinian prisoners at Ansar camp were killed "in an accidental burst of gunfire by a guard, the Israeli military said." In March, Israeli troops fired at about 1000 Palestinians protesting detention of relatives at Ansar, wounding one women (AP, *Boston Globe*, March 17, 1983). Reporting is very scanty.
156. *Ha'aretz*, Dec. 6, 1982.
157. Israel Segal, "Like Animals," *Koteret Rashit*, March 16, 1983.
158. Interview with Meir Pail in *Yediot Ahronot*, April 4 1972, translated in Shahak, *Begin And Co.*; Jon Kimche, *Seven Fallen Pillars* (Secker and Warburg, London, 1950, pp. 217ff.), in Khalidi, ed., *From Haven to Conquest*.
159. See p. 102; Love, *Suez*, p. 689.
160. *Ha'aretz*, Oct. 19, 1982; *Israleft News Service*, Nov. 1.
161. See Yoseph Shavit, "Lieut. Col. (Res.) Yirmiah: 'From war to war we become less human'," *Yediot Ahronot*, Oct. 8, 1982.
162. *Zu Haderech* (the journal of the Israeli Communist Party, which appears to have been the only Israeli journal to report this important meeting), Oct. 27, 1982. See also *Israel & Palestine* (Paris), December 1982.
163. Amiram Cohen, *Hotam* (Mapam) Oct. 29, 1982.
164. *Hotam*, July 16; *Al Hamishmar*, Aug. 5, 1982, the latter written in response to claims by military authorities about the excellent care for the population in Lebanon; *My War Diary*, privately printed, Tel Aviv (1983), with an introduction by Aryeh Lova Eliav, one of Israel's most prominent doves; to be published in English translation by South End Press, Boston. Also Aharon Meged, *Davar*, Aug. 6, 1982.
165. Robert Fisk, *London Times*, June 28, 1982.
166. Charles T. Powers, *Los Angeles Times*, Aug. 29, 1982.
167. *Davar*, July 28, 1982.
168. Hirsh Goodman, *Jerusalem Post*, Oct. 1, 1982.
169. Charles T. Powers, *Los Angeles Times*, August 29, 1982.
170. John Kifner, *New York Times*, Aug. 29, 1982.
171. Ze'ev Schiff, *Ha'aretz*, June 24, 1982.
172. "Beirut Curtain Call," *New Republic*, Sept. 13, 1982.
173. George Orwell, *Homage to Catalonia* (Beacon, Boston, 1952, pp. 171, 54). POUM was regarded by the Communists as Trotskyite, an allegation that it vigorously denied. It was, however, anti-Stalinist, presumably the grounds for the *New Republic* fabrications.
174. See note 134; Editorial, *New York Times*, July 7; Ariel Sharon, Op-Ed, *New York Times*, Aug. 29, 1982.
175. H. E. Mr. Ghassan Tueni, "The Apocalyptic Realities of Today," *New Outlook* (Tel Aviv), August/September 1982.
176. Ghassan Tueni, "Lebanon: A New Republic?," *Foreign Affairs*, Fall 1982.
177. *Monday Morning*, June 14-20.
178. Robert Fisk, *London Times*, June 15, 1982; Jumblatt, interview, *Monday Morning*, June 21-27, July 12-18.
179. *Ibid.*
180. *Ibid.*, June 21-27.
181. *Ibid.*, June 28-July 4.
182. *Ibid.*, Aug. 2-8; Aug. 23-9 (a review of events of August).

183. Cited in a survey of TV news by the Anti-Defamation League of B'nai Brith, to which we return.
184. *Monday Morning*, Aug. 23-29, Sept. 13-19.
185. *Ibid.*, Sept. 6-12.
186. *Ibid.*, July 5-11, July 26-Aug. 1.
187. William Stewart, *Time*, August 16, 1982.
188. Amnon Rubinstein, Special to the *Boston Globe*, July 11, 1982.
189. Yigal Lev, *Ma'ariv*, Dec. 3, 1982.
190. Menachem Rahat, *Ma'ariv*, Dec. 29, 1982.
191. Edward Walsh, *Washington Post—Boston Globe*, Aug.28,1982, reporting a poll conducted between August 10 and 19.
192. AP, *Boston Globe*, Sept. 1, 1982.
193. *New York Times*, Aug. 29, Sept. 9, 1982 (my emphasis).
194. On this matter, see *TNCW*, particularly chapters 1, 2, 4.
195. Gideon Hausner, *Jerusalem Post*, July 11, 1982.
196. Amir Oren, *Davar*, June 28, 1982, an interview with a paratrooper who had returned from the front.
197. Mordechai Bar-On, "The Palestinian Aspect."
198. Meir Pail, "A Military Analysis."
199. Henry Kamm, "Israelis and Germans Doubt Bulgarian Link in Attack on Pope," *New York Times*, Dec. 18, 1982; Norman Kempster, "Israelis Expect Sharp Rise in Anti-Jewish Terrorism," *Los Angeles Times*, Dec. 12, 1982.
200. Ze'ev Strominsky, *Davar*, July 19, 1982.
201. Yoav Biran, Minister Plenipotentiary, Embassy of Israel, letter, *Manchester Guardian Weekly*, July 25; *ibid.*, Aug. 1, 1982.
202. Shlomo Shmelzman, letter, *Ha'aretz*, August 11, 1982; *Israleft News Service*.
203. Meir Pail, "A Military Analysis"; Boaz Evron, "Strength, Strength, Strength" (chapter 4, note 175).
204. Martin Peretz, "Lebanon Eyewitness," *New Republic*, Aug. 2, 1982. More on this contribution below.
205. Meron Benvenisti, "Letter to Professor Avineri," *Ha'aretz*, July 22, 1982.
206. Rabbi Balfour Brickner, "How I (a Rabbi) Spent My Summer," *CALC Report*, Nov./Dec. 1982.
207. Shlomo Avineri, *Los Angeles Times*, June 27, Aug. 20, 1982; Raanan Weitz, "Meeting Israeli and Palestinian Needs," Op-Ed, *New York Times*, Aug. 18, 1982.
208. Embassy of Israel, "THE THREAT INHERENT IN THE PLO'S CONTINU- ANCE AS A POLITICAL BODY," Washington DC, July 26, 1982.
209. Amiram Cohen, "Why was Labor silent?," *Hotam*, Sept. 3, 1982.
210. Norman Kempster, *Los Angeles Times*, Sept. 16, 1982.
211. Henry Fairlie, *New Republic*, July 12, 1982.
212. Barbara Tuchman, Op-Ed, *New York Times*, July 25, 1982.
213. Jacob K. Javits, Op-Ed, *New York Times*, July 5, 1982.
214. Michael Walzer, *New Republic*, Sept. 6, 1982; his emphasis. See also his articles in the *New Republic*, July 5, August 16.
215. Morris B. Abram, *New York Times*, Aug. 24, 1982. For those who believe that UN General Assembly Resolutions, such as the one recommending the forma- tion of a Jewish state in 1947, have some standing, it might be noted that the right that the Palestinians had forfeited in the eyes of American Zionists such as Abram has regularly been endorsed by the UN, including the U.S., within the context of a negotiated settlement, which U.S.-Israeli rejectionism has effectively blocked in recent years.
216. *Boston Globe*, Aug. 11, 1982.

217. Artilleryman Avi Tsarfati, explaining why he refused to return to serve in Lebanon, at the Tel Aviv meeting at which Col. Yirmiah spoke; see note 162.
218. Editorial, *Washington Post;* reprinted in the *Manchester Guardian Weekly,* Aug. 29, 1982.
219. Editorials, *New York Times,* June 23; July 7, 11, 21; Aug. 5, 20, 1982.
220. Op-Ed, *New York Times,* June 30, 1982.
221. Elizabeth Mehren, *Los Angeles Times,* Aug. 29, 1982.
222. Charles Hoffman, *Jerusalem Post,* June 29, 1982.
223. Noah Kliger, *Yediot Ahronot,* March 7, 1982.
224. Yehuda Stav, *Yediot Ahronot,* July 4; *Davar,* July 7, 1982.
225. James M. Markham, *New York Times,* July 5; *Washington Post,* July 3; Will Thorne, "Hayden, Hawkins [Hayden's Republican opponent for State Assembly in the Santa Monica area] agree on major Mideast issues," *Santa Monica Evening Outlook,* July 10-11, 1982.
226. *Jewish Post & Opinion,* April 30, 1982; Support letter, Jewish Community Committee for Tom Hayden, no date.
227. *Al Hamishmar,* Dec. 5, 1982.
228. Uri Avneri, *Ha'olam Haze,* Dec. 22, 1982; Rafik Halabi, *Koteret Rashit,* March 16, 1983; Chaim Bermant, *Jerusalem Post,* March 22, 1983.
229. *Los Angeles Times,* Dec. 14, 1982.
230. Norman Podhoretz, Op-Ed, *New York Times,* June 15, 1982.
231. Statement of the Ad Hoc Committee for Lebanese Freedom, signed by a distinguished group of Nobel Laureates, Law Professors (Joseph Bishop, Alan Dershowitz, etc.), writers (Czeslaw Miloscz, Marie Syrkin, Hilton Kramer, etc.), *New Republic* editors and others.
232. "Lebanese Hail Israel's Action as Liberation"; see note 134.
233. Meir Pail, "A Military Analysis."
234. See chapter 4, note 30.
235. Conor Cruise O'Brien, review, *New Republic,* Jan. 24, 1983. O'Brien has in recent years been a strong supporter of Israel, and is one of the most passionate defenders of the Lebanon war, in a manner that is rare in the British press.
236. David Denby, "The Decline of 'The Village Voice,' *New Republic,* Jan. 31, 1983.
237. Sammy Smooha and Don Peretz, "The Arabs in Israel," *J. of Conflict Resolution,* September 1982, a detailed review and analysis of poll results to which we return in chapter 7, where the numbers and their meaning will be further clarified. See pp. 55-6, 61, on the Israeli poll on West Bank attitudes.
238. Gilmour's emphasis. I have replaced Timerman's "incisive" by "decisive," which I presume was Talmon's original wording.
239. Elfi Pallis, review, *New Statesman,* Dec. 3, 1982; David Gilmour, review, *Middle East International,* Dec. 10, 1982. The final comment applies to Timerman's citation, but not in these terms to Talmon's letter, written in 1980.
240. Barry Sussman, *Washington Post-Boston Globe,* Aug. 20, 1982, an analysis of a poll by the *Washington Post* and ABC News (it should be noted that there is considerable apparent disparity in poll results, probably to be attributed to differences in the way questions are formulated); John E. Rielly, *Foreign Policy,* Spring 1983, reporting on a recent national survey of American opinion. On earlier attitudes of the "intellectual elite," and the "triumph of pragmatism" in their qualified opposition to the war (because it didn't work) at the peak period of anti-war protest, when even substantial business and government circles had turned against it, see Charles Kadushin, *The American Intellectual Elite* (Little Brown and Co., Boston, 1974).
241. William Lee, *Middle East International,* Dec. 10, 1982. The poll was commissioned by the AAUG, but is difficult to see how that could have contaminated the results.

242. Daniel Southerland, *Christian Science Monitor*, Nov. 19, 1982.

243. Martin Peretz, "Lebanon Eyewitness."

244. It can easily be extended. Consider, for example, Peretz's statement *(New Republic*, March 31, 1982) that "We axiomatically print letters from organizations and individuals criticized in our pages." In fact, Peretz regularly intervenes to prevent publication of responses to his slanders, a practice on the part of an owner-editor that reveals an unusual degree of moral cowardice. For two such examples, see the introduction by C. P. Otero, editor of my essays in *Radical Priorities* (Black Rose, Montreal, 1981), pp. 15, 51.

245. Pail, "A Military Analysis."

246. Lily Galili, interview, *Ha'aretz*, Dec. 9, 1982. As a journalist of integrity, he refused. Peretz is presented here as a "Professor of Political Science at Harvard"—which is false—and a critic of Begin—which is correct; he explains that Begin's "style, manner of speaking, and the contents of what he says" are difficult to defend in an American context, which causes problems for supporters of Israel. It will also be difficult to "defend the annexation of the West Bank." As for Peace Now, Peretz speaks quite disparagingly, though he has "sympathy for them." It has perhaps 2000 American supporters, he says: "radical politics [Peace Now?] in the United States is bankrupt."

247. Emphasis added. Martin Peretz, "Usual Suspects," *New Republic*, July 12, 1982; *Boston Globe*, June 27, 1982. Peretz's revision of the ad was pointed out by Alexander Cockburn in the *Village Voice*, eliciting no response, though perhaps the subsequent reference to Cockburn as "despicable," "a nasty piece of work," etc., is to be understood as the response, a characteristic one for this type of journalism. See p. 273.

248. "An Anti-Defamation League of B'nai Brith Study: Television Network Coverage of the War in Lebanon," released October 21, 1982.

249. Tony Schwartz, "A.D.L. Criticizes TV Over Coverage of Lebanon," *New York Times*, Oct. 21, 1982.

250. Leon Hadar, "Covering the War," *Jerusalem Post*, Aug. 2, 1982. Frank is identified as the son of a prominent American Labor Zionist leader.

251. Peter Braestrup, *Big Story* (Westview, Boulder, 1977, two volumes); see my review in *Race and Class*, 1, 1978, and in a briefer version in the journalism review *More*, June 1978, for extensive documentation. The Braestrup study appeared in an abbreviated version, reprinted by Yale University press (1982).

252. See note 40 and text; Roger Morris, "Beirut—and the press—under siege," *Columbia Journalism Review*, November/December 1982.

253. Norman Kempster, "Israel Mounts a Counterattack to Avoid a Public-Relations Defeat," *Los Angeles Times*, Sept. 12, 1982.

254. Charles Hoffman, interview with Aharon Yariv, *Jerusalem Post*, Sept. 24, 1982.

255. *Ma'ariv*, Nov. 22, 1981; *Economist*, Dec. 18, 1982, Feb. 19, 1983; *Ma'ariv*, March 25, 1982. The number of *campesinos* (mainly Indians) killed from the March 1982 coup to October is estimated at 8000 by the Committee for Justice and Peace, a Guatemalan Christian group, and the Guatemalan Commission for Human Rights; *Human Rights in Guatemala: No Neutrals Allowed*, Americas Watch Report (New York, 1982).

256. Moshe Yegar, "Abuse of Freedom," *Jerusalem Post*, Aug. 20, 1982.

257. Yochanan Manor, "Process of disinformation," *Jerusalem Post*, Jan. 4, 1983.

258. Moshe Sharon, "No friend of Israel," *Jerusalem Post*, Jan. 7, 1983; Yuval Elizur, *Boston Globe*, Aug. 6, 1982. Sharon's article is accompanied by a picture of President Reagan with a rather uncharacteristic ugly leer, presumably showing the true face of America with regard to Israel, which Sharon has now exposed.

259. Curtis Wilkie, *Boston Globe*, June 24, 1982.

260. Kempster, "Israel Mounts a Counterattack."

261. Aryeh Rubinstein, *Jerusalem Post*, June 24, 1982, reporting on Knesset debate.
262. Yerah Tal, *Ha'aretz*, June 25, 1982, citing high IDF officials.
263. Yitzhak Zamir, Letter to AI in London, Aug. 25, 1982, in *Human Rights Internet Reporter*, Washington, Sept.-Nov. 1982.
264. Yegar, "Abuse of Freedom."
265. *Haolam Haze*, August 4, 1982.
266. B. Michael, "The Miracle Child," *Ha'aretz*, August 18, 1982; translated in part in *Middle East International*, Sept. 17, 1982.
267. David Landau, *Middle East International*, Oct. 1, 1982.
268. *Ha'aretz*, Sept. 28, 1982; *Israeli Mirror*.
269. Francis Cornu, *Le Monde*, Dec. 31, 1982. See chapter 6, section 6.5.2, for more details.
270. Ihsan A. Hijazi, *New York Times*, Oct. 1, 1982. See also "After the Vandals," an interview with Sabri Jiryis, *Israel & Palestine*, Dec. 1982 (Paris). Israel's UN representative, Yehuda Blum, assured the UN that the "real scholarly material" would be returned, though not material determined by Israel to have nothing to do with "the Palestinian cultural heritage." The UN, however, was "not satisfied with this announcement," and passed a resolution requesting Israel to return all of the material to UNESCO. Yoseph Priel, *Davar*, Dec. 19, 1982. One is entitled to be skeptical as to whether anything will be returned.
271. J. Michael Kennedy, *Los Angeles Times*, Sept. 27, 1982. See also AP, *Monday Morning*, Oct. 4-10, reporting that the apartment of the bureau chief of the French press agency was vandalized and ransacked, and that equipment worth half a million dollars was stolen at the Lebanese airline offices, where, according to the manager, everything movable was stolen and "the Israelis defecated all over..."
272. Rebecca Trounson, *Boston Globe*, Oct. 19, 1982.
273. *New York Times*, June 11, 1982; dispatch from Jerusalem. See pp. 224*, 225, 237f.
274. Phyllis Sutker, National President, Pioneer Women/Na'amat, letter, *New York Times*, July 5, 1982.
275. *Al Hamishmar*, July 25, 1982 *(Israeli Mirror)*, which reports that the couple are "still awaiting permission from the Israeli authorities to visit Israel with the aim to return and live there," obviously a tricky question.
276. "Israeli Aid Group Plays Active War Relief Role," *New York Times*, Aug. 8, 1982.
277. Ilan Shchori, *Ha'aretz*, June 23, 1982.
278. Edward Grossman, "The quantity of mercy," *Jerusalem Post*, June 25, 1982.
279. See *TNCW*, p. 331, and pp. 462-5 for a few examples of what is contained in this important material.
280. See *TNCW*, chapters 1 and 2, for discussion of this and several other examples.
281. Eliahu Zehavi, "Do not tell us about flowers and rice," *Ha'aretz*, June 27, 1982. Zehavi adds that the Danish foreign minister issued a criticism of the Israeli invasion that was unprecedented in its harshness.
282. *Hotam* (Mapam), July 2, 1982.
283. Timerman, *The Longest War*.
284. See my *At War with Asia* (Pantheon, New York, 1970, chapter 4).
285. Yaakov Erez, *Ma'ariv*, Dec. 17, 1982.
286. Trudy Rubin, "Israelis stuck in Lebanese mire?," *Christian Science Monitor*, Jan. 12, 1983.
287. Hirsh Goodman, *Jerusalem Post*, Feb. 18, 1983.
288. AP, *New York Times*, March 21, 1983.

289. Flora Lewis, *New York Times*, Aug. 6, 1982. The same image appears in Arthur Goldberg's contribution, discussed above, and elsewhere repeatedly. Its origin appears to be Peretz's "Lebanon Eyewitness."

290. For evidence on this matter from Israeli and Lebanese sources, see *Israel in Lebanon*, p. 77

291. Trudy Rubin, *Christian Science Monitor*, Aug. 5, 1982; John Yemma, "Few Palestinians have been able to flee west Beirut," *Christian Science Monitor*, Aug. 9, 1982.

292. John Kifner, *New York Times*, Aug. 14, 1982.

293. Marvine Howe, *New York Times*, Aug. 8, 1982.

294. B. Michael, *Ha'aretz*, Aug. 15, 1982.

295. "Terror tactics"; see note 100.

296. Yigal Sarnah, *Kol Ha'ir*, interview with Meir Pail, Aug. 10, 1982.

297. Martin Peretz, "Lebanon Eyewitness."

298. Aharon Abramowitz, *Ma'ariv Supplement*, June 25, 1982, an interview with the mother of a battalion commander of the paratroopers, killed in action, reporting her son's views; *Israleft News Service*. There was similar testimony from others.

299. Bar-On, "The Palestinian Aspect."

300. Victor Ciegelman, "West Bank View," *New Outlook*, August/September 1982.

301. Tony Clifton, *Monday Morning* (Beirut), Aug. 30-Sept. 5, 1982.

302. Chris Drake, BBC report, quoted in *Monday Morning*, Aug. 23-29, 1982.

303. Gideon Spiro, *Haolam Haze*, Aug. 18, 1982. See *Israel in Lebanon*, p. 57.

304. Douglas Watson, *Baltimore Sun*, June 28, 1982.

305. "Beirut Curtain Call," *New Republic*, Sept. 13, 1982.

306. Martin van Creveld, "Not Exactly A Triumph," *Jerusalem Post Magazine*, Dec. 10, 1982. See also the long interview with former Paratroopers commander Danny Wolf (Rahav), commenting on the decline of the IDF under the Sharon-Eitan regime, which reached its furthest point in the Lebanon war; Amir Oren, *Koteret Rashit*, Jan. 19, 1983.

6

Aftermath

1 A Chapter of Jewish History

"On the eve of the Easter festival of 1903, mysterious rumors were set afloat in Kishinev [capital of Bessarabia] telling of the murder of a Christian servant girl, whose death was ascribed to the Jews... The goings-on in Kishinev on the eve of that Easter bore the earmarks of an energetic activity on the part of some secret organization which was hatching an elaborate fiendish scheme... Printed hand-bills were scattered about in the city, telling the people that an imperial ukase had been published, granting permission to inflict a 'bloody punishment' upon the Jews in the course of the three days of the Christian Passover. The police made no attempt to suppress these circulars, for, as was subsequently brought out, they were in the conspiracy... On the eve of the festival of Passover, the representatives of the Jewish community waited upon the governor and the Chief of Police, praying for protection, and received the cool reply that the necessary instructions had already been given and that the proper measures for their safety had been adopted.

"The conflagration which was openly prepared by the incendiaries broke out at the moment determined upon. On Sunday, April 6, the first day of the Christian Passover and the seventh day of the Jewish holiday, the church bells began to ring at noontime, and a large crowd of Russian burghers and artisans, acting undoubtedly upon a given signal, scattered all over the town, and fell upon the Jewish houses and stores. The bands were preceded by street urchins who were throwing stones at the windows. The rioters, whose number was swelled by these youthful 'fighters,' seeing that the police made no attempt to interfere, began to break into the houses and stores, and to throw the contents on the street where everything was destroyed or plundered by the festive crowd. But even then the police and soldier detachments who were stationed on the streets remained passive, and made no attempt to arrest the rioters. This attitude served in the eyes of the mob as a final proof that the rumors concerning the permission of the Tzar 'to beat the Jews' were correct. An immense riff-raff, in a state of intoxication, crowded the streets, shouting 'Death to the Zhyds! Beat the Zhyds!'

"In the evening looting gave way to killing. The murderers, armed with clubs and knives, assailed the Jews in the cars, on the streets, and in the houses, wounding them severely, sometimes even fatally. Even then, the police and military remained inactive; only when in one place a group of Jews, armed with sticks, attempted to drive off the murderers, the police stepped in at once and disarmed the defenders.

"At ten o'clock in the evening the looting and killing were suddenly stopped. Rumor had it that the general staff of the rioters were holding a meeting concerning the further plan of military operations, and were making arrangements for a systematic butchery. The 'army' soon received the necessary orders, and in the course of the entire day of April 7, from daybreak until eight o'clock in the evening, Kishinev was the scene of bestialities such as find few parallels even in the history of the most barbarous ages... Throughout the entire day, wagons were seen moving in the streets, carrying wounded and slain Jews to the hospitals which had been converted into field-lazarettes. But even this sight did not induce the police to step in... The governor of Bessarabia, von Raaben, who, on the morning of the second day of the pogrom, was waited upon by a Jewish deputation begging for protection, replied that he could do nothing since he had received no instructions from St. Petersburg.

"At last at five o'clock in the afternoon, a telegram was received from Plehve, and at six o'clock large detachments of troops, fully armed, appeared on the central streets. No sooner had the crowd noticed that the soldiers were ready to act than it took to its heels, without a single shot being fired... It is needless to point out that had this readiness of the police and military to attend to their duty been displayed in Kishinev at the inception of the pogrom, not a single Jew would have been murdered nor a single house destroyed. As it was, the murderers and rioters were given a free hand for two days, and the result was that forty-five Jews were slain, eighty-six severely wounded or crippled, five hundred slightly wounded, apart from cases of rape, the number of which could not be determined... As against the enormous number of Jewish victims, there were only two fatalities among the intoxicated rioters."[1]

"A cry of horror rang throughout Russia and the more or less civilized countries of the world when the news of the Kishinev butchery became known." Leo Tolstoy wrote of his

> burning feeling of pity for the innocent victims of the cruelty of the populace, amazement at the bestiality of all these so-called Christians, revulsion at all these so-called cultured people who instigated the mob and sympathized with its actions. But I felt a particular horror for the principal culprit, our Government with its clergy which fosters in the people bestial sentiments and fanaticism, with its horde of murderous officials. The crime committed at Kishinev is nothing but a direct consequence of that propaganda of falsehood and violence which is conducted by the Russian government with such energy... Like the Turkish Government at the time of the Armenian massacres, it remains entirely indifferent to the most horrible acts of cruelty, as long as these acts do not affect its interests.

Meanwhile, "the revelations in the foreign press were of a nature to stagger all Europe and America." There was a judicial investigation, but the trial was conducted "behind closed doors." "By this act, the blood-stained Russian Government refused in advance to rehabilitate itself before the civilized world, which looked upon it as the instigator of the catastrophe." Only the "hired assassins and plunderers from among the lower classes" were tried and condemned, while "the organizers of the butchery and the ring-leaders of the mob were escaping justice," though one "had blown out his brains before the beginning of the trial." Some were sentenced to "hard labor or penal service," but the real ring-leaders in the government, army and police, were never sentenced by any court, again scandalizing the "civilized world."[2] And naturally the other "principal culprits," the clergy and others who conducted "the propaganda of falsehood and violence" that instigated the mob, escaped unscathed, firm in their conviction of moral rectitude and honored in their society.

The catastrophe had a "long-lasting effect" upon the Jews of Russia. "Neither the pogroms at the beginning of the eighties, nor the Moscow atrocities at the beginning of the nineties can compare, in their soul-stirring effect upon Russian Jewry, with the massacre of Kishinev," Dubnow writes. It was a major factor in the great wave of emigration of Jews from Russia in the following years, primarily to the United States, but also to Palestine, including "the teenage founding fathers of Israel."[3]

The greatest poet of the Hebrew national renaissance, Chaim Nachman Bialik, wrote a series of famous poems in which "he portrayed his people's agony, scourging the craven, dumb submission of the victims and calling forth the very indignation of Heaven,"[4] expressing his anguish and despair over this barbaric massacre, in which 45 Jews were brutally murdered under the watchful eyes of the Russian army and police after they had been assured by a higher authority that "the proper measures for their safety had been adopted." In one of these poems Bialik wrote:

> And if there is justice—let it show itself at once! But if justice show itself after I have been blotted out from beneath the skies—let its throne be hurled down forever! Let heaven rot with eternal evil! And you, the arrogant, go in this violence of yours, live by your bloodshed and be cleansed by it.
>
> And cursed be the man who says: Avenge! No such revenge—revenge for the blood of a little child—has yet been devised by Satan. Let the blood pierce through the abyss! Let the blood seep down to the depths of darkness, and eat away there, in the dark, and breach all the rotting foundations of the earth.[5]

The phrase "no revenge for the blood of a little child has yet been devised by Satan" has been repeated many times in Israel in the past years, by Menachem Begin and many others, with reference to the terrorist acts of the "two-legged beasts."

Memories of the barbarous Kishinev massacre with its 45 victims were soon to be aroused in Israel as the Lebanese war came to an end,[6] though not in the United States, which had assured the people of the Sabra and Shatila camps, "praying for protection," "that the necessary instructions had already been given and that the proper measures for their safety had been adopted." And surely not by the clergy and intelligentsia who had, for so long, "fostered bestial sentiments and fanaticism" in their "propaganda of falsehood and violence" of which the massacres were a "direct consequence," as American peacekeeping forces withdrew in violation of their pledge to protect the defenseless population, and the Israeli army at once invaded West Beirut in violation of its pledges and immediately dispatched its minions to conduct a slaughter of Palestinians for which the proper words are lacking if, indeed, the cowardly and brutal murder of 45 Jews in Kishinev was an act with "few parallels even in the history of the most barbarous ages." On the contrary, the "principal culprits" kept silent, or blamed someone else (even the Palestinians), or rushed to the press to assure the world that nothing *they* had done could have helped form policies and attitudes towards the Palestinians that allowed these events to occur. Within Israel itself, there was a real and meaningful expression of anguish on the part of certain sectors of the population. As we have seen, this reaction had the practical effect of reinforcing the trends towards militarization of Israeli society and domination of the occupied territories as it filtered through the ideological and political structures of the United States, which bears primary responsibility for the events we have described, and those to which we now turn.[7]

2 A Glorious Victory

2.1 The Achievements of Operation "Peace for Galilee"

As the end of August 1982 approached, the government of Israel could look with some satisfaction at its achievements. Its domestic opposition was quiet and Begin's popularity was at an all-time high; as Labor cheerlessly observed, "Nothing succeeds like success." The opposition Labor Alignment was effectively neutralized by the widespread understanding that the U.S. had given the "green light." Those who had qualms, and they were many, were unwilling to be more critical of state policy than the paymasters, though there were others who did not bend to this principle and continued to oppose the war with courage and honor, some refusing to serve in the hideous concentration camps or to serve in Lebanon altogether. In the occupied territories, protest over the invasion and resistance to the forthcoming extension of Israeli sovereignty remained high, but, the Israeli leadership hoped, it was not likely to be effective given Israel's proven capacity for harsh repression throughout the period of the 15-year occupation, and, crucially, given the submissiveness and discipline of articulate American opinion, which had permitted all of this to pass virtually unnoticed, even to be lauded as a benign experiment in Arab-Jewish cooperation that was but one aspect of a magnanimity unique in history as Israel marched forward to realize the democratic socialist dream.

The U.S. government remained solidly behind Israel's actions despite occasional disclaimers, and the flow of military and economic aid was actually scheduled to increase, as it soon did. As for public opinion, all was not as it should be, but the main bastions were holding solidly. Much of Europe was appalled. The Socialist International, which had bent over backwards to support Israel in the recent past,[8] sent a delegation to Beirut that returned with words of harsh condemnation. Mario Soares of Portugal, who headed the delegation, described their "impression of horror" at what they saw in Beirut, adding that "the pictures we have seen on French television are less than the reality" in a city that Israel had used as "an experimental ground for...new techniques of bombardment." The French representative, national secretary of the pro-Israel Socialist Party, stated that "one cannot imagine in France, in Europe, what the bombardments of Beirut were like." He also had the impression that the bombardments were "selective," aiming at such targets as the places of residence of the French ambassador and of journalists and political figures, as part of a "methodical" strategy.[9] But the French Socialist Party was soon to return to its protective stance, and in any event, Europe matters little as long as American opinion remains properly disciplined.

In Lebanon itself, the situation also offered much reason for satisfaction on the part of the government of Israel. Its favored candidate, Bashir

Gemayel, had been elected President under Israeli guns; some were concerned that those who had carried out this semi-coup were capable of doing the same in Israel as well—among them, former Chief of Staff Mordechai Gur of the Labor Party; see p. 262—but their voice was that of a shrinking minority. With the PLO removed from Beirut and the political and cultural center of Palestinian nationalism demolished, the problem of increasingly visible PLO moderation—the "veritable catastrophe" that was causing such "panic"—might well be on its way to solution, and there might even be some hope that the PLO would return to the tactics of hijacking planes, terrorist bombing, killing many Jews, and other actions more welcome to the government of Israel according to the rather plausible analysis of Yehoshua Porath, Danny Rubinstein, and others (see pp. 200-1). Furthermore, it should now be even easier than before to dismiss the allegiance of the West Bank *Samidin* to the PLO and their insistence that the path to a negotiated settlement is through Beirut. The few remaining political figures still tolerated by the occupying army, such as Elias Freij, might continue to repeat that "The P.L.O. is the official representative for the Palestinian Arabs," but with the PLO in disarray, little heed need be given to such minor noises from below, particularly as long as they are unheard or dismissed in the United States.[10] Soon the *Samidin* would be nothing more than drugged roaches in a bottle, as the Chief of Staff was to explain shortly after; see p. 130*.

The situation in Lebanon offered still more cause for self-congratulation. In the course of the civil war, a balance of force had been created between the Muslim-Palestinian coalition and the Israeli-backed Maronite and Haddad forces. The removal of the PLO destroyed this balance; power now rested in the hands of Israel's clients, though it still remained to eliminate the last elements of the Muslim-Palestinian coalition, as was done, shortly after the departure of the PLO fighters, with the conquest of West Beirut in violation of the agreement under which the PLO had left. Israel's clients would now be free, it could be hoped, to impose their will by the methods at which they had proven so adept in the past, as in Karantina, Khiyam and Tel al-Zaatar. Things seemed well on their way to the "new order" in Lebanon to which Israel aspired, and the danger of Palestinian self-determination in the occupied territories—the feared "dagger poised at the heart of Israel"—also seemed to have been overcome.

As for the government of the country that had officially been liberated, it announced casualty figures of close to 20,000 killed and over 30,000 wounded, almost 7000 in Beirut where about 80-90% were civilians, very likely underestimates for reasons already discussed. The wounded included a large number of amputees and many victims of cluster and phosphorus bombs, a tribute to American technology and munificence. Many thousands, including much of the remaining teen-age and adult male population of Palestinians and also many thousands of Lebanese and others, were in Israeli concentration camps in Lebanon and Israel where they could be brutalized in peace, with little concern in what Dubnow called "the more or less civilized countries of the world." In the south of Lebanon, the refugee camps had been destroyed by bombardment or bulldozed after the refugees had been removed. The two-legged beasts who had infested the area, most of them since 1948 when they had fled or were driven from their homes, had once again been demoralized and dispersed; their villages demolished, they remained without sustenance, shelter, health and social services, or protection after the male population had been removed. The army of occupation had no plans for them at that time except to "drive them East," in the words of the responsible senior official, Ya'akov Meridor, who was busy denouncing the U.S. and European media, following their "regular policy of toeing the PLO line," for their "lies" about casualties and destruction, and could not concern himself with the fate of the people in his charge. Many had, in fact, been driven East. In these respects too, then, there was ample reason for satisfaction.

Meanwhile, Israeli troops were moving into positions well north of Beirut from which they could launch an attack on Palestinian and Lebanese "terrorists" who had not yet been eliminated, and on the remaining Syrian troops to the north and east. As few could fail to observe, Damascus was within range of Israeli heavy artillery. Further bombings in September destroyed the strategic Beirut-Damascus highway behind Syrian lines, "effectively cutting off Syrian troops west of the central mountain chain from reinforcements and supplies."[11] The basis had been laid for the next stage in dispersing the refugees and extending Israel's regional power, though the plans were soon to be upset by unanticipated factors.

2.2   The Syrian Phase of the War

In this connection, something should be said about a topic so far put aside, the Syrian phase of Israel's Lebanon war. The nearest that we have to a definitive account of this topic was provided in a series of detailed articles by military analyst Ze'ev Schiff in *Ha'aretz*. He dismisses the claim, a "new invention" offered in justification for Operation Peace for Galilee after the fact, that Syria was planning an attack on Israel that was forestalled by Israel's preemptive move. Defense Minister Sharon's claims to this effect, he argues, entirely lack foundation; "it is known today" that the Syrian command had no such plans under present circumstances, and were emphasizing "defensive measures." Phalangist initiatives had led to a Syrian response to protect their lines of communication, something that no army could have failed to undertake. It was the view of Israeli intelligence and others that these Phalangist "provocations" had the "intention of causing us [Israel] to come into military conflict with the Syrians." Further conflict resulted from Sharon's "large plan," namely, to impose his "new order" in Lebanon by "driving the Syrians out of Lebanon" and installing Bashir Gemayel, the head of the Phalangist Lebanese Forces, as President, blocking Syria's anticipated attempt to place its favorite, former Maronite President Suleiman Franjieh, in power as it had done six years before with Elias Sarkis. Recall that the election was scheduled for August-September, quite probably a factor in the timing of the Israeli invasion, a conclusion that Schiff does not draw here (but see pp. 196, 203), but that is reinforced by his analysis. "Syria made efforts to avoid conflict" with Israel, but was unable to do so, because of the very nature of Sharon's "large plan," which was put into effect at once, as the Labor opposition was aware despite a pretense of shock and outrage at Begin's "duplicity" (see chapter 5, section 6.3).

Israel could easily have avoided conflict with Syria, Schiff continues, concentrating its attack on the PLO in the western sector, a project that he seems to regard as legitimate. The Syrians would have "curbed the terrorists" in the areas they controlled as they had done before. "Before the war they warned the terrorists to refrain from actions that would bring Israel into conflict with them [Syria]," and they would have persisted in this policy. The war was not limited in this way because of Sharon's intention "to drive the Syrians from Lebanon" in accord with the "large plan," the establishment of the "new order." Despite its efforts to avoid conflict, Syria was "forced to respond" to Israel's attacks, just as "any other army would have done in their circumstances," as Israel moved "to surround the Syrian army in the Bekaa valley." In fact, the Syrian high command did not comprehend that Israel was bent on attacking Syrian forces. "They only understood too late that the war was not for south Lebanon but rather for all of Lebanon," not "limiting itself to terrorist targets." Syria did not even undertake a mobilization of reserves until June 9 and orders were given not to fire or even to respond to Israeli shelling, Schiff asserts. Israeli forces advancing on Syrian positions barely met with artillery fire at first. "The Syrians remained in defensive positions from the first moment, and if we had wished we could have avoided any large-scale ground fighting against them." There is no truth to Begin's assertion in the Knesset on that Syria rejected Israel's cease-fire request, necessitating an Israeli response.* Syria even refrained from employing its

---

* Returning soldiers told much the same story in the Israeli press. See, for example, *Yediot Ahronot*, July 5, 1982 *(Israeli Mirror)*, where Moshe Savir, who "had been among the conquerors of Beaufort castle" in south Lebanon, reports on the lies told by the Begin-Sharon-Eitan triumvirate, among them their radio appeal to the Syrians to refrain from opening fire, an appeal made after "we had already been given orders to draw the Syrians into the war and to settle accounts with them, irrespective of what they themselves did." See also p. 222.

missiles against Israeli aircraft. Until they were attacked directly on June 9, "not one missile was fired against our aircraft," which were operating freely "in great numbers" in Lebanon. The Israeli attack against the Syrian missiles was unprovoked; it was motivated by the "large plan," since Israeli troops attacking Syrian forces would require air cover. "In all of this there may be military logic, but it is the logic of Sharon's larger strategic plan, aimed at removing the Syrians from Lebanon along with the PLO and placing Bashir Gemayel in power." This plan "in its very essence" necessitated "an intentional military attack" against the Syrians—who, it may be recalled, were in Lebanon under an Arab League mandate that was to expire in July 1982, having initially been at least tacitly welcomed by the U.S. and Israel because they were fighting against the PLO-Muslim coalition.[12]

With this background, Israel's actions on the northern and eastern fronts in late August and early September take on a certain significance, in fact, a rather broad significance, to which we will return in the next chapter.

With regard to Schiff's analysis, two points should be noted. In the first place, he is generally considered to be Israel's most knowledgeable military correspondent and is a military historian of distinction, who has followed the affairs of the IDF at close range from its origins. In general, he is considered the prototypical "moderate" who holds "the middle ground," journalist Nahum Barnea observes, noting that when Peres and Begin appeared in a television debate on the eve of the 1977 elections, they chose Schiff to be the moderator. Second, Schiff regarded the war in Lebanon as a disaster for the State of Israel. Sharon, in his view, "is ruining Israel": Sharon might be a proper commander "for the Tartars" who overran Asia and Eastern Europe under Genghis Khan, but not for Israel.[13]

2.3 The West Falls into Line

Returning to the state of affairs as of late August, the situation in the United States was not as favorable as Israel's leaders might have hoped despite the "green light," the projected aid increases in recognition of Israel's achievements, and the range of apologetics across the broad spectrum already discussed. There had been some erosion of the automatic support for Israeli actions and neglect of its atrocities, a fact that aroused much outrage in circles accustomed to more complete obedience and committed to the doctrine that control over thought and expression must be total, so that even slight deviations, even mere reporting of some of the facts, is an intolerable affront, evidence of a "double standard" if not outright anti-Semitism. But despite the slight departure from the norm, the situation was, in fact, well under control. The basic assumptions of Israeli propaganda were quite widely accepted: Israel had the right to invade Lebanon in "self-defense"; to demolish Palestinian population centers; to destroy what must be destroyed and arrest whoever must be arrested, in the words of the Chief of Staff (see p. 155); to scatter the remaining population; and to bomb Beirut to drive out the PLO hijackers, who were holding the civilian population hostage. The subsequent fate of the two-legged beasts aroused little interest or comment here. If Israel had been driven to harsh actions, it was the fault of the PLO, which had never veered from its single-minded commitment to the destruction of Israel and the fostering of international terrorism, always rejecting U.S.-Israeli offers of a fair political settlement. In the occupied territories, Israel was organizing "moderate" elements, now free from PLO intimidation, and the "radicals" were being silenced. Dissent in the United States was unprecedented, but the center—and a very broad one at that—was holding.

In fact, in the West quite generally Israel was being granted the dispensations ordinarily reserved for Western violence. For example, few eyebrows were raised when Henry Kissinger rambled on in his charmingly empty-headed fashion in the London *Economist*, explaining how thanks to the war some "reasonable Palestinians" might finally "come to a Sadat-like insight that they must co-exist with Israel in some form," though surely not the PLO (which had come to that insight years before, though Kissinger could no more comprehend that fact than he could understand Sadat's peace offer of 1971 or the stance of the Arab states at the time that he was successfully blocking State Department moves towards a political settlement; see pp. 65-6); while as for the PLO, the Reagan plan must not be turned into "a subterfuge for rehabilitating" it or for "introducing the PLO in its present form and with its present concepts on the West Bank" (where these "concepts," as discussed in chapter 3, include a two-state settlement in accordance with the international consensus). One particular sin of the PLO is its persistent attempt "to upset the equilibrium on the West Bank," that is, to oppose the Israeli occupation that Kissinger helped to implant, a clear demonstration of PLO "radicalism." Of course, we should "return to the overwhelming majority of Arabs living on the West Bank and Gaza a controlling voice in facing their own future," while blocking the "rehabilitation" of the PLO, which they regard as their political representative, even those officially designated as "reasonable," e.g., Elias Freij. In short, self-determination along the lines of the traditional American conception: namely, in the form that *we* will determine, since we are plainly the authentic representatives of the Palestinians—as of the Filipinos, the Nicaraguans, the Greeks, the Vietnamese, the Chileans, the Salvadorans, and many others who have been privileged to enjoy our beneficent attentions.

Kissinger also warned that "opposition to Israel must not become a congenital feature of our foreign policy," an imminent threat as all can see. We should not permit Arabs to gain the impression that "across-the-board opposition to Israel is built into us, so to speak," as they might conclude, for example, by looking at the flow of aid. We might "harass" Israel "into emotional and psychic collapse" unless it "feels compassion on. our side, maybe even affection, rather than unremitting pressure." Furthermore, "some Arabs" now "seem to imagine that they can achieve their maximum programme [i.e., destruction of Israel] in return for nothing more than simple recognition of Israel"—a pronouncement that appears to mean that some Arabs feel that they can achieve their goal of destroying Israel by nothing more than recognizing it, a most intriguing concept. And so on, all regarded with at least mock seriousness by his sophisticated international audience.[14]

Kissinger argues that we should oppose "the creation of another radical state with irredentist aims towards both Jordan and Israel," a Palestinian state dominated by the PLO, as "irreconcilable with the stability of the Middle East." A saner view, expressed by Assistant Secretary of State Veliotes, is that a Palestinian "ministate would look at Jordan and Israel as superpowers"[15]—though from this rather different perception he draws the same conclusion: we should oppose such a ministate as harmful to "stability," now because of its weakness rather than its irredentism. We see here an example of the beauty of political orthodoxy, as of certain other religious doctrines: since the desired conclusions are necessary truths, they can be derived from whatever premise we choose to put forth.

While support for Israel at all three levels—diplomatic, material and ideological—remained high, nevertheless the purposes of the invasion were well-understood, at least in some circles. In *Foreign Affairs*, the Israeli-American military historian and strategic analyst Amos Perlmutter wrote that

> Begin and Sharon share the same dream: Sharon is the dream's hatchet man. That dream is to annihilate the PLO, douse any vestiges of Palestinian nationalism, crush PLO allies and collaborators in the West Bank and eventually force the Palestinians there into Jordan and cripple, if not end, the Palestinian nationalist movement. That, for Sharon and Begin, was the ultimate purpose of the Lebanese war.

He does not add that the dream entails crushing the overwhelming majority of the population of the West Bank (the allies and collaborators of the PLO), but perhaps that is implicit; or that the same "dream" is shared in essentials, and was being implemented, by the Labor Party, a fact commonly ignored.

In the same issue, Harold Saunders, Assistant Secretary of State for Near Eastern and South Asian Affairs under Carter and previously a member of the National Security Council staff with responsibility for Middle East matters, writes that

> With a fragmented and dispersed PLO, Israeli leaders foresaw the Palestinian population in the West Bank and Gaza— deprived of outside moral support—coming to accept permanent Israeli control there, in a situation in which much of that Palestinian population could be induced (or gradually coerced) to migrate across the Jordan River into Jordan... Thus, the Israeli-Palestinian War [in Lebanon] was fought mainly over whether an organized Palestinian movement would survive in order to negotiate peace between Israelis and Palestinians as two people with equal rights. It was not fought only to determine how many Palestinian fighters should be where in Lebanon... The Israeli invasion of Lebanon, to repeat, was designed to destroy once and for all any hope among the people of the West Bank and Gaza that the process of shaping the Palestinian people into a nation could succeed. It was designed to break any final resistance to total Israeli control and to pave the way for making life so difficult for those who valued their freedom and political self-expression that they would eventually leave for Jordan.

By the late 1970s, he adds, "there is little question that [support for a West-Bank Gaza state "in land from which Israel had withdrawn under Security Council Resolution 242] remains the mainstream view of the Palestinian people as endorsed by the Palestinian National Congress" of the PLO, a position "reinforced" by the Lebanon war.[16]

Perlmutter envisages a virtual partition of Lebanon, with an Israeli-backed alliance dominated by the Phalange and Haddad holding 2/3 of Lebanon and Syria holding the rest, and a "prolonged Israeli military presence" since "the Christians cannot survive as a political force without the protection and presence of Israel." This might provide "an opportunity for a Syrian-Israeli rapprochement." Syria is a "status quo power," as revealed by its passive acquiescence in the Israeli conquest; in fact, Rabin's Labor government had "somewhat reluctantly" encouraged Syrian occupation of parts of Lebanon and "encouraged Syria to come close to Israel's northern border" so as to "pacify the Israeli-Lebanese border in the same way that the Israeli-Syrian border had been pacified after 1973." As for Sharon, he ousted the Israeli settlers from the Sinai "because, pragmatically, a quiescent Egypt was needed for any future course of action in Lebanon"; and by the time he took over the Defense Ministry, "Israeli generals were already busy planning a large-scale invasion of

Lebanon," planning to reach Beirut from the first moment of the war. As for "the scope of Sharon's New Order in Lebanon and for the Middle East," Perlmutter believes that it virtually excludes a stable Lebanese central government (an unlikely prospect at best because of Lebanon's internal strife), and "the so-called New Order, when looked at imaginatively and correctly, provides some leverage for the United States" to turn Syria towards the Western camp and to "reassert...some U.S. control over events in the Middle East." The U.S. should not, however, act "as the PLO's Salvation Army in West Beirut," he wrote in the summer of 1982. Saunders looked forward to U.S. efforts to bring about "an Israeli-Palestinian peace process," but with little hope, it seems.

So matters stood in late August. In summary, the government of Israel had good reason, in its own terms, to feel satisfied with its achievements, at home, in Lebanon, and also in the United States despite some residual problems. The euphoria was not to last very long, however, and the events of the subsequent weeks were to impose at least a change of timetable, if not of longer-term plans for the "New Order for Lebanon and for the Middle East." We turn to these longer-term questions in the next chapter.

3 The Taste of Victory Turns Sour

The events that followed in September 1982 were traumatic and complex. The construction that seemed so pretty in late August began to crumble, temporarily at least. Reagan's peace initiative, announced on September 1, seemed to steal the fruits of victory from the Israeli government. It called for a freeze on new settlements, some vague form of autonomy short of self-determination for the inhabitants of the occupied territories, and a Jordanian solution. These proposals were sharply in conflict with one primary war aim of the government of Israel: to lay the basis for the extension of Israeli sovereignty over the territories. Meanwhile, conflicts were developing between Israel and Bashir Gemayel, who was assassinated shortly after. Israel at once invaded West Beirut, violating the terms of the agreement negotiated by Philip Habib under which the PLO had left. This aroused only mild criticism in the United States, where the U.S. pledge to Lebanon and the PLO that Israel would not enter Beirut was quickly forgotten, but the massacres that followed were harshly condemned. The crumbling Labor opposition in Israel hoped to receive a new lease on life, and its image as upholding peace and justice and conciliation was hastily resurrected by American supporters of Israel. If only Begin and Sharon, who had destroyed the "beautiful Israel," could be removed, then all would be well. Let us now turn to a closer analysis of these crucial events and their significance.

3.1 Reagan's Peace Plan

Reagan's peace plan called for a settlement freeze and stated that the U.S. would not support new settlements during the transition period. The transition was to lead to a form of "autonomy" in which "domestic authority" would be transferred "from Israel to the Palestinian inhabitants of the West Bank and Gaza." At best, the call for a settlement freeze would have been of limited significance, as was quickly noted in Israel, because of the character of the settlement programs that had been instituted, in part under Reagan's initiative. [17]

Reagan's program was explicitly rejectionist: it excluded the PLO, that is, denied the right of the inhabitants of the territories to select their political representative, thus undermining its own rhetoric concerning "self-government." It also opposed "the establishment of an independent Palestinian state in the West Bank and Gaza," thus rejecting the international consensus and the near-unanimous sentiments of the inhabitants of the occupied territories, including even Israel's chosen quislings. It also stated that the U.S. "will not support annexation or permanent control by Israel"—exactly what the U.S. had been supporting and continued to support after September 1 with the newly increased military and economic aid. The "self-government" to be achieved would be "in association with Jordan." The question of boundaries was left vague. [18] As discussed earlier, Reagan's proposal was somewhat analogous to a hypothetical proposal of 1947 offering "autonomy" to the Jewish community of Palestine, but without a state or the participation of the Zionist Organization, and under the rule of some European country in which their experience had been less than happy. Nevertheless, this rejectionist program was considerably more favorable to the Palestinians than the alternatives that had previously been advanced by those with real power in the region: primarily, the U.S. and Israel. Given the objective constraints established by U.S. power, a case can perhaps be made that the wisest course for the Palestinians would have been to accept the Reagan proposals, thus committing national suicide but at least raising some obstacles to the U.S.-backed Israeli takeover of what remains outside Israel's complete control in the occupied territories.

Reagan's proposals were rejected angrily by the Begin government, which announced that it would have absolutely nothing to do with them. The Reagan plan was therefore stone dead from the first moment, unless the U.S. would have chosen to put some pressure on Israel, or more accurately, to withdraw its material support for Israel's settlement programs in the occupied territories. The U.S. at once made clear that it would not limit this support, and in fact extended it shortly after, increasing aid to new heights while maintaining the unique arrangements that permit U.S. aid to be used without supervision, hence for settlements in the occupied territories (in violation of the aid legislation). In short, the U.S. and Israel immediately killed the Reagan plan.

Obviously the actual facts do not constitute an acceptable version of history. Rather, it must be—whatever the facts—that it was the fault of the Arabs, particularly the PLO, that this noble American endeavor failed, though it is also permissible, within the doctrinal system, to assign a portion of the blame to the boorish Begin with his Oriental Jewish constituency. Crucially, no blame may be attached to the United States or to the western-oriented Labor Party, which is preserving the legacy of the "beautiful Israel." These tasks were carried out with customary dispatch and elegance. In the subsequent months, the burden of discussion in the U.S. was shifted to the PLO and Hussein, on the assumption that the fate of the Reagan plan rested on PLO authorization of Hussein to take part in negotiations over the plan that Israel had rejected out of hand with American support. The required conclusion was established without noticeable difficulty while the actual facts of the matter were dispatched to their deserved location, Orwell's memory hole.

A few points of clarification may be in order. First, Israel would have been more than pleased to have Hussein join negotiations over the plan it had rejected, thus tacitly accepting the crucial Israeli principle that the Palestinians have no national rights, that they "are not a party to the conflict" as Israeli courts have ruled and "have no role to play" in any peace settlement, in the words of Labor Party dove Abba Eban (see p. 52). Then Israel could have proceeded to take over the territories, with constant U.S. support, while the negotiations dragged on meaninglessly, or perhaps its extension of sovereignty might even be ratified in some form. No other outcome was possible, given American support for a Greater Israel, which persisted, in fact was reinforced in the months that followed. Second, it should be noted that if the PLO had adapted itself more successfully to the norms of western hypocrisy, pursuing a more intelligent diplomatic course, this would have marginally complicated the task faced by American propagandists: namely, to show that the failure of the plan was the fault of the Arabs and the PLO. The problems they would then have faced would have been comparable to the problems posed by Sadat's 1971 peace offer or the two-state settlement proposed by the PLO and the Arab states in January 1976; that is, it might have taken a day or two to restore the Party Line to full effectiveness. It is difficult to imagine any other outcome, despite much nonsense that has been written about the matter. Let us now review the subsequent events, which followed their predictable course.

Reagan's proposals, while flatly inconsistent with the Likud program, did lend themselves to an interpretation that is at least partially in accord with Labor's rejectionist stance, and were received with cautious approval by the Labor opposition. As we have seen, the leaders of the

Labor Party also made it clear that the program was completely unacceptable to them, but this conclusion was expressed either in the Hebrew press or in circumlocutions which, it was rightly assumed, would be ignored by their well-disciplined American audience. The plan also evoked a partially favorable response by a number of Arab states and the PLO. The Palestine National Council, the governing body of the PLO, met a few months later, in February 1983, and reached a compromise position on the matter. One senior PLO official quoted in the *New York Times* described the Council's stance as "saying yes and no at the same time" to the Reagan plan. PLO spokesman Ahmed Abdel Rahman said that the PLO would continue to support the Arab peace plan adopted in Fez in September 1982, which endorsed the international consensus, calling for a two-state settlement and peaceful coexistence among Israel, the Palestinian state in the West Bank and Gaza, and the other states of the region. The Council also declared that it "envisages the future relationship with Jordan to be a confederation between two independent states," one Palestinian and one Jordanian.[19]

In fact, the PLO reaction was rather similar to that of the opposition Labor Party in Israel: neither acceptance nor outright rejection, with room for maneuver to adjust the terms of Reagan's proposal to their own wishes—the international consensus in the case of the PLO, the rejectionist Allon Plan in the case of the Labor Party. Furthermore, the PLO position appears to be closer to the literal sense of the Reagan plan than the rejectionist stance of the Labor party, though the plan is so vague that one cannot state this with any security.

Commentary on the Reagan plan in the United States was highly favorable, including such predictable responses as that of the *New York Times*, explaining that the U.S. government is now working to persuade the Arab states and "Palestinians who will listen that the P.L.O's rejection of Israel and reliance on terror are at a bloody dead end" and that "such extremists" as the PLO "must no longer be held out by the Arab League as the 'sole' negotiators for Palestinian rights." A brief look at their own files would have sufficed to reveal the intellectual and moral quality of these remarks, and the fuller history should not have been entirely beyond their reach. As for Israel, its "true spirit" will "be revealed," the *Times* assured its readers, if the Arab leaders "offer Israel firm security guarantees in exchange for an unthreatening Palestinian domain in the West Bank and Gaza." The certainty of the *Times* editors was undiminished by the fact, which once again they suppress, that any such notion has consistently been rejected in the clearest and most unequivocal terms by both major political groupings in Israel and also by the U.S., as in the case of the U.S. veto of the January 1976 Security Council resolution to this effect, a resolution backed by the "confrontation states" and the PLO, actually prepared by the PLO if we can believe the current President of Israel, its

1976 UN Ambassador. "The Israelis who marched into Lebanon have never heard the word peace except from Egypt," the *Times* added, with comparable veracity. See chapter 3.

The *Times*'s harshest critic of Israel's expansionist policies, Anthony Lewis, wrote that in its "wisdom" and "shrewdness," Reagan's initiative "has set the agenda for peace" and that it should appeal to "the sensitive democracy of Israel" as shown by the fact that it was "quickly welcomed" by the leader of the Labor Alignment, Shimon Peres. However, though Lewis and others who commented similarly did not discuss the point, Peres was adamantly and unequivocally opposed to the program as Lewis outlines it: namely, transition to Palestinian self-rule in the West Bank and Gaza Strip without "Israeli control over that land." In fact, Peres regards any proposl that entails loss of such control as "threaten[ing] Israel's very existence" (see p. 75*), among many other statements to the same effect, a position from which he has never deviated. Thus Peres "welcomed" the plan in a rather special sense: with an interpretation that is quite inconsistent with its meaning, at least as Lewis understands it.

Comment elsewhere was similar. Reagan's peace proposals, whatever they meant exactly ("Never mind the details," as the *Times* editors put it), were taken as the basis for further discussion among right-thinking people. The general response served to eliminate the international consensus with its intolerable assumption that Palestinians have the same human rights as Jews, while removing from sight the actual diplomatic history with its record of the extreme rejectionist stance of both Labor and Likud, and crucially, the United States. But that, by now, is familiar fare.

The PLO National Council met in February and gave its official response to the Reagan plan, and in April Jordan announced that it had not received PLO authorization to represent the Palestinians and therefore would not enter the negotiations. These events gave the media a further opportunity to display their assumptions and insights. After the February PLO National Council meetings, the *New York Times* delivered an editorial reprimand under the heading "The P.L.O. Versus the Palestinians," declaring that what the PLO "really rejects is reality, diplomacy and, as always, Israel." It has once again "betrayed" the cause of the Palestinians. A Palestinian state in the occupied territories, "if ever attainable, is certainly not attainable now... By demanding the impossible, the P.L.O. continues to obstruct the plausible: self-government for a million Palestinians"—what the term may mean, the *Times* does not say ("never mind the details," especially when it is someone else's life that is at stake). The international consensus is thus dismissed as "impossible"—as indeed it is, in the face of U.S. rejectionism. The *Times* adds that "even if a small, new Palestinian nation were desirable, it could only evolve over time"—there is no Palestinian nation, the *Times* pronounces, echoing the Likud and Labor Party, mimicking Arab extremists who reject Jewish claims to national rights (a "small, new Jewish nation may not be desirable," some anti-Semite might declare). The PLO is "irrelevant," since it does not conform to U.S. wishes.[20]

What the *Times* fails to say is as revealing as its own words. Thus, Israel is not "irrelevant" even though its rejection of the Reagan plan is far more extreme than that of the PLO. The Labor opposition is not "irrelevant"—indeed, it is the hope of the future—even though its reaction to the Reagan plan is approximately on a par with that of the PLO, and its position is in clear and explicit contradiction to the "self-government for a million Palestinians" which the *Times* professes to advocate. The United States is not "irrelevant," though it gave the coup de grace to the Reagan plan by continuing—in fact, increasing—its support for settlement in the occupied territories. Other commentary in the press was not very different at the time, and remained so in coming months.

The *Times* editors might argue that to criticize them along these lines is unfair, since a crucial premise has been omitted which serves to eliminate the absurdities, distortion of the historical record, egregious double standard and blatant inconsistencies: namely, that the task of the "newspaper of record" is to be a servant of external power, an outlet for state propaganda. On this assumption, the stance of the editors makes perfect sense: the U.S. government has determined that Israel is to be supported as a "strategic asset" and that the inhabitants of the conquered territories have no valid claim to the human rights accorded to Jews. Given the overriding principle just enunciated, then, the *Times* reaction is quite logical. The *Times* cannot fairly be accused of a double standard, as in the previous comments, since it is consistently following its single standard of service to the state.

On April 10, 1983, Jordan announced that it had not received the authorization it has requested from the PLO, and that "we leave it to the P.L.O. and to the Palestinian people to choose the ways and means for the salvation of themselves and their land, and for the realization of their declared aims in the manner they see fit." The *New York Times* pronounced the Reagan plan "a worthy but tragic failure." "King Hussein rejected coexistence not with Israel but with the P.L.O."; he "proved Yasir Arafat incapable of compromise." Israel, which had "predicted failure for Mr. Reagan's plan from the start," now "feels vindicated for its resistance to a West Bank deal." In the news columns, where editorializing is more effective since it is slightly concealed under a mask of objectivity, David Shipler explained that "no tangible alternative exists to the [Israeli] Government's determination to hold the West Bank forever." Various Labor Party spokesmen are quoted as saying that "There's no one to yield the West Bank to," "Jordan still hasn't succeeded in disconnecting herself from the extremist Arab world," etc. The "moderate noises" in the Arab world have been shown to be meaningless, Shipler concludes, and in

Israeli Government circles "there was a strange irony of bitter satisfaction in having known all along, more clearly than the Americans could ever understand, that the Arabs were too hateful to negotiate with and recognize Israel." Begin is vindicated: "there is nothing now to challenge him. He stands surrounded by a vacuum."

Obviously, in *New York Times* news reports, it cannot be observed that there is in fact someone "to yield the West Bank to" (and also the Gaza strip, long tacitly conceded to Israel by the *Times*), namely, the population, which has clearly indicated that its political representative is the PLO. Similarly, it cannot be reported that the Reagan plan, which according to Shipler was "torpedoed" by "Arab intransigence," was in fact torpedoed by the U.S. when it at once confirmed its intention to support Israel's rejection of its own rejectionist plan.

The *Times* also added a lesson in political theory and history. "Israel's assault in Lebanon," the editors explained, had "dramatized the impotence of the PLO," a version of the new Arthur Goldberg theory of political legitimacy (see p. 272). Nevertheless, "the P.L.O. remains frozen in fantasy, of victory over Israel culminating in a Palestinian state." Like all other Arabs, Sadat was at first loyal to the "pan-Arab cause," and in the service of this "ideological commitment," he went to war in 1973, establishing himself as "the faithful heir of Nasser's pan-Arabism." "Only then could he escape the ideological stranglehold of the P.L.O. and break ranks with the Arab League." But the other Arabs, and crucially the PLO, refuse any settlement short of "victory over Israel" so that "Americans, for all their zeal" for political accommodation, can do nothing. Since these are the "facts" as determined by the Party Line, it is irrelevant that Sadat offered Israel a peace treaty in 1971 (with no mention of Palestinian national rights, during the period when he still could not "escape the ideological stranglehold of the P.L.O."), an offer rejected by Israel with U.S. backing; that Sadat went to war in 1973 after warning repeatedly that the U.S. and Israel gave him no choice with their refusal of a political solution and with the Labor Party settlement program in northeastern Sinai; that the Arab states and the PLO subsequently made repeated offers of political settlement, e.g., the January 1976 two-state proposal prepared by the PLO, furiously denounced by Israel, and vetoed by the U.S.; etc., as described in chapter 3. All of this is beside the point; it is as "irrelevant" as the PLO, or the Palestinians in the conquered territories, for the loyal priesthood of the state religion.

The *New York Times* does permit itself to refer to Israel's rejection of the Reagan plan, though the U.S. is above criticism. In contrast, the *New Republic* attributes the failure of this "bold American initiative" entirely to the PLO, which will be satisfied with nothing short of the surrender of Tel Aviv, and to Hussein's cowardice. Naturally it cannot mention the Labor Party's interpretation of the Reagan Plan—to understand that would require half a minute's thought—but it is interesting that it cannot even bring itself to mention the government of Israel's rejection of the plan. Nor is the United States subject to any criticism for offering still another rejectionist plan and then offering Israel full support for its immediate rejection of it; the failure was "no fault of the United States." The editors further explain that only a "willful misreading of the facts" could lead to the "paradoxical" idea that the U.S. should invoke "economic sanctions to stop Israeli settlements on the West Bank" (to translate into real world terms, that the U.S. should stop paying Israel to establish these settlements). These settlements "are not an obstacle to peace in the Middle East," but are rather "Hussein's overriding *inducement* to enter negotiations." It presumably follows that we should offer Israel even more support for its rapidly expanding settlement program, to strengthen the inducement.[21]

These reactions approximately delimit the range of articulate reaction to the failure of the rejectionist Reagan plan that had been killed in early September by Israel's rejection with U.S. support. The task of constructing a more acceptable history was therefore successfully concluded, with admirable efficiency.

3.2   The Israeli Response

Returning to September 1, 1982, it was to be expected that Israel would undertake some action to deflect any pressure to consider the Reagan proposals and to reduce the likelihood of conciliatory Arab moves that would induce the usual "panic." There were, in fact, two immediate responses, one well-publicized, the other less so.

3.2.1 The Incorporation of the Occupied Territories

The well-publicized response of the Begin government was its immediate announcement that in defiance of Reagan's request, many new settlements would immediately be established in "Judea and Samaria."*

---

* Similarly, on the same day that Jordan announced that it would not join in Reagan's "peace initiative," "Israeli officials revealed plans for massive Jewish settlement in the occupied West Bank in defiance of Reagan's call for a freeze on new outposts," while expressing "oblique satisfaction" that the Reagan "peace process has suffered a severe blow." The plan, formulated by the World Zionist Organization, called for 57 new settlements in the West Bank and Gaza within four years, and was announced two days after the U.S. "indicated it would pressure Israel to halt settlements to get Hussein into the Mideast peace process." Congress responded in the customary fashion. A House Foreign Affairs subcommittee headed by Democrat Lee Hamilton voted to increase the military and economic aid requested by the Reagan administration for 1984 to even higher levels, without opposition. The Administration made no effort to block the increase. Yuval Elizur, *Boston Globe*, April 11 (Jerusalem); *New York Times*, April 14, 1983. For further details on the World Zionist Organization plan, see David Richardson, *Jerusalem Post*, April 10,

Within a few days, a headline in *Ha'aretz* read: "The Construction of Seven New Settlements has been Authorized in Judea and Samaria," while the subheading reports the government's announcement that "with no connection to the Reagan plan, a new settlement will be established in the northern part of the Gaza Strip." On September 2, Amos Levav reported in *Ma'ariv* that "a new city and four towns will be established in Samaria." In fact, just prior to the announcement of the Reagan plan, "the Ministers of Finance and Development, Mr. Yoram Aridor and Professor Yuval Ne'eman, worked out yesterday methods of raising 500 million Shekels for development activities in Judea and Samaria." In a significant parallel move, Justice M. Ravid "ruled categorically that Israeli companies registered in Israel but operating primarily in the territories are exempt from taxation." Two new settlements (one a kibbutz) were announced in the Golan Heights; and five new Nahal (paramilitary) settlements were announced in Samaria.[22]

Levav reviewed plans laid down by the Zionist Organization Settlement Branch to settle 400,000 Jews in Samaria by 2010, in the planned city and towns; there were 5000 at the time. The Arab population is expected to reach 5-700,000. The development plan includes six highways that will break up the area, circumventing Arab cities such as Nablus. The Arab population will be confined in a "limited area in the heart of the region," at double the current population density. Various measures will be adopted to prevent the expansion of Arab towns and villages, including road construction, building bans, and intensive efforts to purchase lands for Jewish settlement. A Defense Ministry official in charge of settlement confirmed that these plans were already being put into effect in Judea and Samaria.

A few months later the government announced another step towards putting these plans into effect: the "Green Patrols" will be extended to the West Bank.[23] The Green Patrols were established under the Rabin (Labor) government with alleged ecological concerns, under the "Authority for the Preservation of Nature" headed by General (Res.) Avraham Yoffe, a Greater Israel enthusiast. They were directed by Ariel Sharon during his tenure as Minister of Agriculture under the first Begin government, gaining notoriety for their cruelty as they turned to terrorizing Bedouins in the Negev (Israeli citizens who serve in the armed forces, for what that may matter) to prevent them from encroaching on "national lands," that is, lands reserved for Jewish use. Working together with the Border Guards and police, they forcefully evacuated Bedouins from their

1983. The plan is intended to bring the Jewish population of the West Bank to 1.3 million in 30 years, by vast government subsidies and "severe restrictions on construction in Israel's main urban centres..." It is, of course, tacitly assumed that the American taxpayer will bear the cost; a reasonable assumption, given the history and the U.S. government reaction. See also p. 65.

homes to areas where they are to be concentrated, terrorizing women and children, shooting animals, destroying tents, and in general behaving in the manner that has typified the bloody and brutal career of their director from its origins in the early 1950s.[24] Now they are to turn their attention to the West Bank as well. Barel reports that they will be concerned with "illegal construction by Arabs in state lands or areas intended for [Jewish] settlements." The "state lands" are those that have been taken over by Israel under one or another legal ruse, to satisfy the needs of American civil libertarians. Shortly after, the government announced that the new "Land Patrol," similar in character to the "Green Patrol," will "take action to destroy structures built without an appropriate permit" (permits are regularly denied to Arabs), and to prevent the "increasing Arab movement of settlement on state lands," which are to be reserved for Jews in "Judea and Samaria." See note 23. It can be predicted with fair confidence that these Patrols, operating in their customary manner, will expedite what the approved history books will describe as "the voluntary sale of lands" by Arabs who have so far proven recalcitrant, and in general will act to ensure that Israel will take what it wants from the helpless *Samidin*, while the U.S. remains silent and provides the funds.

In a statement on Israeli radio dismissing the Reagan Plan immediately after it was announced, Defense Minister Sharon stated: "Not only will Israel not accept it, it will not discuss it." Reagan's plan has "no chance," Sharon continued, and "The United States could have saved itself a lot of embarrassment and frustration" by not proposing it. "In the end the United States will have no choice but to back down because its plan cannot be implemented." Meanwhile Jordanian and PLO sources, while expressing interest in the plan though with reservations, remained skeptical about the Administration's determination. One Jordanian stated "that unless the United States showed the same forcefulness in acts that Mr. Reagan had shown in words, 'nobody in the region will take it seriously'." Another added the following comment, "reflecting official Jordanian thinking":

> The crucial question is whether Mr. Reagan has the will and the power to back up his words. If Sharon starts a new series of settlements tomorrow, will Washington stop arms supplies or financial aid to Israel, will it go to the Security Council, recognize the P.L.O.?[25]

The question was surely rhetorical, and the answer to it was given very quickly. Israel "started a new series of settlements," going out of its way to express its contempt for the settlement freeze request. And Reagan responded, as we have seen, by advocating an aid increase while maintaining the arrangements that permit the funds to be diverted to settlement in the occupied territories (as they would be, in some manner, arrangements or not), only to have the terms of the aid improved still further by Congressional liberals. The rational response to these events, given a few weeks later, has already been quoted from the *Jerusalem Post:* "the American Government has been financing the very policies it denounces with such consistency that one doesn't have to be an Arab to wonder if the denunciations are sincere."[26] The following months led to increasing conflict between Israel and the U.S. at the rhetorical level and even occasional direct military confrontation between U.S. marines and the IDF in Beirut. The verbal response of the U.S. government was critical, while at the same time it proposed that the phenomenal level of military aid for 1983 be maintained for the fiscal year 1984, thus indicating its true intentions, while Congress moved to increase the aid still further as usual.*

In case Americans didn't get the point, Reagan's settlement freeze request evoked a virtual frenzy of announcements and advertisements about new settlements and other developments in the occupied territories. By the year's end the projected population in Judea and Samaria by 2010 had risen to 1.3 million, according to the calculation of the head of the Jewish Agency's settlement department, Mattityahu Drobles. This should yield a Jewish majority, he added, when we take into account the expected "emigration of Arabs from the territory." In early December, the government announced its plans to build 35 additional urban settlements in Judea and Samaria in addition to those already publicized, and shortly after, Deputy Minister of Agriculture Michael Dekel raised this figure to 42 new settlements, most of them urban, in the next four years.[27] Meanwhile Minister of Science and Development Yuval Ne'eman announced that Samaria will become Israel's Silicon Valley, with "the most advanced section of Israeli industry" concentrated there, and a new "science city" established near the new town of Ariel in the center of Samaria, where the Arab population is concentrated. Other industrialists are also "streaming into Samaria," including a French-financed electronics factory, military industry, and many others. Industry is encouraged to move there by the "easy development loans and even grants" from the government (ultimately, the U.S. government). Amnon Rubinstein "demonstrated" that all of this "is in contradiction to the Fourth Geneva Convention, which Israel signed,"[28] but such considerations may be left to those who are now derided in Israel as "beautiful souls."

Meanwhile, other regions were not being neglected. On the first anniversary of the virtual annexation of the Golan Heights, *Ha'aretz*

---

* Bernard Weinraub, *New York Times*, Feb. 5, 1983. See p. 348*. The timing of the proposal for the 1984 fiscal year was striking, coming as it did at a point of considerable diplomatic conflict between the U.S. and Israel over the fate of Lebanon and immediately after a well-publicized incident when an American marine drew his pistol to stop movement of Israeli tanks into an area that the marines understood to be under their control.

observed that 1000 settlers had moved in and efforts were being made to bring 5000 more in four new settlements now planned. And in the Gaza strip, about 800 million shekels of the national budget have been invested in the past 6 years for 8 settlements with 300 settlers, with a ninth being planned along with a large tourist center. Asked at a press conference about the huge investment for so few settlers, Housing Minister David Levi responded that "there are national-political aims which a state may invest in not on the basis of the number of settlers, but according to its need to develop these places in our country,"[29] a policy that may be undertaken with particular dispatch when the "investment" is provided by a generous donor from abroad.

The fate of Gaza is generally ignored in discussion of the occupied territories, perhaps because it has already been tacitly granted to Israel. The Gaza region was "pacified" with extraordinary brutality by Ariel Sharon under the Labor government in the early 1970s. Since then, Israel has ruled with an iron hand. As an indication, the military courts opened 3853 new cases in the year April 1980 to March 1981, having found 3458 people "guilty" and 180 innocent in the preceding year. The domain of the military courts under what is called "the civilian administration" is quite broad, extending, for example, to merchants who refuse to pay special value-added taxes that they regard as reflecting Israeli claims to sovereignty. Half the working population—about 40,000 people—travel to work in Israel,* some with a working day from 3AM to 8PM, because, although Arabs are encouraged to perform the "dirty work" at extremely low wages in the Jewish state (in fact, conditions are designed so that there are few alternatives), they are not permitted to sleep there (see pp. 140-1). These official figures are surely an underestimate, as is indicated, for example, by the occasional study of illegal child labor.

The Gaza strip is vastly overcrowded and the population is rising rapidly. No opportunities are provided for development. On the contrary, the only land reserves have been expropriated for potential Jewish use. Since the only means of survival are service in Israel's cheap labor force, and since regular commuting is virtually impossible, workers find ways to sleep illegally in Tel Aviv and elsewhere. In Tel Aviv, each worker is picked up by the police several times a year on the average. Workers sleep in fruit stalls in the open markets or in rotting rooms or cellars in slums where they are lined up wall-to-wall, sleeping in their work clothes with no sanitary facilities or showers, waiting for the knock of the police. The rough estimate is that thousands of Arab workers live this way, though no

---

* Danny Tsidkoni, *Davar*, Jan. 16, 1983. There is little reporting from the region, as Tsidkoni explains, in part because the military administration regards journalists as "the enemy" and keeps them away. His report is based on "official information" of a sort rarely released.

one knows. While the police are empowered to prevent Arabs from sleeping in Tel Aviv, there are no laws establishing minimal conditions for their survival.

Within the Gaza Strip itself, the most serious problem is water. Local sources are already overused, leading to increase in salinity and other contamination which threatens to become a "catastrophe." To prevent this catastrophe, water utilization is controlled and local Arabs are punished if they go beyond their ration or dig wells. But, Rafael Gaon reports, "the law concerns only the former [i.e., Arab] residents of the region. The new settlers [Jews]—that is a different story entirely." For their projects— e.g., profitable raising of fruit for the European market—local water supplies are provided in quantities far beyond anything available for Arab agriculture or other Arab use. Apart from the profitability for the Israeli economy (to which the captive market also contributes), this has the added advantages of compelling local Arabs to serve as a superexploited labor force for Israeli enterprises (including kibbutzim), and of permitting foreign visitors to be amazed by Israel's remarkable achievements in making the desert bloom. In short, the usual story—for the Arab citizens of Israel itself, the drugged roaches in the occupied territories, and perhaps, before too long, the residents of the "North Bank" as well.[30]

Like the industrialists, many Israeli citizens are being drawn to "Judea and Samaria" with their empty spaces (the Arabs being properly confined to "limited areas"), cheap land, and generous government loans and grants. Leah Etgar describes how, particularly since Reagan's call for a settlement freeze, the roads to Samaria are clogged as families drive out to tour the area on the Sabbath, "a national sport," in endless rows of cars. There are many Arab villages, but one driver said that there is "no reason to be afraid of them." "Once they threw a stone in Kalkylia, and after that got their market closed down for two weeks. Now they don't even peep outside." Just *Samidin*, trying to hold on to what they have left as the strangers walk through their walls. Besides, there are plenty of Border Guards, so the pleasant family outings will not be disturbed.

Many of the families are searching for land or houses in the new settlements that are springing up everywhere, so rapidly that often only the local Arabs can direct the drivers to them. One particular tourist attraction is a mansion on a hill belonging to Moshe Ser, a wealthy graduate of a religious youth movement. Tourists watch the "Arab workers rushing back and forth, carrying mountains of cement"; the Rabbis have no doubt found an appropriate dispensation to permit the beasts of burden to work on the Sabbath. Here and in the surrounding areas buyers are helped with government funds. "Whenever the money runs out, the Defense Minister comes to visit us with a group of Americans," one middleman in the new settlement of Karnei Shomron explains. "He climbs on Moshe Ser's hill and shows them how near Natanya [in

Israel] is to the guns. That persuades them and they pull out the cheque books." In such ways wealthy American Jews are enabled to fulfill their fondest dream: to contribute to turning Israel into South Africa.*

Israeli soldiers, meanwhile, continue to report their current activities and the attitudes of their officers: arbitrary search and imprisonment, looting, punishment, degradation, general harassment of the population. An IDF officer, a man of considerable culture, breaks into a discussion of a Mahler symphony with this comment to his troops: with regard to the local Arab population,

> There are two alternatives, to live with them or to destroy them. Personally I hate them. They stink. They do not share our culture. They sleep with goats. It is necessary to vaporize them, to turn them to a gas.[31]

Once again one observes the curious, almost pathological drive to imitate the posturing of those we do not "dare to mention by name" (as Abba Eban put it in his comments quoted earlier), to the point of grotesque caricature.

The reaction to all of this in the United States was to increase the funding that makes it possible. One reason is that what is happening in the occupied territories is not really happening, as Jeane Kirkpatrick explained after a visit to Israel: contrary to what has been reported at length in the Israeli press, the U.S. Ambassador to the United Nations "said Israeli settlements on the predominantly Palestinian West Bank were not on the verge of changing the region's character."[32] Another reason may be the one explained by Henry Kissinger: we must show Israel "compassion" and "maybe even affection" or we might "harass it into emotional and psychic collapse." Fortunately, the *Samidin* are a tougher breed, so no such solicitude is required with regard to them.

The fact that Israel reacted to President Reagan's call for a settlement freeze with a huge expansion in the settlement program was partially

---

* Israel has recently devised a method to enable them to fulfill this dream more directly. At a meeting organized by Americans for a Safe Israel in New York in March 1983, Israeli government officials outlined to 300 prominent American Jews the ways in which they could purchase land on the West Bank themselves, without moving there. A brochure entitled *Purchasing Land in Samaria* explains how Arab lands can be bought by Americans through an Israeli institution established in the West Bank "in areas to be developed in the near future." It is a good investment, given the vast government (ultimately, U.S. government) subsidies and the cheap land—which will remain "cheap," and "available," thanks to the Land Patrols, the Border Guards, and other mechanisms of persuasion, no doubt. The State Department professed to be "shocked." Rowland Evans and Robert Novak, *Boston Globe*, April 9, 1983. In a letter to the *Boston Globe*, three officers of Americans for a Safe Israel deny that any Israeli government official discussed the program (it was a private organization, they claim) and state that Arabs in Judea and Samaria "are jumping at an opportunity" to sell their lands. Michael I. Teplow, Mark Espinola, and Josef E. Teplow, letter, *Boston Globe*, May 2, 1982. On the facts concerning the willingness to sell land, see p. 105.

reported here. It must have made the President feel rather powerful, given that the only precedent for such an upsurge in settlement was in response to his earlier pronouncement that settlement in the occupied territories is not illegal, as had previously been maintained. See also p. 348*.

3.2.2 The March on West Beirut

There was also a second Israeli response to the President's peace initiative, one of much greater short-term significance than the expansion of settlements. On September 3 and 4, Israeli forces crossed the cease-fire lines, violating the Habib agreements that had just been reached under which the PLO had departed from Beirut. They moved towards the Sabra and Shatila "refugee camps"—actually urban neighborhoods, now surrounded by the expanded city of Beirut. The Israeli forces cleared mines and established observation posts overlooking the camps, which had been heavily damaged by the bombardment from early June. "Observers noted that the Israeli road-clearing operation might have been aimed at clearing a path for a later advance by an armored column on the Sabra and Chatilla refugee camps."

On September 2, Lebanese national police had taken control of most of West Beirut peaceably as leftist militiamen voluntarily withdrew. "Lebanese forces rumbled through the bombed-out streets in trucks, collecting ammunition and weapons from Palestine Liberation Organization depots," now abandoned, though some had been turned over to the Lebanese Muslim Mourabitoun militia. The commander of the Mourabitoun, Ibrahim Koleilat, said he had "agreed to withdraw and 'dilute our military appearance' in an attempt to give national reconciliation a chance," though his men would not turn in their weapons until Israel pulled out of Lebanon.[33] As was soon to be learned, the Israeli penetration beyond the cease-fire lines was not an innocent one. It was largely ignored at the time, and also in the reconstruction of events after the subsequent massacres; it is, for example, not mentioned in the Israeli government Kahan Commission Report, to which we return.

Israel was not satisfied with the new arrangements in West Beirut:

> Israeli officials have said that the Mourabitoun, the largest Moslem paramilitary organization here, must leave the Lebanese capital because it is the P.L.O's staunchest Lebanese ally... Moslems were outraged by the Israeli demand and rallied to the Mourabitoun's side. Moslem leaders, including moderates such as former Prime Minister Saeb Salam, said Israel wanted to empty Lebanon of its Moslem inhabitants.[34]

Salam's reported comment is too strong, but its general import was to the point. What Israel wanted was to leave the "terrorists"—a term now extended to Palestinians and all Lebanese who were allied with them—

under the domination of its Lebanese clients, the murderous Phalange, Haddadists, Guards of the Cedars, and Chamounist forces. With the PLO gone and the balance of force that had been achieved broken, the Muslim population was now to be at their mercy, in the New Order. Israel's insistence on disarming the last remaining paramilitary force of the "terrorists" would remove the final obstacle to a renewal of massacres such as those at Karantina and Tel al-Zaatar in 1976, or Khiyam in 1978, the last directly under Israeli military occupation. The demand that PLO "allies" leave Beirut simply reflected Israel's not-so-hidden agenda in Lebanon: to ensure the rule of minority Christian groups allied with Israel, a goal that dates back to the first days of the establishment of the state, indeed before, as we have seen.

The significance of Israel's moves was well-understood by the potential victims. The Sunni-dominated Muslim "National Movement" held that its weapons were needed "for the struggle to end Israeli occupation here." The "leading Shiite Moslems have expressed a similar settlement," Hijazi adds. Nabih Berri, head of the Shiite militia Amal that fought alongside the PLO, "has said that if the Israelis do not leave 'we would become the new Palestinians who will fight them'." "A genuine Lebanese is the one who fights Israel," he added, warning that a peace treaty signed under Israeli guns would "lead to partitioning Lebanon." And the spiritual head of the Shiites, the largest of Lebanon's religious groups, "issued a religious edict declaring that collaboration with Israel is a sacrilege." Once again, the people who had just been liberated were failing to express their gratitude for their salvation, though as we have seen, true believers here continued to uphold staunchly the doctrines of the faith, as convinced about what they had seen on their guided tours as were earlier visitors observing happy peasants in the Gulag. See chapter 5, section 8.2.2.

3.3   Ungrateful Clients

Meanwhile, things were not going well between Israel and its chosen candidate for President, Bashir Gemayel. Whatever else Gemayel may have been, he was a Lebanese nationalist and intended to maintain Lebanon's position within the Arab world. There had long been a split within the Lebanese Maronite community over the question of alliance with the Zionist movement against the local Muslim majority, dating back 40 years, as we have seen. The split appears to have re-emerged in August 1982. Although the Phalange had welcomed the Israeli invasion, they had held back from direct participation in it. There were two probable reasons. The first is that it was much more convenient, and safer, to rely on their Israeli "mercenaries" (in Ze'ev Schiff's phrase) with their overwhelming firepower rather than to face Palestinian fighters directly; their courage could be manifested later after the fighting forces had departed. The second reason is that Gemayel probably did intend, as he asserted, to unify Lebanon with Muslim support. Israel had assumed that Gemayel, whom they had placed in power, would be "their man." By early September, however, only a few days after his election as President, "disappointment was increasing in Jerusalem" concerning Gemayel, the Israeli press reported, for several reasons: he had refused to sign an imposed peace treaty and had threatened to bring Major Saad Haddad, Israel's puppet in the south, to trial on charges of desertion from the Lebanese army.[35]

Citing "informed security sources," Ze'ev Schiff reported that "the threat of the new Lebanese government to bring Major Haddad to trial is a hint to Israel that the new regime under Bashir Gemayel strongly opposes Israel's plans to establish a military presence in southern Lebanon in the future or to extend the Haddad enclaves, over which Israel rules indirectly." Phalangist sources alleged that Israel had caused the rift with the Phalange by its insistence on extending "the area of [Haddad's] rule in southern Lebanon and preventing Phalangist forces from penetrating the south." Official sources indicated that Gemayel's "new government, which includes Muslim and Druze elements of various circles, is unwilling to accept a definite Israeli presence in southern Lebanon as it had been in the Haddad enclaves." They also reject "imposed security arrangements." Israel's assessment is that Gemayel will not refrain from a conflict over this matter, which will "strengthen his position among Muslim circles in Lebanon and with the moderate Arab governments."[36]

Government officials in Jerusalem stated that a "harsh" discussion had taken place between Begin and Gemayel, the central issue being "the Lebanese refusal to sign a peace treaty in the near future and primarily, their refusal to permit the establishment of a security zone ruled by Saad Haddad in southern Lebanon in a 40-50 kilometer strip." Begin made clear that Israel would not permit Haddad to be removed from "the Lebanese stage" after his "significant activities." The same sources stated that "Israel's intention is to keep the [southern] region under the arrangements that prevailed before Operation Peace for Galilee, that is, under the control of Saad Haddad's forces, with Israeli direction and support but not direct Israeli command, without deployment of major [Israeli] forces in the region."[37] These are essentially the arrangements that the Lebanese government was compelled to accept a few months later; see pp. 425f.

As for the "harsh" discussion, this took place in Nahariya in northern Israel according to Israeli radio. It appears that Gemayel was summoned to the meeting, and that the fact was then leaked to cause him embarrassment (he denied that the meeting had taken place) after his refusal to go along with the demands of the new overlords. A further sign of Israel's displeasure with its ungrateful client was the banning by Israeli authorities of a rally of Christian followers of President-elect Gemayel in Sidon "after they refused to come out publicly in favor of a peace treaty with Israel.

The rally had been called to celebrate the PLO's evacuation from Lebanon." A Phalangist official interviewed on Israeli TV in Sidon "said the Israelis pressured the Christians to include words of thanks to the Israeli army, in their speeches, for driving the PLO out of the city, and to call for a peace treaty with Israel," but the official stated that "Peace is not something that can be forced on the Lebanese people." Further evidence of Phalange ingratitude was the failure of President-elect Amin Gemayel to invite IDF personnel to a celebration to mark the unification of Beirut after the Israeli soldiers withdrew. "Invited were the U.S. Marines, the French and Italian army personnel, everyone, in fact, with the exception of the army that had paid such a heavy price in blood in the Lebanon war, the Israeli army," so the American Jewish press lamented, clinging to the official doctrine of Israeli liberation and unconscionable Lebanese ingratitude.[38]

Shortly after his election, Bashir Gemayel had had a "historic" and apparently successful meeting with the leader of the Muslim coalition, former Prime Minister Saeb Salam, and "the Muslims rebuked and virtually disowned former President Suleiman Franjieh and former Prime Minister Rashid Karami* for their outright rejection of the new regime."[39] "In the three weeks between his election and his murder [Bashir Gemayel] managed to persuade many Moslem leaders, notably the former prime minister, Saeb Salam, leader of West Beirut's mainstream Moslem politicians, to accept the Phalangist victory for the sake of Lebanon."[40] In short, in Lebanon too the grand design was beginning to crumble. We have already cited the subsequent reporting in Israel indicating that Bashir Gemayel was no friend of Israel, contrary to what had been hoped, and perhaps was "no better" than his brother Amin, who replaced him after the assassination (see p. 186).

No doubt in response to these developments, Sharon announced on September 4 that Israel might establish a "special status" security zone in southern Lebanon if Gemayel refused to sign a peace treaty. Shortly after, Major Haddad stated "that his Israeli-backed militia intends to control a 30-mile-deep strip of territory north of the Israeli border until the Beirut government signs a peace treaty with Israel," adding that "there are no regular Lebanese army units allowed in this area," and no members of the Phalangist militia.[41]

These arrangements had in fact been evident during the fighting itself. By mid-July, it was announced that Haddad's forces would rule the area up to the Awali river just north of Sidon, 55 km. north of the Israeli border. Haddad had already established his office in the rooms of the former Lebanese authorities for the Sidon region. A few weeks later,

---

* Franjieh and Karami are allied to Syria, whose army controls their domains in north Lebanon.

Yehuda Tsur reported in *Al Hamishmar* that Israel is not only help
to take control of this area but is "preventing the Phalangists from penet
ing the region under [Haddad's] control" as part of "the struggle for the
establishment of a new order in Lebanon" (even here, in the journal of the
dovish-left of the Labor Alignment, the term is used without comment or
embarrassment). Tsur adds that the Haddad forces are the only Lebanese
elements to have cooperated with Israel in the fighting. "It should be
noted that in the early days of the Beirut siege the Phalangists attempted
to attack a terrorist position, but were driven back and in the battle a
number of Gemayel's soldiers were killed. From then on they refused any
involvement in active fighting."[42] Their turn would come later.

In short, during the fighting Major Haddad had already been established as "overlord of all southern Lebanon south of the Awali river,
which runs just north of Sidon." He is "Israel's creation, entirely dependent and therefore entirely dependable." Israel had permitted the civilian
Lebanese administration to remain in Haddad's territory "because it
barely functions," but "to ensure Major Haddad's authority, Lebanese
army troops have been ordered out of their barracks in southern towns,
disarmed and replaced by the Haddad militia." Israel was thus acting to
ensure that no central Lebanese authority could exist except under its
control, a crucial aspect of the liberation. Small wonder, then, that "there
are strains between the president-elect [Bashir Gemayel] and his Israeli
sponsor."[43]

4 The Invasion of West Beirut

4.1 The Gemayel Assassination

On Saturday September 11, the last units of the force of U.S. marines
that was to guarantee the safety of the Palestinians after the departure of
the PLO were withdrawn (the decision to withdraw the marines led to the
departure of the rest of the international force), two weeks before its
30-day mandate had expired. On Tuesday September 14, Bashir Gemayel
was assassinated by a bomb that demolished the central Phalange headquarters. Muslim leaders denied any part in the assassination, as did his
known Maronite enemies. The *Economist* reported that the building was
"the most heavily, and until now the most efficiently, guarded place in all
Beirut," so that "the assassins needed the support of an insider." There
was also a heavy Israeli troop presence visibly nearby. The *Economist*
speculated that some Maronite group, perhaps a group within the Phalange that is more pro-Israeli than Gemayel, might have planted the
bomb. Helena Cobban reported that others also suggested that Phalangists close to "the Israeli-Haddad-Chamoun axis" may have been responsible. Numerous other suspicions have been voiced. The Phalangists

nounced that the assassin had confessed; he is reported to
ied foreign connections," possibly Syrian, Palestinian,
iet, while other reports allege that he was in the Phalangist
ratus. The Phalange appear to have settled on the conclusion
under Syrian direction. The Phalange investigation was
car. by Elie Hobeika, who Israel identified as the officer responsible for the Beirut massacre.[44] Existing evidence is too untrustworthy to hazard any judgment. The truth will probably never be known.

4.2 "To Prevent Bloodshed and Acts of Revenge"

At about 10:30 PM on Tuesday, Israel received confirmation that Bashir Gemayel had died, after a 5PM report of the explosion. According to testimony presented before the official Israeli inquiry, the Kahan Commission, Begin at once advised that the IDF should enter West Beirut "in order to prevent acts of revenge by the Christians against the Palestinians." Defense Minister Sharon informed Chief of Staff Rafael Eitan that evening that the Phalange would enter the Palestinian refugee camps, not the IDF. At 3:30 AM on Wednesday the 15th, Eitan informed the Phalangists of the invasion plans and their intended role. At 5AM the Israeli invasion began. At 8AM Sharon gave the orders to send the Phalangists into the camps. At 9:30 AM, Prime Minister Begin informed U.S. envoy Morris Draper about the Israeli move, undertaken "in order to prevent bloodshed and acts of revenge," in his words. At 10PM General Drori, the senior commander in Lebanon, met with the Phalangist leaders to arrange final plans. He stated to the official inquiry that "he warned them to act humanely, and not to harm women, children and old people."[45]

We return to what happened, merely noting now the precise character of the story that was finally settled on after numerous trial balloons: Israel entered West Beirut to prevent acts of violence by the Phalange against the Palestinians, and therefore decided from the first moment to send Phalange troops into the Palestinian camps, now defenseless. Even the governor of Bessarabia and the Czar were not that brazen—but then, they could not count on their supporters abroad to applaud on command, whatever story they might concoct.

The official Israeli justification for the invasion, issued on Thursday September 16, was that Israeli forces entered West Beirut "in order to prevent the danger of violence, bloodshed and anarchy."[46] Up to that point, there had been no violence, bloodshed, anarchy, or even disorder, and the Lebanese government expressed its firm belief that peace could be maintained under the control of the Lebanese army, which, according to Sharon, was under orders from the Lebanese Prime Minister "to open fire on Israeli soldiers entering west Beirut."[47] The Lebanese army did not do so, for obvious reasons. As an Israeli colonel stated, "If they [the Lebanese army] shoot at us, we will kill them."[48] Another phase of the liberation begins.

"Beirut's moderate Moślems pleaded for some response from Washington." The Prime Minister said: "We are waiting, the whole world is waiting." "The Moslem leadership was infuriated... Saeb Salaam, the elder statesman who had worked closely with the United States on the plan that led to the PLO's evacuation from Beirut, sent President Ronald Reagan a personal letter, saying, 'We urge you to halt the Israeli army and to protect the population of Beirut'." Both Salam and Prime Minister Wazzan stated that Washington had assured them "that Israel would not invade West Beirut and would not bother Palestinians in the refugee camps once Yasser Arafat and his forces had left Beirut,"[49] assurances that they apparently believed, with startling naiveté. Recall the assurances of the governor of Bessarabia.

Given the speed with which explanations replaced one another in the face of international reaction to what happened next, it is useful to recall that in announcing its original intention to enter West Beirut, the Israeli government added emphatically that the military thrust was aimed solely at maintaining order following the Gemayel assassination. "This has nothing to do with the terrorists still there," a Government official stated: "...as far as Israel is concerned the evacuation ended with the departure of the last boat."[50] The "terrorists still there" were an alleged 2000 PLO guerrillas who have cropped up repeatedly in Israeli *hasbara*, but have not been discovered elsewhere.

This story was abandoned in the flurry of attempts at self-justification and evasion of responsibility after the subsequent massacres. Sharon referred to the official government statement, cited above, as "a camouflage for something else," insisting that "Our entry into West Beirut was in order to make war against the infrastructure left by the terrorists" (i.e., the remnants of the Palestinian community and their Lebanese Muslim allies, one must assume). Sharon's admission caused a furor in Israel and "is regarded as having embarrassed the Government," not because it is false, but because it is undiplomatic to expose such truths.[51] The same explanation of the decision to invade West Beirut was repeated matter-of-factly by the military command itself, e.g., by Maj. Gen. Amir Drori, the senior Israeli commander in Lebanon.[52]

The IDF quickly conquered the area, killing or scattering the lightly-armed largely teen-aged defenders, leaving 88 killed and 254 wounded according to the independent Lebanese journal *An-nahar*, an estimate supported by a *New York Times* survey.[53] Its instructions were clear enough; in the words of Chief of Staff Eitan, already quoted: "What must be destroyed—we will destroy. Whoever must be imprisoned—we will imprison."[54]

Israel then proceeded to disarm the Muslim militias and to "the cleaning out of terrorist nests," in Sharon's words in his Parliamentary testimony. The Lebanese government demanded that Israel withdraw, as did the UN Security Council by unanimous vote, specifically noting Israel's violation of the cease-fire agreements and previous Security Council resolutions. The Israeli delegate "made clear his country had no intention of obeying any Council demand for an immediate withdrawal," in accordance with Israel's customary practice since 1948 of defying UN resolutions, stating that Israeli troops will "relinquish their positions in west Beirut when the Lebanese armed forces are ready to assume control over these positions in co-ordination with the Israeli Defense Forces in order to insure public order and security." He also maintained that it was the PLO, not Israel, that had violated the Habib agreements, referring to the mysterious 2000 terrorists.[55] By this time the first official explanation for the invasion had been quietly abandoned and forgotten.

Israel had attempted to enter West Beirut on August 1 under cover of a 14-hour land, sea and air bombardment that was the fiercest, so far, of the war—at a time when, according to Maronite President Elias Sarkis, "negotiations for the evacuation of the guerrillas were moving ahead." The Israeli attack, led by tanks, began pushing towards the Palestinian refugee camps, but was halted after a few hundred yards "by a combined force of Palestinian guerrillas, Syrian troops and Shiite militiamen fighting alongside the Palestinians"[56]—i.e., "terrorists" in official jargon. On August 4, the IDF again attempted a ground attack but withdrew after heavy casualties, including 19 soldiers killed (see p. 241). After that, it kept to safer tactics: bombing and shelling of the defenseless city. Now, however, the PLO had been evacuated as a result of the Habib negotiations and the IDF could enter "a largely undefended city," encountering "little return fire."[57] The IDF broke into the Soviet Embassy grounds, seizing the consulate building and holding it until late Friday,[58] a gratuitous provocation that was passed over a bit too casually here; we return to the matter. Israeli armor also surrounded the Sabra and Shatila camps, where the population was now completely defenseless.

These two camps, along with the third major Palestinian camp (Bourj el-Brajneh), had been mercilessly bombarded from June 4, when Sabra and Shatila were subjected to a 4 hour attack with many casualties (see p. 197) in alleged "retaliation" for the attempt by an anti-PLO group with not as much as an office in Lebanon to assassinate Israel's Ambassador to England. "The Sabra and Shatila refugee camps had been so battered by Israeli attacks in the last three months that most people found them uninhabitable," though thousands had returned to "their shattered huts in the last few weeks."[59] Shatila and Bourj el-Brajneh had also been the main targets of the 10-hour non-stop air raids of August 12, when "the Israelis poured high explosive bombs on to the two Palestinian camps in west Beirut yesterday in an apparent attempt to destroy them before Palestinian guerrillas begin to evacuate the city." "From the weight of bombs dropped over Chatila and Bourj el-Brajneh camps, it was difficult to imagine how anyone could survive the raids," which included bombs "never previously seen over such heavily residential districts, projectiles that streaked from the aircraft and exploded at 50 ft. intervals in the sky in clouds of smoke, apparently spraying smaller bombs in a wider arc around." The raids were so severe that the newscaster of the Lebanese radio "broke down while recalling the events of the morning and screamed: 'the Israelis are neo-Nazis and they are murdering our people'." The Prime Minister, who with the President had appealed to President Reagan to intervene, shouted: "If the Israelis want to kill us all, let them do it and let us get it over and done with."[60] It may be recalled once again that these are the people who, according to Conor Cruise O'Brien and others in the *New Republic, New York Times*, and elsewhere, were welcoming their liberation, though they were too ungrateful to allow the liberators to reap the fruits of their humanitarian rescue mission.

The official justification for the raids was that they were necessary to drive the PLO from Beirut, a goal assumed in the U.S. to be the legitimate prerogative of the Israeli army. Many journalists, however, noted that this was a cynical fraud—even if one accepts the remarkable conception of Israel's rights—since negotiations were reaching their final stage, and as the Lebanese Prime Minister observed, "We have offered all the concessions requested from us for the PLO evacuation, and we have even reached the stage of defining the PLO's departure routes."[61] Shatila and Bourj el-Brajneh were declared unfit for human habitation, the latter almost completely destroyed, "which means that the 24,000 Palestinians there are either dead or—for the most part—living now as squatters in northwestern Beirut," where they were also subjected to vicious bombardment by IDF pilots, much admired here for their heroism in bombing undefended civilian areas.

The smaller camps were also not spared. Colin Campbell reports that a refugee camp at Mar Elias, a small camp inhabited by Palestinian Christians who had fled or had been expelled from their homes in 1948, was struck more or less incidentally by Israeli forces advancing on West Beirut on September 15. Israeli tanks "blasted away" at a school and destroyed the homes of 35 families, who "took refuge in a virtually demolished Lebanese Army barracks" after the liberators had passed through with a typical exhibition of the doctrine of "purity of arms." Elders of the Greek Orthodox Church nearby agreed with camp residents that there were no guerrillas and no armed guards, no weapons or munitions (as an Israeli patrol searching the area confirmed), and no fire from the camp. Refugees remained without water or electricity and only a few days' food, and pleaded with visitors for help. Among them were victims of the Israeli-backed Phalange attack on Tel al-Zaatar in 1976, in which thousands were massacred.[62] The refugees at Mar Elias were the lucky ones, however.

5   A Chapter of Palestinian History

Nothing further appears to have happened in the ruins of Bourj el-Brajneh, where the Lebanese army had taken control, but matters were different at Sabra and Shatila, which were "sealed off" by the IDF so that "no one could move in or out" and under direct Israeli observation from nearby command posts.[63] Extensive and detailed reporting by many journalists tells essentially the following story.

On Thursday September 16, truckloads of Phalange and Haddad troops entered the camps, coming from behind Israeli lines to a staging area that Israel had established and following carefully prearranged and marked routes. The Phalangists appear to have been drawn largely from the Damouri Brigade, which had been operating behind Israeli lines since June. These units consisted of "some of the more extreme elements in the Christian militia," "with a well-documented record of atrocities against Palestinian civilians," coming from villages that had suffered brutal PLO retaliation for Phalangist massacres in 1976. The Haddad militia is "virtually integrated into the Israeli Army and operates entirely under its command."[64]

The forces that Israel had mobilized were sent into the now defenseless camps for "mopping up" and "to clear out terrorist nests" (Sharon). For anyone with a minimal acquaintance with the circumstances, it was not hard to imagine what would happen, and by Thursday night it was clear that these expectations were being fulfilled, with ample evidence that a massacre was in progress. Throughout Thursday night, Israeli flares lighted the camps while the militias went about their work, methodically slaughtering the inhabitants.* The massacre continued until Saturday, under the observation of the Israeli military a few hundred yards away. Bulldozers were used to scoop up bodies and cart them away or bury them under rubble. One "mass grave that has been specially bulldozed" was directly below an Israeli command center, with a view from an Israeli rooftop position "directly onto the grave and the camp beyond." IDF troops "stationed less than 100 yards away, had not responded to the sound of constant gunfire or the sight of truckloads of bodies being taken

---

* Phalangists allege that apart from providing flares, Israeli artillery also supported them on Thursday night by softening up a "problematic area in the camp" where there had been some resistance. They also claim that they were accompanied by Israelis in Phalangist uniforms. See "One Day in the life of a Phalangist," *Ha'aretz*, Feb. 18, 1983; translated from *Der Spiegel*, Feb. 14, 1983. See p. 399*.

away from the camps," and told Western journalists that "nothing unusual" was going on while mingling with Phalangists resting between missions inside the camps.[65]

On Friday afternoon Chief of Staff Eitan and Generals Drori and Yaron met with the Phalangist command. Eitan congratulated them on having "carried out good work," offered them a bulldozer with IDF markings removed, and authorized them to remain in the camps for another 12 hours. The killing continued. At 5AM Saturday morning the murderers began to leave the camps, and after 36 hours, the slaughter ended. On Saturday morning, "reporters entered the camp long before any Israeli soldiers,"[66] and the full story began to reach the outside world. In fact, according to Defense Minister Sharon's report to the Knesset, Israeli soldiers did not enter Sabra until Sunday, well after news of the massacre had reached the outside world, and did not enter Shatila at all, a fact that did not prevent the Israeli government from officially taking credit for bringing the massacre to a halt, when the international response began to come in; see below.

It is obvious from the circumstances and the troop deployments that the IDF was well aware of what was happening in the camps to which it had dispatched the gangs of murderers it had organized, just as the Czar's police and army could not have failed to know what was happening in the Jewish quarter of Kishinev. Military correspondent Hirsh Goodman of the *Jerusalem Post* reported that "The senior command of the IDF knew on Thursday night that civilians were being killed by Phalange troops in the Shatilla refugee camp." IDF commander General Yaron received a radio communication from the Phalange commander in Shatila stating that "300 civilians and terrorists have been killed," one of a series of facts that are in "direct contradiction" to public statements by Defense Minister Sharon and Chief of Staff Eitan that there were only "suspicions" until Saturday morning.[67] Further evidence that Yaron was aware of the massacre by Thursday evening was provided by the Kahan Commission of Inquiry, to which we turn below. According to the *Jerusalem Post*, American intelligence provided "hard intelligence information...confirming that Israeli military officers in Beirut were well aware of the brutal killings many hours before the Israeli Defence Forces actually went into the camps," which was well after journalists had done so. "'They simply sat on their hands,' one well-placed U.S. source said, referring to high-ranking Israeli military authorities waiting outside the camps in West Beirut. 'They did nothing to stop the carnage'." U.S. officials said that Sharon and Eitan regarded the operation as "justified" because of "the supposedly greater need to 'purify' all of the Lebanese capital of terrorists. If innocent people have to die, that's the price of all wars."[68] Perhaps the Czar's officers harbored similar thoughts.

By 10PM Thursday, medical workers reported that 2000 terrified civilians had reached their hospital seeking refuge and crying "Phalangists, Haddad, Israel," pointing to their necks to indicate that people were having their throats cut. By 5:30 AM Friday morning Israeli intelligence received further information that 300 "civilians and terrorists" had been killed, transmitting the information to the Defense Ministry. By 8AM Israeli soldiers informed their commanding officers "that they saw Phalangist soldiers killing civilians in their homes," while others were being beaten and kicked. The soldiers were informed by superior officers: "we know, this isn't to our taste, but we are not to become involved."[69]

By Friday journalists were reporting the atrocities. Loren Jenkins of the *Washington Post* reported that "although a tight Israeli Army security cordon tried to keep outside observers from the Palestinian refugee camps in the southern suburbs, there were reports by civilians who managed to escape of violent reprisals by the militiamen," giving details.[70] Colin Campbell of the *New York Times* reported on Friday that

> With Israeli tanks standing guard outside, Israeli-backed Phalangist militiamen moved by foot and jeep into the battered Sabra and Shatila camps. Automatic weapons fire could be heard from within, and women weeping hysterically began appearing in downtown west Beirut and saying that their husbands and sons had been taken away by armed Phalangists.[71]

On Friday morning, Ze'ev Schiff learned of the atrocities and reported the fact to government officials, though he did not make it public. "It is not true," he wrote subsequently, "that the crime was known to us—as official sources claim—only by noon on Saturday after the reports of foreign correspondents in Beirut. On Friday morning when I learned of the slaughter in the camps I passed the information on to a high-ranking official [Minister Mordechai Zipori], and I know that he acted immediately"—in fact, he informed Foreign Minister Shamir, who claimed before the Kahan Commission that he did not understand the message. Schiff added that "this affair will haunt us. Now it will be claimed that we disarmed the Mourabitoun and the leftist militias and detained the Palestinian men in order to enable the Phalangists to annihilate their children, women and old people without resistance."[72]

While the atrocities were in progress, only the soldiers in the Israeli observation posts had a view of what was happening. Friedman points out that the mass graves could be seen with the naked eye from "the site of the telescope and binocular-equipped Israeli observation post," but "whether the Israelis actually looked down and saw what was happening was unknown." What is known is that IDF soldiers "lounged about...reading magazines and listening to Simon and Garfunkel music." "It is not clear whether the Israelis had any inkling of what was happening in the camps, although from their observation posts it would not have been difficult to ascertain not only by sight but from the sounds of gunfire and the screams coming from the camp."[73] It is also not clear whether this is intended as irony.

Newsweek correspondent Ray Wilkinson measured the distance from the Israeli command post to the camps at 250 paces and examined the line of sight from the Israeli command post. The camps are "plainly visible," he reported, down to the "smallest detail," with binoculars. Israeli soldiers equipped with high-powered binoculars could observe what was happening from this command post atop a 7-story building and from a Lebanese army outpost "which provided a view straight down into the camps." There they watched, and "stood by as the murderers dug a 50-square-yard mass grave and dumped Palestinian bodies into it—all within the direct line of sight of the Israeli observation post," while bulldozers "rumble[d] out of Sabra, their scoops filled with bodies."[74] This was before Chief of Staff Eitan authorized provision of another bulldozer, with IDF markings removed, on Friday afternoon as he sent the Phalange back into the camps to continue their "good work."

During the slaughter, *Newsweek* correspondent James Pringle was prevented from entering the Sabra camp by Israeli soldiers and Haddad militiamen:

> As rifle fire crackled inside the camp, Pringle asked one of Haddad's men what was going on. "We are slaughtering them," the militiaman replied cheerfully. Nearby an Israeli colonel who identified himself only as "Eli" said that his own troops would not interfere to "purify the area." Asked whether he was afraid that Haddad's men might commit atrocities, the colonel replied: "We hope they will not do anything like that."[75]

Loren Jenkins of the *Washington Post* stood on top of a mass grave looking up at the Israeli Army main observation post,

> a place where before their own advance into the city, they had set up giant telescopes for spotting snipers. And as I stood there Saturday morning looking up, there were six Israelis looking straight down at me. They stood and watched throughout this whole horrible tragedy as people were brought here, shot, dumped in this grave and packed up. This was a basically undefended civilian camp.

ICRC representatives in Shatila and Lebanese Army soldiers also commented that it is impossible to imagine that the IDF "could not see what is happening here. It is right under the Israelis' noses." And soldiers reported that on Thursday evening, Palestinian women "hysterically told them that the Phalangists were shooting their children and putting the men on trucks." The commanding officer, informed of this, responded: "It is OK, do not worry."[76]

The reader might want to keep these eyewitness investigations and reports in mind, as we turn to the much-lauded Report of the official Kahan Commission of Inquiry later on.

An investigation by ABC news revealed that at least 45 Israeli officers knew by Friday afternoon that a massacre was in progress—that is, at the time when the Chief of Staff was authorizing the Phalangists to return to the "good work" for which he congratulated them. On Friday afternoon, Palestinian women who escaped from the camps were filmed pleading with Israeli troops to intervene to stop the massacre, but were told by the soldiers that they could not leave their posts; the women were sent back into the camps. A few hours earlier, Norwegian journalist John Hambro attempted to enter the camp but was blocked by a bulldozer with the scoop filled with dead bodies. An Israeli officer confirmed that "It is certain, beyond any doubt, that by Friday afternoon everyone knew. I know that on Friday afternoon it was already known that people were being killed in Shatila." A doctor at the nearby Gaza hospital reported that "the patients—the victims—are virtually all women and children," suffering from gunshot wounds.[77]

Testifying before the official Commission of Inquiry, General Amos Yaron, who commanded Israeli forces in the Beirut area, described the replacement of the Phalangists with fresh troops Friday afternoon and "indicated that Eitan showed no reluctance to allow the militia units to remain in Sabra and Shatila until the next morning. He testified that the main reason the Phalangist units were ordered out of the camps on Saturday, September 18, was not fear of civilian deaths but because unnamed American officials were pressing the Israelis to have them removed."[78]

U.S. officials were in fact pressing Israel to stop the massacre. Shortly after the Phalange troops were withdrawn but before the journalists entered the camps, U.S. special envoy Morris Draper demanded that

> You must stop the massacres. They are obscene. I have an officer in the camp counting the bodies. You ought to be ashamed. The situation is rotten and terrible. They are killing children. You are in absolute control of the area and therefore responsible for that area.

The evening before he had warned of "horrible results"—already achieved—if the Phalangists were permitted to enter the camps.[79]

General Yaron's testimony indicates that the IDF did make an effort to rescue people from the gangs of murderers it organized and sent into the camps. He testified that at 6AM on Saturday he saw a group of people "with blond hair" being taken away by the Phalangists—doctors and nurses from the Gaza hospital. "General Yaron ran to them and ordered them to free the prisoners at once."[80] It would, then, be quite unfair, further evidence of a double standard if not outright anti-Semitism, to assert as some do that Israeli forces made no attempt to stop the slaughter.

Without pursuing the matter any further—and this merely scratches the surface—it suffices to remark that the similarity to the Kishinev massacre is uncanny, apart from scale, and putting aside the preceding 10 weeks of increasingly severe bombardment alongside of which the Sabra-Shatila massacres pale into insignificance.

What was the scale of the operation and the casualties? After many falsehoods and evasions which we may omit, the government of Israel finally conceded that it had sent Phalangists into the camps, settling on a figure of 100-150; 150 according to the Kahan Commission. The final official story was that they were sent in for the purpose of "cleansing" the camps of 2000 heavily-armed terrorists left there by the PLO in violation of the Habib agreements. In *Ha'aretz*, B. Michael comments: "So heroic as this are the Christian fighters!" Edward Walsh reports Begin's official reply to the Commission of Inquiry in which he "reiterated his assertion that there was no reason to anticipate a massacre and said the government had 'authoritative information' that about 2000 Palestinian guerrillas were concentrated in the area." Walsh comments: "But no one has publicly explained how the Israelis expected 100 to 130 Phalangists to defeat such a force of Palestinians." Robert Suro of *Time* magazine visited the camps a few days before the attack, and found no military presence there.[81] The 2000 terrorists have proven elusive indeed.

Of course, there are some other questions too, beyond the one that Edward Walsh raised in the *Post*. It is claimed that the 100-150 Phalangists were sent in to avoid IDF casualties in what was expected to be fierce fighting. How credible is this claim, considering the size of the force that was introduced into the camps? And once this claim is dismissed as the obvious nonsense that it is, what remains as the plausible explanation for Israel's decision to send Phalangists of the Damouri Brigade and Haddad troops to enter defenseless Palestinian camps, knowing perfectly well what they had done in the past, and would do again? Recall again the official claim that Israel invaded West Beirut to protect Palestinians from Phalangist terror.

The 2000 heavily-armed Palestinian terrorists seem to have been singularly inept. The 150 Phalangists sent in to overcome them reported 2 killed—exactly the number of casualties suffered by the murderers at Kishinev, by macabre coincidence.[82] It is, in fact, unclear whether these two were killed or wounded; see below.

Turning to the number of casualties suffered by the 2000 terrorists, Defense Minister Sharon testified that based on "the figures of the Army Intelligence Branch," between 700 and 800 people had been killed,[83] almost 20 times the scale of the Kishinev massacre, 375 terrorists for each Phalange fighter. This figure was accepted as the most probable estimate by the Kahan Commission, relying on Israeli intelligence and ignoring Lebanese sources. The Lebanese government alleges that 762 bodies were actually recovered and that 1,200 more were buried privately by relatives, so that the death toll would be about 2000. Perhaps these are the "2000 terrorists" of Israeli *hasbara* exercises.[84]

Thomas Friedman subsequently found that "it has now become clear that at least a quarter, and possibly many more [of those killed], were Lebanese Shiite Moslems," and that most of the Palestinians came from Israel's Upper Galilee and Jaffa in 1948—which means that they were very likely expelled by force. Nine Jewish women were also reported killed.[85] Citing Palestinian and independent medical sources, Friedman added that several hundred men rounded up during the massacres were removed to the Israeli prison camp in Ansar. There had, in fact, been earlier indications that this was so.

As the massacres came to an end, the IDF at once displayed the efficiency of which it is capable when it so desires, turning its attention to those who had somehow survived the slaughter. Early Saturday morning, as the killing ended, Israeli troops outside the camps are reported to have used loudspeakers to order survivors to a nearby stadium where they "were separated into small groups and interrogated, witnesses said." Most were released, "but some, called PLO suspects by the Israelis, were detained." A few days later, the State Department "indicated there was a new source of Administration concern over reports that, after the massacre of the Palestinians in the Beirut camps, Israeli forces rounded up a large number of Arab men in West Beirut, presumably on suspicion of being Palestinian guerrillas, and deported them to detention camps in southern Lebanon." Israel confirmed that "yes, there have been interrogations and, yes, there were large numbers of people held." At the same time, "Heavy weapons captured by the Israeli army in its invasion of Moslem West Beirut are being turned over to the Christian militia forces whose units have been implicated in the massacre of Palestinian civilians in the capital's Sabra and Shatila refugee camps."[86]

One wonders whether the Czar could have carried it off with such grace and elegance.

Ze'ev Schiff reports an "authorized investigation" after the massacres which showed that they were not a case of "revenge killings" after the Gemayel assassination (a rather implausible assumption in the first place, since it was hardly credible that the Palestinians had killed Gemayel), but were "a premeditated attack which was designed to cause a mass flight of Palestinians from Beirut and from the whole of Lebanon." David Shipler reports that as early as mid-June, "Israeli officials were speaking privately of a plan, being considered by Defense Minister Ariel Sharon, to allow the Phalangists to go into west Beirut and the camps against the Palestine Liberation Organization. The calculation was that the Phalangists, with old scores to settle and detailed information on the Palestinian fighters, would be more ruthless than the Israelis and probably more effective."[87] As noted earlier (p. 359), the Phalangists did make one such move, but quickly withdrew in the face of PLO fighters, much as the IDF itself did. It is likely that Sharon's plan was now implemented, once the impediment, armed resistance to the terror, had been removed.

Israel's first response to the reports of atrocities by journalists on Saturday September 18 was that "we do not know anything of these alleged massacres" (IDF spokesman). The expression of anger by the U.S. over the killings in the camps was denounced in Jerusalem as "hypocrisy." Subsequently a variety of excuses were attempted (the Phalangists entered through an area not under Israeli control, etc.), but these were soon dropped as it became evident that there were simply too many credible eyewitnesses. Worldwide outrage was extensive. The General Assembly of the United Nations voted 147 to 2 with no abstentions to condemn the massacre, the United States and Israel alone in opposition as usual.[88] But in the United States too there was outraged condemnation, to which we return, as there was in Israel as well, most notably, in the huge protest demonstration with a reported 400,000 in attendance, which was quickly exploited in the U.S. to increase American support for Israel's new settlements in the occupied territories and its military actions in Lebanon, as already discussed.

The charge of hypocrisy levelled by spokesmen for the government of Israel has considerable merit, once again. There had been no such anger over the murderous bombardments of the camps from June 4, which caused far more casualties than Israel's replay of the Kishinev massacre on a far larger scale, or over the war itself. What is more, earlier massacres in the aftermath of Israeli aggression, as in Gaza in 1956, evoked no outrage, though in that case it was IDF soldiers themselves who did the killing (see p. 102). Hence it is unclear, at first, why the Beirut massacres should have evoked such expressions of horror. In scale, the massacre falls into the category of other recent examples that have not exactly seared the conscience of the West, for example, the Kassinga massacre in Namibia in 1978, when over 600 people were killed by bombing by French-built Mirage jets and by paratroopers transported in U.S.-built Hercules troop carriers.[89] Or the Rio Sumpul massacre in El Salvador in May 1980 which signalled the onset of the mass murder of peasants that constituted one of the final chapters of the Human Rights Administration.[90] Or the massacre of 300 unarmed villagers by U.S.-built fighter-bombers and crack U.S.-trained counterinsurgency forces in San Vicente province in El Salvador in late August 1982, leaving "a mountain of people—children, old people and women," according to survivors.[91] Or the massacre of 300 Indians on July 17, 1982 by Guatemalan troops arriving by foot and in helicopters (thanks to the U.S., and to their Israeli arms suppliers and advisers), who killed every man, woman and child in the village except for three men who managed to hide in the woods, according to interviews arranged for the press by Roman Catholic priests.[92] In none of these cases was there any noteworthy response.

The message is clear enough. Israel had violated a cardinal rule of international etiquette: if you intend to engage in mass murder, then do so when there are not too many reporters in the vicinity or when the editorial offices at home understand the virtues of silence. When Israel speaks of Western hypocrisy, it has a powerful case. As for the Soviet reaction while Russian forces are massacring at will in Afghanistan, or that of the Arab states—for example, Syria, which had just successfully murdered thousands in Hama, or the blood-stained murderers who run Iraq—or Khomeini's Iran, nothing more need be said.

The story finally settled upon, as noted, was that some 100-150 militiamen were sent into the camps to root out 2000 heavily-armed Palestinian terrorists, with replacements on Friday afternoon to consummate the task. As for the constitution of these forces, there is dispute, since everyone insists that they were not involved. There seems little doubt that the forces were primarily Phalangists, with some Haddad troops as well, perhaps 1/3 or 1/4 of the attacking force, though on this matter reports vary, and Israel has repeatedly insisted that these forces, which are virtually part of the Israeli army, were not involved.

Israeli sources alleged that the Phalange troops were commanded by Elie Hobeika, chief Phalange intelligence officer, who had "previously commanded the so-called Damour Commando, a reconnaissance unit which killed Palestinians in revenge for the murder of thousands of Lebanese Christians in the town of Damour, south of Beirut, in 1976."[93] The figure of thousands murdered in Damour appears to be an invention of Israeli propaganda.* In the New York Times, David Shipler again identified Hobeika on the basis of Israeli and Lebanese sources, describing him as the architect of the Tel al-Zaatar massacre, who "had assembled a special unit of commandos, among them former members of the Damuri Brigade, which included Christians whose families had been massacred in Damur and who were bent on revenge." He was well known to the Israeli Mossad and the CIA, Shipler reports.[94] Citing "highly placed sources," The ABC News investigation reported that three Phalange leaders "bear direct responsibility for the massacre": Fady Frem, Phalange military commander; Hobeika, Phalange chief of security and military intelligence; and Joseph Edde, leader of the elite Phalange commandos. "Of all Phalange factions responsible for the massacre, those who emerged from the wreckage of the Christian town of Damour are perhaps the most vengeful."[95] Loren Jenkins of the Washington Post

---

* Colonel Yirmiah gives the figure of 250 killed, in his War Diary. See chapter 5, note 164.

concluded that the main actor was Hobeika, "the chief contact of the Lebanese Forces [the Phalange] with Mossad, the Israeli secret service, as well as with the U.S. Central Intelligence Agency," and that along with Hobeika's special security units "there was also a handful of men who appeared to belong to the militia of Saad Haddad." Frem and Hobeika are reputed to be the leaders of the most strongly pro-Israel section of the Phalange. Thomas Friedman provides extensive evidence from which he concludes that Haddad forces were involved, along with the Phalange.[96]

Survivors attributed the killings primarily to Haddad forces. Every refugee interviewed by the *Christian Science Monitor* "insisted the massacre was carried out by the forces of Maj. Saad Haddad,"[97] and numerous other sources report their direct participation, among others, the U.S. State Department and General Sharon, who testified before the Commission of Inquiry that Haddad forces "had committed acts of murder or harmed the population" in the camps, and that one Haddad militiaman was killed and two others taken prisoner by an IDF paratroop unit outside the camps.[98] A Danish TV crew filmed militiamen wearing Haddad uniforms on Friday outside of Shatila, preventing women from leaving the camp, herding them into trucks, and capturing Lebanese army regulars who approached the camp.[99] Residents of the camps taken to the nearby sports stadium claim to have been interrogated by members of Haddad's militia; and a Lebanese army officer at a post overlooking the camp identified Haddad forces, as did a Norwegian surgeon at the Gaza hospital who had served in the south and was familiar with the distinction between Phalangists and Haddadists, and other medical personnel there, who stated it it was Haddad's militia that had ordered them out of the hospital. A Shiite girl at the Acre hospital identified a Haddadist from her own village in southern Lebanon. Scores of survivors said that the militiamen spoke with southern Lebanese accents and used typical Shiite Muslim names (there are few if any Shiites in the Phalange forces but about half of Haddad's militia are southern Shiites).[100] David Lamb and others report that terrified refugees were screaming "Haddad is coming back" when rumors circulated that the militiamen were returning, repeating "the one word that to them is synonymous with death, 'Haddad'." One Palestinian boy was reported to be sitting on a Haddad Land Rover, his cheeks slashed by bayonets, forced "to reiterate his crime, 'I am a Palestinian'," before being killed.[101] Villagers in the south in Haddad areas reported that "trucks and jeeps marked with Haddad's militia's insignias began pouring into [a village], to turn down an Israeli Army-controlled road that leads to Israeli military positions" near the airport.[102] As noted, Israel denied that Haddad troops participated, claiming that none were "in the area of Beirut," while the Israeli TV military correspondent reported that the Phalange killers wore Haddad uniforms to conceal their identity. Chief of Staff Eitan also denied that these forces were involved.[103] We return to the

Commission of Inquiry interpretation of the evidence of participation of Haddad forces, of which the above is a small sample.

The exact truth will probably never be known. What is clear is that the atrocities were carried out by militiamen brought in by Israel who, furthermore, had "a well-documented history of atrocities against Palestinian civilians"—a fact which raises a "question," as Israeli commander Maj. Gen. Amir Drori conceded.[104]

The exact constitution of the forces is hardly of crucial significance. As David Bernstein comments in the *Jerusalem Post*, "In the final analysis, the question is largely irrelevant, as both Haddad and the Phalange are Israel's creatures, having been armed and trained over the past eight years by the IDF."[105] That they were under IDF control as they were organized to enter the camps, and under its observation as the operation was carried out, is hardly in serious doubt.

Not everyone is convinced. Parts of the Israeli press have suggested a rather different version of what took place. The Labor party press, *Davar*, ran a story in early November under this headline: "The Massacre in the Refugee Camps was Organized by the KGB in order to Persuade the World of Israel's Guilt." The story is by the *Davar* Paris correspondent, Gidon Kutz, and is based on an exciting new book that had just appeared in Paris and his interview with the author, "a well-known Jewish historian and journalist," Annie Kriegel, who explained to him her theory that the killings in the camps were organized by the KGB (who were also responsible for the Gemayel assassination), and carried out by German terrorists associated with the PLO. The American intelligence agencies are aware of all of this, but are keeping quiet, because they are interested in bringing down the Begin government and removing Israeli forces from Beirut. The purpose of the KGB-organized massacres in the camp is plain; they assumed correctly that Israel would be blamed. This was a part of the general Soviet commitment to international terrorism and the undermining of Israel, a program in which they are aided by the educated classes in the democracies, who, as the author writes in her book, have "abdicated all capacity of intellectual and spiritual resistance" in the face of "verbal aggression" aimed at destroying Israel, including the campaign of "intimidation" and "disinformation" directed by the USSR which has taken on "the dimensions of a veritable psychological war" launched against Israel in the summer of 1982.[106]

As noted earlier, in addition to the qualifications just mentioned, Kriegel is a recently-converted high functionary of the French Communist Party, known as a hard-line Party loyalist, who had made the familiar and, from an ideological point of view, quite easy switch to the extreme right. *Davar* reports that her book was published with extreme rapidity by the well-known French publisher Laffont, "thanks to the Jewish origin" of the publishers, as a "national duty."

It will be recalled that it was Kriegel's impressive study that convinced the director-general of the Department of Information of the
World Zionist Organization that the media had been duped by the powerful forces of Wafa and the International Communist Conspiracy (see pp.
291-2). As far as the book itself is concerned, it is of interest only to those
who are amused by the latest antics of Paris intellectuals. More interesting, perhaps, is that it could be taken seriously in Israel, though they were
realistic enough not to use this fascinating material for *hasbara* beamed to
an American audience.

6   Who is Responsible?

6.1   The Background for the Inquiry

When the reports of the massacre reached the outside world, Israel
denied any knowledge of what had happened. This pretense was quickly
dropped in favor of outraged denial of any responsibility. The official
reaction of the government was announced on September 19, and
appeared in a full page advertisement in several American newspapers.[107]
The heading was "BLOOD LIBEL," a reference to traditional anti-
Semitic incitement. It is a reflex reaction to accuse critics of Israel of
anti-Semitism, a device of proven effectiveness to deflect any rational
discussion of the issues; see pp. 15-6.

The official government statement then went on to assert that "there
was no position of the Israeli army" in the area where "a Lebanese unit
entered a refugee camp in order to apprehend terrorists hiding there." It
claimed further that "As soon as the IDF learned of the tragic events,
Israeli soldiers put an end to the slaughter and forced the Lebanese unit to
evacuate the camp." These shameful lies were silently abandoned later on.
The second is not only contradicted by the eyewitness reports of numerous journalists, but also by General Sharon's direct testimony in the
Knesset a few days later, as already noted.[108] The IDF entered Sabra long
after the killings ended and did not enter Shatila at all. The only alleged
"intervention" cited by Sharon was a Friday order to the Phalangist
liaison officer to stop the killings; even if one can believe Sharon's statement, it merely deepens the responsibility of the IDF, since at a later
meeting that day the Chief of Staff congratulated the Phalange on their
"good work" and sent them back into the camp to complete it. As for the
claim that there was no position of the Israeli army in the area completely
surrounded by IDF soldiers who could not only observe what was happening but were so close by that they "must have heard the screams of the
massacred all night,"[109] no comment is necessary. Subsequently, there was
a temporary pretense that the camps had been only partially encircled by

the IDF and that the militiamen must have entered, unknown to the IDF, through the unguarded eastern sector, but this too was dropped as the press, including the Israeli press, reported the opposite, even citing earlier official IDF statements that the camps were completely encircled.[110] Shortly after, the full range of pretenses was dropped, as unsustainable in the face of massive counter-evidence. Apart from a few journalistic hold-outs and Paris ex-Stalinists performing their "national duty," the basic facts were soon uncontested.

The refusal of the Begin government to permit a full independent inquiry raised a new furor. Sharon, in his Knesset testimony, accused the Labor opposition of simply playing politics when it called for an investigation. A look at the Labor critique tends to confirm his judgment. In his speech to the Knesset the same day, Labor Alignment leader Shimon Peres qualified his call for an investigation in the following terms:

> And in the name of the unity of the nation I call upon all members of this house to exclude the Israel Defense Forces from this discussion. Let us leave aside our sons who are serving their nation faithfully. Let us not include the great and important organization that carries out orders, and which is blameless altogether; let us leave them out of this painful political controversy. We are sure that the Israel Defense Forces did not lend its hand to this spilling of blood.[111]

In short, the "full independent inquiry" that the Labor opposition was calling for according to the American press was to exclude the IDF, which is blameless *a priori*, and to keep to "political controversy," i.e., to the role of the Likud government. An inquiry that excluded the role of the IDF in organizing the militias and sending them into the camps it had encircled, standing by in the manner of the Czar's police while they did their work, would be no inquiry at all, but rather, merely an attempt to score political points against the Likud. Within a few days, the opposition to a serious inquiry on the part of both Likud and Labor was swept aside in the political currents within Israel, and the Commission of Inquiry headed by Chief Justice Yitzhak Kahan was established. We return to its report and the reception it received, an interesting story in itself.[112]

Note that the issue was not whether IDF forces were involved in the massacre. No credence was ever given to the occasional reports from Lebanon intimating that Israeli soldiers participated, though one well-known apologist—Martin Peretz—claimed otherwise, stating: "I resent the alacrity with which some people have rushed to arrange the facts so that it seems the Israelis did the murdering, not the Christians."[113] It is always a useful device, when in difficult straits, to concoct an opponent who can be refuted easily, as when critics of orthodox ideological distortions are "refuted" on the pretense that they are pro-Communist,* or when opponents of a strategic weapons build-up are dismissed with arguments against unilateral disarmament. But the conditions that Labor attempted to impose on the inquiry went far beyond the non-issue that Peretz raises, a fact that was overlooked in the outrage focussed upon Begin and Sharon.

6.2 The Charges

The government of Israel blamed the Phalange for the massacre. Sharon, in his Knesset testimony, argued that Israel cannot "choose our neighbors in the Middle East"; if they are savages, it is not Israel's fault. As Begin put it in a widely-quoted statement, "Goyim kill goyim, and they immediately come to hang the Jews,"[114] another sign of the ineradicable anti-Semitism of world opinion. The U.S. government blamed the Christian militias, assigning Israel indirect responsibility for failing to do enough to prevent the massacre. The Labor opposition blamed Begin and Sharon. American supporters of Israel also rushed to blame Begin and Sharon, who had defiled the "beautiful Israel" of earlier years. The Arab states and the PLO blamed the U.S., which they regarded as directly responsible for Israel's actions, virtually a partner in them. The efforts of the Israeli government to dissociate itself from the work of its hired guns have already been discussed. The other charges merit further examination.

Before examining them, it is worth noting that each of these charges had a clear purpose. The Labor Alignment hoped to discredit the Likud government; the huge post-massacre demonstration was the first one supported by the Labor Party, which maintained its silence, with the exceptions already noted, throughout the earlier carnage. Supporters of Israel who had watched similar or worse atrocities in silence in the past, blaming the Palestinians when they are oppressed or massacred, had to find a way to justify their longstanding practice that helped lay the basis for this unusually visible atrocity—which, again, did not compare in scale to the slaughter of civilians by Israel's bombardment of defenseless civ-

---

* Walter Laqueur, for example, fulminates that "The inability to accept the permissible limits of rewriting history was the undoing of Cold War revisionists," adding that "It is one thing to admire Stalin, it is another to depict him as a great humanist whose sole aspiration was to cooperate with the West in a spirit of goodwill, peace and mutual benefit" ("Visions and Revisions," *Times Literary Supplement*, March 5, 1982). He cites no examples of rewriting of history, admiration of Stalin, or the rest; as noted several times, it is a convention of scholarship and intellectual life in general that no evidence is necessary in denunciation of those who dare to question Higher Truths—for Laqueur, that "Unlike the Soviet Union, The U.S. does not want to convert anyone to a specific political, social, or economic system" (Laqueur and Charles Krauthammer, *New Republic*, March 31, 1982), etc. For some further examples of his interesting doctrines, see Chomsky and Herman, *Political Economy of Human Rights*, vol. I, pp. 87f.; *TNCW*, pp. 48, 190.

ilian targets, in the Sabra and Shatila camps and elsewhere, a few weeks earlier. The American government hoped that if Labor were returned to power and the Arab states could be brought into line, Reagan might succeed in imposing the American plan for the region, including the "peace plan" already discussed, thus bringing about the long-sought regional strategic consensus under American power. As for the Arab charges, in this case they strike uncomfortably close to home.

6.3   "We" and "They": Defiling the Beautiful Israel

The attempt to focus blame on Begin and Sharon took various forms. The *New York Times* was positively ecstatic about the fact that "the people of Israel have broken the resistance of their Government to force a full and fair inquiry," ignoring the attempt by the Labor Alignment to forestall such an inquiry. By doing so, the *Times* editors continued, Israelis have "affirm[ed] their humanity,...shame[d] the killers of their own children,...expose[d] the hypocrisy of many of their critics."[115] We have already seen how the genuine revulsion of many Israelis over their government's role in the massacre was converted by supporters here into a device to intensify settlement in the occupied territories and militarization of Israeli society (see p. 109). Commentary of the sort just quoted made its effective contribution to this process.

Within days after the report of the massacre, the U.S. press was flooded with letters and statements by people who had accepted what came before with silence or acclaim, in some cases, with occasional qualms during the Begin-Sharon intensification of the oppressive practices of the Labor government in the occupied territories and the Peace for Galilee Operation. Daniel Bell, Irving Howe, Seymour Martin Lipset and Michael Walzer wrote that "All of us must now say to the Begin-Sharon Government: 'You are doing grave damage to the name of Israel, long associated with democracy, *conciliation and peace*'."[116] On the same day, Howe added in a separate statement that "This has not changed my attitude toward Israel but it has certainly confirmed and strengthened my opposition to the Begin and Sharon Government." The following day, in his third statement on the massacres in two days in the *New York Times*, Howe explained the difference between "We" (opponents of Begin-Sharon) and "They" (the evil pair):

"We" believe in negotiating with any Palestinians who openly acknowledge the legitimacy of Israel, in the hope of reaching a settlement that secures Israeli borders and grants Palestinian rights. "They" regard the Palestinians simply as the enemy to be smashed and "mopped up." Such differences point to a fundamental divergence within Jewish ranks. We are experiencing a conflict between the values of democratic conciliation and the goal of imperial domination, between the visions personified by Chaim Weizmann's liberal Zionism and Vladimir Jabotinsky's ultra-nationalist Zionism. We are in the midst of a struggle over the character of Jewish life, both in Israel and the Diaspora... it is the bad policies and misconduct of Begin-Sharon that provide the most substantial help to the enemies of Israel... So this is where some of us stand: warm friends of Israel, open critics of Begin-Sharon.[117]

Just before the massacres, Nat Hentoff, who had been sharply critical of the Israeli invasion of Lebanon and the silence of American Jews concerning it,* had written:

From the start of the Jewish state, there has indeed been a tradition, *tohar haneshek* ("purity of arms" or "morality of arms"), in the Israeli armed forces. Until now, Israeli soldiers had to be very, very careful about injuring civilians, let alone killing them.[118]

A *Boston Globe* editorial explains:

There is little understanding of the way in which Begin's right-wing revisionist Zionism differs from the Zionism of a David Ben-Gurion or even a military man like Moshe Dayan. Traditional Zionism sought peace between Arab and Jew and empathized with the Palestinian quest for a homeland.[119]

Addressing the Knesset after the massacre, Shimon Peres stated:

But the Prime Minister and the Defense Minister were struck dumb. Their silence thundered as it pained. The fate of Israel, David Ben-Gurion said, is dependent on its strength and its righteousness. Righteousness, not just strength, has to guide our deeds.[120]

---

* A committed civil libertarian who has written widely on civil and human rights issues in the U.S. and abroad, taking a strong and uncompromising stand, Hentoff writes here of his fear that Israel will not "remain a Jewish state" if it continues to rule over 1.3 million Palestinians. It is apparently his view, then, that there is no problem in its being "a Jewish state" with a smaller minority of non-Jewish citizens, say 15%. One wonders whether he would have the same attitude towards a proposal to convert the United States into a "White state" or "a Christian state," with a legal and administrative structure of the sort that defines Israel as "a Jewish state." To my knowledge, he has never addressed this issue in his many writings on Israel and Zionism, a standard oversight among civil libertarian supporters of Israel (not to speak of those who simply deny the facts; see *TNCW*, chapter 9, for some examples). It is also noteworthy that Hentoff has expressed great admiration for committed opponents of civil rights—Alan Dershowitz of Harvard Law School, for example—as long as this opposition is restricted to the Israeli context. See chapter 4, pp. 142-3 and notes 145, 107.

This statement appeared in the *New York Times*, evoking not shock and amazement but respect—and general dismay over the passing of the righteousness of Ben-Gurion's Israel. Examples can be freely multiplied.

The fact that such statements as the ones just quoted could be made, and regarded seriously, once again provides evidence of the remarkable successes of our system of indocrination, of what Walter Lippmann called "the manufacture of consent," among the intelligentsia who are its agents and, not infrequently, its most credulous victims. Enough has already been said to dismiss the claim that the name of Israel has been associated with "conciliation and peace" or that the Zionism of the Labor Party "empathized with the Palestinian quest for a homeland." One can only hope that some day, honesty will lead to the recognition of the contribution made by such outlandish claims as these to allowing both Labor and Likud to undertake their policies of consistent rejectionism and oppression, exactly as Israeli doves have been lamenting for many years.

As for Howe's "we" and "they," he fails to mention that "they" include the Labor Party governments of which he was an ardent supporter, and the current Labor opposition as well, which he continues to support. Labor has never departed from its refusal to deal with any Palestinians on any political issue or to negotiate with the PLO even if it were to renounce terrorism and recognize the state of Israel. While in power, Labor rejected every peace proposal that offered the hope of reaching a settlement that secures Israeli borders, even ones (e.g., Sadat's in 1971) that made no mention of Palestinian rights, and has maintained the same position since, even criticizing Begin for agreeing to abandon the northeast Sinai settlements that Labor established; it has called for transfer of Arabs to East of the Jordan; it supports continued settlement (which Labor initiated) as long as it falls within the framework of its planning and says little about severe repression (also its legacy) in the occupied territories; etc. Hence "we" are a small group indeed; it is, in fact, difficult to see how the Irving Howe of the years 1967-82, whose contributions were discussed above, can form part of this "we."

Howe's implied message is that if only "they" can be removed and the Labor Party returned to power, then "we" can proceed to realize the vision of "Weizmann's liberal Zionism" (as he construes it), an illusion that flies in the face of the entire history of the political grouping that he contrasts to Begin-Sharon. Furthermore, Weizmann's "liberal Zionism" had breathed its last by 1946, when Weizmann returned to London from the Twenty-Second Congress of the World Zionist movement "beaten and embittered. It was the end of an epoch. Militant Zionism had come out on top after a decade-long struggle between giants"[121]—a struggle between Weizmann's "liberal Zionism" and the "militant Zionism" of Ben-Gurion, the leader of the Labor Zionist faction that Howe sees as "we." What is more, a look beyond the obvious would reveal the true nature of Weizmann's "liberal Zionism," "Weizmann's legacy" as Zionist historian Simha Flapan termed it, with its "lasting impact," namely, the rejection of any Palestinian rights within the Land of Israel, except as part of some temporary tactical maneuver.*

In the same connection, the journal that Howe edits, *Dissent*, subsequently cited a 1975 interview with Ben-Gurion, published after his death, in which he called for return to the pre-1967 borders so as to ensure "an unassailable Jewish majority" in Israel ("the Arabs drastically outbreed us") and because the country "belongs to *two* races—the Arabs of Palestine and the Jews of the world—each of whom, first the Jews and then the Arabs, have controlled it for some 1,300 years apiece." This is published under the heading "Ben-Gurion on peace," presumably justifying the association of Howe's "we" with the Labor Zionism of Ben-Gurion. Whatever one thinks of Ben-Gurion's 1975 statement, it hardly serves the purpose. Ben-Gurion's political career ended in the early 1960s. In the 1961 election he was "an electoral liability" and by then he was "to all intents and purposes...a defeated man," Lucas observes. He resigned from office in 1963 and was expelled from Mapai (the Labor Party) in 1965. "In the course of the Six Day War [1967]," his biographer Bar-Zohar writes, "Ben-Gurion grasped that his active involvement in Israeli politics was at an end," and by 1970 he "withdrew from public life" completely. His estrangement from his former Labor Party associates was further revealed by the statement quoted in *Dissent*, which placed him in complete opposition to their outspoken rejectionism.[122] While the citation given was quite beside the point, it would have been in place to cite Ben-Gurion's views while he was the leading figure in the Labor Party, for example, his position that the indigenous Arab population had no particular tie to their homes and hence no real place in Palestine so that transfer would be quite in order on moral grounds, his commitment to a Greater Israel that could be created by one or another method (not excluding conquest) after the tactical and temporary acceptance of partition had laid the basis for state power, his plans to dismember Lebanon, etc. Nothing of this has appeared in *Dissent*, though it would surely be relevant to a proper understanding of "we" and "they."

Some further attention should be given to Howe's demand for acknowledgement of the "legitimacy of Israel" as a precondition to negotiation. The wording is so common here as to pass unnoticed, but a little thought will show that it constitutes still another device of American and Israeli rejectionists to block any possibility of a peaceful political settlement. There is no relevant concept of "legitimacy" or "right to exist" in

---

*On "Weizmann's legacy" and the actual positions taken by the "liberal Zionism" of Weizmann and the "militant Zionism" of Ben-Gurion, see p. 52 and further discussion in chapters 3, 4, and references cited.

diplomatic interactions or international law. States are recognized because they exist and function, not because they are "legitimate" or have a "right to exist." The U.S. would certainly not declare that the USSR is "legitimate" or has a "right to exist" in its present form, or that the governments of its satellites are "legitimate." In fact, the U.S. officially rejects the forcible incorporation of the Baltic states into the USSR, to this day. Nevertheless, the U.S. recognizes the USSR and its satellites. There are others who regard no state as legitimate, but they do not thereby oppose the mutual recognition of existing states with whatever rights are accorded them within the existing international system, though no abstract "right to exist." Note that the demand that Palestinians recognize the "legitimacy" of Israel goes well beyond the demand that Israel recognize the PLO as the "sole legitimate representative of the Palestinians," as Palestinians have insisted with remarkable near-unanimity and as Israel has of course always refused to do. One can recognize that some group regards a particular institutional structure (state or organization) as its legitimate representative without thereby according it "legitimacy" as an institution. There is no more reason to expect Palestinians to accept the "legitimacy" of Israel—that is the "legitimacy" of their dispossession from their homes—than there is for Israel to accept the "legitimacy" of Syria under Alawite tyranny, or for Mexico to accept the "legitimacy" of the United States, which stole much of its land; etc. To impose this unprecedented demand is simply to place still another barrier in the path of eventual negotiations and political settlement. Israelis may regard their state as presently constituted as "legitimate," and Palestinians may regard the PLO as their "sole legitimate representative," but these commitments need not be adopted by others who, nevertheless, recognize the fact of these commitments and accept the right to self-determination, whatever their attitude towards the institutional structures that result from the fulfilment (partial and distorted as always) of this right.[123]

What of the idea, expressed by Hentoff and Peres, that prior to Begin and Sharon Israeli soldiers had to be careful about injuring civilians, or that David Ben-Gurion insisted on righteousness not merely strength and—as is implied by Peres's remarks—would have been appalled at the efforts of Begin and Sharon to evade responsibility for what happened in Beirut? Do these statements give a fair assessment of the period since 1948 when "we struck the civilian population consciously, because they deserved it," in Ze'ev Schiff's paraphrase of the remarks of the Chief of Staff, a relative dove? Or of Ben-Gurion's doctrine that it is necessary to strike defenseless innocents "mercilessly, women and children included," in reprisal actions?[124] American Zionists may plead ignorance of the facts. Peres, however, knows them very well.

Peres knows, for example, that this is not the first time that an Israeli government has been forced to resort to such deceit to cover up the

terrorist violence of Ariel Sharon. The first well-known occasion
October 1953, when Unit 101 commanded by Sharon attacked the
danian village of Qibya in alleged "reprisal" for the killing of a mother and
two children in an Israeli village. Jordan had condemned the murders and
offered its cooperation to track down the criminals; the murderers had no
known or suspected connection with Qibya. UN military observers who
reached the scene two hours after Sharon's commandos had finished their
work described what they found: "Bullet-riddled bodies near the doorways and multiple bullet hits on the doors of the demolished houses
indicated that the inhabitants had been forced to remain inside until their
homes were blown up over them. . . Witnesses were uniform in describing
their experience as a night of horror, during which Israeli soldiers moved
about in their village blowing up buildings, firing into doorways and
windows with automatic weapons and throwing hand grenades."[125]

The Qibya attack evoked harsh condemnation, with even the American Jewish and strongly pro-Israel press comparing it to the Nazi massacre at Lidice; in contrast, the massacre is lauded as a major achievement in
the official Israeli history of the paratroopers, which states that "it washed
away the stain" of earlier defeats that the IDF had sustained in "reprisal
operations." The public stance was different. Concerned over the international reaction, Ben-Gurion, speaking in the name of the Government of
Israel, rejected "the ridiculous and fantastic" claim that Israeli military
units were involved in the raid; it was, he claimed, a spontaneous retaliation by "border settlers in Israel, mostly refugees, people from Arab
countries and survivors from the Nazi concentration camps," who
attacked the village of Qibya "that was one of the main centers of the
murderers' gangs," the kind of reprisal that Israel had "feared." Foreign
Minister Sharett was opposed to the deception, feeling that "no one in the
world will believe such a story and we shall only expose ourselves as liars."
He felt that "the stain would stick to us and will not be washed away for
many years to come." "Seventy corpses were found in the rubble," according to Ben-Gurion's biographer Bar-Zohar, "including dozens of women
and children." Ben-Gurion later "confess[ed] to one of his confidants that
he had lied," Bar-Zohar continues, but justified this act with a literary
reference (Victor Hugo) to a nun who had lied to protect a hunted
prisoner. Bar-Zohar also repeats the standard Israeli claim that "it never
even entered the paratroopers' minds that they were unwillingly perpetrating a massacre" as they blew up house after house in the undefended
village—just as the political and military leadership never dreamed that
the Phalangists they sent into Sabra and Shatila might not behave as
perfect gentlemen. Recall what was found by the UN military observers.[126]

Purity of arms? Care about injuring civilians? Conciliation and
peace? Righteousness, not just strength, and "pain" at the evasion of
responsibility?

I said that Qibya was the first "well-known" example of Sharon's terrorist career. It was not the first example. We find out more from Hebrew sources, for example, the history of the paratroopers, where we learn that Sharon was involved in the abduction of two Syrian officers in the early 1950s, and that the "first attack" of his Unit 101 was in August 1953. The target was the El-Bureig refugee camp south of Gaza, with 50 refugees reported killed according to the Israeli history; other sources give lower numbers, 15 or 20. UN commander Major General Vagn Bennike, reporting to the UN Security Council, described how "bombs were thrown through the windows of huts in which the refugees were sleeping and, as they fled, they were attacked by small arms and automatic weapons." Again, the justification was "reprisal."[127] See also p. 106*.

Qibya is the incident that at once comes to mind—as it surely came to Shimon Peres's mind—when tales about purity of arms, conciliation and peace, righteousness and honor are told to contrast Begin with his Labor Party predecessors. El-Bureig and Qibya launched Sharon's career. Conceivably, the Beirut massacres may end it. His career includes many ugly episodes in between, for example, the repression in Gaza and the brutal treatment of the inhabitants of northeastern Sinai under the Labor government. The responsibility of the Israeli army was far clearer and more stark in the earlier case of Qibya than in the Beirut massacres, as was the deception. The same is true of the massacres in Gaza after the 1956 war, and much else, crucially including the huge slaughter of civilians in Sabra and Shatila, and elsewhere in Lebanon, in June-August 1982.[128]

When Sharett feared that "the stain would stick to us and will not be washed away for many years," he was wrong. In fact, the record has been erased from memory, as the quotes just given indicate, or successfully prettified. Thus, the well-known Israeli-American military historian Amos Perlmutter, writing in the *New York Times Magazine*, describes the activities of Sharon's Unit 101 in the following terms:

> Every time terrorists were captured in Israel, they would be interrogated to determine where they had come from. Then an Israeli force would return to the terrorists' villages and retaliate against them, an eye for an eye—or, more often, two eyes for an eye.[129]

Hardly a proper account of the Qibya operation, or many others.*

Today, Israel's leading journal, *Ha'aretz*, writes that "the stain of Sabra and Shatila has stuck to us, and we shall not be able to erase it."

---

* The implications of Perlmutter's account are in some ways even more appalling than the reality—which is that Israel's "retaliations" were undertaken largely without concern for the source of the terrorism, as in Qibya. Terrorists are not known to tell their interrogators where they had come from, except under torture. Note furthermore that even in his version, the victims of the "retaliation" are innocents. There is also the usual question of the chicken and the egg.

This reference to the Sabra-Shatila massacres repeats virtually the very words used by Moshe Sharett after the Qibya massacre 30 years earlier. Citing this statement, *Newsweek* adds that the Beirut tragedy caused "a wound to Israel's soul [that] went deeper than lamentation over a massacre," a "feeling among many Israelis that over the years their country had strayed somehow from the ideals of Zionism," a feeling that its military successes "had sapped its moral authority, transforming the nation from an underdog into a bully."[130] The same issue of *Newsweek* has a picture of Ben-Gurion, who endorsed the Qibya massacre (among others) and sought to conceal it with lies. He is depicted as a man of peace, "Casting a light unto the nations." Recall the highly selective and politically irrelevant reference to Ben-Gurion's views in *Dissent* (see p. 381). It has been no service to Israel to wash away these many stains, and to have established the conditions under which new and greater ones will appear. It is no service now to pretend that Begin and Sharon have introduced something radically new into Israeli social or political culture or military practice in West Beirut, or before. There are differences between the Likud and its predecessors, important ones, but they are nothing like those presented in contemporary debate. By laboring to cover up the real history of Israel, and the U.S. contribution to it, its supporters have encouraged precisely the tendencies whose fruition they now deplore as the facts become too well-publicized to suppress.

The crucial point, already copiously illustrated, is that over the years Israeli political elites have learned that they will be protected from exposure in the United States, and that, as the *New York Times* editors recommended once again while much of West Beirut was being smashed to rubble, the U.S. will pay for their exploits, as long as U.S. interests are protected. Given this historical experience, Begin and Sharon had every reason to believe that the same tactics would work once again when they sent the forces they mobilized into the refugee camps. Their judgment may in fact prove correct, as memories fade and the inevitable reconstruction of recent events proceeds, a process that was well underway within a few months of the massacre, as we shall see directly when we turn to the Report of the Kahan Commission of Inquiry and its reception.

6.4   On "Moral Idiocy"

The typical reaction in the U.S. to the Beirut massacres was as just illustrated: criticism of Begin-Sharon, resurrection of fantasies concerning the "beautiful Israel" that was, of course, what its supporters had been backing all along; euphoria as Israel showed its profound moral convictions by lamenting the massacre; and to celebrate the triumph of humanitarianism, an aid increase for the further militarization of Israeli society and for new settlements in the occupied territories. There were, however, other reactions. Norman Podhoretz bewailed the "great slide down the slippery slope to moral idiocy" on the part of those who "began denouncing the Jews" when "Christians murdered Moslems for having murdered Christians"—essentially Begin's reaction, at the same time. The "moral idiots" were effacing the responsibility of Yasser Arafat, who was "directly responsible for the deaths of the Lebanese babies behind whom he hid his forces in Beirut," just as his followers "had murdered Israeli babies at Maalot" (on the Ma'alot killings, see p. 189, above; recall also how the Jewish Defense forces—Haganah—"hid behind Jewish babies" during the Jerusalem siege and before; see pp. 311-2). The moral idiots failed to see that it was, once again, the PLO, far more than Israel, who bore a major responsibility for the Sabra-Shatila massacres.[131]

There was also a reaction from Elie Wiesel, who is much revered internationally and in the United States for his writings on the Holocaust and on moral standards and has been proposed many times for the Nobel Peace Prize for these writings, again for 1983, by half the members of Congress according to the secretary of the Norwegian Nobel Committee.* Wiesel's position was that: "I don't think we should even comment on [the massacre in the refugee camps] since the [Israeli judicial] investigation is still on." "We should not pass judgement until the investigation takes place." Nevertheless, he did feel "sadness," for the first time, he explains; nothing that had happened before in the occupied territories or in Lebanon had evoked any sadness on his part, and now the sadness was "with Israel, and not against Israel"—surely not "with the Palestinians" who had been massacred or with the remnants who escaped. Furthermore, Wiesel continues, "After all, the Israeli soldiers did not kill"—this time at least; they had often killed at Sabra and Shatila in the preceding

---

* In 1983, Wiesel was awarded the 1983 International Literary Prize for Peace in Liege, Belgium, perhaps in recognition of his observations through 1982 on Israel's policies in the occupied territories and in Lebanon. *Boston Globe*, April 24, 1983. He was selected as chairman of the Holocaust memorial, as the "only one person of sufficient stature." In his speech at the April 1983 gathering of Holocaust survivors, he emphasized support for Israel in the face of military and "political" threats. *Washington Post*, April 12, 13, 1983. Wolf Blitzer comments from Washington in the *Jerusalem Post* (April 15, 1983) that the organizers "were always careful, in their public statements, to characterize it as a nonpolitical event. But from the start, those involved in the operation fully recognized the automatic political spinoff for Israel...Israeli officials and sympathetic American Jewish political activists agreed that raising public awareness of the Holocaust...was bound to generate heightened sympathy and support for Israel. Only the most fanatically pro-Arab and anti-Israel advocates could fail to appreciate the relationship." The organizers chose a low-keyed approach; they "did not have to use a sledgehammer to press their point for strong U.S. backing for Israel...Thus, without much advertisement or fanfare, Israel's cause automatically received a major boost. Israeli diplomats were very well aware of the fact." He goes on to explain how U.S. government officials "hesitated" to criticize Israel and "its West Bank settlement policy" because of the Holocaust gathering, joining Wiesel in their silence. Recall Nahum Goldmann's remarks on exploitation of the Holocaust for political ends, an act of "sacrilege." See p. 98.

weeks, arousing no "sadness" on Wiesel's part, even "sadness with Israel." Therefore, Israel is basically exempt from criticism, as were the Czar and his officials, military forces and police at the time of the Kishinev massacre, by his exalted standards.

Recall Wiesel's unwillingness to criticize Israel beyond its borders, or to comment on what happens in the occupied territories, because "You must be in a position of power to possess all the information." Generalizing the principle beyond the single state to which it applies for this saintly figure, as we should if it is valid, we reach some interesting conclusions: it follows, for example, that critics of the Holocaust while it was in progress were engaged in an illegitimate act, since not being in positions of power in Nazi Germany, they "did not possess all the information."

At a rather different moral level, the Israeli novelist A.B. Yehoshua responded to the massacre by saying that "the German soldiers also did not know what was happening":

> What happened in the refugee camps in Beirut is the logical consequence of all that took place in the past months. A logical consequence, and almost an unavoidable one. What can one say? Even if I could believe that IDF soldiers who stood at a distance of 100 meters from the camps did not know what happened, then this would be the same lack of knowledge of the Germans who stood outside Buchenwald and Treblinka and did not know what was happening! We too did not want to know.

Others too were unwilling to accept facile evasions of the Elie Wiesel type, for example, Professor Yeshayahu Leibovitz of the Hebrew University, editor of the *Encyclopedia Hebraica*, who wrote:

> The massacre was done by us. The Phalangists are our mercenaries, exactly as the Ukrainians and the Croatians and the Slovakians were the mercenaries of Hitler, who organized them as soldiers to do the work for him. Even so have we organized the assassins in Lebanon in order to murder the Palestinians. [132]

Historian Barbara Tuchman reacted to the massacres by recalling her earlier concern that "Israel's determination to wipe out the Palestine Liberation Organization" in pursuit of its "justifiable aim" of "elimination of the P.L.O. threat" would "encounter difficulties," because the "complications of the Arab world are not such as the Israelis can control." As quoted, she had no further comment on the massacres except to say that "What concerns me is the survival and future of Israel and of Jews in the Diaspora—myself among them." In contrast, Rabbi Arnold Wolf was "crushed and terrified by the massacre," adding that "I think all of us have bloody hands."[133]

6.5   "Putting a Snake into a Child's Bed": The United States and its Commitments

6.5.1 The Defenseless Remnants

Consider finally the last of the series of charges of responsibility cited above: the charge of U.S. complicity. Recall the feeling of the Labor opposition during the war itself that they could not act after the U.S. had given the "green light" for the invasion. The initial U.S. response to the Israeli entry into West Beirut was tempered. White House spokesmen refrained from condemning the move, describing it as "limited and precautionary," and "Israeli diplomatic sources expressed satisfaction last night over the moderate American reaction to the Israeli move into West Beirut," in violation of the Habib agreements and the U.S. pledge to the Lebanese and Palestinians. "Despite persistent questioning, however, U.S. officials declined to criticize the movement of Israeli troops into West Beirut or to insist on their quick withdrawal."[134] The President, in fact, explained that "what led [Israel] to move back in [sic] was the attack after the assassination of the elected President by some of the leftist militia that is still there in west Beirut." Reagan's "justification for the Israeli move stunned officials in Washington," who commented privately that even the Israelis hadn't made that claim, though White House press secretary Larry Speakes conjured up some "private claims" by the Israelis that they were "provoked" by some fire "by leftists." One can sympathize with the officials whose job it is to cover up after the President's various random shots. Reagan also dismissed questions concerning Israel's partial occupation of the Soviet Embassy ("Oh, you know the Russians. You can't believe anything they say").[135]

Israeli officials maintained that the privately-expressed U.S. view "was considerably less demanding of Israel than the public statement Thursday accusing Israel of violating the agreement under which the Palestine Liberation Organization withdrew from west Beirut." They expressed anger over the official statement which "came only hours after a much more 'understanding' American line had been presented by Mr. Draper in private." "The Israelis firmly believe that the private position is the authentic one," and that the "tough statement" is for show, "because of Arab pressure."[136] The Israeli interpretation is not at all implausible. We have seen the same pattern with regard to settlement in the occupied territories, the invasion of Lebanon, and the sharp intensification of the attack on West Beirut in August. Throughout, Israel has held—not unreasonably, given the concrete facts of diplomatic and material support—that whatever public show of anger there may be, they are being privately informed to proceed.

The official U.S. reaction to the massacre was also quite restrained. After the massacre reports had been made public, U.S. officials assigned

Israel "indirect responsibility" for having failed to stop the massacre, and the President's official statement noted only that Lebanese Army units were "thwarted" in their effort to establish control "by the Israeli occupation that took place on Wednesday."[137] Israel was blamed for having failed to prevent the tragedy, not for its role in implementing it. At the UN, the United States stood alone against the entire world, along with Israel, in refusing to condemn the massacre. See p. 371.

U.S. perfidy on this matter is in fact far deeper. During the Habib negotiations, the United States gave explicit assurances to the Lebanese and Palestinians that the safety of the Palestinians would be guaranteed after the departure of the PLO fighters; Habib wrote the Lebanese Prime Minister that "my government will do its utmost to ensure that these assurances [on the part of Israel] are scrupulously observed." Citing the Habib letters, Milton Viorst observes that the American commitments "were crucial to the PLO's agreement to evacuate Beirut," leaving the civilian population unprotected. The text of the agreement had been quoted earlier by Alexander Cockburn:

> The Governments of Lebanon and the United States will provide appropriate guarantees of the safety...of law-abiding Palestinian noncombatants left in Beirut, including the families of those who have departed... The U.S. will provide its guarantees on the basis of assurances received from the Government of Israel and the leaders of certain Lebanese groups with which it has been in contact.[138]

An implied commitment was that Israel would not enter Beirut after the peaceful withdrawal of the PLO.

The American peace-keeping force had the dual obligation of overseeing the departure of the PLO and safeguarding the civilian population, in accordance with the explicit American commitment. It withdrew after the first of these tasks was performed, two weeks before its original mandate ran out, effectively terminating the multinational commitment to protect the civilians left in peril. The ABC News *Closeup* investigation cited earlier states: "The multinational force is committed to protect civilians for 30 days, but the Americans insist on leaving Beirut two weeks ahead of schedule, which forces the French and Italians to pull out as well." Shortly after, the IDF moved into Beirut and the massacre took place. The killers are called "Israeli-backed," Cockburn comments, "but they should, with equal accuracy, be termed 'U.S.-sanctioned' since their onslaught on the camps was only possible in the event that the U.S. flouted a specific guarantee."

Viorst was informed by the State Department that the U.S. had "never formally lodged a protest, either for the occupation of Beirut or for what happened at Shatila and Sabra."

6.5.2 The "Brought-in"*

Viorst also cites a second Habib letter, no less significant, concerning Palestinian prisoners, urging that they be accorded humane treatment. "American officials acknowledge, nonetheless, that very little has been done to follow up on the letter's pledges." According to Viorst, the Israeli government announced that there were 8000 such prisoners in Israel in addition to the 6-7000 in Lebanon. (Note that this estimate accords with the Red Cross figures reported by Israeli journalist Danny Rubinstein; see p. 221). Viorst cites a Red Cross spokesman who stated "that the Israelis have permitted no visits of facilities in Israel, and otherwise decline to cooperate with the Red Cross, so it has no idea of what it is happening there." We have already had a glimpse of what is happening in the Lebanon "concentration camps," as Israeli eyewitnesses term them, where the Red Cross does have some access, and in the Israeli military command post in Sidon. The State Department could cite no specific case of American intercession on the prisoner issue, despite the Habib commitment. In a sense, this is not surprising, since the American press, public, and even humanitarian organizations have also shown no signs of concern over this major atrocity, the exact dimensions of which are not yet known, and may never be known.

It should be noted that reports months after the war from European groups concerned with the scandalous issue of the IDF's prisoners have been shocking (I know of no reports from American groups). They incidentally cite credible information that apart from the wholesale round-up of the male Palestinian population and many Lebanese men, women were also imprisoned, some possibly tortured. This additional atrocity was revealed when Israeli lawyer Felicia Langer appealed for the right to visit Maryam Abdel-Jelil, who had been detained and interrogated in the Israeli military compound in Tyre and then removed to a women's prison in Israel after her arrest on November 1, 1982 at a refugee camp near Tyre where she was a teacher and social worker (Palestinians imprisoned in the Peace for Galilee Operation—and subsequently—are not granted the right to see lawyers, or to be visited at all, another fact that arouses no interest among the American civil libertarians and humanists who are helping to finance these operations). According to the same sources, she was secretly released after Langer's inquiry and found in a Tyre hospital, in a physical and mental condition that indicated that she had been brutally treated. Since then other cases have been discovered. The same sources also allege that in a number of cases the women arrested

---

* The many thousands of people carted away to Israeli prisons and concentration camps are not referred to as "prisoners," which would raise questions about international conventions and other human rights considerations. Rather, a new Hebrew word has been coined to refer to them: they are the ones "brought in."

and deported were the last remaining support for the families who survived in the devastated camps.[139]

Dr. Israel Shahak, Chairman of the Israeli League for Human and Civil Rights, reports that according to information he has received the total number of prisoners at the end of 1982 may have reached 19-20,000, more than 3/4 of them Lebanese. The 4000-4500 Palestinians were all in the Ansar camp in Lebanon, apart from seven women in the Neve Tirza women's prison in Israel. The Lebanese appear to be held in camps scattered in remote areas in Lebanon, under atrocious conditions. There were thousands of prisoners in Israel a few months earlier, as Viorst reported, but with few exceptions they were returned to camps in unknown locations in Lebanon, or freed after the brutal treatment that they have reported on their release; see chapter 5, section 5.3 for a few examples. Many Palestinian men have disappeared in the zones controlled by Israel's client Major Haddad.* Given the general lack of interest in this matter by Westerners who would be concerned if the victims were human beings rather than Palestinians, and who would be evoking images of the Nazis if the victims were Jews, it is impossible to offer a fuller accounting.

6.5.3 More on Hypocrisy

Returning to the charge of "hypocrisy" expressed by Israel with regard to angry U.S. unofficial reactions, one can again perceive its merit. The initial U.S. response encouraged Israel to proceed into West Beirut, and it was only reasonable to expect that some version of Sharon's procedures would be implemented once the population was left defenseless by Israeli military operations.

The essential point was expressed quite accurately by Meron Benvenisti, the former deputy mayor of Jerusalem whose research on the settlement programs was discussed in chapter 4:

What's our Army if not the product of American aid? Didn't Reagan proclaim Jewish settlements on the West Bank "not illegal?" Didn't Haig sanction the first phase of the Lebanese invasion? Everything that has happened in Israel until now has carried the stamp of American approval, or at least it was tolerated by your governments. If the genie is out of the bottle, it was Washington that helped to turn him loose.[140]

---

* Personal communication. For more information, see the references cited in note 139 and chapter 5, section 5.3; also "Women at risk," *Middle East International*, March 4, 1983, describing the techniques used to force women left alone with their families to inform on their husbands or pressure them to surrender to the Israelis, for example, the case of Abla al-Hassan, taken to an Israeli prison leaving her four children (one an unweaned infant, one a mongoloid) without care.

His remarks are just. It is, he correctly says, "just too slick to say that Israel has lost its soul and leave it at that." It will not do for Americans to blame the Phalange, or Begin-Sharon, or their silent partners in the Labor Alignment, or Israeli rejectionism, expansion and oppression over many years. Without crucial American support at every level, matters would have been quite different, not only in the past few months. In short, the circle of responsibility cannot be so narrowly drawn, convenient as it may be to do so.

Commenting on the massacre, the Israeli writer Amos Elon makes this observation:

> A man who puts a snake into a child's bed and says: "I'm sorry. I told the snake not to bite. I didn't know snakes were so dangerous." It's impossible to understand. This man's a war criminal.[141]

He therefore judges Begin and Sharon to be war criminals, as did a number of other Israeli commentators.* The argument cuts deeper, however. What about those who gave the "green light" when Israel invaded West Beirut, or when Israel invaded Lebanon in the first place to "clean out terrorist nests"? Or those who applauded these and earlier ventures or remained silent about them? Did they not know that snakes are dangerous?

6.6   The "Principal Culprits"

At the time of the Kishinev massacre, Tolstoi extended the circle of responsibility to the "principal culprits" with their "propaganda of falsehood and violence." One of Israel's most courageous journalists, Uri Avneri, did the same. "Every child now killed in the bombardment of Beirut, every child buried under the ruins of a shelled house, is being murdered by an Israeli journalist," he wrote during the bombing of Beirut. His reasoning extends to the present case as well, and applies with no less—perhaps more—force in the United States than in Israel, where many outstanding journalists have in fact reported much that has often been concealed and distorted here, over many years. Avneri's point is that in Israel the Palestinians have been thoroughly dehumanized, as when the press announces that "terrorist nests have been bombed and shelled in Beirut," knowing that it is "a lie" and that "The bombs hit civilians, women, men, children and the aged." Furthermore:

---

* See also the comment by Ze'ev Schiff: "whoever allowed the Phalangists to enter the refugee camps on their own can be compared to one who allows a fox into the chicken coop and then wonders why the chickens were all eaten"; *New Outlook*, October 1982. Also "Tales of Foxes and Birds," *Davar*, Sept. 29, 1982, by Yizhar Smilansky, one of Israel's

Terrorists have no "nests." Animals have nests, birds too. People—good or bad—have houses, offices, headquarters.

The "original sin" of Israeli journalists was the very use of the word "terrorist" (or to be more precise, the new term, "mehablim," invented for the purpose) to include "all PLO fighters" and later "all PLO members— diplomats, officials, teachers, physicians, nurses in the Palestinian Red Crescent," and finally "the whole of the Palestinian people," so that "we bomb 'terrorist camps,' meaning Palestinian refugee camps in which PLO fighters may or may not be located." When Palestinian refugees become "terrorists," they can "be bombed, shelled, expelled, denied their human- ity... The ruins of Beirut, with the bodies of the women, men and children buried underneath, serve as the memorial" of this journalistic practice.[142]

A. B. Yehoshua made the same point after the Beirut massacres, six weeks later: "When they speak of extermination and cleansing, when they call the Palestinians two-legged beasts—it is no wonder that a soldier permits such horrors to take place right next to him." The point had been made before by others, among them a group of Israeli doves who pub- lished a statement in June entitled "Life and Death in the Hands of the Language," which discusses such phrases as "nests of terrorists" (like nests of insects), "purification" of these nests (with its religious connotations, understood by every Israeli), "extermination" (as of insects) and "two- legged beasts" for the "terrorists" inhabiting the "nests," expressions that have been devised and used to dehumanize the Palestinian enemy and justify whatever has been done to them, again, a practice that is not without its antecedents in Jewish history, with roles reversed.[143] The effect was once again evident in the following weeks.

The "ideological support" for Israel in the United States, with its systematic falsification of the historical record and its practice of defam- ing the Palestinians and ignoring their torment, merits similar words. The Palestinians have been deprived of their humanity and left as fair game for the atrocities that they have suffered, and will continue to suffer. Nothing is easier than to shed responsibility, to condemn the crimes—often real— of someone else. There is much that could have been done to present a fair and honest picture of what was and had been happening, and to change the U.S. policies that have predictably led to the rise of a Greater Israel that is a threat to its own citizens, to those subject to its military power, and to many others as well, and that lie behind the specific events of 1982. To the extent that we do not do what can be done, we have only ourselves to blame for the consequences. If these are truisms, and they are, they nevertheless will bear repetition so long as they are ignored.

outstanding novelists, responding to the radio comment by Minister Yosef Burg: "Chris- tians killed Muslims; How are the Jews guilty?"

6.7   Reactions: Israel and Elsewhere

Israel surely suffered a deterioration in its image abroad as a result of the war. A dramatic example was given by Yoel Marcus of *Ha'aretz*, who regards the war "from its beginning to its end (which is not yet on the horizon [in October]) as the fulfillment of the most terrifying prophecies that one could imagine." He reports on a visit to South Africa, where he had expected to find "the last island of popular sympathy remaining for us in the world" in "our second most important ally after the United States." The bombings of Beirut were condemned, and also the massacres. "Who would have believed that even in the eyes of the state that is denounced as the most immoral in the world, Israel is regarded as immoral?" "We carry out a policy of Apartheid, we oppress the Blacks, not giving them a decent education, and their wages are miserable—but we do not murder women and children,"* he was told by a South African editor.[144]

Marcus exaggerates; in the United States, and Europe as well, the strongly pro-Israel bias of the past and the dehumanization of the Palestinians persists. A clear indication is the lack of concern for the thousands of people taken to Israeli "concentration camps," or the fate of the Palestinians whose civilian society was demolished by the conquering army, or the *Samidin* of earlier conquests.

Within Israel itself, reactions were mixed. As noted earlier, support for Begin and Sharon ran high by late August, when the successes of Peace for Galilee seemed considerable. An early September poll showed 82% satisfied with Begin's performance, while 78% approved of Sharon's, figures that dropped to 72% and 64%, respectively, after the Beirut massacres. As choice for Prime Minister, no other candidate even came close to Begin in popularity in a poll taken after the massacre; see p. 254*. The support for Sharon immediately after the massacre that he had engineered is particularly striking.

The huge anti-government demonstration called by the Labor Party, estimated by some as reaching 400,000 people, revealed the strength of anti-government feeling on the part of a significant sector of the population, but as historian Jonathan Frankel observed, "the protest movement represented not the exposed tip but almost the entire bulk of the iceberg—while another, separate, and larger iceberg remained intact, albeit submerged . . . the massacres made a far greater impact on the 'formal' political world—the government, the Knesset, the media—than on the mass of the people, the 'silent majority'." Others drew the same conclusion, observing that "Premier Begin's supporters have not been shocked by the revelations of the Beirut massacre that have emerged so far—and they are unlikely to be shocked by future revelations."[145]

---

* This is, of course, a lie, though Marcus does not mention the fact. For just one example, see p. 371.

After the reports of witnesses in the open sessions of the Commission of Inquiry began to appear, Yoel Marcus wrote a column entitled "The Commission will Finish—the Government will Remain," giving his assessment:

> In the matter of Sabra and Shatila—a large part of the community, perhaps the majority, is not at all troubled by the massacre itself. Killing of Arabs in general, and Palestinians in particular, is quite popular, or at least "doesn't bother anyone," in the words of the youth these days. Ever since the massacre I have been surprised more than once to hear from educated, enlightened people, "the conscience of Tel Aviv," the view that the massacre itself, as a step towards removing the remaining Palestinians from Lebanon, is not terrible. It is just too bad that we were in the neighborhood.[146]

The attitude towards Palestinians has taken on the form of race hatred in significant circles in Israel. It is, I think, too facile to consider the cause to be simply Palestinian terrorism. The scale of Israeli terrorism over many years is one of many reasons to question this conclusion; no PLO terrorist act in Israel compares with Qibya, to mention only one example. I suspect that the roots are deeper. As long as any trace of an organized Palestinian presence remains anywhere nearby, the legitimacy of the Israeli national rebirth may somehow appear to be in question. "We cannot stand a symmetry of claims," Meron Benvenisti remarks: "Israelis have a profound feeling that once they accept the symmetry that the other side is also a legitimate national movement, then their own feeling about their own right and legitimacy will be dimmed."[147] Benvenisti deplores this sentiment, which has often been voiced over the years.* Israelis know well that it is possible to cherish memories of one's homeland for a long, long time, if an organized social existence remains somewhere. Therefore it must be extirpated, just as even the rubble of the hundreds of deserted Palestinian villages in Israel must be removed from sight, and from memory. Any manifestation of cultural life or independent political structures must be eliminated in the territories under Israeli occupation; and

---

* Rabbi David Hartman rejects Benvenisti's view that Israelis should accept the legitimacy of the claims of the indigenous population that they have displaced. He argues that there is no reason for him to feel "morally responsible to someone who denies my own existence," and since the Palestinians refuse to concede that "the Jewish people are indigenous to this land, then don't ask me to enter into a moral dialogue with them." Every society has its ugly extreme, here exemplified in the case of Israel: the religious moral philosopher standing with his boot on someone's neck and complaining that his victim does not recognize his legitimacy. In the *New York Times*, Hartman is highly regarded; he is identified as "a philosopher who has spoken of the need for morality in public policy" (see note 147). His thoughts on "integrating Judaic morality with national power" and the renewal of the "moral health" of Israeli society with the Kahan Report are spelled out further in his article "The Covenant in Israel," and he is again featured on the same day in Shipler's "Israel: Voices of Moral Anguish," *New York Times Magazine*, Feb. 27, 1983.

even beyond, nothing may remain, except insofar as this may serve Israel's policy, to which we return, of intensifying communal strife within Lebanon—or, of course, insofar as the Arab labor force from Gaza, the West Bank, and perhaps later on the North Bank, is to be exploited as a cheap and unorganized labor force, in the manner already described.

Despite Marcus's comment, there is no doubt that much of the population was appalled by the war and particularly the subsequent massacre, and expressed this sentiment in many ways: in demonstrations, press conferences, public statements, refusal to serve in a war of aggression. Examples have already been cited, and there were many more. References to the early days of Hitler Germany were not uncommon. Among the many statements of protest, one was a letter describing the war in Lebanon as a moral "disaster," written by 35 members of the elite military unit that carried out the Entebbe rescue. In an interview along with Uri Avneri in Paris, Gen. Mattityahu Peled stated that "the Israelis have become the Mongols of the Middle East, who sow destruction and misery," while condemning the Labor opposition for supporting Sharon. Avneri's newspaper ran without comment diary excerpts based on a book by a German officer on the Nazi invasion of Poland in 1939. Later Peled and Avneri, along with PLO spokesman Issam Sartawi, called on American and European Jews to pressure Begin and Reagan to lift the siege of Beirut and withdraw Israeli forces from Lebanon, citing Arafat's endorsement of the principle of mutual recognition by Israel and the PLO.[148] A number of Israel's leading intellectual figures, including the philosopher Asa Kasher, novelist Yizhar Smilansky, and many others, spoke out strongly against the war. Soldiers, including many officers returning from the front, were among the most outspoken and influential in conveying a picture that had been withheld by censorship and distortion.

Just prior to the news of the Beirut massacres, A. B. Yehoshua, the well-known Jerusalem-born novelist, wrote that "now there are no more complaints against Begin in connection with Deir Yassin. He succeeded in involving all of us in a different kind of Deir Yassin," Yehoshua also comments that "it is possible to say many harsh things about this government, but one thing it is impossible to say about it: that it is an innovative government." In fact, it was following the traditional Labor policy from "the years when Golda [Meir] was in power: 'do not move, do not speak, do not change anything'." Israeli rejectionism does not derive from Begin and Sharon. As for Israel's claim "to be a light unto the nations," they have "felt our light in Beirut, the light of the bombings and the flares dropped by the planes." Like other Israeli doves, Yehoshua had some harsh words for the Jews of the diaspora, "who sit and wail about anti-Semitism when anyone says a word of criticism" about Israel, which for them is "like a second home, against which it is forbidden to say a single critical word," no contribution to the health of Israel, he believes.

As for the "politically motivated" Lebanon war, its "deeper purpose" was "to return the Palestinians in the West Bank in political terms to their status in the days of the Turks."[149] He was far from alone in these feelings, and after the massacres, they received still more articulate expression, some already quoted.

Other views were also expressed, for example, those of a long list of Israeli Rabbis for whom what had happened was "the true sanctification of G-d's name in the world" while "the latest wave of anti-Semitism, in the guise of moral indignation directed at us for an act of vengeance committed by one Gentile community against another, is but one link in the centuries old chain of anti-Semitic expression," the source of which, as Maimonides explained, "is jealousy of our unique sanctity and true ethical superiority, a sanctity and superiority that find special expression in the wars we have waged, wars whose essence has been the demand for fairness and righteousness and the eradication of evil and injustice."[150] A group of more than 1000 American Rabbis chimed in, urging Begin, Sharon and Eitan to be faithful to their task and "continue to save Israel," dismissing the "traitors" of the Peace Now movement (mocked with a childish distortion of their name) and the Labor Alignment who cooperate with "the worst among the enemies of Israel" and are attempting to destroy Israel with their "poisonous propaganda," etc.[151] It is not at all impossible that they really do speak for the "silent majority," as they allege.

Which of these voices will prove to have a significant impact on policy in Israel will depend, in large measure, on the response in the United States, as always.

At least some notice should be taken of the protests among the Arab citizens of Israel in the wake of the Beirut massacres. In this case, the response of the authorities was somewhat different. "Scores of [Israeli] Palestinians who protested the Sabra and Shatila massacres, from Um al-Fahm, Taibeh, Acre, Arrabeh are still in jails and police detention centres, one month after the wave of protests swept the Galilee and Triangle areas. They face charges of demonstrating, inciting, stoning military vehicles and supporting the PLO."[152]

6.8 The Commission of Inquiry (the Kahan Commission)

The Report of the Israeli Commission of Inquiry into the Beirut massacres appeared on February 8, 1983 (see note 112). It evoked new raptures among the faithful. The *New Republic* wrote that this "great and grim document" set a "sublime standard of moral and political action" in "this extraordinary country," this "brilliant democracy." It was "a philosophical and political triumph," with its "moral seriousness and intellectual scrupulousness." Under the heading "Cry of Conscience," the *New*

York Times wrote: "Painfully and convincingly, Israel has raked through the horrors of Sabra and Shatila and judged itself, harshly, by 'the fundamental principles of the civilized world'." "How rare the nation that seeks salvation by revealing such shame."[153] Now that this "cry of conscience" has been expressed and salvation has been found, the U.S. can proceed with no qualms to pay the costs of the Lebanon invasion as the *Times* had recommended while the attack was reaching its peak of ferocity, meanwhile also funding the concentration camps and prisons, the settlements in the occupied territories, the oppression there, and whatever will come next.* The *Times* is incidentally quite correct in saying that Israel acquitted itself nobly by the standards of the "civilized world"—for example, the standards adopted by the *Times* with regard to U.S. aggression in Indochina, the U.S. overthrow of the democratic government of Guatemala and its support for a series of neo-Nazi murderers since, and much else. By civilized standards, however, a rather different judgment may be in order.

The Kahan Commission stated that "The main purpose of the inquiry was to bring to light all the important facts relating to the perpetration of the atrocities; it therefore has importance from the perspective of Israel's moral fortitude and its functioning as a democratic state that scrupulously maintains the fundamental principles of the civilized world."

The central section of the Report, dealing with "The Direct Responsibility," opens as follows: "According to the above description of events, all the evidence indicates that the massacre was perpetrated by the Phalangists..." The section goes on to state that "No other military force aside from the Phalangists was seen by any one of the witnesses in the area of the camps... It can be stated with certainty that no organized military force entered the camps at the aforementioned time beside the Phalangist forces." "No basis was found" for the "rumors" that Haddad forces were involved; indeed, this is "inconceivable," and there is no "hint" of their cooperation with the Phalangists in the venture. "We can therefore assert that no force under the command of Major Haddad took part in the Phalangists' operation in the camps, or took part in the massacre." As noted earlier, the participation of Haddad forces would be a considerable embarrassment for Israel since they are virtually a part of the Israeli army and are expected to play a central role in the New Order that Israel intends to establish in Lebanon.

---

* Columnists Jack W. Germond and Jules Witcover observe that "Israel's supporters" hope that the Report "will help arrest 'the waning of enthusiasm' toward Israel" in Congress, and "make it easier for [friends of Israel in Congress] to give their support and encourage Americans to do the same." *Boston Globe*, Feb. 15, 1983. It may, then, serve the same function as the demonstrations in Israel after the massacres, when filtered through the American ideological system.

The opening sentence, quoted above, is true but rather misleading. In the "above description of events," and apparently in its deliberations as well, the Commission was scrupulous in avoiding the evidence that runs counter to Israeli government claims on this issue, apart from a few passing phrases dismissing it without inquiry.* As we have seen in what was only a partial review, there is extensive evidence of the participation of Haddad forces, and where the Commission did choose to investigate, it regularly found that the government's claims were false, and indeed that its "incorrect and imprecise reports intensified the suspicions against Israel and caused it harm." The Israeli witnesses also proved to be of limited credibility, as the Commission noted. The proper procedure, clearly, would have been to review the evidence of Haddad participation and inquire directly into the composition of the forces that entered the camp by interrogating the leadership and even the participants—a task that should not have been beyond feasibility, given that "we could give them orders," as Chief of Staff Eitan stated with reference to the Phalange while explaining why they were chosen to enter the camps instead of the Lebanese army. The Commission simply avoided the topic, apart from hearing the testimony of Haddad, who, like everyone else, denied participation. Perhaps an honest inquiry into these facts would have led to the conclusion that although there is extensive circumstantial evidence based on a wide variety of eyewitness reports that Haddad forces were involved, nevertheless the conclusion is incorrect. Instead of inquiring into the matter, the Commission chose to renounce any intent to "bring to light all the important facts," and to make it clear from the outset that it was abandoning its mandate.

The Commission was careful to lay out the ground rules for its investigation. With admirable caution, it refrained from concluding that "from a legal perspective" the territory occupied by the IDF in West Beirut was "occupied territory." Thus the IDF is absolved from any of the legal obligations of occupying armies.

The Commission also states that there is no basis for the accusation that the IDF had "prior knowledge" that a massacre would take place. There is "no doubt" that no individuals from the "Israeli political echelon or from the military echelon" were engaged in any "conspiracy or plot"

---

* One of the witnesses, British doctor Paul Morris who worked at the Gaza hospital, subsequently alleged that his testimony was ignored and distorted by the Commission. In an interview with the Beirut weekly *Monday Morning*, he stated that he had testified that IDF soldiers at the forward command post had "told us repeatedly that the armed irregulars were Haddad men." He also claims to have provided evidence that Israeli soldiers were with the "irregulars" who entered the camp, and that the IDF soldiers "could see everything [in the camps] with the naked eye or with binoculars and night-sight devices." The Commission, he charged, "selected words and phrases from my testimony for their report and avoided other parts that could possibly suggest that the IDF has a direct responsibility for the deaths of innocent people in the camps...[My testimony] was deliberately ignored, willfully left out in order not to implicate any Israeli national in any of the murders in the camps." *Israel & Palestine* (Paris), March 1983. See p. 364*.

with the Phalangists "with the aim of perpetrating atrocities in the camps." On the basis of assurances provided by these "echelons," the Commission determined that what they said was true: "We assert that in having the Phalangists enter the camps, no intention existed on the part of anyone who acted on behalf of Israel to harm the non-combatant population, and that the events that followed did not have the concurrence or assent of anyone from the political or civilian echelon who was active regarding the Phalangists' entry into the camps." It need hardly be observed that to "assert" this on the basis of the evidence they review—testimony from the people involved—simply serves as a further indication that the Report is not intended to be taken seriously among rational people.

To underscore the latter point, the Commission provides a fair amount of evidence that higher authorities did indeed expect a massacre. The intelligence unit in closest contact with the Phalange, the Mossad, "heard things from [Bashir Gemayel] that left no room for doubt that the intention of this Phalangist leader was to eliminate the Palestinian problem in Lebanon when he came to power—even if that meant resorting to aberrant methods against the Palestinians in Lebanon... Similar remarks were heard from other Phalangist leaders." There were also "reports of Phalangist massacres of women and children in Druze villages, as well as the liquidation of Palestinians carried out by the intelligence unit of Elie Hobeika" (who was assigned the task of entering the camps by the IDF). "These reports reinforced the feeling among certain people—and especially among experienced intelligence officers—that in the event that the Phalangists had an opportunity to massacre Palestinians, they would take advantage of it." Chief of Staff Eitan expected "an eruption of revenge" and thought there might be "rivers of blood." If the IDF was not present, "it will be an eruption the likes of which has never been seen; I can already see in [the Phalangists'] eyes what they are waiting for... they have just one thing left to do, and that is revenge; and it will be terrible... the whole establishment is already sharpening knives..." The Commission also cites reports in the Israeli military journal that the refugee camps "were liable to undergo events exceeding what had happened" at Tel al-Zaatar, the worst massacre of the civil war. The Commission itself observes that "no prophetic powers were required to know that concrete danger of acts of slaughter existed when the Phalangists were moved into the camps without the IDF's being with them in that operation... The sense of such a danger should have been in the consciousness of every knowledgeable person who was close to the subject." They also cite Prime Minister Begin's official statement that the IDF entered West Beirut "in order to protect the Moslems from the vengeance of the Phalangists," a statement that simply leaves no doubt that at the highest level, it was clearly understood what would happen if Phalangists were sent into a Palestinian camp.

In short, the Commission presents sufficient evidence that the top leadership fully expected a massacre when they sent the Phalange into the camps. They justified the entry into West Beirut as an effort to prevent a Phalange massacre, and then proceeded to send the Phalange into the homes of their worst enemies—but with no intent to harm the population, the Commission "asserts" without equivocation. Again, one can only conclude that the Report is designed for true believers, not for people capable of independent thought.

The Commission incidentally reveals its own moral standards when it states that "it was not incumbent upon the Prime Minister to object to the Phalangists' entry into the camps or to order their removal," even though he sent the IDF into West Beirut "in order to protect the Moslems from the vengeance of the Phalangists." In short, though the Prime Minister fully expected a massacre, it was not his duty to do anything to prevent it. Truly an expression of "sublime" moral standards.

The Commission also "determined" that "events in the camps, in the areas where the Phalangists entered, were not visible from the roof of the forward command post. It has also been made clear that no sounds from which it could be inferred that a massacre was being perpetrated in the camps reached that place." That takes care of the reports of journalists who investigated the scene; for example, those who stood at the site of a mass grave and looked up to the Israeli command posts where they saw IDF soldiers watching them. It takes considerable talent to be able to refute on-the-scene investigations in Beirut from chambers in Jerusalem. In fact, when we look back to see what was actually "determined," we find that it was carefully circumscribed. The Commission determined, as is no doubt true, that "it was impossible to see what was happening within the alleys in the camp from the roof of the command post." But this was not the evidence cited by journalists on the scene who concluded, as was no doubt also true, that the IDF observers on the command post could see that a massacre was in progress, watch the bodies being dumped into the mass graves, and so on. See the direct reports sampled above.

No less interesting is the explanation of why the IDF sent the Phalangists into the camp: the decision

> was taken with the aim of preventing further losses in the war in Lebanon; to accede to the pressure of public opinion in Israel, which was angry that the Phalangists, who were reaping the fruits of the war, were taking no part in it; and to take advantage of the Phalangists' professional service and their skills in identifying terrorists and in discovering arms caches.

These considerations are reiterated later, and described as "weighty," perhaps sufficiently so as to justify sending the Phalangists into the camps even in the expectation of a massacre.

The phrase "further losses" refers to Israeli losses. As we have seen, Israel had made attempts to enter West Beirut in August but withdrew after heavy losses, turning to terror bombings instead, then entering the city after the PLO fighters had departed with an American guarantee that Israel would not enter West Beirut and that the defenseless population would be protected from harm. Some 100-150 Phalangists were sent into the camps, a clear indication that the IDF expected no serious resistance; and in fact, journalists who had visited the camps had seen no indication that there could be resistance in these heavily bombed civilian areas. The talk of "2000 terrorists" can hardly be taken seriously, and as we have seen, was ridiculed by Israeli journalists who noted the size of the Phalangist force. As for the Phalangists' "professional skills," the only such skills that they had revealed were in murdering defenseless people. However, journalists and others had been much impressed by Israel's extensive infiltration of the Palestinian and Lebanese resistance movements as well as the Arab communities in Beirut and elsewhere, which provided remarkably detailed knowledge of what was taking place in Beirut and in the camps. It is difficult to see why these and similar "professional skills" would not have sufficed in the undefended Palestinian camps—where, it will be recalled, the Phalangists suffered *two* casualties—two killed, one part of the Report says, two injured, another part indicates, quite possibly the same two. As for the Commission's sense of "public opinion in Israel," it virtually reeks of anti-Semitism. The Commission is stating that Israeli public opinion would be satisfied somehow if the fox were sent into an undefended and heavily bombarded chicken coop to "clean out terrorist nests," after having refrained from taking part in the actual fighting; see p. 392*.

The Commission states that the IDF received "heavy fire" from Shatila and light weapons fire from both camps when it entered West Beirut. Contradicting itself, it also reports without comment the IDF spokesman's announcement that "The entry of the I.D.F. forces was executed without resistance" and the Chief of Staff's report to Begin that "there was no resistance in Beirut." If evidence existed of "heavy fire" from the camps, thus confirming the claims about the "2000 terrorists," it is reasonable to suppose that it would have been presented. It does not appear to have been reported in the press, and the Commission offers no evidence. The Commission also claims that "there were armed terrorist forces in the camps," possessing arms that they had used against IDF forces: "It is possible to determine that this armed terrorist force had not been evacuated during the general evacuation," but had stayed behind "to protect the civilian population" (clear proof of their terrorist intent) and to renew terrorist activity later on. No evidence is provided to support any of these claims. Nor is there any explanation of why these armed terrorist forces that were directing heavy fire against the IDF were unable to resist or even inflict more than token casualties on 150 Phalangists who previously had been noted for their strict avoidance of combat (see p. 359). Again, it is difficult to believe that any of this is intended to be taken seriously.

Recall that in addition to "asserting," in defiance of its own evidence and plain common sense, that there was no intent to harm the civilian population when the murderous gangs were sent in, the Commission also "asserts" that "the events that followed did not have the concurrence or assent of anyone from the political or civilian echelon who was active regarding the Phalangists' entry into the camps." They pointedly exclude here the "military echelon," though without drawing any specific conclusions from this exception. They also make the unqualified assertion that "No intention existed on the part of *any* Israeli element to harm the non-combatant population in the camps" (my emphasis). Let us look further into how the selection of evidence to which the Report restricts itself bears on these assertions and exceptions.

The Commission recognizes that "the Chief of Staff told the Minister of Defense things about the conduct of the Phalangists that could have led the Minister of Defense to understand that the Phalangists had perpetrated the murder of civilians in the camps," though he "expressed his satisfaction with the Phalangist operation and agreed to their request to provide them with tractors so that they could complete their operations," also authorizing them to stay on in the camps (on Friday afternoon, at a time when the massacres were common knowledge, as noted earlier). The Commission discovered that on Thursday evening, September 16, shortly after the Phalangists had entered the camp, Brigadier General Amos Yaron, who was in command in the Beirut area, received information "that the Phalangists were killing women and children in the camps"; "it became known to Brigadier General Yaron that the Phalangists were perpetrating acts of killing which went beyond combat operations, and were killing women and children as well." Beyond alleged warnings to Phalangist liaison officers, "he did nothing to stop the killing." No order was issued to prevent the Phalangists "from replacing forces on Friday," and in fact the Chief of Staff ordered this replacement Friday afternoon.

What was the evidence available to General Yaron, according to the Commission? One hour after the Phalangist entry into the camps at 6PM on Thursday, an Israeli officer intercepted a radio message ordering the killing of 50 women and children and transmitted the information to General Yaron at once. An hour later another radio communication indicated that 45 people captured were to be killed. At the same time, 8PM, a Phalange liaison officer "told various people" that about 300 people had already been killed by the Phalangists (later he reduced it to 120). About an hour later the Divisional Intelligence Officer of the IDF presented his "intelligence survey" in which he said that

> The impression is that their [the Phalangists'] fighting is not too serious. They have casualties, as you know—two wounded, one in the leg and one in the hand... And they, it turns out, are pondering what to do with the population they are finding inside. On the one hand, it seems, there are no terrorists there, in

the camp; Sabra camp is empty. On the other hand, they have amassed women, children and apparently also old people.

He added the report from a Phalange officer indicating that these people should be killed. Note that the elusive 2000 terrorists had pulled their disappearing act once again, refuting what had been "determined" by the Commission, as just quoted, namely, that the "armed terrorist force" had not been evacuated. On Friday, additional evidence of atrocities was accumulated, as revealed in a report that the Phalangists had "butchered" civilians (early Friday morning) and direct observation of Phalangist murders. The murderers were then sent back in to complete their work—in fact, they were ordered to leave the following morning only "due to American pressure," according to the Chief of Staff.

In short, it is quite impossible to believe that there was no "concurrence or assent" in the events that followed the entry of the Phalangists into the camps on the part of the "military echelon," and the Defense Minister, from the "political" echelon, had been apprised of the facts.

The picture that emerges from the Kahan Commission Report is therefore quite clear. The higher political and military echelons, in their entirety, expected that Phalangists would carry out massacres if they were admitted into Palestinian camps. Furthermore, they knew that these camps were undefended, so they were willing to send in approximately 150 Phalangists known for their unwillingness to engage in any conflict with armed men. Within 1-2 hours after the Phalangists had entered on Thursday at 6PM, clear evidence reached the command post 200 meters away from the camps and overlooking them that massacres were taking place, and that there was no serious resistance. At the command post, the IDF and Phalange commanders and their staffs, including intelligence and liaison, were present and in constant contact. The IDF then provided illumination, and the next day, after receiving further corroboratory evidence that massacres were in process and that there was no resistance, sent the Phalange back into the camps, with tractors, which the IDF knew were being used to bury bodies in the mass grave which they could observe (the latter fact is ignored by the Commission). The Phalange were selected for this operation because, as the Chief of Staff stated, "we could give them orders whereas it was impossible to give orders to the Lebanese army." And in fact, the IDF did give the Phalange orders, from the moment they sent them into the camps to conduct their murderous operations, to the time when they were sent back in on Friday afternoon to complete them, to Saturday morning when they were withdrawn because of American pressure, at which time the IDF began rounding up those who had escaped and sending them to Israeli concentration camps (again, this fact is not discussed by the Commission). That is the story as it emerges from the Commission Report (with the exceptions noted). What will a rational person deduce from this record?

Despite the overwhelming evidence of high level planning and complicity in the massacre, in the advance planning and as it was running its course, the Commission rejected these conclusions. It did, nevertheless, assign some limited "indirect responsibility," basing its recommendations on "the obligations applying to every civilized nation" and crucially, the fact that "the Jews in various lands of exile, and also in the Land of Israel when it was under foreign rule, suffered greatly from pogroms perpetrated by various hooligans; and the danger of disturbances against Jews in various lands, it seems evident, has not yet passed," so it is only prudent to note the responsibility of authorities who do not kill with their own hands.

One may be interested in comparing the tempered and limited critique given by the Commission with the passionate denunciations of those who stood by while hooligans murdered 45 Jews in Kishinev, or of British authorities during the Hebron massacre, or of Nazis who let Ukranian and Croatian anti-Semites rampage. One might also compare the rapturous response to the Kahan Commission's recommendations with Dubnow's report of the horrified reaction of the "civilized world" to the Czar's judicial inquiry, which "was conducted with a view to obliterating the traces of the deliberate organization of the [Kishinev] pogrom," and to court proceedings that sentenced a score of murderers to hard labor and penal service, but not those who instigated or failed to halt the crime. We derive a certain measure of the progress of civilization in the past 80 years.

The Commission states that all concerned "were well aware that combat morality among the various combatant groups in Lebanon differs from the norm in the I.D.F., that the combatants in Lebanon belittle the value of human life far beyond what is necessary and accepted in wars between civilized peoples." There was no more of a "war" when the Phalange entered Sabra and Shatila than when Sharon's Unit 101 entered Qibya, or when IDF forces massacred hundreds of people in the Gaza region after hostilities ended in 1956. Nothing more need be said about the "norms" exhibited during the destruction of Ain el-Hilweh or the siege and bombing of Beirut while there was "a war," of a certain sort. So much for "civilized peoples."

Israel's responsibility, the Commission determined, is "exhausted" by the failure to give adequate attention to the possibility that there might be massacres (though the "weighty considerations" already noted might have justified sending in the Phalangists even in the light of such expectation) and the failure to take "proper heed" of the reports that something unpleasant might be happening. "No complaints could be addressed" to Defense Minister Sharon for sending the Phalange into the camps "if such a decision had been taken after all the relevant considerations had been examined," and no "responsibility should be imputed to the Defense Minister for not ordering the removal of the Phalangists from the camps when the first reports reached him about the acts of killing being committed there"—Friday evening, the Commission alleges, that is, well after numerous journalists, officers and soldiers knew of the facts, an incredible conclusion. It was not Sharon's duty to order the Phalange to leave the camps even when he learned of the facts, again a demonstration of sublime moral standards. One might ask—as several Israeli journalists had already done—whether the IDF would have taken a similarly casual attitude, with the support of the distinguished Commission, if it had learned that PLO terrorists were killing hundreds of Jews in Kiryat Shemona or Tel Aviv.

The Commission recommended that Sharon resign—as he did, to be replaced by Moshe Arens, who basically shares his views, remaining in the cabinet as Minister without Portfolio and joining two important committees, the steering committee directing the negotiations with Lebanon and the Ministers' Committee for Security, a decision that led *Ha'aretz* to comment editorially that the government managed to sabotage "the most important recommendation made by the Commission of Inquiry."* As for Chief of Staff Eitan—who expected massacres and ordered the Phalange back into the camps well after he learned that his expectations had been fulfilled—the Commission made no recommendation, on the grounds that he was soon to retire. General Yaron, who knew of the killings Thursday evening and did nothing, was to be relieved of field command for three years; shortly after, he was given a higher level appointment as head of army manpower and training. The director of military intelligence is to step down. So justice is done; Israel has achieved "salvation" and again demonstrated its"sublimity."

The Commission recognizes that some will not be satisfied with its Report, "those who have prejudices or selective consciences, but this inquiry was not intended for such people." It is certainly true that the inquiry was not intended for people who have a prejudice in favor of truth and honesty, but it will more than suffice for its intended audience, as the reaction to it illustrated. A number of commentators were quick to point out that the Report would help to broaden support for Israel in Congress and among the public, as it did (see p. 398*). If one may deduce intent from rational expectation of consequences, then it would seem fair to say that the intent of the Commission was realized.

The logical conclusion from the episode is that Israel would be well-advised to arrange further massacres, then to produce a "cry of conscience" of the sort just reviewed, so that military and economic aid can be increased still further in recognition of its sublimity and salvation.

One can learn a good deal more from the Report. The historical section is quite revealing. It describes the civil war that "began with

---

* Editorial, *Ha'aretz*, Feb. 21, 1983 *(Israeli Mirror)*. Amir Oren predicts that Sharon will be returned as Defense Minister, citing the opinion among the leadership that the Kahan Commission Report did not exclude this possibility and their reported analogy to soccer matches, where a player can be penalized but then returned to his position. *Koteret Rashit*, Feb. 23, 1983. On Yaron, see *New York Times*, May 17, 1983.

clashes in Sidon between the Christians and Palestinian terrorists." The reference is presumably to a Lebanese army operation against a strike of Lebanese fishermen in Sidon shortly before the event that actually initiated the civil war, an attack by the Phalange on a busload of Palestinians and Lebanese in a Beirut suburb in April 1975, which goes unmentioned.* The war "was waged primarily between the Christian organizations on the one hand, and Palestinian terrorists, Lebanese leftist organizations, and Muslim and Druze organizations of various factions on the other." Throughout, the participants are, on the one hand, people (Christians, Muslims, Lebanese leftists, Druze), and on the other hand, "terrorists," i.e., Palestinians, as the quotes just given illustrate. This usage reflects again the race hatred and profound indoctrination already noted; to the Commission, Palestinians are not people, as distinct from Christians, Muslims, Lebanese, Druze. This passes unnoticed in the commentary on the Report, simply because the assumption is so widely shared. Israel breaks no new ground in this respect. Thus, Israel's Guatemalan friends refer to the victims of the death squads and army terror operation as "subversives," while the Russians in Afghanistan (like the Americans in Greece in the late 1940s) refer to the resistance simply as "bandits." Jews have also been subjected to such usage in the past, with consequences that we recall.

The history continues at an equally revealing level. It refers to the fact that there were massacres in the civil war, giving the example of Damour, where Christians were killed by Palestinians—but, in the typical Israeli propaganda style, omitting the fact that this massacre was in retaliation for Christian massacres in Karantina and elsewhere. It states that Bashir Gemayel's forces "became the central element in the Christian forces," not mentioning how this was done (by murdering the Maronite opposition) or who supported him (Israel). Haddad's army is simply "a separate armed force" in south Lebanon; nothing about its auspices, origin, or command structure. The Israeli role throughout is ignored. Turning to the 1982 war, little is said though it is noted that during the weeks of negotiations on the "evacuation of the terrorists and the Syrian forces" from West Beirut, "various targets in West Beirut were occasionally shelled and bombed by the I.D.F.'s Air Force and artillery." This stunning and shameful comment would suffice in itself to discredit this Report beyond repair among civilized people.

The immediate postwar background to the massacres is also ignored. Thus, as noted earlier, the Commission makes no reference to the fact, reported at once in the press, that in early September Israeli forces violating the cease-fire agreements advanced on the camps, clearing mines

---

* See chapter 5, section 3.3.1 and references cited; also James A. Reilly, "Israel in Lebanon, 1975-82," *MERIP Reports*, September/October 1982.

and setting up observation posts, a fact that does not seem obviously irrelevant to what transpired next. See section 3.2.2. This is only a small sample of what might have been reported by a commission that took its announced mandate seriously.

Also interesting is the statement by Israeli Intelligence, reported without comment by the Commission, that "the IDF's entry into West Beirut was perceived as vital not only by the Christians but also by the Muslims, who regarded the I.D.F. as the only factor that could prevent bloodshed in the area and protect the Sunni Muslims from the Phalangists." This is absurd. Recall the outraged denunciations of the Israeli attack on West Beirut from all segments of the Muslim population (p. 361; also pp. 355-6). But the Commission is willing to believe anything that reaches it on high authority, so it appears.

The reaction in the U.S., indeed the West quite generally, to this dismal performance should be carefully noted.* It reveals, once again, how easy it is to believe what it is convenient to believe. In the U.S., it is crucial to believe that Israel is one of us, a western democracy (though not all would consider it so "brilliant" as the *New Republic* acolytes), therefore capable of no wrong, only error. The Palestinians are an irritant to be removed. The reaction to the Kahan Commission Report is entirely predictable, given these facts, just as from comparable facts one can deduce the reaction in the West to the Bertrand Russell Tribunal on the U.S. in Vietnam. It should, incidentally, be noted that in the more honest world of Israeli journalism, the obvious absurdity of the conclusions drawn by the Commission from its evidence did not go unnoticed. An excellent analysis by Uri Avneri (see note 153), reviewing the evidence surveyed above, reaches the only plausible conclusion: no one believed the "fable of the '2000 terrorists'"; The Phalangist units were organized and sent into the camps with the expectation that they would commit murderous acts in order to cause a mass flight of Palestinians (recall that the international response was surely unanticipated); the IDF, intelligence, and the political echelons cooperated in the massacre throughout, at

---

* I have omitted the critical commentary on the report, for example, by Samson Krupnick, Jerusalem correspondent for the liberal *Jewish Post & Opinion*. The report was extremely unfair, he concludes, since "it ignored completely the totally immoral tactics of the PLO terrorists within the camps wherein 'civilians,' if any, including women and children may be armed and working closely with the terrorists." "The Commission appears not to have a sufficient appreciation of the house-to-house fighting necessitated in these 'camps' with everyone there either a PLO terrorist or a collaborator and potential combatant." Furthermore, the Commission failed to consider that Friday was "a short working day for staff, and was also the eve of Rosh Hashonah, and obviously a day difficult to reach all parties quickly." The Commission "has blown this minor battle of the Phalangists versus the PLO terrorists far out of proportion"—it was "minor in character." The correct conclusion is "that reasonable care was exercised by all concerned." Those so inclined might want to determine whether any of the Czar's apologists sank to this level of degradation at the time of the Kishinev massacre during the Easter holiday.

the command post and elsewhere. Repeating Amos Elon's image, Avneri observes: "When someone places a poisonous snake in the bed of a child, and the child dies after it is bitten—there is no need to prove that whoever put the snake there wanted the child to die. The burden of proof is on someone who denies this intention." The Commission did not accept this burden of proof, but simply adopted unquestioningly the hypothesis that those who put the snake in the child's bed were "insensitive" and failed to give adequate attention to what they should have known. Those who accept this reasoning, or regard it as "sublime," reveal a good deal about themselves.

One additional point should be made, however. Despite the fact that the Kahan Commission Report is disgraceful from an intellectual and moral standpoint, still it is rare for any country to produce even a document of this sort in connection with atrocities for which it bears responsibility, or which it conducts outright. In the United States, for example, only the Mylai massacre, which was merely a footnote to the record of American atrocities, merited a governmental inquiry in the course of the Vietnam war, and even that is more than one could expect from most states, including those that are "civilized" by their own account.

7   Elsewhere in Lebanon

One aspect of the propaganda that has accompanied the Commission of Inquiry is the contrast regularly drawn between Israel's seeking (then attaining) salvation through critical self-analysis and the complete failure of the Phalangist government that had been placed in power by the Israeli conquest to do the same. This is supposed to illustrate the sublime moral qualities of Israel as contrasted with the evil Arab nature. A few points are missed in this comparison. For Israel to resist an inquiry would have been impossible, given its reliance on material and ideological support from the U.S., and the inquiry was sure to carry little cost, indeed, to serve to restore some of the prestige that had been lost by the much too visible massacre in September—exactly what ensued. For the Phalange government to conduct an inquiry into the atrocities conducted by the Phalange militia, which now dominates the sectors of Lebanon under central government control as a result of the Israeli conquest, would have been a task of a rather different order, quite evidently. In fact, it would have destroyed what minimal possibilities may exist for the restoration of a Lebanese state.* Perhaps one can draw some conclusions from the fact that

---

* Other questions too come to mind. The forces sent into the camp were under Israeli, not Phalangist orders, if we can believe the testimony of Chief of Staff Eitan and others, so it should be the responsibility of Israel to judge those who killed with their own hands—at least, if Israel wished to rise to the level of the Czar's judicial inquiry. Certainly Israel knows

the forces to whom Israel turned over effective control of Beirut will not permit an inquiry into their bestial acts, but these will not quite be the usual ones drawn in American commentary that contrasts the behavior of the Israeli and Lebanese governments.

7.1   The South

In West Beirut, there were many reporters present when the massacres took place, and they also witnessed and reported the considerably more brutal massacres carried out by the IDF in the preceding months. But few reporters ventured to southern Lebanon, and few international aid officials were present either. Conditions there were not very different from West Beirut after Israel had eliminated the PLO and its Lebanese Muslim allies. As noted earlier, the few reports indicate that virtually no males of ages 16-60 are to be found. The Palestinian camps had been destroyed by the advancing Israeli army, though many refugees had drifted back to the ruins, having nowhere else to go. At least temporary control over the area had been handed over to Haddad's forces, supervised by the regular Israeli army to the extent that they chose to exercise their control. Early in the war, the Israeli press reported that Haddad's soldiers "pass from house to house in the villages which were conquered by the Israeli army and exterminate the last nests of terrorists." Haddad's soldiers were reported to be "very busy" since they were "awakened to life with the beginning of the 'Peace for Galilee' war... And do not ask in what they are busy."[154] Since few have asked, one can only speculate. Israel Shahak offers one speculation:

> A killing of the Palestinians in Lebanon, specially of males, has begun and is being carried on. There is very little doubt that many of the Palestinians who were "arrested" or who "disappeared" will not be seen again, and their very existence will be denied.[155]

Shahak recalls the fate of the Lebanese village of Khiyam, subjected to Israeli bombing from 1968, its population finally reduced to a few dozen people who were massacred by Haddad forces in 1978 after the IDF swept through the area.[156] There were no reporters in Khiyam, so all of this

---

who were the officers in charge, and according to former intelligence chief Shlomo Gazit, it also knows the names of 10-20 of the direct murderers *(Ma'ariv,* April 10, 1983). It would of course, be difficult to subject any of these men to judicial proceedings while avoiding the responsibility of the "political and military echelons" within Israel. They might plead that they were simply following orders, like the officers on the West Bank who were charged with brutal treatment of civilians; see pp. 128f. In general, no state is in the habit of charging its own war criminals. It might be noted, incidentally, that the majority of Israelis regard the Kahan commission's conclusions as too harsh, specifically with regard to Sharon and Eitan (Sarah Honig, *Jerusalem Post,* April 1, 1983).

passed in silence, as would have happened in Sabra and Shatila too had they been better placed.

Shahak's speculation does not appear to be too far-fetched; we know very little, nine months after the war's official end, about the Palestinians in the south or the thousands of Palestinians and others "brought in" by the IDF, and the little that is known is hardly very reassuring. On August 7, 1982, Phalangist gunmen had set fire to the homes of Palestinians, mostly Christians, in the Miya Miya refugee camp near Sidon; several thousand fled. The camp had put up no resistance to the Israeli onslaught and was undamaged. Israeli troops nearby "made no effort to prevent the Phalangists' assault." "The Red Cross and UNRWA know about the attack, but are staying quiet. They already face severe harassment from the Israelis, who want as few independent observers as possible in the region and have therefore done all they can to limit international relief operations. The aid agencies fear that if they speak out, they will be ejected."[157] Reporting the same event, Marvine Howe states that the IDF sent soldiers, but too late (another case of unexplained inefficiency), and quotes a foreign human rights worker who said: "It seems the militias are deliberately trying to drive the Palestinian refugees out of the Sidon area."* The refugees fled to the ruins of the Ain el-Hilweh camp near Sidon, "which was practically obliterated during the Israeli attack on the city last June," with 8000 killed according to a representative of a religious aid organization (citing refugee reports), 1500 killed according to the Red Cross. One of the women who fled, showing bruises still visible from beatings in the August 7 attack, asks: "Where can we go? Who will protect us now that we don't have our menfolk?"[158]

"In a clear case of Israeli-inspired lawlessness at 2 am on the night of 2 September, two armed men forced their way into the home of an elderly Palestinian woman in Sidon's Ain al Hilweh refugee camp," beating the woman with a rifle butt, dragging her off to the home of one of the gunmen for further beatings, then taking her to the IDF military head-quarters for further "interrogation," and finally leaving her barefoot and far from home, at dawn. "The fact that she was taken to the Israeli headquarters leaves little doubt that the plain-clothed gunmen were acting with Israeli support." The story is familiar from the West Bank, as we have seen. A few days later Haddad militia seized two teenaged Palesti-

---

* For more information on what he calls the "Phalangist murder and harassment campaign against the Palestinians," see Charles Hoffman, *Jerusalem Post*, Feb. 2, 17, 1983. See also Robert Fisk, *London Times*, March 1, 1983, reporting from the Miya Miya camp, which "almost oozes fear." He describes the killings of Palestinians in the vicinity and the threats by the Christian terrorists who run the area under IDF auspices, which "make an average skin creep." "The record of murder and intimidation this past month does not do much credit to the occupying authorities whose duty it is to protect civilians in Sidon" and the nearby camps, he concludes, with a certain understatement. It also does not do much credit to the paymasters and their media, which provide little information about the matter.

nian boys near the Miya Miya camp, beating and torturing them. Others abducted a 25-year-old Lebanese "with leftist connections"; he has not been seen since. Two other Lebanese leftists were seized the same night. One has disappeared. The body of the other was recovered from an East Beirut (Phalange) hospital. "An official government doctor confirmed that he had died by strangulation, that his genitals had been bleeding, and that he had been tortured with a hot kebab skewer."[159] All of this was well before the Phalange and Haddad militiamen were sent in to "purify" Sabra and Shatila, where the Israeli command professed to be shocked at their behavior, having anticipated only the most gentlemanly conduct.

The Lebanon Project Officer for Oxfam, Dan Connell, stated a few weeks later that reports of abduction, torture, murder and rape had been increasing through August and September in southern Lebanon—though again, little is known, since foreign observers are few. At the same time, David McDowell, Oxfam field director in Lebanon, issued a statement calling on international bodies to monitor human rights violations in the south. The statement "cited examples of intimidation, torture, forcible expulsion and appropriation of charitable foundation property by the militia forces," alleging that the IDF was allowing Phalange and Haddad militias "to act without restraint, especially against Palestinian civilians."[160]

Haddad, of course, denies that there are any atrocities under his rule, which he claims includes 100,000 Palestinians: "I defy anyone to tell me that a Palestinian (civilian) was killed by one of our soldiers."[161] In the same issue of the *Los Angeles Times* where Haddad's assurances are reported, a social scientist teaching at the U.S. Military Academy at West Point, who worked in southern Lebanon in 1980-1, tells a rather different story. In addition to well-publicized PLO atrocities, he writes, "Israeli hands were also involved in a series of outrages that have escaped public notice" before the June invasion, with Haddad serving "as a useful facade behind which Israeli agents could direct and control events." The press was absent and "the urbane Lebanese of Beirut" were unconcerned, so "houses could be demolished, political opponents murdered and tribute exacted by the Israeli-supplied, directed and trained militia of Haddad." Israel blamed "the excitability and uncontrollability of their Lebanese clients," but "for anyone who cared to check, the involvement of Israeli agents was easy to detect." "Israeli complicity with earlier Christian excesses" is consistent with the early reports of "Israeli involvement in the terror-killings in Chatilla and Sabra."[162]

Just prior to the Sabra-Shatila massacres, the Beirut correspondent for a British journal observed that the Palestinians left behind by the PLO fighters now "face the prospect of being victims of [Bashir Gemayel's] Phalangist militia out for revenge." He reports that "Misery is greatest in the south where, after destroying their homes and imprisoning their men, the Israelis have unleashed Haddad and the Phalangists upon them... A tacit division of labour allocates the daily dirty work of population control to the Phalangists or Haddad's men, allowing the Israelis to seem uninvolved, even arbiters." He reports, specifically, the murder of a Palestinian family on August 31 by Phalangist militiamen; the mutilated bodies of three women were "dumped near the Museum crossing between east and west Beirut as a grim advertisement." "Half the cases of human rights violations [in south Lebanon] recorded recently involve Lebanese." For the Palestinians, the situation is worse than 1948, when most of them arrived after fleeing from Palestine, "with much of the Maronite community itching to hit the Palestinians now that the fighters have gone," either sent to Israeli concentration camps or driven to Beirut, then sent away, and the economy and social structure demolished.[163] As the report appeared, the IDF was offering the militias under their control a chance to demonstrate their bravery in the camps in Beirut.

Quite apart from the possibility of massacre and atrocities, we might ask what is to become of the hundreds of thousands of Palestinians who were driven out of their "camps" by the invading Israeli forces—over 400,000, according to the calculation of Israeli correspondent Danny Rubinstein in early September.[164] Israel at first blocked any reconstruction of the bombed and bulldozed camps, though in its mercy, it later permitted UNRWA to bring in tents and subsequently offered assistance in reconstructing permanent dwellings, after a policy shift to which we return. Few wage-earners remained, and the rather substantial economy created by the PLO had been destroyed along with the PLO network of social services, its workers either killed, imprisoned somewhere, or dispersed. There is no shelter, no employment, no protection, and nowhere to go.

Articles soon appeared in the U.S. press on the problems faced by the Israeli occupying army, compelled to spend the harsh winter in Lebanon. The *New York Times* expressed much concern about their grim fate. Under the subheading "All Those Jewish Mothers," the following paragraph appears:

> A Jerusalem man, a reservist himself and the father of a soldier, wondered how the army would react "to all those Jewish mothers worrying about their sons freezing in the hills." He laughed, but then said it could represent a real problem.[165]

And all those Palestinian mothers, whose circumstances are perhaps marginally more severe, and who are not part of an invading army backed and supplied by the United States? From the coverage in the *Times* and elsewhere we must assume, again, that they must be made of sterner stuff, or perhaps they simply do not feel pain, as was alleged by some American sophisticates with regard to Vietnamese peasants, not long ago.

In Israel, Col. Dov Yirmiah, whose reports from Lebanon were discussed on pp. 237f., wrote at the end of August that "The Israeli government has done nothing yet to ease the misery of the Palestinian refugees, the victims of the war, and their fate in the coming winter is cause for alarm... The Prime Minister, who is so sensitive to memories of our own people, should remember what it means for families to be divided by war, the torture of not knowing what happens to relatives." His government is following a policy of "cruelty for its own sake," refusing even to permit communication among divided families—that is, families with members imprisoned.[166] Nine months later, that still remained true—but it is perhaps unfair to accuse the Prime Minister of moral inconsistency, as Yirmiah does, since there is after all a difference between people and two-legged beasts.

Some urged that Israel undertake humanitarian efforts for "pragmatic" reasons. Moshe Kol, a former Minister from the Independent Liberal Party, observed that the refugees in the camps destroyed by the IDF "are living in sub-human conditions—in orchards, on the streets, in shattered buildings, corners and cellars." He suggests that "This is not the time to explain to the world that these camps were PLO centers and therefore Israel had to destroy them. Israel would substantially improve its image abroad, which suffered a sharp deterioration following the massive bombing from the air and the sea, if it addressed itself to this humane task."[167] This message was apparently heeded. After the complex events of September, including the cooling of relations with the Phalange and the international reaction to the Sabra-Shatila massacres, the policy of dispersing the refugees shifted and Israel began to provide cement for rebuilding the homes that had been destroyed and prefabricated houses—though "Israel's publicised offer of prefabricated houses for all turned out to be not quite what people had expected," the *Economist* correspondent observes: "some Israeli manufacturers did indeed put exhibition prefabs on display, but at prices that no refugee could afford,"[168] another fact passed over silently here.

The situation of the Palestinians remained grim, if not hopeless, however. In Ain el-Hilweh, Trudy Rubin reports, "self-appointed leaders who claim influence with Israel but are suspected by many camp dwellers of being opportunists or worse" began to appear, while "any genuine leadership left here is afraid to speak out lest the Israelis suspect them of PLO affiliation and arrest them," one "respected camp resident" added. A report in the British journal *Middle East International* provides more details. A "social and humanitarian committee" was set up in the ruins of the camp. Its founder, Dr. Fikry Faour, is suspected of having had connections with Lebanese intelligence and with Israel in the past. One of the first acts of the committee was to beat up an UNRWA official responsible for distributing land plots, a man "known to be efficient and incorruptible." The presence of Israeli troops nearby "suggests protection for the aggressors, not the victim." UNRWA had refused to deal with the committee, calling it "self-appointed." Israel "wants an UNRWA that will not resist its policies—a tamed UNRWA." "Attempts to impose the committee on the people of Ain Helweh have been backed up by threats and arrests—and worse. The Ansar concentration camp is used as a recruiting ground, with prisoners promised release in return for working with the committee." Refugees concerned about arrest or about their current plight are sometimes offered help by the occupying army; "The price: cooperation with the committee." The similarity to practices on the West Bank is striking. Dr. Faour is reported by committee members to have had a meeting with Mustafa Dudin, head of the Israel's West Bank Village Leagues. Israel is reported to have offered arms to the committee "for defence against the Phalangist militia," "a real embarrassment for the committee, which attaches as much importance to its relations with the Lebanese rightists as with the Israelis." These reports are confirmed by others. Robert Fisk interviewed villagers in the south and reported their account of how Israeli soldiers force them to pay protection money to Haddad forces and of the effective use of the concentration camps: prisoners in Ansar, the villagers were told by the IDF, would be held there until the villagers paid the money. Such reports as these suggest that Israel is considering exploitation of communal strife and imposition of a network of collaborators as methods—of a classic sort—to enable it to maintain control after eventual partial withdrawal.

Urban middle-class Palestinians have also been subjected to threats, violence and terror by Phalangists, and though "the Israeli-Phalangist relationship continues to be quite close, even since the Beirut massacre," it is unclear "how much leverage the Israelis will be willing to exert on Phalangists who want to harass Palestinians." The Lebanese government appears to believe that Israel has some leverage. A week later it "asked the United States to intervene with Israel to halt a campaign of intimidation against Palestinians in southern Lebanon by Christian militiamen." Prime Minister Wazzan, describing this appeal to U.S. mediator Philip Habib, stated: "We are exerting every effort to stop the campaign of intimidation against Palestinians and Lebanese in southern Lebanon." The occasion for the appeal was the discovery of 15 bodies, most believed to be Palestinians, near Sidon. "The intimidation campaign was also said to have been directed against Shiite Moslems." Nabih Berri, leader of the Amal Shiite militia that fought alongside the PLO, described incidents in which Shiites were driven from their homes or killed in areas where "Israeli-backed Lebanese Christian militiamen arrived . . . on the heels of the Israelis." The Christian militia involved are alleged to be Haddadists and from the ultra-right Guardians of the Cedars. The State Department had no comment.[169]

As had long been predicted, by early 1983 Israel appeared to be laying the basis for domination of southern Lebanon, which may sooner or later become its "North Bank" if the U.S. continues to provide the wherewithal. It will hardly be a great surprise if sooner or later work begins on a canal linking the Litani river to the Israeli water system. Israeli officers began to distribute an elaborate questionnaire throughout southern Lebanon, *Ha'aretz* reports, citing a copy that reached the AP office in Beirut. This is to be the first census in the region since 1932; it requests detailed responses to questions about the male population between 13 and 65, pregnant women, children and grandchildren in every family, use of electricity and water, the names of the wealthy and village notables, etc. AP reports that "A Western diplomat who studied the questionnaire said it seemed designed to obtain intelligence information that the Israelis could use whether they stay in southern Lebanon or withdraw after transferring security duties to right-wing Lebanese militiamen with whom they are allied." At the same time the Israeli government argued in Israel's Supreme Court that it has the right to continue the war against the PLO, even after the fighting has ended, by destruction of the local economy. The issue arose when a Christian Lebanese brought to the Court a protest against the IDF's destruction of a plastic factory he had purchased from Palestinians near Damour.[170]

Throughout the region, Israel began to arm militias that compete with one another and with Israel's client Haddad. Israel may have realized something that a number of well-informed Lebanese had long observed. Haddad is a dubious client, since he has little standing even in any local region in Lebanon, and furthermore, as a Christian (Greek Orthodox), he is not the optimal choice as Israeli-imposed suzerain in the largely Shiite south. A more efficacious policy is to encourage communal strife, exploiting the crazy quilt of local loyalties and fiefdoms in Lebanon. This will serve the dual purpose of justifying an Israeli "peace-keeping" presence and placing barriers in the way of restoration of a central authority, now unwelcome after the problems that arose with Bashir Gemayel and later his brother Amin. And if Israel is some day compelled to withdraw, a network of antagonisms and dependencies may be in place that will permit its indirect domination of the area. Some of the militias are reported to have been encouraged to infiltrate the areas controlled by the United Nations force (UNIFIL), which Israel would prefer to see removed, since it impedes the expansion of its control. As noted above, after relations with the Phalange began to cool in early September, Israel switched its policy towards the Palestinians; instead of "driving them East," it began to encourage a degree of reconstruction under the control of collaborators. Some observers regard this modification of policy under the changed circumstances as part of an effort to enhance communal conflict and block imposition of a central Lebanese authority over the future North Bank.

Nevertheless, Haddad has surely not been abandoned. In February 1983, he was encouraged to take over control of a 40km-wide section of southern Lebanon, backed by Israeli-supplied tanks, armored personnel carriers and cannons. The Lebanese Foreign Minister stated that Israel held the area by "force of arms." Relations between Israel and the Maronites had now soured to the point that Pierre Gemayel, founder of the Phalange in the 1930s, pleaded with Lebanese Muslims to join in blocking Israel's moves towards partition, moves also condemned by another Maronite elder statesman, Camille Chamoun. Meanwhile, the *Economist* reports, "the pro-Israeli faction in the Phalange militia," led by Fady Frem (one of the architects of the Beirut massacre), expressed their support for Sharon in opposition to the Gemayel central government. A few weeks before, Shimon Peres, head of the Labor Alignment, expressed his view that Haddad should take over a 40km "security zone" inside Lebanon,[171] yet another indication of the fundamental agreement on policy between Labor and Likud.

At the same time, Israel began to implement what it calls "normalization," specifically, flooding south Lebanon with Israeli goods, including agricultural products that may undermine Lebanese agriculture and ultimately provide Israel with another cheap labor force. In September, the Israeli press reported that hundreds of agricultural workers would be brought in from Lebanon in the coming harvest season. By January, it reported that Israeli exports to Lebanon might amount to $1 billion a year, flowing to the Arab world through Lebanon; exports in December were reported by Israeli army spokesman Col. Aaron Gonen and by the Lebanese government to have reached $20 million. Lebanese authorities attempted to put a stop to these practices, but to no avail. The Minister of Economy, Commerce and Tourism, Ibrahim Halawi, commented that the "flow of illegal goods into Lebanon" will rob farmers of their livelihood and spread unemployment in the industrial sector, though it is impossible for the Lebanese government to take action against these illegal practices "with the Israelis still there." The Minister of Health issued similar warnings, reporting also a ban on purchase of medical equipment from Israel or other acts that would amount to *de facto* recognition, again noting the impossibility of implementing policy because of the Israeli occupation. In March 1983, senior IDF officers warned the Tyre chamber of commerce that "its members must immediately stop threatening merchants trading with Israel." According to economist Peter Franck of the American University of Beirut, Israel has effectively exploited its military power and the destruction caused by its attack to penetrate the economy of the south. Israel has even begun to establish counterparts to the West Bank "Village Leagues." Villagers who refuse to join are threatened with imposition of outside militias, or given incentives, the promise of future economic assistance or of release of relatives held in the concentration camp at Ansar.[172]

These practices recapitulate what developed more slowly in the West Bank and Gaza. "Normalization" sounds fair enough, when one neglects the circumstances and implications given the balance of force. It will mean subjugation of at least southern Lebanon to Israeli domination, and in the context of a full peace treaty, would amount to ratification by Lebanon not only of these arrangements but also of the extension of Israeli sovereignty over the occupied territories. Naturally, the government of Lebanon has resisted pressures for "normalization" and a "peace treaty," though the reasons are much obscured in American commentary on the subject,[173] only one of them being regularly noted, namely, that such "normalization" would lead to isolation of Lebanon within the Arab world, as long as Israel persists in its rejectionism.

7.2   The Chouf

In the northern parts of the area occupied by the IDF, the Chouf region southeast of Beirut, communal conflicts began immediately after the IDF conquered the area and have continued since. This region had miraculously escaped the civil war, being recognized as the Druze homeland:

> Although there are Maronites in the Chouf, the Phalange did not try to assert its political presence south of the Damascus highway during or after the civil war of the mid-1970s. All the communities in these hills—Druzes, Maronites, Greek Orthodox, Shias—lived blessedly at peace with each other throughout that war.* It was only after the Israeli army occupied the Chouf last June [1982] that the Phalange, then led by Amin's thrusting brother Bechir Gemayel, began to try to assert its presence in the Chouf and immediately met with vigorous armed resistance from the Druzes... For the Phalange these clashes are part of a much larger pattern of attempted domination. The Sunni Moslem and left-wing forces in Beirut and southern Lebanon have been disarmed and rendered impotent by the Israelis and by the Lebanese army. The Shia Moslems are split between Israeli- and Syrian-occupied areas. The Greek Orthodox have been cowed. Thus the Druzes are the only Lebanese obstacle between the powerful Phalange militia and its domination of Lebanon. The stakes are real and high.[174]

* While it is true that the Chouf region escaped the civil war, it did not completely escape violence. Charles Glass comments that after Druze leader Kamal Jumblatt was assassinated in March 1977, the Druze "went on a rampage, killing hundreds of Christians, with the Syrian Army—much like the Turks 117 years earlier—standing idly by. Many Christians sought refuge in Beirut, their young men joining the Phalange and swearing revenge. Others remained, but the Shouf was quiet until the Israeli occupation." "Victors and Vanquished: Baedecker to the Three Lebanons."

The Phalange incited armed conflict and also carried out numerous atrocities, sometimes reported in the Israeli press.[175] Shmuel Segev reports that although the Phalange were heavily armed by Israel and western countries, the Druze prevailed in the military conflicts that took place as the Phalangists followed the IDF into the Druze homeland. But "in contrast to the results of open battles—in incidents of kidnapping and murder the Christians [Phalange] held the upper hand—while in 90% of the incidents the Druze return Christian captives healthy and well, there have been 36 incidents in which the Christians did not return the Druze captives—or their bodies"; though, as we have seen, they sometimes returned parts of the bodies; see p. 253. In the early stages of the war, Segev continues, Israel tried to cultivate Druze (the Arslan family) who had been traditional rivals of the Jumblatts and the current Druze leader Walid Jumblatt, the leftist "collaborator with the PLO and the Syrians." But the belief among the Druze that "Israel is helping the Christians" has overcome the conflicts among the Druze, and they are now appealing to Syria to allow Syrian Druze to come to their assistance. Within Israel, there has been much agitation among the Druze (who are treated differently from other Israeli Arabs, and serve in the IDF), which "might drive the Druze of the State of Israel right into the arms of the most extreme Arab elements." Earlier, Druze reservists in the IDF threatened to refuse their mobilization orders unless they were sent to serve in the Druze villages of the Chouf, and six Druze sergeants were arrested for attacking Phalangists. Israeli Druze complained that the IDF disarmed the Druze in Lebanon while arming the Phalangists. "We are part of the Israeli army," a Druze leader in Israel said, "but we cannot just stand by and watch it arming the Phalangists who are murdering our kin."[176]

Christian and Druze leaders as well as Prime Minister Shafik Wazzan accused Israel of arming both sides* in an effort to fuel hostilities and justify a continued Israeli presence.[177] A number of Israeli journalists agreed, adding substantial detail. Aharon Bachar commented on the fact that in the early stages of the negotiations at Khalde (Lebanon) and Kiryat Shemona (Israel), when the Lebanese were refusing to accept Israeli demands, the relations between the IDF and Walid Jumblatt's Druze supporters (who had formed part of the PLO-Muslim coalition) became highly "correct." In fact, Druze artillery was able to shell near Khalde, where the negotiations were in process, though it was evident that the IDF could have immediately silenced it had they chosen to do so. Bachar takes this to have been a message from Sharon to the Lebanese government that unless it accepted Israel's terms, Israel would back the Druze who "are

---

* A Western diplomat confirmed that Israel is arming the Druze, basing himself on information from a Druze militia official "who told him the Israelis were selling the Druze a variety of weapons, including heavy artillery" (Rebecca Trounson, *Boston Globe*, Feb. 15, 1983).

able to turn Amin Gemayel from the President of Lebanon to the Mayor of East Beirut in a week," with tacit IDF backing. He also notes that protest by Israeli Druze over Phalange actions in the Chouf had "suddenly stopped," and that the Lebanese government, "caught in the trap that the Israelis had set for them in the Chouf mountains," had no choice but "to take part in the peace comedy in Khalde and Kiryat Shemona," referring to the negotiations between Israel and Lebanon.[178]

By the end of January 1983, Lebanese police reported that 115 people had been killed in the Phalange-Druze fighting in the Chouf. Twenty-five more Phalange fighters were reported killed a week later, when Druze militiamen seized the town of Aley. The Phalange again accused the Israeli army of helping the Druze, alleging that they were operating from positions next to those manned by Israeli troops, who kept Christian militiamen in their barracks. The Lebanese representative at the Khalde negotiations criticized Israel for permitting the Chouf fighting to continue. Israel responded by stating that the IDF had imposed a cease-fire and would not permit anyone to bear arms in the Aley or Chouf mountain regions.[179] The fighting continued, however.

7.3   Beirut after the Israeli Invasion

In Beirut itself, conflicts continued between the Amin Gemayel government and its "undeclared opponents—the Israelis and the hardcore Christians," including the Guardians of the Cedars and the Lebanese Forces militia that had been formed and led by Bashir Gemayel with Israeli assistance. Its pro-Israeli leader Fady Frem, identified as one of the leaders of the September massacres, spoke at a Phalangist rally in favor of "cultural and special ties" between the minorities in the Middle East, that is, between Israel and the Maronites, a call that "could only be seen as an ominous challenge to President Gemayel."[180]

Immediately after Israel conquered West Beirut, the Muslim population was disarmed and the confiscated arms were either taken to Israel or handed over to the Phalangists, whom Israel had just accused of the Beirut massacres, or the Lebanese army, according to IDF spokesmen. "The Muslims of West Beirut now fear most a rampage through their part of the city by the well armed and equipped Falangists who have been their blood enemies since the 1975-76 civil war."[181] A few days later, the Lebanese army, now under Phalange influence, cordoned off large areas of West Beirut to search for weapons and "illegal residents," some foreigners but primarily Palestinians and Muslims who had fled to Beirut during the past decade, driven from their homes by the Israeli bombings from the early 1970s, the Phalange policy of clearing Muslims out of areas under their control during the civil war, the 1978 invasion, the subsequent heavy bombings and finally the "Peace for Galilee" operation. A Shiite ghetto, populated by poor refugees from the south, was bulldozed, and the squatters who lived there were denied permission to reconstruct. Hundreds of people were rounded up, including Lebanese Muslims. Most of those rounded up were probably Palestinians, whose number may have reached several thousand within the following months. David Ottaway reported that "The government has already made clear that it wants the vast majority of the estimated 500,000 Palestinians in Lebanon to leave as soon as possible." He reports that a French officer of the international peace-keeping force saw 60-100 Palestinian men taken from one part of the Sabra camp. The *Economist* reported that "fear and uncertainty in the camps today are even greater than they were when the Israelis briefly occupied west Beirut."*

There was at first a pretense that after the Muslims of West Beirut were disarmed, the Lebanese army would turn to East Beirut and disarm the militia there. That never happened. The Lebanese army did take over East Beirut in February 1983, though the Phalange militia kept their arms and a pier in Beirut harbor that they used for imports without government control, then turning it over to the government after a reported agreement that they would receive funds collected at the port. Muslims who had welcomed Amin Gemayel's election, recalling his reputation for concilia-tion and diplomacy as contrasted with the militant fanaticism of his Israeli-backed brother Bashir, now fear that "instead of Amin using the state and the army to curb the Maronite militants, the latter appear to have hijacked the state and the army for their own purposes," in the words of one "disillusioned Moslem professor" interviewed by Helena Cob-ban.[182] Exactly what is happening within the Phalange government, with its apparent split between Israeli-oriented and more independent ele-ments, it is difficult to ascertain.

The torture of Palestinians under Phalange rule continued. A team of Italian medical volunteers had attempted to reconstruct the services for Palestinians and poor Lebanese in the Acre hospital, where, according to Professor Walter Cavallari of a Rome hospital who headed the ortho-pedic unit of the team, "medical personnel had been kidnapped, killed, tortured, raped." Following the practice of the IDF during the "Peace for Galilee" operation, the Phalange government expelled the Italian team, leaving severely injured patients unattended and closing down virtually the last medical center for Palestinians and Lebanese poor. Dr. Cavallari reports that kidnappings and illegal arrests continue, and that in the

---

* See also Robert Fisk, *London Times*, Feb. 9, 1983, reporting the vicious beating of a Druze woman by Phalangists in Beirut, who justify the act (meanwhile, explaining that "we are not violent people"), also explaining that "we need the Israelis and we dare not lose their help. We are too few here in Lebanon. We have just been driven out of Aley by the Druze. The Israelis let that happen to teach us that we cannot do without them . . . We are patriots and we are not brutal but we are all alone."

camps, fear of "disappearance," Latin America style, is "very terrible." The people live in the ruins of the bombardment, while the government refuses to permit them to reconstruct their homes or the productive enterprises that had provided employment. The Italian doctors say that ill and wounded patients had begun to come to the hospital from other areas of Lebanon as well to receive medical assistance from the Italian team. They are now abandoned, some in the course of surgery, without help and without hope. The Palestinian Red Crescent, which had provided free medical services to the poor, Palestinians and Lebanese, is denied legal status and unable to function (there is no other free medical service in Lebanon). The Italian government made no protest.[183] The U.S. government had no protest to make, since there were no medical volunteers or equipment from the country that had backed and financed the operation that had created this situation.

The one PLO institution in West Beirut that had survived the Israeli invasion and its aftermath was the PLO Research Center. As noted earlier, its 25,000 volume library and microfilm collection was looted and carted away by Israeli soldiers, but it was being restored by its Director, Sabri Jiryis. On February 5, the Research Center was destroyed by a bomb that killed at least 20 people, including Jiryis's wife. Reporting this incident from Beirut, Trudy Rubin notes also that in November the Lebanese army had confiscated a quarter-million dollars worth of medicine donated by foreign charitable agencies and that it was creating visa difficulties for foreign medical volunteers who made up the bulk of the staff of the Palestinian Red Crescent hospitals after the expulsion of the PLO, killing or arresting their staffs. She cites reports of 1-3000 Palestinians imprisoned by the Lebanese government, and reports plans by Lebanese government officials to expel many Palestinians, perhaps all but 50,000 of the approximately 500,000 who remain.[184]

A glimpse of what the invasion has created was given by AP reporter Paola Crociani, arrested and expelled, charged with "contacts with undesirable elements" (Palestinians). In prison, she was shown a room with hundreds of men piled on top of one another, "a huge heap of human bodies with exhausted desperate faces," without food or water, unable to move; "the stench was unbearable." She saw torture victims and heard "terrible screams—screams of pain of men subjected to torture during interrogation." More recruits into the ranks of the disappeared.[185]

By early 1983, the multinational peacekeeping force in Beirut was coming under attack. Apart from continuing conflicts between Israeli forces and the U.S. marine contingent, which elicited harsh comment from marine commandant Gen. Robert Barrow,[186] there were also attacks on Italian, Dutch and French forces by unknown assailants, all in Shiite neighborhoods. Lebanon's army commander, Gen. Ibrahim Tannous, accused unnamed "non-Lebanese parties" of "masterminding and staging" the attacks in a campaign to drive the international peace force out of

Lebanon. Some have speculated that the attackers might be from a dissident wing of Amal (the Shiite militia) with Iranian contacts. "Shiite religious and political leaders, however, have charged the Israeli secret service engineered the attacks to show that the Lebanese army and the international force was incapable of maintaining security in Lebanon."[187] Meanwhile Israeli forces continued to come under guerrilla attack.

7.4   Under Syrian Control

The remainder of Lebanon remains under Syrian control. Bitter communal fighting broke out in the fall of 1982 in Tripoli, with many killed, and factional conflicts of varied sorts continue, involving pro-Syrian groups, Palestinians, and a variety of others. What is happening in this region is obscure; the one extended description that I have seen remains unpublished.[188]

8   Israel's Moral Lapse

As of April 1983, the Lebanese-Israeli negotiations continued in limbo. Israel had little reason to bring them to a conclusion unless its basic terms could be imposed. Asher Maniv points out that "They drag their feet on Lebanese negotiations not because they want to stay there, but because they want to stay in the West Bank." Since Washington had linked the West Bank and Lebanon negotiations, Israel had an incentive to delay the latter so that it could continue with the intensive programs leading to extension of Israeli sovereignty in the occupied territories, derailing any "territorial compromise."[189] Maniv underestimates the Israeli interest in remaining in Lebanon, either directly, under some temporary form of *de facto* partition with Syria (until the next round), or indirectly, after some form of conditional withdrawal, through the system of collaborators and dependent institutional structures that it is imposing. Either way, Israel will have its "North Bank" and can proceed, as circumstances permit, with further integration.

As for the Reagan administration, at least at the rhetorical level it continued to press for a quick settlement and withdrawal of foreign troops from Lebanon, which, it is hoped, can then become an American client state, part of the American-sponsored "strategic consensus" in the region.* Reagan even discovered that "there's a certain moral point that

---

* Like his predecessors, Reagan is having some difficulty in convincing the Arab states that Russia is the enemy they must fear. They have been much more concerned with threats closer to home: Israel and Iran. Shortly after the Soviet invasion of Afghanistan, the well-known Egyptian journalist Mohammed Heikal wrote that "Any Arab leader who tried to stir his people's religious conscience by invoking the sanctity of Kabul to condemn an occupation that is 13 weeks old would only remind them of the occupation to which their

we think the Israelis are neglecting or not observing. And that is the new Government of Lebanon, after all these years of revolution and upheaval, has asked all the foreign forces to leave. For them not to leave now puts them technically in the position of an occupying force, that they are there by force in this country that has said to them, 'We now want you to depart'."[190]

Again, the press was disciplined enough to refrain from the obvious comment, though it may be that the process of self-indoctrination had reached such a point that it did not even come to mind. Throughout the summer of 1982, from June 5, the government of Lebanon had been demanding in the clearest and most vigorous terms that the invading army withdraw forthwith, citing the Security Council Resolutions calling for Israel's immediate and unconditional withdrawal. That did not place Israel "technically in the position of an occupying force," for quite a simple reason: since at that time the U.S. was backing the aggression, Israel was then not an "occupying force" but was rather engaged in self-defense, just like Americans in South Vietnam, Russians in Afghanistan, Germans in Belgium, and all aggressors, by their own lights.

In October, immediately after his election as president, Amin Gemayel spoke at the United Nations, where he again referred to the Security Council Resolutions of early June calling for the unconditional withdrawal of Israel's invading army:

> These resolutions did not lead naturally to the liberation of Lebanon, and they did not put an end to the continuing and recurrent invasion. However, they condemned the act of aggression, firmly established the legitimacy of our rights, supported the sanctity of our soil, and contributed to the preservation of the unity and the sovereignty of our country within its internationally-recognized boundaries... Contending with the Israeli invasion of March, 1978, the United Nations peacekeeping forces in South Lebanon were shocked, as we all know, because they were prevented from performing their mission fully, either through the provocation of one party or through the obstructions set up by another... [In June 1982] Israel violated the [1949 Armistice] agreement by invading Lebanon once more in circumstances known to all. The withdrawal of Israeli forces constitutes today the fundamental objective called for by your resolutions, and this objective must be achieved.

holy city of Jerusalem had been subjected for 13 years" (Op-Ed, *New York Times*, April 2, 1980). Rejecting U.S. warnings about the Soviet threat, the Kuwaiti journal *Al-watan* observed: "At a time when the Israeli dagger is thrust deep in the Arab heart and U.S. planes are bombing thousands of Palestinians, we will not accept the argument that the threat comes from the Black sea" (June 18, 1982; *The Middle East*, July 1982).

Lebanon similarly awaits the simultaneous withdrawal of all non-Lebanese forces present on its territory.[191]

Still, the IDF had not yet become an "occupying force," even "technically." They were not missing any subtle "moral points" during the events of the summer, or afterwards, though by early February 1983 a certain moral lapse could be detected, as they began to refuse American orders. The moral lapse becomes clearer when in a negotiating session, Israeli Maj. Gen. Avraham Tamir declares: "Nobody is going to influence us on matters of our defense. We will do what we please."[192] Israel is entitled to "do what we please," by the approved moral code, only when that is also what pleases its paymaster and sponsor. By early 1983, that was not completely the case, though it is difficult to imagine that in the short term at least, the United States will put any significant barriers in the way of Israel's objectives—at least, so long as no political force appears in the United States committed to an end to U.S. rejectionism and dismissal of Palestinian rights.

In May 1983, Secretary of State Shultz's "shuttle diplomacy" led to a Lebanese-Israeli agreement that Israel accepted over Labor Party opposition, signed on May 17.[193] As for the Lebanese government (in effect, the government of Beirut, as David Shipler observes; a government that was "unable to negotiate forcefully," "with most of their country under occupation," the *Times* continues), it appears to have agreed to the terms under duress, feeling that "the draft agreement contained so many concessions to the Israelis that Lebanon could not afford to agree to it,"[194] though it did, having little choice. In fact, the agreement was presumably a welcome one, considering the alternatives. The terms of the 11-page agreement with its 11-page military annex, side letters, and "clarifications" were leaked by Israeli sources, who claim that the pact is "tantamount to a peace treaty," portraying it as "a wide-ranging document constituting the second major agreement between Israel and an Arab country," thus neutralizing Lebanon along with Egypt in tacit acquiescence to the Israeli takeover of the West Bank, Gaza and the Syrian Golan Heights. The Israeli sources report that a 30-mile strip of southern Lebanon is to be under the control of a "territorial brigade" composed of the Haddad militia and other local forces, with Haddad himself in a command position that is not specified precisely. The exact terms are to be kept secret, reportedly at the request of the Lebanese government. "Israeli officials stress that the real test of the agreement will come not in its language but in its application." Given the actual distribution of power, there is every reason to expect that Israel will ensure that the "application" conforms to the intent outlined by the sources cited, which would effectively place the region under Israeli control. Furthermore, Israel is permitted to conduct joint patrols with the Lebanese army beyond this region, to the Awali river north of Sidon. The Israeli interpretation of the accords corresponds rather closely to their demands on Lebanon in September 1982; see p. 357. It is also consistent with the published segments. Shipler adds that the "high-sounding pledges in the accord... appear to constitute a quasi-legal arrangement under which Israel could intervene again in Lebanon if the agreement's terms were broken... Israel could interpret a subsequent violation [or from another point of view, subsequent resistance to its interpretation of the terms of the imposed agreement or to the integration of the occupied territories] as clearing the way for renewed Israeli military action in Lebanon." United Nations troops are restricted to the right to "surveil and observe" the Palestinian camps;[195] they cannot patrol these areas, which means that they cannot provide a barrier to further killings in the camps. This possible consequence is not noted in the *Times* news reports, which keep to the official Israeli line: that the UN had been unable to prevent "a PLO buildup," which means, under recent and current conditions, a reconstruction of political, social and economic life under the organization that the Palestinians regard as their representative. Two designated entry points are established for Israeli goods, and negotiations on future mutual relations are to start six months after an actual withdrawal of Israeli forces begins.

The *Times* commented editorially that the result "would come close to ending in a Greater Israel. A pro- American coalition of Egypt, Saudi Arabia, Jordan and Lebanon would then acquiesce in the destruction of the P.L.O. and Israel's absorption of the West Bank and Golan Heights [and, we may add, the Gaza Strip]. And the coalition would use its financial strength to make Syria acquiesce as well." It then concludes that "Syria holds the key to Lebanon's independence... And if the Syrians refuse to budge and cause Israel to stay in southern Lebanon, the onus for a tragic partition will be where it belongs," while "The P.L.O., Jordan and Saudi Arabia have to accept their historic responsibility for rejecting the Reagan plan and losing the territory."[196] We have already discussed the latter point; see chapter 6, section 3.1. The import of the former is also clear enough: unless Syria accepts a Greater Israel within an American-dominated regional alliance, as the *Times* accurately outlines it, they bear the onus for partition of Lebanon and what may happen next.

All of this again reflects the assumptions revealed throughout. As an American client, Israel inherits the right of aggression, so that the call for its unconditional withdrawal by the government of Lebanon and the United Nations may be dismissed as absurd—or to be more accurate, is not even noticed. Specifically, Israel had the right to destroy the society of the Palestinians and much of Lebanon as well; to impose the rule of its right-wing Christian allies along with "Moslem privileged classes" (Thomas Friedman; see p. 212); and to use its power to compel them to sign a virtual treaty that in effect endorses the takeover of the West Bank, the Gaza Strip and the Syrian Golan Heights while establishing arrangements in southern Lebanon that secure Israel's long-term dominance and that pave the way for new massacres and perhaps mass expulsion of the Palestinians, now defenseless in the face of the most brutal terrorist groups to have appeared in Lebanon, with Israel's constant support. Having achieved these goals, the conquerors were persuaded to agree to a partial withdrawal, a concession hailed by the paymasters as yet another proof of Israel's honor or even "sublimity." If Syria rejects the arrangements imposed on Lebanon by Israel with U.S. assistance, that will stand as further proof of Arab perfidy; naturally one would not expect the Israeli invaders to withdraw unconditionally after a comparable Syrian-Lebanese agreement imposed under the Russian aegis, but it is irresponsible to apply to ourselves or our clients the standards demanded of others (putting aside here the different circumstances of the entry to Lebanon of these foreign forces, discussed earlier;* the question of the occupied territories; and the question, now unanswerable, of whether Syria would have withdrawn its forces in the summer of 1982 when its six-year mandate expired, had Israel not chosen that moment to invade).

Similar logic applies in other situations. Shortly after Israel announced its magnanimity in agreeing to a partial withdrawal from Lebanon under the conditions reviewed, the USSR announced that "Kabul has expressed its readiness, in agreement with the USSR, for withdrawal of the total, limited Soviet contingent from [Afghan] territory and even expressed their willingness to give a timetable in this regard." The USSR is of course prepared to withdraw completely in conformity with the wishes of the legitimate government of Afghanistan, though there remains the problem of "guaranteeing nonintervention in Afghanistan from the terrorities of other states," intervention which "is taking place every day, which should be stopped," the Soviet spokesman asserted—referring to "intervention" by U.S.-backed guerrillas based in Pakistan, who carry out violence and disruption. We are all supposed to be deeply impressed.[197]

Note that Israel has not only succeeded in realizing the basic goals of its invasion of Lebanon and in imposing its September 1982 demands, but also in separating the Lebanese question from the problem of the occupied territories, which it can proceed to take over without interference; see p. 53. This result was achieved thanks to the success in interpreting Israel's rejection of the rejectionist Reagan plan with U.S. support as the fault of the PLO and the Arab states, as already discussed.

---

* Recall tnat Syria entered Lebanon at the request of the government and with the acquiescence of the U.S. and Israel, since Syria intervened to fight against the Lebanese Muslim-Palestinian coalition, later turning against the Phalange and carving out an area under its own control. See chapter 5, section 3.2; and section 6.2, on the Lebanese reaction to the Israeli invasion.

A side benefit, for the U.S. government, is that Moscow can now be denounced for having "again cast itself as a spoiler of the American peace initiative for the Middle East" while Secretary of Defense Weinberger issues stern warnings to the USSR and its "proxies." The negotiations pointedly excluded Syria. Syria was simply presented with a *fait accompli* which, it could be presumed, would be unacceptable, in substance and in manner. It would surely have been possible to conduct these negotiations in a framework that included Syria, with an eye to realizing the scheduled Syrian withdrawal that was aborted by Israel's invasion and its attack on Syrian forces (see section 2.2). It would also have been possible to engage the Soviet Union in the arrangements, in accord with the express wishes of the government of Lebanon,[198] again a step that would have enhanced the possibilities of mutual withdrawal. Instead of pursuing such options, Shultz chose instead to adopt a course that was designed to ensure an immediate Syrian rejection, with the political capital that could be gained from it, and also to minimize the likelihood of eventual Syrian compliance, thus increasing the probability that Israel will not withdraw and that a state of confrontation will persist.

While the Reagan Administration would no doubt be pleased to see Syria withdraw under the conditions it has established (in effect, following American orders) and may even try to facilitate such withdrawal in the longer term, nevertheless the Syrian refusal guaranteed by the framework for negotiations accords well with its broader aims. From its outset, the Administration has sought international confrontations— anywhere will do—that can be blamed on the "Great Satan" and its "proxies." The reasons derive in part from the domestic programs of transferring resources to the wealthy and expanding the Pentagon system of state intervention in the economy, a topic that would take us too far afield.[199] As in the case of the Reagan plan for the occupied territories, so also in the case of the "Shultz plan" for Lebanon, a program designed to minimize the chances for success has considerable utility if it can be presented in such a way as to place the blame for failure on official enemies and thus to restore eroding support for the U.S.-Israel military alliance, with all that goes with it, while also shoring up the statist-militarist consensus at home. A further gain may be that the PLO might adopt a more militant posture, abandoning its unwelcome evolution towards political accommodation (now perceived as having been effectively blocked by U.S.-Israeli rejectionism), which was becoming something of a problem for the leaders of the rejectionist camp; see chapter 5, section 4.6.1. American diplomacy, as expressed in the Reagan and Shultz plans and the means by which they were pursued, has thus attained its short-term goals, thanks to the effectiveness of the ideological institutions, with the price to be paid by the Palestinians and, given the implications for the region and indeed far beyond, ultimately many others as well.

It is intriguing to see how the terms of discussion have shifted since Israel invaded Lebanon in June 1982. The May 1983 agreement is based on the principle that Israel need not withdraw its military forces unless Syria and the PLO withdraw. In the United States, this principle is accepted as just, virtually without question. Given this assumption, if the agreement is not implemented, Israel will also have the right to undertake what will be called "security measures" in the area under its control, gradually integrating the "North Bank," if it so desires. Notice that if indeed Israel has a right to maintain military forces in Lebanon as long as Syria and the PLO do, as is now assumed, then Israel presumably had a right to introduce these forces into Lebanon in 1982 to bring about the conditions now recognized to be legitimate; that is, it had the right to invade Lebanon and take over the territory it now holds, merely because of the presence of Syrian and PLO forces in Lebanon. This proposition was then advanced by no one, apart from elements regarded as extremist. A principle from which it follows is now adopted by virtually everyone, without question. This radical shift in assumptions demonstrates, once again, the utility of force and violence in international affairs, at least, its utility within the ideological system of the patron who backs and finances the aggression.

In fact, *any* concession that Israel would have been able to extract as a condition for its withdrawal would amount to a ratification of its right of aggression; and indeed, the acceptance of what it has already accomplished and the dismissal without comment of the demand of former Prime Minister Saeb Salam and others that Israel pay reparations for the consequences of its aggression already amount to a ratification of this right.

If there is a massacre and expulsion of defenseless Palestinians as a further result of the "Peace for Galilee" operation and the imprisonment of much of the male population, that will stand as additional proof of PLO cynicism and Arab barbarity, an additional reason why Israel cannot withdraw from the occupied territories. One can virtually write the articles and editorials in advance. Throughout, the claim has been that Israel has the right to impose conditions on Lebanon for its own "security." It is by now completely ignored that the 1981 Habib cease-fire effectively guaranteed Israel's security, one of the main reasons why Israel felt that it had to invade Lebanon to undermine the increasing political legitimacy of the PLO (again, putting aside much else, such as the actual history of the 1970s in southern Lebanon, discussed earlier). It is, in fact, another striking testimony to American racism on this issue that it is Israel, not the Palestinians, that is considered to be facing a security problem that must somehow be overcome.

One may anticipate that Syria will not willingly accept the arrangements outlined in the *New York Times* editorial cited above, that "terrorism" (or resistance) will continue in areas of Lebanon occupied by the IDF and its clients, and perhaps even that "terrorism" will continue or increase in "the Land of Israel," as has, in fact, already been reported.[200] We turn in the next chapter to possible further consequences.

Notes—Chapter 6
Aftermath

1. S. M. Dubnow, *History of the Jews in Russia and Poland* (Jewish Publication Society, Philadelphia, 1920), vol III, chapter XXXIII.
2. *Ibid.*
3. *Ibid.;* Lucas, *Israel.*
4. Max L. Margolis and Alexander Marx, *A History of the Jewish People* (Jewish Publication Society, Philadelphia, 1927, pp. 710-11).
5. Chaim Nachman Bialik, "On the Slaughter," translated by T. Carmi, ed., *The Penguin Book of Hebrew Verse* (New York, Viking, 1981)
6. See Yehoshua Sobol, "History Repeats Itself," *Al Hamishmar weekly*, Sept. 24, 1982; *Israel Press Briefs*. See also B. Michael, "We Only Kill Children by Accident," *Ha'aretz*, June 18, 1982 *(Israeli Mirror)*, a bitter commentary on "purity of arms" beginning with a quote from Bialik's poem "City of Slaughter," another poem on the Kishinev massacre.
7. See pp. 109-110.
8. For a particularly shameful episode, which outraged Israeli doves, see Mattityahu Peled, *New Outlook*, March 1981; *TNCW*, pp. 271-2.
9. *Le Monde*, Aug. 28, 1982.
10. Elias Freij, Mayor of Bethlehem, the last remaining elected mayor of a major town; *New York Times*, Jan. 26, 1983. The *Times* devoted 100 words to his comments, emphasizing his advocacy of negotiations between Israel and the PLO on the basis of the Reagan plan, and his advice to the PLO to announce their acceptance of this position.
11. *Manchester Guardian weekly*, Sept. 19, 1982.
12. Ze'ev Schiff, "An Excuse in Justification of the War," "Three Separate Wars," *Ha'aretz*, Jan. 10, 11, 1983.
13. Nahum Barnea, "The Mood of the Center: Schiff against Sharon," *Koteret Rashit*, Dec. 1, 1982.
14. "After Lebanon: a conversation," interview with Henry Kissinger, *Economist*, Nov. 13, 1982. For more on this odd figure of twentieth century America, see the references of chapter 3, note 68, and Seymour M. Hersh, *The Price of Power: Kissinger in Nixon's White House* (Summit, 1983), a welcome departure from the hagiography to which much of even the allegedly critical commentary descends.
15. Nicholas Veliotes, Assistant Secretary of State for Near East and South Asian Affairs, Hearing before the Subcommittee on Europe and the Middle East of the Committee on Foreign Affairs, House of Representatives, Ninety-Seventh Congress, First Session, Oct. 21, 1981 (U.S. Govt. Printing Office, Washington, 1982, p. 25).
16. Amos Perlmutter, "Begin's Rhetoric and Sharon's Tactics"; Harold H. Saunders, "An Israeli-Palestinian Peace," *Foreign Affairs*, Fall 1982.
17. See chapter 4, note 57 and text.
18. For the text of President Reagan's address, see *New York Times*, Sept. 2, 1982. Also Sept. 9, 1982, for the text of the "Talking Points" sent to Menachem Begin. Charles Mohr reports *(New York Times*, Sept. 3) that the State Department indicated that the U.S. plan envisioned some withdrawal from the Golan Heights.
19. On Labor's initial public reaction, see *New York Times*, Sept. 4, 1982. On Labor's actual views, see pp. 70, 75*, 108, 112-3, 164, 202. On the PLO reaction see Henry Tanner, *New York Times*, Sept. 5, reporting "a favorable if guarded

response" on the part of PLO spokesmen, including Arafat's statement that a federation with Jordan was acceptable in principle. "Most Arab experts are convinced that Mr. Arafat is looking for a peaceful solution of the Middle East conflict," Tanner adds. He also cites Palestinians who were in Beirut through the war on Arafat's enhanced status within the PLO, as a result of the war. The *New York Times*, Sept. 6, published the text of a letter from Elias Freij to the White House, expressing his support for the plan, and the President's reply. On the Palestine National Council reaction, see Thomas L. Friedman, *New York Times*, Feb. 22, 23; wire services, *Boston Globe*, Feb. 22; Trudy Rubin, *Christian Science Monitor*, Feb. 23; Jonathan C. Randal, *Washington Post*, Feb. 23, 1982.

20. Editorial, *New York Times*, Sept. 5, 1982; Anthony Lewis, "Down the Middle," *New York Times*, Sept. 6, 1982; editorial, *New York Times*, Feb. 24, 1983. There is an excellent and balanced discussion of the matter by Stephen Chapman, "The PLO and the Reagan Plan," *Chicago Tribune*, Feb. 27, 1983, the only one I found in the mass media. Chapman observes correctly that the *New York Times* reaction to the PLO's position would have been applicable in the same terms to positions taken by the Zionist organization in its early years, and takes note of the PLO steps towards political accommodation (specifically, the January 1976 proposal that has been erased from history elsewhere) and the harsh rejection of their conciliatory efforts.

21. *New York Times*, April 11; for some background discussion, see Trudy Rubin, *Christian Science Monitor*, April 11. *New York Times* editorial, "A Worthy but Tragic Failure," and David K. Shipler, "In Israel, Relief for Begin: Hussein's Decision Has Ended Any Debate on Possibility of Giving Up the West Bank," April 12; *New York Times* editorial, "The Jordan Door Slams Shut," April 17; *New Republic*, "The Death Of A Plan...," May 2, 1983; The same issue contains a noteworthy review by Kenneth Lynn lauding a novel ridiculing Islam and the entire "Arab world" (including Iran!), written in approximately the style of *Der Stuermer* on Jews and Judaism; whether the novel by Richard Grenier is accurately represented, I do not know.

22. *Ha'aretz*, Sept. 6, 1982; Amos Levav, *Ma'ariv*, Sept. 2, 1982. See also "Israel to Finance More Settlements in Occupied Lands," *New York Times*, Sept. 6, 1982, reporting the approval of ten new settlements "ignoring President Reagan's call for a freeze" and also the "strongly worded statement" by the Reagan Administration condemning the new settlement plan. On Aridor, Ne'eman and Ravid, see *Ha'aretz*, Aug. 31; Zvi Barel, *Ha'aretz*, Aug. 26; *Ha'aretz*, Aug. 25, 1982 *(Israeli Mirror).*

23. Zvi Barel, "Green Patrol also in the [West] Bank," *Ha'aretz*, Jan. 28, 1983; *Yediot Ahronot*, international edition, Feb. 11, 1983.

24. Many examples are given in testimony recorded by the Ad Hoc Committee for the Investigation of Bedouin Problems (Beersheva) and the Association for Civil Rights in Israel. There has also been extensive reporting in the Hebrew press. See also Yitzhak Bailey, "Contrary to our Ideals," *Jerusalem Post*, June 6 1978; Lesley Hazleton, "Forgotten Israelis," *New York Review*, May 29, 1980, and many other reports. See also pp. 105f., 194.

25. AP, *New York Times*, Sept. 5; Henry Tanner, "Jordan Welcomes the Reagan Plan," *New York Times*, Sept. 3, 1982.

26. Chaim Bermant, *Jerusalem Post*, Dec. 19, 1982 (see p. 109).

27. Ze'ev Strominski, *Davar*, Dec. 30, 1982; Eliezer Levin, *Ha'aretz*, Dec. 8, 1982; Gaby Kessler, *Ma'ariv*, Dec. 30, 1982.

28. *Davar*, Dec. 7, 1982 *(Israeli Mirror);* Eliezer Levin, *Ha'aretz*, Dec. 22, 1982; *(Israleft News Service).*

29. *Ha'aretz*, Dec. 14, 1982, Jan. 7, 1983; *Israeli Mirror*.

30. Yosef Valter, *Ma'ariv*, Jan. 14, 1983; Rafael Gaon, *Al Hamishmar*, Jan. 10, 1983. Valter's detailed account of the conditions of Arab workers is based on interviews and a tour with a police patrol.

31. Leah Etgar, *Yediot Ahronot*, Dec. 26, 1982 *(Israeli Mirror)*; Rafik Halabi, "In the Service of the Homeland," *Koteret Rashit*, Jan. 26, 1983. The final statement was allegedly added "in jest."

32. *Washington Post—Boston Globe*, March 18, 1983.

33. Wire services, *Los Angeles Times*, Sept. 5, 1982. David Lamb, *Los Angeles Times*, Sept. 3, 1982.

34. Ihsan A. Hijazi, *New York Times*, Sept. 5, 1982.

35. Ilan Kfir, *Ma'ariv*, Sept. 8, 1982. In the same issue, Yosef Vaksman reports Knesset Member Geula Cohen's response to the report that Gemayel is planning to bring Haddad to trial: "it is necessary to bring to trial those who did not do in central and northern Lebanon what Haddad did in the south."

36. Ze'ev Schiff, *Ha'aretz*, Sept. 8, 1982.

37. Yehuda Litani, *Ha'aretz*, Sept. 8, 1982.

38. Special, *New York Times*, Sept. 4, 1982; *Monday Morning* (Beirut), Sept. 13-19; "Israelis not Invited to Gemayel Party," *Jewish Post & Opinion*, Feb. 2, 1983.

39. T. Elaine Carey, "Lebanese hopes of national reconciliation dealt heavy blow; Assassination [of Gemayel] and Israeli push [into West Beirut] dismay Lebanese," *Christian Science Monitor*, Sept. 16, 1982.

40. Colin Campbell, *New York Times*, Sept. 26, 1982.

41. Norman Kempster, *Los Angeles Times*, Sept. 5, 14, 1982.

42. *Ma'ariv*, July 15, 1982; Yehuda Tsur, *Al Hamishmar*, Aug. 10, 1982.

43. *Economist*, Sept. 4, 1982.

44. Ihsan A. Hijazi, *New York Times*, Sept. 16; *Economist*, Sept. 18; Claudia Wright, *New Statesman*, Sept. 17; Helena Cobban, "Maronites split over ties with Israel," *Christian Science Monitor*, Sept. 21; David B. Ottaway, *Washington Post*, Oct. 2, 1982; *Washington Post—Boston Globe*, Jan. 22, 1983, again reporting the Phalange allegation that Syrian intelligence was behind the assassination. See also Trudy Rubin, *Christian Science Monitor*, Sept. 22, 1982, reporting the conviction of "many ordinary Lebanese" that Israel was in some way involved because of Gemayel's refusal to sign a peace treaty, suspicions that "are likely to continue to cloud Maronite-Israeli relations" unless the "ongoing internal Phalange investigations turn up the culprit."

45. Gidon Alon, "The Slaughter in the Camps—Hour after Hour," *Ha'aretz*, Jan. 11, 1983, a detailed chronology based on the public hearings of the official Israeli Commission of Inquiry, including 24 out of 58 witnesses, the other sessions being secret. Recall Dubnow's comment on the Czar's secret inquiry. We return to the official Report of the Commission in section 6.8.

46. Reuters, *New York Times*, Sept. 17, 1982.

47. Address by Defense Minister Sharon to the Israeli Knesset, excepts translated in the *New York Times*, Sept. 23, 1982.

48. David Lamb, *Los Angeles Times—Boston Globe*, Sept. 17, 1982.

49. *Ibid.*

50. Reuters, *New York Times*, Sept. 17, 1982.

51. David K. Shipler, "Israeli Issue: Sharon," *New York Times*, Sept. 27, 1982.

52. Thomas L. Friedman, *New York Times*, Sept. 27, 1982.

53. Colin Campbell, *New York Times*, Sept. 20, 1982.

54. See p. 155.

55. Bernard Nossiter, *New York Times*, Sept. 18, 1982.

56. Thomas L. Friedman, *New York Times*, Aug. 2, 1982.

57. David Lamb, *Los Angeles Times*, Sept. 16, 1982.
58. David Lamb and J. Michael Kennedy, *Los Angeles Times*, Sept. 18; *Newsweek*, Sept. 27, 1982.
59. Colin Campbell, *New York Times*, Sept. 18, 1982.
60. Robert Fisk, *London Times*, August 13, 1982.
61. *Ibid.*
62. Robert Fisk, *London Times*, Aug. 14, 17, 1982; Colin Campbell, *New York Times*, Sept. 27, 1982.
63. Thomas L. Friedman, *New York Times*, Sept. 26, 1982, a detailed record of the week's events, expanding on his earlier September 20, 21 account; reprinted in *The Beirut Massacre* (Claremont Research and Publications, New York, Oct. 1982), a collection of press and broadcast reports from U.S., British and Israeli sources. See also Michael Jansen, *Battle of Beirut, Israel in Lebanon*, and Amnon Kapeliouk, *Enquete sur un massacre* (Seuil, Paris, 1982).
64. Friedman, *New York Times*, Sept. 20, 21, 26, 27.
65. David Lamb, *Los Angeles Times*, Sept. 20, 1982.
66. Alon, "The slaughter in the camps"; Friedman, *New York Times*, Sept. 20.
67. Hirsh Goodman, *Jerusalem Post*, Sept. 24; Alon, "The slaughter in the camps."
68. Wolf Blitzer, *Jerusalem Post*, Sept. 24, 1982; report from Washington.
69. Alon, "The slaughter in the camps."
70. Loren Jenkins, *Washington Post*, Sept. 18, 1982.
71. Colin Campbell, *New York Times*, Sept. 18, 1982.
72. Ze'ev Schiff, "War Crime in Beirut," *Ha'aretz*, Sept. 20 (translated in *Israel Press Briefs*). See also Alon, "The slaughter in the camps"; David K. Shipler, *New York Times*, Sept. 21, 1982.
73. Friedman, *New York Times*, Sept. 26, 20.
74. *Newsweek*, Oct. 4, 1982.
75. *Newsweek*, Sept. 27, 1982.
76. Loren Jenkins, interview, "All Things Considered," National Public Radio, Sept. 20, 1982 (reprinted in *The Beirut Massacre); Ha'aretz*, Sept. 23, 1982 (reprinted in *The Beirut Massacre* from FBIS).
77. ABC news *Closeup*: "Oh, Tell the World What Happened," Jan. 7, 1983, 10PM.
78. Edward Walsh, *Washington Post—Boston Globe*, Nov. 8, 1982.
79. Testimony of Israeli Foreign Ministry official Bruce Kashdan before the Commission of Inquiry; Norman Kempster, *Los Angeles Times*, Nov. 22, 1982.
80. Alon, "The slaughter in the camps."
81. B. Michael, *Ha'aretz*, Nov. 12; Edward Walsh, *Washington Post—Boston Globe*, Dec. 26, 1982; Robert Suro, *Time*, Oct. 4, 1982, cited in Jansen, *The Battle of Beirut.*
82. Alon, "The slaughter in the camps."
83. David Richardson, *Jerusalem Post*, Dec. 12, 1982, noting that Sharon's October 25 testimony under oath in open session contradicts his claim in New York in early December that 479 had been killed. On the 700-800 figure, which does appear to be the Israeli intelligence estimate, see William E. Farrell, *New York Times*, Nov. 18, 19, 27, and the Kahan Commission Report, discussed below.
84. *Christian Science Monitor*, Oct. 14, 1982.
85. Thomas L. Friedman, *New York Times*, Jan. 30, 1983; *Jerusalem Post*, Sept. 30, 1982.
86. J. Michael Kennedy and David Lamb, *Los Angeles Times*, Sept. 19; David Binder, *New York Times*, Sept. 27; Loren Jenkins, *Washington Post—Boston Globe*, Sept. 23, 1982.
87. Ze'ev Schiff, *Ha'aretz*, Oct. 28; David K. Shipler, *New York Times*, Sept. 19, 1982.

88. *Ibid.;* Louis Wiznitzer, *Christian Science Monitor*, Sept. 27, 1982.

89. See Chomsky and Herman, *Political Economy of Human Rights*, vol. I, p. 363. This massacre received virtually no press coverage, apart from the British *New Statesman*.

90. Reported at once by the international press and church groups, this American-made massacre was apparently concealed by the U.S. press for over a year; see *TNCW*, p. 389.

91. AP, *Los Angeles Times, Boston Globe*, Sept. 8, 1982; *Guardian* (New York), Sept. 22, 1982, citing an AP report and a press conference held by the Salvador Human Rights Commission in San Salvador where three women gave graphic testimony.

92. UPI, *Los Angeles Times*, Oct. 14, 1982.

93. Eric Silver, Jerusalem, *Manchester Guardian weekly*, Oct. 3, 1982, citing "reliable Israeli sources."

94. David K. Shipler, *New York Times*, Oct. 18, 1982.

95. ABC News *Closeup* (see note 77).

96. Loren Jenkins, *Washington Post—Boston Globe*, Sept. 30, 1982; *New York Times*, Sept. 26, 1982.

97. Trudy Rubin, T. Elaine Carey, *Christian Science Monitor*, Sept. 20, 1982.

98. Bernard Gwertzman, *New York Times*, Sept. 19; Excerpts from Defense Minister Sharon's testimony before the judicial Commission of Inquiry, *New York Times*, Oct. 26, 1982. See also Robert Fisk, *London Times*, Sept. 20; *Manchester Guardian weekly*, Sept. 26; and numerous other sources providing direct and credible evidence of the participation of these forces.

99. *New York Times*, Sept. 23, 1982.

100. Thomas L. Friedman, *New York Times*, Sept. 19, 20, 26; Carey, *Christian Science Monitor*, Sept. 20; *Newsweek*, Oct. 4, 1982.

101. David Lamb, *Los Angeles Times*, Sept. 21, 1982.

102. Loren Jenkins, "Witnesses Describe Militiamen Passing Through Israeli Lines," *Washington Post*, Sept. 20, 1982.

103. William E. Farrell, *New York Times*, Sept. 24; Yuval Elizur, *Boston Globe*, Sept. 21; David K. Shipler, *New York Times*, Sept. 20, 1982.

104. Thomas L. Friedman, *New York Times*, Sept. 27, 1982; interview with Gen. Drori.

105. David Bernstein, *Jerusalem Post*, Sept. 21, 1982.

106. Gidon Kutz, *Davar*, Nov. 5, 1982; Annie Kriegel, *Israel: est-il coupable?* (Laffont, Paris, 1982). See also the notice by Yeshayahu Ben-Porat, *Yediot Ahronot*, Dec. 17, 1982. It should be noted that the book, though hardly worth discussion, does not go quite as far as the interview in *Davar*, either because the author was less cautious or the interviewer a bit imaginative.

107. "BLOOD LIBEL," *New York Times*, Sept. 21, 1982.

108. *New York Times*, Sept. 23, 1982; see note 47.

109. Yehuda Litani, *Ha'aretz*, Sept. 21, 1982, citing American sources.

110. See, for example, Avraham Tal, *Ha'aretz*, Sept. 20, 1982.

111. Excerpts from Shimon Peres's speech to the Knesset, *New York Times*, Sept. 23, 1982.

112. The Commission Report was released on February 8, 1983. The full official English translation appears in the *Jerusalem Post*, Feb. 9, 1982. Substantial excerpts appear in the *New York Times*, February 9. See section 6.8 for discussion.

113. Martin Peretz, *New York Times*, Sept. 22, 1982.

114. David K. Shipler, *New York Times*, Sept. 24, 1982.

115. "Israel Finds Its Voice," Editorial, *New York Times*, Sept. 29, 1982.

116. Letter, *New York Times*, Sept. 22, 1982; my emphasis.
117. Irving Howe, Op-Ed, *New York Times*, Sept. 23, 1983.
118. Nat Hentoff, *Village Voice*, Sept. 14, 1982.
119. "An end to unnatural silence," Editorial, *Boston Globe*, Sept. 26, 1982.
120. *New York Times*, Sept. 23, 1982.
121. Bar-Zohar, *Ben-Gurion*, in effect, Ben-Gurion's official biography. Any other reputable source will provide essentially the same information and conclusion.
122. *Dissent*, Winter 1983, citing the *New York Times*, Feb. 8, 1975; Lucas, *Israel;* Bar-Zohar, *Ben-Gurion*.
123. On this rarely-discussed topic, see G. H. Jansen, "Can Israel demand the 'right to exist'?" *(Middle East International*, Jan. 7, 1983).
124. See pp. 181, 182*.
125. E.H. Hutchison, *Violent Truce* (Devin-Adair, New York, 1956), cited by David Hirst, *The Gun and the Olive Branch.* Commander Hutchison was an American UN observer.
126. Hirst, *The Gun and the Olive Branch;* Livia Rokach, *Israel's Sacred Terrorism*, based on Moshe Sharett's personal diary; Bar-Zohar, *Ben-Gurion*.
127. Uri Milshtein, *Milhamot Hatsanhanim* ("Wars of the Paratroopers," 1969, "The creation of Unit 101'), cited by Israel Shahak, *Begin And Co.;* Kennett Love, *Suez;* Hirst, *The Gun and the Olive Branch.*
128. For substantial documentation on the remarkable double standard of the U.S. media with regard to Israeli and Arab terrorism over many years, see Alfred M. Lilienthal, *The Zionist Connection* (Dodd, Mead, 1978), a book that could hardly be reviewed in a major U.S. journal. See also *TNCW*. For a broader perspective on the entire question of "terrorism," see Edward Herman, *The Real Terror Network*. On the role of the Israeli government and its overseas associates in preparing the groundwork for the shift from "human rights" to "international terrorism" as the primary slogan of U.S. foreign policy ("the Soul of our foreign policy," in Jimmy Carter's memorable phrase), see Philip Paull, *International Terrorism: The Propaganda War*, MA Thesis, International Relations, San Francisco State College, June 1982.
129. Amos Perlmutter, "Ariel Sharon: Iron Man and Fragile Peace," *New York Times Magazine*, Oct. 18, 1981. There is a critical article on Perlmutter's piece by Lesley Hazleton in the *Nation* ("The Moderating of Arik Sharon," Nov. 14, 1981). Nothing is said about Unit 101, or Perlmutter's version of it. See Herman, *The Real Terror Network*, for further comment.
130. *Newsweek*, Oct. 4, 1982.
131. Norman Podhoretz, "The Massacre: Who Was Responsible?" (*Washington Post*, Sept. 24, 1982).
132. Elie Wiesel, "Israel Represents Jews of the World," *Jewish Post & Opinion*, Nov. 19 (see p. 16 for further elaboration of his views in the same interview); "Wiesenthal, Wiesel listed for 1983 Nobel Peace Prize," *Jerusalem Post*, Feb. 4, 1983; A. B. Yehoshua, Yeshayahu Leibovitz, *Haolam Haze*, Sept. 22, 1982. The contributions by noted Israeli intellectuals to this "what are they saying" section, in response to the Beirut massacres, may usefully be compared with the reactions by their American counterparts in the *New York Times* on the same day, some already cited, one cited directly below.
133. *New York Times*, Sept. 22, 1982.
134. Bernard Gwertzman, *New York Times*, Sept. 16; Yuval Elizur, *Boston Globe*, Sept. 16; John M. Goshko, *Washington Post—Boston Globe*, Sept. 16, 1982.
135. Bernard Gwertzman, *New York Times*, Sept. 18; Curtis Wilkie, *Boston Globe*, Sept. 18, 1982.

136. David K. Shipler (Jerusalem), *New York Times*, Sept. 18, 1982.
137. *New York Times*, Sept. 19, 1982.
138. Milton Viorst, "America's Broken Pledge to the PLO," *Washington Post*, Dec. 19, 1982; Alexander Cockburn, *Village Voice*, Nov. 9, 1982. The text had previously been cited by Thomas Friedman of the *New York Times* on the basis of information provided by the PLO, correctly, as Cockburn notes. See also Loren Jenkins, *Washington Post*, Nov. 13, 1982 (reprinted in *Palestine/Israel Bulletin*, Dec. 1982), citing explicit guarantees from Habib concerning "the security of the camps."
139. *The Dawn (Al Fajr)*, Jan. 28, Feb. 4, 1983; Report of the Information Center for the Defense of the Palestinian and Lebanese Civilian Population, Prisoners, Deportees and Disappeared, Rome (c/o Lelio Basso Foundation), Jan. 11, Feb. 4, 1983; also Livia Rokach, "Palestinian women from Lebanon in Israeli jails," March 1983, Information Center report, discussing the case of Maryam Abdel Jelil and others; *Al Fajr*, March 25, 1983.
140. Meron Benvenisti, *Newsweek*, Oct. 4, 1982.
141. Amos Elon, cited by David K. Shipler, *New York Times*, Sept. 27, 1982.
142. Uri Avneri, *Haolam Haze*, Aug. 4, 1982.
143. A. B. Yehoshua, *Haolam Haze*, Sept. 22, 1982; see p. 387 for what precedes. "Liberated Territory: Life and Death in the Hands of the Language," advertisement, *Ha'aretz*, June 25, 1982. The latest example is a government order to Israeli television and radio to stop using the Hebrew word "ishim" ("personalities") to refer to leading personalities in the PLO; AP, *New York Times*, March 7, 1983. *Ha'aretz* reports (March 7) that "a careful investigation" conducted by the authorities "in sources and in current usage of the word 'ishim' revealed that indeed there is a positive weight of respect." Putting aside the silliness, the implications concerning the occupied territories (where the population overwhelmingly regards these ex-personalities as their political leadership) are obvious enough.
144. Yoel Marcus, "The End of Sharon," *Ha'aretz*, October 1, 1982.
145. "Begin and Sharon Get Less Backing in Poll," *New York Times*, Sept. 30, 1982, citing a poll of the Dahaf Research Institute (the headline of this brief item has a rather plaintive ring); Jonathan Frankel, "Israel: The War and After," *Dissent*, Winter 1983 (these comments are dated October 25, 1982); Yosef Goell, *Jerusalem Post*, Oct. 1, 1982.
146. Yoel Marcus, Nov. 19, 1982.
147. David K. Shipler," *New York Times*, Feb. 20, 1983.
148. *Kol Hair*, July 9, 1982; *Libération*, June 17, 1982; *Haolam Haze*, June 30, 1982; Ronald Koven, Paris, *Boston Globe*, July 21, 1982.
149. Levi Yitzhak Hayerushalmi, interview with A. B. Yehoshua, *Maariv*, Sept. 17, 1982.
150. "The Truth, and Peace for Galilee," Advertisement signed by 35 Rabbis, *Jerusalem Post*, Nov. 19, 1982.
151. International Rabbinical Committee for the Safety of Israel, New York, Advertisement, *Ma'ariv*, Sept. 14, 1982. They refer to an earlier advertisement of theirs in the *New York Times*, July 2, 1980.
152. *The Dawn (Al Fajr)*, Oct. 29, 1982.
153. Editorial, *New York Times*, Feb. 9, 1983; *New Republic*, March 7, 1983. I noticed only one discussion that raised any question about the Commission Report, namely, Patrick J. Sloyan, *Newsday—Buffalo News*, Feb. 13, 1983, which makes the point that the evidence presented by the Commission on foreknowledge of massacre is not easy to reconcile with the Commission's

conclusion that there was no intention to harm the noncombatant population. There is an excellent analysis of the Commission Report, drawing the reasonable conclusions, by Uri Avneri, *Haolam Haze*, Feb. 16, 23, 1983; we return to it directly.

154. *Ha'aretz*, June 11; *Yediot Ahronot*, June 18; cited by Israel Shahak, letter, *Economist*, July 10, 1982.
155. *Ibid.*
156. See p. 191; *TNCW*, pp. 396-7.
157. Alan George, *New Statesman*, Aug. 27, 1982.
158. Marvine Howe, *New York Times*, Aug. 19, 1982.
159. Alan George, "Israeli law and order," *New Statesman*, Oct. 22, 1982.
160. Dan Connell, public talk, MIT, Sept. 22, 1982; *Monday Morning*, Beirut, Sept. 13-19, 1982.
161. Norman Kempster, *Los Angeles Times*, Sept. 24, 1982.
162. Augustus Richard Norton, *Los Angeles Times*, Sept. 24, 1982.
163. Special correspondent, *Middle East International*, Sept. 17, 1982.
164. Danny Rubinstein, *Davar*, Sept. 3, 1982, report from Lebanon.
165. James Feron, "Israeli Troops Dig In for Tough Winter in Lebanon," *New York Times*, Oct. 3, 1982. See Shimon Weiss, *Davar*, Oct. 18, 1982, on the measures taken to ensure proper housing and heat for IDF soldiers.
166. Dov Yirmiah, letter, *Ha'aretz*, Aug. 30, 1982.
167. Moshe Kol, *Davar*, Aug. 29, 1982 *(Israel Press Briefs)*.
168. James Feron, *New York Times*, Oct. 14; *Economist*, Oct. 30; David Hirst, *Guardian* (London), Oct. 30; John Yemma, *Christian Science Monitor*, Nov. 3, 1982; Trudy Rubin, *Christian Science Monitor*, Jan. 10, 1983.
169. *Ibid;* special correspondent, Beirut, *Middle East International*, Feb. 4, 1983; Robert Fisk, *London Times*, March 4, 1983; see also David Hirst, *Manchester Guardian Weekly*, Feb. 13, *Washington Post*, March 11, and others for similar reports. David K. Shipler, *New York Times*, Feb. 6, 13; special, *New York Times*, Feb. 14; *Economist*, April 16, 1983.
170. *Ha'aretz*, March 11; for the AP report, see the *Los Angeles Times*, March 14, 1983. Shmuel Mittelman, *Ha'aretz*, "The Government in a declaration to the High Court of Justice: the IDF is finishing off the foundations of the PLO economy in Lebanon," March 14, 1983.
171. Francis Cornu, *Le Monde*, Dec. 31, 1982; William E. Farrell, *New York Times*, Jan. 17, 1983; Charles Glass, "Victors and Vanquished: Baedecker to the Three Lebanons," (manuscript, January 1983); Samir Kassir, *Le Monde diplomatique*, February 1983; UPI, *Boston Globe*, Feb. 17; *New York Times*, Feb. 13; *Economist*, February 12; *Ha'aretz*, Jan. 26, 1983 *(Israeli Mirror)*.
172. *Yediot Ahronot*, Sept. 12, 1982; *Yoman Hashavua* (Likud), Jan. 21, 1983; J. Michael Kennedy, *Los Angeles Times*, Dec. 12, 1982; *Boston Globe*, Jan. 23, 1983; *Monday Morning*, Nov. 1-7, Nov. 22-28, 1982; Israel Shahak, report on Israeli trade regulations concerning occupied Lebanon, Nov. 1, 1982, reprinted in *Palestine/Israel Bulletin*, December 1982; *AJME News*, March 1983; Robin Wright, *Christian Science Monitor*, Feb. 8, 1983. See also the references of notes 169, 171.
173. See, for example, "Give Normalization a Chance," *New Republic*, Jan. 31, 1983, an analysis that refutes a series of irrelevant arguments against "normalization" and a "peace treaty," omitting crucial factors that are actually operative.
174. "Blood in the Chouf," *Economist*, Nov. 13, 1982. See also G. H. Jansen, *Middle East International*, Dec. 23, 1982.
175. See, for example, p. 253; Yosef Tsuriel, "Law and Order in the Chouf," *Ma'ariv*, Nov. 12, 1982 *(Israeli Mirror)*; Rafik Halabi, *Koteret Rashit*, Dec. 29, 1982.

176. Shmuel Segev, "The Tragedy in the Chouf Mountains," *Ma'ariv*, Jan. 4, 1983; *Ma'ariv*, Oct. 17, 1982 *(Israeli Mirror)*.

177. *Monday Morning*, Nov. 15-21, 22-28, 1982; *Los Angeles Times*, Nov. 15, Dec. 12, 1982.

178. Aharon Bachar, *Yediot Ahronot*, Dec. 31, 1982.

179. AP, *Boston Globe*, Feb. 1; wire services, *Boston Globe*, Feb. 7; Thomas L. Friedman, *New York Times*, Feb. 8, 1983.

180. Jim Muir, "Challenge to Gemayel," *Middle East International*, Dec. 10, 1982.

181. J. Michael Kennedy, "Captured Guns Given to Falangists, Israeli Says," *Los Angeles Times*, Sept. 23, 1982.

182. J. Michael Kennedy, *Los Angeles Times*, Oct. 6, 9; William E. Farrell, *New York Times*, Oct. 6, 7, 9; AP, *Boston Globe*, Oct. 9, 11, *New York Times*, Oct. 10; UPI, *Boston Globe*, Oct. 10; David B. Ottaway, *Washington Post—Boston Globe*, Oct. 12; *Economist*, Oct. 9; Ihsan A. Hijazi, *New York Times*, Feb. 16; Robin Wright, *Christian Science Monitor*, March 9; Helena Cobban, *Boston Globe*, Jan. 24, 1983.

183. Livia Rokach, *The Dawn (Al Fajr)*, Jan. 7, 1983; see also her article of Jan. 21; Report of the Information Center for the Defense of the Palestinian and Lebanese Civil Population, Prisoners, Deportees and Disappeared (Rome, L. Basso Foundation), Jan. 17, 1983.

184. Trudy Rubin, *Christian Science Monitor*, Feb. 10, 1983. See also Thomas L. Friedman, *New York Times*, Feb. 6, 1983.

185. Testimony of Paola Crociani in Rome, May 4, 1983. Information Center (see note 139).

186. Richard Halloran, *New York Times*, March 18; David K. Shipler, *New York Times*, March 19; AP, *New York Times*, March 19, 1983.

187. AP, *Boston Globe*, March 19, 1983; also Jonathan Randal, National Public Radio, March 17, 1983.

188. See Glass, "Victors and Vanquished."

189. Asher Maniv, "Blaming the U.S.," *Jerusalem Post*, Feb. 4, 1983.

190. Steven R. Weisman, "Reagan Accuses Israelis of Delay On Withdrawal," *New York Times*, Feb. 8, 1983.

191. Official translation of Amin Gemayel's address to the UN Security Council, *Monday Morning*, Oct. 25-31, 1982.

192. Editorial, *Christian Science Monitor*, Feb. 7, 1983.

193. Thomas L. Friedman, *New York Times*, May 10, 1983. For the text of the agreement, see *New York Times*, May 17, 1983. Parts remain secret.

194. David K. Shipler, *New York Times*, May 11; Bernard Gwertzman, with David K. Shipler and Thomas L. Friedman, *New York Times*, May 10, 1983. The agreement was opposed by the Progressive Socialist Party of Walid Jumblatt and by Amal, along with pro-Syrian groupings. *Economist*, May 21, 1983. Jumblatt's party is "the dominant group in the Druze community," and Amal, headed by Nabih Berri, is "the mainstream organization of the Shiite community," the largest religious group in Lebanon. *Middle East Reporter*, April 30, 1983.

195. Shipler, "Israelis Call Pact a Virtual Treaty," *New York Times*, May 11, 1983; also Shipler, May 10, 18; and text, May 17, 1983. General Benjamin Ben-Eliezer (Fuad), former commander of the southern Lebanon region who established the original relations with Haddad, "said that to the best of his knowledge there is a great difference between the published paragraphs [of the accords] and what was decided, and that in any event Haddad will remain in his command position as before for a long time." Shimon Weiss, *Davar*, May 8, 1983. Nahum Barnea reports that Israel has informed Haddad "to disregard what he had heard on the

radio and television or read in the newspapers. There is, in fact, no connection between the reports about the agreement, which provides for the dismantling of Haddad's independent force, and the reality in the field. Out there, Israel is continuing to build up Haddad as the commander of the southern region." *Koteret Rashit*, May 11, 1983; *Middle East International*, May 27, 1983. Barnea's report is particularly plausible in the light of the historical record, discussed earlier: the capture of Eilat after the 1949 cease-fire; the immediate encroachments into the demilitarized zones driving out the inhabitants in the south and subsequently along the border with Syria, setting off conflict in both regions; the capture of the Golan Heights after the cease-fire; the immediate violation of the Habib agreement under which the PLO had left and the subsequent invasion of West Beirut in violation of these agreements; etc. More generally, recall the explicit position of Weizmann, Ben-Gurion and others that agreements are only tactical maneuvers, to be overturned by force if necessary when it becomes convenient to do so. There is little reason to expect any modification of this traditional pattern.

196. Editorial, *New York Times*, May 10, 1983.
197. AP, *Boston Globe*, May 20, 1983.
198. John F. Burns, Sam Roberts, *New York Times*, May 14; Thomas L. Friedman, *New York Times,* May 17, 1983.
199. For discussion, see *TNCW*, introduction and chapters 7, 8.
200. *Ha'aretz* reports (March 30, 1983) that in the past year "terrorist attacks" increased 50% over the preceding year in the "central police region," from Rehovoth to Natanya. On the same day, it reported that IDF and Haddad troops increased their surveillance over villages in Lebanon (particularly, "Shiite villages"), "where incitement against the IDF and the Haddad forces is being carried out."

7

The Road to Armageddon

1 The Fateful Triangle

The United States, Israel and the Palestinians—three national entities so disparate in power that it seems absurd to link them in a single
phrase. The United States is the world's most powerful state. Israel is
ranked as the world's fourth greatest military power, a status that it can
maintain as long as the United States adopts it as a "strategic asset" and
preserves it as such. The Palestinians, in contrast, have scant hope even of
national survival. Nevertheless, these three parties have become locked
into a fateful triangular relationship, and within it they are drifting
towards disaster.

2 The Threat to the Local Parties

With regard to the Palestinians, the fact is too obvious for further
comment to be necessary. For Israel and the United States, the threats are
of different sorts, but they are real enough.

2.1 The Logic of Occupation

Since shortly after the 1967 war, Israel has set itself on a course of
endless oppression and military conflict. As was obvious at once, and
predicted at once, this course entailed international isolation, alliance

with pariah states, and service to the interests of its sole protector. The U.S. has been more than pleased to acquire a militarized dependency, technologically advanced and ready to undertake tasks that few are willing to endure—support for Guatemalan genocide, for example— while helping to contain threats to American dominance in the most critical region in the world, where "one of the greatest material prizes in world history" (in the words of the State Department) must be firmly held. A partnership has evolved in which Israel takes on such tasks while the United States maintains it in an artificial state of dependency. Increasingly, the values implicit in these tasks become internalized, reinforcing values that are ever more firmly implanted in a state controlling a conquered population by force in territories it intends to take for its own use, and founded on the principle of discrimination against "the minorities." The problems of dealing with the inherent contradiction in the concept of a democratic Jewish state with non-Jewish citizens were taxing enough; they become insurmountable under these conditions of moral decay and constant threat to survival, by now in large part self-generated.

Sooner or later Israel will face military defeat—it came close in 1973—or the need to resort to a nuclear threat, with consequences that one hesitates to imagine. Short of that, it will drift towards internal social, moral, and political degeneration. While Israel has chosen this course since 1967, it has done so under pressures that have strongly influenced the choice, particularly the pressures imposed by its supporters—more precisely, the supporters of Israel's moral degeneration and ultimate destruction. Repeatedly, alternative paths have been blocked by the "support" that has been the despair of Israelis who had a different vision of what their society might become.

We have seen some examples of what this "support" has meant for the society and culture of Israel. Some of the consequences are captured, often movingly, by soldiers returning from the occupied territories and the latest conquest, as in this "soldier's lament" by a reservist returning on leave to his kibbutz:

> They arrive home on leave miserable and depressed, young in years but old in spirit, tired and battle-weary. They smile, say "everything is fine," but when you catch them off guard you find bitterness and what are almost guilt feelings. As one soldier puts it: "You are asking me how I feel? If I tell you I feel shitty, will you understand? You here in the kibbutz, can you understand what we, the soldiers, are undergoing out there"?

> "Take me as an example," he says. "I was called up, sent to a training camp and then straight on to patrol Nablus, to chase demonstrating school girls. Then I was transferred to Beit Sahur [also in the West Bank], where we watched the beatings

and the other ways in which the Arabs were maltreated. Then on to Yamit, into the war of Jews against Jews, against the opponents of the withdrawal. So you get hardened, and just as you have come to terms with it all you are sent off to Lebanon. Let me just throw a few names at you. Names like Beaufort castle, Ain el-Hilweh, Damour. Do they mean anything to you? After that came al-Uzai, West Beirut. All the time there is shelling and shooting, there are dead and wounded. So you look in at your mates, you attend the funerals, and you feel increasingly empty inside. Everything passes you by. I have become totally insensitive, I am an emotional cripple, though not a physical one...

"Do you really believe there is any hope of ending this war? Arik [Sharon] claims that the Fatah has withdrawn from Lebanon. Do you believe it? Come and observe our alert there and the fear in our eyes. Even the Lebanese girls long ago stopped smiling at us. Every carrier bag in Lebanon looks like a time bomb to me...

"When I am on leave I try to have fun, to relax so that I can return to Lebanon without that tension, but it never works out. Meanwhile, yet another bus is attacked here and another one over there, and Arik tells us that we have 'destroyed the terror.' Tell me, you civilians, can't you do anything about it? One demonstration of 400,000 and that's it? Is that all you are going to do? Are you waiting for us to return in our coffins?"[1]

The consequences are revealed in other ways as well; for example, when a Peace Now demonstration calling upon Ariel Sharon to resign as the Kahan Commission recommended is "taunted, heckled, shoved and occasionally attacked with fists by young men chanting 'Begin! Begin!' and singing 'Begin, King of Israel!'," and when Emil Grunzweig, a mathematics teacher from Kibbutz Revivim, is killed by an Israeli Army assault grenade while angry men wearing yarmulkes shout at a group of women demonstrators: "You are Arab women! You should have been in Sabra and Shatila," and others shout: "They shouldn't have rescued you from Hitler in 1945!"*

* *New York Times*, Feb. 11, 1983. There is more detailed reporting in the Hebrew press. The demonstration was violently attacked with many injured even before the grenade blast that killed Emil Grunzweig and wounded others nearby. When Grunzweig, already dead, and the wounded arrived at the hospital they were again attacked and beaten, as were doctors on the scene, by men screaming "Next time we will finish you off," "Arik [Sharon] King of Israel," "A shame only one was killed," and so on. Marchers—some of them from elite fighting units, including one who took part in the Entebbe raid and other secret operations "not openly discussed"—were beaten and denounced as traitors, "Arafat's children," who should be sent to crematoria. Journalists who participated wrote of the early days of Hitler Germany and warned of impending civil war, condemning Begin—the "King" of the hordes—for making no move to restrain them.[2]

The consequences are revealed in a different though complementary way in the pages of the *Jerusalem Post*, where Mordechai Nisan, a political scientist at the Hebrew University who has elsewhere expressed his approval for Jewish terrorism, writes the following lines,[3] which are treated with respect and proudly exhibited to the international audience of "supporters of Israel":

> At the very dawn of Jewish history, contact with the Land of Israel established the principle that the presence of non-Jews in the country is morally and politically irrelevant to the national right of the Jews to settle and possess the Land... The Bible states the Jewish right regardless of non-Jewish presence. Much later, the Rabbinic sages expounded on the patriarchal promise and articulated the following principle:... Dwelling in the Land is the Jewish priority and it is in no way restricted, let alone nullified, by a non-Jewish majority population in any given part of the Land. This principle was later codified by Maimonides in his legal work, thus lending his outstanding *halachic* [religious legal] authority to this Abrahamic national imperative... [The view that rejects the legitimacy of Jewish settlement in Judea and Samaria] is a direct denunciation of Abraham, the first Jew, the Father of the Jewish people ...[who] set the precedent and model for settling there in spite of the fact that "the Canaanite was then in the Land." The Jewish presence in the Land has always had to contend with, and at least partially overcome, an indigenous non-Jewish element in the Land.

As we read in the genocidal texts of the Bible, an implicit reference that his Israeli readers will understand. He continues:

> In the democratic age we live in, it is a difficult task to openly adopt what seems like a non-democratic position. But it is nowhere provided that non-Jews will enjoy full equal rights as a national community. After all, the Land is the eternal possession of the Jewish people alone... The tasks of politics, often involving the use of violence, can at times only be achieved by sacrificing the purity of the soul. It is this reality which Zionism raised to the plane of modern Jewish historical experience in the State of Israel, and it is clear that some people have yet to understand this, or have yet to accept it.

> Yet, this inexorable reality will move on and impress itself more deeply on the Israeli consciousness. This would become a smoother process if people realized that pouring Western liberal ideas into Jewish vessels, and serving them up as Jewish, is dishonest and dangerous.

> It is not my contention that such people err in their humanity, but rather in their claim that their personal views are an authentic reflection of Tora teaching, Jewish morality and Israeli interests. Even our era of intellectual and ethical relativism cannot sanction this forgery.

Western Enlightenment is, in effect, a heresy that should be put aside in favor of "Tora teaching."*

The sense that the age of the Enlightenment is over and that it was based on fundamental misconceptions of human nature and needs has significant roots in Zionist thinking, even among liberal Zionists. One of the most noted of these, long a spokesman for a liberal humanist perspective, wrote in 1934, in Berlin, that the coming to power of the Nazis (the "German revolution") signifies the end of the liberal era: "The development from the *unity of man* of the Enlightenment to the *unity of nation* of the present contains within itself the principle of the development from the concept of mankind to the concept of the nation," a development that he appears to regard as a desirable and progressive one, and that places the "Jewish question" in a new light. Assimilation was natural in an era of liberalism and under the impact of the mistaken ideals of the Enlightenment. But for the present era, what is needed is the principle of "recognition of the Jewish nation and the Jewish race." As for the Nazi State, "A state which is built upon the principle of the purity of nation and race can have esteem and respect for the Jews only when they identify themselves in the same manner," as people "of one nation and one race," abandoning Enlightenment errors.[4]

Similar conceptions are found in many national movements. They are particularly striking in the case of Zionism because of the Jewish contributions to 19th and 20th century intellectual and artistic culture and to the Enlightenment ideals; and also, of course, because of what the "principle of purity of nation and race" soon came to mean for the Jews of Europe. Throughout the history of the Zionist movement, these issues have been central ones, and they only took on new forms with the establishment of Israel as "the sovereign State of the Jewish people." This act raised the question of "Who is a Jew?" to one of law and national policy, along with the question of the status of "national institutions" devoted to "the benefit of people of Jewish race, religion and origin" rather than citizens of the state, and including Jewish citizens of other states. With the decline of secularism and the growth of religious-chauvinist tendencies in the expansionist post-1967 period, these questions are once again reformulated, often in an ugly way. Mordechai

---

* The author of these lines is a lecturer at the Hebrew University school for overseas students, where he teaches the moral foundations of Zionism to American Jewish students coming to Jerusalem to discover their heritage. On his support for terrorism, see the *American Zionist*, May/June 1976, cited in *TNCW*, p. 304.

Nisan's version is one example. Western left-liberal "supporters of Israel," many of them of the post-1967 variety, have sought to suppress these issues, insisting that the society was tending towards secularism, egalitarianism and democratic socialism precisely at the time when exactly the opposite was true as a direct consequence of the state policies that they were supporting. Typical examples have been cited above; the consequences of this "support" should by now at last be clear.

We have seen, in chapter 4, the expression of ideas of the sort that Nisan again puts forth from the pens of religious-chauvinist extremists in their own journals (see, e.g., pp. 123-4). As this and many other examples indicate, however, such "Khomeinism" is far broader. A further indication of its scope is given by the Israeli writer Amos Oz in a series of articles in *Davar*, based on interviews. One group is from the settlement of Tekoah south of Bethlehem in the occupied West Bank, a "detestable area," one settler explains, because the Arabs "raise their heads" here. A recent American immigrant from a religious family in New York tells him that she hopes for a war or a "terrible disaster to the Jews abroad" so that "they shall be persecuted" and come to Israel. There will never be peace, she says:

> The hatred the Gentiles feel towards the Jews is eternal. There never was peace between us and them except when they totally beat us or when we shall totally beat them. Maybe if they will give someone like Sharon the chance to kill off as many of them as possible, destroy their countries, until the Arabs will understand that we did them a favor in letting them remain alive...
> We are powerful now and power should talk now. The Gentiles only understand the language of power.

Those who have had the pleasure of addressing an audience of young American Zionists, chanting their slogans and waving their Anti-Defamation League handouts like Little Red Books, will recognize the mood and the sentiments, which are having their own corrupting effect in Israel.

Her husband, from Aden, considers himself "far more extreme," but knowing the Arabs, he sees possibilities of living with them. "We know that the Arab is an obedient good creature as long as he is not incited and no one puts ideas into his head... He just has to be told exactly what his right place is... They must understand who the master is. That's all." A recent immigrant from the U.S. with degrees from Yeshiva and Columbia Universities, now teaching social science at Bar Ilan University, adds his contribution. "Western culture is not for us," he explains, echoing Khomeini: "The Torah is far more modern than western culture," giving a person "freedom without permissiveness." "The ways of God are great" and "gradually all our opponents will understand that they are mistaken."

As for the Arabs, they are "a trial," but if we are "strong and obstinate, it will be the beginning of salvation. All the difficulties are the pains of the coming of the Messiah. . . One must be totally blind not to see that [the settlement in the occupied territories] is the beginning of true salvation."

An unidentified settler in a Moshav—a well-established farmer, educated, of western origin, apparently a person of some distinction who speaks with a sense of authority—takes a rather different stand.* In his view, Israel should be "a mad state," so that people "will understand that we are a wild country, dangerous to our surroundings, not normal," quite capable of "burning the oil fields" or "opening World War III just like that," with nuclear weapons if necessary. Then "they will act carefully around us so as not to anger the wounded animal." Essentially, Richard Nixon's "madman theory." The Lebanon war was fine, but didn't go far enough ("it's a pity we didn't wipe that wasps nest completely off the ground," referring to Ain el-Hilweh; "we should have done it with our own delicate hands," referring to Sabra-Shatila, instead of leaving it to the Phalange—"can you call 500 Arabs a massacre"?). "We shall open another similar war, kill and destroy more and more, until they will have had enough." One great achievement of the Lebanon war was that it aroused anti-Jewish passions throughout the world, so that now "they hate all those nice Zhids" (an anti-Semitic slur) who write books and play music, all those now often derided in Israel as "beautiful souls." He is pleased with the designation "Judeo-Nazi" used by Professor Yeshayahu Leibovitz in a despairing indictment of what he fears Israel is becoming. This man's goal is "to kill as many Arabs as necessary, to deport them, to expel, to burn them, to make us hated by all, to make the ground unstable beneath the feet of the Jews in the Diaspora so that they shall be forced to rush here crying." He wants to imitate the Australians who exterminated the natives of Tasmania, or Truman who destroyed hundreds of thousands with two bombs. If instead of writing books, Jews had come to Palestine and "killed six million Arabs, or one million," then they would now be a people of 25 million, "from the Suez canal to the oil fields." It was a mistake that should not be made again. Afterwards, there will be time for culture and civilization.[5]

If things continue on their present course, within the constraints that are at least induced, if not imposed, by "support" from the United States of the sort tendered in recent years, there is reason to expect that these will sooner or later become the authentic voices of Israel. Note that contrary to many oversimplified accounts, these are not the voices of Sephardic slum-dwellers from the Arab countries, but of educated people of western orientation and origin.

---

* This man's views are taken quite seriously by Oz and many others. See, for example, Boaz Evron, "The Nightmares of C" (as he is identified in Oz's interview), *Davar*, Feb. 4, 1983, a detailed point-by-point refutation of his arguments, which are by no means dismissed as idiosyncratic.

2.2   The Next Round

As 1983 began, concerns were mounting about the next round. Katyusha rockets again fell near the northern settlements, something that had not happened until Israeli violence destroyed the 1981 Habib cease-fire. Galilee settlements were advised to introduce special alerts for an expected intensification of terrorist attacks.[6] Meanwhile, "Diplomatic sources in Damascus said yesterday that Syria has rebuilt its army in Lebanon's eastern Bekaa Valley in expectation of an Israeli attack in late spring or early summer." The USSR installed a new and more advanced air defense system in Syria, locating the bases near Damascus and staffing them with Russian personnel. Israel's new Defense Minister, Moshe Arens, warned that Israel "could resort to a pre-emptive strike against Syria if the buildup of long-range Soviet SAM5 [anti-aircraft] missiles continues there and the Israelis conclude they are faced with a 'mortal threat'." The USSR has warned Washington that it would intervene directly in the event of an Israeli attack on Damascus, and "placing Soviet military men in Syrian bases would make this warning a great deal more credible," the London *Economist* observes. Ned Temko reports from Moscow that the USSR has warned Israel not to strike the SAM-5 missiles. John Yemma adds from Lebanon that

> the underlying fear is that Israel may be tempted towards a preemptive strike against the Soviet missiles in Syria. And if this were to occur, the Soviet soldiers manning the installations might be harmed. This, in turn, could precipitate heavier Soviet intervention in Syria and possibly a crisis between the two superpowers.

If there are clashes between Israel and Syrian soldiers in Lebanon, as may occur if no serious withdrawal plan involving both Syria and Israel is developed and implemented, the Israelis will want air cover "and, to achieve it, Israeli warplanes might go after Syria's Soviet antiaircraft missiles."[7] These prospects are not remote, and will remain threatening in the absence of a comprehensive political settlement.

Israeli military experts believe that as a result of the Lebanon war Syria has intensified its arms acquisitions and military training programs, and by the end of 1983 will have the operational capacity to undertake offensive action—an analysis which, whether valid or not, is likely to elicit a preemptive Israeli strike. One result of the war in Lebanon, Ze'ev Schiff writes, was to prompt Syria to create a larger and more mechanized army. He also notes that in ground combat Syrian units fought well, though they were heavily outnumbered, and that their confidence increased for that reason. "By seeking a general land engagement with the Syrian army in Lebanon in order to expel it from that country," Israel has "accelerated a process detrimental to ourselves." Schiff reports further that General Amos Gilboa expects that "one of the Arab lessons from the [1982] war will be to obtain nuclear weapons," perhaps in alliance with Pakistan.[8]

Long-term predictions in the volatile Middle East are a risky proposition. In early 1983, however, Syria probably viewed its strategy of supporting Iran against Iraq and maintaining its military position in Lebanon as relatively satisfactory; and in fact, its options are limited as long as return of the Golan Heights is not part of the "peace process" as envisaged by the United States. Even under the most optimistic assumptions concerning Lebanon, the chances that another war will erupt are not small.

3   The Threat to the United States and the World

3.1   The Risk of Superpower Confrontation

The disasters threatening the Palestinians and Israel are evident enough. It also does not take a great deal of thought to perceive the risks to the United States, and in fact the entire world, from the unresolved Israel-Arab conflict. The world contains many trouble spots, but none pose such dangers of superpower confrontation as the Middle East, and of the many conflicts in this region, none approaches the Israel-Arab conflict—and at its heart, the conflict between Israel and the Palestinians—in the threat it poses of global, nuclear war. In comparison, the threat of a superpower confrontation in Europe, or elsewhere, seems slight.[9] Sheer self-interest alone, apart from anything else, should make it a priority item for Americans—or for anyone interested in survival—to seek a resolution of this conflict. The question is a particularly urgent one for Americans to address in the light of the role of U.S. rejectionism in perpetuating the conflict and undermining the possibility for political settlement.

The risk that a nuclear war might erupt from a Middle East conflict is nothing new. When Eisenhower sent U.S. forces to Lebanon in 1958, it was his judgment that there was a risk of "general war with the Soviet Union" (Eisenhower's words, in his memoirs), an opinion shared by some of his advisers, for example, Loy Henderson, who felt that "we should face the risk now as well as any time."[10] At the time of the 1967 war, the "hot line" between Washington and Moscow was used for the first time. There was apparently another close call, one that is never listed in the records of the all-too numerous occasions when a nuclear war may have been imminent. When the *U.S. Liberty* was attacked by Israeli planes and torpedo boats during the June 1967 war, F-4 Phantom jets were dispatched from a Sixth Fleet aircraft carrier to defend the ship, "authorized to use force including destruction if necessary" (Smith, quoting the official court of inquiry), nuclear-armed and recalled only by a direct order from Secretary of Defense McNamara and the Chief of Naval Operations in Washington, according to James Ennes. It was unclear at the time who the attackers were; Ennes, who observed all of this as an officer on the *Liberty*, writes that the jets "might have saved the ship, or they might have initiated the ultimate holocaust." In 1973, the U.S. called a strategic nuclear alert in the final stages of the October war. Reviewing this incident, Blechman and Hart conclude that "there was a serious threat of military conflict between the United States and the Soviet Union."[11] This is, in fact, a typical example of how a nuclear war is likely break out, sooner or later, possibly through inadvertence or mistaken judgment as to intent.

During the 1982 Lebanon war, American nuclear forces were not alerted, so far as we know, but the danger of superpower confrontation was not slight. In their sharp condemnation of the Israeli invasion, the foreign ministers of the European Community warned that it posed the risk of "leading to a generalized war" (see p. 27). The U.S. and Soviet fleets were present in force in the Eastern Mediterranean. A senior Soviet official "expressed concern the Mideast fighting may provoke a full-scale confrontation between Israel and Syria, triggering greater Soviet involvement," and it has been alleged that "the Russians had threatened to intervene militarily, if the fighting [between Israel and Syria] did not stop."[12] If Israel's attack on Syrian forces had continued and the fighting had escalated a notch or two higher, the USSR might have made some move in defense of its Syrian ally, a step that surely would have brought about a U.S. military response and possibly a superpower confrontation. As noted earlier, the USSR has warned that it would become directly involved if Damascus were attacked, and the war might well have escalated to Israeli bombing or shelling of Damascus. By September, Israeli forces were deployed north of Beirut and Syrian forces in Eastern Lebanon had been cut off, with Israeli artillery in a position to shell Damascus. It is possible that further steps would have been taken in what military analyst Ze'ev Schiff describes as Israel's war "to expel Syria from Lebanon," had it not been for the unexpected international reaction to the Beirut massacres. It is, in short, not impossible that the victims of this atrocity saved the world from nuclear confrontation.

Even apart from the Syrian phase of the war, the risk of superpower involvement was considerable. The Soviet Embassy was hit on several occasions and was "heavily damaged" during the Israeli shelling of West Beirut. Furthermore, during the Israeli invasion of West Beirut, Israeli troops occupied parts of the Soviet Embassy and held them for two days, a gratuitous act of defiance in the course of the conquest of a virtually undefended city.[13] Assistant Secretary of Defense Richard Perle disclosed subsequently that Israeli jets killed 11 Russians whom they observed investigating a downed Israeli reconnaissance plane in Lebanon.[14]

All of this was passed over calmly here, because we take it for granted that the USSR will back down in any confrontation apart from its immediate borders. Luckily for the world, this expectation once again turned out to be correct. But this should not prevent us from perceiving the seriousness of the provocation. Suppose that the situation had been reversed. Suppose that a Cuban army had invaded Costa Rica or Guatemala, purposely killing 11 American advisers, shelling the U.S. Embassy and occupying it in the course of conquering the capital city. How would the U.S. have reacted? Of course, the question is academic, since at the first appearance of Cuban forces we would have blockaded or bombed Havana or perhaps even Moscow. But as we interpret the rules of the game, the Russians are expected to accept passively affronts that the U.S. would never tolerate for a moment. And so far they have, or we would not be here to discuss the matter.

The Soviet Embassy was, incidentally, not the only one to have been occupied during the Israeli takeover of West Beirut. The governments of Iran and Algeria reported that their Embassies had been taken over as well, with safes broken into and documents and official papers taken.[15] As noted earlier (see p. 299), Lebanese sources allege that all embassies and other major institutions of governments that Israel regarded as unfriendly were shelled, looted, or otherwise damaged.

3.2   The Evasions of the Peace Movement

When the Ambassador of Lebanon, Ghassan Tueni, spoke at the UN Disarmament session on June 22, 1982 (see chapter 5, note 175), he observed that "the war in Lebanon was becoming a danger not to Lebanon alone, but to others as well, and probably to the entire world." His statement was by no means exaggerated, and the fear was shared by many others. It is a startling fact that this quite obvious threat was ignored by the organizers of the huge antiwar demonstration mounted in New York in connection with the UN disarmament session that took place shortly after Israel's invasion of Lebanon. To be more accurate, the issue had been discussed, but it was decided to suppress it, though not all participants in the demonstration remained silent on the point.

There have been many examples of a similar sort. Let me give just one personal experience. My article on directions for the disarmament movement cited in note 9 was excerpted in *Worldview*, a journal published by the Council on Religion and International Affairs. The main point of the article was that it was crucial for the disarmament movement to focus attention on situations in which local conflicts or outside intervention might come to engage the superpowers, leading to global nuclear conflict. Indeed, one would think that this question would receive top priority among people concerned to avert this catastrophe. I listed five examples of such conflicts, the fifth and by far the most significant being the Israeli invasion of Lebanon with U.S. backing. The first four cases appeared in the published excerpts; the fifth and most important case was omitted. One can only conclude that for the editors, the threat of nuclear war is a relatively insignificant matter when measured against the importance of protecting the policies of Israel from scrutiny and evading the question of the U.S. role in the Middle East.[16] All of this is surely to be understood as simply another facet of the "ideological support" for Israel discussed earlier, and of the still more general tendency to deflect critical analysis of one's own state and its policies and actions.

The unwillingness of major segments of the peace movement to face this issue—and more generally, to confront the question of how a nuclear war is likely to break out as a result of tensions and conflicts in the Third World to which the U.S. often makes a significant contribution—deserves some thought. It is a stance that reflects a curious arrangement of priorities on the part of people who are committed to reducing the likelihood of nuclear war.

4   Prospects

The dangers to the partners in this triangular relationship are therefore clear enough. There can also be no serious doubt that U.S. policies and actions will have a significant effect on what comes to be, as in the past. The current prospects are for a continuation of past tendencies: "support for Israel" at the material, diplomatic and ideological levels, combined with conflict at the meaningless rhetorical level. If this remains so, what evolves will, in significant measure, reflect the workings of Israel's social and political order. Let us first consider that question and then turn finally to the possible consequences of a move away from the rejectionist positions of the past in the United States.

Before entering into these two crucial questions, we might take note of some that are secondary in the present connection. As for the third partner in the triangular relationship on which attention has been focused here, the Palestinians, they are so weak and their options are so few that their impact on events will be slight. As discussed earlier, they have already approached or joined the international consensus, though one might also note, again, that both their actions and their propaganda (and their almost complete failure to reach an American audience, not wholly their own fault) have often been self-destructive, and particularly in earlier years, intolerable. Those marginal groups in the West that have given the PLO the kind of "support" that the overwhelmingly dominant groups and institutions have given to Israel merit the same reaction as do the latter, though the phenomenon is so slight in comparison with the "support for Israel" as to be barely worth comment. There are, of course, other actors in the Middle East: Europe, the Arab states, the USSR, and others as well. But in present circumstances their role is secondary at best, and in any event, of far less significance for Americans than the role of the U.S. and U.S.-supported Israel, for transparent reasons, which merit comment, if at all, only because of the constant pretense of inability to understand them: it is the policies of the U.S. that we can hope to influence, and indirectly, the policies of others that are shaped to a degree by U.S. action.

4.1   Assuming U.S. Rejectionism

4.1.1 The Spectrum of Israeli Political Thinking

As has been made abundantly clear, the two major political groupings in Israel are alike in their rejectionism, but differ in the means by which they choose to implement it. Both intend to hold on to the Golan Heights and Gaza Strip. As for the West Bank, Likud advocates an extension of Israeli "sovereignty" while Labor prefers that Israel maintain control over its resources and a substantial part of its territory while overcoming the "demographic problem" by leaving the population stateless or under some form of Jordanian administration but Israeli military control. Neither position can be reconciled with the rather vague rhetoric of the Reagan plan, though Labor's position comes closer. For this and other reasons, the U.S. government and a good part of the press appear to favor the return of Labor to power.

Poll results indicate that none of the current Labor leaders come close to Begin in popularity. Consequently there has been some hope that former President Yitzhak Navon, a Labor Party veteran who is of Sephardic origin and who ranks considerably higher in the polls,* will agree to lead the party in the next elections. Whatever illusions there might have been about this dovish alternative were—or should have been—dissipated by his visit to the U.S. in January 1983, arranged with considerable fanfare as affording a closer look at the alternative to Begin. Navon emphasized that Labor and Likud do not disagree on the legality of settlements in the West Bank and Gaza, but "mainly on where Israelis should settle and at what pace"; in other words, should new settlements be established in accord with the program of Likud or Labor as to how to integrate the territories within Israel? As for withdrawal of troops from

---

* See p. 254*. Some early 1983 polls indicated that if the Labor Alignment were led by Navon, it would draw even with Begin's Likud, though few political analysts in Israel appear to attach much credence to this possibility. On poll results in Israel in this period, see Khalik Nakhleh's essay in *The Palestine-Israel War of 1982*, Institute for Arab Studies (Belmont, Mass.), forthcoming.

Lebanon, Israel requires "tangible expressions of peace" from the country it invaded before agreeing to withdraw—a position that is not regarded as unreasonable within the remarkable framework of assumptions that constrains discussion in the United States. He refused to accept a freeze on settlement in the West Bank as a means for drawing King Hussein into the Reagan "peace process." At a meeting in Boston, Navon "strongly defended Mr. Begin after a university professor criticized the Prime Minister." "Those of us who thought that there would be massive shifts in Israeli policy if Begin were gone had better think again," a "Washington-based Jewish activist said."[17] In fact, there was no basis for any such view before, and if recent history is any guide, the view will be maintained despite this disillusioning experience, and in fact, in complete disregard of whatever the facts may be.

There is a rather detailed analysis of Israeli opinions on crucial political questions by Sammy Smooha of Haifa University and the State University of New York (Binghamton) and Don Peretz of the latter institution, which provides useful background for these matters.[18] They base their conclusions on polls taken in July 1980. The prime focus of their investigation is the Arab population within Israel (Israeli Arab citizens), but more relevant to our concerns here are the comparative results they present concerning Israeli Jews. Israeli Arabs tend towards support of the international consensus as described earlier, no great surprise, since this position is virtually uniform outside of the United States and Israel. As for the PLO, 68% of Israeli Arabs believe that Israel should recognize it as the representative of the Palestinians (an additional 22% "under certain circumstances") and half regard it as a representative for Israeli Arabs, while "58% justified Fedayeen actions in which Israeli Jews are killed" (resistance activities from their point of view, terrorism from the point of view of those who hold the occupied territories by force).

Turning to the Jewish population of Israel, 46% favor settlement in the occupied territories without reservations, an additional 27% with reservations. 1% favor a political settlement on the Green Line (pre-June 1967 borders), an additional 8% "with certain modifications." 57% favor a settlement on the current borders "with certain modifications," while an additional 33% favor "present borders with willingness to compromise also in Judea and Samaria." Among "dovish leaders," 3% favor a settlement on the Green Line, an additional 44% "with certain modifications," and 53% favor present borders with compromise in the West Bank. 86% of the public and 77% of the dovish leaders oppose a peace settlement if it would entail giving up annexed East Jerusalem—an annexation recognized by virtually no one, not even the U.S. On "Israel's recognition of a Palestinian nation," 11% of the Jewish public was in favor, an additional 35% "under certain circumstances," with 54% entirely opposed under any circumstances. The corresponding figures among dovish leaders were

59%, 27%, 15%. On recognition of the PLO as the Palestinians' representative, among the public 3% approved, an additional 13% under certain circumstances, while 85% opposed recognition under any circumstances. Among dovish leaders, the corresponding figures were 21%, 27%, 53%. As for a Palestinian state in the West Bank and Gaza, 5% of the public approved, an additional 18% under certain circumstances, and 77% were opposed under any circumstances. Among dovish leaders, the corresponding figures were 15%, 29%, 56%.

It is clear, then, that massive changes would have to take place within Israel, and considerable changes among the dovish leaders, before any departure from far-reaching rejectionism would become a significant force. As to what the distribution of responses would be if the United States had not backed Israeli rejectionism with such consistency and commitment, one can only speculate.

4.1.2 "From Coexistence to Hegemony"

Given the state of opinion within Israel, and still assuming unchanging U.S. "support for Israel," what long-term policies is Israel likely to pursue, apart from continued steps towards integration of the occupied territories in either the Likud or Labor style? Surely Israel will not tolerate any military build-up in the surrounding region that it considers a potential threat, and there will be no end to such threats if there is no political settlement, a prospect virtually guaranteed by U.S.-Israeli rejectionism. Furthermore, the costs of a permanent state of war are immense, and mounting, costs that Israel is increasingly unable to bear and that cannot be reduced as long as tension exists and its adversaries are not crushed.* Hence the inducement to undertake a preemptive strike will always be high, and with it, the likelihood of regional or even global war. It is only natural to expect that Israel will seek to destabilize the surrounding states, for essentially the reasons that lead South Africa on a similar course in its region. In fact, given continuing military tensions, that might be seen virtually as a security imperative. A plausible long-term goal might be what some have called an "Ottomanization" of the region, that is, a return to something like the system of the Ottoman empire, with a powerful center (Turkey then, Israel with U.S.-backing now) and much of the region fragmented into ethnic-religious communities, preferably mutually hostile.

---

* For a recent analysis of these costs, see Zvi Kassler, "The True Cost of the Lebanon War," *Koteret Rashit*, Feb. 23, 1983. Until the 1967 war, Israel's military expenditures amounted to about 10% of GNP, rising to 18% at the time of that war and to 33% with the October 1973 war. After a decline to below 25% in late 1978, they began a steady rise, reaching 36.6% with Operation "Peace for Galilee," and are expected to remain at about that level, if not higher. The plausible conclusion, which Kassler draws, is that Israel will have to seek "new solutions," perhaps regular "small wars" to keep potential enemies weak or (as others have proposed) reliance on nuclear weapons. There is, of course, little reason to be confident that "small wars" will remain small.

A clear version of such a picture was presented just prior to the Lebanon war by Oded Yinon, who was formerly in the Israeli foreign service, in the ideological journal of the World Zionist Organization.[19] Yinon argues that Israel must restore the status quo that reigned in the Sinai before the "mistaken peace agreement" with Sadat. Egypt is weak ("a corpse") and events will lead to Israeli reconquest of the Sinai. Furthermore, the dismemberment of Egypt should be "the political goal of Israel in the 1980s on its Western front." On the other fronts, Lebanon, Syria, Iraq and the Arabian peninsula must also be dismembered into smaller "factors," religious and ethnic, as in the Levant during the Ottoman period. Jordan will be handed over to the Palestinians and the population of the occupied territories will emigrate there: "the Arabs to Jordan and the Jews to the territories to the west of the river." With the separation of the two peoples, there will be "true peace." All of this is encased in ideological and geopolitical fantasies concerning the collapse of the West before the Soviet-Third World onslaught, an upsurge of anti-Semitism in the West that will make Israel the "last refuge" for Jews, etc. Israel alone has the power to resist these awesome challenges as the humanistic European civilization of the post-Renaissance period is collapsing, Yinon explains, with extensive reference to neo-Conservative literature here and other sources.

In this publication and other current developments, the Israeli writer Amos Elon perceives "the spreading of irrationalism in our collective existence."[20] Instead of recognizing and dealing with the phenomenon, American "supporters of Israel" prefer to deny that it exists, and to protect the facts from scrutiny by defamation of those who are concerned with them. In fact, the views that Yinon expressed in the official ideological journal of the World Zionist Organization are not those of the Zionist mainstream, but of an extreme fringe of Israeli politics, the Tehiya party, essentially; the journal is, incidentally, not likely to feature the views of the other type of "extremists," those who support the international consensus. Shortly afterwards, Tehiya Knesset Member Yuval Ne'eman, who had written in the *Jerusalem Post* in favor of a "new order" in which southern Lebanon would be incorporated in some fashion into Israel, was offered a major cabinet position with responsibility and ample funding for settlement and development in the occupied territories.

Extreme these views may be, but they are not out of the political mainstream, and they may sooner or later come to dominate it in the natural course of events. The entire history of Zionism and later the State of Israel, particularly since 1967, is one of gradual shift towards the positions of those formerly regarded as right-wing extremists; consider, for example, the general attitude in earlier days towards the current terrorist leadership, Begin, Shamir, *et al.*, and their actions and doctrines.[21] Furthermore, in this case the conceptions of the Labor Zionist leadership were not radically different. Recall Ben-Gurion's strategic aims when the state was established in May 1948: to smash Transjordan and Syria, annex southern Lebanon and set up a Christian state in what remained, bombing Egypt if it resists, and to proceed towards realizing the longer-term "vision," by force if necessary, once a state was established under the partition agreement as a preliminary step; see chapter 4, pp. 162-3 and elsewhere.

In fact, much of what Yinon discusses is quite close to mainstream thinking. Both major political groupings agree that Jordan is "the Palestinian state," though Labor wants it to take over areas of heavy Arab population concentration in the occupied West Bank as well so as to relieve Israel of the "demographic problem." Both political groupings look forward to an eventual transfer of large parts of the Arab population to Jordan, reflecting ideas that have deep roots in Labor Zionist thought, as documented earlier. The "new order" that Israel is attempting to impose in Lebanon is based on a conception not unlike what Yinon expresses, and there is every reason to suppose that similar ideas with regard to Syria may seem attractive to the political leadership. With regard to Iraq, Ze'ev Schiff observed just before the Lebanon war that it would be in Israel's interest for it to be divided into three states, Sunni, Shiite and Kurdish—and it is difficult to see why Israel would refrain from seeking this objective.

Schiff's comments were a response to information that Israel was selling weapons to Iran,* and it is indeed likely that Israel's support for Iran (in silent partnership with Syria and Libya) is aimed in part at weakening Iraq, eventually splitting it up into separate states as Schiff and Yinon recommend. There is more involved, however. In an interview with the *Boston Globe*, Israeli Ambassador Moshe Arens, now Sharon's replacement as Defense Minister, stated that Israel had provided arms to the Khomeini regime "in coordination with the U.S. government...at almost the highest of levels." "The objective," he stated, "was to see if we could not find some areas of contact with the Iranian military, to bring down the Khomeini regime." Publication of this report elicited official U.S. government denials, and as Arens told the *Globe:* "I caught a little flack from the State Department." Arens then reiterated his statement about coordination with the U.S. government, but qualified the account

---

* Recall that Israel was closely allied to Iran prior to the fall of the Shah. The nature of this alliance was revealed in part after the Shah's fall by discussion in the Israeli press, particularly, the account by former Israeli Ambassador Uri Lubrani, who reports that "the entire upper echelon of the Israeli political leadership" visited the Shah's Iran, including David Ben-Gurion, Golda Meir, Abba Eban, Yitzhak Rabin, Yigal Allon, Moshe Dayan, and Menachem Begin, and who describes the warm relations that developed between Israel's Labor leaders and the Shah's secret police (SAVAK), who hosted these visits, taking time off from torturing prisoners.[24]

of the "objective": the arms flow was too small to bring down the Khomeini regime; rather, "The purpose was to make contact with some military officers who some day might be in a position of power in Iran."[22]

More information on Israeli ideas with regard to Iran was presented in a BBC program of February 1982 concerned with Israel's arms shipments to Iran and what the moderator, Philip Tibenham, calls "one of the most closely-guarded secrets in the Middle East—Israel's attempt to trigger a military coup in Iran."[23] The first person interviewed was Jacob Nimrodi, head of Mossad (the Israeli CIA, in effect) in Iran under cover as Israeli military attaché under the Shah. He is described as the Israeli closest to the Shah and his military staff during the period of the Israeli-Iranian alliance. Nimrodi states that "I think that we can do with the West together of course something to save Iran from this regime," namely, stage a military coup, which he thinks is possible and "important...for the West." Unless there is a coup, "Iran will fall into the hands of the Communists," first into the hands of the Tudeh (Communist) Party, "and after that in the hands of the Soviet Union." Former Ambassador to Iran Uri Lubrani adds:

> I very strongly believe that Tehran can be taken over by a very relatively small force, determined, ruthless, cruel. I mean the men who would lead that force will have to be emotionally geared to the possibility that they'd have to kill ten thousand people.*

Israel's purpose in sending arms to Iran is to find, maintain contact with and support such men, and then to re-establish the Israeli-Iranian alliance that was considered the foundation of American domination of the region in the 1970s, as discussed in chapter 2. David Kimche, head of Israel's Foreign Office and former deputy director of the Mossad, emphasized that Israel wants the Iranians to be strong so that there may

---

* Lubrani's background is with the Labor Party. He was a member of the kibbutz-based strike force of the Haganah (Palmach) in the pre-state period, and was later secretary to the dovish Foreign Minister Moshe Sharett (later Prime Minister), adviser on Arab affairs in the Ben-Gurion government, and a high official of the Levi Eshkol Labor government in the 1960s. He served as Ambassador to Ethiopia and Uganda before being sent to Iran, where he was a strong supporter of the Shah's regime (for his positive views on the Shah, at the end of his rule, see *TNCW*, p. 455). In Iran, he was close to American Ambassadors Richard Helms and William Sullivan. After he was appointed Defense Secretary, replacing Sharon, Moshe Arens recommended Lubrani for the new position of coordinator of Israeli activities in Lebanon, to replace David Kimche after negotiations on partial withdrawal are completed, and he was appointed by Begin, who had been "impressed by the Ambassador at the time of his [Begin's] secret visit to the Shah in Teheran" in February 1978. Reporting these facts, Shmuel Segev observes that Lubrani's experience in Iran in the last days of the Shah's rule should stand him in good stead in arranging Israel's affairs with various groups in Lebanon, including the Phalangists but also, he says, the Druze leader Walid Jumblatt with whom closer relations have been established (see chapter 6, section 7.2) and Shiite leaders in the south. *Ma'ariv*, April 22, 1983.

be an army takeover. "To encourage just such a takeover," Tibenham adds, "the Israelis embarked on a series of totally secret deals to supply arms to the Iranian military," establishing contacts through a Paris trading firm with the assistance of "a French government agent." The thinking is rather like that of *New Republic* editor Martin Peretz, who in this as other respects, as noted earlier, lines up with right-wing Israeli hardliners. His view is that it was the "timidity" of Jimmy Carter and Cyrus Vance that led to the fall of the Shah and stood in the way of the "U.S.-backed military coup" that he advocated when the Shah's regime was endangered.*

Israel's drive for a kind of Ottomanization of the region has been noted by others, among them, Boaz Evron, who describes Sharon's plan as "a revival of the Ottoman Empire's 'millet' system," that is, a system in which each religious-ethnic group (Druze, Armenians, Maronites, etc.) has its own internal administration but under Ottoman (Turkish) rule. "Sharon is now offering to set up a 'millet' of the same religious-ethnic kind, but one that is armed and tyrannising its own oppressed population. Moreover, since the 'millet' is not territorial, but organized along religious and ethnic lines, it can have no clear boundaries." This plan aims at a breakdown of the national state system which was imposed by the colonial powers on the Middle East, as elsewhere, and is indeed an alien implantation, a fact that has given rise to endless turmoil and suffering; recall what happened during the hundreds of years when the national state system was consolidating itself in Europe, without the contributions of external force.

In Lebanon, Evron continues, the plan is to set Maronites, Sunnite and Shiite Muslims and Druze against one another. Israel will help each group to maintain itself in the "perpetual civil wars" that will result, based ultimately on "the main, basic dispute between the ruling groups and the oppressed Muslims," extending this system beyond Lebanon into Syria, which will also be "dismembered." He also points out that the policy derives from earlier Zionist thinking across the political spectrum, including labor leader Yigal Allon, with the goal of creating an "alliance between the Hebrew nation or the Jewish state (depending on the authors of the different versions of the same idea) with the other ethnic and religious minorities in the region, such as the Druze and the Maronites." This alliance would be aimed "against the supremacy of Sunni Muslim Arabism." Evron believes that Israel too is retreating "from the concept of a

---

* Martin Peretz, "Illusions," *New Republic*, Oct. 14, 1982. He also denounces the "*gauchistes* and mindless ones (the *Nation* and [columnist] Carl Rowan, for example)" who are "furious at Sadat for trying to keep Egypt from recapitulating the experience of Iran," referring, presumably, to the objections of these mindless types to the corruption, increasing class divisions and repression that were among the factors that alienated much Egyptian opinion while Sadat became a hero in the United States.[25] The title of Peretz's piece is a rather appropriate one. On the facts concerning the alleged "timidity" of Carter and his advisers, see *TNCW*, pp. 378-9, and references cited.

state" in the modern sense, undermining "its own civil structure in favor of Jewish religious and ethnic chauvinism" as a reflection of the system it is attempting to introduce into the whole region, in which, of course, it is assumed that Israel will reign supreme. He believes that "The deeper we will sink into this quagmire, the more our national base will disintegrate, and we ourselves will break up into rival ethnic groups. Since the structure of the state of Israel is also becoming increasingly ethnic-religious, this is entirely probable."[26]

One might see the beginnings of the fulfilment of Evron's prophecy in the rise of religious-chauvinist fanaticism to a position of some prominence in Israel and the internal ethnic-religious conflicts, as when Sephardic Jews riot against their Ashkenazi oppressors, shouting that they should all have been sent to Nazi extermination camps. But as the examples cited earlier indicate, it would be an error to draw the lines too sharply in terms of Arab or Western origin; some of the most extreme elements are recent American and Russian immigrants, generally with a religious background, and of the two chief Rabbis (replaced in early 1983), the Sephardi had not adopted the Khomeinist stance of his Ashkenazi counterpart, among many other examples that might be cited. Evron himself comes from an old Jerusalem family

Evron is highly critical of the concept he outlines. Others, who are well within the mainstream, advance something like it, not in such explicit terms as Oded Yinon in the Hebrew ideological journal of the World Zionist Organization, but in a more measured form, for an American audience. Consider the study edited by Daniel Elazar, president of the Jerusalem Institute for Federal Studies, published by the American Enterprise Institute, which I have cited several times.[27] In his summary remarks for this collection of scholarly essays, Elazar argues that "ethnoreligious communities," not states, are the natural form of organization in the Middle East: any general political settlement must remain "dubious about those who claim statehood on the basis of fifteen or thirty or even fifty years of national self-identification." A possible model is the Ottoman millet system, he suggests. He rules out returning the occupied territories to Jordanian or Egyptian rule, or the establishment of a Palestinian state. The latter option ignores "the Palestinian character of Jordan." Furthermore, "even disregarding Israel's own need for secure borders, such a state would be too small and poor relative to its neighbors to be viable," and "hence it would be extremely vulnerable to extremist control" and would be unable to "control its 'crazies'"—as Israel, the USSR, the U.S., and other states have so successfully done. The reasoning is not transparent. It is not obvious why a small and weak state should not, rather, fall under conservative control, fearing its more powerful neighbors and dependent for survival on their goodwill and on the support of the most conservative forces in the region among the Arab oil producers. But let us proceed.

Elazar also rules out "territorial compromise" on the Labor model. What he advocates is a "federative solution." He claims without reference that in 1969 Shimon Peres "endorsed the pursuit of federative options" and later elaborated "a plan for a redivision of the entire Cis-Jordanian area into multiple Jewish and Arab cantons" while others within the Israeli political leadership also advanced federative solutions, though unfortunately "none of these plans nor those produced by others outside of political life such as this writer [Elazar], produced any echoes in the Arab camp... Israel found no partners," the familiar tragedy in Israel's constant search for a peaceful political settlement. But now, perhaps, partners can be found, though he is unclear about what the arrangements will be—surely not the "Israel-Palestine federation, which is sometimes proposed by well-meaning people." In the "federative solution" that he outlines, Israel and Jordan "will maintain their own independence and status as politically sovereign entities," and the status of the Palestinians remains obscure.

It is difficult to believe that Peres or anyone else in Israeli political life, or Elazar, seriously proposed a cantonal arrangement—which entails the abandonment of the concept of a "Jewish state"—but were rebuffed by Arab refusal, though it is true that Peres made vague remarks about some form of "federation" after the 1973 war had undermined Labor's plans for integrating the occupied territories in its preferred manner. Some did make such proposals; I did, for example (recalling suggestions by Ben-Gurion and others from the early 1930s), during the period before the 1973 war, though by then, as I also noted, the possibilities that might have existed before no longer did.[28] These proposals led to considerable outrage in Israel, across the political spectrum, and much more so here. If such proposals were serious, they might well have been reasonable, and might be resurrected—so I believe, in fact. Elazar says little about what he has in mind, but enough to indicate that his proposal is not serious. In fact, it is simply a proposal for Israeli domination over the Palestinians, who are to be deprived of national self-determination. It will be noticed that there is one crucial exception to his remarks on the inappropriateness of the state system to the Middle East. While we are to remain "dubious" about those states that have emerged in the past decades, Israel is free from these doubts; and as for Jordan, it can claim sovereignty, but as a state with a "Palestinian character," with obvious implications for the Palestinians in the occupied territories. The dissolution of the state system, hinted at though not explicitly proposed, in favor of a patchwork of "ethno-religious communities," will leave Israel in a hegemonic position, and will leave the Palestinians with nothing other than a form of Begin's "autonomy" under Israeli rule. The rest is plainly window dressing. The interest of the article is to illustrate, once again, the appeal of the "Ottomanization option" to the Israeli political imagination.

There can be little doubt that from shortly after the 1967 conquest, Israel has been moving in the directions indicated earlier: international isolation apart from pariah states, dependence on the U.S. with the concomitant pressure to serve U.S. interests, militarization of the society, the rise of religious-chauvinist fanaticism, the internal "feed-back" from the policies of oppression and domination, an increasing sense of the inevitability of permanent conflict and with it, the perceived need to disrupt the region and establish a form of Israeli hegemony under the U.S. aegis. These tendencies have been widely noted within Israel. As a last example, consider a thoughtful analytic article by Yoram Peri—former Adviser to Prime Minister Rabin and European representative of the Labor Party, and a specialist on civil-military relations in Israel—in the Labor Party journal *Davar*, just after the fighting in Lebanon came to a probably temporary end.[29]

Peri describes a "true revolution" that has taken place in Israel's basic "military-diplomatic conception," one that he dates to the political victory of Begin and Sharon, though the shift seems to me to have been more gradual and more deeply-rooted than as he describes it. The earlier conception was based on the search for "coexistence" and maintenance of the status quo. Israel aimed at a peaceful settlement in which its position in the region would be recognized and its security achieved. The new conception is based on the goal of "hegemony," not "coexistence." No longer a status quo power, having achieved military dominance as the world's fourth most powerful military force, and no longer believing in even the possibility of peace or even its desirability except in terms of Israeli hegemony, Israel is now committed to "destabilization" of the region, including Lebanon, Syria, Saudi Arabia and Jordan. In accordance with the new conception, Israel should now use its military dominance to expand its borders and "to create a new reality," a "new order," rather than seek recognition within the status quo.

The first step was the invasion of Lebanon designed to "destroy the Palestinian national movement" and "establish a new order in Lebanon." Next will come the overthrow of the Hashemite state in Jordan and its conversion to a Palestinian state while the occupied territories are absorbed within Israel, with consequences that he does not elaborate as regards the Arab population in the occupied territories. The next steps will be Damascus, Saudi Arabia, and who knows where else, as Israel strives to become "the hegemonic power in the region," or as Begin sees it, "to organize the whole world."

Peri is concerned that this program—apart from its general madness—will sooner or later set Israel in opposition to the U.S., on which it now depends for its existence as well as its position as the world's fourth greatest military power.* The reason is that the U.S. is basically a status quo power itself, opposed to destabilization of the sort to which Israel is increasingly committed. The new strategic conception is based on an illusion of power, and may lead to a willingness, already apparent in some of the rhetoric heard in Israel, to undertake military adventures even without U.S. support. The illusions become obvious when one considers the reality of contemporary Israel, "dependent on others." He cites a recent report that Israel is 92nd in a list of 114 countries ranked in order of the danger of serious economic problems by international banks, considered barely more healthy economically than Angola, Haiti, El Salvador. It has one of the largest foreign debts per capita. Begin is "a Napoleon" in a balloon that will quickly burst if Israeli policy leads it into conflict with American objectives, a consequence inherent in the new drive for regional hegemony, he believes. Others too feel that Begin and Company are treading on thin ice as they come to believe their own propaganda about Israeli power, pursuing an independent imperial mission, abandoning the traditional conception that Israel must act in alliance with some major power—in practice, the United States, if possible, in the framework of a regional arrangement such as Ben-Gurion's periphery pact or the Israeli-Iranian alliance of the 1970s.

4.2   Assuming an Abandonment of U.S. Rejectionism

4.2.1   The Effect on Israeli Policy

These considerations lead to the final question. Suppose that the United States does modify or abandon its support for Israeli rejectionism, either because of a conflict in regional goals as Peri fears, or because the U.S. comes to join the international consensus which recognizes the right of Israel *and* the Palestinians to national self-determination within secure and recognized borders. How would Israel react to such a radical shift in the American stand? It would at first glance appear that the impact should be decisive, that Israel is incapable of resisting U.S. pressure. From its origins, Israel has relied heavily on outside support, and now its economy

---

* Elsewhere Peri has expressed the fear that parallel developments within Israel itself may lead to a "military democracy" (*Between Battles and Ballots*, final chapter: "The Begin era: will there be a military coup?"). This might happen, he envisions, if international pressures "force Israel to sign a peace settlement with the PLO, involving evacuation of the areas occupied in 1967 and establishment of a Palestinian state," leading to a "state of national emergency" and a call to the military to take over. On the basis of the troubled history of civil-military relations and the high level of "penetration by former senior army officers into the top political echelons," he questions "the proposition that Israel is a stable democracy immune to military participation in Government" and ends his study by stating that "an upheaval should not be ruled out."

and military strength are highly artificial, crucially dependent on American largesse. One might assume, therefore, that Israel would have to bend to the U.S. will, since the alternative would be economic collapse and military defeat.

4.2.2 Israel's Secret Weapon

Some years ago, this line of argument might well have been valid. Perhaps it still is, though there are now other factors that cannot be ignored. By the late 1970s, some U.S. military analysts began to fear that Israel's military power had reached such a high level, thanks to U.S. assistance programs, that the state could no longer be controlled and might pose "a major national security problem" for the U.S. by carrying out aggressive actions on its own contrary to U.S. interests.* Yoram Peri's observations, expressing concerns felt by many others, carry this analysis a step further, viewed now from an Israeli perspective.

Quite apart from the question of hegemonic aspirations and a commitment to "destabilize" the surrounding region in accordance with the new "strategic conception" that Peri quite plausibly outlines, there have on occasion been barely disguised hints from Israel that if it is pressured towards a political settlement it might respond by military actions that would severely harm U.S. interests. A case in point was the reaction to the Saudi (Fahd) peace plan of August 1981 (see chapter 3, notes 105-7 and text). Daniel Bloch wrote in the Labor Party journal *Davar* that "all the handstands attempted by our propagandists will fail to dispel [the] impression" that the Fahd plan is "a sign of open-mindedness and moderation" on the part of the Saudis, a shift towards commitment to a political settlement (in fact, the shift had taken place well before, but let us put that aside). Bloch interprets Israel's reaction—provocative military flights over Saudi Arabia which "spell out our position" to "international forces" after the failure of "our propaganda campaign against the Fahd plan" to persuade them—as "the continuation of diplomacy by other means": "Jerusalem seems to believe that if rational arguments fail, we must threaten irrational behavior in order to discourage the world, and especially the United States, from putting any pressure on us." What is the "irrational behavior" that is threatened?

> Last week both Begin and [Foreign Minister] Shamir gave strong hints that the adoption of the Fahd plan by the world might cause Israel to reconsider various policies, among them

---

* Anthony H. Cordesman, *Armed Forces Journal*, Oct. 20, 1977. For daring to raise this question, Cordesman was denounced as "anti-Israel and anti-Jewish" by the Anti-Defamation League of Bnai Brith, consistent with the general practice of what was, at one time, a civil libertarian organization.[30]

the planned evacuation of the rest of Sinai. This [and crucially, the military flights over Saudi Arabia] must have caused many foreign intelligence agencies to reach for old files containing statements by Israeli generals about Israel's capacity to bomb the Saudi oil fields. After the bombing of the Iraqi reactor [June 7, 1981], Israel is thought capable of such acts.[31]

This analysis recalls the observation of the moshav farmer interviewed by Amos Oz (see p. 447) that Israel should act as a "wild country, dangerous to our surroundings, not normal," quite capable of "burning the oil fields" or even starting a nuclear war. This is a form of "self-defense" of a novel sort, one that cannot be easily dismissed. The threat is in this case directed primarily against the United States, but indirectly against the rest of the world as well. With this new style of "self-defense," the special relationship takes on a more complex form, under the conditions that have been created by American "support."

In early 1983, the executive director of the officially-registered Israeli lobbying organization AIPAC (American Israel Public Affairs Committee), Tom Dine, returned from a visit to Jerusalem where he met with senior Israeli government officials and policy-makers, with some further threats to deliver. Wolf Blitzer outlines them in the *Jerusalem Post*. Dine explained that sanctions against Israel might force it "to consider sweeping measures to eliminate the [Arab] threat while the IDF is still comparatively strong":

> The upshot of Dine's ominous message was clear: a possible
> preemptive strike by Israel against its Arab adversaries designed
> to cripple their military capabilities for a long time to come.
> Don't get Jerusalem too nervous, Dine implied.

This is the real import of Kissinger's absurd comments, cited earlier (p. 339), on the danger of "harassing" Israel "into emotional and psychic collapse" unless it "feels compassion on our side, maybe even affection, rather than unremitting pressure."

"If [Dine's] intention in outlining these views" of top Israeli policy-makers "was to scare senior White House officials," Blitzer adds, then "he succeeded."[32] The fear has little to do with concern for the Arab victims of another Israeli attack; rather, with two factors of considerably greater significance to White House officials: U.S. relations with the oil producers, and the threat of global war, not an unlikely prospect if Israel moves on to attack its major current military adversary, Syria. See section 2.2.

Blitzer suggests that "Dine's warning" may have been the reason why the Reagan administration, in "proposing another large scale economic and military aid package for Israel" for the coming fiscal year, refused to attach any "political conditions"—meaning, any condition that Israel slow down its rapid absorption of the West Bank or that it withdraw from Lebanon. Testifying before Congress, Assistant Secretary of State Nicholas Veliotes was specifically asked about tying U.S. aid to a retreat from the policy of expanding West Bank settlement in defiance of Reagan's plea for a settlement freeze, but he "steadfastly refused to accept the notion of attaching political conditions for the assistance"—or to be more precise, the notion that the U.S. should not pay Israel to establish these settlements. Blitzer's speculation is not implausible.* The "secret weapon" that the U.S. has supplied to Israel is a powerful and ominous one.

Nuclear threats are also not to be dismissed. I referred earlier to a recent study of Israel's nuclear strategies and capacities by a group of Israeli and American specialists: Amos Perlmutter (Professor of Political Science at American University in Washington, military historian and strategic analyst, formerly a member of the Israeli delegation to the UN and the Israeli Atomic Energy Commission), Michael Handel (military historian at the Harvard Center for International Affairs, formerly of the Hebrew University), and Uri Bar-Joseph (formerly in the Israeli air force, involved with training and tactical planning).[33] As noted earlier, they allege that Israel threatened to use nuclear weapons, and in fact prepared to do so, in the early stages of the October 1973 war, in order to compel the U.S. to provide "a massive shipment of conventional weapons" to Israel. Again, the threat was directed at the United States: "The Israeli signals would make it clear to the decision-makers in the White House, the Pentagon and the State Department that any more delays might bring catastrophe to the Middle East."

The authors then proceed to review the nuclear capabilities that Israel has developed in cooperation with South Africa and Taiwan. They cite reports, which they present as presumably accurate, that Israel has about 200 "operational nuclear warheads" (attributed to the CIA), including a tactical and strategic arsenal, and is working on a neutron bomb. The September 1979 incident in which American and Soviet spy satellites detected a suspected nuclear explosion over the Indian Ocean was in actuality the explosion of a nuclear shell launched from a cannon in a joint experiment of South Africa and Israel that involved "one of the most advanced tactical nuclear systems to be used anywhere in the world." Cruise missiles are under development, jointly with South Africa and Taiwan, with a 1500 mile range, sufficient to hit "many targets in southern USSR." Israel has "a variety of launching systems," including American and Israeli-made planes, surface-to-surface missiles, and soon to come, a nuclear gun and cruise missiles.

---

* There are, however, other reasons as well for U.S. support (rhetoric aside) for Israel's settlement policies, as discussed earlier.

Whether these reports are true or not it is impossible to know.[34] But it is reasonable to suppose that they reflect what Israel would like others to believe. It may also be surmised that nuclear-tipped missiles that can reach southern Russia are not really intended to deter the USSR, but rather to put U.S. planners on notice, once again, that pressures on Israel to accede to a political settlement may lead to a violent reaction that will bring the USSR into the Middle East, setting it in inevitable confrontation with the United States, with a high probability of global nuclear war. One might even speculate as to whether Israel had something similar in mind in its provocative actions against the USSR in Lebanon in 1982, discussed earlier: a hint to the U.S. about what it could do, if pressed. Israel's "secret weapon," which may compensate for its extraordinary economic, military and diplomatic dependence on the United States, is the threat that it may act as a "wild country," if pressed.

While these tendencies are now becoming too visible to be disregarded, they are not without precedent. In his personal diaries, the dovish Prime Minister Moshe Sharett recorded in October 1955 his fears concerning Defense Minister Pinhas Lavon of the Labor Party. Lavon, he wrote, "has constantly preached in favor of acts of madness and taught the army leadership the diabolic lesson of how to set the Middle East on fire, how to cause friction, cause bloody confrontations, sabotage targets and property of the Powers [and perform] acts of despair and suicide."[35] The occasion was the terrorist operation mounted by Israel in Egypt against U.S. and British installations and public buildings, with the aim "to break the West's confidence in the existing [Egyptian] regime" and thus "to prevent economic and military aid from the West to Egypt," in the words of the instructions given by the head of Israeli military intelligence at a time when Israel was concerned over the apparently close relations between the U.S. and Nasser.[36]

The growing threat has been recognized within Israel. Yaakov Sharett writes that the greatest danger facing Israel now is the "collective version" of Samson's revenge against the Philistines—"Let me perish with the Philistines"—as he brought down the Temple in ruins, killing more Philistines than he had during his lifetime.[37] He cites the Sharett diaries, the entry just cited and another one, where Defense Minister Lavon is quoted as stating: "we will go crazy" ("nishtagea") if crossed. Again from the diaries, he cites Labor Party official David Hacohen after the attack on Egypt in 1956, who tells Moshe Sharett that "we have nothing to lose so it is better that we go crazy; the world will know to what a level we have reached," and presumably will be afraid to interfere, a position that Moshe Sharett found appalling.[38] This "Samson complex" is not something to be taken lightly. Aryeh (Lova) Eliav, one of Israel's best-known and most influential doves, writes that the attitude of "those who brought the 'Samson complex' here, according to which we shall kill and bury all the Gentiles around us while we ourselves shall die with them," is a sign of the same sort of "insanity" that was manifested in the violent counter-demonstration in which Emil Grunzweig was killed—see p. 443—and is a phenomenon of some significance in contemporary Israel.[39] It is rein-forced by the feeling that "the whole world is against us" because of its ineradicable anti-Semitism, a paranoid vision that owes not a little to the contribution of supporters here, as we have seen.

In short, Israel's "secret weapon," which renders rational calcula-tions somewhat questionable, is that it may behave in the manner of what have sometimes been called "crazy states" in the international affairs literature. The concept was developed by the Israeli scholar Yehezkel Dror of the Hebrew University. He writes that "I am more sensitive to the possibilities and implications of seemingly irrational political behavior than either American strategists or the American public in general," referring to "the dangers facing my own country."[40] He regards "possible crazy states" as "a main danger—to the world, to the United States, and to each country," noting particularly the Samson complex and the special danger of nuclear crazy states. The text is so abstract that one can only guess as to what exactly he may have had in mind, but the usual reference is to such states as Libya or Iraq, an equally obvious example being pointedly omitted. This kind of "secret weapon" is one to which a state that sees itself as threatened and dependent may resort, and it becomes an extraordinarily dangerous one in the hands of the world's fourth greatest military power, equipped with an extremely efficient and powerful air force capable of bombing the oil fields and nuclear weapons and missiles that can reach the USSR, and undergoing internal social and political developments of the kinds that have taken place in Israel since the 1967 conquest—thanks to U.S. "support."

Would Israel actually resort to its increasingly visible "secret wea-pon" if faced with American pressure to accept a political settlement in which it would lose the conquered territories? Whether it would hazard this under duress might depend on its assessment of the state of American opinion. If it feels that it can count on its supporters to stand firm, it might very well go beyond its reaction to the Saudi peace threat in 1981 and the threat posed by the PLO's reliance on political means in 1982, perhaps employing its ultimate secret weapon. Sooner or later, the time will come when even a switch in U.S. policy away from the rejectionism of the past years will be too late, either because the worst will have happened, or because Israel will be able to rely on its secret weapon to resist pressures to join the international consensus, or because the consensus itself will have eroded under the impact of U.S. power and the Palestinians will have gone the way of the American Indians.

Meanwhile, at least this much seems clear. As long as the United States remains committed to an Israeli Sparta as a strategic asset, blocking the international consensus on a political settlement, the prospects are for further tragedy: repression, terrorism, war, and possibly even a conflict that will engage the superpowers, eventuating in a final solution from which few will escape.

Notes—Chapter 7
The Road to Armageddon

1. *Al Hamishmar*, Jan. 10, 1983 *(Israeli Mirror; Middle East International*, Feb. 4, 1983).
2. Shulamit Har-Even, *Yediot Ahronot*, Feb. 14; Baruch Meiri, *Ma'ariv*, Feb. 13; Dan Ben Amotz, *Koteret Rashit*, Feb. 23; Eliahu Salpeter, *Ha'aretz*, Feb. 14; Amnon Dankner, *Ha'aretz*, Feb. 11, 18, 1983.
3. Mordechai Nisan, "Judaism and Politics," *Jerusalem Post*, Jan. 18, 1983.
4. Joachim Prinz, *Wir Juden*, Berlin, 1934, pp. 150-57.
5. Amos Oz, *Davar*, Dec. 3, 17, 1982.
6. Menachem Horowitz, *Ha'aretz*, Feb. 6, 1983; *Ha'aretz*, Dec. 7, 1982 *(Israeli Mirror; Middle East International*, Feb. 4, 1983). See chapter 6, note 200.
7. AP, *Boston Globe*, Feb. 6, 1983; Jack Nelson, *Los Angeles Times—Boston Globe*, Feb. 23, 1983; *New York Times*, Feb. 24, 1983; *Economist*, Jan. 8, 1983; Ned Temko, John Yemma, *Christian Science Monitor*, March 17, 1983; also William Beecher, *Boston Globe*, Jan. 28, 29, 1983, on concerns in Washington over these developments.
8. Ze'ev Schiff, *Ha'aretz*, Dec. 31, 1982; Jan. 7, 1983 *(Israeli Press Briefs)*. See also Thomas L. Friedman, "Syrian Army Said to Be Stronger Than Ever, Thanks to Soviets," *New York Times*, March 19, 1983.
9. For further discussion of this topic, see my essay "What Directions for the Disarmament Movement?," in Albert and Dellinger, eds., *Beyond Survival*, and the briefer version in the *Michigan Quarterly Review*, Fall, 1982. Also my "Priorities for averting the holocaust," *Guardian* (London), July 12, 1982; "The United States and Israel: A Case Study for the Disarmament Movement" *END Papers Special*, Spokesman Pamphlet no. 81 (Nottingham), 1982, and a briefer version in *MERIP Reports*, September-October 1982; and articles by Eqbal Ahmed and Joseph Gerson in *New England Briefs for Middle East Peacework*, Winter 1983. On the role of the Middle East in current U.S. nuclear strategy, see Christopher Paine, "Rapid Deployment and Nuclear War," *MERIP Reports*, January 1983. Similar ideas have been presented by Daniel Ellsberg. See his "Call to Mutiny," in E.P. Thompson and Dan Smith, *Protest and Survive* (Monthly Review, New York, 1981).
10. Cited by William Quandt, in a review of the 1958 Lebanon crisis in Barry M. Blechman and Stephen S. Kaplan, *et al., Force without War: U.S. Armed Forces as a Political Instrument* (Brookings Institution, Washington 1978).
11. Yoram Peri, *Between Battles and Ballots*, p. 244; James E. Ennes, *Assault on the Liberty*, p. 78; Richard K. Smith, "The Violation of the'Liberty'" (see chapter 2, pp. 31-2 and note 39); Barry M. Blechman and Douglas M. Hart, "The Political Utility of Nuclear Weapons," *International Security*, vol. 7, no. 1, 1982.
12. Ned Temko, *Christian Science Monitor*, June 23, 1982; Claudia Wright, *New Statesman*, June 18, 1982.
13. AP, "Soviet Embassy Heavily Damaged by Israeli Shells," *New York Times*, July 8, 1982. See p. 362.
14. *New York Times, Christian Science Monitor*, Dec. 2, 1982. It is not clear from the news reports whether the incident that Perle describes was during or prior to the Lebanon war.
15. J. Michael Kennedy, *Los Angeles Times*, Sept. 23, 1982.
16. *Worldview*, February 1983.
17. Judith Miller, *New York Times*, Jan. 16, 1983.
18. Sammy Smooha and Don Peretz, "The Arabs in Israel," *J. of Conflict Resolution*, September 1982. The figures presented below are rounded, so they may not add up to 100% precisely.

19. Oded Yinon, "Strategy for Israel in the 1980s," *Kivunim*, February 1982; published by the World Zionist Organization's Department of Information. A partial English translation appears in the *J. of Palestine Studies*, Summer/Fall 1982, and a full translation in Israel Shahak, *The Zionist Plan for the Middle East* (AAUG, Belmont, Mass., 1982). For earlier comment on this analysis, see my articles in the *Guardian, MERIP Reports* and END Papers, cited in note 9; and in *Middle East International*, July 16, 1982 and *Inquiry*, August 1982; also Alexander Cockburn and James Ridgeway, *Village Voice*, July 27, 1982, and Georges Corm, "La Balkanisation du Proche-Orient," *Le Monde diplomatique*, January 1983. For perceptive comment on the general topic, see Edward Said, *Covering Islam* (Pantheon, New York, 1981, pp. 137ff.).

20. Amos Elon, *Ha'aretz*, May 14, 1982.

21. In this connection, we might note the observation by Zionist historian Ben Halpern that the 1942 decision of the Zionist organization to adopt the goal of a Jewish state "was in many ways the kind of definition of the aim of sovereignty long demanded by the Revisionists," the right-wing political group that is the predecessor to Begin's Herut party (*The Idea of the Jewish State*, Harvard, Cambridge, 1969, p. 39). See p. 94, above.

22. Ze'ev Schiff, "The Israeli interest in the Iraq-Iran war," *Ha'aretz*, June 2, 1982; David Nyhan, *Boston Globe*, Oct. 21, 23; Robert Levey, *Boston Globe*, Oct. 22, 1982.

23. *Panorama*, BBC-1 at 2010, February 1, 1982. I quote from the transcript.

24. See *TNCW*, pp. 455-6. For more on the alliance and its background, see *TNCW*, chapter 11, and sources cited there.

25. On these matters, see David Hirst and Irene Beeson, *Sadat* (Faber and Faber, London, 1981).

26. Boaz Evron, "Castle of Sand," *Yediot Ahronot*, Aug. 9, 1982; *Israeli Mirror*.

27. Daniel J. Elazar, ed., *Judea, Samaria, and Gaza*.

28. There is extensive discussion of these matters in my *Peace in the Middle East?* (Pantheon, New York, 1974); also *TNCW*, chapter 9, originally published in 1975.

29. Yoram Peri, "From Coexistence to hegemony," *Davar*, Oct. 1, 1982.

30. Tillman, *The United States in the Middle East*, p. 155.

31. Daniel Bloch, *Davar*, Nov. 13, 1981 (*Israeli Mirror*); see chapter 3, note 106.

32. Wolf Blitzer, "Opening salvoes in Israel aid battle," *Jerusalem Post*, March 4, 1983.

33. Amos Perlmutter, Michael Handel, Uri Bar-Joseph, *Two Minutes Over Baghdad* (Vallentine, Mitchell & Co., London, 1982). Most of the book is devoted to the attack on the Iraqi reactor, which the authors consider a highly meritorious achievement.

34. See chapter 2, note 53 and text, note 41, and references cited.

35. October 1, 1955; quoted in Rokach, *Israel's Sacred Terrorism*.

36. *Ibid.* See chapter 2, p. 20 and note 36, and references cited.

37. *Judges*, Chapter 16.30.

38. Yaakov Sharett, "A Great Danger is Coming," *Davar*, Nov. 3, 1982.

39. "Emil and the murderers," *Davar*, Feb. 13, 1983.

40. Yehezkel Dror, *Crazy States* (Heath Lexington Books, Lexington, MA 1971). The acknowledgments cite, among others, Michael Handel, his former assistant at the Hebrew University, co-author of the work on Israel's nuclear capacity cited in note 33.

Index